מסורה

ArtScroll Halachah Series®

Rabbi Nosson Scherman / Rabbi Meir Zlotowitz
General Editors

NISHMAT
MAN AND HIS DISEASES
MAN AND HIS DISEASES
שלחן ערוך
Published by
Mesorah Publications, ltd

AVRAHAM

VOLUME I: ORACH CHAIM

Medical Halachah for doctors, nurses, health-care personnel and patients

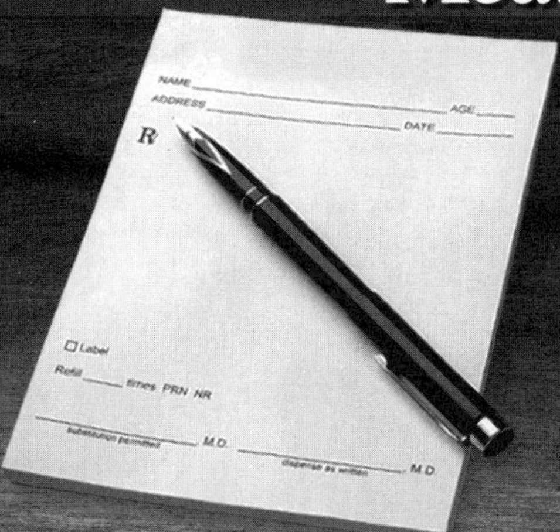

Translated From The Hebrew *Nishmat Avraham*
by its author

ABRAHAM S. ABRAHAM M.D., FRCP

FIRST EDITION
First Impression . . . December 2000

Published and Distributed by
MESORAH PUBLICATIONS, Ltd.
4401 Second Avenue
Brooklyn, New York 11232

Distributed in Europe by
LEHMANNS
Unit E, Viking Industrial Park
Rolling Mill Road
Jarrow, Tyne & Wear NE32 3DP
England

Distributed in Australia & Zew Zealand by
GOLDS WORLD OF JUDAICA
3-13 William Street
Balaclava, Melbourne 3183
Victoria Australia

Distributed in Israel by
SIFRIATI / A. GITLER — BOOKS
6 Hayarkon Street
Bnei Brak 51127

Distributed in South Africa by
KOLLEL BOOKSHOP
Shop 8A Norwood Hypermarket
Norwood 2196, Johannesburg, South Africa

THE ARTSCROLL SERIES®
NISHMAT AVRAHAM
VOL. 1 — ORACH CHAIM

4401 Second Avenue / Brooklyn, N.Y. 11232 / (718) 921-9000 / www.artscroll.com

---

ISBN: 1-57819-575-6
(hard cover only)

Printed in the United States of America by Noble Book Press Corp.
Bound by Sefercraft Quality Bookbinders, Ltd., Brooklyn, N.Y.

This book is dedicated
to the memory of
my dear parents z"l

אדוני אבי מורי ועט״ר

ר׳ אליהו ב״ר נחמיה ז״ל

נפטר ח׳ אלול תשכ״א

ואמי מורתי ועט״ר

מרת חנה כתון בת רחל ז״ל

נפטרה י״ט אייר תשי״ד

ת.נ.צ.ב.ה.

To My Dear Friend,

Robert Schulman, MD

Sylvia and I wish to thank you and Susie for the many years of deep and true friendship that you have shown us and for your exceptional hospitality whenever we visit New York. It is a source of happiness to us for which we are grateful.

Bob, I know that this translation would never have got off the ground but for you. For some time now you have been encouraging me to do this; you had the vision and determination to want to see the Hebrew Nishmat Avraham become available to the English reading public, putting your heart and soul into each stage of the project to ensure that it should become a reality. I know that uppermost in your mind is the wish to spread Torah to publicly glorify Hashem's Name; may Hashem grant you your wish. May He, the source of all reward and blessing, bless you, Susie, your mothers and families with long lives of health and happiness and may you both continue to have much joy from your children and grandchildren.

Mesorah Heritage Foundation *and*
The Association of Orthodox Jewish Scientists
express their gratitude to the following physicians of the Syrian Jewish community of Brooklyn for their vision and generosity in helping bring this monumental work to the English-speaking public.

RABBI ELIE ABADIE, MD
in memory of his father Rabbi Abraham Abadie

MAYER BALLAS, MD
in memory of Esther Ballas bat Nazira and Richard Grego ben Sultana

RICHARD V. GRAZI, MD
in honor of his parents Sally and Joseph Grazi

VICTOR M. GRAZI, MD
in honor of Burton Garfinkel, MD, with love and gratitude

DR. AND MRS. MARTIN (MORDECHAI) AND MIRIAM GROSSMAN
in memory of Herschel (Tzvi) Grossman and David H. Tawil Me'Eli HaCohen

ALBERT MATALON, MD
in honor of his father Robert Matalon, MD, "whom I strive to emulate"

ROBERT MATALON, MD
in memory of his parents Ely and Becky Matalon

STANLEY S. SCHREM, MD
in honor of his parents Jean and Ezra Schrem

Introduction

Hashem, how can I thank You, how can I express my gratitude to You? For even if I knew all the words of all the languages of the world, I still would not be capable of doing so. You have bestowed upon me so much lovingkindness; the merit of being born to parents who sacrificed so much for me and who showed me what love of Torah and mitzvot mean, the merit of being born in Jerusalem, the merit of being able to treat the ill in Jerusalem and of writing my sefarim; and so much more. Your Divine Providence guided me throughout my years as a doctor, and, together with my wife Sylvia, we have the privilege to live in Jerusalem where I have practiced medicine these past thirty years. How else would I have been able to meet and learn from the Gaon, HaRav Shlomo Zalman Auerbach ztz"l and from my teacher and mentor, HaRav Yehoshua Neuwirth shlita and be able to write my sefarim Lev Avraham and Nishmat Avraham? How much more so is my gratitude to You when I know that all of this comes not because of any personal merits but only from the merits of my parents z"l. May it be Your Will that my sefarim together with this present volume lead to the sanctification of Your Name and the glorification of Your Torah — the timeless and Divine manifestation of Your Will and bring my parents z"l even closer to Your divine Presence in the World of Truth.

For some twenty-five years I had the immense privilege of learning from Rav Auerbach ztz"l. Whether by telephone, in writing or in person, I learned from him many times each week. All that I wrote in my sefarim was seen by him and his comments, corrections, novella and insights made Nishmat Avraham what it is. Divine Providence willed it so for which my gratitude is boundless.

My teacher and Rav, Rav Yehoshua Neuwirth shlita, the author of Shemirat Shabbat Kehilchata, has given me unstintingly of his time for the past thirty years. Every page, every paragraph, every sentence of my sefarim was scrutinized by him. He discussed them with me, taught and corrected, edited and criticized both before and after they were seen by Rav Auerbach ztz"l. Even now, his blessing and encouragement has enabled me to undertake the tremendous task of translating the original Hebrew version of Nishmat Avraham, Orach Chaim (taken from volumes 1, 4 and 5).

The world-renowned poskim Rav Yosef Shalom Eliashiv shlita, Rav Eliezer Yehudah Waldenberg shlita and Rav Ovadiah Yosef shlita adorned my sefarim with their great insights, comments and rulings.

Hashem gave me the rare privilege and merit to be present at the formulation and evolvement of much of modern Medical Halachah by these spiritual giants of our age and an even greater merit to be able to transmit their words to Am Yisrael through Nishmat Avraham. For this alone I am and will be eternally grateful to Him.

My wife Sylvia's constant encouragement and help throughout the years, and now the countless hours that she has spent reading and rereading, editing, advising and criticizing has made this translation possible. Rebbe Akiva said it all when he praised his wife to his twenty-four thousand students (Ketubot 63a): Mine and yours are hers. May Hashem give her all the blessings of the Torah that is so dear to her.

Rabbi Meir Zlotowitz and Rabbi Nosson Scherman of ArtScroll, Mesorah Publications have revolutionized Torah learning among the English-speaking public throughout the world and it is indeed a privilege for me to have a small part in their endeavors. Rabbi Avrohom Biderman coordinated this project and has kept everything running smoothly. My thanks to Rabbi Shea Brander for his graphic skills in dealing so successfully with the very complicated task of converting my manuscript into this book and Rabbi Eli Kroen for his artistry with the cover. I thank Professor Yaakov Petroff of Jerusalem who spent much time editing, advising and checking the manuscript and

Mr. Shmuel Blitz of the Jerusalem office of Art Scroll for all his help at this end. It has been a pleasure to work with all of them.

I am grateful to Rabbi Moshe Wein of New York for his help in facilitating the publication. Drs James DiPoce and Barry Levitt of New York spent many months studying Nishmat Avraham and preparing a draft translation of the first part of this volume. I used their basic material to work on when I began my translation and thank them for their help. I hope that our correspondence was helpful to them in elucidating various aspects of Medical Halachah.

I pray that this book should also be a merit for the souls of my wife's parents, HaRav Yehoshua Dov ben HaRav Moshe Shimon Turetsky z"l and his wife Frada bat Reb Dovid Friedman z"l, and for her brother HaRav Moshe ben HaRav Yehoshua Dov Turetsky z"l.

And finally, my prayer to Hashem that He should give me the merit to publicly glorify His Name and spread His Torah to my Jewish brethren throughout the world.

Abraham S. Abraham, MD, FRCP
Jerusalem

חשון תשס"א / November 2000

◆§ A Word Of Thanks

I wish to express my sincere thanks to my esteemed colleagues Dr. Robert Matalon and his son, Dr. Albert Matalon, for their encouragement of this project. It is their effort that brought together the Physicians of the Syrian community of Brooklyn, whose generous support has allowed the translation of the Nishmat Avraham to become a reality.

My grateful thanks also to those anonymous donors who helped towards the initial stages of the translation.

I pray that Hashem reward you all for your generosity and bless you and your families with long lives of health and happiness.

To My Colleagues

To you my colleagues, the doctors, nurses and all the other health-care personnel who make up the patient's caregivers:

This book is not meant to be a handbook of answers. Its purpose is to provide you with material for study, preferably together with a Rav. To know what is permitted and what is not permitted in every situation can only come from a Rav and Posek; a man who has had many, many years of intensive study and experience, preceded by and coupled with the fear of God and an implicit and unwavering belief in the words of our Sages and Torah giants. We all have the duty to learn and understand; that does not mean that we have the ability or right to decide on halachic problems involving the life of a patient or, for that matter, our souls.

The Torah cautions us (Deuteronomy 8,17) from believing that it is our power and efforts that bring us success. We should remember this each time we save a patient's life. Not because of our knowledge and experience will a patient live; but because Divine Providence decrees that he should be so ill and because Divine Providence also decrees that he should live. We have to thank Hashem that he gives us the merit and privilege of being His messengers to carry out His Will.

About the Book

This translation is built on the same format as the original Hebrew version: (1) the Shulchan Aruch, (2) its relationship to modern Medical Halachah — the Nishmat Avraham, and (3) the sources on which these Halachot were based. Nevertheless, since the book has been written especially for those who may not necessarily be accustomed to learning in Hebrew, or are not sufficiently versed in the language of our Sages, or who are uninitiated in the intricacies of Halachah, not all the sections of the Shulchan Aruch quoted in the original Hebrew text have been fully translated here. Much thought has been given to what should and what should not be translated, both from the Shulchan Aruch and from the Hebrew Nishmat Avraham; the final decisions were reached after discussion with my teacher, HaRav Yehoshua Neuwirth shlita and with his approval.

Names of authors or their books, and words and phrases requiring explanation appear in the Nishmat Avraham section in italics, and are to be found in the Glossary. There, Hebrew words and phrases are explained and authors' names and dates of death are given, where possible, so as to give the reader an idea of the era in which they lived.

Contents

Siman refers to the _Siman_ of the _Shulchan Aruch_

CHAPTER 5
LAWS OF *BIRCHOT HASHACHAR*

CHAPTER 6
THE LAWS OF BLESSINGS

CHAPTER 7
LAWS OF *KERIYAT SHEMA*

CHAPTER 8
LAWS OF PRAYER

CHAPTER 9
LAWS OF THE PRIESTLY BLESSING

CHAPTER 10
LAWS OF READING THE TORAH

CHAPTER 11
LAWS OF THE SYNAGOGUE

CHAPTER 12
LAWS OF RITUAL HAND WASHING

CHAPTER 13
LAWS REGARDING HOW ONE SHOULD ACT DURING A MEAL

CHAPTER 14
LAWS OF *BIRKAT HAMAZON*

CHAPTER 15
THE LAWS OF THE BLESSING OVER FRUITS

CHAPTER 16
THE LAWS REGARDING THANKSGIVING BLESSINGS

CHAPTER 17
THE LAWS OF BLESSINGS

CHAPTER 18
THE LAWS OF *KERIYAT SHEMA* AT NIGHT AND *MAARIV*

CHAPTER 19
THE LAWS OF *SHABBAT*

CHAPTER 20
THE LAWS OF *ROSH CHODESH*

CHAPTER 21
THE LAWS OF *PESACH*

CHAPTER 22
THE LAWS OF *YOM TOV*

CHAPTER 23
THE LAWS OF *CHOL HAMOED*

CHAPTER 24
THE LAWS OF *TISHAH B'AV* AND OTHER FASTS DAYS

CHAPTER 25
THE FAST DAYS

CHAPTER 26
LAWS CONCERNING *ROSH HASHANAH*

CHAPTER 27
THE LAWS OF *YOM KIPPUR*

CHAPTER 28
THE LAWS OF THE *SUCCAH*

CHAPTER 29
LAWS OF THE *LULAV*

CHAPTER 30
LAWS OF *CHANUKAH*

CHAPTER 31
LAWS OF THE *MEGILLAH*

NISHMAT AVRAHAM

CHAPTER ONE:

Laws of Conduct on Awakening in the Morning

SIMAN 1: LAWS OF RISING IN THE MORNING

§1: A man should be strong like a lion to arise in the morning (A)and serve his Creator – he should awaken the dawn. GLOSS: *At worst, he should not arise after the time that the community prays.*

GLOSS: (B)*"I have set Hashem before me always"*[1] *– this is a fundamental tenet of the Torah and among the attributes of the righteous. The actions and activities of a man alone at home are*

NISHMAT AVRAHAM

SIMAN 1

(A) and serve His creator: The *Mishnah Berurah* states it was for this purpose that man was created. Even if one's impulse entices him saying, in the winter: "How can you arise in the morning? It's so cold." And in the summer: "How can you get up? You still haven't slept enough." One should overcome it and refuse to give in. Rather, one should think: "If I were called to serve a human king, how careful and quick I would be to arise early to get ready to serve him. How much more so should I do so when serving the King of Kings, the Holy One, Blessed be He."[2]

(B) I have set Hashem before me always: The *Teshuvah MeAhavah*[3] interprets this verse as follows: I have always imagined that *Hashem* is opposed to me, whether things seem to be going well for me or not. For example, if things were going well for me and I had wealth and possessions I said to myself: Perhaps *Hashem* considered me a sinner and my good fortune represented the fulfillment of the verse: "And He pays His enemies to their face," immediately in this world, so He may destroy them in the world to come.[4] If things were going badly for me and I was poor and destitute, I feared that my misfortune represented the fulfillment of the words of *Chazal*:[5] A person does not become destitute in this world unless he has already become destitute in his Heavenly accounts. With this attitude, one will create within himself a constant fear of *Hashem* and scrutinize his actions at all times.[6]

Furthermore, continues the *Teshuvah*

1. תהלים טז:ח
2. ס״ק א
3. הקדמתו לחלק ב
4. דברים ז:י
5. סנהדרין קג ע״ב
6. וכן מצאתי באבות דרבי נתן סופ״ט: דבר אחר, אל תתיאש מן הפורענות. כיצד, בזמן שאדם רואה מה שבידו מצליח, אל יאמר בשביל שזכיתי נתן לי המקום

not his actions and activities when in the presence of a great king; nor are his speech and freedom of expression the same within the family circle and to kin like his speech in the presence of the king. How much more so when he bears in mind that the King, The Holy One, Blessed be He, Whose glory fills the entire world, is present and sees his actions at all times; as it is written: "If man hide in hidden places, will I not see him? says the Lord."[7] *He will then immediately feel awe and humility in his fear of Hashem, and be abashed before Him always. And he will not feel embarrassed by anyone who scoffs at him for his service to Hashem, Blessed be He. In private too, and when lying in bed, he should know in Whose presence he is lying. Immediately upon awakening, he should rise with alacrity to serve his Creator, Blessed be He.*

NISHMAT AVRAHAM

MeAhavah: It was for this reason that the *Tur* and the *Shulchan Aruch* called the first volume by the very appropriate name of *Orach Chaim,* the Path of Life. Like a table set in front of *Hashem* where we eat, drink, and behold His greatness, it contains practices and laws that a man should perform and thus merit everlasting life in the World to Come. He will not be like a man who has eyes but does not see and eats without washing his hands and without saying blessings. If only they would learn *Orach Chaim*! It opens your eyes enabling you to see, and no longer be likened to one who is dead. Do not be like those I see who pursue a career, who learn a page of *Gemara* each day and do not even know the laws of *birkat hanehenin.*

The *Tur* himself, in his introduction, states that he called his first book *Orach Chaim,* the Path of Life, because it will protect those who walk in its ways from deadly pitfalls.

If the above is true for one who is healthy, how much more so for one who is ill. Indeed, *Chazal* stated:[8] The Holy One, Blessed be He, said: There is no illness for which a complete cure is not already present. If one wishes to avoid suffering, let him engage in Torah study which is a remedy for the entire body. And they also said:[9] If one has a headache, let him engage in Torah study; if one has a sore throat, an internal disorder, aches in his bones, let him engage in Torah study; if illness pervades his entire body, let him engage in Torah study. And furthermore we have:[10] Rav Chama bar Chanina says: "Great is repentance for it brings healing to the World." Similarly, the *Gemara Nedarim* states:[11] Rav Chiya bar Abba said: "One who is ill will not be cured until all his sins are pardoned. For it is said:[12] 'He Who pardons all your sins, He Who heals all your maladies.' "

מאכל ומשתה בעולם הזה והקרן קיימת לעולם הבא, אלא יאמר אוי לי שמא לא נמצא לי לפניו אלא זכות אחד בלבד, נתן לי מאכל ומשתה בעולם הזה כדי שיאבדני לעולם הבא

7. ירמיה כג:כד

8. תנחומא יתרו ח

9. עירובין נד ע״א

10. יומא פו ע״א

11. נדרים מא ע״א

12. תהלים קג:ג

CHAPTER TWO:

Laws of Washing One's Hands in the Morning

SIMAN 4: LAWS OF WASHING ONE'S HANDS

§13: If one has remained (A)awake all night, it is questionable as to whether he must wash his hands in the morning both in order to pray and to remove *ruach ra'ah* from them. GLOSS: *One should wash them without a blessing.*

§19: (B)One from whom blood has been drawn who does not wash his hands afterwards should be apprehensive for seven days.

NISHMAT AVRAHAM

SIMAN 4

(A) awake all night: Such as a duty doctor or nurse. There are some *acharonim* who disagree with the opinion of the *Rama,* and feel that when one has been awake the entire night a blessing should nevertheless be said upon the ritual hand washing. Other *acharonim* agree with the *Rama's* ruling. However, most agree that if one relieves oneself prior to praying in the morning, a blessing of *al netilat yadayim* (as well as *asher yatzar*) would be required upon washing one's hands. Moreover, these commentators feel that after being awake the entire night one should use the bathroom, wash one's hands and say the blessings of *al netilat yadayim* and *asher yatzar* before the morning prayers, so resolving the doubt.[1] It must be noted that there are *acharonim*[2] who disagree with this and rule that if one has been awake the entire night the blessing of *al netilat yadayim* should not be made. However, the hands should be ritually washed in the morning. After using the bathroom, the blessing of *asher yatzar* is said, with the blessing of *Elokai neshamah* following.

(B) One from whom blood has been drawn: The *Mishnah Berurah* raises the question as to whether a person (i.e. the patient[3]) from whom blood is drawn, using a leech or heated suction cups, is also required to wash his hands. He concludes that it is better to adopt a strict approach and do so.[4]

The *Shulchan Aruch* only discusses the need for a patient to wash his hands when

1. מ״ב ס״ק ל בשם הגהות רעק״א. ועיין בביה״ל ד״ה ויטלם
2. ברכ״י סי׳ מו ס״ק יב, שו״ת רב פעלים ח״ד או״ח סי׳ א, בן איש חי שנה א פ׳ תולדות סע׳ יג, כף החיים סי׳ מו סוס״ק מט וליקוטי קול סיני שבט תשל״א עמ׳ 39 (הגר״ע יוסף שליט״א)
3. ראה כף החיים ס״ק צב
4. ס״ק מח וכ״כ הפמ״ג א״א ס״ק כב

§20: (C)If one washes his face and does not dry it well, the skin will develop cracks or boils; the treatment for this is to wash it often with a lot of beet juice.

NISHMAT AVRAHAM

the bloodletting is being used for treatment. A clinical setting where this might arise is therapeutic phlebotomy for *Polycythemia Vera* or other hyperviscosity syndromes. It is not clear, however, whether there is a need for a patient to wash his hands after he has blood drawn for diagnostic purposes only. The *Leket HaKemach HaChadash*[5] concludes that since there is no definite ruling for such a situation, one should take the strict approach, and wash one's hands regardless of the reason for which the blood was drawn. *Rav Shlomo Zalman Auerbach zt"l* told me that, in his opinion, the patient needs to wash his hands only when the bloodletting is performed for therapeutic purposes, and not as a diagnostic procedure. He reasoned that where practices, such as bloodletting, done in the times of *Chazal* as a *segulah* are concerned, we may today only learn from those instances explicitly discussed in the *Talmud*. As bloodletting in the times of *Chazal* was only performed for therapeutic purposes, the requirement to wash one's hands should be limited to such situations. *Rav Auerbach zt"l* also felt that a blood donor need not wash his hands, for it is possible that since he is not donating blood for his own use, but rather is assisting in the treatment of another, he is performing a *mitzvah*, and therefore he will not come to any harm.[6]

(C) If one washes: It is generally accepted that it is prohibited to make use of medical treatments discussed in the *Talmud.*[7] There are various explanations given for this prohibition:

i) The natural order of the world has changed since the times of *Chazal*, so that the treatments offered in the *Talmud* are not effective nowadays.[8]

ii) It is impossible for us to correctly identify the exact nature of the medications mentioned; and their doses and method of usage are not specified.[9]

iii) It is impossible for one to fully grasp the nature of the medical treatment offered by *Chazal*. Therefore, if attempts are made to use them and they fail to achieve the desired results, one may come to deride the words of *Chazal*.[10] For this reason also, it is prohibited to make use of these medical practices.[11]

iv) Other reasons are also given for this prohibition,[12] but *Rav Shlomo Zalman Auerbach zt"l* wrote to me[13] that the explanations given here for not using the medical knowledge of *Chazal* are the main ones.

---

5. ס״ק פא

6. ראה קהלת ח,ה

7. עיין בשדי חמד מערכת הרי״ש כלל נד

8. תוס׳ מו״ק יא ע״א ד״ה כוורא, ע״ז כד ע״ב ד״ה פרה, חולין מז ע״א ד״ה כל, יש״ש חולין פ״ח סי׳ יב. ועיין בכסף משנה פ״ד מהל׳ דעות הי״ח, החיד״א בברית עולם על ספר חסידים סי׳ תעז. ועיין גם בתפא״י בועז שבת פי״ט ס״ק א. או״ח סי׳ שלא סע׳ ט ואהע״ז סי׳ קנו סע׳ ד בהגה, מג״א סי׳ קעג ס״ק א וסי׳ קעט ס״ק ח, חזו״א נשים סי׳ כז ס״ק ג ויו״ד סי׳ ה ס״ק ג

9. שו״ת חות יאיר סי׳ רלד

10. כף החיים (פאלאג״י) סע׳ נ חי׳ רעק״א יו״ד סי׳ שלו ס״ק א,

11. יש״ש חולין פ״ח סי׳ יב

12. אוצר הגאונים חלק התשובות גיטין סח ע״ב סי׳ שעו. ועיין במאירי נדה יז ע״ב ד״ה זהו. רבינו אברהם בן הרמב״ם במאמר על אודות דרשות חז״ל, מודפס בריש עיון יעקב ד״ה דע כי אתה חייב לדעת

13. לב אברהם ח״ב עמ׳ יט

SIMAN 7: THE LAW TO RECITE THE BLESSING *ASHER YATZAR* AFTER VOIDING

§1: (A)After one has used the lavatory, he should recite the

NISHMAT AVRAHAM

SIMAN 7

(A) After one has used the lavatory: The blessing *asher yatzar* is a blessing of praise to *Hashem* for being able to relieve oneself. The *Elef Lecha Shlomo*[1] was asked if a person who is incontinent of urine is required to recite the blessing *asher yatzar* after each episode of incontinence. Perhaps, since such a person does not have full control over his bodily functions, it would be considered inappropriate to offer praise to *Hashem.* His conclusion was that the blessing *asher yatzar* is a general blessing for the wisdom with which *Hashem* created the human body, affording one the ability to relieve oneself. Therefore, even if one does suffer from urinary incontinence, this would not preclude giving praise to *Hashem* regarding the greatness of the creation of the human body, and a blessing should be recited.

There are a number of *halachic* issues that arise regarding the patient with a urinary catheter. The *Har Tzvi*[2] feels that although such a patient's urine exits the body via a foreign construct, this would not constitute a *chatzitzah* that would prevent reciting the blessing. Such a patient is required to recite the *asher yatzar* blessing thanking *Hashem* for allowing his catheter to function properly, since there are times when the catheter tubing may become obstructed and cause problems.[3]

The proper time to recite the *asher yatzar* blessing might depend on the kind of catheter being used. When the patient can control the flow of urine from the catheter (i.e. by means of a stopcock), the blessing must be made each time the patient voids. However, the catheter may be attached to a bag where there is a constant flow of urine into the bag. The patient should then recite the *asher yatzar* blessing along with the morning blessings only, and bear in mind to exempt himself from saying the blessing for the rest of the day.[4] The *Tzitz Eliezer*[5] qualifies that a person with such a catheter should not say the *asher yatzar* blessing while there is urine actively flowing in the tubing, but should wait until the flow has stopped. The same *halachot* would apply to a person with a suprapubic catheter.[6] (See *Siman* 76:5 regarding the patient with a urinary catheter, praying and studying Torah.)

When one gives a urine sample for analysis, a blessing of *asher yatzar* is required.[7]

If one takes a laxative or other compound which causes diarrhea, when should he recite the blessing of *asher yatzar*? Some feel that the blessing should not be recited until he is certain that the

1. או"ח סי' ב
2. או"ח ח"א סי' ו
3. וכן כתב הציץ אליעזר ח"ח סי' א סע' ג
4. לקח הקמח החדש ס"ק ב*. וכן שמעתי מהגרש"ז אויערבאך זצ"ל
5. ח"ח סי' א
6. שם
7. שו"ת מנחת יצחק ח"ו סי' לח אות ג

blessing (B)*asher yatzar* and not *al netilat yadayim,* even if one wants to study Torah or pray immediately afterwards. GLOSS: *Even if urine dirtied his hands, one should not recite al netilat yadayim after washing them.*

NISHMAT AVRAHAM

effects of the laxative have subsided.[8] However, others feel that the blessing should be recited after each bowel movement.[9] The accepted custom follows the latter opinion; however, when one is suffering from severe diarrhea and constantly feels the urge to defecate, it is prohibited to recite the *asher yatzar* blessing.[10] (See *Siman* 78 regarding prayer and *Siman* 92 regarding Torah study. For a patient with an *ileostomy* or *colostomy,* see *Siman* 76:5 regarding praying and *Siman* 301:13 regarding carrying the attached bag outdoors on the Sabbath.)

(B) *asher yatzar*: The *Midrash*[11] says: Fortunate are you Israel who were given a *mitzvah* for every part of your body. For man has 248 parts in his body. That is why we say each day, "Blessed are You, Hashem, our Lord, King of the universe, Who has made man with wisdom, and created in him many openings and many cavities." The numerical value of the letters that make up the words *chalulim chalulim* (many cavities) is 248 – the number of parts in the human body.

8. שו״ת הלכות קטנות ח״א סי׳ פו, שו״ע הרב סע׳ ו, קיצור שו״ע סי׳ ד סע׳ ו

9. היד אהרן מובא בבאר היטב, ברכ״י ס״ק ב, שע״ת ס״ק א

10. מ״ב ס״ק ב בשם השע״ת ס״ק א

11. תנחומא פ׳ שמיני ח, פסוק זאת החיה. וראה ביחזקאל כח:יג ותרגום שם

CHAPTER THREE:

Laws of Tzitzit

SIMAN 24: WEARING *TZITZIT* AND THEIR REWARD

§4: There are those who look at the *tzitzit* when they reach the phrase "and you shall see them" (in the third paragraph of the *Shema*) and place them (A)over the eyes. This is a fine custom and shows love for the *mitzvah*.

GLOSS: *There are also a few who kiss the tzitzit when they look at them, because of their love for the mitzvah.*

NISHMAT AVRAHAM

SIMAN 24

(A) over the eyes: In the *parshah* of *tzitzit* in the Torah we find: "And it shall be *tzitzit* for you and you shall *see* it and remember all the commandments of *Hashem* and perform them."[1] Though the verse speaks of seeing the *tzitzit*, the *Mishnah Berurah* states that a blind person should nevertheless only hold the *tzitzit* in his hand during the reading of the *Shema*, because others can see them as they are being held. But he should not pass the *tzitzit* over his eyes, as this might seem to make a mockery of the custom.[2] In contrast to this ruling of the *Mishnah Berurah*, the *Kaf HaChaim*[3] states that there is no difference between one who can see and one who is blind with regard to this custom since it is merely symbolic. (See *Siman* 38H for the obligation to wear *tzitzit* when one is blind.)

1. במדבר טו:לט
2. ס״ק ז. וכ״כ השו״ת שבות יעקב ח״ב סי׳ לח
3. ס״ק טז בשם שער הכוונות וסידור הרש״ש

CHAPTER FOUR:

Laws of Tefillin

SIMAN 27: LAWS OF *TEFILLIN;* WHERE AND HOW THEY SHOULD BE WORN

§1: The *tefillin shel yad* should be placed on the left biceps which is the bulging muscle between the elbow and the armpit. It should be tilted a little toward the side of the body so that when the arm is extended downwards, the tefillin will be facing the heart to fulfill the phrase, "Let these words be (A)upon your heart."

GLOSS: *One must place the tefillin shel yad at the end of the bone nearest the elbow and not on the half closest to the armpit. (B)A person who has no hand, but has an upper arm, should place tefillin without a blessing. (Tosafot, Perek HaKometz, wrote that such a person is obligated to wear tefillin but the Or Zarua wrote that he is exempt.)*

NISHMAT AVRAHAM

SIMAN 27

(A) upon your heart: Even though the *tefillin shel yad* should face the heart, a person who has dextrocardia (born with his heart in the right side of the chest) should still wear the *tefillin* on the left arm. The fact that the *tefillin shel yad* will not face the heart does not preclude this person from wearing *tefillin* on his left arm. The basis for this is the ruling that a person who is left-handed wears *tefillin* on the right arm, even though the *tefillin* does not face his heart. Furthermore, the *halachah* that the *tefillin shel yad* belongs on the "weaker arm" is based on an exegetic interpretation of the word "your hand" and this takes precedence over having the *tefillin* near the heart.[1] (For laws of *tefillin* pertaining to the person who is left-handed, see *Shulchan Aruch, Siman.* 27:6 and the *Mishnah Berurah.*)

(B) A person who has no hand:

i) If one's left arm has been amputated but the biceps muscle is still present, there are those who rule that he is still obligated to place the *tefillin* on the left arm with a blessing.[2] Others, however, rule that he is completely exempt from

1. שו״ת דובב מישרים ח״ב סי׳ מו, יסודי ישורון ח״א עמ׳ פג

2. תוס׳ מנחות לז ע״א ד״ה קיבורת. ועיין במחצית השקל ס״ק ג וביה״ל ד״ה בלא

NISHMAT AVRAHAM

wearing *tefillin.*[3] Because of this difference of opinion, he should put on *tefillin shel yad* without a blessing.[4] The *Magen Avraham*[5] believes that he should put on *tefillin shel yad* on the right arm without a blessing. When he puts on the *tefillin shel rosh* he does say a blessing. However, *Ashkenazim* and *Sephardim* do not follow the same custom. An *Ashkenazi* says two blessings on the *tefillin shel rosh* – the blessing of *lehani'ach tefillin* and *al mitzvat tefillin.*[6] A *Sephardi* says the blessing *al mitzvat tefillin* only.[7]

ii) If he has part of the left forearm, everyone agrees that he should put on *tefillin* on the left arm with a blessing.[8]

iii) If the left arm was amputated so that no part of the biceps muscle remains, some completely exempt him from wearing *tefillin* even on the right arm.[9] Others rule that he should wear the *tefillin shel yad* on the right arm and only make the blessing upon putting on the *tefillin shel rosh*[10] (see above, **i).**

iv) In contrast to an amputee, if one was born without any part of the left arm, he should wear the *tefillin shel yad* on the right arm, saying the blessing only upon putting on the *tefillin shel rosh* (see above, **i).**[11]

v) If one's third finger of the left hand was amputated, he should wear the *tefillin shel yad* in the regular fashion and wrap the strap three times around the index finger instead.[12]

vi) Although there is an opinion[13] that when one lacks a right arm he is exempt from wearing *tefillin shel yad,* the *Mishnah Berurah* rules that he is obligated to wear it, and he asks others for assistance in putting it on.[14] (See below as to whether a woman may assist him.)

vii) If the right hand was amputated but the forearm remains, there is an opinion that the right arm has now become his "weaker arm."[15] The *Mishnah Berurah*[16] definitively rules that, in such a case, one should wear the *tefillin* on the right arm.

In a situation where one's right arm remains dominant but lacks fingers, one should wear the *tefillin* on the left arm.[17] There is an opinion[18] that he should wear the *tefillin* on the right arm during prayer services in *shul,* making the blessing upon putting on the *tefillin shel rosh* (see above, **i)** and, upon returning home, should again put on *tefillin,* placing the *tefillin shel yad* on the left arm without a blessing.

When the later *halachic* authorities[19] discuss the problem of one's hand "drying up," they appear to be describing a situation with atrophy of the arm which *halachically* is similar to a paralyzed arm (see below).

One whose left arm is paralyzed is obligated to wear the *tefillin* on the left arm in the usual fashion.[20] Notwithstanding, the *Chesed LeAvraham Teomim*[21] makes a distinction between a person who is permanently paralyzed and one who will

---

3. אור זרוע הל׳ תפילין סי׳ תקעז
4. סע׳ א ברמ״א. ועיין בביה״ל ד״ה בלא
5. ס״ק ג בפי׳ התוס׳
6. רמ״א סי׳ כו סע׳ ב
7. שו״ע שם
8. מ״ב ס״ק ה
9. שו״ת רמ״א סי׳ קכב, ב״ח, א״ר, הגר״א ס״ק ו ושו״ת פנים מאירות ח״ג סי׳ יא
10. שו״ת שבות יעקב ח״א סי׳ ג, שו״ת שאגת אריה סי׳ לז, מ״ב ס״ק ו ושעה״צ ס״ק ז וכף החיים ס״ק ו
11. שו״ת שבות יעקב שם
12. שו״ת חלקת יעקב ח״ג סי׳ קג
13. שו״ת בשמים ראש סי׳ ק
14. מ״ב סוס״ק ו
15. פמ״ג סי׳ תרנא א״א ס״ק י
16. ס״ק כב וביה״ל ד״ה ואיטר יד. ומה שפסק בס׳ ו שמניח בשמאלו, צ״ל שמדובר במי שאין לו קיבורת – כתב לי הגרא״י וולדיברג שליט״א וכן שמעתי ממו״ר הגרי״י נויבירט שליט״א
17. שו״ת צמח צדק החדש או״ח סי׳ ה
18. ר׳ מאיר מלובלין בשו״ת ארץ צבי סי׳ ח, מובא בלקט הקמח החדש ס״ק יז*
19. שו״ת אבני נזר סי׳ א, שו״ת אג״מ או״ח ח״א סי׳ ח, שו״ת אמרי יושר ח״ב סי׳ יד
20. שו״ת אג״מ שם
21. סי׳ ג

NISHMAT AVRAHAM

recover from the paralysis. A patient with permanent paralysis of the left arm should put on (with help) *tefillin shel yad* on the right arm without a blessing (and say the blessing upon putting on *tefillin shel rosh* as stated above, paragraph **i**). After praying, the person should put on *tefillin shel yad* on the left arm, also without saying a blessing. If the patient's paralysis of the left arm is likely to be temporary, even though the arm at the moment is without use, he is obligated to wear the *tefillin shel yad* on the left arm with a blessing. The *Beit Shlomo,*[22] however, rules that even a person with permanent paralysis is not considered "lacking the limb" and he should put on the *tefillin shel yad* on the left arm in the usual fashion.

One whose right arm is paralyzed is obligated to wear *tefillin.* However, there is a dispute regarding the arm on which the *tefillin* should be placed. The *Mishnah Berurah,*[23] quoting the *Dagul MeRevavah,* states that he should wear the *tefillin shel yad* on the right arm since it has the *halachic* status of the "weaker arm." In contrast, the *Imrei Yosher*[24] states that regardless of whether one will recover the use of the right arm or not, *tefillin* should be placed on the left arm in the usual fashion. He clarifies the position of the *Dagul MeRevavah* as follows: A man with a paralyzed right arm attains the *halachic* status of one who is "left-handed" only when he masters the use of his left hand so skillfully that upon regaining the use of his right, he still prefers to continue using his left. It is for such a one that the *Dagul MeRevavah* stated that he should continue putting on the *tefillin* on the right arm. *Rav Shlomo Zalman Auerbach zt"l* wrote[25] that even if the right arm is so infirm and weak that he must use his left, nevertheless he should continue wearing the *tefillin shel yad* on the left arm so long as the doctors believe he will regain the use of his right arm. However, if they think that he will never recover the use of his right arm, it becomes his "weaker arm" with regard to *tefillin.* In such an instance, he should don the *tefillin shel yad* on his right arm.

When both arms are paretic, *tefillin shel yad* should be placed on the left arm with the appropriate blessing.[26] *Rav Yehoshua Neuwirth shlita* told me that this was not to be compared with the ruling of the *Magen Avraham* (above, **i**) that a blessing is not said. In that situation, there is a doubt as to which hand the *tefillin* should be put on, whereas here, since both arms are paretic, the *tefillin* are certainly put on the left arm.

A patient with a paretic dominant arm who dons *tefillin* on his other arm (as above), will need assistance in putting on *tefillin.* If there is no man present to help him, a woman may do so.[27] However, there is a disagreement amongst the *poskim* with respect to saying the blessings.[28] These variant views depend on whether or not an assistant in a *mitzvah* must have the same level of obligation to perform the *mitzvah* as the one who is being assisted. Therefore, since women are not obligated to wear *tefillin,* it may be inappropriate for the man to say the blessing on the *tefillin* when a woman puts them on him.[29] The *Mishnah Berurah*[30] rules that it is better

22. אהע״ז סי׳ קמח, מובא בלקט הקמח החדש ס״ק ט

23. ס״ק כב

24. ח״ב סי׳ יד

25. לב אברהם ח״א עמ׳ טו

26. לקט הקמח החדש ס״ק יב

27. שו״ת מהר״ם שיק או״ח סי׳ טו, שו״ת מהר״י אסאד או״ח סי׳ יט, דעת תורה סי׳ כז סע׳ ז וסי׳ לט סע׳ ב, שו״ת יד הלוי או״ח ח״ב סי׳ א, שו״ת ציץ אליעזר חי״ג סי׳ ז

28. המהר״ם שיק פוסק שיברך ולעומת זאת היד הלוי כותב שלא יברך

29. תוס׳ גיטין מה ע״ב ד״ה כל. וכן דעת המג״א סי׳ יד ס״ק ג

30. סי׳ יד סע׳ א ביה״ל ד״ה להצריך וסי׳ תרמט ס״ק יד. ולכאורה אפשר היה להביא ראיה מהא דע״ז לט ע״א באשת חבר שהיתה קושרת לו תפילין על ידו.

§4: Nothing should come between the *tefillin* and the skin of the wearer, both with respect to (C)the *shel yad* and (D)the *shel rosh.*

NISHMAT AVRAHAM

to have a man assist in putting on the *tefillin;* however, if there is no alternative, he may say the blessing. [31] *Rav Neuwirth shlita* told me that although the *Mishnah Berurah* discusses the problem of a woman preparing the object of a *mitzvah,* such as tying on the fringes to a *tallit* or tying together the *lulav* to the myrtle and willow branches for a man, her actually doing the act of a *mitzvah* for him is more problematic.

(C) the *shel yad*: The *Mishnah Berurah,* [32] based on a number of sources, concludes that one may place the strap of the *tefillin* over bandages which are on one's upper arm and say the blessing, if the *bayit* (the box containing the parchments of the *tefillin*) rests directly on the bare skin (regarding the bandaged head, see below). However, the *Mishnah Berurah* urges that he should make certain that the *tefillin* are covered (with his sleeve or *tallit*), in order to fulfill the commandment: "They should be a symbol for you and not for others."[33]

If the entire area of the biceps is bandaged, one may place the *tefillin* on the bandage, but since the bandage intervenes between the *bayit* of the *tefillin* and the arm (and not just the straps), he cannot say the appropriate blessing (regarding the blessing on the *shel rosh,* see below). Here again, as above, the *tefillin* should be covered. If there remains an area on the biceps on which the *bayit* of the *tefillin* can be placed directly onto the skin, the *tefillin* should be placed there with the blessing.[34] In all such instances, it is forbidden to place the *tefillin* on top of the shirt-sleeve instead of over the bandage.[35] Thus, if one has a cast on the arm where he normally wears *tefillin,* he puts on the *tefillin* on the arm with the cast and not on the other arm.[36] If the *bayit* of the *tefillin* rests on the arm, he says the blessing.[37] If, however, the *bayit* does not come in contact with the upper arm, but rests on the cast, he should not say the blessing.

Often, patients in a hospital have an intravenous line inserted in their arm. Even if such a device does not allow one to wrap the strap of the *tefillin* around the forearm seven times as is customary, he should nevertheless put on *tefillin* with a blessing. He wraps the strap around the upper arm as usual, and then passes it over to the middle finger, without wrapping it around his forearm.[38] If, for any reason, he cannot wrap the strap around the middle, or any other finger, he should still place the *tefillin* on the upper arm as usual, and say the blessing.[39]

(D) the *shel rosh*: The *Mishnah Berurah*[40] writes in the name of the *Magen Avraham* and the *Chayei Adam,* [41] that when the straps of the *tefillin shel rosh* lie

---

אולם עיין בתוס׳ מנחות לה ע״ב ד״ה משעת, ברא״ש פ״א דחולין סי׳ יב ובהגהות מיימוניות הל׳ ציצית פ״א ס״ק ט דהיתה רק מסייעת לו. ועיין ברא״ש הל׳ תפילין סי׳ יג בשינוי גירסא

31. שמעתי ממו״ר הגרי״י נויבירט שליט״א

32. ס״ק טז. חיי אדם כלל יד סע׳ יד

33. מנחות לז ע״ב. חיי אדם שם. וע״ע ברמ״א בסוף הסימן ובמ״ב ס״ק מז

34. שעה״צ ס״ק כא

35. מ״ב ס״ק יח

36. שו״ת חלקת יעקב ח״ב סי׳ מג, שו״ת מנחת יצחק ח״ב סי׳ מו

37. מהא דמג״א ס״ק ו ו־ח

38. מהא דסע׳ ח כאן

39. שמעתי ממו״ר הגרי״י נויבירט שליט״א

40. ס״ק טז

41. כלל יד סע׳ יד

GLOSS: *This is specifically so as far as the tefillin are concerned; however, one need not be careful about the straps.*

§7: If the (E)area where the *tefillin* are placed is affected, he should nevertheless wear them since there is enough room on the arm to wear two *tefillin*. This is because the whole of the lower half of the upper arm down (F)to the elbow is considered appropriate for putting on *tefillin*.

NISHMAT AVRAHAM

on a bandage but the *bayit* lies directly on the head, one may place the straps on top of the bandage and say the blessing. However, if the *bayit* will rest on the bandage and not directly on the head, he should nevertheless don the *tefillin shel rosh* but without a blessing (see above, **Bi**).

If one wears a toupee or a wig, since such a hairpiece is easily removable, and is indeed commonly removed at various times throughout the day, it is not considered part of one's body. Therefore, it constitutes an intervention (*chatzitzah*) between one's head and the *tefillin*. Though the *halachah* does not require him to remove a hairpiece in *shul,* since this can be embarrassing, nevertheless, when putting on the *tefillin shel rosh* in *shul,* he should not say the blessing (see above, **Bi**). Instead, when he comes home, he should remove the hairpiece and put on *tefillin* again, this time saying the blessing on the *tefillin shel rosh* if he is an *Ashkenazi*.[42] If, however, by the time he would return home it would be too late to say the *Shema,* he should wear them first at home with the blessing (without his hairpiece), and only then put on his hairpiece under the *tefillin* before going to *shul*.[43]

There is an interesting question in the *poskim* regarding Siamese twins who are joined at the head. The *Shevut Yaakov*[44] felt that since each twin is considered a separate being, capable of performing cognitive and physical tasks independently, they are to be considered two distinct individuals, each of whom is obligated to put on *tefillin* on his respective head.

(E) area where the *tefillin*: There is a dispute among the *poskim* whether or not one may place the *tefillin* on the upper half of the biceps muscle or only on its lower half.[45] Although the latter is the generally accepted view, if one has an affliction on the lower half of the biceps muscle, he may place the *tefillin* on the upper half.[46] In such a situation, most authorities feel that the blessing should be said, although there are others who disagree.[47] If one has a large, very painful wound on the arm, and it is too uncomfortable to don *tefillin,* even though there is room, he is exempt from putting on the *tefillin shel yad* and is only obligated to wear the *tefillin shel rosh*.[48]

(F) to the elbow: The *Mishnah Berurah*[49] explains that the *Shulchan Aruch* means the lower half of the biceps muscle. However, all *halachic* authorities agree that the area of the arm between the lower end of the biceps and the elbow is not suit-

42. אג"מ או"ח ח"ד סי' מ סע' יח
43. שמעתי ממו"ר הגרי"י נויבירט שליט"א
44. ח"א סי' ד וראה במנחות לז ע"א, טור יו"ד סי' שה ובית הלל שם בריש הסימן ושו"ת הלכות קטנות סי' רמה. וע"ע באור זרוע הל' אבלות סוסי' תכד
45. מ"ב ס"ק כט. ועיין בסע' א ביה"ל ד"ה בראש
46. מ"ב ס"ק ד, בן איש חי שנה א פ' חיי שרה סע' ו
47. ערוה"ש סע' ד משמע שיברך ואולי כן הוא גם דעת המ"ב. אולם שמעתי מהגרי"ע יוסף שליט"א שלא יברך. ועיין בשו"ת יביע אומר ח"א סי' ג אות כ ו־כא
48. מ"ב ס"ק כט
49. מ"ב שם

SIMAN 37: WHEN SHOULD ONE PUT ON *TEFILLIN*

§2: The mitzvah is to wear *tefillin* all day. However, one requires a *guf naki,* that is, he should not flatulate while wearing them; and they should be constantly on his mind. Since most people cannot be so careful, the custom is not to wear *tefillin* all day. However, one should (A)wear *tefillin* (B)when he says the *Shema* and *Shemoneh Esrei.*

SIMAN 38: WHO IS OBLIGATED TO WEAR *TEFILLIN* AND WHO IS EXEMPT

§1: (A)One who has diarrhea (B)is exempt from wearing *tefillin.*
GLOSS: *Even if at the time he is not experiencing (C)discomfort.*

NISHMAT AVRAHAM

able for wearing the *tefillin,* and should one put it there, he has not fulfilled the obligation to put on *tefillin.*[50]

SIMAN 37

(A) wear *tefillin*: Although it is forbidden to wear *tefillin* when one must flatulate or when his attention wanders from them, it is assumed that he can control himself for the short time needed for these two essential prayers.[1]

(B) when he says: If for some reason he was unable to put on *tefillin* at the proper time for saying the *Shema* or *Shemoneh Esrei,* either because he did not have *tefillin,* or was sick at the time (i.e. with severe diarrhea), he is obligated to put them on later in the day when he can do so. For any time of the daylight hours is suitable for putting on *tefillin,* and he must not let a weekday go by without fulfilling the *mitzvah* of *tefillin.*[2]

SIMAN 38

(A) One who has diarrhea: Just as one suffering from a naturally occurring diarrhea is exempt from wearing *tefillin,* since it is assumed that he cannot maintain a *guf naki,* so, too, one who takes a laxative is exempt.[1] *Rav Shlomo Zalman Auerbach zt"l* wrote to me that only if he already feels the effects of the medication and suspects that he will not be able to withhold himself for 72 minutes[2] should he desist from putting on *tefillin.* However, if he does not yet feel the need to defecate, he must put on *tefillin.*

(B) is exempt: He is exempt because he cannot maintain the required *guf naki* while wearing *tefillin.*[3]

(C) discomfort: One should not be too exacting to put on *tefillin* in these circum-

50. מ״ב ס״ק ד ו־כט
1. מ״ב ס״ק ה
2. מ״ב ס״ק ו

1. מ״ב ס״ק א
2. סי׳ צב סע׳ א ומ״ב ס״ק ד
3. מ״ב ס״ק ב

However, (D)ill people in general (but not suffering from diarrhea) who are uncomfortable because of their sickness, and therefore cannot concentrate well on the tefillin, are exempt; otherwise they must put on tefillin.

§2: If one is certain that he will not be able to (E)pray without flatulating, it is better to allow the set time for praying to pass, rather than pray without a *guf naki* (see *Siman* 80). However, if he feels that he will be able to maintain a *guf naki* while reciting the *Shema,* he should put on *tefillin* between the blessing of *ahava* and the *Shema* and say the appropriate blessing on the *tefillin.*

§8: Those who write *tefillin* and *mezuzot,* (F)those who sell them, and all those who are involved in "sacred" tasks are exempt from wearing *tefillin* the whole day, except at the time of *Keriyat Shema* and *Shemoneh Esrei.*

NISHMAT AVRAHAM

stances, except for saying the *Shema* and the *Shemoneh Esrei* and then only if he is certain that he will maintain a *guf naki.*[4]

(D) ill people in general: See § 9 below.

(E) pray: When one prays the *Shemoneh Esrei,* he should consider himself to be standing before the King.[5] If he knows that he will be unable to prevent himself from flatulating during this time, and will have to pause until the odor dissipates, he should not start the *Shemoneh Esrei* – even if this means that the set time for reciting the prayer will pass. On the other hand, he may say the *Shema* with its blessings, for when he says the *Shema* it is not as if he stands before the King. However, though one normally recites the *Shema* in the morning while wearing *tefillin,* he should, in this situation, recite the *Shema* without wearing them.[6]

It is improper to flatulate in particular when the *tefillin shel rosh* is still on his head, and he must consider carefully if he will be able to avoid flatulating while wearing it. If he feels that he will be able to remove the *tefillin shel rosh* before flatulating, he should put on *tefillin,* even though he will only have time to take the *tefillin shel rosh* off – and not the *tefillin shel yad* – before flatulating.[7] The emphasis is on the *tefillin shel rosh* because it has the letter *"Shin"* on the *bayit,* representing the Name of *Hashem.*[8] He can, also, easily cover the *shel yad* with his sleeve or *tallit.*[9] However, the *Pri Megadim*[10] is unsure of this ruling.

(F) those who sell them: The general rule is that while one is occupied with a *mitzvah,* he is exempt from performing other *mitzvot.*[11] This is the basis of the

4. ראה סע׳ ב ומ״ב ס״ק ד
5. סי׳ צא מ״ב ס״ק א
6. מ״ב ס״ק ז
7. מג״א ס״ק ב
8. אבל דל״ת ויו״ד שברצועות לא חשיבי כמ״ש התוס׳ שבת סב ע״א ד״ה שי״ן – מחצית השקל ס״ק ב
9. מחצית השקל שם
10. מובא במ״ב ס״ק ט
11. ראה סוכה כה ע״א

GLOSS: *If their work must be done, even at the time of Keriyat Shema and Shemoneh Esrei, they are exempt from reciting the Shema and Shemoneh Esrei and from wearing tefillin. This is because when one is involved in performing a mitzvah, he is exempt from performing another simultaneously, if it will be difficult for him to do so. However, when both mitzvot can be done at the same time without any difficulty, then both should be performed.*

NISHMAT AVRAHAM

halachah stated here by the *Shulchan Aruch*. However, there is an exception to this rule. Sometimes one must forgo the *mitzvah* with which he is currently involved and perform the other *mitzvah*. This happens when the second *mitzvah* is transient and must be performed within a limited time. The individuals discussed in this *halachah* are currently involved with the *mitzvot* of writing *tefillin* and *mezuzot*, and are exempt from wearing *tefillin* the entire day, which was the custom in the times of *Chazal*. However, since there are set, limited, times for the *mitzvot* of reciting the *Shema* and *Shemoneh Esrei*, they must forgo the *mitzvah* at hand in order to perform these *mitzvot* in their proper time and manner. Nevertheless, when the *mitzvah* with which one is presently involved must be performed immediately without any delay, the *Rama* says he may forgo the performance of even a transient *mitzvah*.

There is a discussion among the *acharonim* as to the guidelines for this *halachah*. The *Magen Avraham*[12] feels that only if a man's intentions are purely directed to the performance of the *mitzvah* at hand can he be considered occupied with a *mitzvah*. Then he would be exempt from performing another *mitzvah*. However, if he began a *mitzvah* with other motives in mind, then he would not be exempted from performing a different *mitzvah* that arises. Thus, if the seller of *tefillin* does not have it in mind that he is providing someone with the opportunity to perform the *mitzvah* of *tefillin*, but is rather only interested in selling them in order to make a profit, then according to the *Magen Avraham* such a seller would be obligated to perform another *mitzvah* which arises. The *Biur Halachah*[13] qualifies the opinion of the *Magen Avraham*. He says that if he had both the intention to perform the *mitzvah* and another motive in mind while performing the *mitzvah*, he would be exempt from another *mitzvah*. Besides, there are *mitzvot* such as the writing of *tefillin* or *mezuzot* which are done over a period of time. In such instances, the *Biur Halachah* thinks that although he may have had making money in mind by writing a pair of *tefillin* when he started, this is irrelevant. In the course of his work he will certainly be thinking and concentrating on the actual writing rather than on the profit.

Based on this opinion of the *Biur Halachah, Rav Yitzchak Zilberstein shlita* derived a *halachah* regarding health-care personnel. He states that although people may enter the medical profession solely for the purpose of earning a livelihood, this cannot define their intentions for the rest of their professional career. Everyone involved in the medical profession is occupied with a *mitzvah*. Certainly at the time that he is involved in patient care, he is only aware of the task at hand and is not motivated by the eventual financial reward. Therefore, since a doctor at work is

12. מובא במ״ב ס״ק כד

13. ד״ה הם

§9: (G)One who is uncomfortable or one whose mind is not in a settled ordered state is exempt from wearing *tefillin* since he is not allowed to remove his attention from them.

§13: An excommunicated person and (H)a person who has *tzara'at* are prohibited from wearing *tefillin*.

NISHMAT AVRAHAM

constantly occupied with a *mitzvah,* he is exempt from other *mitzvot* that may arise while he is working.

Rav Shlomo Zalman Auerbach zt"l wrote to me qualifying the opinion of *Rav Zilberstein*. He wrote that only if a doctor is involved in an activity that must be performed immediately does he have the status of "one involved in a *mitzvah.*" In such a situation it would be forbidden for him to stop in order to recite the *Shema* or the *Shemoneh Esrei*. If, however, he did stop, it is possible that he has not fulfilled his obligation of *Shema* or *Shemoneh Esrei* since their recitation when he is actively involved in urgent patient care is a transgression. However, if the doctor's present activities are not pressing and can be delayed, he is obligated to stop whatever he is doing to recite the *Shema* and put on *tefillin* before returning to his work, unless doing so will be troublesome.[14]

(G) One who is uncomfortable: The general words of the *Shulchan Aruch* imply that even if he suffers minor discomforts (if he is cold[15] or achy[16]), he would be exempt from putting on *tefillin*. This *halachah* does not apply in our days because we are not capable of the requisite concentration anyway.[17]

One who is preoccupied with an important issue is not necessarily exempt from wearing *tefillin* and he must, if possible, try to clear his mind from anxiety and don them.[18] The *Leket HaKemach HaChadash*[19] discusses the instance of a father who was very preoccupied with his only daughter's grave medical condition which required surgery. Although he was suffering greatly and thought he would be unable to concentrate properly while wearing *tefillin,* the *responsum* concludes that even here, he would be obligated to don *tefillin*. The *Levush*[20] and the *Pri Megadim*[21] write that since one can fulfill one's obligation to wear *tefillin* even if they are worn for only a short time, he must do so since he can certainly concentrate on them for this short period. This leads the *Orchot Chaim*[22] to wonder why one who suffers from diarrhea or one who feels that he cannot concentrate properly, is not obligated to put on *tefillin* for a moment, thereby fulfilling his obligation. *Rav Neuwirth shlita* wrote to me that with regard to the person with diarrhea, the issue is not whether he has difficulty concentrating, but rather that he cannot maintain a *guf naki*. Since this possibility always exists, it is forbidden for him to don *tefillin* even for a minute.

(H) a person who has *tzara'at*: It is prohibited to erase or cause any disrespect

14. ואמנם יל״ע מסי׳ ע מ״ב ס״ק יח וסי׳ תעה שעה״צ ס״ק לט, אך י״ל שכאן מדובר בדבר ״נחוץ עכשיו״ כפי שכתב הרב זצ״ל
15. מג״א ס״ק יא ומ״ב ס״ק ל
16. ערוה״ש סע׳ יד
17. מקור חיים לבעל החות יאיר. וראה גם בערוה״ש כאן סע׳ יח שכותב ומימינו לא שמענו לפטור עצמו מן התפילין מפני זה
18. מג״א ס״ק יב, שו״ע הרב סע׳ ח, ערוה״ש שם
19. ס״ק כד
20. סי׳ לז סע׳ ב
21. סי׳ לז א״א ס״ק ב
22. סי׳ לח ס״ק א

NISHMAT AVRAHAM

to the written Name of *Hashem.*[23] When a Jewish patient requires isolation because of an infectious disease, hospital policy may demand that any object which came into contact with the patient be destroyed prior to his discharge. Many *acharonim* were asked whether such a patient could bring his *tefillin* into the isolation room. Since the *tefillin* which contain the Name of *Hashem* would later be destroyed by the hospital authorities, perhaps he should be prohibited from bringing them into the isolation room? When the *Gaon from Tshubin*[24] was asked this question, he ruled that such a patient is forbidden to put on *tefillin.* He based his ruling on the *Rashba,*[25] who states that where an action would definitely, though indirectly, lead to erasure of the Name of *Hashem* it should be prohibited. Here the *tefillin* will certainly be destroyed upon discharge from the hospital. Thus, it is as if the patient will by bringing the *tefillin* into the hospital to erase *Hashem's* Name with his own two hands. The *Yesodei Yeshurun*[26] quotes a letter from *HaGaon Rav Tuviah Yehudah Tevyomi* who ruled that it was forbidden and added that *Rav Issur Zalman Meltzer zt"l* and the *Chazon Ish* also agreed with this ruling. The *Igrot Moshe*[27] also concurs with this ruling. The *Minchat Yitzchak*[28] agrees that such a patient should not bring his *tefillin* to the hospital since he would be responsible for the erasure of *Hashem's* Name when the *tefillin* are destroyed. However, in another *responsum*[29] he writes that if the patient's condition might deteriorate because of his mental anguish and heartache at not being able to put on *tefillin,* there is room to rule that they be brought in, preferably by a non-Jew.

On the other hand, the *Chelkat Yaakov*[30] rules that one should not dismiss the obligation to wear *tefillin* so as to avoid the possibility of indirectly causing the erasure of *Hashem's* Name. And besides, it is by no means certain that the parchments containing *Hashem's* Name will be destroyed; they could be removed from their boxes prior to the destruction of the *tefillin.* Since it is possible to do this, there is only a remote possibility of *Hashem's* Name being erased. And this is not a sufficient reason for not wearing *tefillin.*

◆§ One who is blind

The *Rosh*[31] cites the *Sefer HaItim* that one who is blind is exempt from the *mitzvah* of *tefillin* and *tzitzit.* For just as he is exempt from wearing *tzitzit,* because it is written: "and you shall see them,"[32] so he is similarly exempt from putting on *tefillin.* However, the *Rosh* himself thinks that the verse relates specifically to *tzitzit,* and not to *tefillin.*[33] However, the *Shulchan Aruch*[34] rules that a blind man must wear *tzitzit,* and the *Mishnah Berurah* adds that he should do so with a blessing.[35] The *Ben Ish Chai* has the same opinion.[36]

◆§ One who is dumb and one who is deaf

The *Sefer Chasidim* writes that one who is deaf but speaks or dumb but hears must perform all *mitzvot* including wearing *tefillin.*[37] The *Knesset HaGedolah*[38]

23. יו"ד סי' רעו סע' ט
24. שו"ת דובב מישרים ח"א סי' צט
25. חי' שבת קב ע"ב
26. ח"א עמ' קב
27. או"ח ח"א סי' ד־ז וח"ד סי' ח
28. ח"ג סי' ג
29. ח"ד סי' ח
30. ח"ג סי' מב־מד
31. מובא בב"י כאן
32. במדבר טו:לט
33. וכ"כ הפמ"ג א"א ס"ק א
34. סי' יז סע' א
35. שם ס"ק א
36. שו"ת רב פעלים ח"ב סי' יז, וחולק על השו"ת לב חיים ח"א סי' ק מכוח המנהג הפשוט
37. סי' תשעד
38. מובא בכף החיים ס"ק ג ואו"ר ס"ק א

NISHMAT AVRAHAM

learns from this ruling that a deaf-mute who neither speaks nor hears has no obligation to wear *tefillin;* however, he writes that he saw deaf-mutes putting on *tefillin* and the Rabbis in Constantina did not stop them from doing so. He rules, therefore, that the *Sefer Chasidim* obligates one who is only deaf or only dumb to don *tefillin,* whereas a deaf-mute, although exempt (as he is from all *mitzvot*), should not be prevented from doing so if he wishes to. *Rav Neuwirth shlita* wrote to me, wondering about this ruling of the *Knesset HaGedolah.* For since *halachically* the deaf-mute has the same status as one who is severely mentally retarded, he should be exempt, because we cannot be certain that he has a *guf naki.* Nevertheless, *Rav Shlomo Zalman Auerbach zt"l* wrote to me that a deaf-mute may don *tefillin* since there are those who are capable, like children, of maintaining a *guf naki.* Moreover, *Rav Eliezer Yehudah Waldenberg shlita* wrote to me[39] that in contemporary society where deaf-mutes are taught to communicate, there are great *poskim* who believe that such deaf-mutes may even be obligated to put on *tefillin* and perform other *mitzvot* as well. *Rav Waldenberg* goes on to quote the *Shevet Sofer*[40] who writes that his father, the *Ketav Sofer,* once visited a school for children who were deaf-mutes and was so impressed with their ability to communicate and with their level of education that he thought they could possibly be obligated to perform all the *mitzvot.* And, writes the *Shevet Sofer,* it seems that he instructed the school administrators to purchase *tefillin* for the boys. The *Mahari Shtief* [41] writes that a deaf-mute who wishes to don *tefillin* may be allowed to do so. The *Nachalat Binyamin*[42] goes even further and writes that a deaf-mute who dons *tefillin* and prays morning and evening from his prayer book (in whatever language he understands), may even be counted as part of a *minyan.* However, *Rav Waldenberg shlita* writes that many disagree with this ruling that he can be counted as part of a *minyan. Rav Waldenberg* concludes that one should try to buy such deaf-mutes *tefillin* and encourage them to don them. (See also *Siman* 55:2 for more on this issue.)

Rav Auerbach zt"l[43] writes: Regarding a deaf-mute, we must accept the rulings of the *poskim,* that even if he is extremely clever and talented, knows how to pray and is able to conduct his business affairs and sign his name, nevertheless he is considered a complete *shoteh.* Although it is difficult for us to understand how *Chazal* knew that he should be exempted from all *mitzvot* without any apparent basis in the Written Torah or *halachah,* nevertheless, since this is the truth, we are obligated to accept that they, with their superior knowledge, knew that a deaf-mute cannot be considered as someone who is responsible for his actions. Hence we cannot take cognizance of his actions even though he behaves normally with intelligence and knowledge. However, if he has been taught to speak their language with lip movements and is absolutely normal in his understanding and behavior, it would seem that he should be considered as a normal person. Indeed both I and *Rav Eliashiv shlita*[44] were asked about such a person who even had a companion for

---

39. הערה בסוף כרך א של נשמת אברהם ושו״ת ציץ אליעזר חט״ו סי׳ לב

40. חאהע״ז סי׳ כא

41. סי׳ רלט

42. סי׳ לא

43. מנחת שלמה ח״א סי׳ לד

44. בספר בית דוד ח״ב עמ׳ כח כותב הגריי״ש אלישיב שליט״א: עלינו לנקוט להלכה כהני תלתא סבי גדולי המורים ז״ל הדברי חיים (אהע״ז סי׳ עב), בית שלמה (או״ח ח״ב סי׳ צב) ומהרש״ם (ח״ב סי׳ קמ) שלא נחתו לחלק בכך וחשבוהו למדבר גם כשלמד לדבר לאחר שנתחרש. וכותב הגרש״ז אויערבאך זצ״ל שם עמ׳ לג בנד״ד נראה שאם הוא מדבר באופן כזה שסתם בני אדם יכולים להבין כוונתו אף אם תנועות השפתים הן שונות משל כל אדם

NISHMAT AVRAHAM

Torah learning and we both agreed that he was to be considered a normal person. Not that *Chazal* made a mistake in their evaluation of a *shoteh,* Heaven forbid, but since in their time the deaf-mute could not be taught, their evaluation was entirely correct. Today, when we know how to teach them and expand their knowledge and abilities, we can compare this to *Chazal*'s evaluation of an eight-month premature baby. Although such a baby was compared by them to a stone, this of course is no longer applicable because of the advances in the treatment of premature babies. In conclusion, it is extremely difficult in practice to rule against those great Torah giants who have discussed this question at length and from whom we imbibe our knowledge. On the other hand, it is just as difficult to, Heaven forbid, prevent them from performing *mitzvot.* In a further *responsum,*[45] the *Rav zt"l* writes that such a one who wears a hearing aid and can answer "*Amen*" can also be part of a *minyan.* However he should not be called up to the reading of the Torah since he is unable to say the blessings in the normal manner (see also *Siman* 55B).

אפי״ה מסתבר דשפיר חשיב כמדבר ואינו שומע שדינו כפקח לכל דבר. אך אם רק האנשים שרגילים לדבר אתו יודעים ומבינים כוונתו ולא אחרים, אינני יודע להכריע אם חשיב כמדבר או לא

45. שם ח״ב סי׳ ד אות ל

CHAPTER FIVE:

Laws of Birchot HaShachar

SIMAN 46: LAWS OF *BIRCHOT HASHACHAR*

§8: If one is not obligated to say any one of these blessings, for example, if he did not hear the crow of a rooster, did not walk, did not dress, or did not fasten on his belt, he should still say the appropriate blessings but without mentioning the Name of Hashem.

GLOSS: *There are those who say that even if he is* (A)*not obligated to recite them he should still do so since they do not necessarily relate to himself, but are a recognition that the Holy One, Blessed be He, created all of the necessities of life. This is the accepted custom and it should not be changed.*

NISHMAT AVRAHAM

SIMAN 46

(A) not obligated: Some *acharonim* feel that a blind person should say the blessing: "giving sight to the blind."[1] However, the *Magen Avraham* believes that it is inappropriate for a blind person to say this blessing.[2]

A deaf person should say the blessing: "Who gave the rooster understanding to distinguish between night and day" although he cannot hear the crowing of a rooster at dawn.[3] The *Chayei Adam*[4] advises one who is deaf to wait until sunrise before saying this blessing. However the *Kaf HaChaim*[5] rules, in the name of the *Ari z"l,* that since these blessings were instituted for the world as a whole, even if a particular blessing does not apply to someone, he is still obligated to say it.

1. ברכ"י בשיורי ברכה ס"ק יד. בן איש חי שנה א פ' וישב סע' ה. מ"ב ס"ק כה
2. ס"ק יד
3. מג"א שם. מ"ב שם. בן איש חי שם סע' ד
4. מובא במ"ב שם
5. ס"ק נ

CHAPTER SIX:

The Laws of Blessings

SIMAN 47: LAWS OF *BIRKAT HATORAH*

§12: Even if one studies Torah at night he need not repeat the birkat haTorah as long as (A)he has not slept, since the night is considered to be a continuation of the day that passed with regard to this *halachah*.

NISHMAT AVRAHAM

SIMAN 47

(A) he has not slept: The *Chayei Adam*[1] rules that one who remained awake all night (such as a sick person or a doctor on call) need not recite *birkat haTorah* in the morning. Others[2] argue that the blessings should be said. They think that since *Chazal* established these blessings each day like the other *birchot hashachar,* the *halachah* should be the same for it as for the others (see *Rama* 46:8). However, the *Mishnah Berurah* concludes that because there is no consensus and the issue remains in doubt, one should adopt the lenient position and refrain from saying the blessing.[3] However, he advises one who was awake all night to try to listen to someone else say the blessings. He should ask the one saying the blessings to have the two of them in mind, and he should have in mind that he is fulfilling his obligation by listening. He then answers "*Amen*" and says some verses to fulfill the obligation of engaging in Torah study in conjunction with the blessing. If he does not discharge his obligation to say the blessing in this way, he has another option. When he says *ahavah rabbah* before the *Shema,* he should bear in mind that he is fulfilling the obligation of *birkat haTorah* at the same time. After finishing the morning prayers, he should immediately engage in Torah study.[4] The *Shulchan Aruch HaRav,*[5] on the other hand, rules that if he was unable to listen to someone else recite the *birkat haTorah,* he may say the blessing himself.

Saying *birkat haTorah* in the morning exempts one from saying the blessing when engaging in Torah study the entire day. However, if a "*halachic* interruption" occurs, he would be required to repeat the blessing prior to resuming Torah study. Daily activities do not constitute a "*halachic* interruption" of Torah study, since he should always bear in mind that he will resume his Torah study as soon as time becomes available.[6] However, if he slept a *sheinat keva* (a regular sleep instead of a

1. חיי אדם כלל ט סע׳ ט
2. א״ר ס״ק ט. מג״א ס״ק יב
3. ספק ברכות להקל
This is because of a general rule that where there is a question about the obligation to say a blessing, we adopt the lenient view.
4. מ״ב ס״ק כח
5. סע׳ ז
6. סע׳ י ו־יא. וראה בבית הלוי פ׳ יתרו

§13: He who gets up before daybreak to engage in Torah study, should recite *birkat haTorah;* he need not repeat the blessing when he arrives at the synagogue. He who gets up before daybreak should recite all of the *birchot hashachar* except for *"hanotein lasechvi vinah"* and *parshat hatamid* which should be recited only after daybreak.

GLOSS: *Preferably, one should wash one's hands before saying the blessings for studying Torah. If water is not available, it is permis-*

NISHMAT AVRAHAM

nap) in bed, even in the early part of the night, this is considered an interruption. Then, everyone agrees that he should repeat *birkat haTorah.*[7]

If he slept a *sheinat keva* during the day and was awake all of the following night, *Rav Akiva Eiger*[8] rules that he must recite *birkat haTorah* the following morning. The blessing of *ahavat olam* which he said the previous night at *Maariv* cannot exempt him for the following day, unless he engaged in Torah study immediately after *Maariv.* However, *Rav Ovadiah Yosef shlita*[9] points out that among the *Sephardim* (based on the opinion of the majority of *poskim*) one who has been up all night nevertheless recites *birkat haTorah* in the morning (see next paragraph). It is common for a doctor on overnight call to find himself in such a situation.

As to *birchot hashachar,* the *Mishnah Berurah* quotes the *Eliyah Rabbah* who ruled that one who was awake the entire night should not say the blessings of *"Elokai neshamah"* or *"hama'avir sheinah."*[10] The *Sha'arei Teshuvah*[11] ruled that he should listen to someone else saying these two blessings with the intention of exempting himself, answering *"Amen"* afterwards. *Rav Moshe Feinstein zt"l*[12] agrees with this ruling of the *Mishnah Berurah.* However, the *Rashash z"l,* quoting a custom of the *Ari z"l,* rules that one remaining awake all night should recite all of *birchot hashachar* after the *halachic* midnight (midpoint between sunset and sunrise) and postpone the recitation of *birkat haTorah* until after dawn. In addition, there is no obligation to say the blessing *"al netilat yadayim"* in this setting.[13] If, however, one slept for "sixty breaths" (half an hour[14]), everyone agrees that he must recite all of the *birchot hashachar.*[15]

7. מ״ב ס״ק כח

8. מובא במ״ב שם

9. הערה בסוף כרך א של נשמת אברהם. וראה בשו״ת יביע אומר ח״ה חאו״ח סי׳ ו אות ה

10. סי׳ מו ס״ק כד

11. מובא במ״ב שם

12. אג״מ או״ח ח״ד סי׳ ג

13. כף החיים סי׳ מו סוס״ק מט

14. ראה בסי׳ ד סע׳ טז וביה״ל שם שמביא שלוש שיטות, י״א שלוש שעות, י״א חצי שעה וי״א שהוא מעט יותר משלוש דקות וכותב הביה״ל ובעל נפש יחמיר לפי כחו. וראה בארה״ח סע׳ טז ובאר״י ס״ק י די״א דהוא שש שעות וי״א דהוא פחות מד׳ שעות. ועיין בחיי אדם כלל ז סי׳ ח דשיעור ששים נשימות הוא מהלך מאה אמה דהוא חלק ס״ז משעה בקירוב, דהיינו פחות מדקה, עיין סי׳ מד בט״ז ס״ק א ובמ״ב ס״ק ד. וקיצור שו״ע סי׳ ב סע׳ ח הכריע דהוא לערך חצי שעה וכ״כ בשו״ת אור לציון ח״ב סי׳ כה וכן בספר יעלהו יבול סי׳ מז בשם הגרש״ז אויערבאך זצ״ל – כל זה מספר אשי ישראל פ״ב הערה קח ופ״ו הערה סו. ומובא שם בשם הגרש״ז אויערבאך זצ״ל והחזו״א דאם ישן בבגדיו, אפילו בלילה (אפילו במיטה) לא נקרא קבע וא״צ לברך ברכת התורה. ואמנם כשישן את שינתו הרגילה בלילה אפילו ישן בבגדיו כתב בשו״ת מהרש״ם ח״ג סי׳ שלז דהוי שינת קבע וצריך לברך

15. סי׳ מו מ״ב ס״ק כד

sible [B]*to study Torah or to say the blessing (of birkat haTorah) in the same way as one is allowed to say all the other blessings before washing one's hands (as mentioned earlier in Siman* 46).

SIMAN 49:
ONE MAY RECITE *KERIYAT SHEMA* BY HEART

§1: Even though one is not permitted to recite verses from the [A]**Written Torah by heart, everything which is habitual**

NISHMAT AVRAHAM

(B) to study Torah or to say the blessing: If one awakens in the middle of the night and needs to say a blessing or to engage in Torah study, the *Mishnah Berurah*[16] rules that he should wipe his hands on something, even the wall, before saying the blessing. On the other hand, the *Birkei Yosef,*[17] quoting the *Zohar,* rules that one is allowed to say a blessing only after the hands have been ritually washed with water.[18]

The *Taz*[19] rules that one who wakes up in bed and is thirsty, but cannot wash his hands, should think through the blessing in his heart (though not express it vocally) and then drink.[20] The *Eliyah Rabbah*[21] disagrees and says that he should wipe his hands on anything available, even the wall. The *Birkei Yosef*[22] rules like the *Taz.*[23] Certainly, when one is ill and cannot get out of bed to obtain water to wash his hands (and lacks any other method to clean them), he may rely on the *Taz.*[24]

SIMAN 49

(A) Written Torah: Even though the general rule is that written material from the Torah should be read from the text and not recited by heart, it is permissible, in extenuating circumstances, to do so.[1] A blind person may recite verses by heart.[2] One who is imprisoned (or in a hospital) and cannot obtain a *Chumash,* is also permitted to recite lines from the Torah by heart.[3] The *Tosafot*[4] states that the *halachah* that one must not say written material by heart, only applies to the *Chumash* and not the rest of the *Tanach.* The *Kol Bo*[5] quotes the *Yerushalmi* that this rule applies only to one who is reading from a *Sefer Torah* and reads part of it by heart thus giving the impression that the *Sefer Torah* is incomplete. However, this is permissible while praying. In addition, this prohibition applies only when one is discharging another person from his obliga-

1. עיין יומא סח ע״ב ותוס׳ ישנים שם על ע ע״א. תענית כח ע״א. ועיין בב״י או״ח סי׳ קמד ד״ה וכן ובביה״ל כאן ד״ה כגון. ועיין בערה״ש סע׳ ב בשם הזוהר הקדוש, בשדי חמד מערכת ד אות מד ובארחות חיים סי׳ מט
2. תוס׳ ב״ק ג ע״ב ד״ה כדמתרגם והובא במג״א. וע״ע תוס׳ שבת קטו ע״א ד״ה לא נתנו ומהרש״א שם
3. מ״ב ס״ק א
4. תמורה יד ע״ב ד״ה דברים
5. סי׳ יג

16. ס״ק לג
17. סי׳ ד ס״ק ח
18. וכן הובא בשע״ת שם ס״ק טו ומ״ב סוס״ק סא
19. שם סי׳ סב ס״ק א
20. וכן הובא שם במ״ב ס״ק ח וחיי אדם כלל ה סע׳ טז
21. ס״ק ד
22. שם
23. וראה בשע״ת סי׳ ד ס״ק יג
24. מהא דמ״ב ס״ק ח

and familiar to everyone, such as *Keriyat Shema, birkat Cohanim, parshat hatamid* and the like, may be recited by heart.

SIMAN 53:
WHO MAY LEAD PRAYER SERVICES

§14: **(A)A blind person may lead prayer services, but may not read from the Torah, because of the prohibition to say it by heart.**

NISHMAT AVRAHAM

tion.[6] The *Mishnah Berurah*[7] following the *Chavot Yair*[8] permits saying the entire book of *Psalms* by heart since it "awakens *Hashem's* pity" and is akin to prayer, and it is also habitual and familiar to "most people." The *Chayei Adam,*[9] however, rules that *Psalms* should not be said by heart since it is not well known to "most people."

SIMAN 53

(A) A blind person: This *halachah* applies also to one who is blind in both eyes, for he is obligated to perform all the *mitzvot.*[1] However, the *Chavot Yair*[2] rules that one who is blind even in only one eye, should not lead prayer services on the High Holidays if there is someone else, equally qualified, to do so. On the other hand, the *Eliyah Rabbah* rules that he may do so.[3] The *Mishnah Berurah*[4] feels that the ruling of the *Chavot Yair* is limited to the initial appointment of the *shaliach tzibbur.* However, if one already appointed to this position later loses his sight, there is no need to remove him. This is also the opinion of the *Birkei Yosef.*[5] (See below, *Siman* 69A and *Siman* 139:3.)

Rav Akiva Eiger ruled that one who is totally deaf should not serve as a *shaliach tzibbur* since it is preferable that a *shaliach tzibbur* be one who can hear his own prayers.[6] The *Mishnah Berurah*[7] writes that *Rav Akiva Eiger's* ruling apparently pertains to the entire year and not just the High Holidays provided that there is no one who is not deaf to lead the services. In contrast, other *poskim* permit one who is deaf to officiate as a *shaliach tzibbur* except for the High Holidays.[8]

As to a person who has an obvious physical blemish serving as *shaliach tzibbur,* the *Maharshal,* the *Sh'lah* and the *Eliyah Rabbah* rule that he would be preferable since *Hashem* "uses broken vessels."[9] In contrast, the *Zohar* forbids this, stating that the concept that *Hashem* "uses broken vessels" refers to one who is exceedingly humble and not to a person with a physical blemish.[10]

---

6. תוס׳ תמורה יד ע״ב ד״ה דברים. ר״ף בשם התוספתא, מובא בכל בו שם
7. ס״ק ו
8. סי׳ קעה
9. כלל ח סע׳ יא

1. מ״ב ס״ק מא. ועיין במגילה כד ע״א וב״ק פז ע״א. רמב״ם הל׳ תפלה פ״ח הי״ב ושו״ת הרא״ש כלל ד סי׳ כא
2. סי׳ קעו מובא במ״ב שם
3. ס״ק י
4. מ״ב שם
5. ס״ק ז
6. חידושי רעק״א כאן מובא במ״ב שם
7. שעה״צ ס״ק לח
8. שע״ת ס״ק יח בשם התשב״ץ ח״ג סי׳ קיג והברכ״י ס״ק ח
9. ראה ערוה״ש סע׳ ט וכף החיים ס״ק סד
10. כף החיים שם

SIMAN 55: LAWS OF *KADDISH*

§8: (A)A deaf or dumb person is considered as having all his faculties and is included in a *minyan,* but a deaf-mute is in the same category (B)as a *shoteh* or a minor.

NISHMAT AVRAHAM

SIMAN 55

(A) A deaf: The *Taz*[1] ruled that a deaf person cannot be included in a *minyan* since he will not know when to answer *Amen* to blessings during the prayer service. However, many other commentators agree with the ruling of the *Shulchan Aruch* that deafness does not preclude being counted toward a *minyan.* If, on the other hand, such a person knows when to answer *Amen* by watching others, everyone would agree that he can be counted toward a *minyan.*[2] This is derived from the *Gemara* in *Succah,*[3] which describes a large shul in Alexandria where people would be seated so far away from the *shaliach tzibbur* that they could not hear his blessings, and would answer only on cue. The *Shulchan Aruch HaRav* rules that as long as the majority of the people counted for the *minyan* can hear, and only the minority are deaf, those who are deaf may be counted for every prayer requiring a *minyan,* even though they may not know when to answer *Amen.* Nevertheless, if the *shaliach tzibbur* prayed his silent *Shemoneh Esrei,* he should not read the repetition of the prayer unless nine people are listening.[4] The *Ben Ish Chai*[5] and the *Aruch HaShulchan*[6] have the same ruling.

(B) as a *shoteh* or a minor: A deaf-mute is like a minor and a *shoteh,* in that he is absolved from fulfilling *mitzvot.*[7] This common denominator serves as the basis for the *halachah* stated here. The *Biur Halachah* writes:[8] In *Siman* 199:10 the *Rama* says that a *shoteh* who demonstrates a certain level of intellect can be counted as part of a *zimun.* At first glance, it would seem that by this ruling we should also permit him to be counted to make up a *minyan.* However, according to the *Magen Avraham,* it appears that this would not be the *halachah.* In fact, if he has only one of the signs of a *shoteh* mentioned below, he would not be eligible for a *minyan.*[9]

Halachah does not distinguish between a congenital deaf-mute and one who became so later in life; the *halachic* limitations apply to both equally.[10] Similarly, when one's mental faculties fluctuate, his *halachic* status is determined by his present state of mind.[11]

The *Gemara*[12] lists various signs of a *shoteh.* These include: one who goes out alone at night, one who sleeps in a cemetery, one who purposely destroys his garments, and one who loses whatever he is given. The *Gemara* adds that these actions must be carried out in a bizarre fashion in order to be considered valid signs of a *shoteh.* If, however, they were done with good reason,

1. סי׳ קכד ס״ק ב
2. מ״ב ס״ק לח. א״ר סי׳ קכד וכ״כ התשב״ץ ח״ג סי׳ קיג
3. סוכה נא ע״ב
4. סע׳ יא
5. שנה א פ׳ ויחי סע׳ ו
6. סי׳ קכד סע׳ ט
7. שו״ע כאן. פמ״ג יו״ד סי׳ א ש״ד ס״ק כב, מובא בביה״ל כאן ד״ה הוא. וראה גם בפתיחה כוללת ח״ב ס״ק ד ו־ה
8. ביה״ל ד״ה הוא
9. יו״ד סי׳ א סע׳ ה
10. שם
11. שם
12. חגיגה ג ע״ב

NISHMAT AVRAHAM

he is not considered a *shoteh.*[13] There is a discussion in the *Gemara* as to whether it is necessary for one to show all of these signs to be defined a *shoteh,* or whether the presence of even one of them is sufficient. The *Beit Yosef*[14] writes that there is a difference of opinion among the *rishonim* regarding the definition of a *shoteh.* Some[15] believe that only those signs mentioned in the *Gemara* constitute true signs of a *shoteh.* In contrast, the *Rambam*[16] rules that the signs mentioned in the *Gemara* are merely examples of how a *shoteh* behaves.[17]

The *Shulchan Aruch*[18] offers examples of people exhibiting fluctuating mental status. One example is a person suffering from a seizure disorder. He would be considered a *shoteh* during a seizure. However, when the episode subsides he regains the *halachic* status of one with full faculties (assuming that such a person normally demonstrates full faculties in the interim). The *Shulchan Aruch* also states that one who is of extremely low intelligence so that he does not understand anything nor realize the difference between two conflicting ideas is also to be considered a *shoteh.* Similarly, one who does things without understanding or realizing the purpose or consequences of his actions is also to be considered a *shoteh.*[19] It would seem that there is no consensus on the definition of the *shoteh* discussed in the *Talmud.* Therefore, every question of a *shoteh* that arises with respect to a patient needs an expert medical evaluation in conjunction with the advice of a *posek* to determine whether he is a *shoteh* who is absolved from performing *mitzvot.*[20]

There is a debate among the *acharonim* regarding the *halachic* status of a deaf-mute who has learned sign language. Some believe that since he can communicate, he has attained the status of one who can speak but not hear, and is thus obligated to perform all *mitzvot.*[21] However, others rule that he maintains his original status and is still absolved from *mitzvot.*[22] *Rav Ovadiah Yosef shlita*[23] believes that once a deaf-mute learns to communicate via sign language, he may be counted toward a *minyan* in order to have *Kaddish* and *Kedushah* recited. He reasons that since the requirement to pray with a *minyan* is a Rabbinic *halachah,* we may be lenient and include him for a *minyan.* However, if the *minyan* is limited to only nine people and him, the silent *Shemoneh Esrei* should be recited out loud until *Kedushah,*[24] but it should not be repeated by the *shaliach tzibbur.*[25] Because there is this difference of opinion between the *acharonim* regarding the propriety of counting a deaf-mute toward a *minyan, Rav Yosef* feels that when there are only ten people present it is best to limit saying the blessings as much as possible.

The *Pri Megadim* rules that the *halachic* status of a deaf-mute is limited only to one who was born so, but he doubts that such a *halachic* definition would apply to one who only became so later in life.[26] However,

---

13. ש״ך יו״ד סי׳ א ס״ק כד ופמ״ג שם. פר״ח שם ס״ק כד. זבחי צדק ס״ק נד

14. אהע״ז סי׳ קכא

15. רבינו שמחה משפירא ורבינו אביגדור, מובאים בב״י שם

16. פ״ט מהל׳ עדות ה״ט

17. וראה גם בריב״ש סי׳ תסח, בשו״ע חו״מ סי׳ לה סע׳ ח ויו״ד סי׳ א סע׳ ה, פתח עינים להחיד״א על חגיגה שם, הכרתי יו״ד סי׳ א ס״ק כח, פר״ח שם ס״ק כג, דעת תורה שם ס״ק מ, דרכי תשובה שם סי׳ קנב, פמ״ג שם ש״ד ס״ק כג ו־כד, זבחי צדק שם ס״ק נא ו־נד וכף החיים שם ס״ק קכו

18. חו״מ סי׳ לה סע׳ ט

19. שם סע׳ י

20. עיין מה שכתב הראי״ה קוק זצ״ל בשו״ת עזרת כהן סי׳ סז ו־סח

21. המהרש״ם ח״ב סי׳ קמ. נחלת צבי ח״א עמ׳ סא

22. שות מהר״ם שיק אהע״ז סי׳ עט. שו״ת דברי חיים ח״ב אהע״ז סי׳ עב, עו ו־עט. שו״ת זכר שמחה סי ט

23. לב אברהם ח״ב עמ׳ יג. שו״ת יחוה דעת ח״ב סי׳ ו

24. ראה סי׳ רלב סע׳ א ומ״ב ס״ק ד

25. ראה סי׳ קכד סע׳ א

26. פתיחה כוללת ח״ב ס״ק ד ו־ה. וצ״ע ממה שכתב ביו״ד סי׳ א ש״ד ס״ק כב

CHAPTER SEVEN:

The Laws of Keriyat Shema

SIMAN 58: LAWS OF *KERIYAT SHEMA* AND ITS BLESSINGS

§3: (A)One who finds himself in extenuating circumstances may say the *Shema* and its blessings after dawn since at this time, the verse "and when you arise" of the *Shema* and "*yotzer or*" of the blessings of *Shema* already apply.

NISHMAT AVRAHAM

the *Sdei Chemed*[27] quoting the *Melechet Charash*[28] rejects this view, and believes that all deaf-mutes are the same *halachically* regardless of when their disability developed. A similar view is held by the *Shoel U'Meshiv*[29] and the *Tiferet Yisrael*[30] (see also 38H).

SIMAN 58

A) One who finds himself in extenuating circumstances: A patient who must undergo surgery very early in the morning and will not have the opportunity to put on *tefillin* and pray that day, should try to act as follows: If possible, he should start praying at dawn[1] until he reaches *yotzer or* – the first of the blessings of *Keriyat Shema*. He should then wait until the time described as "when one can see his friend at a distance of four *cubits*,"[2] and then put on *tzitzit* and *tefillin*, with their blessings,[3] and continue his prayers.[4]

If the surgery is to begin even earlier, before the time when "one can see his friend at a distance of four *cubits*," he is permitted to don *tzitzit* and *tefillin*, albeit without a blessing, and pray the entire morning service from dawn onwards.[5] The *Biur Halachah*[6] suggests that the leniency to begin praying before the proper time may be limited only to the circumstances of having to set out early on a journey. However, in other extenuating circumstances perhaps such leniency is not allowed and one would need to pray at the

27. מערכת חי"ת כלל קג

28. בפתיחה לספר

29. בהסכמתו לספר מלאכת חרש

30. תרומות פ"א אות י

1. ועיין בביה"ל סי' פט סע' א על זמן עמה"ש וכן במג"א שם ס"ק ג. וע"ע בא"ר שם ס"ק א, הגר"א ושו"ת מלמד להועיל סי' ל

2. סי' ח סע' ג ומ"ב ס"ק ט.

This is a time which falls between dawn and sunrise and represents the earliest time one may say the blessings on *tzitzit* or *tefillin* or recite *Keriyat Shema*. *Ashkenazim* customarily wait until 50 minutes and *Sephardim* 60 minutes before sunrise.

עיין סי' ל סע' א ובפמ"ג סי' נח ס"ק ב. כף החיים ס"ק יח ושו"ת אג"מ או"ח ח"ד סי' ז

3. עיין רמב"ם הל' תפילין פ"ד הי"א שאף עובר על לאו אם מניחה בלילה, אולם ע"ע בשו"ע סי' ל סע' ב ומג"א ס"ק א

4. מהא דמ"ב ס"ק יג וביה"ל סע' א ד"ה זמן. כף החיים ס"ק יז. תפא"י ברכות סוף פ"א. ברכ"י סי' נח ס"ק ד. שע"ת סי' תרסד סע' א. שו"ת יחוה דעת ח"ב סי' ח. שו"ת אג"מ או"ח ח"ד סי' ו

5. מ"ב ס"ק טז

6. ד"ה ומי. וראה גם סע' א בסוד"ה זמן

§6: Although the time of *Keriyat Shema* extends until the end of the third hour of the day, if the third hour has passed and one has not recited it, he may still recite the *Shema* and its blessings until the fourth hour, which is one-third of the day. However, the reward for reciting the *Shema* during this time is not the same as the reward for reciting it in its preferred time. (B)After the fourth hour has passed, he may still recite the *Shema* during the entire day, but without its blessings.

NISHMAT AVRAHAM

proper time. Nevertheless, *Rav Neuwirth shlita* rules that a patient who is scheduled for early morning surgery, and therefore will be unable to don *tefillin* and pray at the proper time, can take the lenient approach and wear *tallit* and *tefillin* with their blessings[7] and recite the *Shema* with its blessings[8] at dawn.[9]

Many *rishonim* believe that according to Torah Law, it is permissible to wear *tefillin* at night.[10] In this light, one might think that a man could say a blessing when putting on *tefillin* before dawn. *Chazal,* however, forbade the wearing of *tefillin* at night lest one fall asleep while wearing them. If, however, one is to set out on an early journey, *Chazal* permitted him to don *tefillin* before dawn, since it is very unlikely that he will fall asleep wearing them. Similarly, there is certainly no reason to believe that a person who arises at this early hour to pray and don *tzitzit* and *tefillin* before surgery will fall asleep while wearing *tefillin.* Therefore, he too can don *tefillin* at this time. In spite of this, it would be inappropriate to say the blessing on the *tefillin* which contains the words "and commanded us"[11] since *Chazal* forbade wearing *tefillin* during this time except under extenuating circumstances.[12] The patient awaiting early surgery, however, should not begin praying until after dawn.[13]

B) After the fourth hour has passed: Regardless of the reason why one was unable to recite the *Shema,* once the proper time passes, it is forbidden to say its blessings.[14] However, the *Biur Halachah*[15] cites *acharonim* who feel that one who missed reciting the *shema* at its proper time because of extenuating circumstances, may recite it with its blessings until midday.[16] The *Kaf HaChaim* recommends that from the fourth hour until midday, one should say the blessings without mentioning the Name of *Hashem.*[17] (See *Siman* 108 regarding how one should act when one misses the proper time of saying the *Shemoneh Esrei* because of extenuating circumstances, such as undergoing surgery.)

7. רמ״א סי׳ יח סע׳ ג ופמ״ג א״א שם ס״ק ד
8. שו״ע כאן וביה״ל סי׳ נח סע׳ א ד״ה זמן
9. סי׳ ל סע׳ ב ומ״ב ס״ק ד. כף החיים סי׳ יח ס״ק כ
10. תוס׳, רא״ש וסמ״ג וכר׳ עקיבא מנחות לו ע״ב
11. וברכות אינן מעכבות.

Although "and commanded us" refers to *Hashem,* it was *Chazal* who commanded us to say a blessing before performing a *mitzvah.*

12. דעת מרן סי׳ יח סע׳ ג ומ״ב שם ס״ק ט
13. והסכים מו״ר הגרי״י נויבירט שליט״א עם כל זה
14. והוי ברכה לבטלה – מ״ב ס״ק כו
15. ד״ה קוראה
16. וכ״כ החיד״א בשו״ת חיים שאל ח״ב סי׳ לח סע׳ ע. וצ״ע בדעת הבן איש חי כי שם בפ׳ וארא סע׳ יז פסק כהשו״ע אולם בשו״ת רב פעלים ח״ב סי׳ יב כתב לברך עד חצות
17. ס״ק כה

SIMAN 62:
ONE WHO RECITED *KERIYAT SHEMA* SILENTLY

§4: If due to sickness, or for some other reason beyond his control, one recited the *Keriyat Shema* without vocalizing the words, (A)he has fulfilled his obligation.

GLOSS: *One may even do this in the first instance if he is in a place that is unclean, and cannot clean up the area before reciting the Shema. However, if the place is [halachically] filthy, he may not do so since it is forbidden to even think of words of Torah in such a situation.*

NISHMAT AVRAHAM

SIMAN 62

(A) he has fulfilled his obligation: Certain *mitzvot,* such as the recitation of *Keriyat Shema* require the recitation of specific texts in order to discharge one's obligation. Is it absolutely necessary to enunciate the text; or perhaps, if one is unable to articulate the words, may he fulfill his obligation by contemplating the text only? The general consensus of the *acharonim* is that ideally, one must enunciate the text in order to fulfill the obligation. The *Mishnah Berurah*[1] concludes that one may contemplate the words of the *Shema* in extenuating circumstances, and *Hashem,* "will reward him for this." However, if he later is able to vocalize the words while there is still the proper time to recite the *Shema,* he must do so, since he has not really discharged his obligation. This is unlike the *Pri Megadim*[2] and the *Birkei Yosef*[3] who ruled differently. They believed that such a person would not be obligated to repeat *Keriyat Shema* when he is later able to voice the words since he has already fulfilled his obligation. The *Biur Halachah,*[4] in contradistinction to the *Pri Megadim,* concludes that the majority of *rishonim* believe that one cannot fulfill one's obligation by mere contemplation, and adds that the same ruling applies to *birkat hamazon* and other blessings as well.

Rav Neuwirth shlita wrote to me that since, according to later *poskim,* the obligation to remember the Exodus from Egypt verbally is present the whole day, he must do so when possible even if the time for *Keriyat Shema* has passed. *Rav Auerbach zt"l* also wrote me that one is obligated to say that *Hashem* took us out of Egypt.

A person who is confined in a filthy place (for example, where there are feces) must not even contemplate the *Shema* or any blessing. He should, however, bear in mind that he is obligated to perform the *mitzvah* at this time and wholeheartedly regret that he is unable to do so. *Hashem,* who is All-knowing, will reward him for these thoughts under the extenuating circumstances.[5]

1. מ״ב ס״ק ז
2. מ״ז ס״ק א
3. סי׳ פ ס״ק ב
4. ד״ה יצא
5. מ״ב ס״ק ט

SIMAN 63:
ONE'S POSTURE WHILE RECITING THE *SHEMA*

§1: One may recite the *Shema* while walking, standing, lying down, riding an animal or sitting. However, he should not do so (A)while lying face down or flat on his back. One may recite the *Shema* while lying on one's side.

GLOSS: *(since he is already lying down and it is hard to get up). (B)One may lean on his side to recite the Shema if he is obese or ill and finds it difficult to turn onto his side.*

SIMAN 69:
LAWS OF RECITING THE *SHEMA* FOR THE CONGREGATION

§2: (A)A person who is blind from birth, although he has never ever seen lights, may say the blessing "He who creates lights" for the congregation. This is because he also benefits from the lights since others can see to lead him.

NISHMAT AVRAHAM

SIMAN 63

(A) While lying face down: Although one should not recite the *Shema* lying prone or supine, if one did so in either of these positions, he would not be required to repeat it.[1]

Rav Shlomo Zalman Auerbach zt"l told me that if a patient's shoulders are elevated by pillows or by the raising of the head of the bed, he is considered as if he is sitting.[2] He reasoned that since the *Shulchan Aruch* rules that even a person who only leans to one side fulfills the requirement of "sitting" while reciting the *Shema,* it follows that if the shoulders are raised, this too can be considered as not lying flat.

(B) One may lean on his side: If one is unable even to lean on his side, he may recite the *Shema* while lying flat.[3] However, if he can manage to muster enough strength to lean on his side while reciting the first verse of the *Shema,* he must do so.[4] See also *Siman* 94 and 123.

SIMAN 69

(A) A person who is blind: A person who is blind may serve as *shaliach tzibbur.*[1] In *Siman* 53A we concluded that there are times when it is preferable for a blind person not to act as the *shaliach tzibbur*. However, one must differentiate between the *Shema* and the *Shemoneh Esrei.* With regard to the *Shema* there is no need for the *shaliach tzibbur* to exempt

1. ביה״ל ד״ה אבל בשם הפמ״ג
2. עיין היטב בנדה יד ע״א
3. ערוה״ש סע׳ ה
4. מ״ב ס״ק ד

1. מ״ב ס״ק יט

SIMAN 72: THE LAW FOR THOSE WHO CARRY THE BIER AND ALL WHO ACCOMPANY IT

§2: A corpse should not be taken out to be buried (A)close to the time for reciting the *Shema,* unless the burial can take place before the proper time for reciting the *Shema.* However, if they have already begun to do so, they need not be halted in order to recite the *Shema.*

NISHMAT AVRAHAM

the members of the congregation from fulfilling their own obligation to recite the *Shema,* whereas with the *Shemoneh Esrei* he does exempt them with the repetition of the prayer.[2] Therefore, a blind person would always be eligible to act as *shaliach tzibbur* for *Maariv* (since the *Shemoneh Esrei* is not repeated).[3]

SIMAN 72

(A) close to the time for reciting the *Shema*: Often, when the *Shulchan Aruch* uses the words "close to" a particular time, it refers to the half hour before that time.[1] However, the *Biur Halachah*[2] rules that in this context, "close" does not mean within a half-hour before the proper time to recite the *Shema,* but rather, connotes the time it will take to complete the burial before the time for reciting the *Shema* arrives.

Since one is forbidden to become involved in any activity close to the time when he will recite the *Shema, Rav Neuwirth shlita* wrote to me wondering why a surgeon should be allowed to begin an operation if he knows with certainty that the surgery will take so long that he will inevitably miss the opportunity to recite the *Shema* and *Shemoneh Esrei* at their proper times.[3] The Rav *shlita* questioned why the *Mishnah Berurah* here decided differently from his ruling in *Siman* 70 (23), that one who starts to work or have a bath, haircut, etc. before dawn may continue even when the time to recite the *Shema* and *Shemoneh Esrei* arrive, provided that he will still be able to recite them before the time allotted for them passes.

To answer this question, I must first present some of the background material. The *Talmud,*[4] in discussing the *halachah* stated in this section, gives an exception to the rule: When the one to be buried was an eminent personage, the attendants are permitted to bury him even though they will miss the opportunity to recite the *Shema* at the proper time. The *Chavot Yair*[5] cites many *rishonim* who believe that the "eminent personage" discussed

2. אפילו בזמנינו, לפי דברי האר״י ז״ל מובא בכף החיים ס״ק טו

3. כף החיים שם

1. ראה להלן סי׳ רלב

2. ד״ה אין

3. כשמתחיל הניתוח לפני זמן משיכיר.
The case cited here is somewhat different from the one presented in the Hebrew version of *Nishmat Avraham* vol. 4 pp. 3-4. However, Rav Neuwirth *shlita* was consulted and agreed that the manner in which the case is presented here reflects his true intention.

4. ברכות יט ע״א

5. בספרו מקור חיים על או״ח כאן

SIMAN 74:
THE PROHIBITION TO SAY BLESSINGS WHEN EXPOSED TO AN *ERVAH*

§1: If one is naked underneath his nightgown, and he wishes to recite the *Shema*, (A)he must first tighten the nightgown below the area of his heart. This is because he is prohib-

NISHMAT AVRAHAM

in the *Gemara* does not refer to someone who was considered merely distinguished. Rather, it refers to a man who possessed outstanding qualities as well as scholarship. The *Beit Yosef* believes that nowadays no one has this stature, to qualify for the leniency stated in the *Gemara.* However, unlike the ruling regarding the recital of the *Shema* (of Torah obligation), it would appear that a distinguished person may be buried even if it means missing the time for the recital of the *Shemoneh Esrei* (of Rabbinic obligation only).[6]

If, in fact, a person does achieve the status of an "eminent personage," albeit not because of scholarship only, then it could be that the leniency introduced by the *Gemara* would apply. I suggested to the Rav *shlita* that any patient who must undergo an operation that starts before dawn, and lasts until the early afternoon, can be looked upon as being an "eminent personage" with regard to this *halachah.* The fact that the surgeon is involved in the *mitzvah* of saving his life makes him the object of this most important *mitzvah,* putting him into the category of an "eminent personage" (the same way, for example, that a mundane palm branch is transformed into a "holy" object when used for the *mitzvah* of *lulav*). Thus, even though his status may not be due to his scholarship and outstanding qualities, nevertheless the leniency mentioned in the *Gemara* could apply. Therefore, the surgeon involved in the operation would be permitted to begin the surgery, even if he is certain that, due to this, he will be unable to recite the *Shema* and *Shemoneh Esrei* at their appropriate times. *Rav Neuwirth shlita* concurred with this suggestion.

SIMAN 74

One is prohibited from reciting prayers and blessings, or engaging in Torah study when one is exposed to an *ervah.* The *halachot* of *ervah* are very relevant to the hospitalized patient. Patients who are bedridden often face the problem of praying or saying blessings when either they or others in the room are inappropriately dressed, and they find themselves in the presence of *ervah.*

(A) he must first tighten: When a patient is wearing a hospital gown without a belt, the hospital gown does not provide a separation between the area of the heart and the private parts. In such a situation, he is not permitted to recite the *Shema* because the heart is exposed to the *makom ervah.* This is so even though the *makom ervah* is not visible to the eye. By tightening the garment below the area of his heart, he creates a partition between his heart and his *erva.* Without doing this, he cannot say any blessings or engage in Torah study, since his heart is exposed to

6. מקור חיים שם

ited from reciting the *Shema* so long as his heart "sees" (B)his *ervah.*

GLOSS: *The same law applies when the area of his heart is uncovered in the presence of someone else's ervah.*

§2: Covering the area beneath the heart with one's hands is not considered a covering.

GLOSS: *So too if he covers (C)his head with his hands when saying a blessing, this is not considered covering the head. See below,* Siman 91.

§4: There is an authority who believes that (D)women are permitted to pray when they are wearing only an outer gar-

NISHMAT AVRAHAM

his *ervah* beneath the garment.[1] If, on the other hand, he was wearing a shirt underneath his gown, this would serve as an appropriate covering of the heart, and permit him to say blessings and engage in other Torah activities.[2]

(B) his *ervah*: The *Mishnah Berurah*[3] cites both the *Derech HaChaim* and *Pri Megadim* who believe that one who transgressed this prohibition, and recited the *Shema* or *Shemoneh Esrei* while the area of his heart was exposed to the *makom ervah,* must repeat these prayers. In addition, he must repeat the blessings associated with the recital of the *Shema.* However, other blessings need not be repeated.[4] The *Chayei Adam*[5] agrees that the *Shema* must be repeated. Since the Torah obligates us to recite the *Shema,* we cannot act leniently regarding it. However, he believes that one need not repeat the *Shemoneh Esrei,* since the prohibition is only Rabbinic in nature and there is room for leniency. The *Mishnah Berurah* concludes that one may rely on the opinion of the *Chayei Adam.*

(C) his head with his hands: *Halachah* does not deem one's own hand suitable to serve as a head-covering. Therefore, the *Mishnah Berurah*[6] states that it is not permissible to say a blessing if an appropriate head-covering is unavailable. In contrast, the *Eliyah Rabbah*[7] believes that, in extenuating circumstances, one may rely on those *acharonim* who rule leniently and allow the use of one's own hand as a head-covering. However, he suggests that one should preferably pull his shirt-sleeve onto the palm of his hand and use it to cover his head.[8] However, if another puts his hand on your head it is a covering.[9]

(D) women are permitted to pray: This applies to a woman wearing a hospital gown with no undergarments. The *Bach,*[10] the *Magen Avraham,*[11] the *Chochmat Adam*[12] and the *Kaf Ha-*

1. מ״ב ס״ק ב
2. ביה״ל ד״ה צריך לחוץ
3. מ״ב ס״ק ה. ועיין בביה״ל סי׳ צא ד״ה הואיל
4. במ״ב שם
5. חיי אדם כלל ג סע׳ לג ונשמת אדם כלל ד
6. ס״ק י
7. סי׳ צא
8. מ״ב סי׳ ב ס״ק יב
9. שו״ע סי׳ צא סע׳ ד
10. כאן
11. ס״ק ז
12. כלל קכא סע׳ יד

ment, even though there is no separation beneath between the *makom ervah* and the area of her heart.

SIMAN 75:

ONE SHOULD AVOID HEARING A WOMAN SING OR SEEING HER REVEALED HAIR WHILE RECITING THE *SHEMAH.* IT SHOULD NOT BE RECITED IN THE PRESENCE OF AN *ERVAH*

§1: It is forbidden to recite the *Shema* in front of any part of a woman's body (A)that is normally (B)covered and is now uncovered to the extent of a *tefach,* even if the woman is his wife.

NISHMAT AVRAHAM

Chaim[13] rule that women should say blessings only when there is a separation between the area of their hearts and their *makom ervah,* even if they are wearing an outer garment. In contrast, the *Taz*[14] and *Shach*[15] feel that the prohibition for one's heart to "see" the *makom ervah* does not apply to women. As long as there is some form of covering of her private parts she is permitted to say blessings, even when she is not wearing undergarments. However, the *Mishnah Berurah*[16] believes that it is best to adopt the stringent opinion of the *Bach* quoted above.

SIMAN 75

☙ The Torah forbids one from looking at any part of a woman's body with desirous thoughts.[1] Additionally, the Torah forbids one from reciting the *Shema,* praying, or engaging in Torah study in the presence of her *makom ervah.*[2] However, there is a Rabbinic prohibition to recite prayers when parts of a woman's body that are normally covered are exposed; hearing her sing is also included in this prohibition. It is this Rabbinic category of *ervah* that is most often encountered by the hospitalized patient who wants to perform a religious activity. The *halachot* discussed in this *Siman* speak of the proper behavior one should adopt when he finds himself faced with such an *ervah.* They are of importance both for patients and staff.

(A) that is normally: *Chazal* forbade the recitation of prayers in front of any area of a woman's body that is normally covered, but is currently exposed, since it is likely to generate inappropriate thoughts. See below, §6H.

(B) covered: There are two components to the Rabbinic-level prohibition of *ervah.* There is what we might term "social" *ervah.* Society determines whether a certain mode of dress is appropriate, whether exposure of a certain part of the body is considered immodest. From the point of view of *halachah,* fashion is a factor with respect to the exposure of a woman's face, hands, and the area of the leg below the knee. If it is common practice for any of these areas to be exposed, then it is not considered an *ervah,* and one is permitted

13. ס״ק יז
14. יו״ד סי׳ ר ס״ק ג
15. שם ס״ק א
16. ס״ק טז

1. ולא תתורו וגו׳ אחרי עיניכם – במדבר טו:לט
2. ועיין לעיל בהקדמה לסי׳ עד

GLOSS: *There are some authorities who feel that the measure of a tefach applies only when the woman is his wife. However, with respect to any* (C)*other woman, even if* (D)*less than a tefach is exposed, this is considered an ervah and the prohibition to pray in front of it is in force. It seems from the words of the Rosh that even for a woman, exposure to a tefach of another woman's body that is normally concealed is considered an ervah, prohibiting her from reciting the Shema. However, according to the Rosh a woman is permitted to recite the Shema even if she herself is naked, as discussed in Siman* 74.

NISHMAT AVRAHAM

to pray in its presence. However, if any of these areas is normally concealed, it is an *ervah* on a Rabbinic level, and a man is forbidden to pray in its presence if more than a *tefach* of the part is exposed. We may refer to the second component of the Rabbinic-level *ervah* as the "objective" *ervah*. Regardless of the accepted fashions in a particular culture, the areas in this category are always considered *ervah*. Therefore, one is always forbidden to pray or engage in Torah study if more than a *tefach* of these areas is exposed. These areas include a woman's arm from the shoulder to the elbow, and her leg from the knee to the hip.[3] It is also inappropriate to expose any of the areas defined as an "objective" *ervah* in front of the written Name of *Hashem*. *Rav Shlomo Zalman Auerbach zt"l* noted that patients, male and female, must be aware of any wall hangings that contain the Name of *Hashem*, so as not to undress in their presence[4] (see also *Siman* 263D).

(C) other woman: This *halachah* applies regardless of whether the woman is single or married.[5]

(D) less than a *tefach*: The *Mishnah Berurah*[6] rules that one is forbidden to recite the *Shema* in the presence of his wife even if less than a *tefach* of her thigh is exposed.

I will now briefly discuss closing one's eyes as a solution to the problem of facing an *ervah*.[7]

i) Even though the *Shulchan Aruch*[8] and the *Rama*[9] rule that closing one's eyes is sufficient, there are major *acharonim*[10] who rule that he must turn his back on the *ervah*, before reciting the *Shema* and other prayers. *Rav Ovadiah Yosef shlita*[11] agrees that one should take

3. שוקה, עיין מ״ב, ס״ק ב.

Chazal refer to the area of a woman's leg that is included in the objective category of *ervah*, as the "*shok.*" There is a debate among the *acharonim* regarding the definition of the "*shok.*" The *Mishnah Berurah* believes that the "*shok*" begins at the knee and extends to the hip. However, many other *acharonim* feel that the "*shok*" begins at the ankle and extends to the hip. Included among these is the *Chayei Adam* (4,7), *Bach, Shulchan Aruch HaRav,* and the *Aruch HaShulchan*. Both *Rav Neuwirth shlita* and *Rav Zilber shlita* (*Beit Baruch* on the *Chayei Adam*) feel that it is best to heed the more stringent opinion.

4. ועיין שבת קכ ע״ב ורמב״ם הל׳ יסוה״ת פ״ו ה״ו

5. מ״ב ס״ק ו

6. ס״ק ז

7. קצות השולחן ח״א הערות דף פט עמ׳ ב

8. סע׳ ו

9. מזה שלא הגיה על השו״ע כלום

10. עיין §6H

11. הערות על נשמת אברהם כרך א עמ׳ שלג. שו״ת יביע אומר ח״ג חאו״ח סי׳ ז

§2: One is forbidden to recite the *Shema* in front of a woman's hair (E)which is normally covered.

NISHMAT AVRAHAM

the stringent view with regard to the *makom ervah*. Therefore, one should act in this way. See §6 below for more discussion on this topic.

ii) The *Chayei Adam*[12] wonders whether one may only close his eyes when exposed to a *tefach* or more of a Rabbinically prohibited *ervah*. The *Mishnah Berurah*[13] concludes that if he has not yet said the *Shema,* he should not say it even with his eyes closed. However, if there is no way he could turn so that the *ervah* is behind him, he may rely on the lenient opinions and recite the *Shema* and other prayers with closed eyes. This is also the opinion of *Rav Ovadiah Yosef shlita.*[14]

iii) The *Mishnah Berurah* concludes that one may close one's eyes to avoid seeing a woman's uncovered hair while reciting the *Shema.*[15]

(E) which is normally covered: The Torah requires that married women have their hair covered in public. As already mentioned in the previous section, the Rabbinic-level prohibition of *ervah* includes all areas of a woman's body which are normally covered. Therefore, since their hair must be covered, it attains the status of *ervah* on a Rabbinic level regarding recital of the *Shema,* prayers, etc. This is the basis for the *halachah* stated by the *Shulchan Aruch* in this section.

As in the previous section, the *Mishnah Berurah*[16] explains the *Shulchan Aruch* as describing both an objective and a social component to this prohibition. Even though the Torah requires that a married woman has her hair covered in public, with regard to praying etc. in front of her, her hair has the status of an objective *ervah* on a Rabbinic level, independent of the customs of times and place. Therefore, even if an entire community of married Jewish women choose to leave their hair uncovered, it is still an *ervah,* and one may not recite prayers in its presence. In contrast, any hair that happens to show from underneath a head-covering has a status subjective of a social *ervah*. Therefore, if a community of women are not stringent regarding the exposure of loose strands of hair, and it is normal for such hair to be seen, they are not said to be exposing an *ervah*. However, if the women are normally strict about allowing even loose strands of hair from being seen, then these acquire the status of *ervah,* and one may not recite prayers in their presence.

The *Aruch HaShulchan*[17] condemns the practice of married Jewish women leaving their hair uncovered. But, unlike the *Mishnah Berurah,* he feels that the *halachah* regarding the exposure of all of a woman's hair depends on the fashion of the times, and since it is customarily exposed it will not cause desirous thoughts in the mind of the beholder because it is so commonplace. Because hair is an *ervah* dependent on society's customs, it is not classified as an *ervah* in contemporary society and it is permissible to recite the *Shema* and pray in front of it. This is also the opinion of the *Igrot Moshe,*[18] the *Ben Ish Chai*[19] and *Rav Ovadiah Yosef shlita.*[20] It should be emphasized that this lenient ruling is only with regard to

12. בנשמת אדם כלל ד סי׳ א
13. ס״ק א
14. ראה הערה 11
15. ס״ק ה. נשמת אדם שם. פמ״ג סי׳ עא מ״ז ס״ק ב
16. ס״ק י
17. סע׳ ז
18. או״ח ח״א סי׳ מב ו־מג
19. שנה א פ׳ בא סע׳ יב
20. הערה על נשמת אברהם כרך א עמ׳ שלג. שו״ת יביע אומר ח״ו או״ח סי׳ יג

GLOSS: *Even when the woman whose hair is uncovered is his wife. However, as to a woman who has* (F)*never been married, who is accustomed to go about with her hair uncovered, he is permitted to recite the Shema in the presence of her uncovered hair.*

§5: If one sees an *ervah* through (G)glass, he is forbidden to recite the *Shema,* since it is written, "and He shall not see any immodest thing in you," and this can be seen.

§6: One is permitted to recite the *Shema* in the presence of *ervah* if either he turned his face away from it, or (H)he closed his eyes, or it was at night, or he was blind. For the *ervah* is said to be present only if he can see it and, in all of the above situations, he does not see it.

NISHMAT AVRAHAM

praying in front of a woman's hair; the Torah prohibition of having her hair uncovered in public still stands.

(F) never been married: Since there is no requirement for such women to cover their hair, it is not considered an *ervah. Rav Moshe Feinstein zt"l* rules that since it is customary for non-Jewish women to leave their hair uncovered, one would be permitted to recite the *Shema* even in the presence of a married non-Jewish woman whose hair was uncovered, provided that it does not cause him to have desirous thoughts.[21]

(G) glass: If one can see *ervah* through a glass window, he is forbidden to recite the *Shema.* This is true even when the *ervah* is in a different building. The *Mishnah Berurah*[22] believes that in such a case, if one recited the *Shema,* he would be required to repeat it when the *ervah* is no longer visible. In contrast, the *Kaf HaChaim*[23] believes that we can be lenient in this situation, since the prohibition involved is only Rabbinic in nature.[24] Similarly, one is forbidden to recite the *Shema* where the *ervah,* although covered by a thin garment, is still visible.[25] However, in these situations, he may close his eyes to avoid seeing the *ervah.* Closing one's eyes is normally not sufficient to permit one to pray in front of an *ervah;* however, in these instances it is sufficient, since the *ervah* is covered.[26]

(H) he closed his eyes: Most *acharonim* disagree with this ruling of the *Shulchan Aruch.* They believe that one is permitted to recite the *Shema* only if he has completely turned away from the *ervah.* They interpret the verse "and He shall not see any immodest thing in you,"[27] on which this prohibition is based, to require that one not face *ervah* while praying. Therefore, when one's own *ervah* is exposed, one has no choice but to cover it with a garment.[28]

21. שו"ת אג"מ או"ח ח"ד סי' טו
22. ס"ק כו
23. ס"ק לח
24. לפי שבראיה תלה הכתוב.
Although the *Shulchan Aruch* cites a verse, *Chazal* used the verse on which to base an already existing *halachah.*
25. ס"ק כה בשם הח"א כלל ד סע' ג ו-ט והפמ"ג א"א ריש הסימן ובמ"ז סי' עד סוס"ק א
26. מ"ב שם
27. דברים כג:טו
28. מ"ב ס"ק כט בשם הב"ח, הט"ז, מג"א, הגר"א, שו"ע הרב, דה"ח וח"א. וכן פסקו הברכ"י ס"ק ד, הערוה"ש סע' יא והבן איש חי שנה א פ' בא סע' ו

SIMAN 76:
TO AVOID EXCREMENT DURING *KERIYAT SHEMA*

NISHMAT AVRAHAM

SIMAN 76

Although the *halachot* of reciting the *Shema,* praying, or Torah study when excrement lies nearby are complex, it is important that both the health-care professional, as well as the patient be familiar with them. The following is a summary of some of these *halachot,* as taken from the *Biur Halachah.*[1] Throughout this *Siman,* whenever the prohibition of reciting the *Shema* is discussed, the prohibition of praying, saying a blessing or Torah study is automatically included (see §1A below).

1) The Torah forbids anyone to recite the *Shema,* pray, speak words of Torah, or say any blessing when excrement is four *cubits* or less behind him or to the side (see 79:1). This is based on the verse "and your camp shall be holy,"[2] and the four *cubits* surrounding a person are considered his "camp," and therefore must be kept "holy." If one did not inspect the area when there was reason to suspect that excrement might be present and, after reciting the *Shema,* he subsequently found some, he is required to repeat it.[3]

2) The *halachah* is basically the same for excrement that can be seen in front of one, even though it lies outside of the four-*cubit* limit, as it is for excrement which lies behind him or to his side within the *four* cubits. But the *Rashba* and the *Rosh* differ in their understanding of why what lies before him is not limited to four *cubits.*[4]

The *Rashba*[5] maintains that the verse:[6] "He shall not see any immodest thing in you," which prohibits reciting the *Shema* when one can see *ervah,* applies to excrement also. One is forbidden to recite the *Shema* when *ervah* can be seen, even if it is in a different room; this applies to excrement also.[7] And, if the excrement is more than four *cubits* away, even though he still sees it, he is permitted to think (but not speak) about Torah topics. The *Rashba* derives this from the verse, "He shall not see any immodest thing in you" which speaks of *ervah.* The word *davar* (thing) in the verse, has the same root as *dibbur* (speech). Thus, the prohibition regarding *ervah* is limited to speech, but not thought. And this applies also to excrement which he can see but which is not in his immediate presence (i.e. it lies more than four *cubits* away).

On the other hand, the *Rosh*[8] contends that the verse "He shall not see" applies only to *ervah* and not to excrement; the prohibition to recite the *Shema* in the presence of excrement stems from the verse "and your camp shall be holy." Thus, if the excrement is in a different room from the one in which a man is praying, he may recite the *Shema,* even though the excrement can still be seen. For "your camp" indicates a *halachic* extent of space and another room lies outside of that space. Although the *Rosh* agrees that one is forbidden to recite the

1. הקדמה לסי' עט
2. דברים כג:טו
This verse follows a command that soldiers relieve themselves only outside the camp area and, in so doing, keep the camp holy, allowing the Holy Presence to dwell within the camp.
3. ראה סוסי' עו
4. ברכות כה ע"א
5. ד"ה היה מקום גבוה
6. דברים כג:טו
7. ראה סי' עה סע' ו ומ"ב שם
8. סי' מד

NISHMAT AVRAHAM

Shema when the excrement in his room can be seen, it is unclear if this is a Rabbinic prohibition or forbidden by the Torah. Furthermore, since everything in one's room and within sight is within "your camp," he is forbidden to even contemplate Torah topics because it is either a Rabbinic or a Torah prohibition.[9]

3) The Torah states, "and you shall cover your excrement."[10] This verse teaches us that when excrement is covered, even if it is within four *cubits* from where one stands, he may recite the *Shema* provided there is no odor. According to *Rashi* and the *Rambam,* excrement that is either enclosed in a glass receptacle or even if completely uncovered but separated from him by a glass partition, is considered "covered" for the purposes of reciting the *Shema. Rav Shlomo Zalman Auerbach zt"l* believes that even the *Rashba* would agree with this ruling.[11] As to the proper height of such a partition, see the *Magen Avraham*[12] and the *Nishmat Adam.*[13]

4) A foul *"odor emanating from a source"* has the Torah status of excrement with respect to reciting the *Shema.* Therefore, if one recited it when such an odor was present, he would be required to repeat it. Furthermore, it is necessary to be at least four *cubits* away from the point where the odor can no longer be smelled. There is a major difference between actual excrement and a foul odor which emanates from a source in a different room. If the odor is still smelled, even though one is in a different room from its source, there is only a Rabbinic prohibition to recite the *Shema,* as it is considered an *"odor which does not have a source."*[14] For such an odor, there is no need to be an additional four *cubits* away from where the odor can no longer be detected.[15]

5) The Torah forbids reciting the *Shema* while one is urinating. But when urine is on the ground or on the legs, there is only a Rabbinic prohibition to recite the *Shema,* as long as the urine is not foul-smelling. Nevertheless, one must remove himself from urine that is on the ground just he does for excrement. However, when the urine is foul-smelling, the Torah prohibits reading the *Shema* in its presence.

6) *Halachah* puts any foul-smelling object (such as rotting garbage or meat) in the same category as excrement and the Torah forbids reciting the *Shema* in its presence. One is also forbidden by the Torah to recite the *Shema* in the presence of certain types of urinals or bedpans, even though they are empty. For further details, see *Siman* 87.

The *Biur Halachah*[16] states that it is preferable to refrain from praying if one is unable to remove himself to a proper distance from excrement, for to pray would entail transgressing a prohibition of the Torah. Nor should he even contemplate the words of the prayer in an attempt to fulfill his obligation to pray. Instead, he should think that although he is obligated to pray, he nevertheless cannot do so now. He should agonize over this, and *Hashem,* Who knows what is in his heart, will surely reward him for these thoughts and feelings.[17]

9. ראה פמ״ג מ״ז סי׳ עו ס״ק ב בשם הפר״ח
10. דברים כג:יד
11. וכ״כ המ״ב סי׳ עט ס״ק יד וביה״ל ד״ה אותה
12. סי׳ פז ס״ק ד
13. כלל ג
14. עיין בביה״ל בדעת הלבוש, הגר״א והח״א
15. ובפמ״ג נשאר בצ״ע אם אפילו בהפסקת רשות בעינן ד״א ממקום שכלה הריח
16. כאן סע׳ ה ד״ה צריך
17. מ״ב סי׳ סב ס״ק ט

§1: **It is permissible** [(A)]**to recite *Keriyat Shema* in front of excrement in a glass container even though it can be seen, because the presence or absence of excrement is determined by whether or not it is covered; for the Torah says: "and you shall cover your excrement," and here it is covered, even though it is visible.**

§4. **If one has feces on his** [(B)]**skin and it is covered by his clothing, or if he put his hand into the bathroom but detects no odor, some would permit him to recite the *Shema* while others would forbid it.**

GLOSS: *The same laws apply to semen on the skin.*

§5: **If one has feces on the area of his** [(C)]**anus,** [(D)]**he may not recite the *Shema* according to all opinions, even if the**

NISHMAT AVRAHAM

(A) to recite: The *halachot* regarding the prohibition to recite the *Shema* in the presence of excrement or in the presence of an *ervah,*[18] also apply to the study of Torah, prayer, or the pronouncement of blessings (henceforward described as "religious activity"). This is true regardless of whether the language used is Hebrew or not.[19]

(B) skin: If hands are soiled after wiping following a bowel movement, or after touching perspiration on his body, or after scratching his head, one is forbidden to recite the *Shema* or pray until he washes them. If there is no water to wash his hands, he should clean his hands in the manner described in *Siman* 4.[20]

(C) anus: One who has *hemorrhoids* and, as a result, has a constant odorous discharge, may not recite the *Shema* and the like as long as he has this discharge. However, when there is no odor present, if the discharge is intermittent and occurs because the patient voluntarily contracts his abdominal muscles, it is assumed that it originates from the digestive tract. Such a discharge is therefore considered as excrement, and has the *halachic* status of excrement. He can redress the situation by cleaning the area which is dirty before praying etc. But, if the fluid flows frequently and involuntarily, it is assumed to have originated from the *hemorrhoids.*[21] Such fluid does not have the status of excrement, and he may pray without first cleaning the area.[22]

The *Minchat Yitzchak*[23] rules that a patient with a *colostomy* or *ileostomy* may pray as long as the site is covered, and there is no foul odor. One might think that such a person should be prohibited from praying since it is likely that there is feces on his body. However, since one does not know this for certain and the prohibition is a Rabbinic one, there is room to be lenient and permit him to pray.[24] The *Tzitz Eliezer*[25] agrees with this ruling after the *ostomy* has been cleaned and covered.

---

18. סי׳ עד
19. מ״ב ס״ק ב
20. מ״ב ס״ק י
21. מ״ב ס״ק טז בשם שו״ת הרדב״ז ח״א סי׳ שטו
22. שו״ת הרדב״ז שם
23. ח״ו סי׳ יא ו־יב
24. בהסתמך על הח״א כלל ג סע׳ כה בנ״א ס״ק ו
25. ח״ט סי׳ ו

area is covered and even if the feces can only be seen when he sits but not when he stands.

§8: If one recited the *Shema* (E)in a place where he should have suspected that there may be feces, and then (F)later found feces, he must repeat it. If there was no reason for suspicion, he need not repeat the *Shema*. Urine, however, is not like feces; whether he should suspect its presence or not, even if he finds it, he need not repeat the *Shema*.

NISHMAT AVRAHAM

I also heard this from *Rav Shlomo Zalman Auerbach zt"l.*

Rav Waldenberg shlita rules that a person with an *in-dwelling urinary catheter* may participate in any religious activity (see **A**) as long as there is no foul odor emanating from the urine bag.[26] However, he states that it is preferable to cover the *catheter* tubing and bag, since it has the *halachic* status of a urinal. *Rav Shlomo Zalman Auerbach zt"l,* on the other hand, told me that there is no need to cover the tubing or the bag. Since the *catheter* is disposable, and there is no odor from the urine while it is in the bag, it lacks the *halachic* status of a urine container.[27] *Rav Neuwirth shlita* also told me that the tubing need not be covered since the urine does not remain there but only passes through it.[28]

See *Siman* 7 as to whether one with a *colostomy, ileostomy,* or *urinary catheter* should pronounce the blessing of *"asher yatzar."* See *Siman* 301:13 regarding a *colostomy* or *catheter* and the law prohibiting carrying outside on *Shabbat.*

(D) he may not: If one recited the *Shema* while feces was present in the area of the anus, he must repeat it. However, there is no consensus among the *acharonim* as to whether the same *halachah* applies to the *Shemoneh Esrei.* The *Chayei Adam*[29] writes that this issue needs further investigation. However, the *Eliyah Rabbah, Pri Megadim,* and *Derech HaChaim* rule that he must repeat the *Shemoneh Esrei.*[30]

(E) in a place where he should have suspected: The *Mishnah Berurah*[31] suggests this where there are small children is such a place. It would seem that a room where there are bed-bound patients is similar.

(F) later found: He must only repeat the *Shema* if he found the excrement within four *cubits.* However, if the excrement is further than four *cubits* away, one may adopt a lenient position and not repeat it.[32]

26. שו״ת ציץ אליעזר ח״ח סי׳ א

27. עוד כתב לי הגאון זצ״ל: וגם מכוסים תמיד באופן שבשום פעם לא מרגישים סרחון, וגם מסתבר שזה דומה למתכת וזכוכית, סי׳ פז סע׳ א, ולכן אין עליהם דין של עביט

28. ולכן י״ל דיש לו דין של בית כסא של פרסיים (ברכות כו ע״א ואו״ח סי׳ פג סע׳ ד)

29. כלל ג סע׳ כה

30. מ״ב ס״ק יז ושעה״צ ס״ק יח

31. ס״ק כח

32. מ״ב ס״ק כט וסי׳ פא מ״ב ס״ק יג וכדעה ראשונה בשו״ע שם

SIMAN 77:
ONE SHOULD NOT RECITE THE *SHEMA* WHILE FACING URINE

§1: It is prohibited to recite the *Shema* while (A)facing urine until it is (B)diluted with a *revi'it* of water. Both urine on the ground or in a container may be diluted in this way but not if the container was (C)specifically made for urine *(For the laws regarding a container specifically made for urine, see below, Siman 87).* **It is considered dilution both if water was added to the urine or if the water was already in the container.**

SIMAN 78:
HE WHO NEEDS TO URINATE WHILE RECITING THE *SHEMA*

§1: (A)One who, while reciting the *Shema*, began passing urine,

NISHMAT AVRAHAM

SIMAN 77

(A) facing: All of the laws of putting distance between oneself and excrement discussed in *Siman* 79:1 apply here as well.[1]

(B) diluted: The Torah prohibits reciting the *Shema* while urinating even if the urine does not have a foul odor. For urine on the ground which does not have a foul odor, the prohibition is Rabbinic. Since it is Rabbinic, *Chazal* ordained that adding a *revi'it* of water to any quantity of such urine is sufficient no matter how large a quantity. However, if the urine has a foul odor even after a *revi'it* of water has been added, the Torah prohibits reciting the *Shema* in its vicinity. One would need to add more water until the foul odor disappears.[2]

(C) specifically made for urine: One may not recite the *Shema* near a urinal. Whether or not urine is present it has the status of excrement. Adding water to such a container, even when empty, is not enough to allow for the recitation of the *Shema*. See *Siman* 87 for further details.[3] However, if the urinal is made of glass or the like, if both the inside and outside are cleaned well, and if there is no foul odor, it is permissible to recite the *Shema* in its presence.[4]

SIMAN 78

(A) One who: The laws that apply to reciting the *Shema* also apply to the *Shemoneh Esrei* and engaging in Torah study. One needs to stop praying or studying until the flow of urine ceases — even if this

1. מ״ב ס״ק א
2. ברכות כה ע״א. מ״ב ס״ק ב. ערוה״ש ס״ק א
3. מ״ב ס״ק ה
4. סי׳ פז סע׳ א ומ״ב ס״ק ו

must break off until he stops (B)urinating. He may then continue even though his underwear may be soaking wet, because his (C)outer clothing covers the urine. However, if he urinated onto the ground, he (D)moves away four *cubits* from the urine.

NISHMAT AVRAHAM

means waiting in the middle of the *Shemoneh Esrei* so long that he would have been able to finish the entire *Shemoneh Esrei,* and then, according to the *Rama,* he would have to start again from the beginning.[1] However, according to the *Mechaber,* he may continue from where he had stopped. In a *responsum,* the *Rama* ruled[2] that one who is constantly incontinent of urine and cannot pray because of his condition, and therefore would otherwise be permanently exempt from praying, would certainly be permitted to pray even without a *guf naki.* When urine is flowing, he should stop praying, and after the flow ceases, he should resume even though the urine remains on his clothing. This is because the Torah only prohibits praying while he is passing urine. Therefore, in such extenuating circumstances, one should not act stringently. Nevertheless, he should be scrupulous to keep his outermost clothing clean. He should, however, have an article of clothing or a sponge (e.g. diaper) around his genital area so that the urine will remain as if covered.

This advice is dependent on not feeling the urge to urinate when he begins to pray, even though he knows that he will inevitably pass urine during prayer.[3]

(B) urinating: Even if his legs are still damp from urine, he may recite the *Shema.*[4]

(C) outer clothing: If the outermost layer of clothing is also wet from urine, he must change his clothes or at least cover the soiled area with another garment in order to continue reciting the *Shema* or engaging in other religious activities (see *Siman* 76A). However, if this happened while he was in the middle of the *Shemoneh Esrei,* when it is forbidden to interrupt to change clothing or find a garment, then he should wait until the flow ceases. Even though it is a Rabbinic prohibition to pray near urine, since he is already in the middle of prayer, *Chazal* did not prohibit his continuing the *Shemoneh Esrei.*[5] The *Kaf HaChaim*[6] believes that only if one has already begun the *Shema* can he complete it if the urine has soiled his underwear. However, he is forbidden to start to recite the *Shema* or to engage in other Torah activities if he has soiled his underwear. The *Kaf HaChaim*[7] notes that the elderly often fail to clean themselves adequately after urinating. Because of this, he writes that it is a *mitzvah* to remind them to make sure that they and their clothes are appropriately clean before beginning the *Shema,* praying or pronouncing blessings.

(D) moves away: The *Mishnah Berurah*[8] rules that if this should occur during the *Shemoneh Esrei,* he should move four *cubits* away as as he would for *Keriyat Shema.* However, the *Magen Avraham*[9] and the *Ateret Zekenim*[10] rule that *Keriyat*

1. מ״ב ס״ק א
2. סי׳ צח
3. הובא גם במג״א סוס״ק ב ובמ״ב סוס״ק ד
4. מ״ב ס״ק ב וראה בשעה״צ ס״ק ג
5. מ״ב ס״ק ג
6. ס״ק ד
7. ס״ק א
8. ס״ק ד
9. ס״ק א
10. הגהות על הסעיף

GLOSS: *Or the distance described later in Siman 82, or he should wait until the urine is absorbed into the ground (if unpaved).*

Even if until he stopped urinating he had to wait the amount of time that it would take to say the whole of the *Shema*, he need not return to the beginning of the *Shema*, but may continue from where he left off.

GLOSS: *Some rule that if he waited the amount of time that it would take to finish all of the Shema, he should return to the beginning and start again. This is the preferable way to act as I wrote earlier in Siman 65. The time that it would take to finish reciting all of the Shema is based on the recital time of the individual concerned.*

SIMAN 79:
HE WHO COMES ACROSS FECES WHILE RECITING THE *SHEMA*

§9: If one flatulated, he is forbidden to speak words of Torah until the odor dissipates. If someone nearby flatulated, (A)he may speak words of Torah, for it would be impossible to prohibit this, for while some students are learning aloud others may be sleeping and flatulate in their sleep.

NISHMAT AVRAHAM

Shema differs from *Shemoneh Esrei;* during the *Shema* he may move away, but he may not do so during the *Shemoneh Esrei,* and therefore *Chazal* did not require him to move the four *cubits* when urine is on the ground near him. The *Machatzit HaShekel* explains that when the *Magen Avraham* stated that it is prohibited to move from one's place during *Shemoneh Esrei* in such a situation, he was referring to moving in order to find a change of clothing. Changing clothing involves a considerable interruption of prayer, whereas a move of four *cubits* does not.

SIMAN 79

(A) he may speak words of Torah: Since the prohibition to speak about matters of Torah in the presence of a foul *odor without a source* is Rabbinic, *Chazal* did not prohibit him from speaking about matters of Torah if someone else flatulated. This is because it would take time away from his study of Torah if he must wait for the odor to dissipate.[1]

1. מ״ב ס״ק ל. בן איש חי שנה א פ׳ בא סע׳ כו. ועיין בתהל״ד ס״ק ה

However, it is (B)prohibited (C)to recite the *Shema* until the odor dissipates.

SIMAN 80: HE WHO CANNOT PREVENT HIMSELF FROM FLATULATING

§1: If one (A)is certain that he (B)will not be able to recite the *Shema* and *Shemoneh Esrei* without flatulating, it is better that he allow (C)the proper time for them to pass

NISHMAT AVRAHAM

(B) prohibited: He may not recite the *Shema* while there is still an odor from flatulence because he can leave the area and recite it where there is no odor.[2] Someone, however, who is bed-bound, should wait until the odor dissipates before continuing the *Shema*. The *Magen Avraham*[3] wonders if one who is studying Torah alone should be allowed to continue studying in the presence of the odor if he can leave the area. Perhaps since *Chazal* did not explicitly prohibit one from learning Torah in such a case, he need not leave. The *Shulchan Aruch HaRav*[4] and the *Ben Ish Chai*[5] rule that one who is learning alone need not leave the area since *Chazal* only prohibited reciting the *Shema* in the presence of the odor from flatulence and did not extend their prohibition to learning Torah.

(C) to recite the *Shema*: Not only is it forbidden to recite the *Shema* until the odor from flatulence dissipates, but it is also forbidden to pronounce any blessings.[6]

SIMAN 80

(A) is certain: However if he is only uncertain about his flatulating during the *Shema* and *Shemoneh Esrei,* he should recite them.[1]

(B) will not be able: If one feels that it will be possible to complete the *Shema* and *Shemoneh Esrei* without flatulating, he should recite only these prayers rather than completely desist from praying altogether. However, when flatulation is inevitable even in this short period of time, he should not say even them. This is true even if it entails missing the proper time for their recitation.[2]

(C) the proper time: The *acharonim* believe that the *Mechaber* did not intend to write that the proper time for *Keriyat Shema,* which the Torah itself commands us to recite, should be allowed to pass because of a concern about flatulence. The *Rosh,* who is the source of this ruling, does not include *Keriyat Shema* in his discussion. The *Magen Giborim* explains that the *Mechaber* wrote *Keriyat Shema* because it often occurs in the same context as *Shemoneh Esrei*. When one prays the *Shemoneh Esrei,* it is as if he is standing in front of the King. It would therefore be

2. מ״ב ס״ק לב
3. ס״ק טו
4. שם סע׳ יא
5. שם
6. מ״ב ס״ק לא

1. מ״ב ס״ק א
2. מ״ב ס״ק ב

rather than to pray without a *guf naki.* If the proper time for *Shemoneh Esrei* passes, he is considered as being in an extenuating circumstance and should pray the *Minchah Shemoneh Esrei* twice. If he thinks that he can manage to recite the *Shema* only, without flatulating, he should put on *tefillin* between the blessing *ahavah rabbah* and the first verse of the *Shema.*

GLOSS: (D)*He should pronounce the blessings on the tefillin.*

NISHMAT AVRAHAM

inappropriate to begin praying, even if this means that he will not be able to say the *Shemoneh Esrei* in its proper time. This is so only if he is certain that it will be impossible not to flatulate while saying the *Shemoneh Esrei.* However, with the recital of the *Shema* he is not speaking to the King, but, rather, he fulfills His will and he may say the *Shema* with its blessings.

Even though it is preferable to recite the *Shema* while wearing *tefillin,* in this instance he may recite it without *tefillin* so that he may say it in its proper time. Later, when he is certain of a *guf naki,* he should don *tefillin.*[3] The *Gra* seems to think that he should even pray the *Shemoneh Esrei* (as well as the *Shema*) in its proper time, otherwise he would have to forgo saying it altogether.[4] The *Ben Ish Chai,* on the other hand, rules in accordance with the *Mechaber,* that it is better to miss the appropriate time for *Keriyat Shema* and *Shemoneh Esrei,* rather than pray without a *guf naki.* If the proper time for the *Shemoneh Esrei* does pass, he should recite it twice at *Minchah.*[5]

(D) He should pronounce the blessings: If one feels that he will not be able to maintain a *guf naki* any longer, he should remove his *tefillin* immediately after finishing the *Shema.* However, he need not remove his *tallit* since there is no requirement of having a *guf naki* while wearing it. The *Mishnah Berurah*[6] rules that if he did not wear a *tallit* at the beginning of his prayers, he may put it on, albeit without its blessing, between the blessing of *ahavah rabbah* and the *Shema,* since putting on a *tallit* does not constitute an interruption. In contrast, the *Ben Ish Chai*[7] rules that whereas putting on *tefillin* between *ahavah rabbah* and the *Shema* would not constitute an interruption, putting on a *tallit* would and is therefore prohibited.

The *Shulchan Aruch* rules that one who cannot maintain a *guf naki* is not permitted to pray. If a man suffers from a condition where he may flatulate at any time, it would seem that he would never be able to pray. However, this is not so; he is permitted to pray, even without a *guf naki.* The basis for this leniency is as follows: The prohibition to pray in the presence of the odor of flatulence is Rabbinic, since it is an *odor without a source.* On the other hand, the obligation to recite the *Shema* is a Torah commandment, and the *Shemoneh Esrei,* though Rabbinic in origin, has a greater significance than other Rabbinic ordinances since it is the basis of congregational prayer.[8] Therefore, in order to allow him to fulfill the important acts of

3. מ״ב ס״ק ג ועיין בביה״ל
4. שעה״צ ס״ק א
5. עוד יוסף חי פ׳ בא סע׳ ג
6. ס״ק ד
7. שם
8. מ״ב סי׳ צ ס״ק כח בשם החיי אדם

SIMAN 85:
WHERE IS IT PROHIBITED TO RECITE THE *SHEMA*

§2: It is forbidden (A)to even think about Torah topics while one is in the toilet, a public bathhouse, or a place where either feces or urine are present.

GLOSS: *It is prohibited even to study the laws that pertain to the bathhouse in the bathhouse.*

One may talk about mundane matters in these places, even in Hebrew. So too, one may mention the attributes of *Hashem* such as *Rachum* [The Compassionate One], (B)*Ne'eman* [The Trusted One], or the like, in these places.

NISHMAT AVRAHAM

Keriyat Shema and *Shemoneh Esrei,* the Rabbinic prohibition not to pray in the presence of the odor of flatulence is set aside.[9] The *Pri Chadash* agrees with this ruling, stipulating, however, that one who must flatulate while praying should stop praying until the odor dissipates. The *Ben Ish Chai*[10] agrees with this stipulation but adds that if he waits for as much time as it would take to say the entire prayer, he should repeat it from the beginning.

The *Pri Megadim* suggests further that perhaps he should also be permitted to put on *tefillin,* lest he never be able to perform that Torah commandment. The *Mishnah Berurah,* however, adds that it could be that the *Pri Megadim* was only suggesting that he put on *tefillin* for a few moments in order to fulfill the commandment to wear *tefillin* every day. He would certainly be prohibited from wearing *tefillin* for a longer period, since he cannot maintain a *guf naki.* And if he feels that he cannot prevent himself from flatulating for the amount of time necessary to put on the *tefillin shel yad* and *shel rosh* together, it is better to don them separately at different times. Nevertheless, in such a situation he should not pronounce the blessing upon donning *tefillin* since the *Gemara,* (*Shabbat* 49a) implies that such a person is exempt from wearing *tefillin.*[11]

In emphasizing the severity of flatulating while wearing *tefillin,* I heard from *Rav Auerbach zt''l*[12] that if one did so he has more of an obligation to fast than one whose *tefillin* fell to the ground.

SIMAN 85

(A) to even think about: If it is urgent, he may confess his sins even when feces or urine are present. However, he should not utter the Name of *Hashem* or make reference to His Kingship.[1]

(B) *Ne'eman* [Trusted One]: *Halachah* considers Hebrew to have a higher level of sanctity than any other language. Nevertheless, in a toilet, bathhouse, or other inappropriate place, one is prohibited from speaking words of Torah in any language, and certainly prohibited from

9. מ״ב שם בשם שו״ת רמ״א סי׳ צח
10. עוד יוסף חי שם
11. מ״ב ס״ק ד ושעה״צ ס״ק ט
12. בשם הלכה למשה אות קעה

1. שמעתי ממו״ר הגרי״י נויבירט שליט״א, וראייתו מהא דסי׳ תרו שעה״צ ס״ק כב. והוסיף הגרש״ז אויערבאך זצ״ל, שטוב שלא יכוין למצות וידוי כמו בשופר ראה להלן 588A

However, it is prohibited to mention those Names of *Hashem* which may not be erased.

SIMAN 87:

HOW FAR SHOULD A BEDPAN OR URINAL BE FROM ONE RECITING *KERIYAT SHEMA*

§1: One must remove himself from an earthenware or wooden bedpan or urinal as he would from feces, even if water was poured into it. However, if it is made of metal, (A)glass, or glazed earthenware, he may recite the *Shema* in its vicinity provided it has been (B)washed well.

NISHMAT AVRAHAM

mentioning those sacred Names of *Hashem* which one is forbidden to erase. Even a name such as the English, "God," which may be erased, should not be pronounced in these places, because it is considered disgraceful to make any reference to *Hashem* in an inappropriate place, even in a language other than Hebrew. Similarly, since *Hashem* can be called by the name *Shalom,* it is prohibited to use this word as a greeting in an inappropriate place. This is so even though it is permissible to erase this name and it is not specific to Him.[2] See also *Siman* 206A.

A hospitalized patient who is in a room with others who may relieve themselves by their bedsides must be very careful to cover books on religious topics, even if they are in script (and not in square letters) and are located on a table, like those normally found beside a hospital bed. However, if the dimensions of the table are four by four *tefachim* and the table has solid sides (rather than legs) that are at least ten *tefachim* high, one need not be concerned about covering the books since they are located in a different and distinct space from a *halachic* perspective. The *Taz*[3] warns that whoever is not careful to respect the holiness of printed Torah material will, in the future, be held accountable for it. However, in extenuating circumstances such as these, there are those[4] who feel that one can act leniently if there is no way at all that they could be covered.[5]

SIMAN 87

(A) glass: Today, containers and bedpans are generally made of plastic. One may treat them as one does a glass urinal since the feces or urine are not at all or only minimally absorbed into the plastic.[1]

(B) washed well: Within and without provided that there is no smell. If it does have a smell, it is considered an *odor without a source* and one need only move to a point where there is no odor and not four more *cubits* beyond that. However, if it has not been washed, one must move four *cubits* beyond the point at which the odor is no longer sensed since it is possible that it is still soiled and its odor will be an *odor with a source.*[2]

---

2. מ״ב ס״ק י וראה בנשמת אברהם באריכות
3. יו״ד סי׳ רעא ס״ק ח
4. שו״ת חות יאיר סי׳ קפד. א״ר סי׳ מ ס״ק ב
5. ראה סי׳ מ מ״ב סוס״ק ד ושעה״צ ס״ק יא

1. עיין במ״ב ס״ק ד. וב״ה שזכיתי לכוון לדעתו של מו״ר בשמירת שבת כהלכתה פכ״ב הערה קיג
2. מ״ב ס״ק ו

§3: One may recite the *Shema* in a house where there are feces, urine, or their containers if they stand at the (C)required distance (see *Siman* 79). Similarly, if they are covered, even if in the same room, they are considered as if interred, and he may recite the *Shema* facing them.

NISHMAT AVRAHAM

(C) required distance: If the feces are on the other side of an intervening partition and its odor does not reach him, he may recite the *Shema* and engage in religious activities (see *Siman* 76A). A curtain enclosing an area such as in a hospital room might be sufficient if it meets certain qualifications. It must be at least 80 cm[3] high,[4] 32 cm. wide,[5] and firm enough not to be shaken by a normal wind.[6] A curtain such as is found in a hospital should be fastened at the ceiling and floor to ensure its immobility,[7] or be fixed, top and bottom, to a movable frame.[8] However, as far as a hospital is concerned, one may take the view of the *Chazon Ish*[9] who believed that the curtain need not be fastened at the bottom since there is no wind indoors.[10] In addition, the curtain must either reach, or, at least, come within 24 cm. from the ground.[11]

One should bear in mind that a curtain or a folding partition with the above dimensions may not be erected, moved while open,[12] or opened on *Shabbat*.[13] Rather, it must be unfolded at least 8 cm.[14] before *Shabbat* in order that it may be opened fully on *Shabbat*[15] or *Yom Tov*.[16] This is because such a partition permits religious activities when it separates the person from feces, urine or their containers (that have no odor). However, a curtain or partition may be moved, erected or opened on *Shabbat,* no matter what its dimensions, if this is done only in order that one may sleep or have his privacy.[17]

3. לשיטת הגר״ח נאה זצ״ל ספר שיעורי תורה סי׳ ג סע׳ יח. אולם לשיטת החזו״א צ״ל 100 סמ׳ – ספר שיעורין דאורייתא
4. או״ח סי׳ שטו מ״ב ס״ק י
5. או״ח סי׳ פז סע׳ ג ביה״ל ד״ה מותר. ולשיטת החזו״א 40 סמ׳
6. שמירת שבת כהלכתה פכ״ד סע׳ ל מהא דאו״ח סי׳ שטו מ״ב ס״ק י
7. או״ח סי׳ רמ סע׳ ו בביה״ל ד״ה עד. או״ח סי׳ שטו במ״ב ס״ק ו ו־ט ובשעה״צ ס״ק ו ו־יא
8. או״ח סי׳ שטו מ״ב ס״ק יא
9. חזו״א או״ח סי׳ נב ס״ק יד ד״ה והנה המג״א וסי׳ עז ס״ק ו
10. שמעתי ממו״ר הגרי״י נויבירט שליט״א
11. שמעתי ממו״ר הגרי״י נויבירט שליט״א
12. מחיצה המתרת במקום אחד אינה נחשבת למחיצה מתרת במקום שני. אולם אם מושך את המחיצה המתרת כל שחלק מהמקום הראשון נשארה בו מחיצה, אז אולי לית לן בה, וכן גם להוסיף מחיצה שניה לאורך מחיצה הקיימת כדי להאריכה – מו״ר הגרי״י נויבירט שליט״א. ועיין בשמירת שבת כהלכתה פכ״ד הערה קכז
13. שמירת שבת כהלכתה פכ״ד סע׳ לב
14. ולשיטת החזו״א 10 סמ׳
15. או״ח סי׳ שטו סע׳ א בהגה. וראה גם במ״ב ס״ק י ו־יא. שמירת שבת כהלכתה שם, ועי״ש
16. חזו״א או״ח סי׳ נב ס״ק יד
17. שמעתי ממו״ר הגרי״י נויבירט שליט״א. וראה בשמירת שבת כהלכתה שם סע׳ לא

CHAPTER EIGHT:

The Laws of Prayer

SIMAN 89: THE LAWS OF PRAYER (*SHEMONEH ESREI*) AND ITS PROPER TIME

§3: It is forbidden to engage in one's affairs, or set out on the road until he prays the *Shemoneh Esrei*. (*Some authorities are lenient on these matters and permit them after he has said some of the morning blessings before "Baruch She'amar." However it is better to be stringent.*) **(A)He may not eat or drink in the morning before the *Shemoneh Esrei*. However, (B)he may drink water beforehand whether it be a weekday,**

NISHMAT AVRAHAM

SIMAN 89

(A) He may not eat: *Chazal* cite two verses from which they derive the principle that it is inappropriate to eat before praying. The verse in *Kings*[1] states, "and you have cast Me behind your back." The verse in *Leviticus*[2] states, "You shall not eat with the blood." *Chazal*[3] expound on these two verses and derive the principle that one should not taste anything before he accepts upon himself the yoke of Heaven and prays for his very existence.[4] However, the *Biur Halachah*[5] notes a difference in the handling of these two verses. From the verse, "You shall not eat with the blood," *Chazal* derive the *halachah* that one should not eat before he prays, referring to the recitation of *Shemoneh Esrei*. On the verse, "and you have cast Me behind your back," *Chazal* state that it is as if *Hashem* says: "Only after he ate, drank and was full of pride, did he accept upon himself the yoke of Heaven." Accepting the yoke of Heaven refers to the recitation of the *Shema*. Thus one verse serves as the basis for the prohibition to eat before reciting the *Shema*, while the other serves as the basis for the prohibition to eat before saying the *Shemoneh Esrei*. Because of this difference, the *Mishnah Berurah* feels that one who must eat before saying *Shemoneh Esrei*, such as a person who is ill, should at least recite the *Shema* before eating anything in order to first "accept upon himself the yoke of Heaven." *Rav Shlomo Zalman Auerbach zt"l* believes that one should also offer some form of supplication to *Hashem* prior to eating, even if only to say: "Hear *Hashem* and favor me, *Hashem*, be my support."[6]

(B) he may drink water: The *Mishnah*

1. מלכים א יד:ט
2. ויקרא יט:כו
3. ברכות י ע״ב
4. מ״ב ס״ק כא
5. ד״ה ולא
6. תהלים ל:יא

(C)*Shabbat* or *Yom Tov*. Similarly, (D)food or beverages which are necessary for medical purposes are (E)permitted.

NISHMAT AVRAHAM

Berurah[7] believes that drinking water before prayers does not constitute an act of conceit, since it is common to drink water in the morning to quench one's thirst. However, when one adds sugar to water, this is solely for taste and is considered to show conceit; that is forbidden before praying. The *Mishnah Berurah* allows one to drink coffee or tea before praying if he feels that this will enable him to pray better. Nevertheless, he is not permitted to put milk or sugar into the beverage, for that shows conceit. However, the *Maharsham,*[8] the *Aruch HaShulchan,*[9] and *Rav Ovadiah Yosef shlita*[10] rule that it is permitted to drink tea or coffee with sugar before praying. This is also what I heard from *Rav Shlomo Zalman Auerbach zt"l.* As to adding milk to the beverage, *Rav Ovadiah Yosef shlita* writes that although one should be stringent if possible, nevertheless one who wishes to act leniently may do so, provided that there is less milk than water in the beverage. The *Ben Ish Chai*[11] forbids even water.

(C) Shabbat: The obligation to recite *Kiddush* on *Shabbat* morning does not begin until after the *Shemoneh Esrei.* At that point, it is forbidden to eat or drink anything, even water, until after *Kiddush.*[12] Before the *Shemoneh Esrei,* the *halachah* regarding eating is the same on *Shabbat* as for a weekday, for which see above, **B.** An ill person, who intends to eat a meal before the *Shemoneh Esrei,* is obligated to recite *Kiddush* before he even drinks water.[13] A woman who is unable to pray as usual because of ill-health or weakness, may say the first sentence of the *Shema* followed by a short prayer praising *Hashem,* a brief supplication (such as "make Your Torah always desirable to me")[14] and then thanking Him briefly; she is then permitted to eat after making *Kiddush.*[15] (See *Siman* 289A for a fuller discussion.)

(D) food and beverages which are necessary for medical purposes: The *Biur Halachah*[16] cites *acharonim* who believe that one should make every effort to say the *Shemoneh Esrei* before eating. Therefore, if one is too weak to postpone eating until after the prayer services are completed in synagogue, he should pray at home by himself rather then eat before going to pray in the synagogue. Once he has completed the *Shemoneh Esrei* (recited *Kiddush*) and eaten a small amount (see *Siman* 272B), he should go to the synagogue to hear *Kaddish, barechu,* and other portions of the service which require a *minyan.* The *Pri Chadash* and the *Pri Megadim* state that if he must eat for medical reasons he may eat before prayers, even if he feels that he could wait until after the *Shemoneh Esrei.*

(E) permitted: One may eat food needed for medical reasons before he prays, even if he derives pleasure from it and even if he is not very ill.[17]

---

7. ס״ק כב
8. דעת תורה כאן
9. סע׳ כג
10. שו״ת יביע אומר ח״ד סי׳ יא ו־יב
11. שנה א פ׳ יתרו סע׳ יח
12. מ״ב ס״ק כג
13. הגרש״ז אויערבאך זצ״ל, לב אברהם ח״ב עמ׳ כ. ועיין בפמ״ג א״א סי׳ רפט ס״ק ד
14. ראה סי׳ מז סע׳ יד וביה״ל שם. והוסיף לי מו״ר שליט״א שאין לה חיוב להזכיר את השבת. ועיין בפמ״ג א״א סי׳ רפט ס״ק ד
15. שמעתי ממו״ר הגרי״י נויבירט שליט״א
16. ד״ה וכן
17. מ״ב ס״ק כד. ועיין גם בס״ק כח ובשע״ת ס״ק ג בשם הברכ״י

§4: [F]One who is thirsty or [G]hungry is considered ill regarding the *halachot* of prayer. If he feels that he can concentrate on his prayers he should pray, but if not, he may [H]eat and drink before praying, should he so wish.

§5: If he [I]began to eat before dawn, [J]he must stop at dawn.

NISHMAT AVRAHAM

(F) One who is thirsty: Although one may drink water before prayers (see above in the previous section), the *halachah* here does not refer to a man who wishes to drink water only, but to one who cannot drink without having something to eat with it. If he is thirsty he may eat a small amount of food.[18]

(G) hungry: Only if one is famished is he permitted to eat before prayers. However, if he is merely hungry he should not eat.[19]

(H) eat and drink: Ideally, one should only pray when he is certain that he can concentrate properly on his prayers. Why then does the *Shulchan Aruch* not say that if he cannot concentrate because of thirst or hunger he should eat or drink before praying so that he will be able to concentrate? Instead, he writes, "if not, he may eat and drink before praying." This is because nowadays people do not attain a high level of concentration during prayers anyway[20] and even if one does not eat and drink it will not affect his customary level (or lack) of concentration. Thus the *Shulchan Aruch* permits him to drink and eat only if it will improve his ability to concentrate.[21] The *Eliyah Rabbah,*[22] however, feels that he is forbidden to pray until he eats or drinks, if not eating or drinking will adversely affect his concentration.

(I) began to eat: He may begin to eat at any time throughout the night, up to a half-hour before dawn. If he did begin before the half-hour to dawn he may continue to eat as much as he wishes until dawn. During the half-hour before dawn, however, he is forbidden to begin unless he intends to eat less than a *kebeitzah* (45 grams).[23] This ruling only applies to men; a woman may start at any time and eat as much as she wishes all the way to dawn.[24]

Thus, a doctor or male nurse who is on overnight duty may begin a meal anytime in the night before the half-hour prior to dawn. However, if he only began eating during the half-hour before dawn and consumes more than 45 grams, he must stop eating immediately (a woman may continue eating until dawn). He may begin eating within the half-hour prior to dawn if he eats less than this amount.

(J) he must stop at dawn: According to the *Zohar,* one is forbidden to eat any time after the *halachic midnight.* The *Pri Megadim* says the *Zohar* refers only to one who has slept. However, one who has been awake the entire night may begin to eat until the half-hour before dawn. The *Mishnah Berurah*[25] believes that preferably one should heed the words of the *Zohar.* However, when this is not possible, he may begin to eat until the half-hour

18. ביה״ל ד״ה הצמא, בשם הפמ״ג
19. מ״ב ס״ק כה בשם הלבוש
20. עיין בירושלמי ברכות פ״א ה״ד הובא בתוס׳ ב״ב קסד ע״ב ד״ה עיון. וראה גם בהשגות הראב״ד בסוף הל׳ קריאת שמע
21. מ״ב ס״ק כו
22. כאן
23. מ״ב ס״ק כז
24. הגרש״ז אויערבאך זצ״ל בלב אברהם ח״ב עמ׳ כ. וטעמו הואיל ואין חיוב תפלה שלהן דומה לשל גברים (אולם עיין סי׳ קו מ״ב ס״ק ד – מו״ר הגרי״י נויבירט שליט״א)
25. מ״ב ס״ק כח, ועיין בסי׳ תקסד

(K)Some say that he need not stop.

SIMAN 90: THE PROPER PLACE FOR PRAYER WITH THE CONGREGATION

§9: One should always try to pray in a synagogue (A)with the congregation. If, (B)because of extenuating circumstances,

NISHMAT AVRAHAM

before dawn, even if he has slept a part of the night.

(K) Some: According to this opinion, one is not required to stop if he began eating before dawn. However, the *Mishnah Berurah* qualifies this ruling. When one begins his meal during the half-hour before dawn, he is required to stop in order to put on *tefillin*[26] and recite the *Shema,*[27] since both are commandments of the Torah. However, he is not required to pronounce the blessings of the *Shema* or pray *Shemoneh Esrei* then, since they are only Rabbinic requirements. After completing these *mitzvot,* he is permitted to resume his meal, without having said *Shemoneh Esrei.* Once he has finished eating, he should recite the daily prayers, repeating the *Shema,* now with its blessings, and say the *Shemoneh Esrei.* Most *acharonim* believe that the first opinion cited in the *Shulchan Aruch* (in this section) should be followed; namely, he should stop eating at dawn to recite the entire prayer service, including the blessings of the *Shema* and *Shemoneh Esrei.*

SIMAN 90

(A) with the congregation: Parts of the prayer service are essentially meant to be said together with a *minyan.* Some mistakenly think that the most important part of the collective prayer service is to respond to *Kaddish, Kedushah,* and *barechu* together with the congregation. However, this is not true. Rather, it is more important that the individual start his *Shemoneh Esrei* together with the rest of the congregation.[1] Therefore, he should make every effort to arrive at the synagogue in time to say *Shemoneh Esrei* together with the *minyan.*[2] But even if he did not arrive in time to do so, and started after the others, he is still considered, post facto, to have prayed with them.[3] In light of this, one who is ill and is permitted to come to the synagogue for only a short time, should make every effort to be there to pray the *Shemoneh Esrei* with the *minyan* rather than to come to hear the reading of the Torah. However, if he feels that, because of his illness, he would concentrate better if he recited *Shemoneh Esrei* at home, he should do so at the same time as the congregation. After he has completed the *Shemoneh Esrei,* he should go to the synagogue to hear the reading of the Torah.[4]

(B) because of extenuating circumstances: This refers to one who feels too weak to go to the synagogue, even if he is not actually ill.[5]

Rav Chaim Palachi z"l writes[6] that a doctor who is called to tend to a *seriously ill*

26. ביה"ל ד"ה וי"א
27. ס"ק כט
1. מ"ב ס"ק כח בשם הח"א
2. שם
3. שו"ת אג"מ או"ח ח"ג סי' ד
4. שו"ת מנחת יצחק ח"ז סי' ו
5. מ"ב ס"ק כט
6. שו"ת לב חיים ח"ב סי' קמח

he is unable to go to the synagogue, (C)he should try to pray at home at the hour that the congregation is praying. *(This is also true for those who live in a place where there is no minyan. They should nevertheless pray Shacharit and Maariv at the same time that other congregations pray.)* **If because of extenuating circumstances, a person did not pray at the hour that the congregation prayed, he should pray in the synagogue, even if alone.**

§10: When one is praying together with the congregation, he is forbidden to say *Shemoneh Esrei* before they do. However, if the service is long, because of many supplemental prayers or any other reason, and he feels that the congregation will not reach *Shemoneh Esrei* before (D)the proper time to recite it passes, he may pray the *Shemoneh Esrei* before they do. *(If, however, there will still be time to say the Shemoneh Esrei, he should recite the supplemental prayers together with the congregation rather than separate himself from them, even to engage in Torah study. See Siman* 68.)

NISHMAT AVRAHAM

patient must leave the synagogue even if he is in the middle of his prayers or during the reading of the Torah, and even if by doing so the time set for that particular prayer will have passed. *Rav Waldenberg shlita* believes that he must interrupt his *Shemoneh Esrei.*[7] Similarly, a doctor must respond immediately when his beeper sounds, even if he is in the middle of his *Shemoneh Esrei* or during the reading of the Torah. Since it is possible that he is being called for a patient who is dangerously ill and requires immediate assistance, he must not delay his response, even to complete the *Shemoneh Esrei.*

(C) he should try to pray: Nowadays, many Jewish communities have several *minyanim* throughout the morning. Therefore, a doctor or a male nurse who cannot attend synagogue because he must be at work very early, should begin his prayers so that his *Shemoneh Esrei* coincides with sunrise. Since there are many synagogues that have prayers at this time, it is likely that he will say his prayers simultaneously with them, and fulfill the requirement mentioned here by the *Shulchan Aruch.*[8]

(D) the proper time to recite it: The *Gemara* [9] states that one who feels weak may pray at home before the time that the congregation will pray. However, once he is in the synagogue, he is forbidden to pray before the congregation does. However, if one is ill or there are other extenuating circumstances, the *Bach* and the *Perishah*[10] write that he may pray before the congregation, even when he is in the synagogue.[11]

7. שו״ת ציץ אליעזר ח״ט סי׳ יז פ״ז וח״י סי׳ יג
8. מהא דמ״ב ס״ק לא
9. ברכות כח ע״ב
10. סי׳ קיד סע׳ ב
11. מ״ב ס״ק לו ודלא כהב״י עיין מג״א ס״ק כא

§27: If one was praying *Shemoneh Esrei* in the synagogue, and an (E)infant urinated near him, he should (F)remain silent until someone (G)pours water on the urine, or he should move so that the urine is four *cubits* behind him or to his side; or, he can leave the synagogue and complete his *Shemoneh Esrei* outside.

GLOSS: (H)*It is preferable that one move elsewhere, rather than stop his recitation of Shemoneh Esrei in the middle and wait, since he might pause too long and be required to repeat it from the beginning.*

SIMAN 91:
ONE SHOULD BE SUITABLY DRESSED WHILE PRAYING

§5: One should not recite the *Shemoneh Esrei* wearing an external money belt, with his head uncovered, or with bare feet, if the local custom is to wear shoes when (A)in the presence of important people.

NISHMAT AVRAHAM

(E) infant urinated: The same holds true for a hospitalized patient if a fellow patient, sharing the room, urinates nearby while he is praying.

(F) remain silent: Normally, one must not interrupt *Shemoneh Esrei* with an extended pause. However, here he may allow a significant amount of time to elapse while waiting for someone to bring water. Nevertheless, he may not speak during this time. Since the prohibition to pray in the vicinity of a urinal is only Rabbinic (if it is made of glass or plastic — see *Siman* 87:1), a hospitalized patient may continue his *Shemoneh Esrei* after his fellow patient has finished urinating, rather than stop to call a nurse to either cover or remove the nearby urinal. However, if his roommate defecated nearby, the Torah prohibits his praying in the presence of the feces, and he would be forbidden to continue his *Shemoneh Esrei*.[12] See *Siman* 76 for details regarding this *halachah*.

(G) pours water: This is also permitted on the *Shabbat*.[13]

(H) It is preferable: A bed-bound patient who cannot move away from the urine that is within his four *cubits* and fears that if he waits until it is removed he will have waited the time he would take to complete the *Shemoneh Esrei* and thus have to repeat it from the beginning, may depend on the *Rashba's* ruling that he may continue praying. This is because he started to pray when the area was clean and the prohibition to pray in the presence of urine is Rabbinic.[14]

SIMAN 91

(A) in the presence of: When saying *Shemoneh Esrei,* one should envision oneself as standing in front of the King.[1]

12. מהא דמ״ב ס״ק פד ו־פה
13. וכ״כ המ״ב סי׳ שב ס״ק נו שע״ת ס״ק ז.
14. מ״ב ס״ק פה בשם החיי אדם
1. מ״ב ס״ק א

SIMAN 92:
PREPARATIONS BEFORE PRAYING

§9: One who spits should not begin the *Shemoneh Esrei* until the time it takes to walk four *cubits* has passed. One who is praying should not spit until he waits this amount of time. This *halachah* applies only if he spits (A) at will. However, if he suddenly felt the need to spit, he is permitted to do so immediately (*see Siman* 97:2).

SIMAN 93:
ONE MUST TAKE A BREAK FROM WHAT HE IS DOING AND WAIT SOMEWHAT BEFORE PRAYING

§4: One who is involved in communal work is like one involved in Torah study with respect to the *Shemoneh Esrei*. Just as one is allowed to begin the *Shemoneh Esrei* immediately following Torah study, so too, one may begin the *Shemoneh Esrei* immediately following his communal work. Others interpret this statement to mean that one involved in communal work is not required to stop his activities (A) to recite the *Shemoneh Esrei* just as one is not required to interrupt his Torah study to pray.

NISHMAT AVRAHAM

Therefore one is required to be fully dressed as would be considered appropriate for such a situation. He should try, where possible, not to pray in a dressing gown or pajamas since it is not appropriate to stand thus before *Hashem*.[2]

SIMAN 92

(A) at will: A person with a productive cough should keep a tissue or handkerchief on hand to collect his sputum. He is permitted to continue his recitation of *Shemoneh Esrei* immediately, and is not required to wait the amount of time it takes to walk four *cubits*.[1]

SIMAN 93

(A) to recite the *Shemoneh Esrei*: When one is unable to find another to relieve him of his duties, he may continue with his communal work, even if the time to say the *Shemoneh Esrei* will pass. However, if he can find a temporary replacement, he must stop his activities in order

1. עיין במ״ב ס״ק לה

2. מ״ב ס״ק יא בשם החיי אדם. וראה בבן איש חי שנה א פ׳ יתרו סע׳ טו

NISHMAT AVRAHAM

to say the *Shemoneh Esrei.*[1]

Most *acharonim* believe that if one fails to say *Shemoneh Esrei* because of his involvement in communal work, he is not required to make up the prayer by saying it twice the next time he prays.[2] This is only so when he became involved in his activities before the time for that prayer began. If, however, he began his activities after the time to say *Shemoneh Esrei* started, and he failed to say it before its time passed, he must make it up at the next prayer service.[3] Thus, a surgeon who began operating after the time to pray *Minchah* had already arrived, and did not complete his work until nightfall, must recite the *Shemoneh Esrei* twice when he prays the *Maariv* service. The same *halachah* applies to a doctor who is unable to pray because of involvement in patient care.

What does a woman do with respect to making up missed prayers? There is a dispute between the *Rambam* and the *Ramban* about the source of the obligation to recite *Shemoneh Esrei.* According to the *Rambam,* the Torah requires a person to pray once a day. This prayer must consist of supplication and praise to *Hashem.*[4] Although one can fulfill this obligation by reciting any form of praise and supplication to *Hashem,* our Rabbis established the text of *Shemoneh Esrei* to be recited three times a day.[5] However, only men are required to adhere to these Rabbinic guidelines. Since the *mitzvah* of prayer is time-bound, women are exempt from it and are only required to pray once a day. In light of this, according to the *Rambam,* it is not relevant to discuss women making up a missed prayer for, on a given day, they are only required to pray once. Furthermore, since she is only obligated to pray once a day, she cannot make up today for the prayer she missed yesterday.[6]

In contrast to the *Rambam,* the *Ramban*[7] rules that the obligation to pray is Rabbinic. Although the *mitzvah* of prayer is time-bound, nevertheless they obligated women as well to pray *Shacharit* and *Minchah* since the purpose of prayer is to ask for *Hashem*'s mercy. Most women are not accustomed to pray *Maariv;* nevertheless, if she was unable to pray *Minchah* because of extenuating circumstances she should pray *Maariv* that evening and recite a second *Shemoneh Esrei* in place of the *Minchah* that she missed. But, since women are not obligated to pray *Maariv,* she is not required to recite a second *Shemoneh Esrei* at *Shacharit* if she missed a *Maariv* service.[8] It goes without saying that according to the *Ramban,* a woman who forgot to pray *Shacharit* would be required to pray *Shemoneh Esrei* twice at *Minchah* (see also *Siman* 289A).

1. מ״ב ס״ק ח וסי׳ קו ס״ק ג. וע״ע במ״ב סי׳ קח סוס״ק ב
2. הפרישה כאן ס״ק ט, הדרישה יו״ד סי׳ שמא ס״ק ג, הש״ך שם בנקה״כ, המג״א כאן ס״ק ה, הא״ר ס״ק ד, והברכ״י כאן ס״ק ג וסי׳ תרפז ס״ק א. ועיין בכף החיים ס״ק טו
3. סי׳ קח סע׳ ח
4. הל׳ תפלה פ״א ה״א ו־ב וספר המצוות מצוה ה
5. מ״ב סי׳ קו ס״ק ד
6. שמעתי ממו״ר הגרי״י נויבירט שליט״א
7. ספר המצוות מצוה ה. וראה במ״ב שם בשם דעת רוב הפוסקים. וראה באשי ישראל פ״ז סע׳ טו והערות שם
8. ספר הליכות בת ישראל פ״ב סע׳ ה בשם הגרש״ז אויערבאך זצ״ל וראה שם בהערות נ ו־נא

SIMAN 94:
FACING IN THE DIRECTION OF *ERETZ YISRAEL* WHILE PRAYING, AND THE LAW FOR ONE WHO IS TRAVELING ON LAND OR WATER

§5: Someone sitting in a boat or wagon who wishes to say the *Shemoneh Esrei* must, if possible, at least stand up for the parts of *Shemoneh Esrei* where he has to bow and also to take the required three steps back, after finishing.

GLOSS: *Even when one has been sitting for the entire Shemoneh Esrei, if he is able to stand up in order to bow where required and to take the three steps back on conclusion, he must do so. If he is unable to do so, for example, if he is riding on an animal, he should have the animal* (A)*take three steps backward, and it will be considered as if he himself stepped back.*

§6: A sick person may pray even while (B)**reclining on his side, provided he can concentrate.** *(If he cannot pray, he should at least* (C)*contemplate the Shemoneh Esrei in his heart, since it is written, "say in your hearts, on your beds.")*

NISHMAT AVRAHAM

SIMAN 94

(A) take three steps backward: Regarding one who is in a wheelchair, or who cannot stand because of illness, see *Siman* 123.

(B) reclining on his side: See *Siman* 63A for *Rav Auerbach zt"l's* opinion regarding the criteria for reclining while praying, especially for the bedridden patient.

One must stand, if possible, at least for those parts of the *Shemoneh Esrei* where he is required to bow.[1] If he does not know the proper direction to face while saying the *Shemoneh Esrei,* he may face any direction but should direct his thoughts toward *Hashem.*[2] See below, §9.

(C) contemplate the *Shemoneh Esrei* in his heart: The *Mishnah Berurah*[3] takes up the question as to whether one who contemplated the *Shemoneh Esrei* when he was unable to recite it aloud, is required to repeat it if he becomes capable of speaking while there is yet time for the prayer. He cites *acharonim*[4] who believe that contemplation fulfills the obligation of saying the *Shemoneh Esrei*. However,

1. סע׳ ה ומ״ב ס״ק כ
2. סע׳ ג
3. ס״ק כא
4. ראה במ״ב סי׳ סב סע׳ ד ובביה״ל שם. וכ״כ הפמ״ג מ״ז סוסי׳ סב, הברכ״י סי׳ פ ס״ק ב והכף החיים סי׳ סב ס״ק ח וסי׳ צד ס״ק כח

§8: One should be careful not to lean on a column or on someone (D)while praying.

§9: One who must (E)sit while praying (F)must repeat the *Shemoneh Esrei* when he gets the chance to stand up but he is not required to add anything new to the text.

GLOSS: *One who is traveling and finds himself in the vicinity of a non-Jewish hotel, should go to the side of the road to pray, where passing travelers will not disrupt his prayers, rather than pray in the (G)non-Jewish hotel, where the residents may disturb him. However, if he cannot go to the side of the road where he will not be disturbed, he should pray in the hotel, in a private corner.*

NISHMAT AVRAHAM

the *Mishnah Berurah* himself,[5] along with other *acharonim,* believes that one does not fulfill his obligation through contemplation and he is therefore required to recite the *Shemoneh Esrei* if the opportunity becomes available.

(D) while praying: Ideally, one should stand without leaning on anything while saying the *Shemoneh Esrei.* However, a sick person, who is sure that he will be unable to concentrate as required if he would stand unaided, may lean on something while praying, if he believes that this will improve his concentration. However, if he feels that even this will interfere with his concentration, he may recite the *Shemoneh Esrei* seated.[6] One who is seated while saying *Shemoneh Esrei* should nevertheless attempt to sit upright with his head bowed and avoid leaning to his side, lounging with his legs stretched out or sitting with his legs crossed.[7]

(E) sit: See below, *Siman* 123, regarding the proper conduct for one seated in a wheelchair.

(F) must repeat: Most *acharonim,* however, rule that one who recited the *Shemoneh Esrei* while seated is not required to repeat it when able to stand.[8]

(G) non-Jewish hotel: A patient lying in a non-Jewish hospital where the rooms are decorated with crucifixes or statues, must not pray while facing in their direction.[9] If he is bedridden and cannot turn to avoid these objects, he should close his eyes to pray.[10] Such a patient may not bow at the required times during the *Shemoneh Esrei* in the presence of a crucifix, since it might seem that he is bowing to it.[11]

Regarding the recitation of *Shemoneh Esrei* while standing opposite pictures hanging on a wall, see *Tosafot,*[12] *Magen Avraham,*[13] *Pitchei Teshuvah,*[14] *Mishnah Berurah,*[15] *She'arim Metzuyanim BaHalachah,*[16] and *Yechaveh Da'at.*[17]

5. סי׳ סב ס״ק ז
6. מ״ב ס״ק כד
7. כף החיים ס״ק לב. לקט הקמח החדש ס״ק טז
8. מ״ב ס״ק כז. וכ״כ הכף החיים ס״ק לד
9. מ״ב ס״ק ל. ומקור הדין בתרומת הדשן סי׳ ו
10. שו״ת עצי חיים סי׳ א ושו״ת חלק לוי סי׳ מד, מובאים בשערים מצויינים בהלכה סי׳ יח ס״ק ז
11. שמעתי ממו״ר הגרי״י נויבירט שליט״א
12. יומא נד ע״א
13. סי׳ צ ס״ק לז
14. יו״ד סי׳ קמא ס״ק ג בשם שו״ת חת״ס סי׳ קכט
15. סי׳ צ ס״ק עא
16. סי׳ יח ס״ק ז
17. ח״ג סי׳ סב

SIMAN 98:
ONE SHOULD CONTEMPLATE DEEPLY WHILE PRAYING

§1: A person should try to understand the simple meaning of his prayers. He should envision that he is standing before the Divine Presence and focus entirely on his prayers, (A)removing from his mind all extraneous thoughts that bother him. He should realize that were he beseeching a human king, he would certainly organize his words carefully and familiarize himself with his petition in order that he should not falter. How much more so when one is praying to the King of Kings, the Holy One, Blessed be He, Who knows everyone's thoughts. If an outside thought enters his mind while praying, he should wait quietly until it leaves him. He should try to reflect on ideas that cause humility, and direct his thoughts towards his Father in Heaven, shutting out all trivia.

GLOSS: *Before one begins to pray, he should contemplate the loftiness of Hashem, and the lowliness of man, removing all human desire for pleasure from his heart. He is forbidden to kiss his young children while in the synagogue, thus instilling in his heart that nothing can compare to the love of Hashem.*

SIMAN 101:
ONE MAY PRAY IN ANY LANGUAGE

§4: One may pray in any language that he wishes to when praying with a congregation. However, if praying alone

NISHMAT AVRAHAM

SIMAN 98

(A) removing from his mind all extraneous thoughts: One is permitted to pray for a person who is ill while saying the *Shemoneh Esrei*. However, he must not focus his prayers only on the blessing for the sick when praying for him. Rather, he must concentrate fully on the entire *Shemoneh Esrei,* so that the Heavenly prosecutors are not given a chance to claim that he apparently has no other needs but this one. By concentrating properly on all of the blessings of the entire *Shemoneh Esrei,* they cannot allege that he is more concerned with his own needs than with showing proper respect to *Hashem.*[1]

1. ספר חסידים סי׳ קנח. א״ר ס״ק א. אשל אברהם על גליון השו״ע

he should only do so in Hebrew. There are some who rule that this is so only when he asks for his personal needs, for example when he prays for (A)a person who is ill or for any other personal problem. However, if he is reciting a prayer of a text which has been established for the community, then even if praying alone, he may recite it in any language. There are others who rule that even a person praying alone who is petitioning for his own needs may do so in any language, with the exception of Aramaic.

SIMAN 102:
ONE SHOULD NOT PASS IN FRONT OF SOMEONE WHO IS PRAYING

§2: There is an authority who rules that a person who is (A)feeble is permitted to sit beside one who is praying.

SIMAN 108:
ONE WHO DID NOT PRAY BECAUSE OF AN ERROR, EXTENUATING CIRCUMSTANCES, OR BY DESIGN

§1: One who erred, or who, (A)because of extenuating circum-

NISHMAT AVRAHAM

SIMAN 101

(A) a person who is ill: *Chazal* teach us that when one is ill, the Divine Presence is present at his bedside. Therefore, when one prays on behalf of a sick person, he may pray in any language, provided that he is in the person's presence. However, if one is not in the presence of the sick person, he should pray in Hebrew.[1]

SIMAN 102

(A) feeble: This *halachah,* which allows a person who is feeble to sit beside someone who is praying, only applies to one whose inability to stand because of his weakness is obvious to others. Additionally, there are those who only permit such a person to sit beside, but not in front of, one who is praying.[1] Nevertheless, the *Pri Megadim* states that most *poskim* are more lenient and permit one who is feeble to sit even in front of one who is praying.[2]

SIMAN 108

(A) because of extenuating circumstances: For example, if one was unable to recite *Shemoneh Esrei* because he was ill, he must make it up and recite a second one at the next prayer time.[1]

See *Siman* 93:4 for a discussion regarding a doctor or nurse who was unable to pray due to involvement in patient care.

1. מ״ב ס״ק טז

1. מ״ב ס״ק ב
2. שעה״צ ס״ק יד

1. מ״ב ס״ק י בשם הא״ר

stances, did not pray *Shacharit,* should pray *Shemoneh Esrei* twice at *Minchah,* the first for *Minchah*, and the second to make up for the missed *Shacharit.* If he reversed the order and recited the first *Shemoneh Esrei* with *Shacharit* in mind, he has not fulfilled his obligation, and must now recite a third *Shemoneh Esrei* for the one he missed. This ruling applies whenever one must make up for a missed *Shemoneh Esrei.*

§8: One who did not pray because he thought that there would be sufficient time to do so when he completed (B)the activity with which he was involved, and the time set for that *Shemoneh Esrei* passed; or one who was involved with his finances; or one who was too intoxicated to pray; all of these are considered to be extenuating circumstances, and he may therefore make up the missed prayer by reciting a second *Shemoneh Esrei* at the next prayer time.

GLOSS: *Preferably, one should not allow the time set for prayer to pass to prevent financial loss.*

SIMAN 116:

THE EXPLANATION OF THE BLESSING OF *REFA'EINU*

§1: "Heal us Hashem, and we shall be healed." The verse from which this is taken is in the singular, and verses may not be changed from singular to plural. This is true when it is said as a verse. However, when one recites it (A)as a prayer and supplication, he is permitted to change it.

NISHMAT AVRAHAM

(B) the activity with which he was involved: Certainly, one who is involved in patient care is included in this *halachah.*[2] See *Siman* 38:8F and *Siman* 93:4.

One who cannot pray because of inappropriate surroundings is also in an extenuating circumstance.

SIMAN 116

(A) as a prayer: One may include a prayer for an ill person within the blessing of *refa'einu.* When in the presence of the ill person, his name need not be mentioned in the prayer. However, when he is not present, his name must be mentioned

2. שמעתי מהגרש״ז אויערבאך זצ״ל

Nevertheless, if he recites an entire chapter of Psalms, he is forbidden to change singular to plural, or vice versa.

SIMAN 119:

THE LAWS REGARDING ONE WHO WOULD LIKE TO ADD TO THE BLESSINGS DURING THE *SHEMONEH ESREI*

§1: If one wishes to add a prayer to one of the middle blessings of the *Shemoneh Esrei*, he may do so as long as it pertains to the content of the blessing being recited. For example, if there is an ill person in his family (A)he may ask

NISHMAT AVRAHAM

within the prayer.[1] Some *acharonim* say that if one prays for an individual he should include the prayer in the blessing *refa'einu;* others prefer that he put it in the blessing *shomei'a tefillah.*[2] See below, *Siman* 119, for additional discussion regarding prayer for one who is ill.

The main purpose when praying for a complete recovery from illness is that we may be healthy and strong to fulfill our obligation to study Torah and perform the *mitzvot.*[3]

Chazal composed the blessing of *refa'einu* as one of the blessings in the *Shemoneh Esrei.* May it be recited on behalf of a sick person as an independent blessing and not in the context of *Shemoneh Esrei*? The *Chavot Da'at*[4] believes that one is permitted to recite the entire blessing, including the Name of *Hashem,* even when it is not said within the context of the *Shemoneh Esrei.* In his opinion, the same holds true for all blessings; one may recite each separately as praise to *Hashem,* and even mention the Name of *Hashem.* In contrast, *Rav Shlomo Zalman Auerbach zt''l* wrote to me that it is forbidden to recite the blessing of *refa'einu* with the Name of *Hashem* when it is not in the context of the *Shemoneh Esrei.* He felt that the *Chavot Da'at* did not mean that one may recite one of the blessings of the *Shemoneh Esrei* in its original form as a separate prayer, since he who does so shows his low opinion of *Shemoneh Esrei* in his using its blessings at will. Rather, what the *Chavot Da'at* meant was that one does not need to rebuke those who pray, with a different text, for healing and include a blessing with the Name of *Hashem.* The *Taz*[5] rules that one must protest against the use of *Hashem's* Name if, after completing one's prayers, the blessing is said in its original form as in the *Shemoneh Esrei.* However, if *Hashem's* Name is omitted, the prayer would be permitted. The *Chazon Ish*[6] agrees with this ruling of the *Taz.*

SIMAN 119

(A) he may ask Hashem: It is customary when one is praying for an ill person, to mention his and his mother's name and not his father's name.[1] For example, one

1. מ״ב ס״ק ג
2. שעה״צ ס״ק ה
3. אליהו זוטא על הלבוש סי׳ קטו. וראה גם בטור
4. על קונטרס ספק ספיקא של הש״ך, יו״ד סי׳ קי ס״ק כ
5. או״ח סי׳ קלא ס״ק טו
6. ראש השנה סי׳ קלז סוס״ק ה. כן כתב לי הגרש״ז אויערבאך זצ״ל

1. אמרי אפרים מודפס בסוף ספר ארחות חיים בשם הדעת כהן סי׳ קלב והזקו אהרן ח״א סי׳ יא שהביאו

***Hashem* to have mercy on him within the blessing *refa'einu*. If he needs a livelihood, he asks for *Hashem's* help in *birkat hashanim*.**

GLOSS: *When one adds a prayer to a blessing, he should first begin the established blessing and then add his own additional prayer and not say his added prayer before starting to say the established text.*

In the blessing of *shomei'a tefillah*, he may ask for any of his needs, because it encompasses all possible requirements.

NISHMAT AVRAHAM

would say, "*Yitzchak ben Sarah,*" as opposed to, "*Yitzchak ben Avraham.*" Although many *acharonim* believe that this is the most appropriate manner of praying for an ill person, it is not absolutely necessary. Thus, if the mother's name is not known, the father's name can be substituted.[2]

The *Mishnah Berurah*[3] quotes the *Pri Megadim* who believes that one may only include a prayer within the *refa'einu* blessing of the *Shemoneh Esrei* for one who is presently ill. One may not, however, pray asking that someone not, become ill in the future. Nevertheless, within the blessing *shomei'a tefillah,* he may make such a request.

It is normally forbidden to refer to one's father by name. However, if he is reciting a prayer for his father who is ill, he should refer to him by his first name but add "my father."[4]

Is one permitted to pray for a dying patient? For he may have passed away at the time of the prayer and then the prayer is one said in vain. The *Orchot Chaim*[5] quoting the *Meorei Or*[6] rules that one should not recite the prayer. He recommends that if one wishes to recite the prayer then, he should pray that no evil befall the dying person. Such general language can also apply to one who has already passed away. In contrast, the *Sha'arei Teshuvah*[7] quotes the *Nachalat Shivah*[8] who himself recited a prayer on the Sabbath on behalf of a dying person who was in a different town. As long as one believes that the person is still alive, and there is no information to the contrary, a prayer can be recited on his behalf asking that his condition improve.[9]

Within the prayer that is customarily recited for people who are ill, we ask *Hashem* to, "to speedily send a full recovery from above for his 248 limbs and 365 sinews." The *Pardes Yosef*[10] takes up the issue as to whether it is appropriate to recite this part of the prayer for one who has had a limb amputated. The Torah states: "Distance yourself from falsehood,"[11] teaching us that we should not lie and deceive others. Since the person is

בשם הזהר פ׳ לך לך עמ׳ פד. וראה שבת סו ע״ב ורש״י שם וסז ע״א, ע״ז יב ע״ב, וגיטין סט ע״ב. ועיין גם במ״ב ס״ק ב

2. שו״ת יביע אומר ח״ב סי׳ יא

3. ס״ק א

4. כף החיים ס״ק ו בשם כנה״ג יו״ד סי׳ רמ בשם ספר חסידים והגרע״א

5. כאן

6. חלק באר שבע דף כז ע״א

7. סי׳ רפח ס״ק ג

8. סי׳ לט

9. ראה גיטין כח ע״א

10. ספר פרדס יוסף פ׳ משפטים כג:ז

11. פ׳ משפטים שם

SIMAN 123: THE LAWS CONCERNING BOWING AT THE CONCLUSION OF THE *SHEMONEH ESREI*

§1: At the conclusion of *Shemoneh Esrei* one must bow and, while doing so, take (A)three steps backward. After one has taken three steps back, while still bowing and before standing erect, he should turn his face to his left while he says: "*Oseh shalom bimromav,*" and then to his right while he says: "*Hu ya'aseh shalom aleinu.*" Finally he bows forward, like a servant leaving the presence of his master.

NISHMAT AVRAHAM

missing a limb, perhaps it is inappropriate to ask *Hashem* to heal his "248 limbs" when he lacks that number. The *Pardes Yosef* offers a number of reasons why it is unnecessary to change the text of a prayer on his behalf. First: It is known that one's soul is considered to have "limbs" corresponding to the physical limbs of the body and, although he has lost one of his physical limbs, all of his spiritual "limbs" are still intact. Second: In spite of his missing a limb, he has not lost the potential to pass on the gene for that limb to his children; it is as if the limb is still contained within him. Finally: The prayer can be considered as referring to the collective body of the Jewish people and it is therefore irrelevant if it does not apply to a particular individual, since it is not directed at him personally, but rather to the nation as a whole.

Chazal[12] teach us that, in contrast to men who have 248 limbs, women have 252[13] limbs. Because of this the text of the prayer recited for an ill woman was changed to: "and all of her limbs, and her 365 sinews" instead of "248 limbs."[14] However, there are many others who disagree, and believe that the text should not be changed since, in terms of *halachah,* a "limb" is defined as a part of the body which can cause a specific kind of ritual defilement.[15] Since men and women are treated alike with regard to the laws of ritual defilement, only 248 limbs can confer impurity.[16] It is only these 248 limbs, therefore, that are considered significant as limbs, and it is for these limbs that we pray when we recite a prayer for a sick person.[17]

SIMAN 123

(A) three steps backward: The *Talmud*[1] teaches us that if he does not take the three steps it would have been better had he not prayed at all. Since they are given such importance, one confined to a wheelchair should move the chair backwards, a distance of three steps, when he reaches the end of *Shemoneh Esrei*. If he is unable to do so unaided, he should do so

12. בכורות מה ע״א
13. ע״ע ברמב״ם טומאת מת פ״ב ה״ז ובכסף משנה שם
14. אוצר התפלות
15. אהלות פ״א מ״ח. אנציקלופדיה תלמודית כרך א ערך אברים (א) עמ׳ קיד
16. רמב״ם טומאת מת פ״ב ה״ז
17. וראה בירושלמי סוטה פ״ה ה״א, בעל הטורים במדבר ה:יח והחיד״א בדבש לפי מערכת ס או״ק א

1. יומא נג ע״ב

GLOSS: *It is customary to recite the following prayer after one has completed bowing: "May it be Your will that the Temple be rebuilt etc.," since prayers are in place of the sacrificial service. Therefore, we ask Hashem to rebuild the Temple, where we can perform the actual sacrificial service.*

NISHMAT AVRAHAM

with help (see *Siman* 94:5). Also, see *Siman* 63B and *Siman* 94:8, which discuss other relevant *halachot* pertaining to one who has limited mobility.

CHAPTER NINE:

Laws of the Priestly Blessing

SIMAN 128:

LAWS OF THE PRIESTLY BLESSING AND FACTORS WHICH DISQUALIFY THE *COHEN*

§4: (A)When a *Cohen* does not wish to go up to recite the priestly blessing with the other *Cohanim,* he need only remain outside the synagogue at the time the *shaliach tzibbur* proclaims "*Cohanim*" (i.e. calls them to recite the blessing). However, lest the congregation think that he left the synagogue because he is unfit to recite the priestly blessing, it is customary that he only return after the priestly blessing is completed.

§14: The *Cohanim* should not recite the priestly blessing except in Hebrew, while (B)standing with (C)their hands raised, and (D)out loud.

NISHMAT AVRAHAM

SIMAN 128

(A) When a *Cohen* does not wish: He may, for example, feel weak or ill. The *Magen Avraham*[1] writes that the *Cohen* who does not wish to recite the priestly blessing should leave the synagogue before the *shaliach tzibbur* begins the blessing of *retzei* in the repetition of *Shemoneh Esrei.* He reasons that since the congregation is unaware that he feels weak or ill, they might say that he did not join the other *Cohanim* when called up because he is unfit to recite the blessing.

(B) standing: A *Cohen* who is weak and unable to stand without leaning on something may not recite the priestly blessing, because leaning is considered like sitting and sitting is prohibited while reciting the priestly blessing.[2] The *Pri Megadim*[3] rules that one who cannot stand at all without leaning on something should not go up for the priestly blessing and must return, even if he has already gone up. However, the *Kaf HaChaim*[4] rules that if there is another *Cohen* as well, he may listen to him pronounce the blessing preceding the priestly blessing, thus fulfilling the requirement to say the blessing before

1. ס״ק ד ומ״ב ס״ק יב

2. מ״ב ס״ק נא. שו״ת פנים מאירות ח״ב סי׳ קפו. נודע ביהודה מהד״ק או״ח סי׳ ה. ועיין גם בברכ״י שיורי ברכה ס״ק א ובשע״ת ס״ק כה. וע״ע בשו״ת שבות יעקב ח״ב סי׳ א שמיקל

3. א״א ס״ק כב ומ״ז סוסי׳ קכח

NISHMAT AVRAHAM

beginning the priestly blessing. They may then proceed to recite the priestly blessing together even though he is unable to stand without leaning.

It is customary for the congregation to stand while the *Cohanim* recite the priestly blessing. However, if one feels that he is too weak to stand, he may remain seated during the recitation of the priestly blessing.[5]

(C) their hands raised: A *Cohen* who cannot raise his hands may not recite the priestly blessing. Even if he had already recited the priestly blessing, it would not be considered acceptable ex post facto. If his hands could be raised and fastened to a brace attached to his head, he still may not recite the priestly blessing, because the *Cohen* himself must raise his hands.[6] If, however, he is able to do so, he may raise his hands while he says the words of the priestly blessing only, and lower them in between each word when the *Cohanim* customarily chant a melody.[7] The *Ketav Sofer*[8] rules that if a *Cohen* is unable to raise his hands at all without resting them on something, he may still recite the priestly blessing while doing so. However, he should not pronounce the blessing that precedes the priestly blessing but should listen to another *Cohen* pronounce it, thus exempting himself from saying the blessing. However, the *Kaf HaChaim*[9] writes that in the opinion of the *Rambam*[10] if a *Cohen* cannot raise his hands, he may not recite the priestly blessing. This is also the opinion of the *Noda BiYehudah*[11] and such is the opinion of the *Shulchan Aruch* (here) who phrased the *halachah* in the negative: "The *Cohanim* should not recite the priestly blessing, except . . . with their hands raised."

During the recitation of the priestly blessing, the congregation must not look at the raised hands of the *Cohanim*. Therefore, a *Cohen* whose hand has been amputated should not recite the priestly blessing even if he has covered his arms and hand with his *tallit,* because the lack of the hand is noticeable beneath the *tallit* and even people who are familiar with him will look and be distracted.[12] Nevertheless, the *Avnei Nezer*[13] rules that such a *Cohen* may recite the priestly blessing as long as he does not pronounce the blessing that precedes it. He should listen to another *Cohen* pronounce the blessing with the intention of exempting himself from saying it. *Rav Shlomo Zalman Auerbach zt"l* wrote to me that this ruling applies only when the congregants are familiar with his physical impairment and will not be distracted during the priestly blessing.

A *Cohen* who has a band-aid or protective gauze on his hand is permitted to recite the priestly blessing.[14] However, if it is three by three fingers wide or more, it is considered a *chatzitzah,* and he may not recite the priestly blessing.[15]

(D) out loud: The priestly blessing should not be recited in a whisper, but rather in a normal speaking tone. Therefore, it would seem that a *Cohen* who is hoarse and can only speak in a whisper, should not recite the priestly blessing if he is the only *Cohen* present; it is preferable that he leaves the congregation before the *shaliach tzibbur* begins the blessing of *retzei* in his repetition of the

4. ס״ק צ
5. שו״ת ציץ אליעזר חי״ד סי׳ יח. ועיין בכף החיים ס״ק צא
6. מ״ב ס״ק נב בשם הנודע ביהודה שם
7. מ״ב שם בשם השו״ת כתב סופר או״ח סי׳ יג
8. שם
9. ס״ק קעו
10. פט״ו מה״ת הי״א
11. או״ח סי׳ ה
12. שו״ת הרדב״ז שני אלפים קיז
13. שו״ת, או״ח סי׳ לא
14. מג״א ס״ק נד. שערים מצויינים בהלכה סי׳ ק ס״ק ה
15. שערים מצוינים בהלכה שם. יסודי ישורון ח״ב

§30: A *Cohen* who has a blemish on his face or on his hands should not recite the priestly blessing because the congregation will be distracted by it. This also applies to blemishes on his feet, in places where the *Cohanim* recite the priestly blessing without socks. Similarly, one who drools on his beard, whose eyes tear excessively or (E)who is blind, even if only in one eye, should not recite the priestly blessing. However, if he is well-known in his city, and everyone is aware of his blemish, he may recite the priestly blessing. This includes even someone who is blind in both eyes.

§35: A *Cohen* (F)who has killed someone, even accidentally, should not recite the priestly blessing, even if he has repented.

NISHMAT AVRAHAM

Shemoneh Esrei.[16] If, however, there is another *Cohen* present to pronounce the blessing that precedes the priestly blessing, the *Cohen* who cannot speak above a whisper may listen to the blessing from the other *Cohen,* thus exempting himself from pronouncing the blessing before beginning the priestly blessing. They may then proceed to recite the priestly blessing together.[17]

(E) who is blind: Since our custom is for the *Cohanim* to drape their *tallitot* over their face and hands, the blemishes mentioned by the *Shulchan Aruch* would be concealed and would not disqualify a *Cohen* nowadays from reciting the priestly blessing.[18]

A hearing defect is not considered a blemish as far as reciting the priestly blessing is concerned. Therefore, a *Cohen* who cannot hear a normal speaking voice such as that of the *shaliach tzibbur* who calls him to recite the priestly blessing, may still go up to recite the priestly blessing.[19]

The *Pri Chadash* ruled that a *Cohen* suffering from diarrhea should not recite the priestly blessing. Instead, he should leave the congregation before the *shaliach tzibbur* reaches the blessing beginning *retzei.*[20] However, if he has an in-dwelling *urinary catheter,* an *ileostomy,* or a *colostomy,* he is permitted to recite the priestly blessing. See *Siman* 76:5 for more details.

(F) who has killed someone: The *Mishnah Berurah*[21] quotes the *Ritva*[22] who states that a *Cohen* who committed murder may not recite the priestly blessing even if he repented. This is because even though nothing stands in the way of repentance, it is nevertheless inappropriate for the same hands that shed blood to be raised as part of the priestly blessing which have the theme of peace.

A *Cohen* who is a surgeon, and whose patient died because of an error on his part

16. מ״ב ס״ק נג
17. לקט הקמח החדש סוס״ק עח
18. שו״ע סע׳ לא
19. כף החיים ס״ק קעה
20. מ״ב סוס״ק קיא
21. ביה״ל ד״ה אפילו עשה. ומ״ב ס״ק קכט. ועיין בתוס׳ יבמות ז ע״א ד״ה שנאמר. א״ר ס״ק סד. פמ״ג א״א ס״ק נא וכף החיים ס״ק רי. ולגבי גרימת מוות ע״י נהיגה במהירות מופרזת, עיין בשו״ת הרא״ש כלל קא ס״ק ה ורדב״ז בלשונות הרמב״ם סי׳ אלף תרסו (שד)
22. מכות סופ״ב בשם בעלי התוספות

GLOSS: *There are some who rule that if he repented, he may recite the priestly blessing. We should be lenient for one who wishes to repent so as not to turn him away; this is the accepted custom.*

§38: **(G)A *Cohen* who drank a *revi'it* of wine at one gulp may not recite the priestly blessing. If he drank it in two gulps or diluted it with water, he may recite the priestly blessing. If he drank more than a *revi'it* of wine, even though it was diluted and he drank it with many gulps, he may not recite the priestly blessing until after the effects of the wine have worn off.**

NISHMAT AVRAHAM

during surgery, may recite the priestly blessing. This ruling is similar to the ruling of the *Shulchan Aruch* that a *Cohen* who acted as a *mohel* is not disqualified from reciting the priestly blessing even if the baby died subsequent to the circumcision.[23] The basis for these rulings is that the *mohel's* intention to perform the circumcision and the surgeon's to save life, override their possible culpability for the accidental deaths. Therefore, both may continue to recite the priestly blessing.[24] A *Cohen* who performed an abortion not sanctioned by *halachah* is still allowed to recite the priestly blessing since Jewish law does not impose the death penalty for performing a *halachically* illegal abortion.[25] [*Author's note*: *Although according to most opinions aborting a fetus is murder and permitted only to save the mother's life, nevertheless it does not carry the death penalty since the fetus does not have a separate existence*.[26]]

(G) A *Cohen* who drank a *revi'it* of wine: On *Shabbat* or *Yom Tov,* one is forbidden to eat before reciting *Kiddush.* Generally, *Kiddush* may not be recited until one has prayed *Shacharit.* But, a *Cohen* who is unwell and feels that without eating he will be unable to recite the priestly blessing, may recite *Kiddush* over a *revi'it* (86 cc.) of wine before he prays *Shacharit* provided that the *revi'it* of wine is either diluted with water or drunk in two separate gulps. Nor need he drink an entire *revi'it* of wine to satisfy the requirement for *Kiddush;* slightly more than half of it is sufficient and that will not disqualify him from reciting the priestly blessing. He may also substitute a smaller amount of liquor for *Kiddush,* instead of wine, and thus not lose the opportunity to perform the commandment of the priestly blessing.[27] The same *halachah* applies to a *revi'it* of raisin wine.[28] The *Biur Halachah*[29] suggests that since, nowadays, all wine is diluted with water, a *Cohen* who is to recite the priestly blessing during the *Mussaf* service, may make *Kiddush* first, drinking a full *revi'it* of wine. Although the *Magen Avraham*[30] permits a *Cohen* to drink any intoxicating beverage other

23. שו״ע כאן סע׳ לו

24. לקט הקמח החדש ס״ק קלו. ועיין בלב אברהם ח״ב פי״ד סע׳ ה ובהערה שם מהגרש״ז אויערבאך זצ״ל. ועיין גם בשו״ת מהרש״ם ח״ה סי׳ ל

25. מ״ב ס״ק קכט ועיין בשעה״צ ס״ק קא. ולגבי כהן שהרג עכו״ם ראה בשו״ת ציץ אליעזר חי״ד סי׳ ס ובכף החיים ס״ק רח

26. חו״מ סי׳ תכה סע׳ ב. וראה בנשמת אברהם כרך ג חו״מ עמ׳ רכ

27. חיי אדם כלל לב סע׳ ז

28. נשמת אדם שם

29. סי׳ רפו סע׳ ג ד״ה אכילת

30. ס״ק נה

§41: **(H)A *Cohen* who willfully becomes ritually impure from a corpse other than one of his seven close relatives (which is permitted), is disqualified from reciting the priestly blessing and any other benefits of the Priesthood until he repents and accepts it upon himself to avoid any further contact with the dead.**

§45: GLOSS: (I)*One is forbidden to make use of the service of a Cohen,*

NISHMAT AVRAHAM

than wine before reciting the priestly blessing, the *Mishnah Berurah*[31] points out that many *acharonim* disagree with the ruling.

(H) A *Cohen* who willfully becomes ritually impure: A *Cohen* studying medicine who will certainly become ritually impure from a corpse as part of his studies is not allowed to recite the priestly blessing.[32] This is so even if he came into contact with non-Jewish corpses that do not convey ritual impurity to the same extent as Jewish bodies.[33] However, if he repented and avoids any further ritual impurity from the dead, he is permitted to recite the priestly blessing.[34]

(I) One is forbidden to make use: The Torah states that the *Cohanim* have a higher degree of sanctity than others because they have the responsibility of performing the sacrificial service. Even today, although the sacrificial services do not exist, *Cohanim* still retain this higher degree of sanctity and the prohibitions that apply to a *Cohen,* such as not marrying a divorcee and not becoming ritually impure from a corpse, still apply.[35] Furthermore, a *Cohen* must be treated with a higher level of honor; for example, he is the first to be called up to the Torah. However, since this honor given to the *Cohen* is meant for his benefit, he may, if he so wishes, forgo the honor afforded to him. Thus he may permit another to use his services. However, according to the *Taz,*[36] a *Cohen* may not serve anyone unless he receives some compensation for his services. Such compensation includes receiving payment for his services or the pleasure he receives from serving an important person. However, if he does not receive compensation for his services, he may not perform them, even though he is willing to forgo his honor, since he is not permitted to do anything that would lower his status as a *Cohen,* and serving someone without compensation is considered demeaning for a *Cohen.* One should certainly be careful not to use a *Cohen* for menial work.[37] The *Ketav Sofer*[38] rules that even today there is a Biblical prohibition for a person to be served by a *Cohen* unless the *Cohen* is compensated for his service.

It would seem then that a *Cohen* who works as a male nurse either in a private home or in a hospital where ritual impurity from the dead can be avoided, is permitted to perform any duties needed for patient care. These duties might in-

31. ס״ק קמא

32. שו״ת חת״ס יו״ד סי׳ שלח

33. שו״ת מהר״י אסאד סי׳ מז. וראה גם בשו״ת כתב סופר או״ח סי׳ טז ושערים מצויינים בהלכה סי׳ קא ס״ק יז

34. שו״ע כאן

35. מ״ב ס״ק קעד

36. ס״ק לט

37. מ״ב ס״ק קעה ועיין גם בביה״ל ד״ה אסור. וראה בט״ז שם במעשה דר״ת ובערוה״ש סע׳ סו־עב

38. או״ח סי׳ טו. ועיין בשו״ת מהר״ם שיק או״ח סי׳ ס בשם החת״ס ובברכ״י בשיורי ברכה אות ד

even today, because it is likened to the misuse of a holy object, unless he has waived his rights as a Cohen about this.

NISHMAT AVRAHAM

clude washing the patient or aiding him in the bathroom. This is permitted since the *Cohen* is receiving payment for his activities. *Rav Shlomo Zalman Auerbach, zt"l* agreed with my conclusion. However, the Rav *zt"l* noted that it is preferable for a *Cohen* not to enter a profession, such as medicine or nursing, if by doing so he will need to perform any activities which are objectively demeaning for others.

An extensive literature exists regarding the genealogy of today's *Cohanim.*[39]

39. ראה יש"ש ב"ק פ"ה סי' לה, הרמ"א סי' תנז סע' ב ובמ"ב ס"ק כב, השו"ת מהרשד"ם אהע"ז סי' רלה, השו"ת שבות יעקב ח"א סי' צג, הט"ז יו"ד סי' שכב ס"ק ה, הש"ך שם ס"ק ט בשם מהרי"ו תשובה סי' קנג, המג"א סי' רא ס"ק ד, שו"ת המבי"ט ח"א סי' ריט, היעב"ץ שאלה קנה, החיי אדם שערי צדק פי"ד סע' ד, החזו"א שביעית סי' ה ס"ק יב, הבאר היטב כאן ובאהע"ז סי' ו ס"ק ב, הפ"ת יו"ד סי' שה ס"ק יב ושכב ס"ק ג, השדי חמד מערכת כ"ף כלל צב ד"ה הרב וד"ה ואני הדל, השו"ת כנסת יחזקאל סוסי' צו, שו"ת המהרי"ט ח"א סי' קמט, הערוה"ש יו"ד סי' שה סע' נה והגליון מהרש"א שם סע' ח

CHAPTER TEN:

Laws of Reading the Torah

SIMAN 139: THE ORDER OF READING THE TORAH AND ITS BLESSINGS

§3: Since it is forbidden to recite even one letter of the Torah by heart, (A)a blind person should not be called up to the Torah *(The Maharil wrote (B)that nowadays, we may call a blind person up to the Torah just as we call up a person who is unlearned and for whom we read the portion.)*

NISHMAT AVRAHAM

SIMAN 139

(A) a blind person: See *Siman* 53:14 for more *halachot* pertaining to a blind person.

(B) that nowadays, we may call: In the times of the *Talmud* and the *Shulchan Aruch,* the one who was called up to the Torah read from the Torah himself. However, nowadays, the custom is that a designated reader reads from the Torah and those who are called up need only recite the blessings before and after the Torah portion is read. Since a designated reader always reads from the Torah scroll, and never recites the Torah portion from memory, there is no reason why a blind person cannot be called up and recite the appropriate blessings.[1] *Rav Shlomo Zalman Auerbach zt"l* also wrote to me[2] concurring with this ruling since even an unlearned person, who does not know how to read from the Torah scroll together with the reader, is also called up. However, the *Kaf HaChaim*[3] writes that the decision to allow a blind person to be called up to the Torah is determined by the local custom. However, where there is no established custom, one must act stringently in accordance with the ruling of the *Mechaber.*[4]

One who is severely mentally retarded is *halachically* absolved from *mitzvot* and may not be called up to the Torah, since his *halachic* status is less than that of a minor.[5]

1. מ״ב ס״ק יב וכן כתבו המג״א ס״ק ד והט״ז סי׳ קמא ס״ק ג
2. לב אברהם ח״ב עמ׳ יח
3. ס״ק טו
4. וראה בשו״ת יחוה דעת ח״ג סי׳ יא בהערה**
5. פמ״ג מ״ז ס״ק ב

CHAPTER ELEVEN:

Laws of the Synagogue

SIMAN 155: ONE SHOULD GO FROM THE SYNAGOGUE TO THE HOUSE OF STUDY

§1: When one leaves the synagogue, he should go to the House of Study. (A)He should designate a particular time to study Torah as part of his fixed daily schedule, and not allow this time to pass without having studied Torah. This is so even if he thinks that he could be earning a large profit from his business dealings during that time.

GLOSS: *Even one who does not know how to learn Torah well,*

NISHMAT AVRAHAM

SIMAN 155

(A) He should designate a particular time: The *Rambam*[1] states: Every Jewish male is required to study Torah, whether he is poor or rich, healthy or ill, young or very old and weak; a poor man who is supported by charity begging from door to door, or one married with children, all are obligated to set aside time for studying Torah, by day and by night, as the verse states:[2] "and meditate in Torah by day and by night." Furthermore, the *Rambam* writes:[3] Until when is a person obligated to study Torah? Until the day of his death, as the verse says:[4] "and lest they stray from your heart all the days of your life."[5]

From the *Rambam* we see that it is imperative for every Jewish male to spend time studying Torah every day. The *Mishnah Berurah*[6] points out that the study of Torah has no limitation and therefore there is an obligation to study Torah whenever one can. If one does not make use of his free time to study Torah, it is as if he disdains the Word of *Hashem.*[7] Furthermore, *Chazal* tell us that one who only learns Torah at set times even though he has free time in which to learn more, is also in this category.[8] The *Sha'arei Teshuvah*[9] writes that even if one is busy all day with his business dealings, he must nevertheless steal from his own time to study Torah. The *Mishnah Berurah*[10] recommends that a person who can only

1. הל' תלמוד תורה פ"א ה"ח
2. יהושע א:ח
3. שם ה"י
4. דברים ד:ט
5. והובא ביו"ד סי' רמו
6. ס"ק ד
7. סנה' צט ע"א
8. ירושלמי ברכות סופ"ט
9. סוסי' קנו. ועיין במלאכי ג:ח ומפרשים שם. ועיין בר"ה כו ע"ב
10. ס"ק ט. ועיין בשנות אליהו פאה פ"א ובשו"ע הרב הל' תלמוד תורה פ"ב ה"ט

should nevertheless go to the House of Study, thereby receiving a reward through the act of going. Alternatively, he can designate a place for himself to study a little in the area of Torah that he is able to, absorbing its content, and thus acquiring the fear of Heaven.

NISHMAT AVRAHAM

dedicate a small amount of time every day to the study of Torah should focus his studies on *halachah,* in order to know how to conduct himself in his daily activities. However, if he cannot understand the intricacies of *halachah,* he should study those areas of Torah which are within his capacity.

A doctor might make the mistake of believing that the obligation to dedicate time to the study of Torah only applies to other professions. Since he spends his time caring for the sick, reading medical texts and journals, attending lectures and conferences and even doing research, all with the ultimate goal of improving his knowledge and consequently improving the level of care that he can provide for his patients, he might believe that he is exempt from his obligation to study Torah. After all, since he is already involved in a *mitzvah,* should he not be exempted from performing other *mitzvot,* including the study of Torah! This, however, is not so. Every doctor certainly has some free time throughout the day when he is not involved in patient care. If so, why should he not take advantage of this free time and study Torah? As the *Biur Halachah*[11] states: Unfortunately, many people are lax in their study of Torah, and do not designate even a little time during the day for Torah study. This is because they do not know how great an obligation they have to study Torah. As *Chazal* have stated,[12] "The Holy One, Blessed be He, forgave the sins of idol worship, illicit relationships and murder, but He did not forgive the sin of forgoing the opportunity to study Torah."

If one examines the daily schedule of the *Rambam,* as described by him in one of his letters,[13] an incredible lesson emerges. The *Rambam,* who was the official doctor to the royal family of Egypt, writes: Every day I travel to the king's palace to tend to his family and officers. Even if nothing untoward happened I do not return until after midday. I am hungry, and come and find all the anterooms full of patients, Jews and gentiles, important people and common folk, judges and policemen, friends and foe, a large crowd waiting my arrival. I get down from my animal, wash my hands and then go to them to appease them and beg them to forgive me if I ask them to wait a little longer while I take a light snack to eat, my only meal in 24 hours. I then start to examine and treat, writing out prescriptions, explaining and advising until night, and sometimes until 2 hours or more after nightfall. All this time I am lying down from exhaustion until I am so weak that I can no longer speak. Members of the community cannot speak to me nor spend time with me except on *Shabbat.* Then, after the morning prayers, most if not all of the community visit me and I advise them on communal matters for the coming week, and they read a little until the afternoon, when they would leave me. After *Minchah* some would remain behind and they would learn together until nightfall.

11. ד״ה עת ללמוד
12. איכא רבה פתיחתא ב ד״ה רבי אבא בר כהנא
13. מובא בספר רבי משה בן מימון ע״י הרב י.ל. הכהן מימון, מוסד הרב קוק עמ׳ קנב

§2: Before going to the House of Study, one may eat breakfast, if he is accustomed to doing so. (B)It is proper to accustom oneself to eat breakfast.

NISHMAT AVRAHAM

Despite the grueling schedule, in which there seemed to be no spare time for studying Torah, the *Rambam,* the teacher of all Israel, must have nevertheless managed to find time to learn and to review his learning daily. Therefore it would be preposterous for any doctor to claim that he has no time in his schedule for studying Torah. Clearly, it is possible to find the time if one so desires.

A patient too, should apportion time for study for, in addition to learning for the sake of learning, there are many *halachot* that he must know concerning proper conduct in the hospital and at home, both for weekday activities and for *Shabbat* and Festivals. Besides, involvement in Torah study will not only benefit him on a spiritual level, but on a physical level as well; it can heal all ailments and illnesses.[14]

(B) It is proper to accustom oneself: The *Gemara*[15] emphasizes that eating breakfast is very important. It is imperative that one protect his health in order to serve *Hashem* to his fullest.[16] A person cannot appreciate the greatness of *Hashem* and His wonders in this world, if his physical health is failing.[17] Therefore, he should eat healthy foods in moderate amounts, avoid becoming obese[18] and exercise regularly.[19]

Chazal forbade any activity that entails putting one's life in danger. If a person ignores this prohibition, and deliberately places his life in danger, he has committed a serious transgression.[20] Using any narcotic drug is included in this prohibition.[21] See below, *Siman* 511:2 for a discussion of how *halachah* views smoking.

14. סי׳ סא מ״ב ס״ק ו בשם מדרש נעלם
15. ב״ק צב ע״ב
16. מ״ב ס״ק יא
17. רמב״ם הל׳ דעות פ״ד ה״א. וראה גם שם פ״ג ה״ב ו״ג
18. שם פ״ד ה״ב והט״ז
19. שם הי״ד
20. ומכין אותו מכת מרדות– רמב״ם הל׳ רוצח פי״א ה״ה. וראה ביו״ד סי׳ קטז דסכנתא חמירא מאיסורא. וראה בשו״ת נודע ביהודה תניינא יו״ד סי׳ י, הובא בפ״ת יו״ד סי׳ כה ס״ק י
21. הגרש״ז אויערבאך זצ״ל. וכ״כ השו״ת אג״מ יו״ד ח״ג סי׳ לה

CHAPTER TWELVE:

Laws of Ritual Hand Washing

SIMAN 158: LAWS OF RITUAL HAND WASHING BEFORE A MEAL

§2: There is an authority who rules that if one eats (A)less than a *kebeitzah* of bread, he should wash his hands without a blessing.

SIMAN 161: LAWS OF CHATZITZAH DURING RITUAL HAND WASHING

§1: One must (A)be careful to make sure that there is no *chatzitzah* on his hands before ritually washing them. Every-

NISHMAT AVRAHAM

SIMAN 158

(A) less than a *kebeitzah* (45 grams): Although *Chazal* decreed that a person must ritually wash his hands before eating a meal with bread, he is required to pronounce the blessing only when he is to eat at least a *kebeitzah* (two *kezeitim)* of bread, if each *kezayit* (27 grams) will be eaten within the time of *kedei achilat pras* (2 to 4 minutes each).[1] One who knows that he will be unable to eat at least two *kezeitim* of bread within this time, should wash his hands before the meal but without pronouncing the blessing *al netilat yadayim.*

SIMAN 161

(A) be careful: Even though ritual hand washing before eating bread is only a Rabbinical decree, *Chazal* modeled their decrees along the lines of Torah decrees. Therefore, if one has a *chatzitzah* on most of the area of the hand which should be washed, he may not wash the hand. This is so, even if most people are not particular about such a *chatzitzah* on their hands. If, however, the *chatzitzah* covers only a small part of the hand, he may wash provided that most people would not be particular about it.[1] The majority of *poskim* believe that it is sufficient to wash the fingers up to where they join the palm of the hand.[2] Therefore only if the *chatzitzah* covers the greater part of the area of the fingers, will it be prohibited to ritually wash the hands.

1. כתב לי הגרש״ז אויערבאך זצ״ל וכן שמעתי ממו״ר הגרי״י נויבירט שליט״א. וכן מצאתי בקצות השולחן סי׳ לו סע׳ ב. וראה שם בבדה״ש ס״ק ה. וראה בשו״ת שבט הלוי ח״ו סי׳ ס אות ג

1. מ״ב ס״ק א

2. שעה״צ ס״ק ב

thing that is considered a *chatzitzah* for ritual immersion, for example, (B)a bandage or plaster on the skin, is also a *chatzitzah* for ritual hand washing.

GLOSS: *It is possible that we are accustomed to act leniently regarding chatzitzah during ritual hand washing because there are those who rule that it does not apply. However, the accepted ruling is that everything considered a chatzitzah for ritual immersion is also considered a chatzitzah for ritual hand washing.*

SIMAN 162:
RAISING AND RUBBING THE HANDS DURING RITUAL HAND WASHING

§10: If one has a wound on his hand which is bandaged, (A)it is

NISHMAT AVRAHAM

(B) a bandage: The *Shulchan Aruch* rules that if one has a bandage or band-aid (elastoplast) on a finger, the area covered does not require washing,[3] because it is as if the finger was amputated. This ruling only applies when the bandage or band-aid protects a wound and removing it will cause pain. Then it is unlikely that one will remove the bandage or band-aid while eating, allowing the unwashed area to possibly touch food. However, if a bandage or band-aid covers an area where there is no wound, and if removed it would cause no pain, it should be taken off before washing. If it remains in place, it would be considered a *chatzitzah.*[4]

Rav Neuwirth shlita believes that even if one has a bandage on his hand, he may still wash his hands in the normal manner on *Shabbat* without concern for violating the prohibitions of "laundering" or "wringing out"[5] on *Shabbat.* Nevertheless, one should be careful not to dry the bandage vigorously if it becomes wet, lest he wring out any liquid that was absorbed. However, when drying a band-aid, one need not be concerned with violating the prohibition of "wringing out" since it does not absorb water. *Rav Eliashiv shlita* agreed with this ruling.

On the other hand, *Rav Auerbach zt"l* wrote to me that there is a possibility that the water will wash away any dirt that may be on the bandage ("laundering"). He also asked, why should there not be the real possibility that he will squeeze the water out of the bandage ("bleaching")? Therefore he ruled that one should not pour water near a bandage. If this is difficult,[6] he should cover the hand with a glove, wash only the other hand[7] and pronounce the blessing of *al netilat yadayim.*[8] The glove must be left on throughout the meal.[9]

3. סי׳ קסב סע׳ י
4. מ״ב ס״ק ה
5. מלבן – רמב״ם הל׳ שבת פ״ט ה״י וי״א.
The *melachah* is "bleaching." "Laundering" and "wringing out" are both included in the same category.
6. ראה סי׳ קסב סע׳ י
7. מ״ב שם ס״ק סט
8. שמעתי מהגרש״ז אויערבאך זצ״ל
9. שמעתי ממו״ר הגרי״י נויבירט שליט״א

sufficient that he wash (B)the unbandaged part of his hand.

SIMAN 163:

THE LAW REGARDING RITUAL HAND WASHING WHEN FEEDING ANOTHER

§2: One who feeds others bread (A)does not need to wash his hands. However, the one being fed needs to do so even though he himself does not touch the food. This rule also applies to one who eats using cutlery. *(It is forbidden to feed bread to (B)one who did not wash his hands because of the prohibition of "Do not place a stumbling block before a blind person.")*

NISHMAT AVRAHAM

SIMAN 162

(A) it is sufficient that he wash: This *halachah* applies to one who is unlikely to remove the bandage or band-aid (elastoplast) from the wound since it would be painful. Then, the area covered by the bandage is likened to an amputated limb; that is, it is considered absent in terms of washing. Accordingly, the bandage or band-aid is not considered a *chatzitzah* and it is sufficient that he wash the unbandaged part of the hand.[1]

(B) the unbandaged part of his hand: If a patient is unable to wash his hands, he should either wrap a napkin around each hand or wear gloves, to prevent his bare hands from touching the food.[2] See above, *Siman* 161B regarding *Shabbat.*

SIMAN 163

(A) does not need to wash his hands: See also *Siman* 169:2. Even though the one who feeds another comes into contact with the food, only the person who is eating the food must wash his hands if he will be eating bread.[1]

(B) one who did not wash his hands: One must not feed bread to another whom one knows for certain has not washed his hands. But, if one is uncertain whether or not he has done so, he may feed him, particularly in the case of a poor person. However, it is best to encourage him to wash his hands before eating, if he will be partaking of bread.[2] The *Ateret Zekeinim* rules that not only is one forbidden to feed bread to another who has not washed his hands, but he may not even offer it to him. The *Sdei Chemed,*[3] however, differentiates between offering someone non-kosher food which is forbidden, and offering kosher food (with bread) to someone who has not yet washed his hands, which is permitted. That is why the *Rama* only forbids directly feeding bread to someone who has not washed his hands.

The *Magen Avraham*[4] cites the *Bach* who rules that one may offer food to a poor person even though he knows that he will not recite a blessing before eating.[5] However, the *Magen Avraham*[6] himself, quot-

1. מ״ב ס״ק סח
2. מ״ב ס״ק סט
1. מ״ב ס״ק ח
2. מ״ב ס״ק יא
3. מערכת וא״ו כלל כו ס״ק יט
4. סי׳ קסט ס״ק ו
5. עיין גם אשל אברהם בוטשאטש
6. שם

NISHMAT AVRAHAM

ing the *Sh'lah,* rules that if one is certain that this person will not recite a blessing before eating, he must not give him food, since this will constitute a violation of the Biblical commandment, "Do not place a stumbling block before a blind person."[7] The *Eliyah Rabbah* contends that there is no disagreement between the *Sh'lah* and the *Bach.* The *Sh'lah* is speaking about one who adamantly refuses to recite a blessing because he disdains to do so; in such a case the *Bach* would agree that he should not offer food. The *Kaf HaChaim*[8] rules that if one is certain that a person will not wash his hands before eating or recite *birkat hamazon,* he is forbidden to offer him bread. However, if the person is in dire need of food, it is best to feed him food other than bread which would then not require washing or *birkat hamazon.*

Rav Shlomo Zalman Auerbach zt"l[9] wrote to me that one must take into consideration the possible repercussions of not offering food to a person who will not recite a blessing before or after eating, or wash his hands. If one believes that not offering him food will engender hatred toward observant Jews and the Torah, he may offer him food. With this in mind, one may feed an ill patient, if he cannot feed himself, if there are grounds to suspect that not doing so will cause him to hate the Torah and those who follow it. *Rav Neuwirth shlita* wrote to me agreeing, but added that it would be commendable to attempt to teach the patient to recite blessings before eating.

One might add that the offering of food to a person who is ill, even if he will not pronounce a blessing before eating, is an act of kindness which is even more important than giving charity.[10]

---

7. ויקרא יט:יד
8. סי׳ קסט ס״ק טו
9. ראה גם במנחת שלמה ח״א סי׳ לה. וראה תוס׳ חגיגה כב ע״א ד״ה כמאן
10. תוספתא פאה סופ״ד. ירושלמי פאה פ״א ה״א. סוכה מט ע״ב. וראה ברמ״א סי׳ קסט סע׳ ב

CHAPTER THIRTEEN:

Laws Regarding How One Should Act During a Meal

SIMAN 169: LAWS REGARDING THE ONE WHO SERVES THE MEAL

§2: (A)**One may only give food to one who will recite a blessing before eating.** *Some are lenient and permit giving food to a poor person as charity even though he may not pronounce a blessing.*

SIMAN 178: WHAT IS CONSIDERED AN INTERRUPTION DURING A MEAL

§1: **If he was eating at home and, in the middle of the meal, went to another house, or if he was eating and was called outside to talk to his friend, he is required to recite *birkat hamazon* on what he has already eaten when he returns to the table. He must then repeat the blessing of *hamotzi* before continuing with his meal. However, if he spoke with his friend in the same room, even if he moved from one corner to another, he is not required to recite another blessing neither on the food that he has already eaten, nor prior to continuing his meal.**

§2: GLOSS: (A)*Some disagree with the entire ruling stated in this Siman.*

NISHMAT AVRAHAM

SIMAN 169

(A) One may only give: See *Siman* 163:2.

SIMAN 178

(A) Some disagree: In order to summarize the opinions of the *Shulchan Aruch* and *Rama* as clarified by the *Ben Ish Chai* and the *Mishnah Berurah,* I will, with *Hashem*'s help, attempt to summarize these *halachot. Rav Neuwirth shlita* concurred with this summation and its practical applications. These *halachot* are especially relevant to the doctor who may be interrupted in the middle of his meal in order to tend to a patient. It is therefore vital that he be familiar with them, in order to know how to act whenever this happens:

1. *Berachah acharonah*:

A doctor who returns to his meal after tending to a patient is not required to pronounce a *berachah acharonah* on the food that he had eaten, before continuing with his meal.[1]

2. *Berachah rishonah*:

A. If he remained within the same building, even if he moved from one room to another, or even from one floor to another and:

(i) If he has already eaten a *kezayit*[2] (27 grams) of bread, grain products or one of the five species of fruit of *Eretz Yisrael* (whose *berachah acharonah* is *al ha'etz v'al pri ha'etz*),[3] prior to his leaving, he is not required to pronounce a *berachah rishonah* before continuing his meal when he returns to the table. This is true whether or not he has forgotten about his meal in the interim,[4] or even if more than 72 minutes have elapsed from the time he left the table.[5] This ruling applies only when he wishes to eat foods that are normally eaten during a meal together with bread.

(ii) If, however, he wishes to eat, as part of his meal, foods that are not normally eaten as part of a meal, he need not pronounce a new *berachah rishonah,* if he is able to see, from his new location, the place where he had originally eaten. And if, when he began his meal, he thought that he would need to leave the table, he is also not required to pronounce another *berachah rishonah* on returning. However, if neither one of these conditions are met, then, according to the *Ben Ish Chai*[6] he must pronounce a *berachah rishonah* prior to eating, whereas, according to the *Biur Halachah,*[7] he need not.

(iii) If he was eating fruit (not included in the seven species) or drinking a beverage, then, according to the *Ben Ish Chai,*[8] he would be required to pronounce a *berachah rishonah* before continuing, whereas according to the *Biur Halachah*[9] he should not.

B. If, on the other hand, he had to leave the building, then:

(i) If he had already eaten a *kezayit* (27 grams) of bread, grain products or one of the five species of fruits prior to leaving the table, and, when he returned, he wished to eat foods that are normally part of a meal, he is not required to recite a *berachah rishonah* before continuing.

(ii) However, if, while he was away his

---

1. מ״ב ס״ק כו

2. ראה בן איש חי שנה א פ׳ בהעלותך סע׳ ה ומ״ב ס״ק כח ושעה״צ ס״ק כב. וראה שם מה דינו אם יצא לפני שאכל כזית

3. בן איש חי שם סע׳ ג. וכן משמע מהמ״ב ס״ק מה שגם פירות משבעת המינים אפשר להקל עכ״פ בדיעבד

4. כתב לי הגרש״ז אויערבאך זצ״ל: ור״ל אפילו הוא עצמו הסיח דעתו מלאכול עוד ויצא במחשבה שגמר סעודתו. ולכאורה תמוה, הרי מפורש כותב הרמ״א כאן ״מיהו אם הסיח דעתו ודאי צריך לברך״, ואולי הוא סובר כהאבן העוזר שהובא בביה״ל שם ד״ה אם הסיח (וכן בבאר היטב ס״ק ד) שתמה על הלכה זו של הרמ״א, ואולם מובא שם בביה״ל שכמה אחרונים סתמו שלא כדבריו. ונראה שאם יצא לתפלה או לטפל בחולה, אין זה נקרא הסיח הדעת להפוסקים שהליכה אינה מפסקת, עכ״ל. ועיין גם שם סע׳ ו. ועיין בכף החיים סי׳ יח ס״ק ז שהכלל של ספק ברכות להקל הוא אפילו נגד מרן ואפילו נגד הרוב

5. סי׳ קפד מ״ב ס״ק יז

6. שם סע׳ ב ו־ד

7. ד״ה אכל

8. שם סע׳ ד

9. ד״ה בבית אחד

NISHMAT AVRAHAM

mind was so preoccupied that he forgot about his meal, then, upon returning, he is required to wash his hands before eating any bread, albeit without its accompanying blessing.

(iii) If he wanted to eat foods that are not normally eaten as part of a meal, the *halachah* is the same as that stated above **(Aii).**

(iv) However, if he was eating fruits which are not included in the seven species, or if he was drinking a beverage and then left the building, all *poskim* agree that on his return he is required to recite a *berachah rishonah* before eating anything else. This is so even if he did not forget about his meal while he was away from the table.[10]

(v) If he no longer wishes to continue his meal, he should act as follows: If he had been eating bread or other grain products, he is required to return to the table in order to recite *birkat hamazon* or *al hamichyah,* provided that less then 72 minutes[11] have elapsed from when he last ate. If he had been eating one of the five species of fruits, he should try to return to his table in order to recite *al ha'etz v'al pri ha'etz.* However, if he was eating any other food he is permitted to recite *boreh nefashot* where he is, even though he has changed locations.[12] Nevertheless, in all of the above, one should not recite a *berachah acharonah* if more than 72 minutes have elapsed since last eating.[13] See *Siman* 271B regarding the *halachah* of what to do if you must leave the table after reciting *Kiddush.*

10. ראה רמ״א סע׳ א ומ״ב ס״ק ד ו־יב. בן איש חי שם סע׳ ד

11. סי׳ קפד מ״ב ס״ק ב

12. כאן סע׳ ה ומ״ב ס״ק מה

13. סי׳ קפד מ״ב ס״ק ב

CHAPTER FOURTEEN:

The Laws of Birkat Hamazon

SIMAN 185: RECITING *BIRKAT HAMAZON* ALOUD AND ADDITIONAL DETAILS REGARDING *BIRKAT HAMAZON*

§5: If one recited *birkat hamazon* while he was (A)facing excrement or while he was (*completely*) intoxicated, the *Tosafot* and the *Rosh* debate as to whether one needs to repeat it. If one recited *birkat hamazon* while in the presence of urine, one certainly does not repeat it.

NISHMAT AVRAHAM

SIMAN 185

(A) facing excrement: The *Mishnah Berurah*[1] explains that in this instance he recited *birkat hamazon* where he should have suspected that excrement may be present, did not ascertain if this was so, and subsequently found excrement. Although in *Siman* 76 the *Shulchan Aruch* ruled that in such a case one is required to repeat the *Shemoneh Esrei,* and similarly the *Shema,* the *Tosafot* and the *Rosh* wonder whether *birkat hamazon* should be repeated or not, since there are times when the *halachah* is more lenient for *birkat hamazon* than it is for *Shemoneh Esrei.*

Although the *Chayei Adam*[2] rules that in this situation one must repeat the *Shema* and *Shemoneh Esrei* if excrement is found nearby, he believes that one need not repeat *birkat hamazon* or any other blessing. He emphasizes[3] that although *birkat hamazon* is a Biblical command, he is still not obligated to repeat it, even if he recited it knowing that there may be excrement in the vicinity.[4] In contrast, the *Mishnah Berurah*[5] rules that one must repeat *birkat hamazon* if one recited it within four *cubits* of the foul odor.[6] However, if excrement or its odor was further than four *cubits* away when one recited *birkat hamazon,* then, according to all opinions, there is no need to repeat it.[7] It goes without saying that, according to Torah law, it is forbidden to recite *birkat hamazon,* or speak any words of Torah at any time, in the presence of excrement.[8]

1. מ״ב ס״ק ה
2. כלל ג סע׳ לג
3. נשמת אדם שם ס״ק ז. וכ״כ הקיצור שו״ע סי׳ ה סע׳ י
4. ודלא כהע״ת והא״ר
5. ס״ק ז
6. סי׳ עט סע׳ א
7. שעה״צ ס״ק ח
8. מ״ב ס״ק ז

SIMAN 196: EATING NON-KOSHER FOOD

§2: [(A)]One who must eat [(B)]non-kosher food to save his life, should recite a blessing before eating it *(see below, Siman* 204).

NISHMAT AVRAHAM

SIMAN 196

(A) One who must eat: The Torah permits one whose life is in danger to transgress most *mitzvot* of the Torah in order to save his life. Therefore, one whose life is endangered by an illness may eat a food that is normally Biblically prohibited, if it may help towards his recovery.[1] Moreover, the *Levush,*[2] *Magen Avraham,*[3] *Pri Megadim*[4] and *Chayei Adam*[5] believe that one is fulfilling the Biblical commandment to preserve one's life; it is a *mitzvah* to eat such a food and he should pronounce the proper blessing prior to eating it. However, the *Chida*[6] rules that although one whose life is in danger may eat food that is normally prohibited by the Torah, nevertheless, he should not pronounce a blessing. This is also the opinion of the *Bach.*[7] The *Ketav Sofer*[8] basically agrees with the opinion of the *Shulchan Aruch,* but advises one who wishes to act stringently to first pronounce a blessing on a permitted food, and at the same time have the prohibited food in mind. In this way he will avoid the necessity to pronounce a blessing specifically on the non-kosher food. The *Kaf HaChaim*[9] and the *Panim Meirot*[10] agree with this ruling. The *Kaf HaChaim* adds that if one is unable to follow the advice of the *Ketav Sofer,* it is preferable that he contemplate the blessing, rather than pronounce it aloud. Obviously, he should not recite a blessing if the non-kosher food is repulsive to him.[11]

The *Levush*[12] believes that one who may eat a non-kosher food because of his medical condition may be included in the *zimun,* whereas the *Pri Megadim*[13] and the *Kaf HaChaim*[14] disagree.

(B) non-kosher food: Non-kosher food which was chemically altered, and thereby became unsuitable for human consumption, and then, undergoing a further chemical change again become edible, is considered to be an entirely new food. Even a *non-seriously ill* patient may eat it.[15]

1. מ״ב ס״ק ה
2. כאן
3. סי׳ רד ס״ק כא
4. א״א ס״ק כא
5. כלל מח סע׳ יח
6. שיורי ברכה כאן
7. סי׳ רד
8. שו״ת או״ח סי׳ כב
9. ס״ק ח
10. ח״ב סי׳ ו מובא בשע״ת
11. שע״ת שם. מ״ב סי׳ רד ס״ק מח. וכותב השעה״צ שם ס״ק מב, ופשוט
12. כאן
13. מ״ז סוס״ק א
14. ס״ק ט
15. שו״ת אחיעזר ח״ג סי׳ לא ועיין שם חיו״ד סי׳ יא. ראה גם ביו״ד סי׳ קנה סע׳ ג בהגה ושו״ת רדב״ז סי׳ תתקעט (ח״ג סי׳ תקמח), ש״ך יו״ד שם ס״ק יט, הגר״א שם ס״ק כב ואו״ח סי׳ תמה סע׳ ב. וראה גם בשו״ת שבות יעקב ח״ב סי׳ ע. וראה ברמ״א יו״ד סי׳ פז סע׳ י וש״ך ס״ק לג שם ופ״ת סי׳ קנה ס״ק ו

SIMAN 199:
WHO MAY OR MAY NOT JOIN IN A *ZIMUN*

§10: GLOSS: (A)*A deaf person and* (B)*a shoteh who has a certain level of intelligence may be included in a zimun, even though the deaf person cannot hear the blessing that is being recited.*

NISHMAT AVRAHAM

SIMAN 199

(A) A deaf person: The *Biur Halachah*[1] debates whether a deaf person is permitted to lead a *zimun,* or is merely permitted to be included as part of the *zimun,* as mentioned by the *Rama* in this section. A deaf-mute, however, because he is exempt from performing all *mitzvot,* cannot be included in a *zimun.*[2] See *Siman* 55:8 for a discussion regarding the status of one who is a deaf-mute.

The *Pri Megadim*[3] raises the issue of one who is dumb. Is he eligible to be included as part of a *zimun*? Perhaps because he cannot respond to the invitation to the *zimun* he may not be part of it. The *Ben Ish Chai*[4] concludes that he may not be included in a *zimun.*

(B) a *shoteh*: The *Rama* is not referring to a true *shoteh.* For a true *shoteh* is exempt from performing all *mitzvot* and would not be eligible to be part of a *zimun.* The *Rama* is rather referring to one who is not very intelligent, and whom people generally regard as a simpleton. Such a person may be included in a *zimun,* if he demonstrates a sufficient level of understanding and intelligence.[5]

1. ד״ה מצטרפים
2. מ״ב ס״ק כח
3. א״א ס״ק ה
4. שנה א פ׳ קרח סע׳ יב
5. מ״ב ס״ק כט

CHAPTER FIFTEEN:

The Laws of the Blessing Over Fruits

SIMAN 204: THE LAWS OF BLESSING FOR THE OTHER FOODS

§7: One who drinks water (A)to quench his thirst must first pronounce the blessing *shehakol,* and, after finishing his drink, *borei nefashot* (see *Siman* 210:1 for details). However, if he is (B)choking on a piece of meat, (C)and drinks water to dislodge it, he does not pronounce a blessing on the water, neither before nor after drinking it.

§8: (D)A blessing is pronounced before and after eating all foods and drinks that a person consumes for medical

NISHMAT AVRAHAM

SIMAN 204

(A) to quench his thirst: Although the *Shulchan Aruch* seems to imply that a blessing is required only when one drinks water to quench thirst, this should be qualified. Whenever one derives any pleasure from drinking water, he is assumed to be thirsty and he is required to pronounce a blessing both before and after drinking.[1] If he drinks water for medical reasons when he wakes up in the morning, he should not pronounce a blessing unless he is also thirsty.[2] Similarly, he should not pronounce a blessing when drinking water to swallow a pill.

(B) choking on a piece of meat: This *halachah* applies also whenever one drinks water only to dislodge something that has stuck in his throat.[3]

(C) and drinks water: When one drinks water for a reason other than to quench thirst, it is assumed that he does not derive any direct pleasure from the water, and a blessing is not required.[4] However, if he drinks a beverage other than water for this purpose, since the palate savors it we say there is pleasure and he is required to pronounce a blessing. Similarly, if one were to eat a piece of bread to help dislodge something that was stuck in his throat, a blessing is required before and after eating it, as stated in §8.[5]

(D) A blessing is pronounced: The *Rama*[6] states that food that is not normally eaten by healthy people, but only consumed for medical purposes, requires a blessing of *shehakol* before it is eaten. The *Mishnah Berurah*[7] explains that although one may derive pleasure from eating such food, nevertheless, since healthy

1. מ״ב ס״ק מ. וראה גם בשעה״צ ס״ק לד
2. מ״ב ס״ק מב
3. מ״ב ס״ק מא
4. בן איש חי שנה א פ׳ מטות סע׳ יב
5. מ״ב ס״ק מב וכדלקמיה בשו״ע סע׳ ח
6. סע׳ יא
7. ס״ק נד

reasons, (E)if they taste pleasant and are palatable.

GLOSS: *One who is forced to eat a food or drink does not recite a blessing on it, even though it is palatable.*

NISHMAT AVRAHAM

people do not normally eat it, its primary purpose is medical. For such food, it is proper to pronounce the all-inclusive blessing of *shehakol* even on the five species of grain.[8] However, the *Mishnah Berurah*[9] concludes that many *acharonim* disagree with this ruling of the *Rama,* and believe that since one derives pleasure from the food even though he eats it for medical purposes only, he must nevertheless still pronounce the blessing appropriate to it.

(E) if they taste pleasant: Many foods are consumed for their purported medical benefits. However, even if he eats it only for its medical benefits, he is required to pronounce a blessing as long as he derives pleasure from it. But, if he dislikes its taste, no blessing is required.[10] Many *acharonim* agree with this ruling, and add that the basic point is whether or not the food has an unpleasant taste. As long as this is not so, he is required to pronounce a blessing, since some pleasure is derived from it.[11]

Many medicines taste unpleasant. In order to make them more palatable they are often mixed with sugar or other sweeteners. Regardless of whether a sweetener is added, the medicinal substance is considered the main part of the mixture. *Rav Neuwirth shlita* told me that since we always look at the primary part of a mixture to determine the appropriate blessing, no blessing should be pronounced since the main ingredient is bitter and is taken only for medical purposes.[12] However, the *Da'at Torah*[13] and *Rav Ovadiah Yosef shlita*[14] believe that one is required to pronounce the blessing *shehakol* prior to taking the medicine. *Rav Waldenberg shlita* told me that when one says the prayer of *yehi ratzon*[15] before taking a medication it is as if he pronounced a sort of blessing, and is exempt from pronouncing the formal blessing prior to taking it. When we pronounce blessings before we eat we acknowledge the sovereignty of *Hashem.* By doing so we are allowed to partake of foods which He has provided for us. Since the prayer of *yehi ratzon* recognizes *Hashem's* dominion, one who recites it is not required to recite a formal blessing in this situation.

There is an opinion that a person who drinks natural spring water for its therapeutic benefit must pronounce a blessing prior to its consumption, if he enjoys its taste.[16] However, there is another view that he should not pronounce a blessing, since the water is used for medical reasons and not to quench one's thirst.[17]

Rav Shlomo Zalman Auerbach zt"l[18] wrote me that any medicinal tablet that is coated with a sweetener requires a blessing of *shehakol* before it is taken, since one inevitably derives enjoyment from the sugar coating before tasting the bitter

8. שעה״צ ס״ק מה
9. ס״ק נה
10. מ״ב ס״ק מג
11. ארחות חיים כאן ס״ק ט, שו״ע הרב סע׳ יד, שעה״צ ס״ק לז
12. ראה ספר נר ליחזקאל עמ׳ 117. וראה בנשמת אברהם כרך ה חאו״ח סי׳ רד ס״ק א (עמ׳ יא)
13. כאן
14. שמעתי מפיו וכן מובא בשמו בילקוט יוסף סי׳ רד עמ׳ תלו סוף הערה י
15. ראה שו״ע סי׳ רל סע׳ ד
16. שו״ת בנין ציון סי׳ י
17. שו״ת יד הלוי או״ח ח״א סי׳ לה. וראה גם בשו״ת ציץ אליעזר ח״ח סי׳ טו פט״ו אות יז ד״ה אסמכתא
18. נשמת אברהם כרך ד חאו״ח סי׳ רד ס״ק א (עמ׳ ז)

SIMAN 206:

LAWS REGARDING INTERRUPTION AND MISTAKES IN BLESSINGS OVER FRUITS

§3: A man whose (A)head is uncovered is forbidden to pronounce a blessing.

NISHMAT AVRAHAM

medicine. However, if the sweetener is mixed together with the medication (as it is in throat lozenges and cough syrup), one is not required to pronounce a blessing before taking it. Since a healthy person would not take it, it is obvious that it is primarily a medicine and not a food, and does not require a blessing.

Many diagnostic procedures require patients to take various substances to improve the interpretation of their results. For example, patients are asked to swallow barium to ensure better visualization of the gastrointestinal tract. *Rav Shlomo Zalman Auerbach zt"l* told me[19] that one is not required to pronounce a blessing prior to drinking barium, even if it has been mixed with a sweetener, or mixed with bread. Since the barium is the primary substance and the sweetener and the bread are secondary to it, a blessing is not required. However, when the functional status of the gall bladder is evaluated, patients are often asked to eat a fatty food such as an egg yolk to cause the gall bladder to contract. Then, one must pronounce a blessing prior to the eating of such a food. For although he eats the food for medical reasons, he nevertheless derives pleasure from it, and a blessing is therefore in place.

SIMAN 206

(A) head is uncovered: See *Shulchan Aruch Siman* 91:3 for more regarding this topic.

Shalom is used as a greeting among Jews. The *Shulchan Aruch,*[1] the *Magen Avraham,*[2] the *Ben Ish Chai,*[3] and the *Mishnah Berurah*[4] rule that since *Shalom* is considered a Name of *Hashem,* it may not be used as a greeting when one is in a place which is *halachically* unclean;[5] this is not uncommon in a hospital.

Rav Ovadiah Yosef shlita[6] believes that one is allowed to greet a person with the word *Shalom,* even when this person is not wearing a head covering and is likely to respond by saying *Shalom.* Since there is no clear consensus as to whether *Shalom* is one of *Hashem's* Names or not, *Rav Yosef* believes that we may rely on the lenient opinions of those who feel that it is not. It would seem though, that, if possible, one should try to avoid saying *Shalom* to a person whose head is uncovered and, instead, use another greeting, such as "good morning," thus avoiding any potential *halachic* problems. I found a similar suggestion offered by the *Birkei Yosef,*[7] and *Rav Moshe Feinstein zt"l.*[8] *Rav Neuwirth shlita* told me that he is careful to use other greetings.

The above *halachah* is relevant for one who is in a hospital where in many situations it is inappropriate to recite *Hashem*'s Name. Therefore, according to

19. נשמת אברהם שם
1. סי׳ פד
2. סי׳ פה ס״ק ט
3. בספרו בן יהוידע על ברכות יז ע״א
4. סי׳ פד ס״ק ו
5. ראה גם בברכ״י סי׳ קנו ס״ק א
6. שו״ת יביע אומר ח״ו סי׳ טו ס״ק ח ו-ט
7. שם
8. או״ח ח״ד סי׳ מ ס״ק כד

SIMAN 210: THE LAWS REGARDING ONE WHO EATS LESS THEN A *KEZAYIT*

§1: One who eats (A)less than a *kezayit* of bread or any other food, or drinks less then a *revi'it* of wine or another beverage, must recite a *berachah rishonah* that is appropriate for that type of food, but does not recite a *berachah acharonah.*

NISHMAT AVRAHAM

the *acharonim* cited above, one should be careful about saying *Shalom* in such places. And, whenever a Jew is not wearing a head covering, one must also take into account the opinions cited above when considering the proper greeting to offer.

SIMAN 210

(A) less than a *kezayit*: *Chazal* established that one is only obligated to recite a *berachah acharonah* after eating a *kezayit* (27 grams) of food within a span of time, which is called a *kedei achilat pras*[1] (2 to 4 minutes). Therefore, if an old or sick person ate very slowly, taking longer than a *kedei achilat pras* to eat a *kezayit,* he should not recite a *berachah acharonah.*[2] The *Minchat Yitzchak*[3] adds that where possible he should try to listen to someone who is pronouncing the appropriate blessing after eating.

Since one pronounces a blessing when deriving pleasure from the food that he eats, many *poskim*[4] believe that a patient who is fed through a *naso-gastric* feeding tube, or one who is being fed via a *PEG,* should not pronounce a blessing before or after he is fed, since his palate does not derive any pleasure from the food. However, others[5] disagree and believe that as long as one is satiated, he is required to recite a blessing both before and after the feeding. The *Levushei Mordechai*[6] and the *Machazeh Avraham*[7] recommend that in such a situation one should try to listen to another who is pronouncing the appropriate blessing before and after eating and thus exempt himself from his possible obligation to recite the blessing. *Rav Waldenberg shlita*[8] wrote to me endorsing this recommendation.

When a sick person is certain that he will be unable to eat at least a *kebeitzah* (54 grams) of bread with his meal, he should ritually wash his hands before eating but not pronounce the blessing *al netilat yadayim.*[9] If he is certain that he will eat less then a *kezayit* of bread there are

1. מ״ב ס״ק א
2. שמעתי מהגרש״ז אויערבאך זצ״ל. אג״מ או״ח ח״א סי׳ עו. ציץ אליעזר חי״א סי׳ יג. שמירת שבת כהלכתה פ״מ סע׳ צג
3. ח״ג סי׳ יח
4. מנחת חינוך מצוה שיג ס״ק ב. שו״ת מהר״ם שיק סי׳ רנ. שו״ת דברי מלכיאל ח״ה סוסי׳ רמא. שע״ת סי׳ קצו סוס״ק ח. שו״ת חלקת יעקב ח״ג סי׳ סח ושו״ת מחזה אברהם או״ח סי׳ קכט
5. שערים מצויינים בהלכה סי׳ נ ס״ק ח בשם המור וקציעה סי׳ קצו. ומה שמביא שגם האגלי טל מלאכת טוחן ס״ק סב (ב) סובר כן חולק עליו מו״ר הגרי״י נויבירט שליט״א בכוונתו של האגלי טל
6. ח״א סי׳ לב
7. או״ח סי׳ קכט. ועיין שם שדן רק לגבי ברכת המזון
8. לב אברהם ח״א עמ׳ כא ושו״ת ציץ אליעזר חי״ג סי׳ לה
9. סי׳ קנח סע׳ ב

NISHMAT AVRAHAM

acharonim who rule that he is not even obligated to wash his hands before his meal.[10] However, there are others[11] who believe that he must wash his hands, albeit without a blessing. One should therefore act stringently, and wash one's hands even to eat less then a *kezayit* of bread.[12] *Rav Shlomo Zalman Auerbach zt"l* wrote to me that one who knows at the outset of his meal that he will be unable to eat two *kezeitim* of bread (equivalent to a *kebeitzah*), each *kezayit* within a *kedei achilat pras,* should wash his hands before eating, but should not recite the blessing *al netilat yadayim* (see *Siman* 158:2).

10. שם סע׳ ג ובמ״ב ס״ק י
11. מ״ב שם בשם הלחם חמודות, המג״א והא״ר ועוד אחרונים
12. מ״ב שם

CHAPTER SIXTEEN:

The Laws Regarding Thanksgiving Blessings

SIMAN 219: AN INDIVIDUAL'S BLESSING OF THANKSGIVING

§1: Four categories of people are required to give thanks to *Hashem* by reciting the thanksgiving blessing. Those who were on a sea journey must give thanks upon arriving on shore; those who traveled through the desert must give thanks when they reach a settlement; (A)one who was ill (B)and recovered; and one who was imprisoned and then freed.

NISHMAT AVRAHAM

SIMAN 219

(A) one who was ill: *Rav Shlomo Zalman Auerbach zt"l* told me that a patient who undergoes *cardiac catheterization* is required to pronounce the blessing of *hagomel* after the procedure. This is so even when no additional procedures, such as a *balloon catheterization* or *stenting* were performed. Even though the risks involved with *cardiac catheterization* are very low, *Rav Auerbach zt"l* believed that a blessing is required after this procedure. In light of this ruling, I am uncertain as to the level of risk that one must have faced before being required to pronounce this blessing.

(B) and recovered: The *Mishnah Berurah*[1] explains that only one who is fully recovered may pronounce the blessing.

It is customary that women do not recite the *hagomel,* even after emerging from a potentially life-threatening situation. The *Ba'er Heitev,*[2] citing the *Halachot Ketanot,*[3] explains that women refrain from reciting the blessing since it is immodest to do so in front of men (the blessing requires a quorum of ten men – see §3): The *Knesset HaGedolah* believes that a woman may pronounce the blessing from the ladies' section in the synagogue, and the men in the main sanctuary respond to it. The *Ben Ish Chai*[4] and the *Kaf HaChaim*[5] rule that a woman is obligated to pronounce this blessing in the presence of ten men, in order that she can say it with *Hashem's* Name and reference to His Kingship. If she is embarrassed to do so, she should pronounce the blessing privately without making reference to the Name of *Hashem* or His Kingship. *Rav Ovadiah Yosef shlita*[6] also agrees with

1. מ״ב ס״ק ב
2. ס״ק א
3. ח״ב סי׳ קסא
4. שנה א פ׳ עקב סע׳ ה
5. ס״ק ג
6. שו״ת יחוה דעת ח״ד סי׳ טו

§2: Which blessing should these people recite? "Blessed are You, Hashem, King of the universe, (C)Who grants good to the guilty, Who has bestowed every goodness upon me." Those who hear this blessing should respond: "May He Who has bestowed every goodness upon you, continue to bestow every goodness upon you forever."

§4: If one recited the blessing for another who was obligated to say it, and said the following text: "Blessed are You, Hashem, King of the universe, (D)Who has bestowed every goodness upon you," and the person responded "*Amen,*" he has fulfilled his obligation.

NISHMAT AVRAHAM

this ruling. *Rav Shlomo Zalman Auerbach zt"l* wrote to me that he noticed that in Jerusalem, only women who have given birth pronounce the blessing. He believes that in the days when the *Beit HaMikdash* was present, a woman who had a baby needed to bring a sacrifice; today, she recites *hagomel* instead. And generally, since a woman who has just given birth often has many visitors, and among them are her male relatives, she is often in the presence of a quorum and has the opportunity to pronounce the blessing.[7]

The *acharonim* take up the issue as to whether a husband may pronounce *hagomel* to exempt his wife from her obligation to do so. The *Beit Yosef*[8] writes that he may not since he may be taking *Hashem's* Name in vain. On the other hand, the *Darchei Moshe* rules that he may do so, if he so wishes. The *Shulchan Aruch*[9] rules that a person may pronounce the blessing for another; the *Mishnah Berurah*[10] quotes the *Eliyah Rabbah*[11] who rules that he may not and that this is the majority view. However, the *Eliyah Rabbah*[12] rules that a husband may pronounce the blessing to exempt his wife. The *Mishnah Berurah*[13] adds that when he does, the text of the blessing should be as follows: "Who grants good to the guilty, Who has bestowed every goodness upon you," to which she responds, "*Amen.*" If she was not present at the time, the husband says: "Who has bestowed every goodness upon my wife." See, however, **D** below.

(C) Who grants good to the guilty: The meaning of the blessing of *hagomel* is that *Hashem,* in His ultimate mercy, bestows goodness even upon those who are unworthy. By reciting the blessing it is as if he is declaring that although he is among those who are unworthy of *Hashem's* mercy, *Hashem* nevertheless has acted benevolently toward him by saving him from danger.[14]

(D) Who has bestowed every goodness upon you: As mentioned in **C** above, the blessing of *hagomel* connotes that *Hashem* has saved one who was undeserving, and, deserved to suffer. Despite this negative connotation, the *Taz*[15] rules that one is

7. מנחת שלמה ח״ב סי׳ ד אות לא
8. ד״ה וממ״ש
9. סע׳ ד
10. ביה״ל סע׳ ד ד״ה ואין זה
11. ס״ק יא
12. ס״ק יב
13. מ״ב ס״ק ד וס״ק יז וכדלקמיה סע׳ ד
14. מ״ב ס״ק ד
15. ס״ק ג

GLOSS: *This is not considered a blessing pronounced in vain by the one who said it, even though he was not obligated to do so, since the blessing was recited to express his thanks and to praise Hashem for the good fortune of his friend, in which he rejoices.*

§8. One must recite this blessing (E)after any illness, even if it was not life-threatening, or internal. Rather, (F)anyone who was ill enough to take to bed must pronounce the

NISHMAT AVRAHAM

permitted to recite this blessing on behalf of a father or teacher who has recovered from an illness. Although it might seem inappropriate to do so, since he appears to be suggesting that his father or teacher is unworthy, the *Taz* explains that he may do this because the reference to "the unworthy" can be interpreted as referring to the one who pronounces the blessing. It is as if he says that although he himself is unworthy of it, nevertheless, *Hashem* in His mercy, cured or saved his father or teacher. The *Kaf HaChaim,*[16] however, writes that the custom is not to recite the blessing even for a wife, father or teacher.

(E) after any illness: The *Mateh Levi*[17] believes that there are certain *mitzvot* that one cannot perform without placing his life in danger. He believes that if he pronounces the blessing of *hagomel* after performing such a *mitzvah* he displays a lack of faith in *Hashem.* This is because he thought that he would be in danger as a result of performing a commandment, whereas, on the contrary, he should have believed that no harm would befall him while performing the *mitzvah.* Therefore, he rules that a woman who has given birth should not pronounce the blessing of *hagomel* after she recovers. Although her life may have been endangered during the delivery, it is inappropriate for her to pronounce the blessing since she was performing a *mitzvah* by having a child. In this light, it would seem that a male who never underwent circumcision as an infant, and therefore must undergo it as an adult, may not pronounce the blessing of *hagomel* after he recovers. However, *Rav Shlomo Zalman Auerbach zt"l* told me that he is required to do so. *Rav Auerbach zt"l* cites the *Shulchan Aruch* who rules that one who traveled by boat must pronounce the blessing of *hagomel,* even if he traveled in order to perform a *mitzvah,* such as coming to Israel. With regard to a woman who has given birth, see above, **B.** *Rav Waldenberg shlita*[18] also disagrees with the ruling of the *Mateh Levi* and believes that a woman's life is certainly endangered when she is giving birth, and it is appropriate for her to pronounce a blessing of thanks to *Hashem* upon her good fortune of surviving the delivery. In light of this, *Rav Waldenberg shlita* agrees with the ruling of *Rav Auerbach zt"l* that an adult male who undergoes circumcision must pronounce *hagomel* after recovery. I further heard from *Rav Auerbach zt"l* that a proselyte who underwent circumcision does not pronounce the blessing since at the time that he was endangered by the circumcision, he was still a non-Jew.

(F) anyone who was ill enough: According to the *Shulchan Aruch,* only one who had to take to bed because of illness should pronounce *hagomel* after recovery.

16. ס״ק כז
17. שו״ת ח״ב או״ח סי׳ ח
18. הערה לנשמת אברהם כרך ד עמ׳ ריט

blessing when he recuperates, (G)since it is as if he stood before a court to be judged. (H)There is no difference whether he has a chronic condition that recurs intermittently, or whether the onset of his illness is new.

GLOSS: *There are some who say that one should not recite this blessing unless he suffered a life-threatening illness, (I)such as an internal affliction. This is the custom in Ashkenaz.*

NISHMAT AVRAHAM

However, if one has suffered a mild discomfort, such as a headache or a sore throat, he should not pronounce the blessing.[19]

(G) since it is as if: Just as the fate of one who is about to stand trial is unknown, so too, is the fate of a person who is so ill that he has to take to bed. Although at the onset of an illness the condition may not appear severe, one never knows if it will take a turn for the worse and become life-threatening.[20] Therefore, one whose illness was such that he had to take to bed, must pronounce the blessing of *hagomel* when he recovers to thank *Hashem* for saving him from a potentially life-threatening situation.

(H) There is no difference: One might mistakenly think that a repetitive illness is less likely to progress to a life-threatening state and that one need not pronounce *hagomel* after each episode of the illness. However, many chronic conditions progressively worsen, and one may not rely on previous recoveries for his future prognosis during a new attack. Therefore, one with a chronically recurring illness must recite the blessing of *hagomel* after he recovers from each bout of the illness.[21]

(I) such as an internal affliction: Or any life-threatening disease.[22] In contrast to the ruling of the *Shulchan Aruch,* the *Rama* rules that only one who recovers from a life-threatening illness should recite the blessing of *hagomel.* The *Biur Halachah*[23] states that according to the *Shulchan Aruch,* even one who has a mild fever should pronounce the blessing of *hagomel* after the fever subsides, whereas according to the *Rama,* only if he had a high fever with chills should he recite the blessing. It must be noted, however, that although it is often the case that a high fever with chills indicates a severe condition, even a patient who is afebrile or has a low-grade fever may be in serious danger, and thus may be required to recite the blessing of *hagomel* upon recovery.

The *Biur Halachah*[24] clarifies the opinion of the *Rama,* and explains that anyone who has a life-threatening illness, a high fever with chills – or if a doctor believes that his life is in danger – is required to recite the blessing of *hagomel* after he recovers. Furthermore, the *Biur Halachah* believes that in the opinion of the *Taz,*[25] the *Shulchan Aruch* only requires one who was ill for three days to recite the blessing, regardless of whether or not the illness was life-threatening. In contrast to his understanding of the *Taz,* the *Biur Halachah* believes that the *Shulchan Aruch* does not have a minimum requirement of three days before one is obligated to pronounce the blessing. Instead, anyone whose illness forces him to take to bed

19. מ״ב ס״ק כד. ועיין בשעה״צ ס״ק יז
20. מ״ב ס״ק כה
21. שו״ת הרשב״א ח״א סי׳ פב מובא במ״ב ס״ק כו
22. מ״ב ס״ק כח (הראשון)
23. ד״ה כגון
24. שם
25. ס״ק ה

must pronounce *hagomel* upon recovery. The *Ben Ish Chai*[26] agrees with the ruling of the *Taz,* and feels that only one who had to take to bed for three days must pronounce the blessing. The *Mishnah Berurah*[27] reconciles these various opinions by stating that one who had to take to bed, and therefore would be classified as a *seriously ill patient,* must pronounce the blessing only if he was ill for three days. However, if he had a life-threatening illness, he must pronounce the blessing after he recovers, even if the duration of the illness was less than three days.

According to the *Lev Chaim,*[28] one who attempted to commit suicide and failed is required to pronounce the blessing of *hagomel.* In contrast, *Rav Ovadiah Yosef shlita*[29] rules that one who recovers from a failed suicide attempt should not pronounce the blessing of *hagomel,* since he thus recalls his sin of attempted suicide. *Rav Waldenberg shlita*[30] agrees with this ruling. He feels that anyone who knowingly places his or her life in danger should not pronounce the blessing of *hagomel.* However, if he wishes to, he may say the text of the blessing without mentioning *Hashem's* Name or His Kingship.

One whose psychiatric illness endangered his life is required to recite the blessing of *hagomel* upon recovery. *Rav Shlomo Zalman Auerbach zt''l* questioned whether one who denied or ignored his illness, was required to recite the blessing upon recovery. This would include psychiatric illness or a major stroke in which the patient has complete unawareness and neglect of the paralyzed side.

---

26. שנה א פ׳ עקב סע׳ ז

27. ס״ק כח (השני)

28. הגר״ח פלאג׳י, ח״ג סי׳ נג מובא גם בארחות חיים ס״ק י

29. בהערה על נשמת אברהם כרך א עמ׳ שלד, הערה ד

30. בהערה על נשמת אברהם כרך א עמ׳ שמ, הערה ה. שו״ת ציץ אליעזר חי״ב סי׳ יח אות ח

CHAPTER SEVENTEEN:

The Laws of Blessings

SIMAN 223: THE PROPER BLESSING FOR ONE WHOSE WIFE GAVE BIRTH, WHO RECEIVED AN INHERITANCE, WHO BUILT A NEW HOUSE, OR WHO PURCHASED UTENSILS OR CLOTHES

§1: (A)When a woman has given birth to (B)a boy, (C)the husband

NISHMAT AVRAHAM

SIMAN 223

(A) When a woman: If the father was out of town when he heard of his son's birth, he should nevertheless recite the blessing *hatov vehametiv* even though he has not yet seen him.[1] When he sees hisborn son he should then recite the blessing *shehecheyanu*.[2] However, in view of the *Rama's* ruling that many people act leniently and do not recite these blessings, it would be better not to recite them. Rather, he should recite the *shehecheyanu* at the *brit milah* bearing in mind that thereby he is also fulfilling his obligation to have done so at the birth.[3] The *Ben Ish Chai*[4] also rules that the father should say the *shehecheyanu* at his son's *brit milah*. If, however, the father only returns after the *brit*, there are varying opinions regarding the recitation of this blessing, and if he is sure that the prevalent custom of the area is to recite it, he should do so. However, if the custom of the area is not to say it, he should try to say the blessing of *shehecheyanu* over a new article of clothing or fruit when he first sees his son, bearing the auspicious occasion of the birth in mind when he says it. *Rav Neuwirth shlita* wondered whether the father should, perhaps, say *shehecheyanu* according to the ruling of the *Pri Megadim*.[5] However, *Rav Auerbach zt"l* wrote to me that it is not customary to do so, for the father's real joy is in the birth itself.

For *Chazal*, a baby born in the seventh month of gestation is more likely to survive than a baby born in the eighth month. The *Aishel Avraham*[6] rules that where there is reason to be uncertain as to whether a baby was born in the seventh or eighth month of gestation, the father should not recite *shehecheyanu* at the birth, but wait thirty days. One recites *shehecheyanu* at the time of birth only because most babies are likely to survive. However, where there is reason to believe that the baby may not survive, one should not recite the blessing. Rather, he should wait until the *brit milah* in order to say the blessing of *shehecheyanu*. Nowadays, a baby born in the eighth month of gestation is likely to survive, and the blessing may be

1. מ״ב ס״ק א
2. כף החיים ס״ק א בשם שו״ת הלכות קטנות ח״א סי׳ רא. מ״ב סי׳ רכה ס״ק ה וראה שם בשעה״צ ס״ק ה
3. כף החיים ס״ק ו
4. שנה א פ׳ ראה סע׳ ח
5. מובא במ״ב סי׳ רכה ס״ק ה
6. מבוטשאטש, על הגליון כאן

recites the blessing *hatov vehametiv*. She also must recite this blessing.

GLOSS: (D)*If she died during childbirth, he recites the blessing shehecheyanu instead of hatov vehametiv since this blessing only applies to two who share the happy event. Similarly, if the husband dies before his wife gives birth, she recites the blessing shehecheyanu. Some authorities have ruled that since this blessing (shehecheyanu) is not obligatory but rather permissible, the custom is to be lenient and not recite it. As a result, many* (E)*do not recite these blessings*.

NISHMAT AVRAHAM

recited immediately upon birth. However, if the newborn baby has a serious defect which makes it unlikely that he will live for thirty days, the father should wait thirty days to see if he will survive before he recites *shehecheyanu*.

(B) a boy: Since the *poskim* do not mention the requirement to say the blessing of *hatov vehametiv* after the birth of a daughter, it seems that one should not say this blessing upon the birth of a daughter. This is so even if a daughter is born after many sons and thus brings him much joy upon fulfilling his obligation to "be fruitful and multiply." Nevertheless, it would seem that the father should recite the blessing *shehecheyanu* the first time he sees his newborn daughter.[7] The custom, however, is not to do so (see *Rama*). Does one who has many sons and desires a daughter recite the blessing *hatov vehametiv* at the birth of another son? Though the birth of a son is objectively considered a happy occasion, perhaps he, having wanted a daughter, may feel a sense of disappointment upon the birth of the son; it may be inappropriate for him to recite *hatov vehametiv*.[8]

(C) the husband recites: Although it is preferable to recite the blessing *hatov vehametiv* as soon as he is aware of the birth of his son, all of the *poskim* agree that one who failed to do so then, may still recite the blessing later.[9]

(D) If she died: According to some *acharonim*, the *Shulchan Aruch* and the *Rama* disagree on this point. The *Rama* maintains that one does not recite the blessing *hatov vehametiv* if a wife died in childbirth; the *Beit Yosef* (the author of the *Shulchan Aruch*) rules that he should recite the blessing even if his wife died in childbirth.[10] Many *acharonim* accept the ruling of the *Rama*.[11] *The Kaf HaChaim*[12] refers to the *Knesset HaGedolah,* who reconciles the apparent disagreement between the *Beit Yosef* and the *Rama*. He explains that they are discussing two different situations; the *Beit Yosef* speaks of a wife who died <u>after</u> childbirth, but before the birth of his son became known to the father; and the *Rama* ruled that he does not recite the blessing, where the wife died <u>in</u> childbirth.

(E) do not recite: The *Rama* explains that because the *shehecheyanu* blessing is not obligatory, people tend not to recite either blessing. However, the *Mishnah*

7. מ״ב ס״ק ב. וראה במ״ב סי׳ רכה ס״ק ה ושעה״צ ס״ק ה בשם הפרי מגדים. והמנהג לא לברך עיין לעיל
8. ביה״ל ד״ה זכר
9. מ״ב ס״ק ג בשם הפמ״ג
10. ט״ז וא״ר
11. מור וקציעה, לחם חמודות, לבוש וח״א. כל זה במ״ב ס״ק ד
12. ס״ק ז

§2: (F)When one's father dies, he recites the blessing *dayan ha'emet.*

SIMAN 225:
THE BLESSING, "WHO MAKES HIS CREATURES DIFFERENT"

§9: One who sees a person who was born lame, without a limb, blind, or stricken with boils, or whose body is covered with spots, should say the blessing, "Who makes His creatures different." However, if they were afflicted later in life, he should say the blessing *dayan ha'emet.* There is an

NISHMAT AVRAHAM

Berurah[13] states that one should recite them.

(F) When one's father dies: One is required to rend his garment upon hearing of the death of a close relative for whom he is required to mourn.[14] One is also obligated to rend his garment if he is present when a Jew or Jewess dies even though the deceased may have occasionally transgressed a negative commandment because he was unable to control his desires, or did not perform a positive commandment because it was too much trouble to do so.[15] The *Shulchan Aruch*[16] also rules that one is required to rend his clothing in the presence of a *worthy person* who has passed away, anytime before his burial. In contrast, the *Rama*[17] rules that there is no obligation to tear clothing upon the death of a *worthy person* unless one is by his side at the moment of death. In such a case, he rules that one need not tear the outer garment as is required on the death of a close relative. Rather, one may merely rip the corner of his garment.[18]

Doctors and nurses who work in a hospital do not customarily rend their garments when they are present at the side of a Jewish patient at the time of his death though *halachah* indicates that they should. *Rav Waldenberg shlita*[19] attempts to explain this practice. He argues that if observant doctors, nurses and members of the burial committee were required to tear their garments every time they were present at the death of a person, no one would want to be present at the bedside of a dying patient for fear of the financial loss that would be incurred. Furthermore, *Rav Waldenberg shlita*[20] rules that it is also possible that the deceased was not truly a *worthy person*, upon whose death one would be required to tear one's garments. Since one is unsure as to the status of the deceased, one may take the lenient approach and refrain from tearing his garment. Besides, the outer clothing of a doctor or nurse often belongs to the hospital, and the hospital will not approve of the tearing of their property. See *Yoreh Deah Siman* 340:34, and the *Shach*, subheading 50, for further details.

13. ס״ק ז
14. יו״ד סי׳ שמ סע׳ א
15. שם סע׳ ה
16. שם סע׳ ו. וכן באו״ח סי׳ תקמז סע׳ ו
17. יו״ד שם סע׳ ו
18. שם סע׳ ב
19. לב אברהם ח״א עמ׳ כא
20. שו״ת ציץ אליעזר חי״ג סי׳ לה

opinion that the blessing (*dayan ha'emet*) is only recited if he feels pain for the person with the disfigurement. One only recites either of these blessings (A)the first time he sees such a person, because it is then that the disfigurement makes a great impression on him.

GLOSS: *There are some authorities who believe that these blessings should be recited again if he has not seen him for thirty days.*

SIMAN 230:
LAWS REGARDING SOME PERSONAL BLESSINGS

§4: One who is about (A)to have his blood let should recite, "May it be Your will, Hashem, my Lord, that this endeavor shall cure me, (B)for You are the Healer Who takes no fee." After the bloodletting is completed, one should say,

NISHMAT AVRAHAM

SIMAN 225

(A) the first time: The *Chayei Adam*[1] explains that since we are accustomed to see people with the afflictions mentioned in this section, it is not our practice to recite these blessings. The *Kaf HaChaim*[2] recommends that whoever encounters another with any of these afflictions should recite the blessing without mentioning the name of *Hashem* or His Kingship. *Rav Shlomo Zalman Auerbach zt"l* wrote me that one must be very careful that the person with the disfigurement does not hear the blessing, since it will certainly cause him pain.

SIMAN 230

(A) to have his blood let: One should recite this prayer prior to undertaking any medical procedure or treatment.[1] This includes the swallowing of medication of any kind. One must realize that *Hashem* alone is responsible for his medical fate, and not the doctor or a particular mode of treatment.[2] Therefore, one should place his trust in *Hashem* and pray that he be healed.[3] Some *acharonim*[4] believe that for bloodletting one should only recite the concluding blessing, which uses the language of "Blessed—." This is because his life is considered in danger when he undergoes the bloodletting procedure as it was done at the time of the Talmud. However, the first part of the prayer, "May it be Your will—" should certainly be recited in all situations, since it is not a blessing but a supplication to *Hashem*.[5]

(B) for You are the Healer: *Hashem* takes no fee and is still a healer; but of a human doctor who treats for nothing[6] it is said:[7] "A physician who treats for

1. כלל סג סע׳ א
2. ס״ק סה
1. מ״ב ס״ק ו בשם המג״א והחיי אדם
2. יד אברהם יו״ד סי׳ שלו
3. מ״ב שם
4. א״ר ס״ק י בשם הרד״א מובא בבאר היטב ס״ק ה
5. מחצית השקל מובא בשעה״צ ס״ק ח
6. ברכ״י בשיורי ברכה ס״ק ד בשם המהרש״א
7. ב״ק פה ע״א

(C)"Blessed is He who heals the sick."

SIMAN 231:
ALL ONE'S INTENTIONS SHOULD BE DIRECTED TOWARDS HEAVEN

§1: If one is unable to study Torah without first taking an afternoon nap, he should sleep.

GLOSS: *On awakening, he is not required to recite the blessing of Elokai neshamah. There are some who believe that one must recite the prayer of vihi noam, before sleeping.*

The ruling that one may sleep in the afternoon applies only when he will not take a long nap, since he should not sleep during the day for (A)more than half an hour. Even when taking a short nap, he should not do so just to satisfy his physical needs, but rather to strengthen himself in order to serve *Hashem*. Similarly, all the pleasures one derives from this world should be with the intention to serve the Blessed Creator rather than for his own enjoyment, as it is written, "In all of your ways you shall know Him." Our Sages have said that all of one's actions should be done for the sake of Heaven. Even actions that do not fulfill commandments, such as eating, drinking, walking, sitting and arising, engaging in marital relations, speaking, (B)and engaging in any action necessary for one's body,

NISHMAT AVRAHAM

nothing is worth nothing!"

(C) Blessed is He Who heals the sick: The *Mishnah Berurah* says that although one should really include the Name of *Hashem* and His Kingship when reciting this blessing,[8] the accepted practice is not to do so.[9] It is only necessary to include these references to *Hashem* when reciting a blessing. However, the passage which is discussed in this section is a plea to *Hashem* to cure him of his ailment; it is a prayer and not a blessing and this is why it is inappropriate to mention the Name of *Hashem* or His Kingship while reciting this prayer.[10]

SIMAN 231

(A) more than half an hour. See above, *Siman* 47 note 14.

(B) and engaging in any action necessary for one's body: Whatever one does to improve his health, such as exercising etc., should only be done to enable him

8. ב״י, ט״ז ובאר הגולה
9. מ״ב ס״ק ז בשם הפמ״ג
10. שעה״צ ס״ק ט

all of these should be directed to serving the Creator or towards achieving this aim. For example, it is not praiseworthy if one who is hungry or thirsty eats or drinks only for his own enjoyment. Instead, he should eat and drink only what is necessary to enable him to serve his Creator. Similarly, it is not praiseworthy if he associates with the righteous and the pious, and even follows their advice, if he does so only for his own pleasure and gain. Only when he acts with intentions directed towards Heaven are his actions considered commendable. So too, regarding sleep, it is unnecessary to state that one should not sleep away his time, merely because he enjoys sleep, at a time when he could be engaged in Torah study or performing *mitzvot.* On the contrary, even when he is tired, and needs to sleep in order to regain his strength, it is not praiseworthy if he sleeps merely in order to satisfy his needs. Instead, his intention should be to rest his body in order to stay healthy, and to be able to concentrate and remain alert while studying Torah. Similarly, he should fulfill marital relations, a Torah *mitzvah,* with the intention of fulfilling the *mitzvah* or with the intention of having children who will serve the Creator, not in order to satisfy his desires or to derive bodily pleasure; even if he also wishes to have children to serve and inherit him, it is not praiseworthy. Similarly, regarding conversation, even one who wishes to speak words of wisdom should do so with the intention of serving his Creator, or to bring him closer to doing so. In short, man is obligated to examine and assess all that he is about to do, weighing it intelligently, and when he sees that it will bring him closer to the service of his Creator he should do it, and if not, he should desist from doing it. If one acts in this way he will constantly be serving his Creator.

NISHMAT AVRAHAM

to better serve his Creator by studying Torah and performing *mitzvot*, as it is written: "In all of your ways you shall know Him."[1]

1. משלי ג:ו

CHAPTER EIGHTEEN:

The Laws of Keriyat Shema at Night and Maariv

SIMAN 235: THE PROPER TIME FOR *KERIYAT SHEMA* AT NIGHT

§4: One who recites the nighttime *Keriyat Shema* after dawn, albeit before sunrise, has not fulfilled his obligation to recite *Keriyat Shema* at night, unless he did so under extenuating circumstances, for example, if he was inebriated, (A)or ill, or any other such reason. If he was unable to recite the *Shema* because of extenuating circumstances, and does so after dawn, he should not say the blessing of *hashkivenu,* since people do not normally go to sleep after dawn.

GLOSS: *However, he says the two blessings preceding the recitation of the Shema, and the blessing of emet ve'emunah until the blessing of hashkivenu.*

NISHMAT AVRAHAM

SIMAN 235

(A) or ill: Although one who deliberately pushes off the opportunity to perform a *mitzvah*, and then subsequently loses the opportunity to fulfill it, cannot amend his transgression, the *halachah* is different here. If he could have recited the *Shema* at the beginning of the night, yet did not do so, and subsequently became ill and, as a result could not recite it the entire night, he is not considered to have deliberately evaded the *mitzvah*. Since one is permitted to recite the *Shema* the entire night, he obviously thought that he would have time later, and did not intentionally avoid the opportunity to perform this *mitzvah*. Such a person is permitted to recite the *Shema* after dawn, even though it is not the ideal time for its recital.[1]

1. מהא דמ״ב ס״ק לא

SIMAN 238:
ONE SHOULD ESTABLISH A SET TIME FOR TORAH STUDY AT NIGHT

§2: If one has a set amount of Torah that he learns every day, and was too busy during the day to complete that set quota, (A)he must promptly complete it at night.

NISHMAT AVRAHAM

SIMAN 238

(A) he must promptly complete it: Although the summer nights are short, one is still obligated to dedicate time every night to complete his daily quota of Torah study. He should not postpone it until the next day, because he will inevitably fall behind in his studies, and never make up the lost time for studying Torah, thus fulfilling the verse:[1] "A crooked thing that cannot be fixed."[2] Both doctor and patient are obligated to study Torah every day to the best of their ability; see *Siman* 155, and the accompanying discussion.

1. קהלת א:טו

2. מ״ב ס״ק ד

CHAPTER NINETEEN:
The Laws of Shabbat

SIMAN 245:
HOW A JEW WHO HAS A NON-JEWISH PARTNER SHOULD ACT WITH REGARD TO *SHABBAT*

§1: When (A)a Jew and a non-Jew jointly own a field, oven, bathhouse, or mill, or they are partners in a store, and they stipulated from the outset of the partnership that the earnings from *Shabbat,* however small or large as they may be, belong to the non-Jew exclusively, while the earnings from one other day of the week belong exclusively to the Jew, then the partnership and its business transactions are permissible. If, however, they did not make this

NISHMAT AVRAHAM

SIMAN 245

(A) a Jew and a non-Jew: When a Jew and a non-Jew agree to become partners in a medical practice, they must make the following agreement before they officially begin their partnership. The non-Jew must agree that only he will receive the earnings from all work done on *Shabbat*, and, in return, the Jew will receive all the earnings from one of the weekdays, whether large or small. If this arrangement was made before they entered into the partnership, they are permitted to decide later to divide the entire weekly earnings equally, if they should so wish.[1] When such a stipulation was not made before the partnership officially began, *Rav Sherira Gaon* rules that the non-Jew must take all of the earnings from each *Shabbat*, while the Jew receives the earnings from one of the weekdays, whatever they may be. In contrast, the *Ran* believes that when both the Jew and the non-Jew work every weekday, but the non-Jew also works on *Shabbat*, they may divide all of the earnings equally. This is because the non-Jew is working for himself, and not on behalf of the Jew. Therefore, the Jew is permitted to benefit from this type of partnership. Nevertheless, the Jew should take the payment as a lump sum rather than specify which day's earnings he is claiming, for if he did not take a lump sum, it would appear as if he is benefiting from work done on *Shabbat*.[2] The *Shulchan Aruch* adopts the stringent opinion of *Rav Sherira Gaon* whereas the *Rama* follows the opinion of the *Ran*. The *Chatam Sofer*[3] and the *Maharam Shick*[4] also rule like the *Rama*.

1. מ״ב בהקדמתו לסימן
2. מובא בב״י
3. שו״ת או״ח סי׳ נח
4. שו״ת או״ח סי׳ קו

stipulation at the outset, then the non-Jew must take all of the earnings from each *Shabbat*, and the rest of the earnings are divided evenly between the two. If the exact amount of earnings from *Shabbat* are unknown, the non-Jew takes one-seventh of the total earnings, and the rest is divided between them.

NISHMAT AVRAHAM

A Jew is forbidden to help another Jew transgress any prohibition; this is derived from the verse: "Do not place a stumbling block before a blind person."[5] One only violates this Torah prohibition when he assists another to violate a transgression which that other would have been unable to do without his assistance. However, *Chazal* instituted a Rabbinic prohibition which forbids one to assist another in violating a prohibition, although he could have successfully committed the sin even without this help.[6] This becomes especially relevant when considering the permissibility of becoming a partner with a *mumar* (a Jew who, knowingly and willfully, desecrates the Sabbath in public) in a medical practice. If one does so he knowingly condones his partner working on *Shabbat*. The *Mishnah Berurah*[7] believes that with regard to this *halachah* there is no difference between an observant Jew and a *mumar,* and the verse, "Do not place a stumbling block before a blind person," applies to both. Therefore, it would be forbidden to enter into a partnership with such a Jew, for fear of violating the Biblical prohibition of "Do not place a stumbling block." The *Levushei Mordechai*,[8] on the other hand, believes that there is no Biblical prohibition of "Do not place a stumbling block" with regard to a *mumar*; however, there is the Rabbinic prohibition. Therefore, he recommends that, given the choice if one has not already become a partner, he must not enter into such a partnership. The *Chelkat Yaakov*[9] disagrees with both the *Mishnah Berurah* and the *Levushei Mordechai*, basing his view on the opinion of the *Shach*,[10] that there is not even a Rabbinic prohibition when the one who is being assisted in a transgression is a *mumar*. The *Orchot Chaim*[11] rules that if one wishes to enter into a partnership with a *mumar,* he should do so only with a written contract specifying that he (the *mumar*) will not work on *Shabbat*. If, in spite of the contract, the *mumar* later does insist on working on *Shabbat*, the observant partner must first nullify the contract and then make another one in which they agree to divide the weekly workload, whereby the observant Jew will work for the first half of the week (from Sunday to Wednesday afternoon) and the non-observant Jew the second. This is similar to the suggestion of the *Shulchan Aruch* as to the stipulations one must make before taking a non-Jewish partner so as not to benefit from *Shabbat* earnings. The *Melamed LeHo'il*[12] writes that if the partners are unable to determine the amount of Sabbath earnings, the observant partner should forfeit one-seventh of the total earnings to the *mumar*, and the rest of the earnings should be

5. ויקרא יט:יד
6. עיין תוס׳ ע״ז ו ע״ב ד״ה מנין
7. סי׳ תמח ס״ק יא
8. שו״ת לבושי מרדכי וויינקלער מהד״ק או״ח סי׳ מג. יסודי ישורון ח״ג עמ׳ קיז
9. ח״ב סי׳ נד
10. ועיין בש״ך יו״ד סי׳ קנא ס״ק ו
11. כאן ס״ק ב
12. שו״ת או״ח סי׳ לד

GLOSS: *There are some who permit the Jewish partner to accept his part of the total weekly earnings in the event that such a partnership was agreed upon without any such stipulation at the outset. It seems to me that when there would otherwise be a great loss of income for the Jew, he may rely on these authorities. There are others who rule that this only applies to a partnership where each partner works on different days. However, if they work together on all of the weekdays and only the non-Jew works on Shabbat, it is permissible to divide the earnings evenly. This is because the non-Jew working on Shabbat is doing so for his own*

NISHMAT AVRAHAM

split equally between the two.

Most residency programs in the United States are not designed to allow an observant Jewish intern or resident to choose *Shabbat* as his day off from work. Consequently, it is not uncommon for these interns or residents to be "on call" in the hospital on *Shabbat*. *Rav Moshe Feinstein zt"l*[13] rules that one must do his best to receive permission from his superiors to arrange his schedule so that he will not be required to be in the hospital on *Shabbat*. If a doctor does find that he has been put "on call" on *Shabbat,* he must do his best to change with a non-Jewish colleague, even if he will need to do more on-calls or pay him for doing so. *Rav Feinstein zt"l* rules that if there is no alternative he may change with a non-religious Jewish colleague. *Rav Auerbach zt"l*,[14] on the other hand, rules that he may not do so.

Should a doctor make his services available to his patients on *Shabbat*, even though this might require him to violate its laws? *Rav Moshe Feinstein zt"l*[15] rules that when there are other physicians in the area whose services are easily accessible, one must close his office on *Shabbat*. Furthermore, his home telephone number must be unlisted, in order to avoid his being called by a patient on *Shabbat*. However, if one of his patients were to come to his home, he would be required to treat him. *Rav Moshe Feinstein zt"l* was asked: "Is a physician obligated to seek training, employment, or attending-physician status at a hospital where there is a minimal or no conflict between hospital policy and Sabbath observance? Should a house officer seek training at an inferior quality hospital where he is "guaranteed" not to have to work on the Sabbath or should he seek training in a hospital where training and overall patient care is far superior, but where there may be interference with the Sabbath spirit but not with the observance of *halachic* restrictions? Must one compromise one's medical education in order to to simplify Sabbath and *kashrut* observance? Answer: A physician must seek association with the most reputable and prestigious hospital possible to ensure excellent training and continuing education. Comment: Jewish law requires that the physician acquire maximum skill and competence to practice his chosen profession, Therefore, he should forgo the personal comfort and convenience of training in a hospital that is sympathetic to his religious needs in favor of the hospital that will provide him with the best possible training, provided that he is certain of his fortitude in main-

13. שו״ת אג״מ או״ח ח״ד סי׳ עט
14. שמירת שבת כהלכתה פל״ב הערה קכה
15. שו״ת אג״מ שם

benefit and the Jew is not benefiting from this work since he himself is not obligated by the contract to work on Shabbat. Nevertheless, the Jew should not accept any earnings specifically from Shabbat; they should be a part of a lump sum payment for the whole week.

SIMAN 248:
THE LAWS APPLYING TO ONE WHO SET OUT TO SEA OR WITH A CARAVAN ON *SHABBAT*

§4: It is prohibited to set out into the desert with a caravan within the three days before *Shabbat*, since one will thereby be required to desecrate *Shabbat*, as it would be too dangerous to stop on the *Shabbat* in the desert and remain there alone. However, it is permissible to set out on (A)Sunday, Monday, or Tuesday. If, afterwards, he has

NISHMAT AVRAHAM

taining all *halachic* requirements, despite the less favorable environment. **If the superior training is to be acquired at the price of Sabbath desecration, even of Rabbinic ordinances only, the student-physician must forgo the educational advantages of the prestigious hospital** (emphasis mine). It is important to emphasize that residents in non-"*shomer Shabbos*" programs have often found themselves under great stress from hospital administrations and mentors who are unsympathetic to their religous convictions. Open discussion with the training-hospital administration must be initiated before accepting such an appointment."[16]

This ruling I also heard from *Rav Auerbach zt"l*,[17] *Rav Eliashiv shlita* and *Rav Neuwirth shlita*.

In Israel, a religious doctor (or nurse) must not change his (or her) *Shabbat* rotation of duties with a non-religious or non-Jewish doctor (or nurse) should the only reason for doing so be his (or her) unwillingness to work on *Shabbat*.[18]

SIMAN 248

(A) Sunday: According to the *Raza*, these three days are linked to the previous *Shabbat*[1] and therefore, one need not take precautions at this time to prevent dese-

16. עבודה בבה"ח בשבת

Practical Medical Halacha, Rabbi M. D. Tendler and Dr. F. Rosner, Rephael Society of the Association of Orthodox Jewish Scientists, p. 150,1998. In a preface, the authors write: "Because of the far-reaching significance of many of these *halachic* decisions, they were submitted to HaGaon Moshe Feinstein of blessed memory for review."

ועיין היטב בע"ז כו ע"א ותוס' שם ד"ה סבר, ש"משום איבה" מתיר רק ביום חול. ובשבת, רק איסורי דרבנן ולא איסורי תורה. ולכן, לפי הפוסקים הנ"ל, ההיתר שייך רק בדיעבד ובשעת הדחק ואינו מתיר לכתחלה. וראה גם בשו"ע (הגדול) או"ח סי' של סע' ב וביו"ד סי' קנד סע"ב. וכן אמרו לי הגרש"ז אויערבך זצ"ל, הגרי"ש אלישיב שליט"א והגרי"י נויבירט שליט"א

17. ראה בשמירת שבת כהלכתה פ"מ סע' כג ופל"ב הערה קכה

18. שמירת שבת כהלכתה פ"מ סע' כג והערה סה**. וראה שם בח"ג הערה על סעיף זה

1. שיטת הרז"ה מובא בב"י

to break *Shabbat* in order to preserve life, it is permissible and not considered a desecration of *Shabbat*. If one wishes to travel to the Land of Israel in order to settle there, and the only available caravan is on Friday, he may set out with them, since this is a *mitzvah*. However, he should stipulate that they stop traveling on *Shabbat*.

NISHMAT AVRAHAM

crating the coming *Shabbat*. However, the *Knesset HaGedolah* and the *Radvaz* write that if he is certain that it nevertheless will lead to the desecration of the coming *Shabbat*, he is forbidden to undertake a trip or task early in the week.[2]

In *halachah*, nightfall marks the beginning of a new day. However, regarding the undertaking of a trip or task, the *Raza* considers Tuesday night as if it is still within three days of the previous *Shabbat*.[3] In his opinion, one will be permitted to begin such a trip or task on Tuesday night. As to Wednesday, the *Mishnah Berurah*[4] cites the opinion of the *Magen Avraham*[5] that one is prohibited to leave for a trip on Wednesday. However, the *Gra* cites many sources who believe that the phrase "three days before *Shabbat*" includes *Shabbat* itself and therefore, it would be permissible to leave on Wednesday.

What if one did leave for a trip or begin an endeavor during the latter half of the week, and finds that by doing so, he must transgress *Shabbat* laws because of danger to life?[6] The *Chochmat Shlomo*[7] argues that someone who endangered his life through his own negligence has no dispensation to violate *Shabbat* in order to save his life. However both *Rav Shlomo Zalman Auerbach zt''l*[8] and the *Igrot Moshe*[9] rule that he is permitted to do so, even though he was responsible for the situation by transgressing the *halachah*. See also *Siman* 328:2, regarding transgressing *Shabbat* laws to treat someone who attempted suicide.

Following the guidelines outlined above, if one requires non-urgent surgery, it would be best to attempt to have it scheduled for the beginning of the week, thus reducing the possibility of transgressing *Shabbat* laws.[10] If the surgeon who is an expert at a given procedure only schedules surgery for the latter half of the week, it is permissible to undergo the procedure on Wednesday, Thursday, or Friday. This is comparable to the ruling of the *Shulchan Aruch* that one is permitted to perform a *mitzvah* in the latter half of the week even if there is a chance that by so doing he may be required to violate the coming *Shabbat*.[11] In a large hospital where many patients are scheduled for surgery, it is permissible to perform a procedure on Thursday or Friday to minimize the time that patients wait for surgery, and to prevent the possibility that a patient's condition will worsen to the point of possible danger while waiting.[12] *Rav Shlomo Zal-*

2. מ״ב ס״ק כו. וראה גם בט״ז יו״ד סי׳ רסב ס״ק ג וש״ך סי׳ רסו סוס״ק יח ושמירת שבת כהלכתה פל״ב הערה צו
3. ביה״ל ד״ה וביום
4. ס״ק ד
5. ס״ק ב
6. סי׳ שלא שעה״צ ס״ק יז. שמירת שבת כהלכתה שם. ועיין בקובץ הערות יבמות סי׳ כג אות ג
7. או״ח סי׳ שכט
8. מוריה סיון תשל״א עמ׳ לב. מנחת שלמה ח״א סי׳ ז אות ד
9. או״ח ח״א סי׳ קכז
10. שמירת שבת כהלכתה פל״ב סע׳ לג
11. הגרש״ז אויערבאך שם הערה צז
12. שמעתי ממו״ר הגרי״י נויבירט שליט״א. שו״ת ציץ אליעזר חי״ב סי׳ מג, וראה שם סי׳ מו

SIMAN 252:

THE LAWS REGARDING THE PERMISSIBILITY OF BEGINNING WORK ON FRIDAY WHICH WILL ONLY BE COMPLETED ON *SHABBAT*

§5: It is permitted to open a faucet on Friday allowing water to flow into a garden even though it will continue to flow the whole of *Shabbat*. It is permissible (A)to apply (B)a thick eye-salve *(an ophthalmic ointment)* **to the eye on Friday, even though it would be prohibited to do this on *Shabbat*.**

GLOSS: *It is permitted to wind a clock on Friday even though it will sound each hour on Shabbat. (C)This is because everyone knows that the winding of such a clock is usually done the previous day (see Siman* 338*).*

NISHMAT AVRAHAM

man Auerbach zt"l[13] wrote to me that if the patient is in pain, it is a *mitzvah* to perform surgery on his behalf even on Friday. This *mitzvah* is similar to that of a *brit milah* that has been delayed because the baby was ill, which may be performed on Friday (see, however, *Siman* 331:4). See also *Siman* 468B.

When a pregnant woman has reached her due date, she may undergo induction of labor if her doctor believes that otherwise, either she or her baby will be endangered, even if it is probable that by doing so she will give birth on *Shabbat*.[14]

SIMAN 252

(A) to apply: Even though an ointment applied to the eye before *Shabbat* will provide therapeutic benefit on *Shabbat* itself, one may nevertheless apply it before the onset of *Shabbat*. Similarly, one may place a bandage on a wound before *Shabbat*.[1] Water may be poured into a "warm-water" humidifier (vaporizer) before *Shabbat* even though it will be heated and produce steam on *Shabbat*. One may add water to a "cold-water" humidifier (vaporizer) on *Shabbat* itself. However, there is a disagreement among the *poskim* whether one may add water to a "warm-water" humidifier (vaporizer) on *Shabbat* itself for a *non-seriously ill* patient;[2] a competent *halachic* authority must be consulted. (See *Siman* 278D[h] regarding a *seriously ill* patient.)

(B) a thick eye-salve: A clear, soft eye-salve may be applied on *Shabbat* itself if it was prepared before *Shabbat*.[3] See below, *Siman* 328:21.

(C) This is because everyone knows: See below, *Siman* 338:3 for discussion regarding the use of an alarm clock on *Shabbat* for one who is ill.

13. לב אברהם ח״ב עמ׳ כ
14. שמירת שבת כהלכתה פל״ב הערה צח
1. מ״ב ס״ק לו
2. עיין במאמרו של הגרי״י וייס זצ״ל באוצרות ירושלים חלק רכז סי׳ קנה שאוסר. אמנם הג״ר הלוי יצחק הלפרין שליט״א בספר אסיא ח״ב עמ׳ 266 מתיר בתנאי שמוסיפים רק מים רתוחים מערב שבת שעומדים על האש ושהמכשיר מחובר לרשת החשמל מערב שבת ונשאר כך עד מוצאי שבת
3. מ״ב ס״ק לז

SIMAN 263: WHO SHOULD LIGHT THE SABBATH CANDLES

§1: One should take care to prepare a beautiful holder for the *Shabbat* light. There are those who prepare two separate wicks, one representing "*Zachor*" and one "*Shamor*."

GLOSS: *One may add three or four candles and this is our custom.* (A)*A woman who forgot to light the two Sabbath candles should then always light three in the future. This is because one may add to, but not detract from, that (in our case, light) which is used to represent something else (zachor and shamor).*

§2: Both men and women are obligated to have (B)light (C)in their homes on *Shabbat*. Even one so poor that he has

NISHMAT AVRAHAM

SIMAN 263

(A) A woman who forgot: However, a woman who is unable to light candles on *Shabbat* because she was ill, is not required to light an additional candle in the future.[1]

(B) light: A doctor or nurse on hospital duty on Friday evening must light Sabbath candles with a blessing,[2] if there is no one to light them on his behalf at home, because of the obligation to honor the *Shabbat*.[3] If someone at home will light Sabbath candles on his behalf, he has fulfilled this duty. However, he must still make certain, because of the additional obligation of *oneg* (enjoying) *Shabbat*, that there will be light during the Sabbath in all the rooms that he will be using.[4] Furthermore, if he knows that at some point on *Shabbat* night he will be present in his own room (where he will sleep),[5] and thus be able to enjoy their light, he is required to light Sabbath candles in that room and recite the blessing.[6] He must make certain that the candles will burn long enough to allow him to derive benefit from their light once it is dark.[7]

Doctors or nurses may light candles in the dining room near where they will eat. However, each individual has an obligation to light candles. Thus, he or she either pays towards the cost of the candles lit in the dining room, and also lights in the bedroom (as above) without the blessing, or else lights in the bedroom with a blessing.[8] If the hospital authorities arrange for candles to be lit in the dining room, the doctor or nurse has no obligation to light there.[9]

(C) in their homes: If a duty doctor or nurse, or a patient in a hospital is unable to light Sabbath candles, either because the hospital prohibits lighting candles in rooms or because he forgot to prepare

1. מהא דמ״ב ס״ק ז
2. בן איש חי שנה ב פ׳ נח סע׳ ה
3. ראה רמב״ם הל׳ שבת פ״ה ה״א ופ״ל ה״ה
4. ראה מ״ב ס״ק ב ו־כח
5. מ״ב ס״ק ב ו־כח
6. מ״ב ס״ק לב וביה״ל שם ד״ה בחורים
7. מ״ב ס״ק ל
8. שמעתי ממו״ר הגרי״י נויבירט שליט״א. וראה שמירת שבת כהלכתה פמ״ה סע׳ ט
9. או״ח כאן סע׳ ז ומ״ב ס״ק לג

nothing to eat should beg from door to door in order to buy oil for Sabbath lights. This is because light is part of the enjoyment of *Shabbat.*

NISHMAT AVRAHAM

candles before *Shabbat*, may he or she say the blessing for *Shabbat* candles when turning on an electric light (on the eve of *Shabbat*) for this purpose? The *Beit Yitzchak*[10] maintains that one may fulfill the obligation to light Sabbath candles by turning on an electric light and he may therefore recite the appropriate blessing. The *Machazeh Avraham*,[11] *Har Tzvi*[12] and *Az Nidberu*[13] agree with this. If light is already present, *Rabbeinu Tam*[14] rules that one must first extinguish and then relight it to make it apparent that it was lit solely for the honor of *Shabbat*. This is also the opinion of the *Magen Avraham*.[15] *Rav Shlomo Zalman Auerbach zt"l* wrote to me that one would certainly need to turn off and re-light the electric light if it had already been lit before *plag haminchah*.[16]

In contrast, the *Mishpetei Uziel*[17] argues that one does not fulfill the obligation of lighting Sabbath candles by using an electric light since the light would go out if there were an electrical power failure. In such a case, he believes that one would have transgressed the prohibition of reciting a blessing in vain. Even though such power failures may only occur rarely, nevertheless the blessing should not be recited. A basis for this ruling of the *Mishpetei Uziel* may be found in a *responsum* of the *Rashba*.[18] The *Rashba* states that we do not recite a blessing on a *mitzvah* which is not completely within our control. Since we do not have control of the electricity, we should not recite a blessing on the electric light. The *Levushei Mordechai*[19] also prohibits the use of an electric light to fulfill the obligation of lighting Sabbath candles since electric lights do not resemble any oil-based material which normally constitutes a conventional candle. However, in a later *responsum*[20] he is less certain of the prohibition.

The *Yabia Omer*[21] advises that although there is not sufficient reason to believe that one's obligation to light Sabbath candles is not fulfilled with electric lights, nevertheless it is best to act stringently and light a candle as well, if at all possible, and recite the blessing over this candle.

A female patient who spends *Shabbat* in a hospital outside of Israel and is not permitted by the hospital to light a candle in her room, should turn on an electric light beside her bed as a Sabbath candle before *Shabbat* begins. However, she should not recite the customary blessing before doing so, since there is no consensus among the *poskim* as to whether electric lights can serve as Sabbath candles. On the other hand, I heard from *Rav Auerbach zt"l* and *Rav Neuwirth shlita* that a blessing may be said over a battery-powered lamp or flashlight (torch) in these circumstances,[22] if it is certain that the battery is new and will last at least until nightfall.

10. יו״ד ח״א סי׳ קכ או״ק ה וח״ב סי׳ לא או״ק ח
11. או״ח סי׳ מא
12. או״ח ח״א סי׳ קמג
13. ח״ג סי׳ א
14. שבת כה ע״ב ד״ה חובה
15. ס״ק יא
16. ראה שמירת שבת כהלכתה פמ״ג סע׳ לב
17. או״ח סי׳ ז
18. ח״א סי׳ יח
19. מהד״ג סי׳ נט
20. מהדורה שנת תרצ״ז סי׳ יט
21. ח״ב או״ח סי׳ יז
22. ראה שמירת שבת כהלכתה פמ״ג הערה כב

§3: (D)Women have a greater obligation than men to light Sabbath candles since they are generally at home and take care of the needs of the home. If one cannot afford to buy both one candle for *Shabbat* and wine for *Kiddush*, then the Sabbath candle takes precedence. Likewise, if he cannot afford to buy both one candle for *Shabbat* and one candle for *Chanukah*, the Sabbath candle takes precedence because of family harmony. This is because there is no family harmony without light. *(If one cannot afford to buy both wine for Kiddush and light for Chanukah, see below, Siman* 675).

NISHMAT AVRAHAM

(D) Women: The Sabbath candles should be lit where the Sabbath meal will be eaten. A hospitalized female patient who cannot leave her bed should light the Sabbath candles at her bedside since this is where she will be eating her meal.[23] When at home, such a patient should preferably ask her husband, or someone else, to light the Sabbath candles in the room where the Sabbath meal will be eaten.[24] If this is not possible, she may light them at her bedside and have them moved, before *Shabbat*, to the table where the Sabbath meal will be eaten.[25]

An ill woman who has lit candles by her bedside must be careful not to do anything in their presence which would profane the *mitzvah*, such as getting undressed or using a bedpan[26] (see also above, *Siman* 75 end of §B).

The husband of a blind woman should light the Sabbath candles and recite the blessing. If she lives alone, she may light them and recite the blessing. If she lives with others who are also required to light candles, she should light candles without the blessing but she should try to hear the blessing before lighting the candles from another who bears her in mind when saying it.[27]

A woman who must undergo surgery on Friday afternoon, and knows that she will not awaken from the anesthesia until after the candles have burnt out, if she knows that she will be the only Jewish patient in the room, or that she will be in the post-operative recovery room, she should not light Sabbath candles in her room beforehand, since she will not have the opportunity to benefit from their light, and the blessing will have been "in vain."[28] If there is another Jewish woman sharing her room who will be lighting Sabbath candles, she should not light. However, if the other Jewish woman will not be lighting Sabbath candles, she may light them and recite the blessing, since the other woman will derive benefit from the light once *Shabbat* begins.[29] The same ruling applies to a woman who must travel to the hospital on Friday afternoon before dusk. If her husband or other family members will remain at home, she should light the candles at home with a blessing even though she herself will not benefit from them. However, if no one will be at home, she may not do so.[30]

23. מ״ב סוס״ק ב
24. מ״ב ס״ק יא
25. מ״ב ס״ק מח
26. שמירת שבת כהלכתה פמ״ג סע׳ מא
27. שם סע׳ י
28. מהא דמ״ב ס״ק ל
29. ואם המקום כבר מואר ראה בשו״ע כאן סע׳ ח, מ״ב ס״ק לו, כף החיים ס״ק נד ו־נו ושמירת שבת כהלכתה פמ״ג סע׳ לד
30. כתב לי הגרש״ז אויערבאך זצ״ל

§17: There are some authorities who rule that even one who "brought in" the Sabbath for himself well before dusk is permitted to ask a fellow Jew (who has not yet done so) to do otherwise forbidden work for him.

Gloss: *One may benefit from this same work on the Sabbath and certainly so after the Sabbath. Similarly, it appears to me that a person who has delayed praying Maariv on Saturday night,* (E)*or whose third meal has continued into the night, may ask a fellow Jew, who has already prayed and recited Havdalah, to do work for him such as lighting candles or cooking, and benefit from this work.*

NISHMAT AVRAHAM

(E) or whose third meal has continued: The *Mishnah Berurah*[31] explains that if a person, whose *seudah shelishit* (third Sabbath meal) continued after nightfall, said *hamavdil bein kodesh lechol* during the meal, he may perform work that is otherwise forbidden on *Shabbat*. However, it is unclear whether, during the *birkat hamazon* following the meal, he may still include the paragraph beginning *retzei* which is said on *Shabbat*. Perhaps his saying *hamavdil* signifies that *Shabbat* has ended for him? Therefore, it would be inappropriate to say *retzei* during *birkat hamazon* since it is said only on *Shabbat*. *Rav Neuwirth shilta* told me that a doctor whose *seudah shelishit* continued after nightfall should first say *baruch hamavdil bein kodesh lechol* (without mentioning the Name of *Hashem* or His Kingship) before answering the telephone. Basing himself on a *Magen Avraham*,[32] he ruled that the doctor should then include the paragraph *retzei* in *birkat hamazon* at the end of his meal. However, *Rav Shlomo Zalman Auerbach zt"l* wrote to me that it was by no means certain that the *Magen Avraham* could be used as the basis for this *halachah*. It seemed to me that the *Chayei Adam*,[33] basing himself on a different *Magen Avraham*,[34] supports this ruling of *Rav Neuwirth shlita* that one should say *retzei* in such a situation. However, *Rav Auerbach zt"l* wrote to me that the *Chayei Adam's* ruling, based on the *Magen Avraham* is most surprising, since the *Magen Avraham*, is not discussing a situation where he had said *hamavdil* in the middle of his meal.

The *Shulchan Aruch HaRav*[35] rules that if one recited the full *Havdalah* while he was still eating his *seudah shelishit*, it is as if he has prayed *Maariv*, and therefore, he should not recite *retzei* when he says *birkat hamazon*. However, he also rules that even one who only said *hamavdil bein kodesh lechol* should not say *retzei* in *birkat hamazon* since there are those who rule that one never says *retzei* after nightfall.[36]

31. ס״ק סז וכמ״ש השו״ע בסי׳ רצט

32. סי׳ תפט ס״ק ז. וראה בדעת תורה כאן

33. כלל מז סע׳ כד

34. סי׳ רעא ס״ק יד

35. סוסי׳ קפח. וראה בתהלה לדוד סי׳ רסג ס״ק יג שכותב וז״ל: במה שנסתפק המג״א ס״ק לג אם אמר המבדיל בין קודש לחול בלא שם ומלכות אם יאמר אח״כ רצה בבהמ״ז, הרב ז״ל בסוסי׳ קפח כתב דלא יאמר, עכ״ל. וראה גם בתוספת שבת כאן ס״ק מ

36. ראה בכף החיים סי׳ קפח ס״ק מג. ופלא שהוא פוסק נגד מרן וגם נגד הבן איש חי שכותב דאזלינן בתר התחלת הסעודה וכן המנהג פשוט להזכיר של שבת. וכ״כ הגר״ע יוסף שליט״א בהערה על נשמת אברהם כרך ד עמ׳ רכה ובשו״ת יחוה דעת ח״ג סי׳ נה

SIMAN 271: THE LAWS OF *KIDDUSH* OVER WINE

§14: (A)If the one who recited *Kiddush* did not drink from the wine, but another in the group, who also has the obliga-

NISHMAT AVRAHAM

SIMAN 271

(A) If the one who recited *Kiddush* did not drink: One who, for reasons of health, is unable to drink the required amount of wine to fulfil the obligation of *Kiddush* (see next paragraph), should not recite *Kiddush;*[1] he should listen to another's recitation of *Kiddush* in order to fulfill his obligation.[2] If no one else is available to recite *Kiddush* over wine for him, he should recite *Kiddush* over *challah,* rather than recite it on wine and be unable to drink it[3] (see *Siman* 272A).

There is a Biblical obligation (for both men and women) to recite *Kiddush* on Friday night.[4] *Chazal* instituted the practice of reciting *Kiddush* over a cup of wine (containing at least 86 cc. of wine)[5] or grape juice[6] before eating the *Shabbat* meal.[7] There is a specific quantity of wine or bread that must be consumed to fulfill the obligation of reciting *Kiddush.* Ideally, one should eat slightly more than a *kebeitzah* (54 grams) of bread after reciting *Kiddush.* [8] However, if this is not possible, he may eat a *kezayit* (27 grams) of bread,[9] within 2 to 4 minutes,[10] in order to fulfill his obligation. If he is unable to consume this amount of bread, he may fulfill his obligation by eating a *kezayit* (27 grams) of cake made of one of the five species of grain.[11] If this is not possible, he should drink a *revi'it* (86 cc.) of wine, in addition to the *melo lugmav* of wine (44 cc.), that he drank immediately after reciting *Kiddush* – a total of 130 cc.[12] Finally, if even this is not at all possible because of his illness, he can fulfill his obligation by drinking a *revi'it* (86 cc.) only of wine after reciting *Kiddush.* [13]

If one cannot satisfy any of the above conditions, is he required to recite *Kiddush*? It would appear from the *Pri Megadim* [14] that a person who is fasting (or a patient who is unable to eat) on Friday evening is obligated to recite *Kiddush,* and give the wine to someone else to drink. The *Sha'arei Teshuvah,* [15] on the other hand, states that one who cannot drink wine or eat bread is not obligated to recite *Kiddush,* and he therefore should not recite the blessings of *Kiddush* on Friday night. As for the Biblical requirement to recite *Kiddush,* it is fulfilled when he recites the blessing of *Kiddush* in the Friday night *Shemoneh Esrei* (the fourth

1. מג״א סי׳ רעב ס״ק ט ומ״ב שם ס״ק לג. קיצור שו״ע סי׳ עז סע׳ ט
2. מ״ב שם ס״ק לד
3. מ״ב שם ס״ק לג
4. רמב״ם הל׳ שבת פכ״ט ה״א. מ״ב ס״ק ב
5. שיעור רביעית

According to the *Chazon Ish,* this should be 150 cc.; see *Shemirat Shabbat KeHilchatah* Ch. 47:9.

6. ראה שמירת שבת כהלכתה פמ״ז סע׳ ט
7. רמב״ם שם ה״ו. תוס׳ סוכה לח ע״א ד״ה מאי. מ״ב ס״ק ב
8. סי׳ רצא סע׳ א ומ״ב ס״ק ב
9. מ״ב שם ובסי׳ רעא מ״ב ס״ק לה וסי׳ רעג מ״ב ס״ק כא
10. קצות השולחן סי׳ פא בבדה״ש ס״ק ב
11. סי׳ רעג מ״ב ס״ק כה וסי׳ רעד מ״ב סוס״ק ט
12. סי׳ רעג מ״ב ס״ק כז
13. מ״ב שם. סע׳ ה שם ומ״ב ס״ק כב. ועיין גם במ״ב ס״ק כה וסי׳ רפו מ״ב ס״ק ז
14. מ״ז סי׳ רפט ס״ק א וא״א סי׳ תקצז ס״ק ג
15. סי׳ רעב ס״ק ב

tion of reciting *Kiddush,* drank a (B)*melo lugmav,* the obligation of reciting *Kiddush* has been fulfilled. However, the *Geonim* maintain that if the person reciting *Kiddush* did not drink from the wine, the obligation has not been fulfilled, and it is proper to abide by their opinion.

§15: (C)If after reciting *Kiddush* one spoke before drinking the wine, he must recite the blessing *borei pri hagafen* again.

NISHMAT AVRAHAM

blessing), provided that he had this intention in mind when reciting it.[16] The *Pri Megadim*[17] himself seems to agree with this ruling. This, however, only applies to Friday night, when there is a Biblical obligation to recite *Kiddush.* On *Shabbat* morning, however, when the requirement to recite *Kiddush* is entirely Rabbinic, the *Pri Megadim* agrees that one who can neither drink wine nor eat is not obligated to recite *Kiddush* at all.[18]

If a person could not recite *Kiddush* at night because he was unable to eat, but can do so on *Shabbat* morning, he should recite the text of the *Shabbat* night *Kiddush* the next morning before his *Shabbat* meal.[19] However, he should omit the portion of *vayechulu*.[20] *Rav Neuwirth shlita* told me that if one contemplated, but did not say, the blessing on *Shabbat* night aloud,[21] or, if he recited the *Shabbat* night *Shemoneh Esrei,* and had in mind to thereby fulfill his obligation, he is nevertheless required to recite the text of the *Shabbat* night *Kiddush* on *Shabbat* morning (omitting the passage *vayechulu*) if he is able to eat or drink.[22]

A patient who is unable to eat the required amount of bread, or drink the required amount of wine, or who is unable to do so within the allotted time (see above), and who finds no one else from whom he can hear *Kiddush,* is exempt from making *Kiddush* before he eats. He should fulfill his obligation with the passage in the *Maariv Shemoneh Esrei,* as explained above.[23]

A patient who is fed through a tube inserted into his stomach (*naso-gastric tube* or *gastrostomy*), is exempt from *Kiddush,* just as he is exempt from reciting any blessing before and after food or drink which is fed to him in this way. However, it would be good if he could hear *Kiddush* from someone else who is reciting it for himself.[24]

(B) *melo lugmav*: Enough to fill one cheek, i. e. 44 cc.[25]

(C) If after reciting *Kiddush*: A doctor who is called to see a non-urgent case immediately after reciting *Kiddush,* should try to eat at least a *kezayit* (27 grams) of

16. סי' רעא שעה"צ ס"ק ד. ועיין גם בסי' רפט מ"ב סוס"ק י

17. מ"ז סי' רפט ס"ק א

18. מנחת שבת סי' עז ס"ק כב. ועיין שם בהשמטות לגבי מי שהרהר בקידוש ובהערה של הגר"ע יוסף שליט"א בסוף נשמת אברהם כרך א או"ח עמ' שלד ס"ק ה

19. עיין במ"ב כאן ס"ק ב בשם המג"א ס"ק א ובביה"ל סע' א ד"ה מיד. סי' רעא סע' ח ובשעה"צ ס"ק מז וסי' רפט מ"ב סוס"ק י

20. סי' רעא סע' ח ברמ"א ומ"ב ס"ק מ

21. ראה הערה 18

22. שמעתי ממנו ולא כפי שהיה מסופק אז בזמן כתיבת נשמת אברהם כרך א, וכ"כ בשמירת שבת כהלכתה פנ"ב סע' כה. ועיין סי' סב סע' ד ובמ"ב שם ומ"ב כאן ס"ק ב

23. שמירת שבת כהלכתה פ"מ סע' מז

24. שו"ת מחזה אברהם ח"א סי' לב. שו"ת ציץ אליעזר חי"ג סי' לה

25. שו"ע כאן סע' יג

However, he need not repeat the entire *Kiddush*. This is also what he should do if the cup of wine spilled before he drank from it. Then, another cup of wine should be brought to the table and the blessing *borei pri hagafen* only should be recited over it.

NISHMAT AVRAHAM

cake (made with one of the five species of grain) or drink a *revi'it* (86 cc.)[26] of wine, in addition to the mouthful of wine (44 cc.) that he drank for *Kiddush,* i.e. a total of 130 cc. If this is not possible, he should try to drink at least a *revi'it* (86 cc.) of wine. If he was able to fulfill any of these conditions, he is not required to repeat *Kiddush* when he completes his task and returns to the table. However, if the call was urgent and he did not have time to eat or drink these minimal amounts, or if he became so involved in his work that he forgot about his meal, or left the building where he had recited *Kiddush,*[27] he is required to repeat *Kiddush* when he returns to his meal.[28] If he was called in the middle of his *Shabbat* meal, and had already eaten a *kezayit* of bread[29] or cake[30] which obligates him to recite *birkat hamazon*,[31] he is permitted to resume his meal immediately upon returning to the table, and does not recite any additional blessings,[32] even if he had been immersed in what he was doing such that he forgot about his meal.[33] He must, however, ritually wash his hands again if he wishes to eat bread,[34] without reciting the blessing of *al netilat yadayim*.[35] If however, he had touched a portion of the body which is usually covered (his own or the patient's), he says the blessing.[36] On the other hand, the *Ben Ish Chai*[37] rules that even in this situation the blessing is not recited.

If, after his call, he does not wish to eat further, and it is still less than 72 minutes since he ate,[38] he should ideally return to his table to recite *birkat hamazon* or *al hamichyah*.[39] He may, however, eat something where he is and then recite the appropriate blessing there.[40] If, however, 72 minutes have elapsed since he last ate, he does not say *birkat hamazon* or *al hamichyah*.[41]

The busy doctor must also make *Kiddush* on *Shabbat* morning before eating even if he has not yet recited the *Mussaf* service. He may recite *Kiddush* and then eat bread or cake to a maximum of 54 grams or eat as much fruit as he wishes. If he does not have the time to do this, he

26. see Ref. 5

27. מ״ב ס״ק עח בשם המג״א ס״ק לב

28. סי׳ רעא מ״ב ס״ק עח

29. שמעתי ממו״ר הגרי״י נויבירט שליט״א

30. ולדעת הבן איש חי שנה א פ׳ בהעלותך סע׳ ג, וכן ראה באו״ח סי׳ קעח סע׳ א מ״ב ס״ק מה, אף פירות משבעת המינם שברכתן מעין שלוש

31. או על המחיה על מזונות שמעתי מהגרש״ז אויערבאך זצ״ל

32. ואפילו אם הסיח דעתו או עבר שבעים ושתים דקות, עיין לעיל סי׳ קעח הערה 3 ו־ 4

33. ראה נשמת אברהם כרך א או״ח סי׳ קעח (עמ׳ פו) הערה 12 בשם הגרש״ז אויערבאך זצ״ל

34. סי׳ קסד סע׳ ב וסי׳ קע סע׳ א ומ״ב ס״ק ט

35. בן איש חי שנה א פ׳ אחרי סע׳ כא. או״ח סי׳ קסד סע׳ ב במ״ב ס״ק יג ובביה״ל שם וכן לעיל סי׳ קעח ובדברינו שם

36. כתב לי מו״ר הגרי״י נויבירט שליט״א וכן דעת המ״ב שם

37. בן איש חי שנה א פ׳ אחרי סע׳ כא ופ׳ בהעלותך סע׳ ח, כי ספק ברכות להקל

38. או״ח סי׳ קפד מ״ב ס״ק ב

39. ראה שם מ״ב ס״ק ז

40. כתב לי מו״ר הגרי״י נויבירט שליט״א

41. סי׳ קפד מ״ב ס״ק ב

SIMAN 272:
WHAT KIND OF WINE CAN BE USED FOR *KIDDUSH*

§9: **[(A)]If there is no wine available for *Kiddush,* some rule that one should recite *Kiddush* over beer, or any other beverage, other than water. Others rule that when wine is not**

NISHMAT AVRAHAM

should drink a total of 130 cc. of wine and then eat fruit. If he does not have the time even for this, it is sufficient if he drinks 86 cc. of wine.[42] If he cannot make *Kiddush,* he may eat fruit.[43] If this will not suffice, some bread or cake may be eaten as necessary[44] (see *Siman* 289A).

A doctor who was too busy to hear *Kiddush* or to eat bread or cake on Friday night, or to drink the minimum quantity of wine, must recite *Kiddush* on *Shabbat* morning as he would have done the previous night without, however, saying *vayechulu*.[45]

One should use the best available cup for *Kiddush;* a disposable cup should not be used, if possible.[46]

***SHABBAT* AND FESTIVAL MEALS.** Both men and women are obligated to eat three meals during *Shabbat* (one on Friday night and two during the day)[47] and two during the Festival (one at night and one during the day).[48] A doctor, nurse or patient who did not eat a meal on Friday night should eat three meals during the day.[49] If he did not eat on the Festival night he should eat two meals during the day.[50]

SIMAN 272

(A) If there is no wine available: What should a hospitalized patient who is unable to find or drink wine for *Kiddush,* and also does not have or is unable to eat bread, do? The *Mishnah Berurah*[1] states that he should eat his *Shabbat* meal without reciting *Kiddush,* in order to fulfill his obligation of the *mitzvah* of *oneg Shabbat.* However, *Rav Neuwirth shlita* rules that on *Shabbat* night, he should make *Kiddush* on cake (made from one of the five species of grain).[2] If this is not available, he may make *Kiddush* on a beverage such as beer or undiluted juice.[3] However, both the *Chida*[4] and, in our day, *Rav Ovadiah Yosef shlita*[5] write that on Friday night *Kiddush* must only be made over either wine or bread (see also the *Mishnah Berurah*).[6] If, according to both opinions, this is not possible, and he feels that he is too weak to postpone his meal until wine

42. או״ח סי׳ רפו סע׳ ג ומ״ב ס״ק ז
43. או״ח שם
44. מ״ב שם ס״ק ט. שמעתי ממו״ר הגרי״י נויבירט שליט״א
45. או״ח סי׳ רעא סע׳ ח ומ״ב ס״ק מ
46. שו״ת אג״מ או״ח ח״ג סי׳ לט. שמירת שבת כהלכתה פמ״ז סע׳ יא
47. שבת קפז ע״ב. או״ח סי׳ רצא סע׳ א
48. או״ח סי׳ קפח מ״ב ס״ק כו ושם סע׳ ט בביה״ל ד״ה סעודה
49. סי׳ רצא סע׳ א ברמ״א
50. מ״ב שם סע׳ ה. וראה פרטי דינים בשמירת שבת כהלכתה פנ״ו סע׳ ה

1. ס״ק י
2. שמירת שבת כהלכתה פנ״ג סע׳ ז
3. שם סע׳ ט
4. ברכי יוסף ס״ק ח
5. יביע אומר ח״ג או״ח סי׳ יט אות א. וראה במרן כאן. והלכה כי״א בתרא (כף החיים שם ס״ק נ)
6. ס״ק כז שכותב: ולדינא יש ליזהר לכתחלה שלא לקדש בלילה על שום משקה חוץ מן היין או פת אם אין יין בעיר וכו׳. ושמעתי ממו״ר הגרי״י נויבירט שליט״א שהמ״ב מדבר לכתחלה, אך כשאין לו לא יין ולא פת, יקדש על חמר מדינה וכדעה הראשונה בשו״ע

available, he not should recite *Kiddush*. According to the *Rosh,* in the absence of wine on Friday night, he should recite *Kiddush* over (B)bread rather than on beer, whereas on Shabbat morning he should make *Kiddush* on beer, reciting the blessing of *shehakol* before making the blessing of *hamotzi* on the bread. For if he would make *Kiddush*

NISHMAT AVRAHAM

or bread (in the opinion of *Rav Ovadiah Yosef shlita*) or another beverage (in the opinion of *Rav Neuwirth shlita*) can be found, he may eat his meal without making *Kiddush,* relying on the *Kiddush* in the *Shabbat* night *Shemoneh Esrei* to fulfill his obligation of reciting *Kiddush* on *Shabbat* night. Nevertheless, if he is too ill to pray, he is still permitted to eat even though he did not recite *Kiddush* at all.

Rav Neuwirth shlita writes:[7] If he does not have any wine, bread or other important beverage on which to make *Kiddush* on Friday night or Shabbat morning, and if there is no one else from whom he can hear *Kiddush,* he should eat his meal without *Kiddush.*

(B) bread. If wine is not available for the Sabbath night, *Kiddush* is made on two loaves of bread (for *lechem mishneh*)[8] and, if two full loaves are not available, on two slices of bread (each of 27 grams) or even on one slice of bread (27 grams). The blessing *hamotzi* is recited with *Kiddush* in mind.[9] If there is no bread at all, he may make *Kiddush* on cake made from one of the five species of grain. He washes his hands saying the blessing of *al netilat yadayim,* takes two whole cakes for *lechem mishneh* and recites *Kiddush* after the blessing of *hamotzi.* He should eat a quantity which can qualify as a "*set meal*" (an amount of cake equal to the amount of bread one would normally use for a sandwich meal, i.e. 210[10] to 230 grams)[11] and recite *birkat hamazon* after the meal.[12] If only one slice of cake (27 grams) is available, *Kiddush* is still said over it following the blessing of *borei minei mezonot.*[13] The blessing *al hamichyah* is recited afterwards. If even this is unavailable, he should make *Kiddush* over beer or undiluted juice.[14] However, see above, **A,** for a differing opinion regarding making *Kiddush* on anything other than wine or bread.

For the Sabbath morning *Kiddush,* if wine is unavailable, *Kiddush* is recited on beer or undiluted juice.[15] If this is unavailable, *Kiddush* may be recited on milk, coffee or sweet tea.[16] If only water is available, *Kiddush* is recited over bread, as above. However, both *Rav Ovadiah Yosef shlita*[17] and *Rav Abba Shaul zt"l*[18] rule that *Kiddush* should not be made on milk, tea, coffee or fruit juice. *Rav Ovadiah Yosef shlita*[19] adds, however, that if these fluids are all that he has, he may say the blessing *shehakol* on one of them.

7. שמירת שבת כהלכתה פנ״ג סע׳ יד. ועיין שם בהערה או״ק נ
8. סי׳ רעד סע׳ א
9. מ״ב שם ס״ק ב
10. או״ח סי׳ קסח סע׳ ו ומ״ב ס״ק כד. שיעורין דאורייתא בשיעורי המצוות סע׳ כז
11. שיעורי תורה להגר״ח נאה זצ״ל סי׳ ג סע׳ טז
12. שמירת שבת כהלכתה פנ״ג סע׳ יח
13. שם
14. שם פנ״ג סע׳ ז ו־יח
15. שם סע׳ ט
16. שם סע׳ יא
17. שו״ת יביע אומר ח״ג או״ח סי׳ יט אות י־יא. שו״ת יחוה דעת ח״ב סי׳ לב
18. אור לציון ח״ב פ״כ סע׳ יט
19. שו״ת יביע אומר שם אות יא

only over bread and say the *hamotzi* blessing, there would be no obvious difference between the Sabbath meal and a weekday meal which begins with the blessing of *hamotzi*. This ruling of the *Rosh* is very acceptable.

GLOSS: *The widespread custom is in accordance with the opinion of the Rosh. If there is wine available in the city, Kiddush should not be made over bread.*

SIMAN 273:
KIDDUSH MUST BE RECITED WHERE THE MEAL WILL BE EATEN

§1: ***Kiddush* must only be recited (A)where the meal is to be eaten. If one moves from one part of a room to another, it is considered the same place. Therefore, if one recited *Kiddush* with the intent to eat in a certain part of a room, and then changed his mind to eat in another part, even if the room is a very large one, he need not repeat *Kiddush*.**

GLOSS: *If one leaves his house to go to the succah, it is considered like moving from one part of a room to another.*

NISHMAT AVRAHAM

SIMAN 273

(A) where the meal is to be eaten: Both the *Kiddush* recited at night and the *Kiddush* of *Shabbat* day must be where the meal is to be eaten.[1] One should make every effort to begin his meal immediately after reciting *Kiddush*.[2] However, *Rav Waldenberg shlita*[3] believes that one can allow even more than 72 minutes to elapse between the recitation of *Kiddush* and the beginning of the meal,[4] particularly for the *Shabbat* day meal, where the *Kiddush* is only Rabbinic in origin.[5] Therefore, a hospitalized patient who recited *Kiddush* assuming that his meal will arrive shortly, and subsequently waits a long time before the meal actually arrives, is not required to repeat *Kiddush* prior to eating.[6] However, if possible, he should drink a *revi'it* of wine (86 cc.), in addition to the amount he drinks for *Kiddush* (44 cc.), i.e. a total of 130 cc. The addition is considered a meal and by drinking it, he will have made *Kiddush* in conjunction with a meal.[7]

1. סי׳ רפט סע׳ א
2. סע׳ ג בהגה
3. שו״ת ציץ אליעזר חי״א סי׳ כו ולב אברהם ח״ב עמ׳ כו. וכ״כ האשל אברהם (בוטשאטש) ס״ק ג
4. וכבר כתבו דמליל הסדר של פסח מוכח דחשיב מקום סעודה אף שבין הקידוש והסעודה יש יותר משעה וחומש– מאת הגרש״ז אויערבאך זצ״ל
5. ראה במקראי קודש להגרצ״פ פראנק זצ״ל פסח ח״ב עמ׳ קלו וחזון עובדיה עמ׳ קכז
6. מ״ב ס״ק יג וערוה״ש סע׳ ד. שמירת שבת כהלכתה פנ״ג סע׳ טז. וראה בנשמת אברהם כרך א או״ח סי׳ רעג סוס״ק א (עמ׳ קיג) בשם הגרש״ז אויערבאך זצ״ל ומו״ר הגרי״י נויבירט שליט״א
7. חזון עובדיה עמ׳ קכז

There are some who believe that as long as one can see the place where he recited *Kiddush,* even if he goes from his house to the courtyard, he need not repeat *Kiddush.* There are others who believe that if he recites *Kiddush* in one place with the intention of eating in another (*see above, Siman* 178), **he has acted correctly if both places are in one house; for example if he moves from one room to another or from the roof to the ground floor.** (*This is the opinion that one should follow.*)

§4: One (B)may recite *Kiddush* for others even though he will not be eating together with them, since he recites *Kiddush* where they will have their meal. In general, one cannot

NISHMAT AVRAHAM

(B) may recite *Kiddush* for others: In many hospitals and nursing homes, an appointed person goes from room to room to recite *Kiddush* for patients (male and female) who are unable to do so for themselves. The following summarizes the *halachot* for one who wishes to fulfill the *mitzvah* of *Kiddush* by proxy in the proper manner.

1) He who recites *Kiddush* must bear in mind that his recital is meant to have all those who are listening fulfill their obligation to recite it. Furthermore, everyone who is listening must concentrate on the recitation of *Kiddush* and bear in mind that they, too, are fulfilling their obligation.[8] The person reciting *Kiddush* may also recite the blessing of *borei pri hagafen,* even if he himself will not drink any wine after reciting this blessing.[9] This ruling applies to the *Kiddush* of *Shabbat* day also, even though the only blessing that is recited is *borei pri hagafen.*[10]

2) There are some *poskim* who believe that in order to establish a unified group, permitting one of the members to exempt everyone else from their obligation, everyone should seat themselves near the person reciting *Kiddush.*[11] For those who are unable to leave their beds, the person reciting *Kiddush* should sit as close as possible to the beds. Those whose custom it is to stand while *Kiddush* is recited may do so,[12] provided that they are in close proximity to the person reciting *Kiddush,* and do not wander about during its recitation.[13]

3) If the person reciting *Kiddush* has already eaten his *Shabbat* meal, he should drink a *revi'it* (86 cc.) of wine after reciting *Kiddush* for the group. Although normally one is required to drink only a *melo lugmav* (44 cc.) of wine when saying *Kiddush,*[14] he should drink a *revi'it* to be certain that he can then recite the *berachah acharonah* afterwards.[15]

8. כאן סע׳ ו

9. שו״ע כאן

10. רמ״א כאן

11. עיין סי׳ רעא סע׳ י ברמ״א ומ״ב ס״ק מו ושעה״צ שם

12. מטה אפרים סי׳ תרכה באלף המטה ס״ק עד

13. מ״ב שם

14. סי׳ רעא סע׳ יג

15. סי׳ קצ סע׳ ג וסי׳ רי סע׳ א. ולגבי שתיית יי״ש ראה בט״ז סי׳ רי ס״ק א, אשל אברהם (בוטשאטש) סי׳ רעב ומ״ב סי׳ רעב ס״ק ל וסי׳ רעא סוס״ק סח

exempt others from their obligation to recite the blessing over wine (*borei pri hagafen*) if he himself does not drink from it. But here, because the blessing *borei pri hagafen* is required for *Kiddush,* it has the same status as the *Kiddush.* Therefore, one can exempt others of their obligation of this blessing even though he himself will not partake of the wine.

GLOSS: *One may do this even for the Kiddush of Shabbat morning.*

NISHMAT AVRAHAM

4) If, on the other hand, he has not yet made *Kiddush* for himself, he should preferably include himself in the group. After reciting *Kiddush,* he should drink a *revi'it* (86 cc.) of wine in addition to the *melo lugmav* (44 cc.) that he is required to drink.[16] If, however, he does not wish to make *Kiddush* for himself at this time, he may not drink from the wine; a member of the group should drink a *melo lugmav* of the wine.[17] If it is impossible for any of the listeners to drink the amount of a *melo lugmav,* it is sufficient if each one drinks a bit of the wine, and that the total amount of wine consumed adds up to a *melo lugmav.*[18]

5) Ideally, the *melo lugmav* of wine should be consumed in one draft. However, if this is not possible, it should be drunk within a maximum of 4 minutes after saying the blessing.[19] This is true whether only one person drinks the wine, or if many drink from it.

6) Even though the person who recites the blessing drinks the wine, it is nevertheless still commendable for everyone who hears the blessing to try and drink some of the wine also.[20]

7) Both the blessings of *borei pri hagafen,* which is said every *Shabbat,* and *shehecheyanu* which is said on *Yom Tov,* may be said many times, as long as one has the intention to have a new group of people fulfill their obligation with these blessings at the time of their recital. With each group, 44 cc. of wine must be drunk by one of the group, or at least among them.[21]

8) As long as one knows that he will be reciting *Kiddush* for more people in the hospital or nursing home, he should not recite a *berachah acharonah* on the wine that he has drunk. The *berachah acharonah* should be said only when he is certain that he will no longer be required to drink any more wine.

9) One is permitted to accept the *Shabbat* upon himself on Friday afternoon from *plag haminchah* until a few minutes before sundown. This is not commonly done in the winter, since *Shabbat* begins early, but many communities take advantage of this *halachah* on the long

16. סי׳ רעא מ״ב ס״ק עב וסי׳ רעג ס״ק כז

17. סי׳ רעא סע׳ יד

18. שו״ע שם. וכתב הגרש״ז אויערבאך זצ״ל בספר זכרון לרי״י וינברג זצ״ל (עמ׳ 12): מכיון דטעימת כוס אינה אלא משום גנאי שלא יאמרו שלא לצורך הוא ברכה זו (עיין במג״א סי׳ תרכא, וכן ברש״י עירובין מ ע״ב ד״ה ליתביה), אז אם מחלק את הכוס בין המסובין אע״ג דכל אחד שותה רק מעט, מ״מ לאו גנאי הוא לכוס אלא אדרבה מחשיבו בכך וכו׳, ולכן אפילו אם מברך ואינו טועם כלל אין זה ברכה לבטלה, עכ״ד

19. סי׳ רעא מ״ב סוס״ק סח. שמירת שבת כהלכתה פמ״ח סע׳ י ו־יד

20. סי׳ רעא סע׳ יד ומ״ב ס״ק עא

21. שמעתי ממו״ר הגרי״י נויבירט שליט״א

§5: The *Geonim* have written that if one eats enough food or drinks enough wine to require a *berachah acharonah,* this is considered a large enough meal to recite *Kiddush* beforehand. He may then conclude his meal elsewhere. This ruling applies (C)if he ate bread or drank wine, but not if he only ate fruit.

NISHMAT AVRAHAM

summer days and start *Shabbat* early. What if the person reciting *Kiddush* does not wish to begin *Shabbat* early, after reciting *Kiddush* for those who wish to do so at this earlier time? *Rav Shlomo Zalman Auerbach zt"l* wrote[22] that one who recites *Kiddush* for those who accept the *Shabbat* upon themselves early, but he himself does not wish to accept it upon himself with the recitation of *Kiddush,* may act leniently and not take the sanctity of *Shabbat* upon himself if he makes *Kiddush* for a few individuals and does so occasionally. However, it would be preferable if he too would accept the *Shabbat* upon himself when reciting *Kiddush.* If he does, he may still ask a non-Jew to drive him home before sundown, but not pay him until after *Shabbat.* If there is no non-Jew available, he may ask a Jew who has not yet accepted *Shabbat* upon himself to drive him home. However, *Rav Auerbach zt"l* stresses that one should not make a habit of acting in this manner. *Rav Waldenberg shlita* rules likewise.

(C) if he ate bread: One who suffers from *Celiac Sprue,* a gastrointestinal disorder, is forbidden to eat foods containing *gluten* such as bread made from wheat flour. He may suffer from severe diarrhea and gastrointestinal discomfort if he eats a product containing *gluten.* The *halachot* which follow are subject to the consent of the patient's specialist, who knows his case best. I only wish to provide broad guidelines. A gastroenterologist should be consulted in every case. If the patient's condition is so severe that he is unable to tolerate even the slightest amount of bread made from wheat flour without a severe, life-threatening exacerbation ensuing, he is *halachically* forbidden to eat such a product. On *Shabbat* or *Yom Tov,* he should recite *Kiddush,* and drink a *revi'it* of wine (86 cc.) in addition to the *melo lugmav* (44 cc.) which he drinks after completing *Kiddush.*[23] If, however, he can tolerate a small amount of products containing *gluten* without exacerbating his condition, and he occasionally does eat such products (even without the approval of his doctor), he should act as follows: It is preferable, given the choice, that he use oat bread or oat cakes. However, if such products are not available, he should eat a *kezayit* (27 grams) of bread made from wheat flour at the Sabbath night and morning meals (but refrain from eating bread for the third meal).[24] If he will only eat a *kezayit* of bread, he must wash his hands without reciting the blessing of *al netilat yadayim.*[25]

One may eat *matzah* made from any of the five different types of grain which include oats in order to fulfill his obligation to eat *matzah* during the *seder.* Therefore, if one suffers from *Celiac Sprue,* but not to the extent of having life-threatening reactions to *gluten,* he should attempt to ob-

22. מוריה אלול תש"מ, מנחת שלמה ח"א סי' ג
23. מ"ב ס"ק כב
24. סי' רצא סע' ה
25. סי' קנח סע' ב

SIMAN 276: A LIGHT THAT WAS LIT BY A NON-JEW ON *SHABBAT*

§1: If a non-Jew kindles a light for a Jew on *Shabbat,* it is prohibited for any Jew to make use of it, even if it was not lit for him.

GLOSS: *It does not make any difference whether the non-Jew works for a fixed wage, is contracted for a job, or works as a day laborer. The prohibition applies in all instances since the Jew derives benefit on Shabbat from work done on that day.*

However, if the non-Jew kindled the light for his own needs, or for the needs of a Jew who is ill, (A)even if not seriously,

NISHMAT AVRAHAM

tain *matzah* made from oat flour. If he is able to obtain such *matzah,* he should, if his physician permits, eat the five *kezeitim* of *matzah* required by *halachah* during the *seder.* If he is unable to obtain oat flour *matzot,* and knows that he cannot tolerate even the slightest amount of *gluten* products without aggravating his condition, he is forbidden to eat *matzah.* However, if he knows from experience that he can tolerate a small amount of *gluten* without exacerbating his condition, he should act as follows: He should not eat any *matzah* during the entire meal. At the end of the meal he should wash his hands without reciting a blessing, say the blessings of *hamotzi lechem min ha'aretz,* and *al achilat matzah,*[26] and then eat a *kezayit* of normal *matzah* as the *afikoman.*[27] In so doing, he fulfills the Torah obligation to eat *matzah* at the *seder.*

Similarly, since one is obligated to eat bread in the *succah* on the first night of *Succot,* someone suffering from *Celiac Sprue,* but without life-threatening reactions to *gluten,* should attempt to obtain bread that is made from oat flour. If this is not possible, and he knows that he can tolerate a small amount of products containing *gluten,* he should wash his hands without reciting a blessing, and eat a *kezayit* of bread (27 grams) made from wheat flour in the *succah* in order to fulfill his obligation.[28] If, however, he is unable to tolerate even the slightest amount of *gluten* he must not eat bread and cannot say the blessing *leshev basuccah.*[29] However, if possible, he should hear the blessing pronounced by someone else who is saying it for himself and bears him in mind as well.[30]

SIMAN 276

(A) even if not seriously: Anyone may take advantage of the light kindled for a *seriously ill patient,* even if it was lit by a fellow Jew.[1] It is also permissible for a healthy person to benefit from it even when the patient no longer has any need for it.[2] If one suspects that the non-Jew did more than was necessary for the

26. ראה נשמת אברהם כרך ד חאו״ח סי׳ תעה ס״ק א
27. סי׳ תפב סע׳ א ומ״ב ס״ק ו
28. סי׳ תרלט סע׳ ג
29. ראה סי׳ תרלט סע׳ ג ומ״ב ס״ק כא
30. שמעתי ממו״ר הגרי״י נויבירט שליט״א
1. דנר לאחד נר למאה, ביה״ל ד״ה אין בו סכנה
2. ביה״ל סע׳ ד ד״ה אבל

GLOSS: *or for the needs of* (B)*a child, who is halachically considered to be in the category of a non-seriously ill patient,*

it is permissible for any Jew to make use of the light. This is also the ruling if a non-Jew makes a fire for his own needs or for the needs of a sick person. However, (C)there are some who (distinguish between a light and a fire and) rule that it is prohibited to use such a fire. This decree was instituted to avoid using such a fire because the non-Jew might add more fuel to the fire for the benefit of the Jew.

GLOSS: *If a non-Jew kindles a light or fire in the home of a Jew on his own initiative, the Jew need not leave his house even though he does inevitably benefit from it.*

NISHMAT AVRAHAM

patient so that a healthy person would also benefit,[3] or if what he did produced something that was *muktzeh,*[4] a Jew who is not sick is forbidden to make use of it on *Shabbat.* However, immediately after *Shabbat,* he may use it.[5] See *Siman* 318:2 for further details regarding this topic.

(B) a child: See below, *Siman* 328:54 for further details.

(C) there are some: In their opinion, even if the fire was lit for a *seriously ill patient,* a Jew who is not sick is forbidden to warm himself by it, lest the non-Jew add more fuel to it for his benefit,[6] or increase the amount of heat coming from an electric or gas heater. In a time of need, one may rely on the lenient opinion cited by the *Shulchan Aruch,*[7] that anyone may warm himself from such a fire or heater.[8] In countries where it is really cold in winter, one may even ask a non-Jew on *Shabbat* to turn on the heating. If a healthy adult would not feel uncomfortable without heating, but there are little children or old people in the house,[9] it is permissible to ask the non-Jew to turn on the heating.[10]

3. סי׳ שיח סע׳ ב ברמ״א
4. סי׳ שה סע׳ כ ומ״ב ס״ק עא ו־עב
5. סי׳ שיח מ״ב ס״ק יד. שמירת שבת כהלכתה פ״ל סע׳ מג
6. ב״י
7. דעה ראשונה כאן וכן בסע׳ ה
8. ביה״ל ד״ה ויש אוסרים
9. שמירת שבת כהלכתה פל״א הערה כב
10. שם פכ״ג סע׳ כד

SIMAN 278:
ONE MAY EXTINGUISH A CANDLE ON *SHABBAT* FOR AN ILL PERSON

§1: [(A)]One may [(B)]extinguish a light so that a [(C)]seriously ill

NISHMAT AVRAHAM

SIMAN 278

(A) One may: There is a prohibition of Biblical force against extinguishing a candle on *Shabbat* when the intention is to use the charred wick (see below, **C**). However, even if one has no intention of ever using the wick again, there is still a Rabbinic prohibition against extinguishing the flame. The *Biur Halachah*[1] states that we act more stringently with regard to the Rabbinic prohibition to extinguish a flame than we do with respect to other Rabbinic prohibitions. The *Rambam*[2] rules that, given the choice, one should try to find an alternative way to darken the room, without extinguishing the light, so as to enable a *seriously ill patient* to sleep. For example, he should first attempt to cover the light, or move the patient, so that the light will not bother him. But he should only move the patient if he is certain that this will not cause his medical status to worsen. However, if he was concerned that by moving the patient his condition would worsen, and there was no other alternative other than to extinguish the light, he should do so. See below, **C**, regarding the *halachic* status of incandescent light bulbs.

(B) extinguish a light: Once the *seriously ill* patient awakens, one may turn on the light[3] (in an indirect manner, for example, with the back of a finger or hand), if it is needed by him or for his care. If a non-Jew is available to turn on the light, it is preferable that he do so,[4] but only if the patient will not suffer as a result of the delay while waiting for the non-Jew to arrive. One may not increase a flame to create an unnecessary amount of light. This is because we are not permitted to act as if all of the prohibitions of *Shabbat* are set aside when dealing with a patient. Rather one is only permitted to do acts that are necessary for him, and no more. See below, *Siman* 328:16.[5]

(C) seriously ill patient: One is permitted to extinguish a light for someone who is definitely or possibly *seriously ill*. On the other hand, he is forbidden to put it out for a patient whose life is not in danger.[6] However, *Rav Shlomo Zalman Auerbach zt"l*[7] qualifies this latter ruling, basing himself on the *Shulchan Aruch* in *Siman* 334:27, that one may extinguish a burning ember if it is a public hazard. Therefore, *Rav Auerbach zt"l* rules that although one is forbidden to extinguish a flame for a *non-seriously ill patient*, he is permitted to do so when there are three or more *non-seriously ill patients* together in the same room, for when three people are present in one location, they are defined as a crowd rather than as individuals.[8]

1. ד״ה מותר
2. פירוש המשניות שבת פ״ב מ״ה
3. ביה״ל ד״ה לכבות בשם הרמב״ם הל׳ שבת פ״ב הי״א
4. מ״ב ס״ק ב, מסי׳ שכח סע׳ יב בהגה
5. ביה״ל ד״ה לכבות
6. מ״ב ס״ק ג
7. מנחת שלמה ח״א סי׳ ז (עמ׳ מג) וסי׳ יב (עמ׳ קח)
8. עיין גיטין מו ע״א, כתובות עה ע״א ויו״ד סי׳ רכח סע׳ כא שסתם רבים, שלושה. ועיין שם שמעיר גם בכה״ג שהחולה שאין בו סכנה הוא יחידי והוא מצטער מזה שאינו יכול לישון, דלמה לא חשיב כמי

patient [D]can sleep.

NISHMAT AVRAHAM

One may perform acts that are Rabbinically forbidden on *Shabbat* for a *non-seriously ill patient* if they are done in an indirect manner.[9] Therefore, some *acharonim* rule that one is permitted to extinguish a light for such a patient, if it is done in an indirect manner.[10] However, others disagree.[11] As stated above, some *acharonim* believe that we act more stringently with respect to the Rabbinic prohibition to extinguish a light than we do with respect to other Rabbinic prohibitions, and, although other acts which are Rabbinically forbidden may be performed in an indirect manner, we do not do so when it comes to extinguishing a light.[12]

Up to this point, I have been discussing the possibility of extinguishing a flame on *Shabbat* for a person who is ill. There are those who rule stringently when the issue is extinguishing a flame for a *non-seriously ill patient.* They reason that the wick is improved when the flame is put out, because it is easier to light it in the future; they take the *Rambam's* opinion[13] into account, namely that one violates a prohibition of Biblical force when he extinguishes a wick, even if he has no intention to use it again in the future. An incandescent bulb, however, may be *halachically* different from a candle. The metal filament found in an incandescent bulb is not like the wick of a candle. Rather, it more closely resembles the "glowing piece of metal" discussed in the *Gemara.*[14] Even the *Rambam* agrees that if one has no intention of refining the metal by cooling it off, he has not violated the prohibition of extinguishing a flame.[15] One may, then, turn off a light for a *non-seriously ill patient,* if he does it with the back of the hand or finger. However, one should remember that in the opinion of the *Chazon Ish*[16] turning off a light is prohibited because when one breaks a circuit, it falls into the category of "dismantling" (one of the thirty-nine Torah tasks forbidden on *Shabbat*).

Rav Shlomo Zalman Auerbach zt"l rules that the metal filament in incandescent bulbs is similar to the "glowing piece of metal" discussed in the *Gemara,* and not to the wick of a candle. He therefore rules that there is only a Rabbinic prohibition to turn off an incandescent bulb. By this view, one would possibly be permitted to turn off an incandescent bulb that is preventing a *non-seriously ill patient* from sleeping, if he does so in an indirect manner .

(D) can sleep: One may take any measure to prevent a life from becoming endangered. That is why the *Biur Halachah*[17] is puzzled as to why the *Shulchan Aruch* only discusses a *seriously ill patient* when permitting the extinguishing of a candle on *Shabbat* to enable him to sleep. The *Shulchan Aruch* should have stated that one may extinguish a candle for any patient whose life will be endangered if he does not get adequate sleep. However, the *Biur Halachah* explains that the *Shulchan Aruch* chose to phrase the *halachah* in this manner because *Chazal,* and the *Shulchan Aruch,* knew that every *seriously ill patient* requires an adequate

---

שנמצא פרעוש על בשרו, דכתב הרא״ש ריש פי״ד דשבת דדמי לקוץ בר״ה, ויהא מותר לכבות הנר ולהוציאו, ע״ש, שמירת שבת כהלכתה הערה קעה*

9. סי׳ שכח סע׳ יז לפי הדעה השלישית

10. עיין בדעת תורה בשם הגור אריה יהודה, השולחן עצי שטים והמג״א סי׳ שז ס״ק ז

11. קצות השולחן ח״ז עמ׳ לז. מ״ב ס״ק ג

12. קצות השולחן שם

13. הל׳ שבת פי״ב ה״ב

14. שבת מב ע״א

15. הל׳ שבת פי״ב ה״א

16. הל׳ שבת נ ס״ק ט

17. ד״ה בשביל שיישן

NISHMAT AVRAHAM

amount of sleep to recuperate. The *Shulchan Aruch* ruled therefore that it is permitted to extinguish a light on *Shabbat* for a *seriously ill patient* even when it is not known definitively that a lack of sleep will endanger his life. Since an insufficient amount of sleep may worsen his condition, one may set aside the *halachot* of *Shabbat* to prevent this from happening. Nevertheless, if a doctor declares that a *non-seriously ill patient* must have an adequate amount of sleep, otherwise his condition may worsen to the point of possibly endangering his life, the light may be extinguished for him as well. In either instance it would be preferable, where possible, to move the patient (if this can be done easily) or the light (if it is portable and on a long cord) to another room, or to adjust the Sabbath clock that is already switched on, so that the lights will shortly be extinguished.[18] Where possible, it is preferable to dim the light via a dimmer switch rather than to switch it off.[19] Where a non-Jew is available he should be asked to switch the light on or off as necessary.[20]

(a) KINDLING LIGHT.

i. <u>The *seriously ill* patient.</u> One may turn on a light in order to attend to a *seriously ill* patient. If light is needed it should be turned on in an indirect manner, with the back of the finger or hand.[21] One may turn on the light if he is afraid to lie in the dark or feels that otherwise his needs will not be noticed, since this may lead to a possible decrease in his well-being.[22] Even if the patient is blind, a light may be turned on in his room if he is afraid, or so that he should feel that he is under continuous observation.[23] However, this is not permissible for an unconscious patient unless the light is needed for his care.[24] If there are two switches, one which turns on one bulb and the other which turns on two, and one bulb is sufficient, he should use the switch which turns one on. If the electricity must be turned on via a main switch (such as the switch of a Sabbath clock), all the switches in the other rooms should first be turned off and only then the main switch turned on so that lights are not lit unnecessarily. However if time is of the essence, the main switch should be turned on immediately.[25] If a non-Jew has been asked to turn on a light for a *seriously ill* patient and does so via a main switch, there is no need to turn off the other switches first. If, by his turning on a main switch, light is switched on in another room, or an electric stove is switched on heating food or water, a healthy person may benefit from the effect of the electricity.[26] One should preferably turn on the smaller of two lights if that is sufficient for the treatment of the *seriously ill* patient.[27] Light that – has been lit for the *seriously ill* patient – may be used by anyone else. And light in another room that was lit automatically when the main switch was used in order to provide immediate light for the patient – when there was no time to first turn off the other switch – may also be used by all.[28]

Electric or battery operated instruments such as those used for examination

---

18. שמירת שבת כהלכתה פל״ב סע׳ ע
19. שמעתי מהגרש״ז אויערבאך זצ״ל. כי בעת שימוש בעמעם נשאר חוט הלהט שבנורה כשהוא מלובן כולו כל הזמן, וכאשר מגבירים את הזרם, מאיר יותר, ולהיפך, ומשום כך אין כאן איסור הבערה כלל אף לדעת החזו״א
20. מ״ב ס״ק ב וסי׳ שכח סע׳ יב בהגה
21. שמירת שבת כהלכתה פל״ב סע׳ סד
22. שם פל״ב סע׳ סג
23. או״ח סי׳ של סע׳ א
24. כתב לי מו״ר הגרי״י נויבירט שליט״א
25. שמירת שבת כהלכתה פל״ב סע׳ סו
26. שמעתי מהגרש״ז אויערבאך זצ״ל כי פסיק רישא בגוי מותר (ראה שמירת שבת כהלכתה פל״א הערה א), ואין משום שמא ירבה כי יש כאן גופים נפרדים. וראה בשמירת שבת כהלכתה פל״ב הערה קעד
27. שמירת שבת כהלכתה פל״ב סע׳ סז
28. שם סע׳ סט

of the throat, ears or fundus may be turned on (using the back of a finger or hand) to examine a *seriously ill* patient. The battery operated instrument should be turned off (again, in an indirect manner) at the end of the examination rather than leaving it on and replacing the battery when spent. Turning the light off in an indirect manner involves a twice removed Rabbinic law (that is, transgressing a Rabbinic law in a manner which is also only prohibited by Rabbinic law), whereas having to replace a flat battery may involve a Torah law of "building" and should therefore be avoided.[29]

(ii) The *non-seriously ill* patient. A Jew may not turn on a light for such a patient even if it is done in an indirect manner.[30] On the other hand, when necessary for his well-being, it is permissible to turn off a light if this is done in an indirect manner (such as with the back of a finger or hand).[31] A non-Jew may be asked to turn on a light when needed for patient care and then later to turn it off so that the patient can sleep. A bedridden *non-seriously ill* patient may use a non-electric bell to call for assistance. He may only use an electric bell if it is certain that no light is kindled at the same time and immediate help is required. A *non-seriously ill* patient who must use a bedpan should attempt to find someone who can ask for help. If a non-Jewish patient is in the next bed he may ask him to ring the electric bell. However, if there is no alternative and he cannot wait, he may use the electric bell, activating it with the back of his finger or hand, even if a light is also automatically turned on[32] (see also *Siman* 338A).

(b) REFRIGERATOR.

i. The *seriously ill* patient. A refrigerator may be opened in order to take out what is needed for the *seriously ill* patient even if a light inside the refigerator (which was not inactivated before the Sabbath) goes on as a result; food for the healthy may also be taken out at the same time. However, the door may not now be closed since this will cause the light to be switched off. If more food or medication requiring refrigeration may possibly be needed for the patient that *Shabbat,* or immediately after, the door may be closed provided that the food or medication cannot be kept elsewhere (in a neighbor's refrigerator in which the light has been inactivated before *Shabbat,* for example). If the food will not spoil with the door being left open or, if it will but it could be replaced in time, the door may not be closed. If the door is to be closed, the light should first be inactivated (in an indirect manner), even if it is only probable that the refrigerator will be needed that *Shabbat* for the patient. By doing so, only one act (Rabbinic) of extinguishing is done rather than acts of kindling (Torah) and extinguishing each time the door is opened and closed.[33]

ii. The *non-seriously ill* patient. If the light inside the refigerator was not inactivated before *Shabbat,* the refrigerator door may not be opened or closed by a Jew for a *non-seriously ill* patient. However a non-Jew may be asked to open it to remove food or medication for the patient, closing it afterwards. If, however, food or medication will be needed again for the *non-seriously ill* patient, the non-Jew should be asked to inactivate the light before closing the door so that a Jew may

29. שמעתי מהגרש״ז אויערבאך זצ״ל

30. אורח חיים סי׳ שכח סע׳ יז

31. כי מותר לעבור על שבות דשבות עבור חולה שאין בו סכנה, שם ומ״ב ס״ק נז. וראה מה שכתב הגרש״ז אויערבאך זצ״ל בספרו מאורי אש דף פח עמ׳ א, מובא בנשמת אברהם כרך א או״ח סוסי׳ רעה (עמ׳ קיח)

32. משום ״גדול כבוד הבריות״, שמירת שבת כהלכתה פ״מ סע׳ יט. וראה בשער ציון סי׳ שכב ס״ק יב שמעתי ממו״ר הגרי״י נויבירט שליט״א

33. שמירת שבת כהלכתה פל״ב סע׳ עא

be able to open and close the door later.[34]

(c) HEATING and COOLING. See *Siman* 328 §18A.

(d) TELEPHONE.

i. The *seriously ill* patient. A doctor may answer the telephone at home if there is a possibility that his help is required for a *seriously ill* patient. If possible, he should lift the telephone off the hook in an indirect manner,[35] with the back of the hand or finger, together with someone else, or if he is alone, with both hands.[36] He need not restrict his speech (as he would have to do when writing) but he may say whatever he feels necessary for the patient, and also add pleasantries such as thank you and *Shabbat Shalom.*[37] However, he may not hold a conversation which does not pertain to the patient or his care.[38] He should also return the telephone to its place, in an indirect manner.[39] It is preferable for the doctor to telephone for a cab with a non-Jewish driver, rather than take his own car to visit a *seriously ill* patient, even if he only does this so that the cab will wait and return him home after the visit.[40] An attending doctor who is at home some distance from the hospital may phone to ask the duty doctor about a *seriously ill* patient. He may even phone to ask about possible problems with such patients if he is uncertain that the duty doctor will, on his own initiative, ring him for advice.[41]

The same rules apply to a *seriously ill* patient or member of his family who must summon urgent medical help or an ambulance. He (the patient himself or a member of his family) may use the telephone even though the family member could go to call a doctor who lives only a short distance away, if not using the phone means the patient will be left alone and in fear.[42] A non-observant or non-Jewish specialist may be called even if there is a local observant general practitioner available. This is so even if one knows that the non-observant doctor will desecrate the *Shabbat* unnecessarily as a result of the call.[43]

A pregnant woman who feels that labor has started may telephone for an ambulance or cab to take her to the hospital.[44]

Since it is permissible to the telephone for an ambulance or cab in order to take a *seriously ill* patient to the hospital, there is no obligation to trouble a Jewish neighbor to do so in his car, if he may be unable to return home on *Shabbat* or if he must be awakened.[45]

A doctor, living some distance away, was called for a *seriously ill* patient. Before that doctor arrived, another doctor or ambulance crew took care of the patient and there was no longer a need for the doctor who had been summoned. Although the doctor, living at a distance, will need to drive to answer the call and thus will set aside Torah law many times, *Rav Auerbach zt"l* told me that one may not telephone him to prevent him from doing so. For he is permitted to set the law aside since he does so within the framework of saving life and he will be rewarded for it. But he should not be telephoned, because one may not set aside any Sabbath law, even a Rabbinic one, to stop him. However, if a non-Jew is available,

34. שמעתי ממו״ר הגרי״י נויבירט שליט״א
35. שמירת שבת כהלכתה פל״ב סע׳ מז
36. שם סע׳ מ. ראה בנשמת אברהם כרך ה או״ח סי׳ שמז ס״ק א שעדיף בשינוי יותר מ״שנים שעשאוה״
37. שמירת שבת כהלכתה פל״ב סע׳ מא
38. שמירת שבת כהלכתה שם. וראה בנשמת אברהם כרך א או״ח סי׳ שלח ס״ק א (עמ׳ רמב)
39. שמירת שבת כהלכתה שם סע׳ מז
40. שמירת שבת כהלכתה פ״מ סע׳ סט והערה קמט
41. שמעתי ממו״ר הגרי״י נויבירט שליט״א
42. שם פל״ב סע׳ לז
43. שם סע׳ מה
44. שם פל״ו סע׳ ט
45. הגרש״ז אויערבאך זצ״ל שמירת שבת כהלכתה פ״מ סע׳ עב

NISHMAT AVRAHAM

he may be asked to contact the doctor to stop him from coming. *Rav Auerbach zt"l* added that this was applicable even to a non-observant Jewish physician.

ii. The *non-seriously ill* patient. It is forbidden to use the telephone for a *non-seriously ill* patient.[46] However, on the Festivals the telephone may be used for such a patient.[47]

(e) ELEVATORS. A "Sabbath elevator" may be used as necessary. Automatic escalators may be used as necessary.[48]

i. The *seriously ill* patient. If the patient is *seriously ill* and time is of the essence, an elevator may be used as usual.[49] The call-button may be pressed to summon the elevator even if a light is also lit simultaneously. However, wherever possible, this should be done in an indirect manner (with the back of a finger or hand).

ii. The *non-seriously ill* patient. If a "Sabbath elevator" is not available, an elevator that is operated by a non-Jew may be used in order to reach a *non-seriously ill* patient (even if the elevator is not being simultaneously used by others), provided that the doctor does not press the call-button to summon the elevator. An elevator that is operated by a non-Jew may be used to take a *non-seriously ill* patient to receive treatment or undergo tests (even if the elevator is not being simultaneously used by others). A Jew may not press the call-button.[50] The elevator may not be used to take him to the hospital synagogue.

(f) ELECTRICALLY OPERATED DOORS. A patient may not use such a door in order to pray with a *minyan* in the hospital synagogue.

i. The *seriously ill* patient. If he requires a test or treatment he may be taken through by another Jew. A doctor may walk through such a door if he is on the way to answer an urgent call for a *seriously ill* patient. If, however, the call is not urgent, he should wait to walk through with a non-Jew.[51]

ii. The *non-seriously ill* patient. A *non-seriously ill* patient may ask a non-Jew to take him through or pass through with a non-Jew in such a way that it is the non-Jew who causes the door to open and close.[52]

(g) GLUCOMETER. A glucometer may be used as necessary by a diabetic patient receiving multiple insulin injections each day, where each dose of insulin is determined by the blood sugar level at the time. The glucometer should be switched on, whenever possible, by a non-Jew or in an indirect manner, for example with the back of the finger or hand.[53]

(h) VAPORIZER (HUMIDIFIER). A *seriously ill patient* who must inhale humidified air on *Shabbat* may activate either a cold- or hot-water vaporizer as required (whenever possible, if it is a hot-water vaporizer, hot water which has been kept hot before *Shabbat* should be used).[54] See also *Siman* 252A, 301B, 321C, and 322A.

---

46. שמירת שבת כהלכתה פל״ג סע׳ ג. והיום שרוב הנורות שבמערכת הטליפונים הם קרות (מסוג ניאון או L.E.D.) צ״ע אם לא יהיה מותר גם לחולה שאבו״ס ככל תרי דרבנן. וראה במנחת שלמה ח״ב סי׳ יט

47. הגרש״ז אויערבאך זצ״ל שם הערה כג*

48. שמירת שבת כהלכתה שם סע׳ נב

49. שמעתי ממו״ר הגרי״י נויבירט שליט״א. וראה בשמירת שבת כהלכתה פכ״ג סע׳ מט ופ״מ סע׳ מא

50. כתב לי מו״ר הגרי״י נויבירט שליט״א

51. ראה נשמת אברהם כרך ד חאו״ח סי׳ רעח ס״ק א (עמ׳ יט)

52. שם

53. שמעתי מהגרש״ז אויערבאך זצ״ל וממו״ר הגרי״י נויבירט שליט״א

54. שמירת שבת כהלכתה פל״ז סע׳ טו

SIMAN 287: CONSOLING MOURNERS AND VISITING THE SICK ON *SHABBAT*

§1: [A]One may console mourners and [B]visit the sick on *Shabbat*. However, one should not say the usual words of comfort to the patient ("*refuah shelemah*") [C]as one does on weekdays.

NISHMAT AVRAHAM

SIMAN 287

(A) One may console: The *Mishnah Berurah*[1] writes that *Chazal* were reluctant to allow one to visit a patient or console a mourner on *Shabbat* since the visitor may become saddened upon the sight of the patient or the mourner, and one should not be sad on *Shabbat*. Therefore, it is not right to desist from visiting the sick during the week, and leave it for *Shabbat*.[2] Nevertheless, if one is busy during the week, it is a *mitzvah* to visit a person who is ill on *Shabbat* if he knows that the patient will be comforted by the visit. However, if he will be upset by seeing the ill person's suffering, he should not visit him on *Shabbat*, as his enjoyment of *Shabbat* will be marred. The *Biur Halachah*[3] points out that since there is no upper limit to the number of times one may visit the sick, as long as one visits the patient during the week he may visit him again on *Shabbat*. In particular, it is exceptionally praiseworthy to visit a person who is ill, perhaps to give him advice regarding his condition and to raise his morale, even on *Shabbat*.

(B) visit the sick: If a *seriously ill patient* requests that his family members come to the hospital to visit him on *Shabbat*, (and there is a possibility that the patient might otherwise become so agitated that his condition will deteriorate if they do not fulfill his wish,)[4] it is permissible to ask a non-Jew to drive to the family members to ask them to come[5] and a Jew may accompany the non-Jew.[6] However, a Jew may not, himself, transgress any Torah prohibition. Therefore, if there is no non-Jew available, a Jew may not drive to the family members since by doing so he will violate a Biblical prohibition.[7] He may, however, walk, even beyond the city limits,[8] to summon family members. *Rav Shlomo Zalman Auerbach zt"l* qualifies that he may do so only if he walks less than twelve *mil* ($11^1/_2$ km.) outside the city limits, since otherwise, according to many authorities, this constitutes a Biblical prohibition.[9]

One may use a non-Jewish driver to summon the family members to visit a *seriously ill patient*, even if he himself has not requested this[10] (see below, *Siman* 306:9).

(C) as one does on weekdays: Since it is

---

1. ס״ק א ו־ב
2. שע״ת ס״ק א
3. ד״ה וכן יכולים
4. כתב לי הגרש״ז אויערבאך זצ״ל
5. סי׳ שו סע׳ ט
6. שו״ת הר צבי יו״ד סי׳ רצג
7. ילקוט הגרשוני סי׳ שו ס״ק ה. קצות השולחן סי׳ קלה בבדה״ש ס״ק א. שו״ת ציץ אליעזר ח״ח סי׳ טו פ״ט
8. שו״ת חלקת יעקב שם. וראה שם דמשמע שאם החולה שיש בו סכנה יהנה מבקור קרוביו, מותר להם גם לחלל את השבת ככל ספק פקו״נ שדוחה שבת. ועיין בכל בו על אבילות ח״א פ״א סי׳ א סע׳ טו
9. שמירת שבת כהלכתה פל״ח הערה יט
10. שו״ת חלקת יעקב סוסי׳ סד. שו״ת שואל ומשיב מהד״ג ח״ב סי׳ קפ

Instead, one should say: (D)"Today is *Shabbat* and it is prohibited to cry out in supplication; yet a cure is imminent since His mercy is great, and your *Shabbat* rest should be peaceful."

GLOSS: *There are some authorities who rule that it is not necessary to say, "since His mercy is great etc.," and this is our practice.*

SIMAN 288:

PRAYERS AND SUPPLICATIONS FOR A SERIOUSLY ILL PATIENT

§10: Prayers and supplications are made on *Shabbat* for (A)any patient who is seriously ill. It is also the practice to offer

NISHMAT AVRAHAM

forbidden to cause someone to become upset and cry on *Shabbat.*[11]

(D) "Today is Shabbat and it is prohibited to cry out in supplication": The *Ran*[12] explains that one may not "cry out" on *Shabbat* on behalf of a patient since, in doing so, the patient could become saddened and may cry. Instead, one should comfort him and try to raise his spirits.

The *Mateh Ephraim*[13] rules that one who says a *misheberach* in *shul* for a patient on *Rosh Hashanah,* even if it falls on *Shabbat,* does not say: "Today is *Yom Tov* and it is prohibited to cry out in supplication." Rather, he says the prayer as he would on a weekday, because *Rosh Hashanah* is the Day of Judgment,[14] and on such a day, it is appropriate to "cry out." By the same token, the *Katzeh HaMateh*[15] adds that since *Yom Kippur* is a day marked by *Hashem's* compassion, one really should say "Today is *Yom Tov* etc." But the *Mateh Ephraim*[16] wrote that one should say "the Day of Judgment" in the *misheberach,* and all prayer books refer to *Yom Kippur* as a Day of Judgment. Hence it is inappropriate to say, "Today is *Yom Tov* etc.," just as it is inappropriate on *Rosh Hashanah.* The *Shemirat Shabbat KeHilchatah,*[17] basing himself on the *Siddur HaGra,* rules that when one prays for a patient on the High Holy Days, he should pray as he does during the week, even if they fall on *Shabbat,* since one is permitted to cry out and supplicate on these days of penitence and prayer.

SIMAN 288

(A) any patient who is seriously ill: The *Shemirat Shabbat KeHilchatah,*[1] rules that if a *seriously ill patient* asked that the congregation recite *Psalms* on his behalf on *Shabbat,* they may do so, even if he is not in immediate danger. If others, however, make this request, the congregation may not do so.[2] Whereas the congregation should not recite *Tehillim* on behalf of a *non-seriously ill patient* on

11. מ״ב ס״ק ב
12. שבת יב ע״ב מובא בב״י
13. סי׳ תקפד סע׳ כה
14. אלף למטה שם ס״ק ד עפ״י הגמ׳ ר״ה טז ע״א
15. ס״ק לח וסי׳ תריט ס״ק סט
16. סי׳ תריט סע׳ נג
17. פ״מ סע׳ מח

1. פ״מ סע׳ מט
2. שו״ת אג״מ או״ח ח״א סי׳ קה

certain special prayers on *Shabbat* for a patient whose life is in mortal danger.

GLOSS: *It is also permissible to recite a blessing for a patient who is* (B)*in mortal danger on Shabbat.*

NISHMAT AVRAHAM

Shabbat or *Yom Tov,* the patient himself may do so.[3] Furthermore, it is permissible for a healthy person to recite *Tehillim* for himself as a preventive measure to protect him from danger.[4]

(B) in mortal danger: When one recites a *misheberach* for a *non-seriously ill patient,* one should add the words, "Today is *Shabbat* and it is prohibited to cry out in supplication, yet a speedy cure is imminent." A woman having difficulty during childbirth is considered to be in danger, as is a woman during the first week after childbirth, and therefore one may certainly pray on their behalf.[5]

Rav Yosef Karo,[6] the author of the *Shulchan Aruch,* rules that one may recite a *misheberach* on *Shabbat* for either a *seriously* or *non-seriously ill patient* who has pledged a donation so that it be recited on his behalf. He reasons that *Chazal* only prohibited praying on *Shabbat* for a patient if it will cause either him or the person praying to become saddened. However, the *misheberach* prayer is not said as a direct supplication for the patient, but rather, it is a prayer to *Hashem* to send a speedy recovery to the patient as a result of the charity that the person praying intends to give. Thus, reciting the *misheberach* is not disheartening, but, on the contrary, uplifts the spirits of the patient and those who love him, by enlisting *Hashem's* aid.[7] In contrast, the *Ya'avetz*[8] rules very strictly, writing that one should not engage in supplication on behalf of a patient on *Shabbat,* unless he is *seriously ill.* A *non-seriously ill* patient, on the other hand, should not pray for his own recovery in the way he does on a weekday. Rather, he should have faith that by virtue of keeping *Shabbat* his condition will improve.

The *Shaarei Teshuvah*[9] cites the *Nachalat Shivah*[10] who himself recited a *misheberach* on *Shabbat* for a patient who was in a different town more than an hour's distance away. This is in contrast to a ruling of the *Likutei Maharil* that one should not recite a *misheberach* on *Shabbat* for a patient in another town for he may have already died or recovered, and the prayer would therefore have been recited in vain. The *Aruch HaShulchan*[11] agrees that a *misheberach* may be recited on *Shabbat* for a patient in another town and is not concerned that perhaps he may have died, since most patients survive their illness unless they already have the status of a *gosses*. However, if one is praying for a *gosses,* one must be certain that he is alive before reciting a *misheberach.*[12]

3. שמירת שבת כהלכתה שם
4. יו״ד סי׳ קעט סע׳ י
5. מ״ב ס״ק כח
6. שו״ת אבקת רוכל סי׳ יב. ועיין שם סי׳ יג ו־יד מחלוקת בזה
7. ועיין בערוה״ש סי׳ רפז סוסע׳ ב ובהלכות קטנות ח״א סי׳ סב
8. שאילת יעב״ץ ח״א סי׳ סד
9. כאן ס״ק ג
10. סי׳ לט
11. סע׳ יז
12. ועיין גם בשו״ת שבות יעקב ח״א סוסי׳ צ

SIMAN 289: THE SABBATH MORNING *KIDDUSH* AND MEAL

§1: (A)One should not taste any food before *Kiddush,* just as on Friday night. However, one may drink water before the morning prayers since there is not yet an obligation to recite *Kiddush* at that time.

GLOSS: *See above, Siman* 271, 272 *and* 273, *for the laws of Kiddush.*

NISHMAT AVRAHAM

SIMAN 289

(A) One should not taste any food before *Kiddush*: On *Shabbat* morning, one may eat only after he has recited *Kiddush.* However, he is only obliged to recite *Kiddush* after praying *Shacharit.* Therefore, he may not eat any food before he prays *Shacharit,* but he may drink water. A doctor or male nurse on duty who has been awake for the entire night is only permitted to eat and drink until the half-hour before dawn (see below regarding a woman).[1] At dawn, he should ritually wash his hands; if, during the night, he touched parts of his or a patient's body that are normally covered, he should also recite the blessing *al netilat yadayim.*[2] He may then pray *Shacharit,* even before sunrise (if he will not have time to do so afterwards).[3] He is then permitted to recite *Kiddush* and eat, being careful to eat only enough to fulfill the requirement of reciting *Kiddush* at a meal.[4] He may not eat a full meal until after he prays *Mussaf.*[5] This means that after *Kiddush,* he should eat less than 54 grams of bread, cake or cookies, or, if these are unavailable, he may drink a *revi'it* (86 cc.) of wine in addition to the amount required to fulfill the requirement of *Kiddush* (44 cc.).

If a doctor, nurse or patient (male or female) has no wine, *Kiddush* may be recited on beer or undiluted fruit juice[6] and, if these are unavailable, milk, coffee or sweet tea.[7] However, both *Rav Ovadiah Yosef shlita*[8] and *Rav Abba Shaul zt"l*[9] rule that *Kiddush* should not be made on milk, tea, coffee or fruit juice. *Rav Ovadiah Yosef shlita*[10] adds, however, that if these fluids are all that he has, he may say the blessing *shehakol* on one of them. If these are also unavailable, he may make *Kiddush* on two loaves of bread or even two slices of bread, each of 27 grams (two for *lechem mishneh*), or, if he has no choice, even on one slice of bread. If he has no bread, he may use a whole cake or cookie. He says the blessing of *hamotzi* or *mezonot* on the bread or cake respectively, and bears in mind that with the blessing he is making *Kiddush.*[11]

After reciting *Kiddush* and before praying *Mussaf,* one may eat as much fruit as he wishes and, if he feels weak and needs to eat a more substantial meal, he is per-

1. מהא דסי׳ פט מ״ב ס״ק כז
2. סי׳ ד מ״ב ס״ק ל
3. מהא דאו״ח סי׳ נח סע׳ ג ומ״ב ס״ק יב לענין ק״ש וסי׳ פט סע׳ ח לענין תפלה– שמעתי ממו״ר הגרי״י נויבירט שליט״א
4. הגרש״ז אויערבאך זצ״ל
5. סי׳ רפו סע׳ ג. וראה בשו״ת יביע אומר ח״ה סי׳ כב
6. שמירת שבת כהלכתה פנ״ג סע׳ ט
7. שם סע׳ יא
8. שו״ת יביע אומר ח״ג או״ח סי׳ יט אות י־יא. שו״ת יחוה דעת ח״ב סי׳ לב
9. אור לציון ח״ב פ״כ סע׳ יט
10. שו״ת יביע אומר שם אות יא
11. שם סע׳ יב

SIMAN 296:
THE LAWS OF *HAVDALAH* ON WINE

§1: The order of the blessings of *Havdalah* is first on [A]wine

NISHMAT AVRAHAM

mitted to eat even more than 54 grams of bread.[12] If he will have no wine or other beverage for *Kiddush* until after *Mussaf,* but feels so weak that he cannot wait to eat until then, he may eat fruit or cake before *Mussaf,* even though he has not yet recited *Kiddush*[13] (see *Siman* 271C).

If neither wine, nor another permissible beverage nor bread are or will become available for *Kiddush,* he must eat his Sabbath meal without reciting *Kiddush.*[14]

How should a woman conduct herself with regard to *Kiddush*? According to the *Rambam,*[15] the Torah requires both men and women to pray once a day. Although the *Anshei Knesset HaGedolah* established our formal liturgy, only men were required to recite the specific text of prayer of the *Shemoneh Esrei.* Women, however, may fulfill their obligation to pray by offering any form of praise and supplication to *Hashem.* Therefore, a female doctor or nurse may recite *Kiddush* and eat her *Shabbat* meal after she has fulfilled the requirement of praying by reciting the morning blessings, which constitute praise to *Hashem.*[16] In contrast to the *Rambam,* the *Ramban*[17] believes that both women and men only have a Rabbinic obligation to pray every day. When the *Anshei Knesset HaGedolah* instituted the formal liturgy and daily schedule for prayer, both men and women were included in this obligation. However, the obligation of a woman to pray differs somewhat from that of a man in that she is only obligated to pray the *Shacharit* and the *Minchah* services, while he must recite the *Maariv* service as well.[18] Therefore, according to the *Ramban,* since women have the same obligation to pray *Shacharit* as men, they may only, where possible,[19] eat their meal after they have completed the service and recited *Kiddush.* In summary, it is sufficient for a *Sephardi* female to recite a short prayer to *Hashem* (praising Him, adding a short supplication, such as "make Your Torah always desirable to me,"[20] and then thanking Him briefly), prior to making *Kiddush* and eating. On the other hand, an *Ashkenazi* female is obligated to recite the first sentence of the *Shema,* if possible with the *emet veyatziv* blessing, followed by the *Shemoneh Esrei,* before she may recite *Kiddush* and eat her meal.[21]

Rav Shlomo Zalman Auerbach zt"l wrote to me that, in contrast to a man who is only allowed to eat until half an hour before dawn, a woman may eat until dawn.[22]

SIMAN 296

(A) wine: If wine is not available, *Havdalah* may be made on beer.[1] *Rav Moshe*

12. סי׳ רפו ס״ק ט
13. סי׳ רפו מ״ב ס״ק ט ושע״ת ס״ק ג
14. שם סע׳ יד וראה שם בהערה נ
15. הל׳ תפלה פ״א ה״א ו־ב. ספר המצוות מצוה ה
16. סי׳ קו מג״א ס״ק ב. שו״ת יביע אומר ח״ו סי׳ יז
17. ספר המצוות מצוה ה. וראה במ״ב סי׳ קו ס״ק ד בשם רוב הפוסקים. וראה באשי ישראל פ״ז סע׳ טו והערות ס״ק כז, כח ו־נד שם. ולגבי מוסף עי״ש סע׳ טז
18. עיין במ״ב סי׳ קו ס״ק ד
19. הוסיף לי מו״ר הגרי״י נויבירט שליט״א
20. ושמעתי ממו״ר שליט״א שאין צורך שתזכיר את השבת
21. והסכים אתי מו״ר הגרי״י נויבירט שליט״א
22. לב אברהם ח״ב עמ׳ כ
1. שו״ע כאן סע׳ ב

then on fragrant leaves or spices, then on a (B)flame, and finally, the *hamavdil* blessing.

§8: **Women are obligated to make *Havdalah*, just as they are obligated to make *Kiddush*, but there is an opinion to the contrary.**

GLOSS: *Therefore they (C)should not make Havdalah for themselves but hear it from an adult male.*

SIMAN 298: THE LAWS OF THE *HAVDALAH* LIGHT

§13: **(A)A blind man should not recite the blessing over the *Havdalah* light.**

NISHMAT AVRAHAM

Feinstein zt"l[2] and *Rav Neuwirth shlita*[3] rule that if neither wine nor beer are available, *Havdalah* may be made on undiluted fruit juice. However, *Rav Ovadiah Yosef shlita*[4] rules that *Havdalah* may be made only on wine or grape juice but not on fruit juice. According to all opinions, *Havdalah* cannot be made on bread.[5]

(B) flame: The blessing of *borei meorei ha'aish* should not be recited over an electric light.[6]

(C) should not make *Havdalah* for themselves: A female doctor, nurse or patient should try and listen to a man reciting *Havdalah.*[7] If this is not possible, she may recite *Havdalah* herself with the appropriate blessing on wine, then on a fragrant plant or spices, but not the blessing *borei meorei ha'aish* on a flame.[8] Finally, she recites the blessing *hamavdil* but without mentioning *Hashem's* Name or His Kingship,[9] and drinks the wine.[10]

SIMAN 298

(A) A blind man: When one recites the blessing over the *Havdalah* flame, he must look at his hands in the light showing that he derives some benefit from it. Since one who is blind cannot obtain such benefit, he is exempt from reciting this blessing.

The *Mishnah Berurah* rules that he does recite the other blessings.[1] This is also the opinion of the *Magen Avraham,*[2] *Eliyah Rabbah,*[3] *Tosefet Shabbat,*[4] and the *Shulchan Aruch HaRav.*[5] The *Beit*

2. שו"ת אג"מ או"ח ח"ב סי' עה
3. שמירת שבת כהלכתה פ"ס סע' ד
4. שו"ת יביע אומר ח"ג חאו"ח סי' יט, וכותב שאם בירך ברכתו לבטלה
5. שו"ע כאן סע' ב ומ"ב ס"ק ז
6. כף החיים סי' רצח ס"ק עא. וראה בשמירת שבת כהלכתה פס"א הערה קו שכך נוטה גם דעתו של הגרש"ז אויערבאך זצ"ל. וראה מחלוקת הפוסקים בזה סי' רצח סע' טו ביה"ל ד"ה או בתוך ובלב אברהם ח"ב פכ"ה סע' יט
7. מ"ב ס"ק לו
8. ביה"ל ד"ה לא
9. כף החיים ס"ק נה. וע"ע במ"ב ס"ק לה ובשעה"צ ס"ק לד
10. מ"ב שם
1. מ"ב ס"ק לד
2. ס"ק יז. וכ"מ בטור ומרדכי דלא כהרשב"א
3. ס"ק כד
4. ס"ק כה
5. סע' יט. וכן משמע מהבן איש חי שנה ב פ' ויצא סע' יד

SIMAN 299:
ONE MAY NOT EAT NOR DO ANY WORK BEFORE *HAVDALAH*

§10: One may not do (A)any work before making *Havdalah*. If one has said *Havdalah* during the *Maariv* service even though he has not said the *Havdalah* on wine, he may do work. If he needs to do any work immediately after nightfall, before he prays *Maariv,* he should first say (*baruch*) *hamavdil* (*bein kodesh lechol*) without mentioning Hashem's Name or Kingship, before starting to work.

GLOSS: *Women who do not pray Maariv should say (baruch) hamavdil bein kodesh lechol before doing any work.*

NISHMAT AVRAHAM

Yosef, on the other hand, quotes the *Rashba* who believes that since a blind person is unable to recite the blessing over the flame, he is also exempt from reciting the entire *Havdalah.* Rather, he fulfills his obligation of *Havdalah* when he includes the *ata chonantanu* in the *Shemoneh Esrei* that is said at the conclusion of *Shabbat.* The *Kaf HaChaim*[6] rules that since there is no consensus among the authorities regarding the obligation of a blind person to recite the entire *Havdalah,* it is preferable that he listen to the *Havdalah* made by another. In this way he need not recite any of the blessings himself.

SIMAN 299

(A) any work: Although Sabbath ends at nightfall, *Chazal* forbade one to do any work, including moving an object that is *muktzeh,*[1] until one has recited *Havdalah,* either during the fourth blessing of the *Shemoneh Esrei* (*ata chonantanu*) or on wine, or at the very least, by saying *baruch hamavdil bein kodesh lechol* without mentioning *Hashem*'s Name.[2] Thus a doctor, male or female,[3] who is too busy with patient care to pray *Maariv* or make or hear *Havdalah* after nightfall, should say the above before continuing with his work.[4] If, however, he is busy with a *seriously ill patient,* he must continue to treat him and only recite the blessing after he has finished.[5]

A healthy person may not eat or drink before *Maariv* (with the addition of *ata chonantanu*) and before making *Havdalah* on wine.[6]

6. ס״ק סח
1. מ״ב ס״ק לב
2. מ״ב ס״ק לג
3. רמ״א כאן
4. שם ומ״ב ס״ק לד
5. שמעתי ממו״ר הגרי״י נויבירט שליט״א
6. סי׳ רצט סע׳ א ומ״ב ס״ק לה

SIMAN 301: OBJECTS WHICH MAY OR MAY NOT BE TAKEN OUT ON *SHABBAT*

§2: Young people who enjoy jumping and running may do so on *Shabbat*. One may also run to see anything for pleasure. (*It is also permitted to* (A)*go for a stroll.)*

§7: (B)If one goes out with an object that is neither an

NISHMAT AVRAHAM

SIMAN 301

(A) go for a stroll: It is forbidden to exercise on *Shabbat*. Although one may exert himself if it is pleasurable, nevertheless, he may not do so if it is apparent that he is doing so for medical reasons. Therefore, most *acharonim* permit a person to take a walk on *Shabbat,* even if he does so for medical reasons, since it will not be obvious to an onlooker that this is the intention. However, others forbid medically prescribed walking.[1] Therefore, an otherwise healthy person who jogs regularly to prevent a heart attack, should not do so on *Shabbat*. However, one who has already suffered a heart attack, and believes that by jogging daily he will prevent another one, is permitted to jog on *Shabbat*. This type of activity is permissible for him since he is, at the least, in the category of a *non-seriously ill patient* [see *Siman* 328:6 for a discussion of physical therapy (physiotherapy)].

(B) If one goes out with an object: The Torah forbids carrying an object on *Shabbat* from a *private domain* into a *public domain* or vice versa. Furthemore, one may not carry any object for four *cubits* or more within a *public domain*. It must be noted that one oversteps the Biblical prohibition only if he carries it into or within an area that is *halachically* defined as a *public domain*. *Chazal* have also prohibited carrying four *cubits* within a *carmelit* as well as into or from it. A rabbi, who is expert in these matters, must be consulted to determine the status of a particular area where one wishes to carry.

MEDICATION. Many people must carry medication with them whenever they leave the house. This is permitted on *Shabbat* (even where there is no *eruv*) if the following conditions are met: (a) it is carried in a *carmelit* and not in a *public domain;* (b) the patient is going to perform a *mitzvah* such as going to pray or to attend a Torah lesson; (c) it is carried in an indirect manner; and (d) there would be a problem of *kavod habriot,* for instance, one who is ashamed because of his bad breath may go out with a spice in his mouth;[2] or if one would never be able to go out on *Shabbat* if he would be unable to take his medication with him (see also *Siman* 322A regarding medication).

For example, a patient with *angina pectoris* must carry *nitroglycerin* pills, and *diabetics* must carry sugar candies to prevent a possible *hypoglycemic* attack. Many *poskim*[3] rule that a patient who must always have immediate access to his medi-

1. מ״ב ס״ק ז
2. ראה או״ח סי׳ שג סע׳ טו
3. שו״ת משנה הלכות ח״ז סוסי׳ נו. שמירת שבת כהלכתה פ״מ סע׳ ז. ועיין בשו״ת מהר״ש ענגיל ח״ג סי׳ מג

NISHMAT AVRAHAM

cation is permitted to carry it outdoors on *Shabbat* provided that the area into which he is entering (from a *private domain*) is a *carmelit* only and not a *public domain,* and that he is going out to perform a *mitzvah,* such as going to the synagogue or to learn Torah. Furthermore, he should only carry the required amount of medication with him and must do so in an indirect manner. The medication should be carried under his hat or under his shirt. He must try to walk directly to his destination without stopping in the street along the way.[4] *Rav Shlomo Zalman Auerbach zt''l* wrote to me that if the patient needed to take his medication while he was outdoors, he should try to enter a *private domain* to do so rather than take it while still in the *carmelit.* However, if he must take the medication immediately, as he must for *angina pectoris,* he may do so. If he takes it in the *carmelit,* once he resumes his journey he should attempt to walk to his destination without stopping; upon reaching his destination he should leave the medication in a *makom petur* rather than bring it indoors with him. By doing this, he will avoid the problem of transferring something from the *carmelit* where he had stopped to a *private domain.*

Similarly, one who once had a life-threatening allergic reaction to a bee sting may enter a *carmelit* on *Shabbat* with an automatic pre-filled syringe for immediate use, if it is carried in an indirect manner.[5]

Rav Waldenberg shlita[6] disagrees with this opinion and rules that one is forbidden to carry medication where there is no *eruv.*

It is also forbidden to go out into the street with food or medication in his mouth to be swallowed later.[7]

What is the *halachah* for a diabetic who is receiving continuous insulin by means of a battery-driven pump attached to a needle placed under his skin? May he go out into the street on *Shabbat* with the pump clipped to his belt or in a specially designed pocket as he usually does, if there is no *eruv* in the area? *Rav Auerbach zt''l* told me that he may not go out if there is no *eruv.*[8] A patient who has a urinary *catheter, colostomy* or *ileostomy* (see later) is permitted to go out with a bag attached to collect the urine or feces. *Rav Neuwirth shlita* told me that the difference between the two is that the urine or feces is not being carried for any positive purpose, that is, to take an object from one place to another so that it be in a new location.[9] Therefore, only a Rabbinic prohibition is involved. It is like taking out a corpse — that is beginning to smell — from the house into a *carmelit,* which is permitted, because the purpose is not that the corpse be in the *carmelit,* but rather that it not be in the house.[10] It is removed from the house in respect for it and for the people in the house. Such a corpse may be carried out in a bed. Since the bed is secondary to the corpse, we do not carry out the bed for its own sake. That is why there is no desecration of the Sabbath in carrying out the bed.[11]

The *catheter* bag is not needed for its own sake; it is needed to keep the circuit closed and sterile, preventing infection. It also prevents soiling of the person's body. The *ostomy* bag prevents embarrassment from the odor of the feces. Thus these may be taken out. The insulin, on the other hand, is carried for its inherent use, as is the

---

4. ועיין בשמירת שבת כהלכתה שם הערה כג בשם הגרש״ז אויערבאך זצ״ל

5. שמעתי ממו״ר הגרי״י נויבירט שליט״א

6. שו״ת ציץ אליעזר ח״ג סי׳ לד

7. ראה שבת קב ע״ב. רשב״א שם צב ע״א ד״ה מתני׳. תוס׳ שם צב ע״א ויבמות לד ע״א ד״ה והוציאו. ספר חסידים סי׳ רסה. או״ח סי׳ שנ סע׳ ג ומ״ב ס״ק יג. שמירת שבת כהלכתה פי״ח סע׳ ב

8. שמעתי מהגרש״ז אויערבאך זצ״ל

9. אין כאן מלאכה שצריכה לגופה אלא מלאכה שאינה צריכה לגופה

10. סי׳ שיא סע׳ ב

11. שם סע׳ ד ביה״ל ד״ה יש

syringe and pump,[12] and is therefore forbidden where there is no *eruv*. A patient, then, may not go out with the syringe etc. strapped to him in the usual way. However, if it were carried in an indirect manner, for instance, if he were to wear the special pocket around his arm or leg, this would be permitted. *Rav Neuwirth shlita* agreed with this, adding that since he would otherwise never be able to leave his home on *Shabbat,* this, too, is reason to permit him to do so in this way. Because the carrying is done in an indirect manner, it is permitted so that the patient preserves his self-respect.[13]

What is the *halachah* regarding a patient who is on continuous oxygen which he either carries in a cylinder in a shoulder bag or which he wheels in a trolley? *Rav Shlomo Zalman Auerbach zt''l* told me that since the *halachah* only allows one to take out that which is either an ornament or an amulet into the street, but not something that is medicinal, it would not be permissible for him to go out on *Shabbat* with the oxygen. However, if he went out into a *carmelit* and the cylinder was carried or wheeled by a non-Jew this would be permitted. I also heard the same ruling from *Rav Eliashiv shlita. Rav Neuwirth shlita* added that a child should not be asked to carry the cylinder or wheel the trolley.[14] This *halachah* is not comparable to the ruling permitting someone with bad breath to go out with a spice in his mouth.[15] For the spice, in its entirety, is being used to sweeten his breath and prevent his embarrassment. But, only that part of the oxygen which enters his lungs at any given time has a therapeutic effect; the rest has no immediate use. And the cylinder has no therapeutic use; it is merely a means of transporting the oxygen. It may not be taken out, like any other article that is carried out for a positive reason, that is, in order to be in the new location and not just removed from the previous one.[16]

Since asking a non-Jew to do a *melachah* on *Shabbat* is less severe than having a Jew do the same *melachah* in an indirect manner, it would appear that just as a Jew is allowed to take out his insulin into a *public domain* in an indirect manner, it should also be permissible to ask a non-Jew to carry or wheel the oxygen cylinder, not only into a *carmelit* but also into a *public domain. Rav Neuwirth shlita* wrote to me that this is so if the patient is *non-seriously ill,* and, even more so, if he is *seriously ill.*

The reasons prohibiting the taking out of the oxygen and its cylinder into the street all apply to the insulin and syringe discussed above. Nevertheless, *Rav Neuwirth shlita* told me that the insulin and syringe may be taken out by a Jew, because they are not noticeable to the public (being worn under his clothes) and they can be taken out in an indirect manner. Neither point applies to the oxygen cylinder.

A patient may go out into a *carmelit* to attend synagogue or to learn Torah wearing a bracelet containing important personal medical information which could be lifesaving in an emergency, for example, that he is a diabetic or that he is receiving steroid therapy.[17]

(C) ornament: BEEPER. May a doctor

12. מלאכה שצריכה לגופה

13. ראה שמירת שבת כהלכתה פי״ח סע׳ מז הערה קפח בשם השו״ת לבושי מרדכי שאדם מצונן מאד מותר לו לצאת עם ממחטה הכרוכה לו מסביב לידו. וראה בסי׳ שכב שעה״צ ס״ק יב שמשום כבוד הבריות מותר גם באיסורי תורה בשינוי

14. מהא דביה״ל סי׳ רסו סע׳ ו ד״ה הגה ושעה״צ סי׳ שלד ס״ק נד

15. סי׳ שג סע׳ טו

16. שמעתי ממו״ר הגרי״י נויבירט שליט״א

17. שמירת שבת כהלכתה פ״מ סע׳ ז

(C)ornament nor is worn as clothing, he violates a Torah ordinance if he takes it out in the manner that it is usually carried.

NISHMAT AVRAHAM

on call go out with his beeper? The *Igrot Moshe*[18] permitted members of *Hatzalah* to go out into a *public domain* with their two-way radios clipped onto their clothes, since he considered it to be an ornament attesting to their importance in the community and to their good deeds. [*One wonders whether this would be true today when many go out on a weekday carrying upon themselves some means of communication.*] *Rav Feinstein zt"l* ruled that one may carry the radio even when it is not in use since it could be considered as part of one's clothing; obviously it would be permitted when needed. He reasoned, also, that if this were not permitted, it would mean that they would be confined to their homes for the whole of *Shabbat* and this would probably discourage many from volunteering for *Hatzalah*.

Rav Shlomo Zalman Auerbach zt"l, however, told me that a doctor may only go out with his beeper on *Shabbat* into a *carmelit* (and not into a *public domain*), and provided that it was carried in an indirect manner. He added, in a letter to me, that if the doctor had to go into a *public domain* in order to treat a *seriously ill* patient, he would be allowed to take the beeper with him, if he carried it in an indirect manner. The *Rav zt"l* explained to me that a doctor on call would not be allowed to leave his home on *Shabbat,* if he had to carry his beeper into the *public domain*. This would not be permitted even if he carried it in an indirect manner; he would have to stay home in order to take telephone calls. However, once he was called out to an emergency, he could take his beeper with him, even into a *public domain,* carrying it in an indirect manner, if possible, so that he could take other emergency calls.

I asked the *Rav zt"l* if it would be permissible for a doctor on call, living in an area that was Biblically defined as a *public domain,* to leave home on *Shabbat* with his beeper if it was an integral and inseparable part of his belt, made for this purpose (just as a key is carried as the buckle of a belt). *Rav Auerbach zt"l* told me that even though the beeper was not comparable to a key since it contained a battery (which was separate from the beeper), it could be compared to a watch with which people go out, even though it contains a battery. He would therefore permit a doctor on call to go out, even into a *public domain,* wearing his beeper as an integral part of his belt (and not as a detachable unit), if he went out to perform a *mitzvah* such as praying or learning Torah.

STETHOSCOPE. A doctor may not carry his stethoscope or other professional implements from one domain to another if there is no *eruv,* unless he needs them for the examination of a *seriously ill patient.* If possible, they should then be carried in an indirect manner. He may carry them home if there is a possibility that he may need them again for another *seriously ill patient.*[19]

KOSHER FOOD. Suitable arrangements must be made to provide kosher food for a hospitalized patient. If kosher facilities are not available at the hospital, food should be brought in from the outside. If this was not done before *Shabbat* and a *seriously ill patient* does not have enough

18. שו"ת אג"מ או"ח ח"ד סי' פא

19. שמירת שבת כהלכתה פ"מ סע' י

§11: An article that is made both for use and as an ornament, such as beautiful silver keys, may not be carried out since people will think that he is taking them out in order to use them. However, there are those who permit this if they are made of silver.

GLOSS: *One may not, nevertheless, go out with a silver spectacle case since the* (D)*spectacles themselves are considered "a burden."*

§13: A person with a venereal discharge may not go out wearing a (E)**bag to prevent soiling.**

NISHMAT AVRAHAM

kosher food for his needs, it is permissible to bring in kosher food for him on *Shabbat.* Since the patient is *seriously ill* and eating non-kosher food might upset him and possibly aggravate his condition, it is permissible to bring in the food even though it has to be carried through a *public domain.* If possible, the food should be carried in an indirect manner or brought in by a non-Jew (accompanied by a Jew[20]). If, however, the patient's condition is such that he is unaware that he is being given non-kosher food, or he is too young to understand this, food may not be brought in through a *public domain.*[21]

(D) spectacles: It is forbidden to go out with spectacles which rest on his nose only (pince-nez) if there is no *eruv,* since they may fall off and he may pick them up and carry them in the street.[22] However, one may go out, even into a *public domain,* with spectacles which are firmly fixed above or behind the ears.[23] Reading glasses may not be worn in the street but bifocals may.[24] One may not go out into a *public domain* wearing contact lenses until he is accustomed to them since it is quite probable that after a while he may take them out and carry them in the street. However, once he has become accustomed to them it is permissible.[25]

One may not go out into a *public domain* wearing sunglasses even if they are clipped onto his spectacles.[26] This is also the opinion of *Rav Auerbach zt"l.*[27] However, if he has sensitive eyes that easily become inflamed without protection from the sun, he is permitted to wear sunglasses in a *carmelit;* he should be careful not to take them off when he reaches a shaded area. Sunglasses that are hinged onto one's glasses, which the wearer does not remove but merely lifts up when in the shade, may be worn in a *public domain.*[28] Photogrey spectacles that darken in the sun may be worn. Their changing color does not involve the wearer in the *melachah* of "coloring" since he himself does not do anything to cause this, nor is the color change permanent; it can be likened to sunbathing.[29]

(E) bag to prevent soiling: **URINARY CATHETER.** A patient with a urinary

---

20. שמעתי ממו״ר הגרי״י נויבירט שליט״א. וראה ביו״ד סי׳ קיח סע׳ א

21. שמירת שבת כהלכתה שם סע׳ יז

22. מ״ב ס״ק מד בשם הח״א כלל נו סע׳ ג

23. מנחת שבת סי׳ פד ס״ק ו. שו״ת בנין ציון החדשות סי׳ לז. שמירת שבת כהלכתה פי״ח סע׳ טז

24. שמירת שבת כהלכתה שם

25. שם סע׳ יז

26. שמירת שבת כהלכתה שם סע׳ יח ס״ק א. ועיין בשו״ת הר צבי או״ח ח״א סי׳ קעג

27. שמירת שבת כהלכתה שם הערה עא

28. שם סע׳ יח ס״ק ב

29. שו״ת אג״מ או״ח ח״ג סי׳ מה. שו״ת יחוה דעת ח״ב סי׳ מז. שמירת שבת כהלכתה שם הערה * ו־ע

§15: An amputee may not go out with a piece of wood fashioned like a leg and hollowed out at the top to fit his stump. It was not made so that he could walk and so he still requires crutches. Since it is (F)not used for walking, but is meant to have him appear as lame and not as missing a leg, it is forbidden.

NISHMAT AVRAHAM

catheter may go out into a *public domain.* Since it prevents pain and suffering it is considered as clothing or an "ornament." The collecting bag connected to the catheter may also be worn since it helps to prevent a bladder infection.[30] *Rav Auerbach zt"l* also agrees with this ruling but added that though carrying the urine itself is forbidden by Rabbinic law only (since there is no positive intention to carry it from one place to another), nevertheless, the patient must empty the bag, if possible, before going from one domain to another.

A patient with a *colostomy* or *ileostomy* may also go out with a bag into a *public domain* since it prevents embarrassment from the smell of feces.[31] Here as well, *Rav Auerbach zt"l* told me that the patient must empty and clean the bag, if possible, before going from one domain to another.

(F) not used for walking: PROSTHESIS. The reason for forbidding him to go out with this is that he may take it off and come to carry it in the street.[32] However, nowadays with modern prostheses, one may go out with one since it is made for use as a limb.[33]

Similarly, one may go out with a glass eye since it is fixed in the eye socket and it is unlikely that he will remove it in the street.[34]

HEARING AID. The *Har Tzvi*[35] rules that one may not go out with a hearing aid in an area where there is no *eruv,* since it is not considered an article of clothing but "a burden." The *Minchat Yitzchak*[36] first wrote that if the hearing aid is firmly placed so that it cannot fall, and he cannot, under any circumstances, go out without it, it would be permitted. However, if it is possible for him to go out without it, then it would be considered "a burden," and cannot be compared, as are spectacles, to something that is worn. One must weigh well whether he really cannot manage without it. However, in a later *responsum*[37] the *Minchat Yitzchak* retracted his permission after having seen the *Har Tzvi* and writes that it would be forbidden to go out with a hearing aid on *Shabbat. Rav Neuwirth shlita* added that the same ruling would apply to a hearing aid worn behind the ear.

Rav Shlomo Zalman Auerbach zt"l writes[38] that it is possible that a hearing aid is comparable to spectacles. On the other hand, it is also possible that this is not so since it is not like clothes, ornaments or amulets which give direct benefit by their presence. But hearing is achieved through the hearing aid, because the sound waves reaching it cause a mem-

30. שו״ת ציץ אליעזר ח״ד סי׳ נח. ועיין גם בשו״ע הרב סע׳ י וערוה״ש סע׳ סו

31. שו״ת ציץ אליעזר שם. וכן שמעתי מהגרש״ז אויערבאך זצ״ל

32. מ״ב ס״ק נו

33. שמירת שבת כהלכתה פי״ח סע׳ טו

34. שו״ת מהרש״ם ח״ב סי׳ ה

35. שו״ת הר צבי או״ח ח״א סי׳ קעג

36. שו״ת מנחת יצחק ח״א סי׳ לז

37. ח״ב סי׳ קיג

38. שמירת שבת כהלכתה פל״ד הערה קה

NISHMAT AVRAHAM

brane within it to vibrate, so that it should probably be considered "a burden" and not like clothing. However, since there are those who are lenient and consider a watch (when it is itself not valuable as an ornament), as clothing, even though it really is different, then a hearing aid could certainly be likened to an amulet, since once it is turned on and worn, no further action needs to be taken by the wearer in order to hear. In these circumstances where there is no alternative, one could possibly be lenient.

If the hearing aid is completely attached to a spectacle frame, there are those who permit one to go out with it even where there is no *eruv,*[39] while others do not.[40] *Rav Auerbach zt"l*[41] writes that it would appear that even though the hearing aid is hidden in the spectacle frame, making it invisible, nevertheless there is a visible wire connecting it to the earpiece. The hearing aid is certainly not secondary to the spectacles and, on the contrary, is more important or at least equal to it. The reason for the leniency is, as stated above, that it is likened to an amulet which has been tried and proven.

In a later *responsum,* however, *Rav Auerbach zt"l*[42] writes: I have previously written that it would probably be permitted to go out into a *public domain* with a hearing aid since it could be likened to an amulet that has been tried and proven. And so have many great Sages written to permit wearing spectacles in the street for this reason. On the other hand, since electrical changes take place in the hearing aid, it could be that it differs from spectacles, which are more akin to clothes (as is an amulet), where no changes take place and its benefit is obtained merely because it is worn.

Rav Auerbach zt"l later told me that even though he had earlier believed that it would be permissible for a deaf person to go out with a hearing aid, he now believes that one should be strict with both types of hearing aids mentioned above since they really cannot be likened to clothes where no changes take place. He added, in a letter to me, that the hearing aid could also not be compared to a watch, which is worn by many and therefore could be considered part of one's clothing. The hearing aid, on the other hand, is only made for the purpose of hearing and not to be seen and therefore probably does not come under the category of clothing.

Finally, *Rav Auerbach zt"l* wrote that one may go out with a hearing aid containing a battery inside it.[43] [*It is both humbling and educational to see how a man of the stature of the Rav zt"l was not afraid to debate with himself, back and forth publicly, in his search for the truth.*]

Rav Ovadiah Yosef shlita[44] also rules that a deaf person may go out with a hearing aid, even in a *public domain,* since it is firmly fixed in his ear and is considered like clothing. In his opinion, one may go out with a hearing aid for the same reasons that permit one to go out with spectacles.

COCHLEAR IMPLANT. One may go out on *Shabbat* with a cochlear implant even in a *public domain.*[45]

USING A HEARING AID at home or where there is an *eruv.* One may use a hearing aid if it has been turned on before *Shabbat.*[46] Its volume may be adjusted on *Shabbat,* if doing so does not cause any

39. שו״ת הר צבי או״ח ח״א סי׳ קעג. שו״ת מנחת יצחק ח״ב סי׳ קיב וח״ג סי׳ מא
40. שמירת שבת כהלכתה שם סע׳ כח
41. שמירת שבת כהלכתה שם הערה קי
42. שו״ת מנחת שלמה ח״א סי׳ ט הערה 3 מובא בנשמת אברהם כרך ד חאו״ח סי׳ שא ס״ק ב (עמ׳ כג)
43. ראה ח״ג של שמירת שבת כהלכתה על פל״ד הערה קי הוספה מהגאון זצ״ל לחזק את ההיתר שהוא כתב קודם. וכן שמעתי ממו״ר הגרי״י נויבירט שליט״א
44. ספר לוית חן על הלכות שבת אות ל
45. שמעתי ממו״ר הגרי״י נויבירט שליט״א
46. שו״ת יביע אומר ח״א סוסי׳ יט

§16: An amputee who is unable to go out at all except by (G)sitting on a low chair to which he is tied and which he moves by using his hands to propel himself and the chair forward while leaning on his stump, may not go out with a leather pad or piece of wood to protect the stump, since it may fall off in the street. However, he may go out with his chair and hand-rests. If both legs have been amputated, and he walks on his stumps, he may go out with his pads.

NISHMAT AVRAHAM

wire to become red hot when the current is increased or cease to glow when it is reduced.[47]

One may converse with someone who is wearing a hearing aid[48] or cochlear implant[49] even if, as a result, a light flickers, provided that it is either a neon lamp[50] or a light emitting diode (L.E.D.).[51] Expert advice should be sought regarding the technical details of each device.

(G) sitting on a low chair: WHEELCHAIR. A disabled person who can only get around in a wheelchair may be taken out by a non-Jew into a *carmelit* in order to perform a *mitzvah* such as going to pray or to attend a Torah lesson, even if there is no *eruv*. If, however, he can propel himself by turning the wheels of his chair, a non-Jew may be asked to take him out even in a *public domain,* provided that the patient also simultaneously propels the chair forward. Since both the patient and the non-Jew can each, on his own, move the chair, and both do so together (and one is a non-Jew), this is permissible. A Jew may not take him out even into a *carmelit* even though the patient can actively help. If the patient himself can propel his chair all the way without help he may do so. In any event, there should be nothing on the chair that he does not need for sitting; nor must there be anything in his pockets.[52] If there is an *eruv,* a Jew may take him out.

On *Yom Tov* a person may be taken out in his wheelchair by a Jew, even into a *public domain.*[53]

The *Lev Aryeh*[54] permits one who is unable to walk without crutches, or even one who can walk a little but cannot walk as far as the synagogue, to ask a non-Jew to take him in a wheelchair, even in a *public domain.* Since he can walk with crutches (unlike the patient above who is confined to a wheelchair), one may apply to him the phrase "a living person helps to carry himself." Wheeling him even in a *public domain* is only Rabbinically forbidden and is permissible when done by a non-Jew. The *Lev Aryeh* also permits him to place his crutches in the wheelchair to be used later to walk from the *shul* courtyard into the *shul. Rav Neuwirth shlita* forbids this since the crutches in the wheelchair are like shoes that are carried rather than worn. However, he recently

47. שמירת שבת כהלכתה פל״ד סע׳ כח

48. ראה מנחת שלמה סי׳ ט סע׳ ב. וכן שמעתי מהגרש״ז אויערבאך זצ״ל, כי מה שהוא משנה את עוצמת הזרם על ידי דיבורו לאו כלום הוא, כיון שלא נעשה בכך שום כיבוי והדלקה כשהמכשיר כבר דלוק. ועיין היטב בשו״ת אג״מ או״ח ח״ד סי׳ פה

49. שמעתי ממו״ר הגרי״י נויבירט שליט״א

50. מנחת שלמה ח״ב סי׳ יט ד״ה אך יש כהיום

51. ראה גם בשו״ת ציץ אליעזר ח״ו סי׳ ו ובמילואים שם. שו״ת מנחת יצחק ח״א סי׳ לז, ח״ב סי׳ יז, יח וקיג, וח״ג סי׳ מא. שו״ת יביע אומר ח״א סוסי׳ יט

52. שמעתי ממו״ר הגרי״י נויבירט שליט״א

53. שמירת שבת כהלכתה פל״ד סוסע׳ כז

54. שו״ת לב אריה ח״ב סי׳ ז

§17: A lame person who cannot walk without his walking stick may go out with it even if it is not tied to him. However, if he can (H)walk without it and only uses it for extra support, it is forbidden. (*The same rules apply to a patient who has recovered from his illness as to the lame person.*)

NISHMAT AVRAHAM

wrote to me that if he is being wheeled by a non-Jew, he may place his crutches in the wheelchair for later use.

(H) walk without it: An elderly person who walks at home without a cane but, because of his weakness, uses one when he goes out in order to support himself, is forbidden to go out with it. Since he only uses it as a means of steadying his gait in the street, but not at home, it is considered a "burden." However, if he cannot walk at all without it, even at home, he may go out with it.[55] It would appear that one who only needs his cane when going up an incline or stairs, should be forbidden to use it outside, since here, too, there is the possibility that he may carry it when walking on a level surface when he does not need it for support.[56]

What about one who has sustained an injury to his foot and can walk about fifty meters with crutches which he uses only for slight support, but cannot walk beyond that at all without them because of pain? *Rav Neuwirth shlita* at first wrote to me that he would not be permitted to go out with his crutches, that he was like an elderly person who does not need his cane at home, whom I discussed above. Later, he wrote to me that he might be like one who must go to a *seriously ill patient* on *Shabbat* to help at a given time. If he would walk all the way there, he would not make it in time for the patient. He should start to walk, and only when he feels that if he continues walking he will not arrive at the appointed time, may he then take a cab. Nevertheless, if he knows that when he does need a cab it will not be possible to get one, he may certainly take a cab earlier, even though for the first part of the ride he really did not need it. However, *Rav Neuwirth shlita* then wrote that his example is perhaps not applicable to the question in hand, since the lame person is not really obligated to go out as is one going to the *seriously ill* patient.

Rav Waldenberg shlita,[57] on the other hand, permits the patient in question to go out with his crutches, based on the opinions of the *Taz*[58] and the *Aruch HaShulchan,*[59] since he does need the crutches a little even during the first fifty meters. The *Mirkevet HaMishneh*[60] goes further and permits even a healthy person to go out with a cane if he is concerned about slipping and falling on an icy road or on a wet incline in the rain. This is also the opinion of the *Menorah HaTehorah.*[61] Furthermore, *Rav Waldenberg shlita* writes that since he requires the crutches to lean on during the first fifty meters, even those who rule against the *Taz*[62] would agree with him here. They disagree when considering someone who is slightly lame and does not need a cane at all, but takes one as security should he need to walk on a slippery surface. Finally, adds

55. מ״ב ס״ק סד

56. הגרש״ז אויערבאך זצ״ל בשמירת שבת כהלכתה פי״ח הערה נט

57. שו״ת ציץ אליעזר חי״ח סי׳ לד

58. מובא במ״ב ס״ק סה

59. סע׳ ע

60. בספרו שלחן עצי שטים, מלאכת הוצאה

61. הל׳ שבת סי׳ שא בקני המנורה ס״ק כו

62. ראה במ״ב שם

§18: [I]A blind person is forbidden to go out with his cane.

NISHMAT AVRAHAM

Rav Walldenberg shlita, there is the opinion of the *Levush*[63] who writes that the *halachic* prohibition of this section is only Rabbinic and is a precaution lest he come to carry the cane; by Torah law the cane would be considered an "ornament" since he uses it to steady himself. The crutches, in the case under discussion, would therefore be permitted.

Rav Neuwirth shlita, however, wrote to me again pointing out that even though the *Levush* writes that, in his opinion, this is a Rabbinic prohibition, nevertheless the *Levush* himself is only lenient when the person actually uses the cane. However, if he does not, then there is a transgression of a Torah prohibition. Second, even according to the *Levush, Chazal's* precautionary prohibition still stands. Finally, the *Biur Halachah*[64] quotes the *Mordechai* and the *Or Zarua,* both of whom rule that there is a Torah prohibition. Since they are both *rishonom* (early Sages) and no other *rishonim* disagree with them, we surely cannot rule like the *Levush.*

Rav Ezriel Auerbach shlita told me in the name of his father-in-law, *Rav Eliashiv shlita,* that in his opinion also one may not rely on the opinion of the *Taz* in the situation under discussion, and the patient who can walk fifty metres almost unaided would not be allowed to go out with his crutches.

(I) A blind person: A blind person may not go out with his stick unless there is an *eruv.* For he can walk without it and only uses it to walk more surely.[65] This only applies if he goes out into a familiar area where the cane is an extra precaution. However, in an area unknown to him where he cannot go out at all without it, he is like a lame person and may go out with it to prevent him tripping or falling over some obstacle.[66] Nevertheless, since there are *poskim* who do not definitely permit this, a Rav who knows the person's circumstances should be consulted.[67]

The *Lev Aryeh*[68] permits a blind person to go out into a *public domain* with his guide-dog. For since the connecting halter is not carried by the dog alone but is carried simultaneously by both the person and the dog, the Torah prohibition to "cause an animal to work" (among the forbidden tasks is causing it to carry a burden) does not apply, nor has he failed to fulfill the commandment "that your ox and ass might rest."[69] This is so since a *melachah* that can be done by either one of two, all by himself, (in this case the carrying of the harness in a *public domain,*) and is done by both simultaneously, is not prohibited by the Torah. There is not even a Rabbinic prohibition in the case of the guide-dog because whatever is Rabbinically prohibited for a person may be done by an animal even at his master's command.[70] However *Rav Shlomo Zalman Auerbach zt"l* wrote to me[71] that since the halter is for the blind person's benefit only, it would possibly be considered a "burden," since he alone holds the halter while the dog leads him. Again, a Rav who knows the particular circumstances should be consulted.

The *Igrot Moshe*[72] permits a blind person to enter a *shul* with his guide-dog,

63. כאן סע׳ יז
64. כאן ד״ה אבל
65. מ״ב ס״ק סח
66. עטרת זקנים על השו״ע סי׳ תקכב. ערוה״ש סע׳ עב
67. ראה בשמירת שבת כהלכתה פי״ח סע׳ יג והערה שם
68. ח״ב סי׳ ב
69. שמות כג:יב
70. שבת קנג ע״ב
71. לב אברהם ח״ב עמ׳ יח
72. או״ח ח״א סי׳ מה ד״ה ולכן

§22: One may go out with a (J)sponge over a wound. Since it has healing properties it is akin to an ornament. Similarly, one may go out with a band-aid or with a poultice with adhesive plaster over it. However, if they fall off one may not replace them and certainly, one may not put them on the wound on *Shabbat*.

§26: A doctor who says that he is a (K)specialist is believed.

§27: One may go out both on weekdays and on *Shabbat* with a locust's egg, a fox's tooth, etc., and this is not forbidden because of being heathen customs since anything that is done for healing is permitted and is not considered a heathen custom. However, if it is (L)not evident that it is being

NISHMAT AVRAHAM

since otherwise, he will never be able to pray with a congregation. The *Chelkat Yaakov,*[73] on the other hand, forbids this since others would be surprised to see it. Similarly, the *She'arim Metzuyanim Ba-Halachah* writes[74] that since non-Jews are generally very particular not to do this sort of thing in their houses of worship, if they were to see a Jew entering a synagogue with a dog, there would be a desecration of *Hashem's* Name. *Rav Kasher zt''l*[75] also concurs.

(J) sponge: A person may go out with a bandaged wound or with a handkerchief placed directly around a wound.[76] Since the bandage is being used for his bodily needs, it is likened to an ornament. The bandage may be kept in place, but only with something that has no value for the user and which he will discard, together with the bandage, later. Thus a length of string or bandage clips (which come with the bandage) may be used but not a handkerchief or safety pin. Since the bandage itself will be discarded afterwards but not the safety pin, it cannot be considered secondary to the bandage; it is considered a "burden," and is forbidden, at least at the Rabbinic level.[77]

If one binds a bleeding wound only in order to prevent staining of one's clothes, he is forbidden to go out into a *public domain* with the bandage.[78]

It is permissible to go out into a *public domain* with a bandage, plaster cast[79] or sling worn to keep a painful limb at rest.[80]

(K) specialist: See *Siman* 328:6 and 328:10

(L) not evident: One may wear a "copper bracelet" or other such bracelets as a cure and go out with it into a *public domain.*[81] *Rav Auerbach zt''l* told me that since it is common practice to wear these things as a charm, it can be considered as clothing. He also added that even if the charm only works if he actually

73. ח״ג סי׳ פז
74. סי׳ יג ס״ק ב
75. תורה שלמה חט״ו פ׳ יתרו מילואים עמ׳ קמז
76. מ״ב ס״ק עז בשם הגר״א וכן בס״ק קח ושעה״צ ס״ק קל
77. שמירת שבת כהלכתה פי״ח סע׳ יט ועיין שם בהערה עח
78. שם
79. שם פי״ח סע׳ יט
80. שם סע׳ כ
81. שמירת שבת כהלכתה פל״ד סע׳ טו

used for healing, it is forbidden because it is then considered a heathen custom.

NISHMAT AVRAHAM

carries it in his hand (as opposed to wearing it), the *Sefat Emet*[82] ruled that it is permissible, just as a lame person may go out with his stick (see §17). He also pointed out to me that an ornament carried in the hand is only forbidden because such an action will cause others who observe this to misinterpret the *halachah* and carry even things that are forbidden.[83]

CHARMS. The *Rambam*[84] writes: The *halachah* is not like *Rebbe Matya ben Charash* who permits a person bitten by a mad dog to eat of its liver, since this has no effect except as a charm. And the *Chachamim* (majority view) held that one may not transgress *mitzvot* except when the treatment is conventional, etc. To attempt to treat with charms is forbidden since their power to heal is so slight, etc.

The *Chida*[85] writes: From this *Rambam* we can deduce that even though there may be no doubt that a particular charm has been tested and been shown to work, nevertheless the *Chachamim* rule that it is forbidden to use it, if one thereby must desecrate his religion. On the other hand, the *Radvaz*[86] is of the opinion that the *Rambam* means that a charm is not a treatment at all and does not even have a possibility of cure; thus one may not desecrate *Shabbat* in order to use it when a Torah prohibition is involved. Though one may go out with an amulet written by an expert, etc. (see §27), this is only with reference to a Rabbinic prohibition since the amulet is worn and not carried.[87]

However, the *Chida* quotes the *Admat Kodesh*[88] who proves that both the *Ramban* and the *Rashba* do not agree with the *Rambam* and do not differentiate between a treatment that is natural and one that is supernatural. He follows their opinion and even permits (tested) amulets when Torah prohibitions are involved. The *Chida* himself concludes that nevertheless one needs deep study to clarify the opinions of the *Ramban* and *Rashba*. Elsewhere, the *Chida*[89] writes: I saw in an old manuscript that *Rabbeinu Peretz z"l* wrote Holy Names on *Shabbat*, a well-tried charm for women in labor.[90] And again, the *Chida*[91] writes that the *Yad Ramah* (not to be confused with the *Ramah*) in a *responsum* (still in manuscript form) also permitted a well-tried and proven amulet to be written on *Shabbat*. Here again, the *Chida* writes that the matter needs further clarification.

The *Maharsham*[92] discusses whether or not one may set aside Sabbath laws in order to send a messenger to a well-known righteous man to ask him to pray for one who is *seriously ill*. He writes: I know of a case where a Rav permitted that a non-Jew be asked to write the names of a *seriously ill patient* and his mother on *Shabbat*, in order that a messenger be sent for this purpose. *Rav Shlomo Kluger* who was in town vehemently disagreed

82. שבת סב ע״א

83. מג״א ס״ק כז

84. פ׳ המשניות יומא פ״ח מ״ד

85. ברכ״י כאן ס״ק ו

86. לשונות הרמב״ם סי׳ אלף תלו (סג) וסי׳ אלף תקכו (קנג)

87. וכן ראה בחכמת שלמה כאן סע׳ כה

88. ח״א יו״ד סי׳ ו הובא בברכ״י שם

89. שו״ת חיים שאל ח״ב סי׳ לח אות פא

90. כותב הברכ״י (יו״ד סי׳ רצ ס״ק ב) על נכפה שאמרו המומחים לכתוב קמיע על קלף צבי ולא מצא רק מן ספר תורה, צדד הרב שער אפרים סי׳ צ לחתוך מהספר תורה ולגרור הכתב ולמחוק שמות וכו׳.

91. כסא רחמים על מס׳ סופרים פ״ה מי״ד

92. שו״ת ח״ה סוסי׳ רכה

§28: One who has a [M]wound on the sole of his foot may go out with a coin tied over it, since it both protects and [N]heals.

NISHMAT AVRAHAM

(M) wound: One who sprained a joint but is not in severe pain is permitted to bring the joint into a restful position. Thus he may put a hand into a sling or use an elastic bandage.[98] *Chazal* forbid one who is not really ill to take medication, lest he pulverize ingredients (which is a Torah prohibition) to use as medication. They allow only those who fall into the category of at least the *non-seriously ill* to take medication. This holds true today also although the possibility of pulverizing ingredients is remote. They also prohibited any action which is meant to heal or treat, if the same ends could be reached by taking medication. This enactment was to prevent the possibility of someone who had only a *minor illness* from using medication as an alternative.[99] *Rav Shlomo Zalman Auerbach zt"l* explained to me that the sling is different. Since everyone knows that a sling or elastic bandage does not cure, there is no fear that permitting them will lead to taking medication as an alternative. However, if the pain is severe, the patient is classified as a *non-seriously ill patient* and he will be discussed in *Siman* 328:17.

One may not put a compress on a sprain.[100]

(N) heals: The *Mishnah Berurah*[101]

and disqualified the Rav from deciding further *halachic* questions. In such matters, writes the *Maharsham,* one should not be lenient, especially in our generation. It is of such a situation that it says: "Today is *Shabbat* and it is prohibited to cry out etc." (see *Siman* 287:1).

Rav Shlomo Kluger himself writes:[93] Even though the *halachah* is clear that one may set aside Sabbath laws to save life, this is only if the cure is conventional and, even then, only if it has been tried and proven. One may not, under any circumstances, do so with supernatural cures or with prayers. Even if the supplicant is as great a sage as *Rebbe Chanina ben Dosa* (a Talmudic Sage from the *Mishnaic* period, famous for his prayers for the sick), one may not set aside Sabbath laws for this.[94] The *Tzitz Eliezer,*[95] in a number of *responsa,* also rules that it is forbidden to set aside Sabbath laws for this purpose not only at a Torah level but even at a Rabbinic level. If the patient himself demands this, one must use every possible tactic to make him believe that this was done – but not do it.

On the other hand, other *poskim* permit this.[96] *Rav Auerbach zt"l*[97] wrote to me that since the problem remains controversial among the *poskim,* it is obvious that one should avoid doing so.

93. שו״ת ובחרת בחיים סי׳ פז מובא ביסודי ישורון ח״ד עמ׳ רמב

94. ראה גם בשו״ת טוב טעם ודעת מהד״ק סי׳ רלט. שדי חמד מערכת יוהכ״פ סי׳ ג ס״ק כד

95. ח״ד סי׳ ד אות יז, ח״ח סי׳ טו פ״ח אות ז, ח״ט סי׳ יז פ״ג אות א־ג, חי״א סי׳ סא אות ד

96. שו״ת צמח צדק החדשות או״ח סי׳ לח מובא במנחת שבת סי׳ צב ס״ק יח וראה בשיורי המנחה שם, כל בו על אבלות ח״א עמ׳ 18, יסודי ישורון ח״ד עמ׳ רמב וח״ה עמ׳ פא. וראה גם באשל אברהם אופנהיים בגליון או״ח סי׳ שכט סע׳ ג, הארחות חיים סי׳ שא ס״ק ה, שו״ת חת״ס יו״ד סי׳ שלט, הפתחי תשובה יו״ד סי׳ קנה ס״ק ג, הט״ז יו״ד סי׳ פד ס״ק כד, והקצות השולחן סי׳ קלה סע׳ א בבדה״ש

97. לב אברהם ח״א עמ׳ יח

98. שמירת שבת כהלכתה פל״ה סע׳ לה

99. מ״ב סי׳ שכח ס״ק קל

100. סי׳ שכח סע׳ ל

101. ס״ק קח

§36: One may go out on *Shabbat* wearing two similar garments, one over the other, whether for his or for someone else's benefit. It does not matter whether these are two inner or two outer garments, or two belts worn one over the other, even without another garment between them.

GLOSS: *There are those* (O)*who forbid two belts to be worn one over the other unless there is another garment between them and this is how one should act. One may wear two headcoverings or two pairs of slippers (or shoes).*

§51: A person with a wound on his hand or arm may go out with a cloth round his neck (and arm) in order to (P)**rest his arm. Similarly, one may go out with a cloth tied around a wound on his hand or finger.**

NISHMAT AVRAHAM

points out that the *Tur* is of the opinion that if it does not cure but would only protect the wound from further injury, it is forbidden to go out with it. However the *Eliyah Rabbah* rules that even if it does not cure but only protects, it is permissible to go out with it. The *Tosefet Shabbat* in the name of *Rav Shlomo Kluger* also writes this. The *Mishnah Berurah* points out that he has already mentioned[102] that the *Gra* believes this is also the opinion of the *Rambam*. Therefore, he writes, if one cuts oneself and ties a piece of cloth over it to prevent it being rubbed by his clothes, he may go out with it. However, he adds, it is best to follow the opinion of the *Pri Megadim* and use a piece of cloth that he will later discard. For then the cloth is secondary to the wound and, in everyone's opinion, it would be permissible to go out with it. The cut should be washed well to prevent staining of the cloth (as staining involves the *melachah* of coloring).

One may go out with a hernia truss or any other such belt. Since it is used on the person's body, it is compared to spectacles that are worn and are permissible.[103]

(O) who forbid: Regarding going out into a *public domain* with a handkerchief, see the *Mishnah Berurah*[104] and the *Shemirat Shabbat KeHilchatah.*[105] If, however, one has a very bad cold and would be ashamed to go out in public without a handkerchief, the *Shemirat Shabbat KeHilchatah*[106] writes that it would be permissible if he carried it out in an indirect manner, such as carrying it under his hat or around his wrist or neck. When carried in such a way there is a Rabbinic prohibition and that falls away if he would suffer public embarrassment.

(P) rest his arm: One may go out with a sling to rest a painful arm.[107]

102. ס״ק עז
103. שמירת שבת כהלכתה פי״ח סע׳ כ
104. ס״ק קלג
105. פי״ח סע׳ מז
106. שם ובהערה קפח
107. שם סע׳ כ

SIMAN 302: THE LAWS OF LAUNDERING AND FOLDING OF CLOTHES ON *SHABBAT*

§3. One may fold clothes on *Shabbat* if one does so in order to wear them on that same *Shabbat*. This is only permissible if (*one*) person folds them, if they are new and have not yet been laundered, are white, and he has no other clothes to change into. If one of these conditions is not met, it is forbidden. There is an opinion that if the first crease is folded differently, it is permitted in all cases, and (A)this view is acceptable.

SIMAN 303: THE LAWS CONCERNING A WOMAN'S ORNAMENTS

§24: A married woman may go out with a *tekuma* stone (a special stone which prevents miscarriage when worn) or with its counterweight in order to prevent miscarriage, (A)even if she is not yet pregnant.

NISHMAT AVRAHAM

SIMAN 302

(A) this view: One may make up beds on *Shabbat* morning in order to sleep or rest on them the same day.[1] One may not make them up on *Shabbat* in preparation for Saturday night. However, if the bed is visible to others and it would be unseemly for it to be seen in its unmade state during *Shabbat,* it may be made up.[2] Therefore a nurse may not make up a hospital bed on *Shabbat* if she is certain that it will not be used until after *Shabbat*. However, if there are other patients in the room this is permissible.[3] Similarly, if there is the likelihood that a new patient will need the bed, for example in the emergency room or in an intensive care unit, this is also permissible, and even in a private room, in order that there should be no delay in admitting the patient. If the bed needs cleaning, she should be careful to do so with a nylon cloth which does not absorb fluids (thus avoiding the *melachot* of "squeezing" and "laundering").

SIMAN 303

(A) even if she is not yet pregnant: I.e. if she fears that she will become pregnant and miscarry,[1] even though she has no previous history of miscarriage.[2] *Rav Auerbach zt"l* wrote[3] that the *tekuma* stone acts as a charm from the outset to prevent a miscarriage.

1. שבת סו ע״ב. מ״ב ס״ק עח
2. שעה״צ ס״ק סד
3. שמירת שבת כהלכתה פ״מ הערה כ

1. שעה״צ ס״ק כב
2. מ״ב ס״ק יט
3. שמעתי ממו״ר הגרי״י נויבירט שליט״א

SIMAN 306:
WHAT MAY ONE SPEAK ABOUT ON *SHABBAT*

§5: It is forbidden to hire a cantor to lead the services on *Shabbat* but there are those who permit this.

GLOSS: *However, if he was* (A)*hired for a year or for a month it is permissible according to all opinions.*

NISHMAT AVRAHAM

However the *Orchot Chaim* writes that it appears from *Rashi*[4] that if she knows for certain that she is not pregnant, it is forbidden for her to go out with it. The *Pri Megadim*[5] also quotes this *Rashi* and reaches the same conclusion. He continues that although it would appear that she may only go out with it if she has a past history of miscarriage (see *Siman* 301:25), nevertheless, since the *poskim* did not differentiate, it is permissible for her to go out with it even without such a past history. The *Meiri* and the *Chidushei HaRan,* however, specifically write "for example if there is a strong family history." *Rav Auerbach zt"l* wrote to me that an unmarried girl would certainly be forbidden to do so.

The statement of the *Shulchan Aruch* above, "even if she is not yet pregnant" is, at first sight, difficult to understand. Why should it be permissible to break a Sabbath law if there is no necessity? However, it has been shown[6] that twenty-two percent of pregnant women do miscarry even before they themselves realize that they are pregnant. How great were *Chazal,* whose knowledge was so much superior to ours![7]

SIMAN 306

(A) hired: A midwife may certainly take payment after *Shabbat* for services rendered on *Shabbat.*[1] However, her fees may not be discussed on *Shabbat.*[2] The *Mishnah Berurah*[3] also writes that there are those who permit taking fees for doing a *mitzvah* on a weekday, such as digging a grave. He also writes[4] that there are those who say that, according to all opinions, one may be paid (after *Yom Tov*) to bury someone on the second day of *Yom Tov* – a matter which is relevant only outside of Israel. Since *Chazal,* who instituted the second day of *Yom Tov,* made it similar to a weekday with respect to the dead, this will hold true as far as receiving payment for services rendered.

Therefore, a doctor or nurse called privately to treat a patient on *Shabbat* may ask for payment (after *Shabbat*) for their services[5] since the payment is for the *mitzvah* of saving life.[6] This is also the opinion of the *Maharsham,*[7] the *Minchat Shabbat,*[8] the *Har Tzvi,*[9] the *Harei Besamim,*[10] the *Tzitz Eliezer,*[11] the *Yabia Omer,*[12] the *Yesodei Yeshu-*

4. שבת סו ע״ב ד״ה ולא
5. מ״ז ס״ק יג
6. NEJM 319:189 '88
7. ראה ברד״ק ספר יהושע ד, יא בסוף

1. מ״ב סוס״ק כד
2. שמירת שבת כהלכתה פכ״ח סע׳ סז
3. שם
4. שם ס״ק מא
5. שמירת שבת כהלכתה פכ״ח סע׳ סז
6. פמ״ג מ״ז ס״ק ד
7. דעת תורה ס״ק ה
8. סי׳ צ ס״ק יט
9. שו״ת או״ח ח״א סי׳ רד
10. שו״ת ח״א סי׳ נב
11. שו״ת ח״ח סי׳ טו פי״ג
12. שו״ת ח״ה סי׳ כה

§7: One may measure on *Shabbat* if it is for the [B]purposes of a *mitzvah,* for example to ascertain whether a *mikveh* contains the requisite forty *se'ah* of water.

NISHMAT AVRAHAM

run[13] and the *She'arim Metzuyanim BaHalachah.*[14] However, this only applies to a Jewish patient. As to the non-Jewish patient, the *Ritva*[15] feels that fees are taken but not used, since one may not charge for *Shabbat* services. The *Chatam Sofer*[16] says that, on the one hand, one must take payment,[17] but on the other, it is preferable not to benefit by it. Rather, he should give it all to charity. However, *Rav Ovadiah Yosef shlita*[18] quotes the *Pekudat Elazar*[19] permitting the doctor to take fees in the normal way since ultimately it is also for the sake of a *mitzvah.*[20] This is also the opinion of the *Darchei Teshuvah*[21] (see also the *Shemirat Shabbat KeHilchatah*).[22]

A doctor or nurse who demands immediate payment on *Shabbat* for treating a *seriously ill patient,* should, if possible, be given a suitable article which bears the person's name and address as a pledge, so that the doctor need not write them. If such a pledge is not available then one may be given to the doctor even without a name and even if he then writes it.[23] If this is unavailable or is refused, one may pay him but not take change on *Shabbat* and certainly not ask for a receipt, since these have no bearing on the needs of the patient.[24] However, *Rav Shlomo Zalman Auerbach zt"l*[25] writes that it is forbidden to pay the doctor on *Shabbat* even if he is a non-Jew (since it is akin to doing business). If the doctor is a Jew there is an additional Rabbinic, and possibly even a Torah, prohibition of "placing a stumbling block before the blind" and should be avoided unless it will interfere with patient treatment.

(B) purposes of a *mitzvah*: Any measurement which is necessary for the treatment of a patient is permissible. Since the measurement is for the purpose of a cure, this is a *mitzvah.* Nor does the decree of *Chazal* against taking medication on *Shabbat* lest you pulverize ingredients apply since that only applies to treatment by tangible substances such as food or drink.[26] Therefore it is permissible to measure or weigh the amount of food a patient needs. Similarly, it is permissible to take his pulse and blood pressure, to weigh him or to make any other measurement that is needed for his care.[27]

MEASUREMENT OF TEMPERATURE. It is permissible to measure one's temperature on *Shabbat. Rav Auerbach zt"l* writes[28] that the prohibition against measuring on *Shabbat* is because it falls into the category of "weekday activities." However, taking one's temperature can in no way be compared to this[29] and is therefore permitted on *Shabbat* and *Yom Tov.*

13. ח״ד עמ׳ ערב
14. סי׳ צ ס״ק ז
15. ע״ז כו ע״א ד״ה אולודי
16. שו״ת חו״מ סוסי׳ קצד ד״ה והנה
17. משום לא תחנם
18. שו״ת יביע אומר ח״ה או״ח סי׳ כה
19. או״ח סי׳ כט
20. כיון דאיכא איבה הו״ל צורך מצוה
21. יו״ד סי׳ קנד ס״ק ט
22. שמירת שבת כהלכתה פכ״ח הערה קמז
23. שם פל״ב סע׳ נה הערה קמז ובח״ג
24. שם פ״מ סע׳ יב
25. שם הערה לט וראה גם בח״ג
26. מ״ב ס״ק לו
27. עיין שמירת שבת כהלכתה פכ״ט סע׳ לט ופ״מ סע׳ ב
28. מאורי אש דף לג ע״ב
29. דלא שייכא כלל מדידה זו לעובדין דחול והוי רק עובדין דחולי

NISHMAT AVRAHAM

This also the opinion of the *Chelkat Yaakov,*[30] the *Igrot Moshe,*[31] the *Minchat Yitzhak,*[32] the *Tzitz Eliezer*[33] and the *Shemirat Shabbat KeHilchatah.*[34] As to shaking down the thermometer after use, although the *Shevet HaLevi*[35] prohibits this, writing that it may possibly involve the Torah prohibition of "completing work," the *Tzitz Eliezer*[36] permits it, if it will be needed for use again the same day. I heard this also from *Rav Auerbach zt"l* who writes in *Shemirat Shabbat KeHilchatah*[37] that since the thermometer is normally shaken down, such an action is permitted.[38]

A woman who takes her temperature every day in order to ascertain her time of ovulation, may do so on *Shabbat* since this is also included in the *mitzvah* of treatment.[39]

Is the thermometer *mukzteh* when not in use? The *Shemirat Shabbat KeHilchatah*[40] writes, in the name of *Rav Shlomo Zalman Auerbach zt"l,* that even though the *Sha'arei Teshuvah*[41] writes that the tools of a workman are *muktzeh* because of their worth, nevertheless, measuring instruments do not fall into this category, since the prohibition of measuring is only because of "weekday activities." In this case, since the measurement of temperature is only for a specific person at a specific time, it cannot even be classified as a "weekday activity." Furthermore, the thermometer may be considered an instrument used for the performance of a *mitzvah.* True, medications are considered *muktzeh,* but this is because treatment itself is prohibited except for someone who has reached a certain degree of illness (see *Siman* 328) whereas the measurement of temperature is part of performing a *mitzvah* and is not, in itself, treatment. Therefore, the thermometer itself is an "instument whose use is permitted" (as against an "instrument whose use is forbidden") and therefore is not *muktzeh.* That the mercury column expands is also not a cause to prohibit its use since the heat causing it to do so does not reach a temperature that would cause one to pull away his hand lest it be burned (the definition of cooking or heating by Torah law).[42]

The thermometer may be washed in alcohol and then wiped off with dry absorbent cotton. Absorbent cotton that has been soaked in alcohol may not be used to clean it because of the *melachah* of "squeezing."[43] The *Tzitz Eliezer,*[44] however, permits this.

A contact thermometer, on which numbers can be vaguely seen before its use, may be used on *Shabbat.*[45] However, it may not be used on *Shabbat* if it is blank before use and figures become visible only after it has been in contact with the skin, unless the patient is *seriously ill* or is possibly so, and there is no other way to take his temperature.[46] This is also the opinion of the *Minchat Yitzchak*[47] and

30. ח״ג סי׳ כד
31. או״ח ח״א סי׳ קכח
32. ח״ג סי׳ קמב
33. ח״ג סי׳ י
34. פ״מ סע׳ ב
35. ח״א או״ח סי׳ סא
36. חי״א סי׳ לח
37. שם הערה ז
38. וכותב שם אף לדעת החזו״א בסי׳ נ נראה דהכא קיל טפי
39. שו״ת ציץ אליעזר שם. וחי״ב סי׳ מד אות ה. שמירת שבת כהלכתה פ״מ סע׳ ב
40. שם הערה ג
41. סוסי׳ שח
42. וכותב: כיון חשיב כחמה ולא כאש
43. שמירת שבת כהלכתה שם סע׳ ב
44. ח״ח סי׳ טו פי״ד אות יא וח״ט סי׳ יז פ״ב אות לג
45. שו״ת ציץ אליעזר חי״ד סי׳ לא. וכן שמעתי מהגרש״ז אויערבאך זצ״ל
46. שמירת שבת כהלכתה פ״מ סע׳ ב הערה ח* בשם הגרש״ז אויערבאך זצ״ל
47. ח״ז סי׳ כב

NISHMAT AVRAHAM

the *Machazei Eliyahu.*[48] On the other hand, the *Tzitz Eliezer*[49] permits its use. This controversy is based on the definition of "writing" which is forbidden on *Shabbat* by Torah law. *Rav Auerbach zt"l*[50] writes that just as there is a Rabbinic prohibition to hold paper on which one has written in milk or lemon juice over a flame, in order that the letters which were until now invisible become visible, so too in our case there is a Rabbinic prohibition to use such a thermometer even for a *non-seriously ill patient.* True, the letters disappear quickly and the writing is therefore temporary, nevertheless it is possible that even this is forbidden. It is also possible that when the writing becomes visible it is as if one writes afresh each time on the heat-sensitive area of the thermometer. On the other hand, the *Tzitz Eliezer*[51] writes that although writing which is transient is Rabbinically prohibited, this is only if the writing remains for a while as it does when written with milk or lemon juice. However, if it disappears within a short space of time, as happens with a contact thermometer, it is permitted. See also the *Pri Megadim*[52] who writes in a similar vein. In addition, we are discussing a *non-seriously ill patient.* Therefore we may permit the use of this type of thermometer for someone who feels unwell and does not have a regular thermometer available, and certainly where babies and small children are concerned. However, if a regular thermometer is available, it should be used so that the *halachah* should not be misinterpreted or misunderstood by others.[53] *Rav Ovadiah Yosef shlita*[54] also rules that it is permissible to use such a thermometer.

Since in *Rav Auerbach zt"l*'s view, typing onto a computer screen is not considered "writing" by Torah law (see *Siman* 340D), I asked why he forbade the use of a contact thermometer where the figure representing the temperature only becomes visible on body contact (see *Siman* 306B). In both situations only Rabbinic law is set aside and therefore it should be permitted for the *non-seriously ill patient.* The *Rav zt"l* wrote to me that putting the thermometer on the person's body is like writing something that is not permanent. On the other hand, when typing onto a computer screen there is no writing at all; one fires electrons onto an appropriate background. He also told me that for a *non-seriously ill patient* a Jew may only set aside Rabbinic law if he does the action in an indirect manner. Where it is possible to use a regular thermometer, this type of contact thermometer is forbidden. However in a hospital where only this type of thermometer is available, it would be permitted. *Rav Neuwirth shlita* wrote me differentiating between the computer and the thermometer. In the former the figures have no permanency at all and only remain on the screen because of a continuous repetitive firing of electrons, but the figures on the thermometer remain for a short while (even after the contact with the skin is broken); these are like writing on a damp window which is forbidden.[55] Thus it should only be used for a *non-seriously ill patient* if there is no other thermometer available.

48. סי׳ סה־סו

49. חי״ד סי׳ ל־לא

50. שמירת שבת כהלכתה פ״מ הערה ח* מהא דפמ״ג סי׳ שמ מ״ז ס״ק ג

51. שם

52. סי׳ שטו ס״ק ח

53. מראית העין

54. הערה על נשמת אברהם ח״ד עמ׳ רכה. שו״ת יחוה דעת ח״ד סי׳ כט

55. מ״ב סי׳ שמ ס״ק כ

§8: (C)One may think about his business affairs. However, so as not to spoil one's *oneg Shabbat,* it is a *mitzvah* not to think about them at all, but rather he should feel as if all his business affairs have been completed.

§9: It is forbidden to ask a non-Jew to go beyond the *techum Shabbat* in order to call family members to come and eulogize a dead person. However, if a seriously ill patient asks that his family be informed, it is (D)certainly permitted.

NISHMAT AVRAHAM

(C) One may think: The verse[56] says that you should honor *Shabbat* by not doing business or even talking about it on *Shabbat,* implying that it is permitted to think about it. The *Sheilat Ya'avetz*[57] writes that to peruse and think about a written document is forbidden. The *Meiri*[58] writes that since the Torah was not given to angels it does not forbid one to think about one's work. The *Shemirat Shabbat KeHilchatah*[59] deduces from this *Meiri* that this is only true for abstract thinking but not when one ponders over a document.

The *Shaarei Teshuvah*[60] quotes the *Sheilat Ya'avetz* that it is forbidden to attend the operating theater in order to learn. The *Sheilat Ya'avetz*[61] also writes that one should not watch an operation on *Shabbat,* as this is strictly forbidden if the intention is to learn, since *Chazal* have ordained that one should stay away from all work and all "weekday activities." Furthermore, one may come to actually doing a *melachah.* Remember the words of the *Rambam,* who writes that "it is forbidden to study any wisdom during the *Shabbat* except that of *Hashem's* Torah," and certainly one cannot learn something that itself is forbidden on *Shabbat.* See below, *Siman* 307:17D.

(D) certainly permitted: The *Magen Avraham*[62] and the *Mishnah Berurah*[63] both rule that it is permitted to hire a non-Jew who will go many miles to notify the family of a *seriously ill patient* that they should visit him on Saturday night. This is permitted in order to prevent the patient becoming so agitated and upset that it might worsen his condition. The *Levushei Serad* (gloss on the *Shulchan Aruch*) points out that this is included within the *mitzvah* of saving life.

The *Shemirat Shabbat KeHilchatah*[64] deduces from the *Mishnah Berurah* that a Jew is permitted to transgress the sin of *"amirah lenochri"* (asking a non-Jew to do something that the Jew himself is forbidden to do) in this case, since this is a milder transgression than any of the other Rabbinic violations of the Sabbath. The *Aruch HaShulchan*[65] rules that a Jew may not violate Rabbinic laws for this purpose, since it is not part of treating the patient but only prevents the remote possibility of his condition deteriorating should his request not be carried out immediately. However, if the doctor feels

56. ישעיה נח:יג
57. סי׳ קסב
58. שבת קיג ע״ב
59. פכ״ט הערה קעה
60. ס״ק ג
61. סי׳ מא ד״ה לכן אהוב כבני
62. ס״ק ז
63. ס״ק מא
64. פל״ב הערה פב
65. סע׳ ב

that this possibility is real, then Torah laws may also be set aside, as they may be for any *seriously ill patient.* See also the *Shulchan Aruch* (*Even HaEzer*[66] and *Choshen Mishpat*[67]) that only Rabbinic law may be set aside in order to prevent the possibility that a *seriously ill patient's* condition will deteriorate if his non-medical request is not carried out immediately on *Shabbat.*

The *Tzitz Eliezer*[68] also permits the setting aside of Rabbinic law only and not of Torah law. See also the *Maharsham,*[69] *Harei Besamim,*[70] *Machazeh Avraham*[71] and *Yesodei Yeshurun,*[72] all of whom permit the setting aside of Rabbinic law only and, unlike the *Shoel U'Meshiv*[73] (who permits it even if the patient does not himself ask for his relatives), only if the patient himself requests this. See also above, *Siman* 287B.

On the other hand, one may accompany a *seriously ill patient* in an ambulance, so that he should feel calm knowing that someone is close by to help him.[74] This is permitted because it is possible that a Sabbath law is not being set aside by doing so, if the journey is within the city limits.[75] *Rav Neuwirth shlita* told me that if, for whatever reason, he cannot accompany the patient in the ambulance, and he cannot find a non-Jew to drive him, he may himself drive to the hospital. However, this is permitted only if there is a possibility that he will be able to help, for example, if he is needed to provide important details of the patient's history to the doctor.

If complying with the patient's request will lift up his spirits and strengthen him to fight his illness or help in his treatment, then one is not only permitted but obligated to do so on *Shabbat.* Thus one may turn on lights in order that the *seriously ill patient* should not be frightened of the dark,[76] or so that he be satisfied that the treatment given will be more efficient, even if he is blind (see *Siman* 330:1 for details). One may boil water if the patient asks for a hot drink, or in order to wash him and to freshen him and so relieve some of his suffering.[77]

It appears that *Chazal* differentiated between two situations which could result in the *seriously ill patient* becoming upset or agitated or would need to be calmed. In the one, there is a possibility that the resulting depression or agitation would aggravate his already serious medical condition. Here one may set aside even Torah law to prevent this. In the other, his condition would not become worse, and here only Rabbinic laws may be set aside to comply with his request. Thus the *Aruch HaShulchan*[78] rules that if the doctor feels that the patient's medical condition will be aggravated if his request is not carried out, even Torah rules may be set aside. The *Tzitz Eliezer*[79] writes that the difference in the two situations lies in the reason for the patient's request. If his request is for his bodily needs and strength, and not complying with what he believes will help him recover will indeed aggravate him to

---

66. סוסי' קלו

67. סי' רנג ובסמ"ע ס"ק ג

68. ח"ח סי' טו פ"ט

69. ח"ד סי' נד

70. ח"ב סי' קפט

71. ח"א סי' מו

72. ח"ד עמ' רמג

73. מהד"ג ח"ב סי' קפ

74. אגרות החזו"א ח"א סי' קמא. שו"ת אג"מ או"ח ח"א סי' קלב

75. אג"מ שם

76. שמירת שבת כהלכתה פל"ב סע' סג וראה במ"ב סי' רעח ס"ק ב

77. סי' של מ"ב ס"ק יג, סי' שכח שעה"צ ס"ק יא וביה"ל סוד"ה כל. שמירת שבת כהלכתה פל"ב סע' כב,כו,עב,עג ו־פא

78. סע' כ

79. ח"ח סי' טו פ"ט (עמ' קו)

SIMAN 307: THE LAWS OF *SHABBAT* THAT ARE DEPENDENT ON SPEECH

§5: A Jew may ask a non-Jew to do something for him on *Shabbat* that is Rabbinically forbidden if this is for a person who is (A)somewhat ill, if there is great need for it, or if it is for a *mitzvah*. For example, a non-Jew may be asked to bring water through a courtyard which has no *eruv,* in order to wash a patient, but there are those who forbid this.

NISHMAT AVRAHAM

the point of his condition deteriorating, Torah law may be set aside. However, if a request, such as the patient asking to have his family brought to visit him, does not concern his bodily needs and will not readily lead to his condition becoming worse, Torah law may not be set aside.

As to sending a messenger to ask a well-known righteous person to pray for a *seriously ill patient,* the *Minchat Shabbat*[80] deals extensively with the problem. The *Tzitz Eliezer*[81] and *Rav Auerbach zt"l*[82] both forbid the setting aside of any law in order to do so on *Shabbat*. See also above, *Siman* 301L.

SIMAN 307

(A) somewhat ill: The *Mishnah Berurah*[1] writes that for a *non-seriously ill patient* or someone who is in danger of losing a limb, even a Jew may, according to one opinion (see *Siman* 328:17), set aside Rabbinic law (and this is the *halachah*). One should know, however, that only where *Chazal* have explicitly stated that Rabbinic law may be set aside, may one do so. We may not apply a lenient ruling in one situation to another. Thus we see that they forbade a Jew to ask a non-Jew to do a *melachah* (asking him is a transgression of Rabbinic law by the Jew) in the case of circumcision,[2] whereas they allowed asking him when buying a house in Israel.[3]

Rav Akiva Eiger (in his gloss to this section) writes that the *Chavot Yair*[4] was uncertain as to whether there would be any problem in asking one non-Jew to ask another to do a *melachah* (making it a Rabbinic prohibition of a Rabbinic prohibition). The *Shemirat Shabbat KeHilchatah*[5] wonders whether one may ask a non-Jew to do a *melachah* in an indirect manner (also a Rabbinic prohibition of a Rabbinic prohibition) where a *mitzvah* is involved or for a person who is somewhat ill. He writes, in the name of *Rav Auerbach zt"l,* that with respect to freeing a blocked drainpipe,[6] we find those who rule that a Jew doing a *melachah* in an indirect manner is a lesser violation of Sabbath laws than asking a non-Jew to do the *melachah* in the normal manner.[7]

---

80. סי׳ פד ס״ק כט
81. ח״ח סי׳ טז פ״ח אות ז וח״ט סי׳ יז פ״ג
82. לב אברהם ח״ב עמ׳ יח
1. ס״ק כא ועיין שו״ת רמב״ן סי׳ קכג
2. סי׳ שלא סע׳ ו
3. סי׳ שו סע׳ יא
4. סי׳ מו
5. פ״ל הערה מו
6. או״ח סי׳ שלו סע׳ ט
7. תהלה לדוד סי׳ שז ס״ק ה וסי׳ שכח ס״ק נד. חזון איש סי׳ נו סוס״ק ד

GLOSS: *The Mechaber rules leniently in Siman* 587. *See also Siman* 276:3 *that there are those who even permit Torah law to be set aside*.

§17: [B]One may not study on *Shabbat* or *Yom Tov* anything except Torah, and the study of other wisdoms is forbidden, but there are [C]those who permit them. According to this [D]second opinion, one should also be permitted to use an astrolabe on *Shabbat* (*and to adjust and carry it, as in Siman* 308).

NISHMAT AVRAHAM

Even though the *halachah* is not so,[8] nevertheless this can teach us that asking a non-Jew to do a *melachah* in an indirect manner is permissible. The *Shemirat Shabbat KeHilchatah* continues that even if the non-Jew himself then does the *melachah* in the normal manner, it would be acceptable.[9] However, the *Orchot Chaim*[10] rules that asking two non-Jews to simultaneously do a *melachah* which each could do by himself (also an example of a Rabbinic prohibition of a Rabbinic prohibition) is forbidden, even though if two Jews did so, the transgression would only be Rabbinic.

(B) One may not study: This is the view of the *Rambam*.[11]

(C) those who permit: This is the view of the *Rashba* and *Ramban*.[12] The *Mishnah Berurah*[13] writes that this is the accepted ruling. However, the *Eliyah Rabbah* writes that a person who fears *Hashem* should act strictly since both the *Rambam* and the *Ran* forbid this.

(D) second opinion: According to this opinion, one may also study medical texts.[14] *Rav Auerbach zt"l*[15] rules that a doctor may certainly study medical texts and it is considered a *mitzvah*. However, he told me that a medical student must not do so, since he has no responsibility for patient care at this stage.

There is a difference of opinion among the *poskim* regarding learning as a spectator only, for example, as in the operating theater. The *Magen Avraham*,[16] the *Shulchan Aruch HaRav*[17] and the *Chelkat Yaakov*[18] permit this, whereas the *Sheilat Ya'avetz*,[19] (quoted above 306:8C) forbids it. The *Mishnah Berurah*[20] quotes the stringent view, writing that it is only permissible if by chance he happens to be there, but he forbids a planned session. Furthermore, one must be careful not to discuss the operation with the surgeon. However, *Rav Auerbach zt"l*[21] wrote to me that the stringent view only applies to a trade, but to be present in an operating theater and even discuss the details with his teacher is permitted (see

8. עיין קצוה״ש סי׳ קלד סע׳ ד ובבדה״ש ס״ק ו. וסי׳ שכח סע׳ יז וסי׳ תצו בשעה״צ ס״ק ט. וראה גם בב״י סי׳ שלד סוד״ה ומ״ש מצילין ספרים
9. אשל אברהם (בוטשאטש) סי׳ שז סע׳ ה. ועיין בביה״ל סי׳ שטז סע׳ יב ד״ה ואסור
10. סי׳ שז סוס״ק ג
11. פ׳ המשניות פרק שואל
12. שו״ת הרשב״א ח״ז סי׳ רפח שמביא את הרמב״ן
13. ס״ק סה
14. עטרת זקנים. וכן מובא בבאר היטב ס״ק כ
15. לב אברהם ח״ב עמ׳ יח
16. סי׳ שמ ס״ק ח
17. שם סוס״ק ו
18. ח״א סי׳ פד
19. סי׳ מא, מובא לעיל
20. סי׳ שמ ס״ק כא
21. לב אברהם ח״ב עמ׳ יח

SIMAN 308:
WHAT MAY OR MAY NOT BE MOVED ON *SHABBAT*

§41: A woman may help a child walk [(A)] even in a public domain provided that she does not drag him; he should be able to lift one foot after the other. In that way he will be constantly supporting himself on (at least) one foot.

NISHMAT AVRAHAM

Siman 306:8C). As to whether or not medical texts are *muktzeh*, see *Siman* 308:50.

It is forbidden to ask a non-Jew to write a second copy (using carbon paper) of lecture notes on *Shabbat*, even though what he writes is primarily for himself. One may copy his notes after *Shabbat*.[22] It is, however, permitted to ask him to write two copies for himself and then buy one from him after *Shabbat*.[23]

SIMAN 308

(A) even in a public domain: For even if she were to carry him she would only be violating Rabbinic law and so *Chazal* did not decree that she cannot take him out walking. *Chazal* use the expression "a living person carries himself." Since it is well known that it is easier to carry a live person than a corpse, it is as if the carried person assists in being carried. It is as if both are carrying the same object, making the prohibition a Rabbinic one even in a *public domain* since each could have done so by himself.[1] The *Tosafot,*[2] however, argue against this. They feel that since no live animals needed to be carried in order to build the *Mishkan*, carrying live animals on *Shabbat* cannot be forbidden by the Torah (all thirty-nine *melachot* are tasks needed in building the *Mishkan*). The *Tosafot* equate carrying an animal with carrying a human being. However, their view is not the one accepted in practice.

The above *halachah* only holds true if the child can, albeit with difficulty, walk on his own. However, if one carries a sick person or cripple, who cannot walk on his or her own, in a *public domain*, he violates Torah law.[3] Similarly, Torah law would also forbid carrying a baby who cannot walk at all, in a *public domain*.[4]

Based on the above, the *Shemirat Shabbat KeHilchatah*[5] rules that a sick child who can walk on his own, but with difficulty, may be carried in a *public domain* in order to receive medical care. Since the child is considered to be *non-seriously ill*, a Rabbinic prohibition may be set aside for his health. In a *carmelit*, even a sick baby who cannot yet walk may be carried for this purpose.[6] However, one must be careful that the child does not hold in his hand or put in his pocket anything that is not necessary for his treatment. On the other hand, if the child is frightened, he

22. שו״ת מנחת יצחק ח״ה סי׳ לו

23. שמעתי ממו״ר הגרי״י נויבירט שליט״א מהא דאו״ח סי׳ תמח סע׳ ד ומ״ב ס״ק כג, ארחות חיים סי׳ שז ס״ק ה

1. רש״י שבת צג ע״ב ד״ה את. תוספות רא״ש שם צד ע״א

2. שם תוסד״ה שהחי. ועיין בתוס׳ שם קל ע״א ד״ה רבי וע״ע תוס׳ ב״מ עט ע״ב ד״ה השתא

3. מ״ב ס״ק קנג

4. מ״ב ס״ק קנד

5. פי״ח סע׳ נא

6. וראה בשו״ת אג״מ ח״ד או״ח סי׳ צא. וראה בחכמת שלמה כאן ובשו״ת אלף לך שלמה סי׳ קמו

§50: The *Rashba* permits one to move an astrolabe and books of secular subjects (inside the house), whereas according to the (B)*Rambam* this would be questionable.

SIMAN 311:

THE LAWS CONCERNING A CORPSE ON *SHABBAT*

§2: (A)A corpse that is malodorous and thereby a dishonor to the dead while at the same time disgracing the living,

NISHMAT AVRAHAM

may hold a toy to pacify him. If the patient is *seriously ill*, he may be carried through a *public domain* in order to receive medical attention.[7]

When one may carry a sick child to a doctor, he may also take him in a baby carriage (pram), since it has no status of its own and is considered as an additional subsidiary to the child.[8] One must, however, try, wherever possible, not to carry them separately, for example, when going down stairs. Furthermore, everything which is not for the benefit of the child's health must be removed from the baby carriage.[9] Wherever possible, it would be best if the baby carriage were pushed by two Jews simultaneously,[10] or, preferably, by a non-Jew.[11]

(B) Rambam this would be questionable: This opinion, that one is forbidden, on *Shabbat*, to study anything other than Torah, is the ruling of the *Shulchan Aruch* and has been discussed earlier (*Siman* 307:17). By this view books on non-Torah subjects may not be moved, as they would be *muktzeh*. However the *Gra* rules that even according to this opinion, it would be permissible to move them. The *Gra* himself rules like the *Rashba* that one may study other wisdoms on *Shabbat*.[12]

SIMAN 311

(A) A corpse: A corpse is *muktzeh* and therefore may not be moved, nor may any of its limbs be moved.[1] Thus the eyes may not be closed nor the limbs straightened out.[2] However, where it has become customary to do this so that the limbs should not become set in an awkward position thereby dishonoring the corpse, they should be allowed to continue to do so. Nevertheless, where possible, the limbs should be straightened out in an indirect manner, for example, by placing a pillow or garment on the limb and using it, rather than directly straightening the limb.[3] A bandage may be tied around the jaw and head (using a knot and bow and not a double knot) to prevent an open jaw from dropping further open, but it should not be used to close it.[4]

Since the corpse is *mukzteh*, its clothes may not be changed for shrouds.[5] How-

7. עיין שמירת שבת כהלכתה פי"ח הערה ריא בשם הגרש"ז אויערבאך זצ"ל
8. שבת צג ע"ב
9. שמירת שבת כהלכתה שם
10. שם הערה ריב
11. שם פל"ח סע' כח
12. מ"ב ס"ק קסד
1. כאן סע' א
2. סע' ז
3. מ"ב ס"ק כב
4. שם
5. הגרש"ז אויערבאך לב אברהם ח"ב עמ' כא

GLOSS: *there are those who say that even if it does not have an odor yet but there will be one soon,*

may be moved out of the house into a *carmelit*. If, however, the people in the house have somewhere else to stay, they should move out, rather than move the corpse. There are those who say that a corpse may only be moved if another object is placed on it and carried out with it.

NISHMAT AVRAHAM

ever, if the clothes are soiled, and thus dishonor the dead person if left on, they may be changed for shrouds.[6] If the corpse is soiled with blood, for example, one may wash it using plastic or rubber gloves or a plastic cloth but not absorbent cotton, a sponge or washcloth.[7] Infusions, needles, catheters and the like may be removed.[8]

In a hospital, since the bed will be needed for the next admission, the corpse may be moved out of the ward, after placing an object that is not *mukzteh* on it or on the bed to be carried out together with it. If this is not possible, and the corpse is still clad in his own clothes, one may take the lenient position and move it without another object.[9] The corpse may be moved out through a *carmelit* but not through a *public domain*.[10]

Jews should preferably close the eyes, straighten the limbs, wash the corpse, put on the shrouds and move the corpse[11] even if non-Jews are available.[12] However, nothing which is Torah forbidden may be done by a Jew. On the other hand, a nurse may ask a non-Jew to remove the deceased from the ward to the hospital mortuary, even if he will use the elevator or do *melachot* which are forbidden by the Torah, since he does so for his own convenience and benefit.[13]

If the corpse is to be moved out of the ward and hospital by non-Jews, a Jew should, if possible, accompany them even if they use the elevator.[14]

A *Cohen* may not remain under the same roof as a corpse.[15] Thus if, on *Shabbat*, someone dies at home where a *Cohen* also lives, the corpse may be taken out only by non-Jews.[16] However, if the *Cohen* is ill and cannot leave the house, the corpse may be taken out through a *carmelit* even by Jews, after putting an object that is not itself *muktzeh* on the bed.[17]

6. שמעתי ממו״ר הגרי״י נויבירט שליט״א

7. שמירת שבת כהלכתה פס״ד סע׳ ט

8. שם

9. סע׳ ד מ״ב ס״ק טז וביה״ל ד״ה יש

10. שו״ע

11. כי זה הוא כבודו של המת שיהודי יעשה את כל הדברים האלה – שמעתי ממו״ר הגרי״י נויבירט שליט״א

12. כף החיים כאן ס״ק לג. סי׳ תקכו סע׳ א ומ״ב ס״ק ט. שמירת שבת כהלכתה פס״ד סע׳ יב

13. שמעתי ממו״ר הגרי״י נויבירט שליט״א מהא דמ״ב סי׳ רעו ס״ק כז. וראה במ״ב כאן ס״ק יב בשם הא״ר וכף החיים ס״ק כח וסי׳ תקכו סע׳ א ומ״ב ס״ק ו שמתירים לבקש מגוי לעשות איסורי תורה בשביל כבוד המת

14. מעשה רב שראיתי עם מו״ר הגרי״י נויבירט שליט״א

15. יו״ד סי׳ שעב סע׳ א ברמ״א

16. ראה הערה 13

17. מג״א סוס״ק יד. שמירת שבת כהלכתה פס״ד סע׳ יד

SIMAN 313:
ASSEMBLING MANY PARTS TO MAKE A WHOLE

§6: It is forbidden to reassemble and tighten a bed [(A)]made up of parts on *Shabbat*. Such an act would have required the bringing of a sin-offering in the Temple. However, if the bed is (*usually*) **loosely assembled, one may reassemble it on *Shabbat*** (*provided that he does not do so firmly*).

NISHMAT AVRAHAM

SIMAN 313

(A) made up of parts: This *halachah* applies to the assembling of needles with syringes on *Shabbat* and their use for a *non-seriously ill* patient. Needles and syringes are usually packaged separately and the appropriate syringe and needle are assembled immediately prior to use. There are three types of needles and syringes:

1) Both the needle and syringe can be reused after sterilization.

2) Only the needle or syringe may be reused; the non-reusable piece is discarded once used.

3) Both the needle and syringe are for single use only and commonly discarded as a single unit after use.

Rav Auerbach zt"l[1] ruled that the law of the *Shulchan Aruch* permitting reassembly on *Shabbat* was true even if the individual pieces were of no intrinsic value themselves. Therefore, on *Shabbat*, one may use the first two types for a *non-seriously ill patient*[2] even though the needle and the syringe are each of no use without the other. The *Tzitz Eliezer*[3] and *Rav Ovadiah Yosef shlita*[4] also permit the use of the first two types of syringes. The *Shulchan Aruch HaRav* explains[5] that the assembling of items on *Shabbat* is only prohibited if it will definitely not be dismantled on *Shabbat*. Therefore, according to the *Shulchan Aruch HaRav,* there would not even be a violation of a Rabbinic prohibition in assembling such a needle and syringe on *Shabbat* for a *non-seriously ill patient* since it will be dismantled after use. This is also the opinion of the *Chelkat Yaakov*[6] and the *Ben Ish Chai.*[7]

It would appear that the third type, the single-use needle-syringe composite may not be assembled on *Shabbat.* For the law forbids binding the *lulav* together with the *hadassim* and *aravot* on *Yom Tov* of the first day of *Succot*. This, though the knot has a temporary status; it is for the duration of the Festival only. Yet because the *lulav* will be discarded after the Festival with the *hadassim* and *aravot* as a single unit, the knot is *halachically* a "permanent" one, and may not be tied on *Shabbat* or *Yom Tov*. The syringe-needle is not dismantled after use but disposed of as is. Thus its assembly has a "permanence" like the tying together of the *lulav*, *hadassim* and *aravot*.[8]

1. שמירת שבת כהלכתה פל״ג סע׳ ט הערה מג
2. שם סע׳ ט
3. חי״ג סי׳ מו. ועיין גם בלב אברהם ח״ב עמ׳ כו
4. שו״ת יחוה דעת ח״ב סי׳ נו
5. כאן סע׳ כא
6. ח״ג סי׳ קיג
7. שנה ב פ׳ ויקהל סע׳ ה
8. הגרש״ז אויערבאך זצ״ל בשמירת שבת כהלכתה שם הערה מג בשם החזו״א סי׳ נ ס״ק ט ד״ה והא דכתבו. וכ״כ בלב אברהם ח״ב עמ׳ כ. וראה שו״ת ציץ אליעזר חי״ד סי׳ כז ס״ק ה שחולק בדעת החזו״א, וכ״כ בלב אברהם שם עמ׳ כו

SIMAN 316: TRAPPING ON SHABBAT

§7: [A]Catching a snake or other harmful reptile on *Shabbat* to prevent them from biting someone is permissible. However, if he does so for their medicinal properties he is culpable by Torah law.

NISHMAT AVRAHAM

However, the *Maharil Diskin*[9] rules that one does not transgress a *melachah* by tying a permanent knot on *Shabbat* which he will not undo on *Shabbat*, even though when he has no further use for it, he will discard it as is. He explains that a knotted rope that one has no further use for lacks the status of permanency even though it remains knotted indefinitely. As proof, he quotes the *Talmud*[10] which states that *Chazal* decreed that a red band be tied to the horns of the *sa'ir la'azazel* on *Yom Kippur* before it was pushed into the ravine. Since the knot remained long after *Yom Kippur*, it should have been forbidden by Torah law as a permanent knot. Therefore, the *Maharil Diskin* concludes that any knot made on *Shabbat* and left that way after the person no longer requires it, is not a "permanent" knot.

On the other hand, *Rashi*[11] explains that one is forbidden to tie a knot around a *lulav* on *Yom Tov* because it is considered permanent since the *lulav* will be discarded after *Succot* without being untied.

Rav Auerbach zt"l clarifies the difference between the tying of the *lulav* and the assembling of the single-use needle-syringe.[12] The *lulav* must be bound to the *hadassim* and *aravot* either because of the Biblical imperative of beautifying a *mitzvah*[13] or because of a unique ruling that necessitates the *lulav* being joined to the *hadassim* and *aravot*.[14] Thus the knot itself is the goal, without thought as to what will happen to it after *Succot*. On the other hand, when a needle is attached to a syringe, it is done to give the injection and then be discarded. Thus there is no Torah violation of a *melachah* in the use of such a needle and syringe for a *non-seriously ill patient*.[15]

See too the *responsa* of *Rav Weiss zt"l*[16] and *Rav Auerbach zt"l*.[17]

As to the different types of injections (i.e. subcutaneous, intravenous, etc.) see *Siman* 316B.

If any part of a stethoscope becomes completely detached from another it may not be re-attached, and another stethoscope should be used.[18]

SIMAN 316

(A) Catching a snake: One who was bitten by a snake, scorpion (or any dangerous reptile), but managed to kill it should bring it to the hospital even through a *public domain*, so that appropriate treatment can be given on its identification.

9. קונטרס אחרון אות לה
10. יומא סז ע״א
11. סוכה לג ע״ב ד״ה הותר אגדו
12. שמירת שבת כהלכתה ח״ג פל״ה הערה סג
13. זה א־לי ואנוהו – שמות טו:ב
14. מחלוקת רבי יהודה ורבנן סוכה לג ע״א
15. שמעתי מהגרש״ז אויערבאך זצ״ל. וכן פוסק הציץ אליעזר חט״ז סי׳ טו
16. נשמת אברהם כרך א עמ׳ שנה
17. שם עמ׳ שסב
18. שו״ע כאן וראה בביה״ל ד״ה דרכה – שמעתי ממו״ר הגרי״י נויבירט שליט״א

§8: Torah law forbids trapping one of the eight reptiles mentioned in the Torah or causing them any injury that will [(B)]cause them to bleed, even if the bleeding appears as a bruise only.

NISHMAT AVRAHAM

(B) cause them to bleed: Most *rishonim*[1] rule that drawing blood from a patient on *Shabbat* is forbidden by Torah law, no matter how small the amount.[2] It is therefore forbidden to draw blood from a patient who is *not seriously ill* even by pricking a finger. This also holds true for blood drawn from a corpse.[3] If, however, the deceased's diagnosis and cause of death are unknown and examination of his blood or a biopsy of one or more of his organs may help to diagnose and treat another *seriously ill patient*, currently in the department, with the same signs and symptoms, this is permissible.[4]

One may draw blood from a *seriously ill patient* on *Shabbat* even if the results will not be available for a few days (e.g. for blood cultures). But, such a patient who needs blood tests including arterial blood gases, should have all his tests done on a single arterial puncture and not have both an arterial as well as a venous puncture, since each is considered a separate *melachah*.[5] Additional blood for routine testing may not be drawn unless as part of the same procedure. Thus when using a "vacutainer," the tube may be allowed to fill completely even though not all the blood is required for urgent testing and the rest would be used (after *Shabbat*) for routine tests. However, when a syringe is used, only the amount required for urgent testing may be drawn.[6] A non-Jew should be asked to fill in the request form for the lab. If a non-Jew is not available, the doctor should do so, writing only what is absolutely necessary and using his left hand (if he is right-handed).

SERIOUSLY ILL PATIENT: A patient who is possibly *seriously ill* may be examined as necessary on *Shabbat*, including examination of the throat, ears and fundus [see below, *Siman* 378D(i)]. X-ray examination (including CT and MRI), sonography (ultrasound), vascular studies (Duplex, angiography), and all other investigations must be done on *Shabbat* if urgently needed. All urgent endoscopies must be performed. If photographic documentation is necessary for diagnosis or follow-up, this is permitted. Developing the film must be left till after *Shabbat* unless required immediately. Photography is not permitted where done for teaching purposes only.

A patient with neurological signs may have a spinal tap (lumbar puncture). Similarly, an abscess associated with systemic signs may be drained.

NON-SERIOUSLY ILL PATIENT: Physical examination including pulse, blood pressure (using a non-electronic sphygmomanometer) and temperature may be performed even for a *non-seriously ill patient.* No examination or investigation involving the desecration of *Shabbat* may be performed. Ascites, pleural effusion or joint-fluid may be tapped on *Shabbat* for diagnosis or treatment, even from a *non-*

1. רש״י חולין מו ע״ב, רמב״ן רשב״א ריטב״א ומאירי שבת קז ע״א, תוס׳ שבת עה ע״א ד״ה כי וקז ע״א ד״ה שמנה ותוס׳ ריד שבת קו ע״א. ראה ביה״ל ד״ה החובל ומ״ב ס״ק ל
2. מחמת נטילת נשמה שבאותו מקום שחבל, כי הדם הוא הנפש
3. א״א ס״ק טו וסי׳ שלא מ״ז ס״ק א
4. הגרש״ז אויערבאך זצ״ל לב אברהם ח״ב פ״כ סע׳ ה
5. שמירת שבת כהלכתה פ״מ סע׳ כז
6. שמעתי ממו״ר הגרי״י נויבירט שליט״א

NISHMAT AVRAHAM

seriously ill patient since the fluid is considered to be "isolated" from the circulation.[7]

INJECTIONS. Since a subcutaneous or intramuscular injection is not meant to draw blood or cause bruising, it is permitted even for a *non-seriously ill patient.*[8] However, there is no consensus among the *poskim* with regard to intravenous injections. Since one usually withdraws blood into the syringe to make sure that a vein has been cleanly entered before injection, this is forbidden except for a *seriously ill patient.*[9] On the other hand, the *Tzitz Eliezer*[10] rules that since the blood is not used for itself but is a means of making sure that one has entered a vein, this is only forbidden by Rabbinic law and is therefore permitted even for a *non-seriously ill patient.*

One may not insert an intravenous line in a *non-seriously ill patient* to have an "open vein" in case of an emergency, unless one is expected. If a vein is already cannulated, intravenous fluids and injections may be given, even to a *non-seriously ill patient.* (see also *Siman* 313A and *Siman* 328 §17(I).

It is permissible to tear the wrapping off a syringe, medication, IV fluids, gloves etc., including tearing on a perforation. The *melachah* of "cutting to measure" does not apply here since one is not interested where he actually tears and the perforations are there only to make tearing easier.[11] If possible, one should tear between words[12] and not through print.[13] Before an injection, the skin should not be swabbed with absorbent cotton or gauze soaked in alcohol, iodine or other disinfectant, even if it is held by forceps and even if soaked before *Shabbat* because of the *melachah* of "squeezing." One should preferably use nylon (non-absorbent) swabs. If these are not available, the fluid should be poured onto the appropriate part of the body and wiped off with absorbent cotton or gauze[14] (see *Siman* 320A).

A *seriously ill patient* with severe pain may be given intravenous narcotics since whatever may reduce suffering or calm such a patient is included in the duty to save life.[15]

A patient who has difficulty with erection may be taught to inject drugs into his corpora cavernosa (two chambers in the penis which run the length of the organ and are filled with spongy tissue containing blood. A greater amount of blood flows in and fills the open spaces in the spongy tissue to create an erection). Since the area is rich in blood, the injection can be made without the need to first draw blood to make sure that a vein has been entered. Therefore this may be done on Friday night in order to perform the *mitzvah* of having relations with his wife regardless of whether or not he already has children. The non-functioning of any organ falls into the category of *a danger to a limb*[16] and a Jew may do anything for such a patient that would otherwise be forbidden by Rabbinic law, even if he does so in the normal fashion.[17] Since blood does not

---

7. שמעתי ממו״ר הגרי״י נויבירט שליט״א
8. שמירת שבת כהלכתה פל״ג סע׳ ז
9. שמירת שבת כהלכתה פל״ב סע׳ נח והערה קנא בשם הגר״י אברמסקי זצ״ל. הגרש״ז אויערבאך זצ״ל מובא בשו״ת ציץ אליעזר ח״ט סי׳ יז פ״ב ס״ק כ (לו) וח״י סי׳ כה
10. ח״ח סי׳ טו פי״ד, ח״ט סי׳ יז פ״ב, ח״י סי׳ כה פ״א וחי״ג סי׳ מה
11. שמעתי מהגרש״ז אויערבאך זצ״ל. וראה בשמירת שבת כהלכתה פ״ט הערה כה
12. שמירת שבת כהלכתה פ״ט הערה מח
13. שם פל״ג סע׳ ד ופ״ט סע׳ ד
14. שם פל״ג סע׳ י
15. שמעתי מהגרש״ז אויערבאך זצ״ל. וראה בשמירת שבת כהלכתה פל״ב סע׳ ב
16. קצות השולחן סי׳ קלח בבדה״ש סוס״ק יח. שמירת שבת כהלכתה פל״ג סע׳ א ס״ק ה בהערה
17. או״ח סי׳ שכח בדעת השלישת ומ״ב ס״ק מט ו־נז

SIMAN 318: COOKING ON *SHABBAT*

§2: A healthy person or a non-seriously ill patient may not eat on *Shabbat* from food that was (A)cooked on that *Shabbat* for a seriously ill patient (*nor may he benefit from any other usually forbidden act*), since there is a possibility

NISHMAT AVRAHAM

need to be withdrawn from the vein before the injection, the injection itself will be classified, according to all the above authorities, as a Rabbinic prohibition only[18] and would therefore be permitted.

SIMAN 318

(A) cooked: It is permitted to cook on *Shabbat* for a *seriously ill* patient who needs hot food in order to strengthen and fortify him,[1] if such food is not available or is not fresh enough for him.[2] Similarly, it is permissible to boil water[3] on *Shabbat* for drinks or for a bath if hot water is not available.[4] This is so even if a neighbor has hot food or water available, if asking for them will cause the neighbor hardship, for example, if he is asleep and must be awakened, or if he will be left without hot water or hot food on *Shabbat*.[5] Even according to the opinion that *Shabbat* is only "set aside" as opposed to "nullified" for a *seriously ill* patient, there is no obligation for anyone to undergo hardship except in the process of saving life; there is, on the other hand, no need for hardship in order to avoid doing a *melachah* which has been *halachically* permitted. This is similar to the *halachah* that one may kill another who is about to commit armed robbery on a neighbor, without any obligation to first try and buy him off. Even if *Shabbat* is only "set aside" and not "nullified," nevertheless, because of the importance of saving life, it has been almost treated as "nullified" in most cases. There is also the concern that there will be those who may not wish to tend to a *seriously ill* patient if they may have to give him of their own food or drink in order to avoid doing a *halachically* permissible *melachah* on *Shabbat*.[6] See also *Tzitz Eliezer*.[7]

One must only cook the amount necessary for the patient. More food than necessary may not be added, even to the same pot and even if this is done before the pot is put on the fire or the fire lit. However, if time is of the essence, one need not be exact. Similarly, if only a large pot is available, and the pot would spoil if only the small amount required for the patient is cooked, such that there would also not be any hot food for the patient, one may cook as much as necessary to avoid this, to ensure that hot food be available for the patient.[8]

When cooking for a *seriously ill* patient, one should preferably use an electric rather than a gas stove, since a match or other lighter must first be lit for the gas stove, whereas with the electric stove

---

18. ראה שמירת שבת כהלכתה פל״ב הערה קנא
1. עיין ביה״ל סי׳ שכח סע׳ ד סוד״ה כל
2. עיין מ״ב סי׳ של ס״ק יג
3. שעה״צ סי׳ שכח ס״ק א
4. שמירת שבת כהלכתה פל״ב סע׳ עב
5. שם סע׳ עד
6. שם הערה קסו בשם הגרש״ז אויערבאך זצ״ל. מנחת שלמה ח״א סי׳ ז
7. ח״ח סי׳ טו סוף פי״א מובא בשמירת שבת כהלכתה שם הערה קפט
8. שמירת שבת כהלכתה שם סע׳ עה

that more than is necessary for the patient would be deliberately cooked.

NISHMAT AVRAHAM

there is only one act of lighting.[9] If, however, a pilot light is already burning in the gas stove, there is no difference between the stoves.

As to the use of a microwave oven, *Rav Moshe Feinstein zt"l*[10] rules that its use on *Shabbat* is forbidden by Torah law since this is now an accepted manner of cooking even though there is no fire.[11] On the other hand, *Rav Shlomo Zalman Auerbach zt"l*[12] rules that its use in such a situation is not forbidden by Torah law.

Even a *non-seriously ill patient* may not partake of leftover food or drink that has been cooked by a Jew on *Shabbat* for a *seriously ill* patient, unless he has no food or drink and a non-Jew is not available to cook for him (see below).[13] The food may be tasted to make sure that it is palatable.[14] After *Shabbat*, even a healthy person may eat of the leftover food and the pot remains in its previous "kosher" status (see below).[15] If, however, Sunday was a Festival, a healthy person may not eat this food; the water boiled on the *Shabbat* may be drunk on the Festival after it has been allowed to cool.[16]

If the patient became ill, and seriously so, on *Shabbat*, and the food in its original uncooked state was inedible,[17] for example, if it was meat, fish or potatoes, then it is *muktzeh* and may not be moved even after cooking, except for the patient.[18] However, leftovers may be disposed of or put in the refrigerator if leaving them out would attract flies and other insects. However, if the patient was already ill before *Shabbat*, the food may be moved even if not for the patient.[19]

A Jew may heat water for a *seriously ill* patient, if a hot bath or wash would strengthen him and increase his well-being, if hot water is not available or there is no non-Jew to do so.[20] This is so even if his condition would not deteriorate without the bath. If possible, one should heat the water to the required temperature so that the patient may wash or bathe without needing to add cold water, even though this requires the heating of a larger quantity of water.[21]

If hot water is not available, it is also permissible to put on an electric boiler even though much more water is heated than is necessary for the patient's needs.[22] Water may be drawn from an electric boiler even though cold water will inevitably enter the tank in its place. If the patient is to have a bath, the hot-water faucet of the bathtub may be closed. However, if he is to be washed, it may not be closed since this will result in the cold water in the tank being heated. If there is a possibility that the patient may require more hot water that *Shabbat*, the hot-water faucet may be closed.[23]

If a non-Jew was asked to boil the water and a full kettle is on the stove, there is no

9. שם סע׳ עו
10. שו״ת אג״מ או״ח ח״ג סי׳ נב
11. וצ״ע מהמג״א סי׳ שא ס״ק נז ושמירת שבת כהלכתה פ״א הערה קכז
12. שמעתי מפיו
13. שו״ת רשב״א ח״א סי׳ תתיד. מ״ב ס״ק יב. שמירת שבת כהלכתה פל״ב הערה ר
14. מ״ב ס״ק יא
15. מ״ב ס״ק יא. שמירת שבת כהלכתה שם סע׳ עח
16. מ״ב ס״ק ה. שמירת שבת כהלכתה שם הערה רב
17. כף החיים ס״ק כח
18. סי׳ שכח מ״ב ס״ק נח
19. מ״ב ס״ק טו. שמירת שבת כהלכתה שם סע׳ עט
20. כתב לי מו״ר הגרי״י נויבירט שליט״א
21. שמירת שבת כהלכתה פל״ב סע׳ פא
22. שם סע׳ פב
23. שם

GLOSS: *Even if a non-Jew cooked, it may not be used on the Sabbath.*

NISHMAT AVRAHAM

need to first pour out the water that is in excess of the patient's needs, before he lights the flame. If the non-Jew was to fill the kettle, *Rav Auerbach zt"l* told me that he should be asked to fill it only as needed for the patient. A healthy person may not have any benefit from the excess water on *Shabbat.*

The gas or electricity may not be extinguished or decreased after the food or drink has been cooked.[24]

A non-Jew may be asked to turn on an electric boiler, draw water from it or boil water for a *non-seriously ill* patient who requires a hot drink or bath.[25] See also *Siman* 328(19A).

TRAVELING: A doctor may drive his own car (if he cannot find a cab with a non-Jewish driver) to visit a *seriously ill* patient, driving as he would on a weekday.[26] He should have, before *Shabbat*, neutralized the internal light that normally turns on when the door is opened. If this was not done, and there is time, he should do so after having shut the car door.[27] All essential documents such as driving license, insurance etc., may be carried into the car, even where there is no *eruv*, but this should be done in an indirect manner (under the hat, between his shirt and his vest, or inside his shoe). Having reached the patient's home or the hospital, the car keys and papers must be left in the car. If, however, there is a real possibility that leaving the keys in the car would lead to the car being stolen, they may be removed (in an indirect manner, for example, between two fingers) and carried in an indirect manner (as above) even though there is no *eruv*. This is so even if removing the keys from the switch results in dashboard lights or other lights being switched off.[28] If there is an *eruv,* the car key may be carried in the usual manner if it also opens the car door.[29] Car lights may not be extinguished at the end of the journey, unless there is a possibility that the doctor will not be able to travel again that *Shabbat* to help another *seriously ill* patient because of a used-up battery. The car motor should not be turned off if in so doing dashboard and other lights will also be extinguished. If leaving the motor running may give rise to a dangerous situation, such as the possibility of a child entering the car with the motor running, it may be turned off in an indirect manner (e.g. grasping the key between two fingers).[30] A doctor may travel to or from hospital duty or to treat a *non-seriously ill* patient in a car driven by a non-Jew, if the distance is too great for walking.[31] A doctor who lives close to the hospital and is due to come on duty on *Shabbat* morning, may nevertheless spend *Shabbat* eve away from home and be driven to his resident duty by a non-Jew. He may not, however, travel to a point that is more than 11½ km. from the city limits. Similarly, he may not live more than 11½ km. from the city limits and come into the city for resident duty on the *Shabbat*, even

---

24. שמירת שבת כהלכתה שם סע׳ לז
25. שו״ע סי׳ שכח סע׳ יז ברמ״א
26. שמעתי מהגרש״ז אויערבאך זצ״ל
27. ראה בשמירת שבת כהלכתה פ״מ סע׳ נד
28. סופו משום תחילתו באיסור דרבנן, כ״כ לי מו״ר הגרי״י נויבירט שליט״א
29. שמירת שבת כהלכתה פ״כ סע׳ עז. ועיין שם סע׳ פג והערה ער
30. מנחת שלמה ח״ב סי׳ כט,א ד״ה והנה ושם סי׳ ל. שמעתי ממו״ר הגרי״י נויבירט שליט״א. וראה בשמירת שבת כהלכתה פ״מ סע׳ נח־ס
31. ראה שמירת שבת כהלכתה פל״ח סע׳ יג ופ״מ סע׳ כב. וראה נשמת אברהם כרך א סי׳ שכט ס״ק ז (עמ׳ רכג) וכרך ד חאו״ח סי׳ שכט ס״ק א (עמ׳ מד)

NISHMAT AVRAHAM

if driven by a non-Jew.[32] On the other hand, an attending doctor on call may stay outside $11\frac{1}{2}$ km. of the city limits on *Shabbat* or even move to live there, since it is not at all certain that if called he would necessarily have to come in, and even then, it would only be for a *seriously ill* patient. Once he has come in, however, he may not return home even if driven there by a non-Jew.[33] It is preferable to travel, when essential, using a non-Jewish driver, who can also be asked to carry into and out of the car all that the doctor needs in order to treat the patient. One should try and arrange that the driver receive payment after *Shabbat,* even if this means that he is given a handsome tip for his willingness. If, however, he refuses to wait, he should be given an appropriate article as a pledge. If this is not practicable, or he refuses, he may be paid but no change or receipt should be requested.[34] A doctor who drove to visit a *seriously ill* patient may not drive home on *Shabbat*, unless there is a good possibility that he will be needed again at home to treat another *seriously ill* patient.[35] If, however, he was driven there by a non-Jew, he may return home with him, even if only for his convenience, provided he is still within the city precincts.[36] The doctor who is likely to need to drive on *Shabbat* should attempt to deal with a non-Jewish car or taxi service which will undertake to provide immediate service and be willing to receive payment after *Shabbat*. See also *Siman* 329E regarding driving back home.

A patient may be driven to a particular hospital that has his records or which he prefers (for medical but not for financial reasons), even though it is further away than the local hospital.[37] After the patient has left the car, one may not drive any further even if the car is in a "no-parking zone," and will result in a fine. On the other hand, if this might lead to a traffic hazard or prevent another *seriously ill* patient from being brought to the hospital or emergency room, the car must be moved away sufficiently to avoid this. If possible, it should be pushed rather than driven out of the way.[38] A family member or anyone else whom the patient trusts may accompany him to hospital, even if there is already someone present who can render necessary aid and even if the patient does not request this.[39] If there is no room in the car and one may be of help to the patient at the hospital (for example in providing essential information to the receiving doctor), he may drive there in his own car.[40] The patient may take whatever may be necessary for his treatment or well-being to the hospital.[41] If the car enters a courtyard (where there is an *eruv*) at the patient's home and at the hospital, he may take with him whatever he wishes.[42] Where there is no *eruv* the articles must be carried in an indirect manner (as above). The driver or the accompanying person may not return home by any means that involves setting aside *Shabbat* laws.[43]

32. כתב לי מו״ר הגרי״י נויבירט שליט״א, כי הרי לדעת הרמב״ם יש איסור תורה לצאת מחוץ לי״ב מיל

33. שמעתי ממו״ר שליט״א

34. שמעתי ממו״ר שליט״א. וראה בשמירת שבת כהלכתה פל״ח סע׳ יג

35. שמירת שבת כהלכתה פ״מ סע׳ סט. וראה נשמת אברהם כרך ד חאו״ח סי׳ שכט ס״ק א (עמ׳ מד) בשם הגרש״ז אויערבאך זצ״ל והשו״ת אג״מ או״ח ח״ד סי׳ פ

36. שמירת שבת כהלכתה שם

37. שם סע׳ נא

38. שם פל״ב סע׳ נז

39. שם פ״מ סע׳ נז

40. שמעתי ממו״ר שליט״א. וראה בנשמת אברהם כרך ד חאו״ח סי׳ שו ס״ק א (עמ׳ כט)

41. שמירת שבת כהלכתה פ״מ סע׳ ע

42. הגרש״ז אויערבאך זצ״ל שם פל״ו הערה יח

43. כי לא מצינו בש״ס דחוששין על ישראל שיימנע מהצלת נפש (ואין כאן ההיתר של סופו משום תחילתו כדי שלא להכשילן לעתיד לבא), הגרש״ז אויערבאך זצ״ל נשמת אברהם כרך ד חאו״ח סי׳ שכט ס״ק א (עמ׳ מה)

NISHMAT AVRAHAM

If one has to travel to bring essential medication for a *seriously ill* patient, it is preferable, if time is not of the essence, to use public transportation (where the driver is a non-Jew). If the medication needs to be brought through a *public domain* and there is no *eruv*, it should be carried, where practical, in an indirect manner.[44]

It is preferable to telephone for a cab driven by a non-Jew rather than drive one's own car for a *seriously ill* patient. With the use of the cab *Shabbat* laws are set aside only once (making the telephone call), whereas with the use of the car, they are continuously set aside as a result of repeated combustion during driving.[45] However, if time is even only probably of the essence, the patient should be driven immediately to the hospital without waiting for a non-Jewish driver. Since it is permissible to telephone for an ambulance or cab to take a *seriously ill* patient to the hospital, there is no obligation to trouble a Jewish neighbor to do so in his car, if he must be awakened to drive, or if driving may cause him to be unable to return home on *Shabbat*.[46] A *seriously ill* woman who must travel to the hospital may do so even if she will be alone in the car at night with a driver who is not a relative, if the hospital is in the city, or the journey is along a well-used highway. If, however, there is no alternative but to use a deserted highway, she may still do so even though there is no close member of the family to accompany her.[47]

A *non-seriously ill* patient who is discharged from the hospital or emergency room on *Shabbat* and cannot stay in the hospital and be provided with his needs, nor can he walk home, may return home with a non-Jewish driver if it is within the city limits.[48] He should ask the non-Jew to carry whatever he needs. The same applies to a person who is accompanying a *seriously ill* patient to the hospital on *Shabbat* and who must return home.[49] A *non-seriously ill* patient who badly needs treatment on *Shabbat* in a clinic or emergency room and cannot get there on foot, may travel there with a non-Jewish driver either by flagging down a cab — in the Diaspora — or by asking a non-Jew to telephone for one. If there is no *eruv* he may ask the driver to carry whatever he needs for his treatment.[50] A non-Jew may be asked to carry a sick child who is *not seriously ill* through a *public domain* or to drive him to receive medical attention.[51] A non-Jew may be asked to telephone a non-Jewish doctor, to drive a patient to him or to purchase medication that he requires that *Shabbat*. A patient with a severe toothache may go to a non-Jewish dentist to receive treatment. If there is the possibility of an infection then even a Jewish dentist may be contacted.[52]

As to payment, one must attempt to persuade the driver to receive payment after *Shabbat* (even if this means adding a handsome tip). If this fails, he should try to persuade him to take an article as a pledge. If this is not available or if the driver refuses and there is no non-Jewish neighbor who would be willing to pay him, he may show the driver where his purse is and let him take his fee. If this is not practical, he may pay him but may

44. שמירת שבת כהלכתה פל״ב סע׳ נד
45. שם פ״מ סע׳ סט והערה קמט
46. הגרש״ז אויערבאך זצ״ל שם סע׳ עב
47. שמעתי ממ״ר שליט״א. וראה במנחת שלמה ח״א סי׳ צא אות כא, מובא בנשמת אברהם כרך ג חאהע״ז סי׳ כב ס״ק א (עמ׳ צח). וראה היטב בשו״ת אג״מ יו״ד ח״ב סי׳ פב ואהע״ז ח״ד סי׳ סה אות ג
48. שמירת שבת כהלכתה פ״מ סע׳ מג. ושמעתי ממו״ר הגרי״י נויבירט שליט״א שכוונתו לי״ב מיל (כ־11.5 ק״מ או כ־7 מייל), כי אז ישנו ספק איסור דאורייתא עבור היהודי ולא מועיל שהנהג הוא גוי
49. סופו משום תחילתו, שמעתי ממו״ר שליט״א
50. שמעתי ממו״ר שליט״א
51. שמירת שבת כהלכתה פל״ח סע׳ כח
52. שם סע׳ ה

SIMAN 319:
THE LAWS OF CHOOSING ON *SHABBAT*

§3: When there is a mixture of (A)two kinds of food, one may be separated from the other in order to eat it immediately.

SIMAN 320:

THE LAW OF SQUEEZING OR WRINGING OUT ON *SHABBAT*

§17: One may not (A)use a wet sponge for cleaning unless it has a handle, lest he squeeze it.

NISHMAT AVRAHAM

not accept change or ask for a receipt.[53]

SIMAN 319

(A) two kinds of food: The *Pri Megadim*[1] wonders if one who separates one kind of food from another, with the intention of eating both later, violates Torah law. Since both are to be eaten later and one is not separating what will be eaten from what will not, perhaps the *melachah* of "choosing" does not apply. On the other hand, the *Biur Halachah*[2] writes that it appears from the *Rambam* that if he separates one kind from another he transgresses Torah law. However, he may choose one for immediate use, leaving the other as is.[3] Thus, when a doctor receives simultaneously on *Shabbat,* a number of results from the laboratory belonging to different patients, he may not first sort them out by patient name to file each in the appropriate chart. Instead he should look at each result and then file it in the appropriate chart. In this way he has not "chosen" since he first looks at whatever he picks up.[4] Similarly, one may not separate instruments — that have become mixed together — from one another.[5] *Rav Waldenberg shlita*[6] writes that if it is difficult for the doctor to file each result separately, he may separate them from one another by patient name before filing. He writes that we do not find the concept of "choosing" in *Chazal, Rambam, Tur* or *Shulchan Aruch* except with regard to food and things that are thoroughly mixed together. Only the later *poskim,* starting with the *Taz,* apply the concept to such objects as pots and clothes, where each article, although "mixed" with the others, can be recognized as a separate entity (with reference to results it would be the pieces of paper).[7]

SIMAN 320

(A) use a wet sponge: The *Mishnah Berurah*[1] quotes the *Gra* who is of the opinion that the words "lest he squeeze it"

53. שמעתי ממו״ר הגרי״י נויבירט שליט״א. וראה בשמירת שבת כהלכתה פל״ח סע׳ יג

1. מ״ז ס״ק ב

2. ד״ה היו

3. מ״ב ס״ק טו וביה״ל ד״ה לאכול

4. שמירת שבת כהלכתה פ״מ סע׳ לה

5. שם פל״ב סע׳ ס

6. לב אברהם ח״ב עמ׳ כה ושו״ת ציץ אליעזר חי״ב סי׳ לה

7. אור שמח הל׳ שבת פ״ח הי״א

1. מ״ב ס״ק מח

SIMAN 321: PRESERVATION OF FOOD AND TAKING MEDICINE ON CONSECUTIVE DAYS INCLUDING *SHABBAT*

§5: One may not (A)salt cooked meat or a boiled egg in order to eat it later.

NISHMAT AVRAHAM

are a printing error and should read "because of squeezing." This he bases on the *Gemara*[2] which states that when he holds the sponge in his hand it will be impossible for him not to squeeze out some of the water absorbed in the sponge. This is also the opinion of the *Magen Avraham.*[3] That is why the *Shemirat Shabbat KeHilchatah,*[4] writes that one may not use an absorbent cotton swab dipped into alcohol or iodine (even if this was done before *Shabbat*) in order to clean a wound, or to swab the skin before an injection or before putting in an intravenous line on *Shabbat,* since he will certainly squeeze out fluid, resulting, in so doing, in the two *melachot* of "squeezing" and "bleaching."[5] Even if the swab were to be held with forceps or tweezers, this ruling will still apply, for this is not like a sponge with a handle which can be used without necessarily "squeezing"[6] or which may be used because it is like pouring water from a saucer.[7] One may, however, use synthetic material such as a nylon swab, to which liquid adheres but into which it is not absorbed.[8] If this is not available, the antiseptic liquid should be poured on the area and then wiped off with a dry absorbent cotton swab.[9] Paper that has been soaked, even on *Shabbat,* may be used for patient care.[10]

On the other hand, the *Tzitz Eliezer*[11] rules that one may use an absorbent cotton swab since the liquid that is squeezed out goes to waste. However, *Rav Auerbach zt"l* wrote to me that since the liquid squeezed out cleanses the skin or wound in the process, it cannot be considered as going to waste.

"Coloring" the swab or the patient's skin with iodine, for example, is not a violation of a prohibition since there is no intention to dye the swab and, on the contrary, the swab is soiled by the color. Furthermore, there is no Torah prohibition forbidding the coloring of human skin.[12]

SIMAN 321

(A) salt: The *Mishnah Berurah*[1] writes that one may salt fresh meat or fish to prevent them from spoiling. The *Chayei Adam*[2] writes that even though the *melachah* of "preserving" (akin to the tanning of skin) does not apply to food, this is only so with food in the full sense of the word. However, there is an opinion that "preserving" does apply to something that

2. שבת קמג ע״א
3. ס״ק יט
4. פל״ה סע׳ יא
5. הגרש״ז אויערבאך זצ״ל מובא בשו״ת ציץ אליעזר ח״ט סי׳ יז פ״ב ס״ק יט
6. דעת רש״י שבת קמג ד״ה עור בית אחיזה ורמב״ם הל׳ שבת פכ״ב הט״ו
7. דעת הראב״ד הל׳ שבת פכ״ב הט״ו מובא במ״ב ס״ק מז
8. שמירת שבת כהלכתה פל״ג סע׳ י
9. שם פל״ה סע׳ יא והערה יג בשם הגרש״ז אויערבאך זצ״ל
10. שמעתי ממו״ר הגרי״י נויבירט שליט״א, ועיין בשו״ת הר צבי ח״א סי׳ קצ ושו״ת אג״מ או״ח ח״ב סי׳ ע
11. ח״ח סי׳ טו פי״ד ס״ק יא וח״ט סי׳ יז פ״ב ס״ק יט
12. מ״ב סי׳ שג ס״ק עט. שמירת שבת כהלכתה פל״ג הערה מח
1. ס״ק כא
2. כלל לג סע׳ יב

§11: One may water flowers or plants that have been cut off before *Shabbat,* in order to (B)prevent them from wilting.

§18: If one took medicine on Thursday and Friday, he is permitted to (C)take it on *Shabbat* also if necessary, since the cure depends on taking it for seven consecutive days.

NISHMAT AVRAHAM

is not food in the full sense of the word, such as fat.

Rav Auerbach zt"l ruled that it is permissible to take a post-mortem needle biopsy in order to arrive at a diagnosis. He told me that it is also permissible to do so on *Shabbat* if there is another patient present who may benefit from this knowledge. However, in order that the biopsy specimen can be examined histologically later, it must be put into formalin immediately. *Rav Neuwirth shlita* told me (based on the above *Chayei Adam*) that this may not be done by a Jew on *Shabbat* unless the patient who may be helped is *seriously ill. Rav Auerbach zt"l* concurred with this ruling.

A 24-hour urine collection may be made over *Shabbat* for anyone undergoing diagnostic tests even if he has not yet been categorized as a *non-seriously ill* patient. Even though the bottle of urine (which is *muktzeh*) must be picked up each time he needs to urinate into it, *Rav Neuwirth shlita* rules that one may be lenient and permit this. However, if the bottle contains a preservative, it may be forbidden. *Rav Auerbach zt"l* wrote to me that preservation of fluids is not mentioned as being forbidden and there would be no Torah violation. *Rav Neuwirth shlita* then asked that if we permit this for one who is *not seriously ill,* why should the *halachah* of *muktzeh* not apply to one who is as yet not even in that category, since the collection on *Shabbat* is for his convenience only? *Rav Auerbach zt"l* replied that even this would be permitted and the bottle would not be considered *muktzeh* since he had prepared it for this purpose before *Shabbat.* However, he added, the collection may not be done on *Shabbat* if it is only in order to avoid the embarrassment of having to take the bottle to work, since he could take a day off to make the collection on a weekday, even if this meant that he would not be paid.

(B) prevent them from wilting. Contact lenses are put into a special fluid every night to keep them soft and moist. *Rav Neuwirth shlita* asked whether or not this was allowed on Shabbat. *Rav Auerbach zt"l* answered that this was permitted on *Shabbat* and was not to be compared to putting a *lulav* into fresh water on *Shabbat*[3] or to changing the water on *Yom Tov*[4] which is not permitted since such acts put new life into the *lulav* rather than keep it in its present state. However, if the lenses had already dried they would be like the *lulav* and one would not be permitted to put them into the preservative on *Shabbat* as this would be an act of "repairing."

(C) take it on *Shabbat*: A patient who must take medicine for a few consecutive days, including *Shabbat,* may do so according to some opinions.[5] However, others only permit this if omitting the medication on *Shabbat* would cause him harm, or if he would only be cured by taking the medicine a given number of consecutive days which will always include *Shabbat.*[6]

3. או״ח סי׳ תרנד מ״ב ס״ק ג וסי׳ שלו סע׳ יא ומ״ב ס״ק נד. וראה בשו״ת מחזה אברהם סי׳ נד ס״ק ג
4. או״ח סי׳ תרנד סע׳ א
5. שמירת שבת כהלכתה פל״ד סע׳ יז
6. שם הערה עו בשם הגרש״ז אויערבאך זצ״ל. וכ״כ האג״מ או״ח ח״ג סי׳ נג

SIMAN 322: CUTTING TO SIZE ON *SHABBAT*

§5: It is permissible to handle aromatic twigs (that have been cut before *Shabbat*) and their leaves in order to smell

NISHMAT AVRAHAM

Similarly, a woman who must take medicine for a given number of consecutive days in order to help her become pregnant,[7] or alternatively to prevent pregnancy (if she has permission to do so from a recognized *halachic* authority), may take it on *Shabbat.*[8] The same holds true for a bride who must take medication to ensure that she menstruates sufficiently early before her wedding to allow her to go to the *mikveh* before the wedding.[9] Similarly one may continue to take medication to prevent a relapse of an illness[10] (see also *Siman* 278D, 301B and 322A).

Is medication *muktzeh*? The *Minchat Shabbat*[11] writes that once the patient no longer needs the medication, if it is so bitter that neither a human nor an animal would eat it, it may not be moved either to prevent its being damaged or in order to clear the space on which it stands. Even if it is palatable, one should nevertheless be strict and not move it, since it was made only for someone who is unwell. If the patient requires the medication again, it may be moved as necessary. The *Shemirat Shabbat KeHilchatah*[12] writes that if the person was already ill before *Shabbat* and realized that he will require the medication on *Shabbat,* it is not *muktzeh* and may be moved even if the moving is not for his needs.

A *seriously ill* patient may take medication for a concomitant illness even if that illness is unconnected to his basic illness and even if it is not necessary to save his life. Thus he may take analgesics for a toothache even if his basic illness, for example pneumonia, is painless. However, Torah law may not be set aside for this purpose and he may not ask a Jewish doctor to write him a prescription for the analgesics.[13] On the other hand, a *non-seriously ill* patient who may take medication for his illness, may not take medication for a concomitant mild illness which, on its own, would not have categorized him as a *non-seriously ill* patient. Thus, a patient with the influenza, sufficiently severe to make him take to bed, may not take analgesics for a mild toothache[14] (see also *Siman* 278D, 301B and 322A).

A *non-seriously ill* patient may receive sub-cutaneous or intra-muscular injections[15] (see also *Siman* 313A, 316B and 326B). Medication to prevent one from becoming *non-seriously* ill is also permitted, for example to prevent serious migraine attacks.[16]

A patient suffering from *angina pectoris* may take appropriate medication on Friday night to enable him to have marital relations.[17]

---

7. שו״ת חלקת יעקב ח״ג סי׳ כג
8. שמירת שבת כהלכתה שם סע׳ יט. וראה גם בשו״ת ציץ אליעזר חי״א סי׳ לז
9. שמעתי ממו״ר הגרי״י נויבירט שליט״א
10. שמירת שבת כהלכתה שם סע׳ יז
11. סי׳ פח ס״ק טז
12. פל״ג סע׳ ד בהגה
13. שמירת שבת כהלכתה פל״ב סע׳ נו
14. שו״ת אג״מ או״ח ח״ג סי׳ נג
15. שמירת שבת כהלכתה פל״ג סע׳ ז
16. שם פל״ד סע׳ טז
17. שו״ת מנחת יצחק ח״א סי׳ קח

their fragrance or to wave them over the head of a patient. If one wishes to smell them, he may (A)crush them between his fingers, whether they are still fresh or have dried.

NISHMAT AVRAHAM

SIMAN 322

(A) crush them: The *Mishnah Berurah*[1] adds that the text should read "cut and crush them."

Cutting anything to size is one of the thirty-nine *melachot* forbidden on the *Shabbat* ("cutting"). However, if one cuts to destroy or without any intention as to a particular size, he transgresses a Rabbinic prohibition only.[2] Hence, it is forbidden to cut a bandage to size or to cut one end lengthwise in order to be able to tie a knot. Instead, the complete bandage should be wrapped round the wound.[3] Similarly, it is forbidden to cut or tear an adhesive tape to size[4] (see also *Siman* 331).

Tablets may be crushed as necessary. Since they were already in powder form before being made into tablets, crushing them to return them to their previous state is permissible.[5] One may also cut a tablet or suppository in half to use one half of the dose. *Rav Auerbach zt"l*[6] ruled that the *melachah* of "cutting" does not apply even though one is careful to cut it into two exact halves, because: (a) The *melachah* of "cutting" takes place when one intends to use the cut piece and not when he intends to swallow it, since it then is a "food" and this *melachah* does not apply to food.[7] This holds true for a suppository which also enters the body. (b) The patient wishes to obtain the correct amount of medication; he is not interested in the size of the tablet per se. After cutting it into two halves he does not care whether or not the half breaks up into two or three smaller pieces. (c) The patient has no interest in a tablet of a given length, breadth or shape (e.g. it does not matter whether it is a square or rectangle), since he is prepared to cut it along its length, breadth or diagonal. *Rav Auerbach zt"l* told me that even if he cuts the tablet along a line etched on it for this purpose, it is permissible, since the line was only put there for convenience in breaking or cutting it. (See also *Siman* 301B and *Siman* 328 §17I regarding medication.)

Although it is permissible to cut or crush a twig (that has been cut from the tree before *Shabbat*) to smell its fragrance, it is forbidden to do so to use it as a toothpick. If he did so using a knife or scissors to shape it, he will have transgressed Torah law, and Rabbinic law if he did so by hand.[8] To do so with a knife is forbidden by Torah law even if he would be ashamed to be seen with a piece of meat (or other food) stuck between his teeth. The *Sha'ar HaTziyun*[9] adds, in the name of the *Pri Megadim,* that where there is no alternative he may shape it with his fingers. *Rav Neuwirth shlita* told me that this shows us that where the problem of shame arises, not only is a Rabbinic law set aside to avoid this shame, but even a Torah law, if the act is done in an indirect manner. Based on this he rules that a patient receiving intravenous therapy via an electrically operated computerized pump that gives a continuous measured

1. ס״ק יז
2. מ״ב ס״ק יח וראה גם בביה״ל ד״ה אחד
3. שמירת שבת כהלכתה פל״ה סע׳ כא
4. ראה סי׳ שמ סע׳ יג ומ״ב שם ס״ק מא. שמירת שבת כהלכתה שם סע׳ כג
5. רמ״א סי׳ שכא סע׳ כא ופמ״ג מ״ז ס״ק י. שמירת שבת כהלכתה פל״ג סע׳ ד
6. שמירת שבת כהלכתה שם
7. כאן סע׳ ד ומ״ב ס״ק יב
8. מ״ב ס״ק יג
9. ס״ק יב

SIMAN 326: WASHING ON *SHABBAT*

§1: One is forbidden to wash or shower his whole body even if each part is washed separately and even with (A)water that was heated before *Shabbat*. One may wash his face, hands and feet.

§6: One may not put a (B)hot-water bottle on one's abdomen.

NISHMAT AVRAHAM

amount of medication per hour may not disconnect himself on *Shabbat* to use the bathroom. Instead he must ask that a bottle or bedpan be brought to him. However, if there are other patients in the room and he will be ashamed at their hearing him use a bedpan, he may ask a non-Jew to disconnect the pump so that he can use the bathroom. If a non-Jew is not available and he cannot wait, he may disconnect the pump by removing the plug in an indirect manner (e.g. by grasping it between the knuckles of two fingers or by using both hands simultaneously). On his return, he should reconnect the plug, if possible in an indirect manner. The above would also apply if he was attached to a monitor.

A patient, even one who is *not seriously ill* (i.e. in a chronically stable condition), may use an electric bell to call for assistance, if he cannot wait for a nurse to pass and, if the use of the bell will not cause a light to go on simultaneously in the nurses' station. Here, again, human dignity is a factor. Obviously if there is any question of danger to life, these conditions do not apply.

If he needs a bedpan urgently and there is no one available to call a nurse, and a non-Jew who could ring for one is not present (the non-Jew may do so even if this causes a light to go on at the same time), he may ring for the nurse himself, pressing the button with the back of his hand or finger, even if a light is lit up simultaneously.[10]

An intravenous line or cannula may not be removed or changed on *Shabbat* unless leaving it will cause medical complications.[11]

SIMAN 326

(A) water that was heated: *R. Akiva Eiger*[1] writes that someone with a *minor illness* or one who has *aches and pains* may wash his whole body, even though he is not in the category of a *non-seriously ill* patient. He must, however, be careful not to squeeze water out of his hair.[2]

(B) hot-water bottle: The *Tosafot*[3] writes that this is because he clearly does so for a medical reason and *Chazal* forbade it lest he prepare a medicine for himself by grinding herbs (which is forbidden by Torah law), but, if there is great need it would be permitted.[4] However, if he or others are accustomed to use a hot-water bottle even when healthy, he may use it as long as it is not apparent that he does so because he is ill.[5]

10. שמירת שבת כהלכתה פ״מ סע׳ יט
11. משום דימום – שמעתי ממו״ר הגרי״י נויבירט שליט״א
1. הגהות על שו״ע סי׳ שז סע׳ ה, מובא בביה״ל כאן ד״ה במים
2. מ״ב סי׳ שכ סוס״ק נה וכאן ס״ק כא
3. שבת מ ע״ב ד״ה ובלבד
4. מ״ב ס״ק יט
5. שמירת שבת כהלכתה פל״ד סע׳ יא

§10: One may [(C)]**wash his hands with coarse bran.**

GLOSS: *One may not wash with* [(D)]*soap since he causes it to melt and a new object is thereby created.*

NISHMAT AVRAHAM

As to an electric blanket, the *Igrot Moshe*[6] permits its use on *Shabbat* for the following reasons: (a) The blanket itself is not *muktzeh* since it can be used without turning on the current. (b) The wiring is not *muktzeh* except when it is attached to an electric socket and even then, although it is categorized as *muktzeh* because its use is forbidden, it can nevertheless be moved in order to use the blanket. (c) Since healthy people also use electric blankets, the possibility that a patient may come to take medicines, when he is not allowed to, does not apply. However, since there is a possibility that he may inadvertently change the temperature of the blanket, he should cover the switch and the wall plug as a reminder. *Rav Auerbach zt''l* wrote to me also permitting the use of an electric blanket on *Shabbat* since the electric wires do not reach red heat. This is also the opinion of the *Chelkat Yaakov.*[7]

A patient with hypothermia may be put on a heating mattress that is switched on on *Shabbat.*[8]

(C) wash his hands: Hot water from a boiler which automatically refills with cold water may not be used if the patient is in the category of the *non-seriously ill*[9] unless the faucet is opened (and closed) by a non-Jew. It is preferable not to even use hot water from a solar heater.[10] However, if the patient is *seriously ill,* the doctor (or nurse) may open a hot-water faucet (if possible in an indirect manner, such as turning the tap between two fingers or by using two hands) in order to wash his hands before examining or treating him; a non-Jew must be asked to close it.[11] If, however, it is even remotely possible that more hot water will be needed during *Shabbat* for such a patient, the faucet may be closed by the doctor.[12] After the examination or treatment, even of a *seriously ill patient,* a non-Jew should be asked to open (and later close) the faucet in order to enable the doctor (or nurse) to wash his hands.[13]

On *Yom Tov,* hot water from any source may be used as usual.[14] However, a water heater where the flame is extinguished each time one closes the tap may not be used even on *Yom Tov.*

(D) soap: A doctor (or nurse) who must wash his hands before or after examining or treating a patient on *Shabbat* should preferably use liquid soap. If this is not available, he may use ordinary soap preferably under a running faucet.[15] He may even prepare liquid soap on *Shabbat* (if he did not do so beforehand) by putting the soap into a cup of hot water[16] and stirring it, but not by rubbing the soap with his hands in the water.[17] *Rav Ovadiah Yosef shlita*[18] also permits a doctor to use ordinary soap if he has no choice.

6. או״ח ח״ג סי׳ נ
7. ח״א סי׳ מ וח״ג סי׳ קפא
8. שמעתי ממו״ר הגרי״י נויבירט שליט״א
9. ראה שמירת שבת כהלכתה פ״א סע׳ לט
10. כתב לי מו״ר הגרי״י נויבירט שליט״א
11. כתב לי מו״ר הגרי״י נויבירט שליט״א
12. הגרש״ז אויערבאך זצ״ל לב אברהם ח״א עמ׳ טו הערה על פ״ו סע׳ כב
13. שמעתי ממו״ר הגרי״י נויבירט שליט״א
14. שמירת שבת כהלכתה פ״ב סע׳ ז
15. שמירת שבת כהלכתה פ״מ סע׳ יא ועיין שם פי״ד סע׳ טז
16. כלי שני
17. שם פי״ב סע׳ ו
18. שו״ת יביע אומר ח״ד או״ח סי׳ כח

SIMAN 328: THE PATIENT ON *SHABBAT*

NISHMAT AVRAHAM

SIMAN 328

☙ Introduction: Definition of Types of Patients

1.

The seriously (or dangerously) ill patient (this includes those who are definitely seriously ill and those who may possibly be so):[1]

(a) One who feels that he is so even if his doctor disagrees (if, however, the difference of opinion is related to the diagnosis or the treatment of a recognized illness, the doctor's opinion is taken).

(b) One who the doctor believes is seriously ill, or possibly so, even at the stage when the illness is not yet serious, but may become so if not treated on *Shabbat.*

(c) An ambulant patient, who nevertheless may become seriously ill if not treated on the Sabbath; for example, a diabetic patient who has run out of insulin.

(d) One whose state or illness our Sages have defined as being dangerous, even if this is contrary to current medical opinion; for example, a woman during the first seven days following childbirth or abortion which occurs after at least forty days of pregnancy.

(e) One whose limb is in danger. Since almost all cases of danger to a limb, if untreated, may lead to a threat to life, such a patient is also defined in this category (see 17E). If there is a danger of an acute loss of vision, even in one eye, Torah laws may be set aside as necessary since in most situations life-threatening complications may arise[2] (see 9A). Regarding a non-functioning organ or limb, see 17E below.

One must realize that whenever there is the slightest possibility that a patient is or may become seriously ill without appropriate treatment, he is categorized as being seriously ill, and Sabbath laws, even those involving Torah prohibitions, are set aside if necessary for his care.

Treatment. A patient who is or may become seriously ill if left untreated, must be treated immediately if time is of the essence, without hesitation and as on a weekday. It is of such a situation that the *Shulchan Aruch* rules that he who is speedy is praiseworthy while he who takes time to ask (whether a particular act or procedure is permissible), is as if he has shed blood.[3] However, if there is time, a Rav should be consulted as to how and when Sabbath laws may be set aside. If such an authority is not available for consultation on *Shabbat,* then everything that the patient (or his attendant) feels to be essential for his medical well-being must be done even if it involves setting aside Torah law. This is also true whenever there is a doubt as to whether a procedure is *halachically* permitted on *Shabbat* or whether it could wait until after *Shabbat.*[4]

2.

The non-seriously ill patient:[5]

(a) One who must take to bed or feels generally ill; for example, someone with

1. ראה פרטי דינים בשמירת שבת כהלכתה פל״ב סע׳ ח ו־ט ונשמת אברהם כרך ד האו״ח הקדמה לסי׳ שכח (עמ׳ לח)

2. הסכים אתי מו״ר הגרי״י נויבירט שליט״א

3. או״ח כאן סע׳ ב וסע׳ יג

4. שמעתי ממו״ר הגרי״י נויברט שליט״א

5. ראה פרטי דינים בשמירת שבת כהלכתה פל״ג סע׳ א ונשמת אברהם כרך ד האו״ח הקדמה לסי׳ שכח (עמ׳ לה)

§1: One who has (A)aches and pains, if he bears with it and acts like a healthy person, may not have (B)any (C)treatment,

NISHMAT AVRAHAM

influenza.

(b) One who has a high temperature which would prevent most people from going out, even if the patient himself does not take to bed.

(c) One who has severe pain (not internal) that makes him feel weak even if he does not take to bed.

(d) One who, although ambulant, will be forced to take to bed if not given preventive treatment; for example, one who suffers from attacks of migraine or asthma.

(e) One who has been so defined by our Sages; for example, a woman from the eighth to the thirtieth day after childbirth or abortion (which occurs after forty days of pregnancy), or a young child who requires treatment.

(f) A child (see 17K).

Treatment. One may ask a non-Jew to do whatever is necessary for the well being of such a patient, even if it involves setting aside Torah laws.[6] A Jew may set aside Rabbinic law, but where possible the acts should be done in an indirect manner.[7] If this is not possible the act may be done in the usual way.[8]

3.

The patient with a minor illness, or with aches and pains:[9]

Someone with heavy nasal catarrh or an irritating cough or headache, but not severe enough to make him take to bed.

Treatment. A Jew may not set aside even Rabbinic law for such a patient, nor may the patient take any medication. A non-Jew may be asked to do whatever is necessary for the well-being of the patient, if only Rabbinic law is set aside.[10]

4.

The patient with discomfort:[11]

Someone with a mild catarrh, cough or skin ailment, for example.

Treatment. No treatment is allowed on *Shabbat,* even by a non-Jew.[12]

1(A) aches and pains: This includes a slight pain such as a mild headache, or a cold or cough[13] which is not severe enough to weaken his whole body or to force him to take to bed.[14] This varies from one individual to another and will depend on his own reaction to the illness.

If, however, he has real discomfort, the *Tiferet Yisrael*[15] considers him to be in the category of a patient with a *minor illness* whom a non-Jew may be asked to treat provided that only Rabbinic law is set aside.[16] On the other hand, *Rav Yaakov Emden*[17] would consider him to be in the more severe category of a *non-seriously ill* patient. According to him, a non-Jew may be asked to set aside Torah law, and, for example, heat water; a Jew may set aside Rabbinic law if a non-Jew is not available.

1(B) any treatment: Even if no violation of the Sabbath is involved.[18]

1(C) treatment: Even if it is customary to do something for the healthy, it may not be done for him if it is clear that it is done only because he feels ill.[19] Thus *Rav*

6. מ״ב כאן ס״ק מז
7. או״ח כאן סע׳ יז ומ״ב ס״ק נז
8. מ״ב כאן ס״ק קב
9. ראה פרטי דינים בנשמת אברהם כרך ד חאו״ח הקדמה לסי׳ שכח (עמ׳ לד-לה)
10. או״ח סי׳ שז סע׳ ה ומ״ב בסי׳ שכח ס״ק נב
11. ראה פרטי דינים בנשמת אברהם שם (עמ׳ לד)
12. או״ח כאן סע׳ א ומ״ב ס״ג ו-פג
13. ערוה״ש סע׳ יט
14. מ״ב ס״ק א
15. כלכלת שבת דיני אמירה לנכרי סע׳ ז(א)
16. שבות דשבות באמירה לנכרי סי׳ שז סע׳ ה ומ״ב כאן ס״ק נב
17. מור וקציעא סי׳ שכח על המג״א ס״ק ט
18. מ״ב ס״ק ב
19. תו״ש ושו״ע הרב

even that given by a (D)non-Jew, to prevent the possibility of the (E)grinding of herbs.

NISHMAT AVRAHAM

Moshe Feinstein zt"l[20] rules that even though a healthy person may take vitamins on *Shabbat* to prevent illness, this patient may not do so. However *Rav Shlomo Zalman Auerbach zt"l* wrote to me: Why should someone who easily catches cold which may progress to pneumonia or other serious complications necessitating treatment, wait to be treated only when he will be *seriously ill* if he can take treatment now to prevent this from occurring? (see below, 37B).

1(D) non-Jew: He may not perform even Rabbinically forbidden actions.[21]

1(E) grinding of herbs: The source of this *halachah* is the *Talmud.*[22] *Rashi*[23] explains that if treatment were permitted, one would come to prepare medication by grinding herbs, and "grinding" is a *melachah* forbidden by the Torah. The *Rif* and the *Rosh*[24] explain that if one is concerned about his health he may forget that it is *Shabbat* and perform a forbidden *melachah.*

Should this enactment apply in our day and age where the preparation of medication is no longer an individual concern but rather that of a pharmaceutical firm or of a pharmacist in a drug store? The *Ketsot HaShulchan,*[25] in discussing this, points out that the *Tosafot*[26] cited by the *Rama*[27] permits that which *Chazal* once forbade since the reason for the enactment no longer exists. However, he quotes the *Torat Chesed,*[28] who in turn quotes a *responsum* of the *Rosh*,[29] that an enactment becomes null and void only when the real reason for the enactment is known and that reason no longer applies. The *Torat Chesed,* however, wonders how anyone nowadays can have the temerity to decide which enactment is to be considered as one whose real reason is known and which therefore is automatically nullified when that reason no longer applies. In view of this, continues the *Ketsot HaShulchan,* the enactment against medical treatment on *Shabbat* for minor illness remains valid today since the real reason behind the enactment is not known. Moreover, he adds that even though most people do not know how to make medication, nevertheless there are those in some parts of the world who continue to use homemade remedies which they prepare by grinding herbs. This is also the view of the *Pitchei Teshuvah*[30] and the *Tzitz Eliezer.*[31] And although the *Taz*[32] writes that one does finds an example of an enactment of *Chazal* which was nullified when the reason for it no longer existed,[33] the *Pitchei Teshuvah*[34] disagrees. He writes that if the enactment was made for a definite reason that was all encompassing with no exceptions, it remains in force even when the reason no longer exists. However, in the example given by the *Taz,* the enact-

20. שו״ת אג״מ או״ח ח״ג סי׳ נד
21. ב״י ומ״ב ס״ק ג
22. שבת נג ע״ב
23. שם ד״ה גזירה
24. שם. וראה באגלי טל מלאכת טוחן ס״ק טז ושו״ת ציץ אליעזר ח״ח סי׳ טו פט״ו
25. סי׳ קלד בבדה״ש ס״ק ז(2)
26. ביצה ל ע״א ד״ה תנן
27. סי׳ שלט סע׳ ג. ועיין במג״א סי׳ שלח ס״ק א וא״ר שם ס״ק ג
28. שו״ת או״ח סי׳ יז
29. כלל ב אות ח
30. אהע״ז סי׳ יג ס״ק ד
31. ח״ח סי׳ טו פט״ו סוף או״ק ד
32. אהע״ז סי׳ קמה ס״ק ז
33. יו״ד סי׳ קטז
34. אהע״ז שם ס״ק ט

§2: [(A)]It is a *mitzvah* to set aside Sabbath laws (as necessary) for [(B)]a seriously (or dangerously) ill patient. He who does

NISHMAT AVRAHAM

ment was made for a possible reason that was not always a certainty. It is in such a case that an enactment no longer applies once the reason no longer exists.

2(A) It is a mitzvah: The *Magen Avraham*[35] rules that this is only so if the remedy is well known or if it is given on the advice of an expert. This is also the opinion of the *Hagahot Maimoniot.*[36] The *Shulchan Aruch HaRav*[37] adds that even if it is not certain that this particular patient will respond to the well-known remedy, *Shabbat* may be set aside so that he may receive the remedy.[38] The *Shemirat Shabbat KeHilchatah*[39] rules that a doctor may set aside Torah law to give an experimental treatment to a *seriously ill* patient even if the outcome is dubious (see also *Siman* 301 §27).

2(B) a seriously (or dangerously) ill patient:

A fetus: The *Rosh*[40] writes, quoting the *Ramban,* that it appears that the *Ba'al Halachot* rules that Sabbath laws may be set aside for a fetus whose life is in danger even though the mother will not be affected.[41] The *Korban Netanel*[42] adds that this is true even if the fetus is less than forty days old.[43] On the other hand, the *Mishnah Berurah*[44] is uncertain whether one may set aside Sabbath laws for a fetus which is less than forty days old. However, *Rav Auerbach zt"l* rules that since we are discussing a life-threatening situation, Sabbath laws must be set aside where necessary even when the *halachah* is not clear cut.

A baby: The *halachah* today which does not follow the opinion of the *Shulchan Aruch,*[45] is that Sabbath laws are set aside for all newborn babies even if born after eight months of gestation.[46] The *Chazon Ish*[47] explains that this apparent change in *halachah* from that laid down in the *Talmud* and *Shulchan Aruch* is because the prognosis of such a baby has changed as a result of a change in nature (see *Siman* 330 §7 for further discussion). *Rav Auerbach zt"l* told me that a very premature baby must also be treated, even if it is clear that it has only a short time to live.

Sabbath laws are also set aside for a full-term baby with serious congenital defects.[48]

A Jew who profanes the Sabbath: Sabbath laws are set aside for him as necessary.[49]

---

35. ס״ק א מהא דיו״ד סי׳ קנה סע׳ ג בהגה

36. פי״ד ממאכלות אסורות

37. סע׳ ב

38. ראה גם בתהל״ד ס״ק ב ודעת תורה כאן

39. פל״ב סע׳ לו

40. יומא פ״ח סי׳ יג

41. ראה גם בקובץ שיעורים כתובות סי׳ קלה, דעת תורה סי׳ תריז סע׳ א ושו״ת ציץ אליעזר חי״א סי׳ מג

42. על הרא״ש ס״ק י

43. וכן ראה בטואו״ח סי׳ תריז ובב״י שם ובביה״ל סי׳ של סע׳ ז סוד״ה או ספק

44. סי׳ תריז שעה״צ ס״ק א

45. סי׳ של סע׳ ז

46. ראה יסודי ישורון ח״ד עמ׳ רלה. שו״ת מנחת יצחק ח״ד סי׳ קכג

47. יו״ד סי׳ קנה ס״ק ד ואהע״ז סי׳ קטו ס״ק ד

48. שמירת שבת כהלכתה פל״ו הערה כד בשם הגרש״ז אויערבאך זצ״ל. וראה גם בשו״ת ציץ אליעזר ח״י סי׳ כה פכ״ז שמחללין שבת על אדם טריפה

49. ראה חזו״א יו״ד סי׳ ב ס״ק טז וס״ק כח, שו״ת יעב״ץ ח״א סי׳ ל, שו״ת חת״ס יו״ד סי׳ שמא, שו״ת מהר״ם שיק או״ח סי׳ קמ, שו״ת בית יצחק קו״א להלכות טרפות סי׳ כט, שו״ת חלקת יעקב ח״א סי׳ מה, שו״ת מנחת יצחק ח״א סי׳ נג וח״ג סי׳ כ, שו״ת ציץ אליעזר ח״ח סי׳ טו פ״ה ופ״ו וח״ט סי׳ יז פ״ב אות ח, מו״ר הגרי״י נויבירט שליט״א בספר הלכה ורפואה ח״א עמ׳ קס. וע״ע ארחות חיים כאן ס״ק ד, פמ״ג מ״ז ס״ק ו, מ״ב סי׳ שבט ס״ק ט סי׳ נה ס״ק מו וסי׳ שפה ס״ק ג

so (C)immediately is praiseworthy whereas (D)he who delays in order to ask is guilty of shedding blood.

NISHMAT AVRAHAM

Attempted suicide: Sabbath laws are set aside for him as necessary.[50] A psychiatric patient who may be a danger to himself or to others must be treated, even if Torah laws have to be set aside.

2(C) immediately: Desecration of *Yom Tov* vis-a-vis *Shabbat*. A patient on Friday, *Yom Tov,* appears to be in a situation that will almost certainly deteriorate such that he will be *seriously ill* the next day, *Shabbat.* However, there is no absolute medical indication to allow desecrating *Yom Tov* and treating him on Friday; and it will not be too late to wait until *Shabbat* to treat him, if necessary. Should he be treated on *Yom Tov* even though the treatment is not called for, since desecrating *Yom Tov* is a far lower level of desecration than that of *Shabbat*? On the other hand, should one wait until *Shabbat* when the treatment will be essential? For example, a patient has acute renal failure and his deteriorating condition clearly indicates that he will soon require dialysis to save his life. On Friday, *Yom Tov,* there is still no real indication for dialysis. However, with his present rate of deterioration, he will almost certainly require dialysis the next day, *Shabbat.* Should he be dialyzed on *Yom Tov* even without a real medical indication, thus avoiding the need to perhaps having to do so on *Shabbat*? The *Netziv*[51] writes that it is better to carry out a more serious violation when there is a life-threatening situation rather than to carry out a lesser violation when there is not. He continues[52] that when Friday is a *Yom Tov* and there will certainly be a need to desecrate *Shabbat,* one should rather desecrate *Yom Tov,* even though the situation is not yet life-threatening. However, if it is not certain that it will be necessary to desecrate *Shabbat,* one should not desecrate *Yom Tov* unnecessarily.

The *Igrot Moshe*[53] expresses surprise at this ruling of the *Netziv* that one should desecrate *Yom Tov* even though the situation is not yet life-threatening. *Rav Moshe zt"l* thought the *Netziv's* Friday (*Yom Tov*)-*Shabbat* solution could not be derived from the *Talmud*[54] which states that in a life-threatening situation one should try to save life with the least possible desecration. For the *Talmud* pictures a life-threatening situation from the outset, whereas nothing is threatening life on *Yom Tov.* Nor can the *Yom Tov* case be compared to a possibility where a life-threatening situation would arise on a Sunday, and it is uncertain whether one would then be able to avert it, whereas one would be able to do so on *Shabbat.* Then *Shabbat* laws must be set aside, though Sunday was an ordinary weekday and the situation on *Shabbat* was not yet life-threatening. But the situation portrayed by the *Netziv* involved a Friday (*Yom Tov*) where no life-threatening situation existed and a *Shabbat* following where danger could be averted.

However, the *Shemirat Shabbat Ke-Hilchatah*[55] appears to rule like the *Netziv* and *Rav Neuwirth shlita* (its author) told me that it stands to reason that if on *Shabbat* the situation will almost cer-

50. ארחות חיים סע׳ יט, שו״ת חלקת יעקב ח״א סי׳ עב, שו״ת אג״מ או״ח ח״א סי׳ קכז, שו״ת ציץ אליעזר ח״ח סי׳ טו פ״ד וח״ט סי׳ יז פ״ב אות ו

51. העמק דבר במדבר יז:יב

52. הרחב דבר שם או״ק א

53. או״ח ח״ג סי׳ סט

54. יומא פג ע״א

55. פל״ב הערה קג

§3: Sabbath laws are set aside for internal disease or injury. From (A)the teeth inwards and (B)including the teeth is considered internal. However, aches and pains are not enough.

GLOSS: *However, one who (C)has a toothache sufficiently severe to*

NISHMAT AVRAHAM

tainly deteriorate into a life-threatening one, then on Friday, *Yom Tov,* its cause is already present. Therefore, even though the patient's condition is not yet dangerous, the cause of the danger is already present on *Yom Tov.* Since the patient's condition is deteriorating, it is better to desecrate *Yom Tov* rather than *Shabbat. Rav Auerbach zt"l* wrote to me agreeing with this ruling.

2(D) he who delays: The *Mishnah Berurah,*[56] quoting the *Radvaz,*[57] explains that he does so because of the fear that he may be desecrating the Sabbath unnecessarily and he is unwilling to do so until given *halachic* permission by a Rav. In such a case he sheds blood since in the time wasted, the patient may become weaker and even more *dangerously ill* and the Torah commands us not to stand idly by when blood is about to be shed.[58] The *Talmud Yerushalmi*[59] writes that he who is asked deserves criticism, meaning that a scholar must publicly teach these *halachot* so that all should know them well, that there should be no need to ask in an emergency. The *Mishnah Berurah* and the *Kitzur Shulchan Aruch*[60] add that if the patient himself objects to Sabbath laws being set aside for him because of this same fear, he must be told emphatically that his piety is that of fools.[61] On the other hand, the *Aruch HaShulchan*[62] warns that this is only true if time is of the essence, but if it is quite clear that it is not, one must certainly ask for *halachic* guidance.

Incidentally, it must be clearly understood that when Sabbath laws are set aside with *halachic* sanction for a patient, Sabbath is not "desecrated" but "kept."[63]

3(A) the teeth inwards: And certainly if the gums are involved.[64] No treatment is permissible for a mild toothache.[65] However, if it is severe enough to affect his whole body, Rabbinic laws may be set aside if done in an indirect manner wherever possible.[66] Medication may also be taken and all treatment by a non-Jewish dentist is permissible.[67] If, however, the pain is so severe that one suspects an infection, or if the gums are swollen, even if painless, Torah laws may also be set aside when necessary.[68]

3(B) including the teeth: I am not certain what the disease *"safdena,"* mentioned by *Chazal*[69] and the *Mishnah Berurah,*[70] is (see below, §6).

3(C) has a toothache: The *Mishnah Berurah*[71] writes that a Jewish dentist

56. ס״ק ו
57. שו״ת, ח״ד סי׳ סז (אלף קלט)
58. ויקרא יט:טז
59. יומא פ״ה ה״ה
60. סי׳ צב סע׳ א
61. ראה גם ברמב״ם שבת פ״ב ה״ג, תרומת הדשן סי׳ נח ורשב״ץ ח״א סי׳ נד
62. סע׳ ב
63. אור החיים שמות לא:יג
64. מ״ב ס״ק ז
65. להלן סע׳ לב
66. חיי אדם כלל סט סע׳ יב
67. כאן בהגה וסע׳ יז ומ״ב ס״ק מז וסוס״ק קב
68. מ״ב ס״ק ח
69. ע״ז כח ע״א
70. ס״ק ח
71. ס״ק י בשם הא״ר

wish to have the tooth extracted should [(D)]*ask a non-Jewish dentist to do so.*

§4: One should not be strict in assessing the needs of a seriously ill patient; even if there is no expert guidance avail-

NISHMAT AVRAHAM

should not extract a tooth on *Shabbat* since its medical value is uncertain. Today, however, since this is an accepted treatment, it may be done even by a Jewish dentist, if, in his opinion, the extraction is essential because of a possible life-threatening situation.[72] *Rav Auerbach zt"l* wrote to me that in his opinion a tooth may be extracted even if this would only probably be lifesaving, since the extraction itself is not a dangerous procedure.

3(D) ask a non-Jewish dentist: The Torah[73] forbids one to cut the hair of his head in the style worn by idolators; the prohibition applies to both one who cuts the hair and to the person whose hair is cut.[74] *Chazal* have also stated as a general rule that when one does something that he is capable of doing himself and someone else nevertheless helps him, "such help does not count."[75] Therefore, *Rav Akiva Eiger*[76] asks: "Why should the one having his hair cut be culpable, in addition to the barber, when the barber does the whole forbidden act himself?" The *Chazon Ish*[77] explains that if one moves a part of his body into an unusual posture, such as raising or bowing the head to an uncomfortable degree, he would be considered to be actively helping. Here, the person having his hair cut is considered as if he is actively helping and he, too, transgresses. On the other hand, for example, opening and closing his eyes when a salve is put in (by a non-Jew)[78] is permissible since the prohibition would only apply to the person applying the salve, and opening and closing of one's eyes happens normally.

The *Taz*[79] asks why the extraction of a tooth by a non-Jewish dentist is permissible. The mouth is normally closed; opening it for the dentist should be considered as active help and should be forbidden just as allowing another to cut one's hair in a forbidden fashion is prohibited. This is also the opinion of the *Magen Avraham*[80] and the *Eglei Tal.*[81] The *Radvaz,*[82] the *Teshuvah MeAhavah,*[83] the *Chacham Tzvi*[84] and the *Maharsham*[85] permit the Jew to actively help only if the prohibition is Rabbinic.

On the other hand, the *Rama*[86] apparently does not make any such distinction between "helping" the non-Jew or not. The *Shach*[87] also argues with the *Taz* and rules that the statement of *Chazal* that "such help does not count" is universal except for the prohibition of cutting one's hair in a fashion forbidden by Torah law (see above). The *Mishnah Berurah*[88]

72. שו״ת ציץ אליעזר ח״ח סי׳ טו פ״י וכן שמעתי ממו״ר הגרי״י נויבירט שליט״א
73. ויקרא יט:כז
74. מכות כ ע״ב ויו״ד סי׳ קפא
75. שבת צג ע״א
76. פסקים סי׳ צו
77. חו״מ ליקוטים סי׳ כג על מכות כ ע״ב
78. ביצה כב ע״א
79. כאן ס״ק א
80. ס״ק טז
81. מלאכת טוחן ס״ק לח אות כה ו־כו
82. ח״א סי׳ רמג
83. סי׳ קלד ו־קלה
84. סי׳ פב
85. ארחות חיים סי׳ שכח ס״ק א ודעת תורה יו״ד סי׳ ב ס״ק סה
86. כאן וסע׳ יז
87. יו״ד סי׳ קצח נקוה״כ על הט״ז ס״ק כא
88. ס״ק יא

able and the patient does not request it specifically, one must nevertheless do (A)whatever would be done on a week-

NISHMAT AVRAHAM

rules like the *Shulchan Aruch* and not like the *Taz.*

4(A) whatever would be done: The *Maggid Mishneh*[89] quotes the *Ramban*[90] that one may do whatever should be done with respect to both food and medication, and, he adds, that it would appear that this is so even if his condition would not deteriorate by not doing so. Since the illness itself is serious, should there be a slight need to do something one would normally do on a weekday, he should do it even on *Shabbat.*[91] However, if the need is great, even those who would disagree with this opinion would agree that it is permissible, as the *Gemara*[92] says that one may heat water for him to drink or to wash.[93] The *Tosefet Yom HaKippurim*[94] says the *Gemara* refers to a patient whose condition would not deteriorate if he did not bathe or wash and that this *Gemara* was a support for the opinion of the *Maggid Mishneh.* The same explanation is given by *Rav Abramsky zt''l.*[95] The *Tashbetz*[96] also rules like the *Maggid Mishneh.* See also the *Tzitz Eliezer.*[97]

On the other hand, *Rashi*[98] rules that it is only permissible to set aside Sabbath laws if the patient's progress will be adversely affected by not doing so. If, however, the patient will not be affected by not receiving a particular medication or food involving setting aside Sabbath laws, the act may only be done through a non-Jew.[99] This is also a view held by many other *rishonim.*[100] The *Mishnah Berurah,* summing up, rules[101] that if one needs to set aside Torah law in this situation, this may only be done through a non-Jew. If Rabbinic law is involved a Jew may perform the work, if possible, in an indirect manner.[102]

Rav Ovadiah Yosef shlita wrote to me[103] that he follows the *Shulchan Aruch* and the *Maggid Mishneh,* that Sabbath laws may be set aside even if the need is only slight, if the patient will feel the better for it.[104] The *Shemirat Shabbat KeHilchatah,* on the other hand,[105] writes that whatever will be of some benefit to a *seriously ill patient,* whether it be medication, food or any other need, may be prepared if Rabbinic law only is to be set aside. This is so in a situation where not providing it will not adversely affect him or his prognosis. Wherever possible this must be done in an indirect manner. If, however, there is great need for it, either to ease suffering or to strengthen and refresh him, it is permitted even if Torah law must be set aside.[106] Thus, if hot food or drink which would strengthen him is not available, it may be cooked on *Shabbat.*[107] Similarly, if a hot bath or washing would refresh and strengthen him, water may be boiled for the purpose if it is not available.[108] These

89. שבת פ״ב ה״ה
90. תורת האדם, שער הסכנה
91. מ״ב ס״ק יד
92. יומא פד ע״ב
93. שעה״צ ס״ק יא
94. יומא פב ע״ב
95. חזון יחזקאל, תוספתא שבת פט״ז מי״ב
96. ח״א סי׳ נד מובא בביה״ל ד״ה כל
97. ח״ו סי׳ יד
98. שבת קכט ע״א ד״ה דבר
99. וכן מובא במג״א ס״ק יז
100. ראה בביה״ל ד״ה כל
101. ס״ק יד
102. ראה במ״ב ס״ק קב
103. הערה על נשמת אברהם כרך א עמ׳ שלה
104. שו״ת יחוה דעת ח״ד סי׳ ל
105. פל״ב סע׳ כד
106. שם סע׳ כב
107. שם סע׳ עב
108. שם סע׳ פא

day. However, if the nature of the illness, even a serious one, (B)is known to be such that one may wait and not need to set aside Sabbath laws, one (C)must not desecrate the Sabbath.

NISHMAT AVRAHAM

rulings are applicable even if his condition would not deteriorate by not having the hot food or water.

The treatment of pain. May Sabbath laws be set aside to treat pain in a *seriously ill patient* even if withholding such treatment will not affect his prognosis? The *Shemirat Shabbat KeHilchatah*[109] writes, in the name of *Rav Shlomo Zalman Auerbach zt"l,* that since morphine only treats pain but not the underlying disease, it would appear that giving morphine should be compared to the extraction of a tooth. The *Rama*[110] and the *Mishnah Berurah*[111] rule that this is forbidden since its medical value is uncertain. In spite of this, continues *Rav Auerbach zt"l,* there is room to permit it since pain can increase the threat to the patient's life. Later we heard from *Rav Auerbach zt"l* that anything that will ease the suffering of a *seriously ill patient* and refresh him is part of the *mitzvah* of saving life, even if it helps for a limited period, and one is therefore required to treat his pain.

4(B) is known to be: This is true only if one is absolutely certain that the patient's condition will not deteriorate as a result of the delay.[112] The *Rashash*[113] says that when it is certain at present that the patient requires a given treatment involving setting aside Sabbath laws, but one wonders whether to wait a while to see if the patient's condition will improve and the treatment will not be necessary, the treatment should be given now. For the patient is *seriously ill* now and it is doubtful that waiting would obviate the need to desecrate the Sabbath.

4(C) must not desecrate: This applies to violations of Torah law; however, violations of Rabbinic law are permitted although, where possible, the violations of Rabbinic law should be done in an indirect manner.[114] Hence, surgery or other treatments should be postponed to after *Shabbat* if it is certain that the patient's condition will not deteriorate as a result of the delay. Similarly, all pre-operative preparations, such as laboratory tests, X-rays and shaving the area to be operated on, should be done after the termination of the Sabbath.[115] This ruling only applies to non-urgent treatment. However, at times, urgent surgery must wait until after the termination of the Sabbath to give the patient blood or other fluids to promote the best results. In such a situation, the transfusion, and all other preparations, must be done on *Shabbat,* if postponing them until after *Shabbat* will result in further delay to the surgery. *Rav Auerbach zt"l* told me, however, that in every acute situation which frightens and panics the patient, one is obligated to do whatever is necessary on *Shabbat.* Thus, he must, if necessary, be operated on on *Shabbat* if possible, even if such an operation is sometimes postponed for a day or two during the week because of more urgent cases. The *Shulchan Aruch* refers to a non-acute situation where there is no

109. פל"ב הערה קן
110. כאן סע' ג
111. ס"ק י ו-יב
112. מ"ב ס"ק טז
113. יומא פד ע"ב ד"ה אשר
114. מ"ב ס"ק קב
115. שמירת שבת כהלכתה פ"מ סע' לח. וראה בשעה"צ סי' שדמ ס"ק ה

§5: Sabbath laws may not be set aside for an external illness unless a doctor or the patient himself says that it is necessary to do so or if either feels that there is (A)danger to life (*see below, Siman* 618).

NISHMAT AVRAHAM

urgency to operate immediately; for example, a patient who has a growth which must be removed. Similarly, during childbirth, an episiotomy is done (to prevent excessive damage to the birth canal) which is then sutured after the birth. *Rav Auerbach zt''l* told me that this must be done immediately after the birth to prevent infection of the wound, even if there is no excessive bleeding and even if the Sabbath will terminate in a short while only (see also *Siman* 340 §1).

5(A) danger to life: According to *Rav Akiva Eiger*[116] this should read "possible danger to life." The *Mishnah Berurah*[117] explains that even if there is only a possibility that the patient's condition will deteriorate, leading to a life-threatening situation, the laws may be set aside. This was also the intention of the *Rama* in his gloss to this section. This is also the opinion of the *Ramban* quoted by the *Beit Yosef*.

Tosafot's[118] statement is famous – "the reason why one does not follow a majority where there is danger to life is because of the Torah's[119] injunction 'and you should live by them' (the laws of the Torah), which implies, and not die because of them.[120] Hence one should not in any way come to cause the death of a Jew (as a result of keeping the laws of the Torah)." But the possibility of the loss of life in the future cannot be considered if at the present there is no hint of this,[121] unless the cause of the possible threat to life is already present. If at present there is no such threat, although such a threat is a possibility in the future because of other factors, the patient cannot be considered to be in danger of his life.[122] *Rav Auerbach zt''l* also rules that if the illness, which could become life-threatening, is already present and the patient's condition is deteriorating, he is to be considered as being in a life-threatening situation. If, however, his condition is stable, the Sabbath may not be desecrated, so long as it is certain that the treatment may be given later, with the same results.[123] True, whatever is common practice is permitted even if there is only a slight danger involved. And whatever is commonly considered to be a threat to life must be considered as such.[124] But when there is generally no concern of damage voiced, *Shabbat* is not desecrated; the lack of knowledge is said to invoke *Hashem's* guardianship, as the verse says: *"Hashem* guards simpletons."[125] The *Binyan Tzion*[126] writes that although nothing takes precedent over a threat to life, and even remote possibilities are considered enough to set aside Sabbath laws, nevertheless this is only if a definite threat to life already exists. Thus if a wall collapsed on someone, even remote possibilities are taken

116. הגהות
117. ס״ק יז
118. יומא פה ע״א ד״ה ולפקח
119. ויקרא יח:ה
120. פרט לע״ז, ג״ע וש״ד – יו״ד סי׳ קנז סע׳ א
121. חזו״א אהלות סי׳ כב ס״ק לב ד״ה כפ״ת. שו״ת רעק״א סי׳ ס ד״ה ולענ״ד
122. שבט מיהודה ח״א בהערות נוספות פרקים ח־י, מובא בשמירת שבת כהלכתה פל״ב הערה ב
123. שמירת שבת כהלכתה שם
124. שבט מיהודה ח״א סי׳ יט ס״ק ב. הגרש״ז אויערבאך זצ״ל שמירת שבת כהלכתה שם
125. תהלים קטז:ו
126. סי׳ לז מובא בשמירת שבת כהלכתה שם

§6: One who has a (A)"*makkah*" on the back of his hand or foot, swallowed a leech, was bitten by a rabid dog or by a snake or other such reptile, even if it is only doubtful as to whether it is lethal, is considered like one who has an internal disease.

NISHMAT AVRAHAM

into account for the benefit of the victim. However if an actual threat is not present but merely a future possibility, probabilities are taken into account. Therefore, the *Tzitz Eliezer*[127] rules that for a mild disease such as a cold we consider how the majority of cases will end and do not act on the basis of the small minority in which it may become a threat to life. However, *Rav Neuwirth shlita* told me that even an early pneumonia is to be considered a life-threatening condition unless the patient's condition is stable.

6(A) "*makkah*" on the back of his hand or foot: The *Shulchan Aruch* uses the word *makkah* which could mean either an injury or a disease. The *Tosafot*[128] says that the *Gemara* which is the source of this *halachah* refers to a disease as opposed to an injury. The *Shulchan Aruch HaRav*[129] and the *Kaf HaChaim*[130] include both within the framework of this *halachah*. The *Tosafot*[131] also writes that Sabbath laws are set aside even though the patient may sometimes recover spontaneously from such a *makkah*.

The *Aruch HaShulchan*[132] defines the back of the hand and foot to exclude the fingers and this is also the opinion of the *Ketsot HaShulchan*.[133] Present medical thinking, however, does not differentiate between the back or palm of the hand or foot for identical wounds.

Controversy between *Chazal* and medical opinion on the nature of an illness.

Chazal[134] state that a *treifah* animal cannot live more than twelve months. The *Rashba*[135] writes about a *treifah* animal that ostensibly lived more than twelve months, that whatever *Chazal* have laid down as from Mt. Sinai can never be denied even if there is so-called evidence against them. The *Rivash*[136] writes that one cannot judge the laws and *mitzvot* of our Torah by the standards of lay experts on nature or medicine, since their opinions could lead one to deny the Divinity of the Torah. The *Shach*[137] mentions the *Rashba* but also cites the *Maharshal*[138] who explains that when *Chazal* stated that a *treifah* animal could not live for more than twelve months, they referred to the vast majority of cases. The *Shach* adds, in approval, that it would appear from this that the *Maharshal* would rule that where doubt exists about a particular animal being a *treifah*, if it lived more than twelve months it would be kosher.[139] [*Author's note: The Rashba and the Rivash*

127. ח״ח סי׳ טו פ״ז או״ק ז
128. ע״ז כח ע״א ד״ה מכה שע״ג היד
129. כאן סע׳ ו
130. ס״ק ל
131. ע״ז יב ע״ב ד״ה הבולע
132. כאן סע׳ כה
133. סי׳ קלו בבדה״ש ס״ק א
134. חולין מב ע״א
135. שו״ת ח״א סי׳ צח
136. שו״ת סי׳ תמז
137. יו״ד סי׳ נז ס״ק מח
138. חולין סו״פ אלו טרפות
139. וראה גם ברמב״ם הל׳ שחיטה פ״י הי״ב ו־יג. מאירי נדה יז ע״ב במשנה. רבינו אברהם בן הרמב״ם במאמרו על אודות דרשות חז״ל, מודפס בהתחלת העין יעקב. חזו״א הל׳ אישות סי׳ כז ס״ק ג. תפא״י שבת פי״ט מ״ב. שו״ת מהר״ם שיק יו״ד סי׳ קנב, רמד ו־רמח. שדי חמד אסיפת דינים מערכת המציצה. זוכר הברית סי׳ יב סע׳ לו. שו״ת אבני נזר יו״ד סי׳ שלח. שו״ת דברי

§7: Sabbath laws are set aside for any injury (A)caused by metal, a (B)rectal boil, a furuncle or for a patient with a

NISHMAT AVRAHAM

surely knew that there are at times exceptional cases. But the Shach is relating to practical halachah whereas the rishonim are reflecting the theological side of the problem. The concept that any "evidence" can contradict Chazal and therefore the Torah itself is obviously inconceivable and attacks the very foundation and basis of our belief in Hashem and His Torah. It is this that the rishonim are discussing and hence their sweeping statements.]

7(A) caused by metal: Even if the wound is external and not on the back of the hand or foot (see §6).[140] Sabbath laws are set aside for any wound, no matter how small or superficial, caused by a knife or even a needle.[141] But the *Aruch HaShulchan*[142] is certain that this is only if the cut is deep. *Rav Yaakov Emden*[143] writes that if the cut is superficial and small and does not appear dangerous and the bleeding can easily be stopped by finger pressure, Sabbath laws are not set aside. This is also the opinion of the *Ketsot HaShulchan*[144] and the *Shemirat Shabbat KeHilchatah*.[145] However, if the knife was dirty or if there is a possibility of tetanus, Sabbath laws are set aside as necessary in order to receive treatment.[146] On the other hand, if the injury was close to the termination of *Shabbat*, one should wait until after *Shabbat* for treatment[147] if it is certain that there is no possible danger in doing so.[148]

7(B) rectal boil: A sufferer from hemorrhoids may take medication on *Shabbat* to prevent constipation, since this is not intended to be a treatment, but is meant to prevent further injury to the hemorrhoids (see §23). Even after the hemorrhoids have been cured, he may continue to take laxatives (this is similar to the *halachah* in §27).[149] If they are painful, one may soak them by sitting in a basin of warm water which was heated before the Sabbath. Since a healthy person may wash himself, it is not obvious that he is soaking himself for a medicinal purpose.[150] The *Ketsot HaShulchan*,[151] however, considers that it is apparent that this is a treatment and therefore is only permissible if his whole body is affected by the pain of the inflamed hemorrhoids. Suppositories may be inserted if the hemorrhoids are very painful.[152] A suppository may be cut in half if necessary (see above, *Siman* 322A).[153]

A patient with hemorrhoids that bleed after defecation should wash himself rather than use toilet paper. However, if water is not available, toilet paper may be used. Even though the paper is "colored" by the blood it is also "dirtied" by it.

מלביאל ח״ד סי׳ פז. שערי תשובה או״ח סי׳ תריב ס״ק ז. שו״ת מהר״י אסאד יו״ד סי׳ רנח. שו״ת בית יצחק יו״ד ח״ב סי׳ צח. שו״ת בנין ציון ח״א סי׳ כג ו־כד שו״ת זכר שמחה סי׳ קלד. מ״ב סי׳ שלא ביה״ל ד״ה ופורעין. דעת כהן סי׳ קמ. שו״ת הר צבי יו״ד סי׳ ריד. מנחת שבת סי׳ צב ס״ק לב. שו״ת מנחת יצחק ח״ה סי׳ כד אות ב. יסודי ישורון ח״ד עמ׳ קצ. שו״ת שבט הלוי ח״ב יו״ד סי׳ קל ופמ״ג סי׳ שכח מ״ז ס״ק ב הובא במ״ב ס״ק ח שדנים בענין

140. מ״ב ס״ק יח

141. חי׳ רעק״א. כף החיים ס״ק לד. ביה״ל ד״ה מחמת

142. סע׳ כו

143. מור וקציעה כאן ד״ה ולתת קורי עכביש

144. סי׳ קלו בבדה״ש ס״ק ב

145. פל״ב סע׳ יא ס״ק ז ופל״ה סע׳ לא

146. קצוה״ש שם. שמירת שבת כהלכתה פל״ה סע׳ מ

147. שמירת שבת כהלכתה שם

148. כתב לי הגרש״ז אויערבאך זצ״ל

149. שו״ת ציץ אליעזר חי״א סי׳ לז

150. שם חי״ב סי׳ מד

151. סי׳ קלח בבדה״ש סוס״ק לא

152. שו״ת ציץ אליעזר ח״ח סי׳ טו פ״י אות ה. קצות החושן שם

153. שמירת שבת כהלכתה פל״ג סע׳ ד והערה ל בשם הגרש״ז אויערבאך זצ״ל

(C)very high temperature with chills.

§9: Sabbath laws are set aside for an (A)illness of the eye if there is a discharge, tearing from pain, bleeding or pus.

§10: Sabbath laws are set aside for any illness, even if external, (A)that doctors consider to be serious. (B)If one doctor con-

NISHMAT AVRAHAM

Moreover, the problem of "coloring" is mitigated because he would suffer shame if he were to appear dirty in public.[154]

7(C) very high temperature. The *poskim* differ as to what degree of temperature the *Shulchan Aruch* is referring to. The *Igrot Moshe*[155] permits Sabbath laws to be set aside for a temperature of 101°F (about 37.9°C), or even less if the patient fears that he is *seriously ill*.[156] Others[157] rule that even with this temperature only Rabbinic laws may be set aside. The *Shemirat Shabbat KeHilchatah*[158] writes that in most cases the fever per se is not dangerous unless extremely high, and medication may be used to bring it down as with any *non-seriously ill* patient. An ice bag or bottle may also be used for this purpose and one may crack ice in order to fill the bag or bottle.[159] Only if the fever is very high, the patient feels ill and the cause of the temperature is uncertain, should the patient be considered *seriously ill*. However, the aged and very young are to be treated as *seriously ill* even if the temperature is not very high if its cause is not obvious.[160]

9(A) illness of the eye: Even though Torah laws are not set aside for a danger to a limb (see §17C), the eye is an exception since the *Talmud*[161] states that it is connected to the heart and a disease in the eye may lead to a danger to life.[162] Thus Torah laws are set aside for any severe acute infection or inflammation, injury, severe pain or sudden deterioration in vision, even if only affecting one eye. Eye drops may be used even for a mild infection.[163] An ointment may also be used since the *melachah* of "smoothing out" does not apply where there is no intention to do so.[164] However, no treatment is permitted for a mildly painful eye.[165]

10(A) that doctors: If the patient demands a particular drug and the doctor says that there is no need for it, one complies with the patient's demands unless the doctor says that he will be harmed by it.[166] If the doctor prescribes a drug (and this involves setting aside Torah law) and the patient refuses to take it, he is forced to do so.[167] Such a *seriously ill*

154. מנחת שבת סי׳ צא ס״ק ל. מג״א סי׳ שכ ס״ק כד. שו״ע הרב סי׳ שכ סע׳ כז. חיי אדם כלל סט סוסע׳ יט. מ״ב סי׳ שכ ס״ק נט וסי שכח ס״ק קמו

155. או״ח ח״א קכט

156. וכ״כ בשמו היסודי ישורון ח״ד עמ׳ רמו

157. קצוה״ש סי׳ קלח בבדה״ש ס״ק לא. שו״ת ציץ אליעזר ח״ח סי׳ טו פ״ז אות ג. הגר״פ עפשטיין זצ״ל בסידור ירושלים בהגהותיו לקונטרס הרפואה הערה 17

158. פל״ב סע׳ יא ס״ק א בשם הגרש״ז אויערבאך זצ״ל

159. או״ח סי׳ שכ סע׳ י. שמירת שבת כהלכתה פל״ג סע׳ טו

160. ראה בשמירת שבת כהלכתה שם

161. ע״ז כח ע״ב

162. מ״ב ס״ק כב

163. שמירת שבת כהלכתה פל״ד סע׳ ח בשם האגלי טל מלאכת טוחן סע׳ יז

164. שמירת שבת כהלכתה שם הערה מ בשם הגרש״ז אויערבאך זצ״ל

165. להלן סע׳ כ ומ״ב ס״ק סד. שמירת שבת כהלכתה שם

166. מ״ב ס״ק כה ו־כו בשם שו״ת הרדב״ז ח״ד סי׳ סו (אלף קלח)

167. מג״א ס״ק ו. מ״ב ס״ק ו בשם הרדב״ז ח״ד סי׳ סז

siders that Sabbath laws have to be set aside and another says they need not, they are nonetheless set aside. There are those who rule that even a (C)layman's opinion that an illness is serious is accepted since (D)everyone has a little knowledge of medicine. Sabbath laws are therefore set

NISHMAT AVRAHAM

patient who acts strictly against the advice of a doctor, is considered to have "shed his own blood" and will be held accountable for his life.[168] The *Shach*[169] points out that the patient has already sworn on Mount Sinai to observe the *mitzvah* of saving his life (along with all the other *mitzvot*).

10(B) If one doctor: If the controversy is between a single doctor on the one hand and two or more other doctors on the other, the opinion of the single doctor is accepted if he is famous for his astuteness and knowledge, if he is the one who says that Sabbath laws must be set aside.[170] The doctor who felt that Sabbath laws need not be set aside must nevertheless do whatever is necessary; he must even set aside Sabbath laws against his own opinion. Because the *Shulchan Aruch* rules that Sabbath laws are set aside, the dissenting doctor must do so since there is now no "desecration" of the Sabbath.[171] This applies if the controversy is about how serious the illness is and how urgent the treatment. However, if the controversy is about the kind of treatment to be given, one doctor suggesting a treatment which does not involve setting aside Torah law and the other suggesting a treatment that will, one cannot demand that the former set aside the Sabbath and administer the treatment which he did not suggest.[172]

The *Biur Halachah*[173] writes that where there is a difference of opinion between the patient and the doctor regarding a particular medication for a known disease, with the patient claiming that it will help and the doctor that it will not, Sabbath laws may not be set aside to comply with the patient's request. However, if the patient claims that in his experience it has helped, or if there is a possibility that he will become so upset and agitated at the refusal to comply with his request that it might further endanger him, Sabbath laws may be set aside. But a patient's diagnosis of his condition cannot be accepted if it runs contrary to that of the doctor. Even though the doctor can be mistaken, the patient cannot be heeded because he is ignorant in this context.[174] *Rav Auerbach zt"l* wrote to me that one should nevertheless take care, as far as possible, to show the patient that his view is being considered, so as not to upset him.

10(C) layman's opinion: This applies only if he claims to be familiar with the disease. His opinion, however, cannot be taken against that of a doctor, even if following his view would lead to a lenient ruling.[175]

10(D) everyone has a little knowledge: Even for an external illness which is gen-

(אלף קלט) וח״ג סי׳ תמד (תתפה). וראה ברמב״ם הל׳ שבת פ״ב ה״ג ורמב״ן מלחמת ד׳ סנה׳ עד ע״א

168. ר״ן יומא פב ע״א ד״ה חוץ

169. יו״ד סי׳ רלח ס״ק ה. וראה גם בלב אברהם ח״ב פ״א

170. מטה אפרים סי׳ תריח באלף המטה ס״ק ב. מ״ב שם ס״ק י. ערוה״ש סע׳ יד. יסודי ישורון ח״ד עמ׳ רלט. שו״ת ציץ אליעזר ח״ח סי׳ טו אות טז

171. יסודי ישורון שם. ציץ אליעזר שם אות יח

172. ציץ אליעזר שם אות יט

173. ד״ה רופא

174. שמירת שבת כהלכתה פל״ב הערה כה בשם הגרש״ז אויערבאך זצ״ל. וראה גם שם סע׳ נב

175. מ״ב ס״ק כז

aside since in matters of life and death we are lenient when the situation is uncertain.

GLOSS: *There is an opinion that this only applies to* (E)*Jews but not to non-Jews who are not doctors.*

NISHMAT AVRAHAM

erally not considered serious. If possible, however, a non-Jew should be asked to do the *melachah* in this situation.[176]

The *Chatam Sofer*[177] writes that if a person who looks healthy, but says he has a pain in his heart, asks for food on *Yom Kippur* or asks that Sabbath laws be set aside for him, we may not comply and answer to his request since he looks healthy, but we may allow him to take food or to set aside Sabbath laws on his own. He[178] bolsters this ruling by noting that the *Mishnah*[179] says that among the miracles that occurred in the Temple, no woman miscarried as a result of an unnatural craving to eat from the sacrificial meat. The *Tosfot Yom Tov*[180] explains, in the name of *Rashi,* that although she hungered for the meat she was not allowed to eat it by Torah law. This explanation is surprising since *Chazal* considered this to be a life-threatening situation and Torah laws are set aside to prevent a miscarriage. Therefore, concludes the *Chatam Sofer,* one must assume that the woman is in the early stages of her pregnancy and it was not yet obvious to others. Hence they could not give her food from the sacrifices. However, *Rav Auerbach zt"l*[181] offers a different explanation. A pregnant woman who craves food is different from anyone else who has the same feeling. She will miscarry if her wish is not fulfilled but there is no comparable danger to anyone else with the same craving. Therefore, if a woman who is not pregnant desires something that is forbidden by Torah law it may not be given to her. However, if she says she is pregnant, even though she is not obviously so, she may be given whatever she craves to eat, be it food on *Yom Kippur* or sacrificial meat, if, for some reason, she is unable to take it herself. Even though her pregnancy is not obvious, we accept this as at least a possibility. Even if she is wont to lie, one cannot be certain that she is lying now. The miracle of which the *Mishnah* speaks must refer to a woman who herself is unaware of her pregnancy, but feels a sudden unnatural craving for the sacrificial meat. Since the forbidden food could not be given to her, a miracle was therefore necessary to prevent a miscarriage. *Rav Auerbach zt"l* concludes that if one fears he is having a heart attack and asks to be driven to the hospital he must not be refused. Even if there are no external signs of a serious illness and we are uncertain if he is indeed having a heart attack, we do not compare this to a situation where someone expresses a desire for forbidden food.

10(E) Jews: The *Mishnah Berurah*[182] also holds the view expressed by the *Rama.* The *Chida*[183] also writes that since all doctors are qualified from recognized institutions we accept them all equally. Other *acharonim*[184] also endorse

176. מ״ב ס״ק כח

177. שו״ת אהע״ז ח״ב סי׳ פב סוד״ה הנה בהאמנת מובא במ״ב סי׳ תריז ס״ק ו

178. שם

179. אבות פ״ה מ״ה

180. שם

181. מוריה סיון תשל״א עמ׳ לא

182. ס״ק ל. וראה גם בתשב״ץ ח״ג סי׳ רעא. תפא״י יומא פ״ח ס״ק כו. הלכתא גבירתא שם מ״ה ס״ק א. שו״ת דברי חיים ח״א יו״ד סוסי׳ לא

183. שיורי ברכה ס״ק א

184. שו״ת פנים מאירות ח״א סי׳ יב. שו״ת שבות יעקב

§11: If it was decided on *Shabbat* that a seriously ill patient required daily treatment for eight days, involving setting aside Sabbath laws, one (A)may not postpone the first treatment till after *Shabbat,* in order that Sabbath laws would only be set aside the following *Shabbat.* Rather, the initial treatment must be given on the first *Shabbat* even though this will mean setting aside Sabbath laws on two Sabbaths.

§12: When one needs to set aside Sabbath laws for a seriously ill patient, he should try not to ask a (A)non-Jew, a child or

NISHMAT AVRAHAM

this view.

The *Sdei Chemed*[185] rules that we may depend on the opinion of a non-religious Jewish doctor, who himself eats on *Yom Kippur,* that a patient must eat on *Yom Kippur.* This is also the opinion of *Rav Moshe Feinstein zt"l.*[186] The *Shemirat Shabbat KeHilchatah*[187] writes that one must do whatever a doctor, religious, non-religious or non-Jewish says is necessary for a possibly *seriously ill* patient, even if Torah law is set aside. One may consult with a non-religious Jewish or a non-Jewish specialist even though a religious Jewish doctor is available who is not a specialist. Although one knows that the non-religious Jewish specialist will desecrate the Sabbath unnecessarily he may still be called preferentially over a religious but non-specialist Jewish doctor.[188]

11(A) may not postpone: This ruling does not contradict the one in §4. Here it is important to start treatment immediately. There, it is certain that the patient will in no way be harmed if one waits until the termination of *Shabbat.*[189]

12(A) non-Jew, a child or a woman: The *Rosh* explains that sometimes a non-Jew or child is not present and precious time may be lost searching for one. If a woman is chosen when men are present, it may lead to a misunderstanding that Sabbath laws may not be set aside for a *seriously ill* patient, and that is why she is asked rather than a man. This misunderstanding will, in turn, lead her to delay and thus cause harm to the patient. Furthermore, she may, through ignorance of Sabbath laws, desecrate the Sabbath in another situation where it is not permitted.[190] These fears, however, do not apply to a nurse[191] or a midwife.[192] If, however, a man is not present, a woman should certainly not hesitate to do whatever is necessary as quickly as possible.[193]

ח״ב סי׳ עו. כף החיים ס״ק מח ו־ס״ק נז בשם האו״ה כלל נט סי׳ ו ותו״ש אות יג. וראה גם בביה״ל סי׳ תריח סע׳ א ד״ה חולה. שו״ת מנחת יצחק ח״א סי׳ קכה ס״ק ו וסי׳ קכז ס״ק ב. שו״ת ציץ אליעזר ח״ח סי׳ טו סופ״ח. שמירת שבת כהלכתה פ״מ הערה א

185. מערכת יוהכ״פ סי״ג ס״ק ה

186. ספר הלכה ורפואה ח״א עמ׳ קל

187. פל״ב סע׳ כא

188. שמירת שבת כהלכתה שם סע׳ מח. וראה שם הערה קכה ו־קכו בשם הגרש״ז אויערבאך זצ״ל

189. מ״ב ס״ק לב

190. מ״ב ס״ק לג. וראה גם שם ס״ק לז. שמירת שבת כהלכתה פל״ב הערה טז. וראה בארחות חיים ס״ק יג

191. סי׳ קלה בבדה״ש סוס״ק ט

192. ר״ן על הרי״ף יומא פ״ח דף ד ע״ב ד״ה ואין. שמירת שבת כהלכתה פל״ב הערה ה

193. מ״ב ס״ק לד

a woman to do so. On the contrary, (B)adult Jews who are intelligent should set Sabbath laws aside.

GLOSS: *There are those who say that if a melachah can be performed (C)in an indirect manner without delay, it should be done in this way. If a non-Jew can do whatever is necessary without any delay, this should be done and (D)this is the accepted custom.*

NISHMAT AVRAHAM

12(B) adult Jews who are intelligent: The *Rambam,*[194] in codifying the relevant *Talmudic* passage,[195] writes that when Sabbath laws must be set aside, this should be done by *gedolei Yisrael* (towering scholars) and the wise. The *Beit Yosef* interprets the *gedolei Yisrael* of the *Rambam* not as the greats of Israel but as the male adults of Israel. But the *Taz*[196] points out the textual difficulties involved and says that the *Rambam* clearly refers to those who are learned and not just adults. The *Orchot Chaim*[197] writes, based on the *Rambam's* commentary to the *Mishnah,*[198] that the *Rambam* in his *Code* refers to those who are renowned Torah scholars; this is also the opinion of the *Tosfot Rid*[199] and the *Maharil.*[200] However, the *Tashbetz*[201] interprets the *Talmud Bavli* as referring to all adult Jews and the *Orchot Chaim* writes that this also appears to be the opinion of the *Talmud Yerushalmi.*

12(C) in an indirect manner: The *Mishnah Berurah*[202] rules that if one can do whatever is necessary for a *seriously ill* patient without setting aside Sabbath laws, they may not be set aside. It would appear, he continues, that if the treatment is not urgent, even if doing whatever is necessary in an indirect manner would lead to a slight delay, this is how it should be done. In this way only a Rabbinic law is set aside instead of a Torah one.

12(D) this is the accepted custom: This is also the ruling of the *Chayei Adam.*[203] The *Taz*[204] however, rules like the *Mechaber* that a Jew must do whatever is necessary wherever possible. This is also the opinion of other *acharonim.*[205] The *Shemirat Shabbat KeHilchatah,*[206] however, adds that if the patient's need is not urgent and a non-Jew is available, it is preferable, wherever possible, to ask him.

But the controversy between the *Mechaber* and the *Rama* may not be as polarized as it would appear. *Rav Abba Shaul zt"l*[207] writes that the *Mechaber* refers to whatever is directly necessary for the patient's bodily needs. However, for something which is not so, such as documentation of his temperature, he, too, would say that one should ask a non-Jew to do it. *Rav Auerbach zt"l* also told me that whatever is not a direct treatment or benefit for the patient, should, even in the *Mechaber's* opinion, be done where possible by a non-Jew, or by a Jew in an indirect manner.

194. הל׳ שבת פ״ב ה״ג
195. יומא פד ע״ב
196. ס״ק ה
197. ס״ק יב
198. שבת פי״ח מ״ג
199. יומא שם
200. הל׳ יוהכ״פ
201. שו״ת ח״א סי׳ נד
202. ס״ק לה
203. כלל סח סע׳ ב
204. ס״ק ה
205. א״ר ס״ק יב. תוס׳ שבת ס״ק טו. שו״ע הרב סע׳ יג. ערוה״ש סע׳ ז. שו״ת ציץ אליעזר ח״ח סי׳ טו פ״ב. שמירת שבת כהלכתה פל״ב סע׳ ו
206. פל״ח סע׳ ב
207. אור לציון ח״ב פל״ו הערה ב

§13: Whoever hastens to set aside Sabbath laws when necessary for a seriously ill patient is praiseworthy, even if there is a by-product to his action; for instance, if he cast a net to save a drowning child and simultaneously caught fish, or (A)any other such example.

NISHMAT AVRAHAM

This would include, for example, documentation of his chart, or turning off a light so that he may sleep. As to putting out an oil lamp or candle so that a *seriously ill* patient can sleep, the *Mishnah Berurah*[208] writes that according to the *Rambam* this may only be done if the patient cannot be screened from the light or moved to another room. However, the *Biur Halachah*[209] notes that the *Meiri*[210] appears to rule that even if the patient can be screened from the light, nevertheless it would still be permissible to extinguish the flame. He feels that this would be true even in the opinion of Rebbe Yehudah (a *Tanna*) who rules that such an act is normally forbidden by Torah law.[211]

The *Maharshag*[212] says that if a *seriously ill patient* must eat a fig to save his life, even if there is one on the table and someone plucked another fig from a tree (transgressing seemingly a Torah prohibition), he would not be guilty of contravening Torah law since he did what he did to save a life. The *Gemara*[213] discusses a case of a *seriously ill* patient who needs two figs to save his life. On a tree there is a twig with two figs and another with three. He should pluck the twig with the two figs since the third fig is not necessary for the patient. The *Avnei Nezer*[214] cites this and says that if there was a twig with two figs and two other twigs with one fig each, it should be permitted to pluck the two twigs, each with one fig, since this is being done for the sake of the patient. The *Kiryat Sefer*[215] writes that when a *seriously ill* patient is required to eat forbidden food, the injunction to prefer the lesser degree of two forbidden foods is only Rabbinic. The *Kovetz Shiurim*[216] adds that if kosher food is available it would be forbidden for the patient to eat non-kosher food. However, to search for kosher food so that he need not eat the non-kosher food is only required by Rabbinic law. For when he eats the non-kosher food, kosher food is not immediately available.

13(A) any other such example: Thus, if a child fell into a pit a person may cut out steps in order to reach him. If a child was locked in, one should not attempt to pacify him until the key is found, lest the child meanwhile die from terror. Rather, he should break the door down to free him, even though the strips of wood from the broken door can be used later for something else. Thus, even if the person will later benefit from the steps and the strips of wood, it is permissible.[217] However, since most *rishonim* rule that it is forbidden for him to have this in mind when saving the child, he should not think of the extra benefits.[218] *Rav Auerbach zt"l,* however, wrote to me that even if he

208. סי׳ רעח ס״ק א
209. סי׳ רעח סע׳ א ד״ה מותר
210. שבת כט ע״ב
211. ומסיים המ״ב ויש לדחות קצת, עכ״ל. ובמאירי שם לכאורה רואים ההיפך וצ״ע
212. שו״ת ח״ב סי׳ יד
213. מנחות סד ע״א
214. שו״ת או״ח סי׳ קנז אות י
215. על הרמב״ם סוף פי״ד מהל׳ מאכלות אסורות
216. כתובות ס״ק יג
217. מ״ב ס״ק לח
218. שעה״צ ס״ק יז

§14: One may (A)ritually slaughter for a seriously ill patient who needs to eat meat, rather than give him meat from an animal that was not ritually slaughtered. However, if he needs the meat urgently, and it would take too long to ritually slaughter an animal, whereas meat from an animal which was not ritually slaughtered is available, he is given the latter.

NISHMAT AVRAHAM

did so, he may still benefit from the by-product. A refrigerator may be opened in order to take out what is needed for a *seriously ill* patient even if the light inside (which was not inactivated before the Sabbath) goes on. Based on the above, *Rav Neuwirth shlita*[219] rules that one may take out food for the healthy when the refrigerator has been opened to take something out for the *seriously ill* patient (see also *Siman* 278D for further discussion on the use of a refrigerator on *Shabbat*).

14(A) ritually slaughter: Since he might feel nauseous at the thought of eating killed (non-kosher) meat and thereby become even more ill. The *Beit Yosef* quotes the *Ran* that since one is punished for every *kezayit* of non-kosher meat eaten, eating such meat is worse than the single offense of slaughtering on *Shabbat*. If Rabbinically forbidden meat was available, the *Mishnah Berurah*[220] rules that the patient should eat that rather than slaughter on *Shabbat* on his behalf. He also raises the question of what to do if the patient says that he would not feel nauseous eating non-kosher meat. Where the patient is a child, rules the *Mishnah Berurah,* it would appear to be preferable to feed him non-kosher meat rather than slaughter on *Shabbat*. This is also the opinion of the *Achiezer.*[221]

The *Tzitz Eliezer,*[222] quoting the *Netziv,*[223] writes that since the forbidden meat will "seal his heart and taint his soul"[224] this would be an additional reason to prefer slaughtering meat on *Shabbat*. Therefore, writes the *Tzitz Eliezer,*[225] one should, in every case, slaughter on *Shabbat* rather than give such a patient non-kosher meat, and this is borne out by the wording of the *Shulchan Aruch.*[226] However, *Rav Auerbach zt"l* wrote to me that the fact that non-kosher meat would "taint his soul" is not, in itself, sufficient reason to desecrate the *Shabbat.*

Should the slaughtered meat be koshered (salted) as demanded by *halachah,* even though salting is forbidden on *Shabbat*? The *acharonim* rule that it should if time permits.[227] The meat need only be salted for 23-24 minutes if the patient cannot wait the full hour.[228]

219. שמירת שבת כהלכתה פל״ב סע׳ עא. ראה גם בביה״ל סי׳ רעו סע׳ א ד״ה אין

220. מ״ב ס״ק לט

221. שו״ת ח״ג סי׳ פא ס״ק י

222. ח״ח סי׳ טו ס״ק כג

223. מרומי שדה על יומא פג ד״ה במשנה

224. עיין יו״ד סי׳ פא סע׳ ז בהגה. ט״ז שם ס״ק יב וש״ך ס״ק כה ו־כו. פמ״ג בש״ד שם. שו״ת מהר״ם שיק או״ח סי׳ קסג. העמק דבר דברים ו,י ובהרחב דבר שם. שו״ת חת״ס או״ח סי׳ פג

225. שם ס״ק כד

226. אך עיין בשו״ת הרשב״א ח״א סי׳ תרפט שכותב דאמרינן לגוי לשחוט. וראה גם בשו״ת חת״ס או״ח סי׳ פב. שדי חמד מערכת חי״ת כלל טו. מקראי קודש הימים הנוראים עמ׳ קנו בהררי קודש

227. שו״ת מהר״ם שיק או״ח סי׳ קלח. ארחות חיים כאן ס״ק יד. שו״ת מהרש״ם ח״ז סי׳ נא ודעת תורה כאן. שמירת שבת כהלכתה פל״ב סע׳ פ

228. שמירת שבת כהלכתה פ״מ סע׳ פז

§15: If the doctor decides that the patient urgently requires to eat a single fig and ten people ran, each to bring him one, none of them are liable even though he was (A)cured after eating the first fig. And they will each be well rewarded by the Almighty.

§16: If it was thought that the patient needed two figs and there were only either two twigs with one fig each or one with three figs immediately available, the latter is plucked. If there were two figs on one twig and three on another, (A)the former is plucked.

NISHMAT AVRAHAM

Wherever possible, a non-Jew should be asked to do the salting, under supervision, to make sure that the requirements of *halachah* are fulfilled.[229]

15(A) cured: Each carried the fig through a public domain (or plucked it from a tree). Even though the patient was already cured after eating the first fig and the other nine set aside Torah law needlessly, they are not liable since each thought that he would be the first. Moreover, not only are they not liable but they will be well rewarded for their good intentions.[230] However, if the need for the fig was not urgent, it would be forbidden for all of them to rush out to bring it.[231]

16(A) the former is plucked: In both cases only one *melachah* is performed (the plucking of a single twig). However, since the third fig is unnecessary, the *melachah* produces more than is required for the patient, and is forbidden. This rule applies to all *melachot,* for instance cooking more than necessary is not permitted.[232] The *rishonim* differ as to whether the above is forbidden by Torah law[233] or Rabbinic law.[234] The *Shemirat Shabbat KeHilchatah*[235] gives several details in this context: (a) There are *melachot* for which one is liable only when he has done an act which involves a particular minimum of material. For example, one is not liable by Torah law for cooking on *Shabbat* if he has cooked less than the amount of a fig. With reference to such *melachot* only that amount which is necessary for the patient can be provided and no more.[236] (b) There are *melachot* for which one is liable no matter how small the act accomplished. There is no minimum amount with respect to the prohibition. With such *melachot* we can speak of sub-categories: i) If two objects are involved: For example it is forbidden to press a switch which turns on two lights simultaneously when there is a switch which turns on only one light, if the patient or his caregiver needs only one light.[237] ii) If a greater or lesser result are both possible: For example one may not turn on a light of higher wattage rather

229. כף החיים כאן ס״ק פט
230. מ״ב ס״ק מב
231. ביה״ל ד״ה ויש
232. מ״ב ס״ק מד
233. ר״ן ביצה יז ע״א ד״ה ומיהא משמע
234. תוס׳ מנחות סד ע״א ד״ה שתים. רשב״א חולין טו ע״ב ור״ן שם. וראה גם בב״י סי׳ שיח ד״ה כתוב בא״ח וסי׳ שלא ד״ה ומ״ש וכן אם היה, מג״א סימן שיח ס״ק ו, תוס׳ שבת שם ס״ק ח, ומ״ב שם ס״ק יג. וראה גם בשו״ת הרמ״א סי׳ עו שמשמע שגם לדעתו הוה מדרבנן
235. פל״ב הערה צ
236. סי׳ שיח סע׳ ב וסי׳ שכח מ״ב ס״ק מד
237. סי׳ שכח סע׳ טז

GLOSS: *If, however, the matter is urgent, these considerations should not be given thought so as not to cause even a minimal delay.*

NISHMAT AVRAHAM

than one of lower wattage, if the patient or his caregiver has no need for the brighter light.[238] iii) If two objects are not involved and there is not a matter of greater and lesser results: Thus one may slaughter equally either a chicken or a cow for a *seriously ill* patient (see above, end of §14A).

When cooking for a *seriously ill* patient, one must be careful to cook only the amount that will satisfy his needs.[239] No more food or water may be added to the pot even if this is done before the fire is lit.[240] Obviously, if the situation is urgent, these considerations should not be given thought.[241] The *Shemirat Shabbat KeHilchatah*[242] adds that *non-seriously ill* patients may not eat food or water that was cooked in a hospital for the use of *seriously ill* patients (see also above, *Siman* 318A).

As to carrying more than is needed, the *Chafetz Chaim*[243] writes that nowadays when most of our streets fall into the category of *carmelit*[244] and not into that of a *public domain,* as defined by the Torah, one could possibly be lenient even according to those *rishonim* (see above, beginning of 16A) who rule that this is forbidden by the Torah. Thus, if necessary, it would be permitted for a Jew to bring food for a *seriously ill* patient and, at the same time, to carry his own food with it.[245] According to these *rishonim* this would not apply in the large cities of the world where there are *public domains* as defined by the Torah.[246] The *Or Same'ach*[247] forbids carrying that which is not necessary for the *seriously ill* patient, together with whatever is necessary for him; the *Har Tzvi*[248] permits it. Both the *Chafetz Chaim* and the *Chelkat Yaakov*[249] permit a soldier, ordered to set out on *Shabbat* for a journey of several days, to carry his *tefillin* (although he is not obligated to take them with him in the line of duty) in his knapsack on *Shabbat* along with those things that he is required to carry in the line of duty.

The *Chafetz Chaim* raises the question as to whether or not the unnecessary articles must be carried in the same hand as those that are necessary. Perhaps if they were carried in separate hands, even the *Rashba* – who considers that carrying the unnecessary along with the necessary is in principle a Rabbinic law – would agree that this would be forbidden by the Torah. But, one could say that since the same individual carries both the necessary and unnecessary articles, it is permitted whether he carries them in the same hand or not. Because the *Chafetz Chaim* is uncertain, he rules that they should be carried in the same hand. *Rav Auerbach zt"l* wrote to me that this issue does not apply to the ruling of the *Or Same'ach* men-

238. עיין שו״ת הר צבי או״ח ח״א סי׳ קעז

239. מ״ב ס״ק מד

240. סי׳ שיח סע׳ ב ומ״ב ס״ק יג. וראה בערוה״ש סי׳ שיח סע׳ טז

241. מ״ב ס״ק מד

242. פל״ב הערה קצג

243. מחנה ישראל פל״א סע׳ ב בהערה

244. אמנם כתוב בשמירת שבת כהלכתה פ״מ סע׳ סה בלשון ״אין לנו רשות הרבים גמורה״ אמר לי מו״ר הגרי״י נויבירט שליט״א שכוונתו לדעה השניה בסי׳ שמה סע׳ ז. וראה בשמירת שבת כהלכתה פי״ז סע׳ ג והערה כא

245. שמירת שבת כהלכתה פ״מ סוסע׳ סה והערה קלח

246. שם הערה קלח

247. הל׳ שבת פי״ח ה״א

248. שו״ת או״ח ח״א סי׳ קעז

249. שו״ת ח״א סי׳ מו

§17: If a person is so sick that he had to take to bed although he is not seriously ill,

GLOSS: *or if he feels unwell throughout his whole body even though he is up and around,*

(A)a non-Jew may be asked (B)to treat him. However, Torah law may not be set aside by a Jew even though there is (C)danger to a (D)limb. As to whether a Jew himself may set

NISHMAT AVRAHAM

tioned above, because the *Or Same'ach* would rule that it would be forbidden by the Torah even if the necessary and unnecessary articles were carried in separate containers in the same hand and certainly so if carried in separate hands. However, it does apply to the ruling of the *Har Tzvi* mentioned above because of the possibility that it would not be forbidden by the Torah since both articles are carried simultaneously by one and the same person.

17(A) a non-Jew may be asked: Only if the treatment is required immediately on *Shabbat*. However if it can wait until after *Shabbat,* it must be postponed till then.[250] *Rav Auerbach zt''l*[251] rules that it is permitted to ask the non-Jew on *Shabbat* so that the treatment will be done as soon after the termination of *Shabbat* as possible.

17(B) to treat him: Even if *melachot* forbidden by the Torah are set aside. One may also ask the non-Jew to see to the patient's other needs, even those that are not directly medical in nature, for example, cooking or baking for him if necessary.[252]

17(C) danger to a limb: A Jew may not set aside Torah law for a patient unless there is a threat to his life[253] even if he does it in an indirect manner.[254] However, there are great *poskim* who permit Torah law to be set aside for a *non-seriously ill* patient provided that it is done in an indirect manner.[255] *Rav Auerbach zt''l* rules[256] that if a non-Jew is not present, one may act leniently in view of the opinion of these great *poskim*. Where there is danger to a limb one may act leniently even if, with some effort, a non-Jew could be found.

The thirty-nine *melachot* forbidden by Torah law on *Shabbat* are based on those used to build the *Mishkan* (the Tabernacle built in the desert). The *Gemara* discusses what the *halachah* would be if one of these *melachot* was done for a reason different from that required for the *Mishkan* (*melachah she'enah tz'richah legufah*). For instance, the flame of a candle or oil lamp wick was snuffed out to produce the charred part. However, if this is done to darken a room, this would be a *melachah she'enah tz'richah legufah*. The *Tanna'im* (Rebbe Yehudah and Rebbe Shimon) in the *Mishnah* differ as to whether *melachah she'enah tz'richah legufah* is forbidden by the Torah or by the Rabbis; the accepted ruling is that it is forbidden by the Rabbis.[257] *Rav Auerbach zt''l* writes[258] that we only find a ruling forbidding a *melachah*

250. מג״א ס״ק יא ומ״ב ס״ק מו
251. שמירת שבת כהלכתה פל״ג הערה יג
252. מ״ב ס״ק מז
253. מ״ב ס״ק מח
254. סי׳ תצו שעה״צ ס״ק ט
255. שו״ע הרב סע׳ יט. אגלי טל מלאכת טוחן סע׳ יח. תהל״ד סוס״ק כב. קצוה״ש סי׳ קלד סע׳ ד בבדה״ש ס״ק ו
256. שמירת שבת כהלכתה פל״ג הערה יז*
257. סי׳ רעח מ״ב ס״ק ג וסי׳ שב סע׳ י בביה״ל ד״ה דלא
258. שמירת שבת כהלכתה שם

aside Rabbinic law for him, there are four opinions: (1) It is permitted even when there is (E)no danger to a (F)limb.

NISHMAT AVRAHAM

she'enah tz'richah legufah for a *non-seriously ill* patient, and the *Mishnah Berurah*[259] does not rule so with certainty. The *Shach*[260] permits Torah law, other than *Shabbat* laws, to be set aside for a patient whose limb is in danger. It would seem then that a *melachah she'enah tz'richah legufah* which is only Rabbinically forbidden may possibly be performed. [*Author's note*: *One may add that many rishonim*[261] *rule that Sabbath laws may be set aside for a patient in danger of losing a limb in the same way as if he were in danger of his life.*]

17(D) limb: If a doctor thinks that there might be a threat to life unless treated, the patient is treated as if he were *seriously ill.*[262] Since present medical opinion is that there is virtually no acute danger to a major limb that does not carry a possible threat to life, Sabbath laws may be set aside inasmuch as is necessary for such a patient.[263] "Danger to a limb" does not only mean the danger of losing the limb. It also includes partial loss of the use of the limb; for example, the need to walk with a limp.[264] However, since there is usually no danger to life, only Rabbinic law may be set aside (see *Siman* 316B).

17(E) no danger to a limb: If, however, there were danger to a limb, all would agree (apart from opinion (4) in the *Shulchan Aruch*) that a Jew may set aside any Rabbinic law for the patient even if he was not in the category of a *non-seriously ill* patient.[265] The *Chayei Adam*[266] rules that whatever another Jew is permitted to do for a *non-seriously ill* patient, the patient may do for himself even though a non-Jew is available.

The *acharonim* discuss whether doing a *melachah* (which is forbidden by the Torah or the Rabbis) in an indirect manner is preferable to asking a non-Jew to do the same *melachah*. The *Minchat Shabbat*[267] writes that it would be better to ask a non-Jew, if one is available, if the *melachah* is only Rabbinically forbidden. However, if the *melachah* is forbidden by the Torah he remains uncertain which of the two should be preferred. He quotes the *Tehillah LeDavid*[268] who writes that it would appear that both the *Maggid Mishneh* and the *Magen Avraham* rule that asking a non-Jew to do a *melachah* forbidden by the Torah is worse than having a Jew doing the same *melachah* in an indirect manner, and this is how the *Tehillah LeDavid* himself rules.[269] Many *acharonim,*[270] however, rule that in such a case it is better to ask the non-Jew to do the *melachah* forbidden by the Torah and this is also the opinion of *Rav Auerbach zt"l.*[271]

17(F) limb: If he is *not seriously ill* and

259. סי׳ שב סע׳ י בביה״ל ד״ה דלא

260. יו״ד סי׳ קנז ס״ק ג

261. תוס׳ סוכה כו ע״א ד״ה ואפילו. תוס׳ הראש שם. אגודה שם דף קמח ע״ג. מאירי ע״ז כח ע״א ד״ה עין. אור זרוע הל׳ יוהכ״פ סי׳ רפ. ואעפ״י שבפסקי התוס׳ סוכה שם מובא ״סכנת עין כסכנת נפשות״ (ולא סכנת אבר) וכן ברש״ש שם כתב על התוס׳ ״ונראה דטעות סופר הוא וצ״ל דסכנת עין כסכנת נפשות״ צ״ע מהראשונים הנ״ל. וראה גם בשו״ת מלמד להועיל ח״ב סי׳ לב ושו״ת יביע אומר ח״ג יו״ד סי׳ כג ס״ק כט

262. פמ״ג מ״ז ס״ק ז. מ״ב ס״ק מט. ערוה״ש סע׳ יח

263. ראה גם בשו״ת ציץ אליעזר ח״ח סי׳ טו פ״י ס״ק ט

264. קצוה״ש סי׳ קלח בבדה״ש סוס״ק יח

265. מ״ב ס״ק נא

266. כלל סט סע׳ יג

267. סי׳ צא ס״ק מג

268. סי׳ שכח ס״ק נז

269. סי׳ שז ס״ק ה

270. קצוה״ש סי׳ קלד סע׳ ד בבדה״ש ס״ק ו. שעה״צ סי׳ תצו ס״ק ט. חזו״א סי׳ נו סוס״ק ד

271. שמירת שבת כהלכתה פ״ל הערה מו

(2) It is permitted only if there is danger to a limb. (3) Where there is danger to a limb, Rabbinic law is set aside (even by direct action). Where there is no such danger, Rabbinic law may be set aside only (G)by indirect action. (4) Even if there is danger to a limb, Rabbinic law, if based on Torah law may not be set aside. On the other hand, Rabbinic law which is not based on Torah law may be set aside even when there is no danger to a limb. Of these four opinions, (H)the third is the most acceptable.

GLOSS: *One may (I)ask a non-Jew to (J)cook for a child who has nothing to eat, since (K)the needs of a child are like those of a*

NISHMAT AVRAHAM

there is no danger to the affected limb, all agree that Sabbath laws may not be set aside except by a non-Jew and then only if they are of Rabbinic status.[272]

17(G) by indirect action: There is no need to first look for a non-Jew.[273] Tablets may be taken in the normal way since there is no practical way to take them in an indirect manner.[274]

17(H) the third is the most acceptable: I.e. where there is no danger to a limb, it is permissible to set aside all Rabbinic laws if done in an indirect manner. On the other hand, if there is danger to a limb, Rabbinic laws may be set aside and there is no need to act in an indirect manner. This is the view of the majority of *poskim*[275] (see, however, 17C above).

17(I) ask a non-Jew: If the child refuses to eat unless fed by his mother, she may do so even if the milk was milked and boiled by a non-Jew and is now *muktzeh.*[276]

17(J) cook: A Jew must be careful not to put the food into the pot (even before the fire was lit) since this is Rabbinically forbidden[277] (also see above, *Siman* 318A).

17(K) the needs of a child: The *acharonim* discuss the age of this child whose needs are equated to the needs of a *non-seriously ill* patient. The *Ketsot HaShulchan*[278] defines him as one who receives food reserved for children even though he is older than three. The *Minchat Yitzchak*[279] puts the age as nine, if no other food is available. The *Tzitz Eliezer*[280] writes that the maximum age is possibly six. The *Shemirat Shabbat KeHilchatah*[281] places the maximum age at nine to ten. However, *Rav Auerbach zt"l* wrote to me that he rules like the *Chazon Ish*[282] that the maximum age is two to three with respect to his food and other requirements. Finally *Rav Abba Shaul zt"l*[283] writes that a child is always defined as under the age of thirteen for a boy (and twelve for a girl). However, each case must be judged on its own merits, and if his needs can be met without setting aside Sabbath laws, these laws may not be set aside even if they are of Rabbinic origin and

272. מ״ב ס״ק נב
273. מ״ב ס״ק נד
274. דעת תורה סי׳ תקלב סע׳ ב
275. מ״ב ס״ק נז
276. מ״ב ס״ק נח
277. מ״ב ס״ק נח בשם החיי אדם
278. סי׳ קלד בבדה״ש ס״ק יח
279. שו״ת ח״א סי׳ עח
280. ח״ח סי׳ טו פי״ב אות ז
281. פל״ז סע׳ ב
282. סי׳ נט ס״ק ג
283. אור לציון ח״ב פל״ו סע׳ ד

non-seriously ill patient. Whatever another Jew may not do, the patient himself also may not do. However, when a non-Jew does something for the patient, (L)he may (M)help him a little since "such help does not count."

§18: One may light a fire to provide heat for someone who (A)became chilled after bloodletting, even in the hot summer months.

NISHMAT AVRAHAM

even by using a non-Jew.[284]

The child may be given any medication necessary, whether external drops (into his eyes, nose or ears), tablets or syrup; the tablets may be crushed and then dissolved in water or juice.[285] Where it is essential, a non-Jew may be asked to do whatever is necessary for the child's health even if Torah laws are thereby set aside[286] (see also *Siman* 308A).

17(L) he may: The *Mishnah Berurah*[287] feels that not only the patient but anyone else as well may help the non-Jew. Other *acharonim*[288] are also of the opinion that there is no difference between the patient himself or another.

17(M) help him a little: This *halachah* applies where a non-Jew can act even without his help. However, if his help is essential, it is not permitted. It would appear that even where the act is forbidden by the Torah, the rule that "such help does not count" still applies (see above, §3D).[289]

18(A) became chilled: During Talmudic times large volumes of blood were removed during therapeutic bloodletting[290] and the patient was then considered to be *seriously ill*. It is in this context that a Jew may light a fire for him, as for anyone *seriously ill* who feels cold since being cold may further jeopardize his health. However, where possible a non-Jew should be asked to light the fire[291] since the danger is not immediate.[292] Therefore, it is permissible to light a fire or electric heater (wherever possible in an indirect manner) for a *seriously ill* patient who feels cold, if a non-Jew is not available to do so. The heat may be turned on only if the patient would feel better with heating than by having extra blankets.[293] It is preferable to turn on an electric heater rather than light a gas heater, since with the gas heater one must first light a match or other igniter, whereas with the electric heater there is only a single act.[294] Similarly, on a very hot day, a Jew may turn on a fan, cooler or air-conditioner, if possible in an indirect manner, if a non-Jew is not available.[295] In *Tosafot*'s opinion[296] heat is more difficult to bear than cold.

If heat from the heater or cold air from a fan or cooler is uncomfortable for a patient or may harm him, a non-Jew may be asked to turn it off. If a non-Jew is not available and the heater or fan cannot be moved away from the patient, or the patient

284. שמירת שבת כהלכתה פל״ז סע׳ ב
285. שם סע׳ ט
286. שם פל״ח סע׳ כד
287. מ״ב ס״ק נט
288. א״ר סוס״ק א. ערוה״ש סע׳ כ
289. מ״ב ס״ק ס
290. רש״י שבת קכט ע״א ד״ה ומוקי, חולין עב ע״א ד״ה רביעית וסוטה ה ע״א ד״ה אדם. וראה בגליוני הש״ס שבת לא ע״ב
291. מ״ב ס״ק סב
292. ערוה״ש סע׳ כח
293. שמירת שבת כהלכתה פל״ב סע׳ פג
294. שם סע׳ עו
295. שם סע׳ פו
296. כתובות ל ע״א ד״ה הכל. ב״ב קמד ע״ב ד״ה חוץ

§19: A non-seriously ill patient [(A)]may be given food cooked by a non-Jew on *Shabbat.*

NISHMAT AVRAHAM

moved to another room, it may be turned down; if this is insufficient, it may be turned off, where possible in an indirect manner.[297]

In countries where the cold is severe enough to cause suffering to the healthy, it is permissible to ask a non-Jew to turn on the heat. If small children or a *non-seriously ill* patient is present, a non-Jew may be asked to turn on the heat even though it is not cold enough to bother a healthy adult.[298] The same rules apply to turning on a fan or air-conditioner during a hot summer day.[299]

19(A) may be given food: Even though other Rabbinically prohibited food may not be given to such a patient,[300] this food is different because it is itself kosher and the patient pronounces a blessing over it as over any other kosher food. Can the food that is left over be eaten after *Shabbat* even by the patient, since fresh food can now be cooked for him by a Jew? The subject turns up in the *rishonim.*[301] The *Ran* in the name of the *Ra'ah* permits it to be eaten after *Shabbat* even by a healthy person, whereas the *Rashba* forbids it even to the patient. The *Rama*[302] rules like the *Ran* as does the *Shach,*[303] whereas the *Taz*[304] and the *Ben Ish Chai*[305] rule like the *Rashba.*

Here the *Mishnah Berurah* sides with those who say that what is left over cannot be eaten after *Shabbat* even by the patient since fresh food can now be cooked for him by a Jew.[306] Elsewhere[307] he writes that the food cooked by a non-Jew on *Shabbat* may be eaten after *Shabbat.* But this is only an apparent contradiction. He allows food cooked by a non-Jew on *Shabbat* to be eaten after *Shabbat* when it is cooked for someone who is *seriously ill.* Since the situation is uncommon *Chazal* did not forbid the food after *Shabbat.*[308] But here, where the patient is *non-seriously ill,* the food is forbidden after *Shabbat.*[309]

As for the pots in which the non-Jew cooked the food, the *Mishnah Berurah* writes that they may only be used after being koshered. Others, however, permit their use.[310] A competent rabbinic authority should be consulted after *Shabbat* about the eating of the remaining food (even by the patient) and about the *halachic* status of the pot in which the food was cooked.[311]

A Jew must not take part in the cooking as he would normally do on a weekday so that it not be considered food cooked by a non-Jew. Even putting the food in the pot before it is placed on the flame, covering the pot (unless the food has been fully cooked) or stirring the food is forbidden.[312]

---

297. שמירת שבת כהלכתה פל״ב סע׳ פה ו־פו

298. שו״ת מנחת יצחק ח״ג סי׳ כג ו־כד. שמירת שבת כהלכתה פי״ג סע׳ לד ו־פל״ח סע׳ ח

299. שו״ת אג״מ או״ח ח״ג סוסי׳ מב. שמירת שבת כהלכתה פ״ל סע׳ יא ו־פל״ח סע׳ ט

300. ראה רמ״א יו״ד סי׳ קנה סע׳ ג

301. מובא בט״ז יו״ד סי׳ קיג ס״ק טו

302. יו״ד סי׳ קיג סע׳ טז

303. נקוה״כ שם וסי׳ קכג ש״ך ס״ק נ

304. יו״ד סי׳ קיג ס״ק טו וסי׳ קכג ס״ק יח

305. שנה ב׳ פ׳ חקת סע׳ כה

306. מ״ב ס״ק סג

307. סי׳ שיח ס״ק יד

308. שו״ת זכרון יהודה מובא בשמירת שבת כהלכתה פל״ח הערה מד

309. דכיון דלא שכיחא, לא גזרו ביה רבנן משום חתנות – שמירת שבת כהלכתה שם

310. ס״ק סג. וראה בשעה״צ ס״ק מא. שו״ת שו״מ מהד״ת ח״ב סי׳ טו. בן איש חי שם

311. שמירת שבת כהלכתה פל״ח סע׳ יא

312. שם

§21: One may soak a salve on Friday in order to apply it to his eyelid on *Shabbat* since (A)he appears to be washing himself when doing so.

§22: One may rub oil into a wound in order to (A)remove the scab, but not solid fat (B)which will melt.

NISHMAT AVRAHAM

On *Shabbat* itself, a healthy person may not eat of this food lest the non-Jew cook a greater quantity for the benefit of the healthy person[313] and because the food is *muktzeh*[314] if it could not have been eaten in its raw state.[315] The food is *muktzeh* as far as the healthy person is concerned even if the patient was already ill before *Shabbat*[316] (unlike the *halachah* concerning milk boiled for a child – see above, §17I). The patient himself may, however, continue to eat of the food on *Shabbat* even though he has recovered from his illness.[317]

21(A) he appears to be: *Chazal* have forbidden anything that is done for a cure on *Shabbat*.[318] However if his intent is not apparent to others it is permitted. Thus the *Igrot Moshe*[319] permits one to add medication in the form of drops to water or other beverage on Friday in order to drink it on *Shabbat* provided that this is the usual way the drops are taken. This is also the ruling of the *Shemirat Shabbat Ke-Hilchatah*.[320] However *Rav Auerbach zt"l* rules[321] that this is only permitted if this is not the usual way the drops are taken. It is forbidden to mix the drops in water on *Shabbat*.[322]

Some antibiotics are sold in powdered form in a bottle. Before use the bottle is filled with water up to a mark so that measured doses can be given to a child (or a *non-seriously ill* patient). This may be done on *Shabbat* since the *melachah* of "kneading" does not apply here.[323] Although there is now enough medicine for the *Shabbat* and subsequent weekdays, the problem of preparing something on *Shabbat* to be used on a weekday does not apply. Since the whole bottle must be prepared at the outset so that the patient can receive the right amount of medication each time and since all the water is added at one time, this is permissible.[324]

22(A) remove the scab: If removing the scab will cause bleeding, it is forbidden[325] (see *Siman* 316B).

22(B) which will melt: A bedridden patient who may develop pressure sores if not given preventive treatment, and certainly one who already has such sores, is a *seriously ill* patient and cream or, if necessary, even an ointment should be applied. Although spreading any ointment evenly on skin is a Torah forbidden *melachah*,

313. רמ״א סי׳ שיח סע׳ ב

314. מ״ב ס״ק נח

315. כף החיים סי׳ שיח סע׳ כח. הגרש״ז אויערבאך זצ״ל לב אברהם ח״א עמ׳ טז

316. שמירת שבת כהלכתה פל״ב הערה רה* בשם הגרש״ז אויערבאך זצ״ל

317. שו״ת ציץ אליעזר ח״ח סי׳ טו פי״א או״ק ג ו־ד

318. מ״ב ס״ק סד

319. שו״ת או״ח ח״ב סי׳ פו. וראה גם בקצוה״ש סי׳ קלח בבדיה״ש ס״ק לא ד״ה כי המנחת שבת

320. פל״ד סע׳ ה הערה כז בשם הגרש״ז אויערבאך זצ״ל

321. שם

322. דעת תורה סע׳ לז סוד״ה וכל. שמירת שבת כהלכתה שם

323. חזו״א או״ח סי׳ נח ס״ק ט

324. עיין במ״ב סי׳ שלו ס״ק לג בשם תוספת שבת – שמעתי ממו״ר הגרי״י נויבירט שליט״א

325. מ״ב ס״ק צ ושעה״צ ס״ק סז

§23: A sponge or a dry new piece of cloth may be put on an [(A)]open wound if it is done to prevent his clothes from rubbing the wound, but not if it is done for treatment.

NISHMAT AVRAHAM

this is only if it remains on the surface and one wishes to spread it evenly. However, where the intention is to completely rub the ointment into the body, as it is with this patient, *Rav Auerbach zt"l*[326] rules that this *melachah* does not apply. The *Tzitz Eliezer*[327] also permits it if the intention is to rub in the cream until it is entirely absorbed. Such a patient may also be put on an air mattress that must be electrically activated on *Shabbat.*[328] Where possible this should be done by a non-Jew or in an indirect manner.

One may rub liquid cream on a *non-seriously ill* patient, doing so in an indirect manner if possible.[329] An ointment may be liquified by putting it first on a hot Sabbath-urn. Although one thereby changes its physical characteristics and a new entity is "born" (*"nolad"*), an act that is Rabbinically forbidden, it is permitted in such a situation.[330]

23(A) open wound: TREATMENT OF WOUNDS. A superficial wound should be cleansed using nylon (non-absorbent) swabs, or by pouring iodine or another disinfectant on it and wiping off the excess with a dry (regular) swab or gauze. If there is suspicion that the wound is infected, it should be cleansed in the usual way (if non-absorbent swabs are not available).[331]

A bleeding wound (including bleeding gums) may not be sucked on *Shabbat* (blood that is visible may not be sucked even on a weekday).[332] The wound should be bandaged only after it has been washed. Continuous bleeding should be stopped by applying pressure using a clean cloth or gauze. The wound is then covered with a band-aid or bandage without ointment.[333] Nose bleeds should be stopped, where possible, by external pressure. If this is unsuccessful, a clean piece of cloth may be stuffed into the nostril until professional help is obtained.[334]

If the patient is in the category of the *non-seriously ill,* ointment may be expressed from a tube directly onto a wound, or applied with a spatula, but not spread. Gauze or a bandage may then be put on it even though this may then cause the ointment to spread automatically. A liquid or cream preparation that is completely absorbed into the body may be used in the normal way even if the patient is *not seriously ill.*[335]

One may bandage a wound, or change a bandage on *Shabbat* without using an ointment (the instances when an ointment may be used and how it is used can be found in the previous paragraph).[336] The bandage should be secured with a single knot and bow, safety pins or special

---

326. שמירת שבת כהלכתה פל״ג באמצע הערה נח בשם הגרש״ז אויערבאך זצ״ל. ראה במג״א סי׳ שטז ס״ק כד ומובא גם במ״ב ס״ק מט. מנחת שבת סי׳ צב ס״ק ל. שו״ת מטה לוי הורוביץ ח״ב סי׳ כא. ודלא כדעת השמירת שבת כהלכתה שם שמותר רק בדרך השלכה

327. שו״ת ציץ אליעזר ח״ז סי׳ ל סע׳ ב וראה גם בח״ח סי׳ טו פי״ד

328. שמעתי ממו״ר הגרי״י נויבירט שליט״א

329. סי׳ שכז סע׳ א ברמ״א

330. שמירת שבת כהלכתה פל״ג באמצע הערה נח*. וראה סי׳ שיח סע׳ טז במג״א

331. ראה בשמירת שבת כהלכתה פל״ה סע׳ ב

332. שם סע׳ יד

333. ראה שם סע׳ יח ו־כ

334. שם סע׳ טו

335. שמעתי מהגרש״ז אויערבאך זצ״ל וראה לעיל הערה 326

336. שמירת שבת כהלכתה שם סע׳ כ

§28: It is permissible to (A)open an (B)abscess on *Shabbat*.

§30: (A)A dislocated joint may not be treated.

§32: One may not (A)gargle with oil for a sore throat.

§34: A woman may not express milk from her breast (A)into a cup or other vessel in order to then give it to her baby.

NISHMAT AVRAHAM

clips, but not with adhesive tape even if one end is stuck to the skin.[337] A bandage may not be cut to size, nor should it be cut partially lengthwise to provide two ends which can be tied together[338] (*melachah* of cutting to measure, see *Siman* 322A). A band-aid may be used on *Shabbat* to cover a wound, but preferably, the protective covering should have been removed and then immediately replaced before *Shabbat.*[339] If this was not done, it may, where necessary, be removed on *Shabbat.*[340]

Adhesive tape may be used to bring together two ends of a cut wound.[341] As to suturing a wound, see *Siman* 340 §2.

A fracture or dislocation may be stabilized using an improvised splint before taking the patient to hospital. A plaster cast that is causing severe pain or discoloration of the limb may lead to life-threatening complications if untreated, and the patient must be taken immediately to the hospital even if Torah laws must be set aside.

28(A) open: It is permissible to extract a splinter, but if possible, one should try to do so without drawing blood.[342] One is also forbidden to scratch himself hard, if he knows that he is likely to bleed.[343]

28(B) abscess: Even if there is blood mixed with the pus it may be opened since the blood is not the result of a fresh wound.[344]

30(A) A dislocated joint: See below, §47.

32(A) gargle: One may not gargle for a sore throat even if he swallows the fluid since it is obvious that he is doing so for medicinal purposes. There are those, however, who permit gargling if he swallows the fluid afterwards.[345]

34(A) into a cup: The *Pri Megadim* *rules* that expressing milk into a vessel is forbidden by Torah law and therefore may not be done for a *non-seriously ill* patient.[346] Although, on the other hand, the *Tosefet Shabbat*[347] rules that this is an act done in an indirect manner (the usual fashion is by suckling directly from the breast) and is therefore only Rabbinically forbidden, the *Mishnah Berurah,*[348] basing himself on *Tosafot,*[349] agrees with the *Pri Megadim.*

337. שם סע׳ כב־כה. וראה בהערה הבא

338. שם סע׳ כא. ושמעתי ממו״ר הגרי״י נויבירט שליט״א שבשעת הדחק כל זה מותר. וכן ראה שם בחלק ג הערה סג ו־סד. וכן מתיר השו״ת ציץ אליעזר ח״ח סי׳ טו פי״ד ס״ק ו כשיש הכרח לכך

339. שמירת שבת כהלכתה שם סע׳ כו. וראה בנשמת אברהם כרך א או״ח סי׳ שכח סוס״ק סב ובהערה 545 ,546 (עמ׳ רד). וראה בשו״ת אור לציון ח״ב פל״ו סע׳ טו שמתיר לכתחילה

340. שמעתי מהגרש״ז אויערבאך זצ״ל

341. שמעתי מהגרש״ז אויערבאך זצ״ל

342. מ״ב ס״ק פח. וראה בשעה״צ ס״ק סג בשם המג״א ס״ק לב ובסי׳ שח סע׳ יא ביה״ל ד״ה הקוץ ותהל״ד ס״ק מז

343. שמירת שבת כהלכתה פל״ה סע׳ לג

344. מ״ב ס״ק פט בשם הפמ״ג

345. מ״ב ס״ק קג

346. ביה״ל ד״ה ותניק וכותב שכן מוכח מכמה ראשונים

347. ס״ק נט

348. שעה״צ ס״ק פא

349. שבת קלה ע״א ד״ה ומפני

§35: If her [A]baby refuses to suckle, the mother may [B]express a little milk to get it to suckle.

NISHMAT AVRAHAM

35(A) baby: All Sabbath rules may be set aside for the medical needs of a newborn infant even if it is clear that he has only a short time to live[350] (see *Siman* 330 Q).

35(B) express a little milk: The *Mishnah Berurah*[351] writes that the milk should be expressed into the baby's mouth since thus it becomes a *melachah she'enah tz'richah legufah.*[352] The *Tosefet Shabbat,*[353] on the other hand, explains that this is permitted because the *melachah* is done in an indirect manner (see 34A above). The *Ketsot HaShulchan*[354] writes that the milk should not be expressed into the baby's mouth but rather into waste; this appears to be the opinion of the *Shulchan Aruch HaRav.*[355] The *Shemirat Shabbat KeHilchatah*[356] rules like the *Mishnah Berurah.* The mother may clean her nipples before feeding her baby, preferably by washing them with liquid soap using her hands or a synthetic cloth; she may not use soaked absorbent cotton.[357]

If she is in pain because of engorged breasts, she may express the excess milk into the sink or onto a cloth which she must remember not to squeeze on *Shabbat.* Alternatively the breast may be dipped into a vessel containing liquid soap and the excess milk expressed into it. If it is difficult for her to express the milk manually, a suction pump may be used, if it is electrically activated by a Sabbath clock or *gramma switch.*[358] Care must be taken to empty the milk from the receptacle of the pump at frequent intervals so as to avoid the collection of a large amount (15 cc.) of milk.[359] Preferably some liquid soap should be put into the receptacle before use; then the amount of milk collected is immaterial.[360]

If the baby is unable to suckle or is hospitalized and the mother must bring him her milk which is the baby's main source of nourishment, daily, she may express, on the Sabbath, sufficient milk for the Sabbath into a vessel, but not what is needed for the baby's feeding after the termination of the Sabbath. This is permitted since the baby might become *seriously ill* if it were given some other milk.[361] She may not express excess milk into a vessel on the Sabbath in order to bring it to a milk bank after the Sabbath[362] since this act is of no use to the baby on the Sabbath itself[363] and can be done after the Sabbath.[364]

A nursing mother may take medication or have injections to treat a breast infection.[365]

---

350. שמעתי מהגרש״ז אוערבאך זצ״ל. וראה בנשמת אברהם כרך ד חאו״ח סי׳ של ס״ק ג (עמ׳ מט)

351. מ״ב ס״ק קיב. אך עיין בשעה״צ ס״ק פא

352. לבוש כאן. וראה בשבת קלה ע״א תוסד״ה מפני

353. ס״ק נט

354. סי׳ קלח סע׳ טז ובבדה״ש ס״ק ל. וע״ע בברכ״י ס״ק יג

355. סע׳ מא

356. פל״ו סע׳ יט

357. שם סע׳ יז

358. כתב לי מו״ר הגרי״י נויבירט שליט״א

359. סי׳ של סע׳ ח ובמ״ב ס״ק לב. שמירת שבת כהלכתה פל״ו סע׳ כ

360. כתב לי מו״ר הגרי״י נויבירט שליט״א

361. שמירת שבת כהלכתה פל״ו סע׳ כא מהא דסי׳ תריז סע׳ א בביה״ל ד״ה עוברות

362. שמעתי ממו״ר הגרי״י נויבירט שליט״א

363. הגרש״ז אויערבאך זצ״ל נשמת אברהם כרך א או״ח סי׳ שכח סוס״ק עה (עמ׳ ריא)

364. כתב לי הגרש״ז אויערבאך זצ״ל

365. שמירת שבת כהלכתה פל״ו סע׳ כב

§37: Whatever is [(A)]not normally considered a food or a beverage may not be eaten or drunk for a cure. This rule applies to someone with a mild illness who is up and around, but if [(B)]he is healthy, it is permissible.

GLOSS: *If one has taken to bed, he, too, is allowed such food and drink.*

§40: A person who has mild stomach pains may put [(A)]an empty hot cup, which had previously contained hot water, on his stomach.

§42: One may not have [(A)]strenuous massage to become tired and sweat.

NISHMAT AVRAHAM

37(A) not normally considered a food or a beverage: Therefore it is forbidden to take laxatives in any form unless his constipation is bad enough to place him in the category of a *non-seriously ill* patient.[366]

37(B) he is healthy: Provided he consumes it because he is hungry or thirsty. However, if he does so in order to augment his health, the *Magen Avraham*[367] rules that this is forbidden even though he is healthy. On the other hand, the *Igrot Moshe*[368] writes that a healthy person who takes it regularly to prevent illness may do so on *Shabbat* as well. As far as taking vitamins are concerned, the *Shemirat Shabbat KeHilchatah*[369] rules that it is forbidden for a healthy person to take them on *Shabbat* even if he takes them daily during the week. On the other hand, if he is *non-seriously ill* he may take them. However, in those countries where it is customary for people to take daily vitamins the *Igrot Moshe*[370] permits them to be taken on *Shabbat* as well. *Rav Auerbach zt"l*[371] adds that this is only permissible if he takes them instead of food, but not if he takes them in order to augment his health. See above, §1C.

Someone who is inebriated may drink strong black coffee since it is also drunk by the healthy.[372]

40(A) an empty hot cup: Similarly, it is permitted to put warm clothes on his abdomen.[373] See *Siman* 326B as to the use of a hot-water bottle and an electric blanket. A non-Jew may be asked to turn on a heating pad so that a *non-seriously ill* patient may put it on his abdomen.[374] He may also be asked to increase or decrease the electric current as required. A Jew is forbidden to do so. The pad may be moved as is necessary for its use.[375]

42(A) strenuous: The *Mishnah Berurah*[376] explains this to mean physical exercise done with the intention of becoming hot and raising a sweat.

366. מ״ב ס״ק קיח ו־קמ

367. מ״ב ס״ק קכ ו־קל בשם המג״א ס״ק מג

368. או״ח ח״ג סי׳ נד

369. פל״ד סע׳ כ

370. שם

371. שמירת שבת כהלכתה פל״ד הערה פה

372. הגרש״ז אויערבאך זצ״ל בשמירת שבת כהלכתה פל״ד סע׳ כא

373. מ״ב ס״ק קכה

374. שו״ת חלקת יעקב ח״א סי׳ מ וח״ג סי׳ קפא. שו״ת אג״מ או״ח ח״ג סי׳ נ

375. שמירת שבת כהלכתה פל״ח סע׳ ז

376. ס״ק קכט

NISHMAT AVRAHAM

PHYSIOTHERAPY (PHYSICAL THERAPY). A patient who has lost the use of a limb may have physiotherapy administered by a Jew on *Shabbat* in the usual way to prevent this loss from becoming permanent.[377] What, however, is the *halachah* for one who still requires physiotherapy to complete his cure but who is no longer in the category of "*danger to limb*" or "*non-seriously ill*"? One may broadly divide physiotherapy into two kinds: (a) Massage used to free painful spastic muscles, such as those experienced by a patient with an acute lumbar disc syndrome. (b) Patients who have a complete or partial paralysis of a limb or limbs who need exercises, with or without the use of weights or springs, to strengthen them. In neither of these categories is there the intention of using force or of making the patient sweat. They cannot be compared to what the *Shulchan Aruch* speaks of. In both the patients are in the category of either the *non-seriously ill* or *danger to limb* since any organ or limb that is non-functioning puts the patient into this category.[378] Physiotherapy is permitted for them on *Shabbat*.[379]

However, what of a later stage when the patient has progressed to walking, albeit with some pain or weakness? *Rav Neuwirth shlita* writes:[380] One may not exercise strenuously on Shabbat nor use springs to strengthen one's muscles. However, simple exercises are permitted even if meant to treat pain. One may not have physiotherapy on *Shabbat* unless he is *non-seriously ill*.[381] *Rav Neuwirth shlita* wrote to me: All treatments that are forbidden on *Shabbat* are based on the enactment of *Chazal* lest one perform the *melachah* of "grinding" (medicinal herbs) (see above §1E). Therefore this enactment holds true only where there is a possibility that it may lead to the *melachah* of "grinding." The second category of physiotherapy for which medication is no substitute would not fall under this enactment of *Chazal* and would therefore be permitted (see *Mishnah Berurah*).[382] Nevertheless, we find that the *Mishnah Berurah* elsewhere[383] probably rules differently. It may also be considered "weekday activity," which is forbidden.[384] And *Rav Neuwirth shlita* notes that there are *acharonim*[385] who, following the opinion of *Rabbeinu Chananel*,[386] do not permit any form of exercise. Yet, since the person is ill and needs rehabilitation, one may be lenient.

However, when one looks closely at the *responsa* of the *acharonim* one finds that they are dealing with something other than physiotherapy. The *Maharshag*[387] speaks of healthy youth who wish to attend a gymnasium on *Shabbat*. The *Seridei Eish*[388] deals with the problem of heavy massage and sweating. The *Tzitz Eliezer*[389] forbids the use of an "expander" since this requires strenuous effort and leads to tiredness and sweating. He does, however, permit the use of simple devices to exercise the hand and fingers, since they do not tire nor do they lead to sweating. Similarly, in another *responsum*,[390] he permits breathing exercises

---

377. מהא דסע׳ יז בדעה שלישית. וראה בקצות השולחן סי׳ קלח בבדה״ש סוס״ק יח דגם איבוד תיפקוד של אבר נקרא סכנת אבר

378. קצות השולחן סי׳ קלח בבדה״ש סוס״ק יח. שמירת שבת כהלכתה פל״ג סע׳ א ס״ק ה בהערה

379. והסכים אתי מו״ר הגרי״י נויבירט שליט״א

380. שמירת שבת כהלכתה פל״ד סע׳ כב

381. שם סע׳ כג

382. ס״ק קל

383. סי׳ שא ס״ק ז ושעה״צ ס״ק ט

384. סי׳ שכז סע׳ ב ובמ״ב ס״ק ז, שם סע׳ ג ובמ״ב ס״ק ח

385. שו״ת מלמד להועיל סי׳ נג. שו״ת מהרש״ג ח״ב סי׳ צג. שו״ת שרידי אש ח״ב סי׳ ל. שו״ת ציץ אליעזר ח״ו סי׳ ד שו״ע הרב סי׳ שכח סע׳ מז

386. שבת קמז ע״א

387. ח״ב סי׳ צג

388. ח״ב סי׳ ל

389. ח״ו סי׳ ד

390. חי״ב סי׳ מה

§47: A [(A)]dislocated joint may be returned to its normal position.

NISHMAT AVRAHAM

for someone who requires speech therapy which was started before *Shabbat,* since there is no intention to cause sweating.

The *Melamed LeHo'il*[391] deals with healthy people exercising. Furthermore, he deduces that *Rabbeinu Chananel* is also referring to the healthy, which is why he forbids exercising on *Shabbat.*

Rav Abba Shaul zt"l[392] permits physiotherapy on *Shabbat,* including the use of devices such as springs and weights, in order to strengthen the muscles of a patient. He also permits massage for a patient with pain when there is no intention of producing sweating.[393]

Finally, *Rav Auerbach zt"l* told me that in his opinion physiotherapy is permitted on Shabbat even if springs and weights are used, to strengthen the muscles of a patient. *Rav Neuwirth shlita* wrote to me that physiotherapy is permitted for a patient who is recovering from a situation where he was *non-seriously ill;* he is like the patient who must to continue taking antibiotics even though he has recovered from his illness.

HOT SPRINGS. It is forbidden to bathe on *Shabbat* in hot springs such as those of Tiberias for the purposes of a cure.[394] *Rav Auerbach zt"l*[395] writes that since it is customary to think that the hot springs of Tiberias are good for health and thus even the healthy use them, it would be forbidden. This would also apply to the Dead Sea.[396]

47(A) dislocated joint: See §30 in which the *Shulchan Aruch* rules that a dislocated joint may not be treated. The *Magen Avraham,*[397] however, writes that if the bone is broken it may be reset, but if the limb is dislocated, it may not be put back into its normal position. A non-Jew, however, may be asked to reposition the dislocated limb. On the other hand, other *acharonim*[398] rule that a completely dislocated joint is a danger to the limb and the limb may be repositioned; they say that §30, above, deals with a partial dislocation only. Since many *poskim* (see §17B and C above) believe that a *danger to a limb* may, in many instances, lead to a danger to life, a Jew may set aside even Torah laws, if necessary, to deal with it. However, if the doctor believes that there is no danger to life and anesthesia is necessary to reposition the dislocated joint, this may be done if only Rabbinic law is set aside.[399]

The *Aruch HaShulchan*[400] expresses surprise that both *halachot* on dislocation of a joint (§30 and here) are missing in the *Rambam's Code of Law.* He answers[401] that since treatment of these conditions are dependent on the patient's situation, it is not possible to lay down hard and fast rules and the *halachah* will depend on the doctor's assessment of the case. Since the *Rambam* himself was a doctor and knew that these situations could sometimes lead to a danger to life, the *halachah* is implied in what has previously been stated above (§2), namely, that it is the doctor who will

391. סי׳ נג
392. שו״ת אור לציון ח״ב פל״ו שאלה יב
393. שם שאלה יא
394. מ״ב ס״ק קלז. וראה גם בביה״ל ד״ה אלא. ומ״ב סי׳ שכו ס״ק ח. שו״ע הרב כאן סע׳ מח. קצוה״ש סי׳ קלח בבדה״ש ס״ק כב. שע״ת סי׳ שכו ס״ק ב
395. שמירת שבת כהלכתה פי״ד הערה כ
396. מ״ב ס״ק קלט
397. מובא במ״ב ס״ק קמה
398. שלחן עצי שטים מובא במ״ב שם. חיי אדם כלל סט סע׳ ז. ערוה״ש סע׳ מ
399. שמירת שבת כהלכתה פל״ג סע׳ יז
400. כאן סע׳ לט
401. סע׳ מ

§48: A piece of cloth may not be put on a bleeding wound since the blood (A)will color it. Since (B)one may not draw blood from a wound, it should first be washed in order to remove the blood before bandaging it.

§49: One may not use a (A)suppository to treat constipation.

NISHMAT AVRAHAM

decide whether there is danger to the person or not.

If there is a severe sprain with pain sufficient to affect the whole body, compresses may be used. A clean cloth is first wrapped around the area and cold or hot water poured onto it. If this is not possible, one may soak the clean cloth in water and then put it on the area of injury.[402] One must be very careful not to squeeze the cloth at any stage. The joint may be bandaged with an elastic bandage.[403]

48(A) will color it: Even though the blood discolors the cloth, nevertheless using the cloth is Rabbinically forbidden. If the cloth is red (where the discoloration is not so obvious) its use is clearly forbidden.[404] Where there is no choice, however, one may be lenient since the cloth is "dirtied."[405] The *Shulchan Aruch HaRav* supports this ruling by pointing out that a woman may use a pad if she started menstruating on *Shabbat.*[406]

48(B) one may not draw blood from a wound: One may not apply pressure to a wound in order to draw blood since this is forbidden as a probable transgression[407] of a *melachah*. Therefore, it may only be done by a non-Jew if necessary for a *non-seriously ill* patient.[408] See above, *Siman* 316 on drawing blood from a patient for laboratory testing.

One may not suck blood from a wound by Torah law.[409] Sucking blood from between the teeth is also forbidden; according to the *Shulchan Aruch HaRav*[410] this is forbidden by Rabbinic law whereas according to the *Magen Avraham*[411] it is possibly forbidden by Torah law.

49(A) suppository: A prepared suppository may be used on *Shabbat.*[412] This ruling does not contradict that of the *Shulchan Aruch* or of the *Mishnah Berurah*[413] since in their times the suppositories were used in a way that led to the pulling out of skin tags or hairs, which is why their use was forbidden on *Shabbat.*[414] The *Tzitz Eliezer,*[415] however, does not permit its use.

A *non-seriously ill* patient may be given an enema, if necessary. Similarly someone who has such severe constipation that it affects his whole body may be given an enema.[416] Wherever possible the enema device should be assembled before *Shabbat* since the *poskim* of our generation

402. שמירת שבת כהלכתה פל״ג סע׳ יט בשם הגרש״ז אויערבאך זצ״ל
403. שם פל״ה סע׳ לה. וכן שמעתי מהגרש״ז אויערבאך זצ״ל
404. מג״א ס״ק נב
405. מ״ב ס״ק קמו וכן בסי׳ שכ ס״ק נט
406. סי׳ שב בקונטרס אחרון מהא דסי׳ שג סע׳ יח
407. מ״ב ס״ק קמז וכן בסי׳ שטז ס״ק ל. שעה״צ ס״ק קי
408. מ״ב ס״ק קמז וסי׳ שטז ס״ק ל
409. סוס״ק קמז
410. סע׳ נד
411. סוס״ק נג
412. שמירת שבת כהלכתה פל״ג סע׳ יא
413. ס״ק קנא וביה״ל ד״ה לשום
414. שמירת שבת כהלכתה שם הערה מט בשם הגרש״ז אויערבאך זצ״ל. וכן הובא בשמו בשו״ת ציץ אליעזר ח״ט סי׳ יז פ״ב ס״ק כה
415. ח״ח סי׳ טו פט״ו ס״ק כ. וראה בקצוה״ש סי׳ קלח בבדה״ש ס״ק יג
416. מהא דמ״ב ס״ק קנ. וכן בשמירת שבת כהלכתה פל״ג סע׳ יב

SIMAN 329: FOR WHOM MAY SABBATH LAWS BE SET ASIDE

§1: Sabbath laws are set aside in every instance of danger to life and whoever hastens to do so is praiseworthy. If a fire broke out in one courtyard and there is a fear that it might spread to another and endanger life, it may be (A)put out before it spreads.

§4: Sabbath laws (B)are set aside for someone who is buried

NISHMAT AVRAHAM

differ as to whether it is permissible[417] or not[418] to assemble it on *Shabbat*. See also the *Yabia Omer*.[419]

SIMAN 329

(A) put out before it spreads: It is forbidden to put out a fire on *Shabbat* unless there is danger to life. A non-Jew may not be asked to do so to prevent monetary loss.[1] The *Magen Avraham*[2] rules that even though a patient or child could be carried to safety via a *public domain*, it is better to put out the fire, since this is a *melachah she'enah tz'richah legufah* and is therefore a *melachah* only in terms of Rabbinic law. On the other hand, since many authorities rule that there are, even today, *public domains* as defined by the Torah,[3] carrying a child or patient out to safety through a *public domain* will mean setting aside Torah law. The *Chayei Adam*,[4] however, rules that it would be better to carry them through a *public domain* rather than to put out the fire.[5]

(B) are set aside: The *Beit Yosef*[6] quotes a *Talmud Yerushalmi*[7] that rules that a person must put himself into possible danger in order to save another who is in certain danger. However, both the *Mechaber* and the *Rama* omit this ruling in the *Shulchan Aruch*. The *Sema*[8] explains that they did not include it because the *Rif*, the *Rambam*, the *Rosh* and the *Tur* all omitted this *Yerushalmi* from their rulings. The *Pitchei Teshuvah*[9] writes that it was omitted because the *Talmud Bavli*[10] rules differently from the *Yerushalmi* (and the *halachah* is usually according to the *Bavli*). The *Radvaz*[11] writes that someone who puts himself into possible danger to save his fellow is acting

417. הגרש״ז אויערבאך זצ״ל והגרי״י נויבירט שליט״א בשמירת שבת כהלכתה שם סע׳ ט והערה מג

418. קצוה״ש סי׳ קלח בבדה״ש ס״ק יד. שו״ת ציץ אליעזר ח״ח סי׳ טו פט״ו ס״ק כ

419. ח״ג סי׳ כא ס״ק ו ו־ז

1. ראה סי׳ שלד סע׳ כה ומ״ב ס״ק סג ו־סח

2. ס״ק א

3. ראה סי׳ שמה סע׳ ז ובביה״ל שם ד״ה שאין

4. כלל מה סע׳ טו מובא במ״מ ס״ק ב. ועי״ש בחיי״א שכותב שצ״ע לפי הפוסקים דבזה״ז לית לן ר״ה, וא״כ ג״כ אינו אלא מדרבנן, והאיסור של כיבוי חמור יותר משאר איסור דרבנן כיון דיש בו צד חיוב לכו״ע (ר״ן על הרי״ף ריש פכ״ב דשבת ד״ה ובמקום, תוס׳ שם מו ע״ב ד״ה דכל, סי׳ רעח במ״ב ס״ק ג) עכ״ד

5. דקטן היודע לילך הרי חי נושא את עצמו – מהגרש״ז אויערבאך זצ״ל

6. חו״מ סי׳ תכו

7. תרומות סוף פ״ח

8. שו״ע חו״מ סי׳ תכו ס״ק ב

9. שם ס״ק ב

10. נדה סא ע״א וסנהדרין עג ע״א. וראה בערוך לנר שם. וראה במהר״ם שיק על המצוות מצוה רלח. שו״ת ציץ אליעזר ח״ט סי׳ מה

11. סי׳ אלף נב (תרכז)

NISHMAT AVRAHAM

with lovingkindness but illogically. However, elsewhere[12] the *Radvaz* qualifies his view and writes that if the possibility of danger to the rescuer is close to certain, and even if the odds are even, he is not required to endanger himself. On the other hand, if the danger to himself is small and the chances of success great, if he fails to attempt to save his fellow he would have set aside the negative Torah command that he not stand idly by when his fellow's blood is being spilled.[13] *Rav Ovadiah Yosef shlita* told me that the *Radvaz*'s first ruling refers to a rescuer who puts himself into a situation where there is at least a 50 percent chance of danger. The *Pitchei Teshuvah*[14] continues that the rescuer must weigh the situation carefully as to whether he will really be putting himself into danger and he should not be overly concerned about himself, and this is also the opinion of the *Shulchan Aruch.*[15] The *Aruch HaShulchan*[16] also writes in the same vein.

The *Tzitz Eliezer*[17] therefore rules that a person may volunteer for experiments on himself for the benefit of another and that this is a *mitzvah,* but only if the doctors assure him that there is no possible danger to himself. The *Igrot Moshe,*[18] however, rules that a person may endanger himself in order to save another. Both the *Tzitz Eliezer*[19] and *Rav Ovadiah Yosef shlita*[20] also permit one to donate a kidney while he is living if doctors assure him that this does not bring certain danger to himself and if the level of medical knowledge is such that there is every good reason to believe that both the donor and the recipient will live.

As far as a doctor is concerned, however, the *Tzitz Eliezer*[21] rules that not only may he endanger himself in order to save the life of a patient with an infectious disease, but it would even be considered a great *mitzvah* for him to do so.[22] *Rav Neuwirth shlita* points out that the case of the patient with an infectious disease is different since it is by no means certain that the doctor will be affected. However when one undergoes an operation (the example discussed by the *Radvaz*), or when one receives an experimental drug which may be dangerous, he leaves himself vulnerable to the side effects of the operation or of the drug.

How much must a person be prepared to spend in order to save the life of another? The Torah tells us not to stand idly by. A negative commandment, such as not to stand idly by, if set aside passively, i.e. by not doing anything, is a less serious offense than a negative commandment which is actively transgressed. *Rav Akiva Eiger*[23] quotes the *Chavot Yair*[24] that since there is no action involved in setting it aside, such a negative commandment has the lesser status of a positive commandment, and there is no obligation for one to spend all of his money to keep a positive commandment.[25] On the other hand, the *Rivash*[26] rules that even in these circumstances, one must give all his money in order not to transgress such a

12. ללשונות הרמב״ם סי׳ אלף תקפב (ריח). וראה בחידושיו של החת״ס על כתובות סא ע״ב ד״ה מ״ט סמכת אניסא. ש״ך יו״ד סי׳ קנב סוס״ק ג. שו״ת ציץ אליעזר ח״ח סי׳ טו פ״י ס״ק יג

13. ויקרא יט:טז

14. חו״מ שם. כאותה שאמרו בב״מ לג ע״א גבי שלך קודם לכל אדם, שכל המדקדק בעצמו כך, סופו בא לידי כך

15. חו״מ סי׳ רסד סע׳ א

16. חו״מ סי׳ תכו סע׳ ד

17. חי״ג סי׳ קא

18. יו״ד ח״ב סי׳ קעד ענף ד

19. ח״ט סי׳ מה וח״י סי׳ כה פ״ז

20. ספר דיני ישראל כרך ז עמ׳ כה

21. ח״ח סי׳ טו פ״י ס״ק יג

22. שם ח״ט סי׳ יז פ״ה

23. יו״ד סי׳ קנז סע׳ א

24. סי׳ קלט

25. עיין במ״ז סי׳ תמו ס״ק ו

26. סי׳ שפז

(C)under rubble even if he is crushed and it is certain that

NISHMAT AVRAHAM

negative commandment. The *Pitchei Teshuvah*[27] quotes the *Pri Megadim*[28] amongst other *acharonim* who rule like the *Chavot Yair*.

The *Chafetz Chaim*[29] writes that although one should not give more than a fifth of one's wealth for charity, this is only where there is no danger to life. However, if there is a possible danger to life, if a prisoner whose life is in danger must be redeemed or if someone might die from hunger, there is no limit to the amount that should be spent to save him. For although it is true that the *Gemara*[30] rules that one's own life comes before that of another, it does not rule that one's wealth comes before the life of another.[31]

However, the *Maharsham*[32] rules that one is not obligated to give all of his wealth to save another's life. He bases this on a *Ra'avad*[33] who says that one need not give more than a fifth lest he himself become poor, and poverty is compared by *Chazal* to death to some extent.[34] Similarly, *Rav Zilberstein shlita*[35] reports in *Rav Eliashiv shlita's* name that one is not obligated to give up more than a fifth of his wealth to save the life of a fellow Jew. *Rav Eliashiv shlita* reasons that the obligation to save life is derived from the Torah's command to return lost property.[36] Since there is no obligation to spend all one's wealth to return lost property – the source – the same applies to the requirement to save life – the derivation. As to the *Chafetz Chaim*'s proof from the *Gemara* (mentioned before), *Rav Eliashiv shlita* takes the *Gemara* which the *Chafetz Chaim* saw as proof that one must spend all he has to save a life, and explains it differently. In the *Gemara,* Rebbe Akiva and Ben Petura speak of two men in a desert, one of whom has just enough water to enable him only to reach safety. Ben Petura rules that he must share the water with his fellow, even if they will both die as a result. Rebbe Akiva rules that the owner of the water may keep it all for himself since his life takes precedence over that of another. This he derives from the Torah's command:[37] "and your brother shall live with you"; this means you are the primary party and he is secondary to you. *Rav Eliashiv shlita* says that Ben Petura also derives his ruling from the same source,[38] but explains "with you" to mean "together with you." Since in practice we accept Rebbe Akiva's opinion that one's own life comes first, this includes one's wealth, for poverty is likened to death to some extent.

I have dealt with the above subject in fuller detail elsewhere.[39]

(C) under rubble: This law is based on a *Mishnah.*[40] However, *Rav Meltzer zt"l*[41] asks: What Torah prohibition is set aside when stones and rubble must be moved to get to the victim? [*Author's note: Surely*

27. יו״ד סי׳ קנז ס״ק ד
28. או״ח סי׳ תרנו א״א ס״ק ח
29. אהבת חסד ח״ב פ״כ ענין חומש ס״ק ב
30. ב״מ סב ע״א
31. וראה גם בערוה״ש יו״ד ריש סי׳ רנב
32. שו״ת ח״ה סי׳ נד
33. מובא בר״ן על הרי״ף סוכה פ״ג ובב״י או״ח סי׳ תרנו
34. וראה גם בתורה תמימה פ׳ ויצא ס״ק כג ומג״א סי׳ רמח ס״ק טז
35. מודפס משיעור שמסר בטבת תשנ״ג. וראה באסיא חוברת נה טבת תשנ״ה עמ׳ 46
36. דברים כב:א. ב״ק פא ע״ב וסנה׳ עג ע״א. רמב״ם פהמ״ש נדרים פ״ד מ״ד
37. ויקרא כה:לו
38. ספרא שם
39. המעין כרך כב ניסן תשמ״ב עמ׳ 31
40. יומא פג ע״א. וראה גם באהע״ז סי׳ ד סע׳ לד
41. אבן האזל הל׳ שבת פ״ב הי״ח

he only has a short time to live. If he is (D)no longer breathing then he is certainly dead and rescue attempts must stop.

NISHMAT AVRAHAM

the Mishnah could have given another more obvious example, such as lighting a fire, to teach us that Torah law may be set aside to save life.] He discusses the possibility that removing rubble in the street comes under the *melachah* of "building" or "dismantling." Another possibility is carrying, the carrying of spades and axes (rescue equipment) through a *public domain.*[42] Further study seems to be required to clarify why the *Mishnah* chose this particular example where the Torah law involved is not obvious.

(D) no longer breathing: It is interesting to note that the *Mishnah Berurah*[43] quotes *rishonim* who write: If found alive, even if his brain is crushed and he only has a short time to live, efforts must be made to rescue him.

Rav Auerbach zt"l told me that this *halachah* was based on the extant medical knowledge at the time. Since there was no treatment for a patient who had stopped breathing, even if his heart was still beating, there was no point in setting aside Sabbath laws for him as there was no way that his life could be saved or even prolonged. Therefore, the question of whether his heart was still beating or not was immaterial. Today, however, since treatment is available, full resuscitation efforts must be made as long as there is even a remote chance that the patient might be saved.

Sabbath laws are set aside for a *gosses* or for someone who has only a short time to live[44] even if this only leads to a slight lengthening of the patient's life.[45]

At first sight this ruling apparently contradicts a *Gemara*. The *Gemara*[46] states that someone who is about to die may be treated even if only to prolong his life for a short while so that he may make his last wishes known as to his estate. Why does the *Gemara* need to give a reason for prolonging his life? Surely this should be done even if there were no such reason? *Rav Eliashiv shlita* told me that the *Midrash* says that Yaakov Avinu prayed that people should not die suddenly (as was customary at the time) but rather should fall ill beforehand so that they would have time to make a will.[47] [*Author's note: The Midrash shows us that Yaakov Avinu saw that making one's last wishes known was important enough for him to pray to Hashem to change the way people died. This being so, it becomes important to tell the gosses to make his wishes known.*] Thus the *Gemara*'s intent is not to tell us that everything must be done to prolong life even if only for a short while, since this ruling is obvious and well known. The *Gemara*'s intent is to tell us that if such time can be gained the *gosses* should be told the importance of making his last wishes known. *Rav Waldenberg shlita*[48] also wrote to me giving a similar explanation. *Rav Auerbach zt"l* explained to me that the *Gemara* gives a picture of a person close to death and suffering whom one did not need to resus-

42. ראה עירובין לה ע״א ו־עז ע״ב

43. ביה״ל ד״ה אלא לפי שעה בשם הסמ״ג וסמ״ק מובא באו״ה

44. ביה״ל שם. שו״ת שבות יעקב ח״א סי׳ יג. שו״ת חת״ס יו״ד סי׳ שלח. אליה רבה ס״ק א. פמ״ג מ״ז ס״ק ב

45. שו״ע כאן. וראה במאמר שכתבתי בספר הלכה ורפואה ח״ב עמ׳ קפה

46. גיטין ע ע״א

47. ב״מ פז ע״א

48. שו״ת ציץ אליעזר חכ״א סי׳ ל

§9: Those who set out to save life [(E)]may return with their equipment.

NISHMAT AVRAHAM

citate *halachically,* since this would add to his suffering without changing the prognosis. However, if the dying person had some important matter to take care of, such as "making a will," this would be permitted.

Sabbath laws are set aside even for someone who deliberately endangered himself.[49]

(E) may return: See *Siman* 318A and 245A. This is permitted lest they would not wish to act in the same way another time.[50] However, only Rabbinic law may be set aside.[51] Therefore a doctor (or anyone else) who drove a car to save life may not drive back home unless there is reason to believe that he will be needed again for another *seriously ill* patient who will contact him at home. He may return home with a non-Jewish driver or by public transportation (if the driver is non-Jewish). *Chazal* permitted the setting aside of Rabbinic law to enable him to return so as to encourage him to set out again if necessary (*sofo me'shum techilato*).[52] However, he may only return home (with a non-Jewish driver) if he lives within the city limits. He must also not carry anything with him unless there is an *eruv.*

Those who work in a hospital in Israel (doctors, nurses, etc.) and whose work is concerned with the care of patients, even *non-seriously ill* ones, may travel with a non-Jewish driver to and from work on their shifts on *Shabbat* (see *Siman* 245A). There is no need for them to try to stay close by on Shabbat to be able to walk to work on *Shabbat.* However, they may use a non-Jewish driver only if it is too far for them to walk, if the weather is bad or for other such reasons.[53] The *Har Tzvi*[54] points out that the *Talmud*[55] permits a midwife, who had come from out of town to deliver a baby, only to walk freely throughout the town (plus 2,000 *cubits* beyond its precincts – the same as is allowed for anyone who lives there). But she is not permitted to set aside any Rabbinic law beyond what the *Talmud* allows in her case (without this special ruling of the *Talmud* she would only be allowed to walk four *cubits* in town after completing her task).[56] At the other end of the spectrum, the *Chatam Sofer*[57] and the *Ya'avetz*[58] both permit Torah law to be set aside. In their view the doctor, and all others who fit into the same category, may return home. The *Igrot Moshe*[59] was asked by *Hatzalah* whether they may return home after answering a call late at night on *Shabbat.* He answered that since it would be dangerous for them to walk back (even if this were physically possible), and they would need to remain there until daybreak, their families would not allow them to go out on another such call and they themselves may not want to do so again under these circumstances. Therefore, he permitted them to drive home although the driver is Jewish. *Rav Auerbach zt"l,* in response to this ruling, wrote to me: It requires study and thought since

49. שו״ת אג״מ או״ח ח״א סי׳ קכז. שו״ת ציץ אליעזר ח״ח סי׳ טו פ״ז
50. מ״ב ס״ק כ
51. שו״ע סי׳ תז. מג״א סי׳ תצז ס״ק יח
52. שו״ת ציץ אליעזר חי״א סי׳ לט. שמירת שבת כהלכתה פ״מ סע׳ סט
53. שמעתי ממו״ר הגרי״י נויבירט שליט״א
54. שו״ת או״ח ח״ב סי׳ י
55. משנה ר״ה כג ע״ב ועירובין מה ע״א. סי׳ תז סע׳ א
56. סי׳ תה סע׳ ו
57. שו״ת או״ח סי׳ רג
58. שאילת יעב״ץ ח״א סי׳ קלב ד״ה ודקשיא
59. או״ח ח״ד סי׳ פ

SIMAN 330:
THE LAWS CONCERNING A WOMAN WHO HAS GIVEN BIRTH ON *SHABBAT*

§1: A woman (A)who has given birth is considered to be (B)seriously ill and (C)Sabbath laws are set aside for her as

NISHMAT AVRAHAM

we do not find that *Chazal* were apprehensive that such a person would not set out again to save life.

Rav Auerbach zt"l writes:[60] We do not have the power to permit setting aside of Torah law to allow a doctor to return home. Even though the *Chatam Sofer* does permit the doctor to return home with a non-Jewish driver, the matter, in my opinion requires understanding. *Chazal* only permitted a midwife who arrived from out of town the same privileges as those living there (normally a person arriving from out of town would only be allowed to walk four *cubits* from where he stands). Thus she is free, after the delivery, to walk around town, and 2,000 *cubits* beyond, in any direction. However we do not find that her privileges stretch beyond this, such as permission to travel back home with a non-Jewish driver. Nevertheless, since a sage as great as the *Chatam Sofer* has permitted this, we can permit the setting aside of Rabbinic law, but surely not the setting aside of Torah law. [*Author's note*: *We find that the Chatam Sofer even permitted Torah law to be set aside.*][61] See above, *Siman* 245A and *responsum Chatam Sofer.*[62]

SIMAN 330

(A) who has given birth: If a woman miscarries after forty or more days following conception,[1] the laws regarding the counting of three and seven days enumerated later in §4 apply to her just as if she had given birth.[2]

(B) seriously ill: If there is any possibility of danger to the fetus and this requires a Cesarean section, this may be done on *Shabbat.*[3] *Rav Neuwirth shlita*[4] quotes *Rav Auerbach zt"l* who rules that the *halachah* does not require one to put himself into possible danger to save another and this applies all the more so if the other is an unborn child. Thus, a mother need not put herself into danger by undergoing the operation in order to save the baby's life. Nevertheless, if she agrees, the operation, if urgent, may be performed even on *Shabbat;* see *Tosafot, Niddah* 44a.[5]

Rav Zilberstein shlita asked *Rav Eliashiv shlita* about a situation where the fetus was known to have a serious heart defect and the mother refused to undergo surgery. Although she could be delivered normally, the Cesarean section would mean that there would be less harm to the child. He asked whether *halachah* would permit or obligate the doctor to operate against her will for the good of the child. *Rav Eliashiv* replied that a mother may not always be permitted to refuse to undergo an operation which is meant to save the life of her unborn baby. Although the *halachah* does not require one to put himself into possible danger to save an-

60. מנחת שלמה ח״א סוסי׳ ח וח״ב סי׳ כט,ו
61. ראה שו״ת או״ח סי׳ רג, ח״ו סי׳ צט ד״ה דאיכא
62. חו״מ סי׳ קצד
1. כף החיים ס״ק ב
2. סי׳ תריז סע׳ ד בביה״ל ד״ה יולדת
3. שמירת שבת כהלכתה פל״ו סע׳ ג
4. שם הערה ד
5. ד״ה איהו

is necessary. A midwife may be called from another town to deliver the baby and (D)a light may be lit in her room

NISHMAT AVRAHAM

other, there are times when a mother is obligated to do so to save the life of her baby. For when a woman marries, it is with the understanding that she is obligated to bear children to her husband and she cannot refuse to do so, because even a normal pregnancy and delivery are not without danger. True, the *mitzvah* of "be fruitful and multiply" does not apply to a woman since there is some danger to her.[6] Nevertheless, if a woman can only have children by Cesarean section, may she deny her husband the right to have children because of the danger of surgery? Surely just as any woman marries understanding that she should have children normally, in spite of the slight danger, so too there is an understanding that she should undergo a Cesarean section where the risk is a little higher. Moreover, the operation is so commonplace these days that it has become a normal form of delivery rather than something out of the ordinary. She is thus obligated to undergo the slightly higher risk of surgery. However, continues *Rav Eliashiv shlita* (as quoted by *Rav Zilberstein shlita*), this only applies where the child will be born healthy. If, on the other hand, there is doubt as to whether the child will live after birth, she may rightfully argue that she is not obligated to take a risk herself when it may well be in vain. And, where there is much doubt as to whether the baby will survive, all would agree with the *Maharit*[7] to the extent that she is not obligated to undergo surgery to prevent the extra danger to the child. *Rav Zilberstein shlita* writes in conclusion that it would seem that although the doctor should try to persuade the couple that she should have the operation, he may not force her to do so. *Rav Auerbach zt"l* told me, however, that in his opinion there is no obligation for a woman to put herself into danger to save her child if she is frightened to do so. The obligation to her husband which she accepted upon herself when they married was to have normal pregnancies and deliveries [see also below, **Q**)].

(C) Sabbath laws are set aside for her: It would therefore be advisable for a woman in her ninth month of pregnancy to prepare, every Friday, whatever she may need were she to give birth on *Shabbat,* to minimize setting aside Sabbath laws.[8] However, she is not obliged to stay close to the hospital in order to avoid traveling there on *Shabbat,* if it is difficult for her to do so.[9] Even if she lives near the hospital and is invited to spend *Shabbat* in another area of the city distant from the hospital, *Rav Neuwirth shlita* told me that she may accept the invitation. If she starts to go into labor on Friday she should not wait until the pains are worse, but should travel to the hospital immediately before the commencement of *Shabbat.*[10]

(D) a light may be lit: Provided it is dark. Although her helpers may be capable of doing whatever needs to be done in the dark, nevertheless *Chazal* knew that she would not feel safe lying in the dark. The *Tosafot*[11] write that even if neither she nor the midwife asks for a light, one must still be lit.[12]

6. משך חכמה פ׳ נח ט:ז
7. סי׳ צט
8. מ״ב ס״ק א
9. שמירת שבת כהלכתה פל״ו הערה יג בשם החזו״א זצ״ל ובשם הגרש״ז אויערבאך זצ״ל
10. קצוה״ש סי׳ קמ בבדה״ש סוס״ק ג
11. תוס׳ ישנים שלהי יומא
12. מ״ב ס״ק ג וראה בביה״ל ד״ה נר

even if she herself is (E)blind. Nevertheless, (F)wherever one can minimize the setting aside of Sabbath law one must do so. Thus, if something must be brought to her it should be carried in an indirect manner.

NISHMAT AVRAHAM

(E) blind: The reason given above (in **D**) does not apply since she does not distinguish between light and dark. Nevertheless, she will feel secure knowing that there is light in the room and her helpers will be able to see if she requires anything. Although the kindling of the light will not help her, nevertheless Sabbath law is set aside, since *Chazal* felt that the lack of peace of mind during childbirth may lead to a danger to life.[13] *The Magen Avraham* questioned this since she would have peace of mind even if she was falsely told that the light had been turned on. However, the *Eliyah Rabbah* overruled this objection since she would sense that she was really lying in darkness when her helpers fumbled in attending to her.[14]

A family member, or anyone else whom she trusts, may accompany a woman in labor to the hospital in the ambulance or car (as for any *seriously ill* patient, see *Siman* 318A). This is permissible although there is already someone in the ambulance who could help her as is necessary.[15] For she should have peace of mind on the way to the hospital and, besides, he may be needed at the hospital to give essential details of her history to the doctor, for example. This is permitted even if the patient herself does not request it.[16] *Rav Neuwirth shlita* told me that if the second reason is true, he may even drive his own car should he be unable to accompany her in the vehicle taking her to the hospital.

If her labor pains stop upon arrival at the hospital, and she is discharged, she may not return home in a car driven by a Jew. However, if there is no place for her to stay at the hospital until after *Shabbat,* she may return home by car if it is driven by a non-Jew and if her home is within the city limits.[17]

(F) wherever one can minimize: The *Mechaber* rules above (*Siman* 328 §12) that where a *seriously ill* patient is concerned there is no need to do whatever is necessary in an indirect manner. Here, however, he follows the view of the *Maggid Mishneh*[18] who rules that since birth is a natural, physiological phenomenon as opposed to disease and since the danger is less than one in a thousand, one should if possible do everything in an indirect manner.[19] However, if time is of the essence it is a *mitzvah* to do whatever is necessary as quickly as possible.[20]

At first sight the *Tosafot*[21] do not seem to agree that the danger is "less than one in a thousand." They write that danger is very common during delivery and that is why the life span of women is less than that of men. The *Meshech Chochmah*[22] deduces from this *Tosafot* that women die at an earlier age than men because of the danger present during childbirth. However, if they live beyond their childbearing age they live longer. The *Rambam*[23] and

13. מ״ב ס״ק ד
14. שעה״צ ס״ק ד
15. אגרות החזו״א ח״א סי׳ קמא. שו״ת אגרות משה או״ח ח״א סי׳ קלב
16. שמירת שבת כהלכתה פ״מ סע׳ ע
17. שם פל״ו סע׳ י
18. הל׳ שבת פ״ב הי״א
19. מג״א ס״ק ג בשם המ״מ שם. וכ״כ המאירי
20. מ״ב ס״ק ה. וראה גם בערוה״ש סע׳ ב
21. כתובות פג ע״ב ד״ה מיתה שכיחא
22. ויקרא כז:ד, על הפסוק ואם נקבה היא
23. פיהמ״ש נדה פ״ה מ״ו

NISHMAT AVRAHAM

the *Ibn Ezra*[24] also write that the life span of the female is usually less than that of the male. Why, then, does the *Mechaber* rule that a woman in delivery is different from any other *seriously ill* patient? Indeed, the *Chavot Yair*[25] writes that the need to do everything in an indirect manner applies only to that which is not directly concerned with danger to life. *Rav Auerbach zt''l,* however, told me that the *Tosafot* did not necessarily mean that women die in childbirth but only that they were in danger then. This weakened them and ultimately resulted in a shorter life span.[26] He also explained that the *Chavot Yair* meant to exclude a complicated delivery where the danger was very real. In such a situation a woman would be treated as any *seriously ill* patient in accordance with the view of the *Mechaber* in *Siman* 328 §12. *Rav Waldenberg shlita*[27] wrote to me that there is no real contradiction between the *Maggid Mishneh* and the *Tosafot.* For the *Maggid Mishneh's* opinion is based on the *Rambam,*[28] and the *Rambam* himself writes slightly later[29] that once bleeding is obvious Sabbath laws are set aside. In the earlier *halachah* quoted by the *Maggid Mishneh,* the *Rambam* has "where possible in an indirect manner"; not so in the later *halachah.* The *Brisker Rav*[30] explains that the ruling – where possible everything must be done in an indirect manner – applies to childbirth only before bleeding is obvious, where the danger is from the painful contractions and is minimal. However once bleeding is profuse, the danger is greater and the woman now has the status of a *seriously ill* patient. The *Chavot Yair* also intended to differentiate between these two periods – before and after she starts to bleed.

This leads us to a new understanding of the *halachah.* The ruling of the *Mechaber* that everything should be done in an indirect manner applies only during labor but before there is bleeding. Once, however, she starts to bleed obviously, or there is any complication, she would be a *seriously ill* patient and, in the opinion of the *Mechaber,* Sabbath laws are set aside as is necessary. *Rav Waldenberg shlita* agreed with this and this is also what *Rav Soloveitchik zt''l* writes.[31]

One more note: The *Rambam*[32] writes that once a woman is about to give birth she is considered to be a *seriously ill* patient. If she needs light during labor, light is kindled for her. He then continues: If oil is required, this is brought for her. However, where it is possible to do so in an indirect manner, one should do so at the time that it is brought. I wondered whether one could deduce from the apparently superfluous words "at the time that it is brought" that it is only here – in the bringing of the oil – that one is required to do so in an indirect manner. For the oil is not needed in the context of danger to life but is probably meant only to reduce discomfort. On the other hand, no change is required in the manner with which light is kindled since it is needed in the context of saving life. The *Gemara*[33] also writes that a change is needed only with regard to the bringing of oil. I conjectured that maybe this was the basis for the opinion of the *Chavot Yair. Baruch Hashem* both *Rav Auerbach zt''l* and *Rav Neuwirth shlita* agreed with me.

24. ויקרא כא:ב
25. בספרו מקור חיים על או״ח כאן
26. עיין בשער המלך הל׳ סוכה פ״ד סוהט״ז דכוונת התוס׳ למיתה דזמן מרובה ומשום טעמא דמסתכנת בלידה, אבל במיתה דבת יומא כההיא דיוהכ״פ איש ואשה שוים וזה פשוט, עכ״ל
27. שו״ת ציץ אליעזר חי״ז סי׳ סה
28. הל׳ שבת פ״ב הי״א
29. שם הל׳ יג
30. קונטרס חידושי רי״ז הלוי סאלאווייציק על עניני קה״ת, יומא וסוכה, תשכ״א בסוף יומא
31. שם
32. הל׳ שבת פ״ב הי״א
33. שבת קכח ע״ב

§3: Sabbath laws are set aside for a woman in labor. She is considered in labor from the time she crouches to give birth, when bleeding is obvious, or when she is unable to walk without aid. If one of these occurs (G)Sabbath laws are set aside.

NISHMAT AVRAHAM

(G) Sabbath laws are set aside: When one of these conditions is present, whatever needs to be done may be done immediately even if it involves the setting aside of Torah law. But if there may be a possible lapse in time before the act can be accomplished, it should be done even before one of these conditions is present, as soon as there is the slightest indication that labor is starting (even if it is doubtful). Thus the midwife must be called even from out of town as soon as labor starts, even before one of the above conditions is present.[34] If necessary she must be driven in.[35]

Therefore as soon as the woman begins to experience regular contractions (even if it is still doubtful whether she will indeed give birth), one may telephone for an ambulance and travel to the hospital where she is registered. She may do this even if there is another hospital close by (within easy walking distance) if she has greater confidence in the more distant hospital or in the obstetrician there. She may not do so if the intention is to save money. But, whatever can be delayed, such as putting on a light in her room, is forbidden unless one of the three conditions mentioned in the *Shulchan Aruch* is present, that is, in modern terms, cervical dilatation prior to childbirth, obvious bleeding (or rupture of membranes) or she is no longer able to walk.[36] An intravenous line can be inserted when there is a dilatation of three to four centimeters, or ablation of the cervix with regular painful contractions (earlier if there are complications). One must be careful to do so in time with a multiparous woman.

One may not induce labor on Friday if the birth would take place on *Shabbat.* Nor may Sabbath laws be set aside in any way to induce labor unless there is any danger to mother or fetus were this to be delayed.[37] On the other hand, if there is a medical indication, augmentation of labor (increasing its efficiency so as to shorten the time of labor) is permitted even on the Sabbath.

An episiotomy should be stitched immediately after the birth as usual and without waiting until the termination of *Shabbat,* even if there is no serious bleeding or there is only a short time to nightfall.[38]

Sabbath laws may not be set aside to rescue a fertilized ovum which is still in the incubator (following I.V.F.), even if this means that another cycle of treatment will be necessary. If, in the preparatory stages, the patient develops the ovarian hyper-stimulation syndrome requiring removal of excess ova lest her life be endangered, this may be done on *Shabbat.* However, Sabbath laws may not be set aside to fertilize these ova.[39]

An abortion (that has been *halachically* sanctioned) may not be carried out on *Shabbat* unless the mother's life is endangered.[40] There is usually no medical indi-

34. מ״ב ס״ק ט
35. שעה״צ ס״ק ז
36. שמירת שבת כהלכתה פל״ו סע׳ ח ו־ט
37. ראה שמירת שבת כהלכתה פל״ב הערה צח
38. שמעתי מהגרש״ז אויערבאך זצ״ל
39. ראה שו״ת שבט הלוי ח״ה סי׳ מז, מובא בנשמת אברהם כרך ג חאהע״ז סי׳ א ס״ק ה3 (עמ׳ טו)
40. פרי מגדים או״ח סי׳ שכח מ״ז ס״ק א

§4: Sabbath laws are set aside for the mother (H)for the first three days following childbirth even if (I)she says that there is no need to do so. From the third day to the seventh day, Sabbath laws are not set aside if she says there is no need. From here on in, up to the thirtieth day, she is considered a non-seriously ill patient and Sabbath laws are not set aside, even if she says that they should be.

NISHMAT AVRAHAM

cation to set aside Sabbath laws for intrauterine death. However, if the condition has brought on or may bring on severe life-threatening depression, Sabbath laws are set aside as necessary.

(H) for the first three days: Does three days mean 72 hours from the moment of birth[41] or only the period up to the beginning of the third day (the opinion of the *Shulchan Aruch*)?[42] The *Mishnah Berurah*[43] rules that the three days means 72 hours, but writes that during the period from the beginning of the third day to the completion of the full 72 hours, a Jew may set aside Sabbath laws when required only if a non-Jew is not available. The *Shemirat Shabbat KeHilchatah*[44] accepts the ruling of the *Mishnah Berurah.* They also take the position that each of these periods (the three days, the seven days and the thirty days) is not made up of days extending from sunset to sunset but of days measured as 24-hour units starting from the birth.

These days commence with the birth of the child[45] and not from the time the placenta is extruded.[46]

Why does the *Mechaber* take the more stringent view that Sabbath laws may be set aside even against her will only up to the third day (and not 72 hours)? Perhaps because he feels, as stated above, that childbirth is a natural, physiological phenomenon and not an illness. Indeed, the source of the *Shulchan Aruch's* ruling is the *Terumat HaDeshen*[47] and he states this specifically[48] (see also *Siman* 617D).

(I) she says that there is no need: The following is a synopsis of the *Mishnah Berurah's*[49] ruling:

(a) For the first three days (72 hours) she is considered a *seriously ill* patient and Sabbath rules are set aside for her if anyone with even a slight knowledge of medicine thinks that it is necessary, and even if the patient disagrees. Certainly if she requests this for her well-being, Sabbath laws are set aside, even if the doctor (or midwife) says that it is unnecessary. However, if both the patient and the doctor (or midwife) say it is unnecessary, Sabbath laws may not be set aside.[50]

(b) During the next four days (96 hours) following the first three days she is still considered to be *seriously ill.* However

41. שו״ת הרא״ש כלל כו סע׳ י. ריטב״א פרק ר״א דמילה. או״ה מובא בא״ר. הגר״א סי׳ תריז סע׳ ד. שו״ת בנין ציון החדשות סי׳ כה. מנחת שבת סי׳ צג ס״ק ו

42. שו״ע סי׳ תריז סע׳ ד (עיין שם במ״ב ס״ק יג). מג״א כאן ס״ק ז. חיי אדם כלל סח סע׳ יז. שו״ע הרב סע׳ ו. קצוה״ש סי׳ קמ סע׳ ו

43. ס״ק י

44. פל״ו הערה כח ופל״ט סע׳ טו

45. מ״ב ס״ק יא. וראה בביה״ל ד״ה כל שלשה ימים וערוה״ש סע׳ ז

46. ראה מה שכתב לי הגר״י זלברשטיין שליט״א (נשמת אברהם ח״א או״ח עמ׳ שמז). וכן שמעתי מהגרש״ז אויערבאך זצ״ל

47. סי׳ קמח

48. ראה גם שדי חמד מערכת יוהכ״פ סי׳ ג אות ג סוד״ה שוב

49. ס״ק יב – טז

50. שמירת שבת כהלכתה פל״ו סע׳ יג

§5: If a woman dies during childbirth (J)a knife may be brought through a public domain and a Cesarean section performed in case the baby (K)may still be alive.

GLOSS: *This is not done in our days even on a weekday since (L)we cannot gauge exactly the point at which the mother dies and the baby can live.*

§6: A fire may be lit for a woman (M)during the thirty days

NISHMAT AVRAHAM

these days are different from the first three, in that Sabbath laws are not set aside at the request of someone who is not trained in medicine, unless the patient requests it. If the doctor (or midwife) requests it, Sabbath laws are set aside. If the patient herself does not express an opinion and a doctor is not present, then Sabbath laws are set aside at the bidding of someone with only a slight knowledge of medicine. If the patient, in contradiction to the doctor's opinion, says that she feels she needs something specific to be done for her well-being, Sabbath laws are set aside, if she is known to hold the sanctity of the Sabbath dear.[51]

(c) From the eighth day after childbirth (i.e. after seven full periods of 24 hours have elapsed) and until the end of thirty days, the patient is considered to be *non-seriously ill.* Whatever she needs for her health may be done for her, in an indirect manner, if only Rabbinic laws are set aside. A non-Jew may be asked to do whatever is required for her health, even if Torah laws are set aside. Should any complication arise, even if it is only possibly life threatening, she is treated like any other *seriously ill* patient.[52]

(J) a knife may be brought: The *Shulchan Aruch* mentions the carrying of the knife through a *public domain;* otherwise there is no violation of Torah law. The surgical procedure itself is not an example of an act forbidden by the Torah, since she is dead.[53]

(K) may still be alive: An unborn baby has not yet established its claim to life. Nevertheless, Sabbath laws may be set aside for it although it is only probable that it may still be alive.[54]

(L) we cannot gauge exactly: She may only have lost consciousness, and the operation would kill her. On the other hand, if one waits until he is certain that she is dead, the baby will not survive.[55]

Nowadays, however, she can be closely monitored and the exact moment that her heart and respiration have ceased completely can be known. One is then obligated to operate to try and save the baby. The *Tzitz Eliezer*[56] writes that the *Rama* also did not mean to contradict the *Mechaber.* That is why he wrote "this is not done in our days" and not "it is forbidden to do so."

See above **(B)** regarding Cesarean section.

(M) during the thirty days: If she feels cold. For this may be dangerous during these thirty days. Therefore if a non-Jew is not available, a Jew may light a fire for

51. שם סע׳ יד
52. שם סע׳ טו
53. מ״ב ס״ק יז
54. מ״ב ס״ק יח. מקור הדין בערכין ז ע״א וכן נפסק ברמב״ם הל׳ שבת פ״ב הט״ו
55. מ״ב ס״ק יט
56. ח״י סי׳ כה פ״ד בשם ספר כורת הברית סי׳ של ס״ק טו

following childbirth even in the hot summer months (*see Siman* 276 *above as to whether others may also warm themselves by this fire*).

§7: Whatever is needed for the newborn baby may be done for him. He is (N)washed and (O)the umbilical cord cut. These rulings only apply to a baby born after nine or seven months following conception. However, if it is born (P)after eight months, or if it is uncertain whether it is seven or eight months after conception, (Q)Sabbath laws may not be set aside unless the baby has hair and nails.

NISHMAT AVRAHAM

her.[57] However many *rishonim* rule that after the first seven days following childbirth she is considered a *non-seriously ill* patient and a fire may therefore only be lit for her by a non-Jew.[58] The *Mishnah Berurah*[59] writes that is very difficult to be lenient and allow a Jew to light a fire during the whole thirty-day period, but in practice the matter needs further study. However, the *Tosefet Shabbat,*[60] *Aruch HaShulchan,*[61] *Chayei Adam,*[62] *Kitzur Shulchan Aruch*[63] and *Shulchan Aruch HaRav*[64] all agree with the ruling of the *Shulchan Aruch.*

(N) washed: The *Mishnah Berurah*[65] writes that Torah laws are not set aside in these instances, since there would be no danger to life by not doing them. However, there are *rishonim* who rule that Torah law may be set aside. Certainly it would be permitted to ask a non-Jew to heat water for the purpose of washing the baby as well as the other things mentioned. The *Aruch HaShulchan* writes that if a non-Jew is not available a Jew may do whatever is necessary.[66]

(O) the umbilical cord cut: Views vary as to whether this involves Torah or Rabbinic law.[67] In practice, the cord is tied twice (each time with a double knot) and cut between the two ties to avoid dangerous bleeding from either the mother or the baby.

(P) after eight months: Since such a baby will certainly not live.[68] See below.

(Q) Sabbath laws may not be set aside: Since we are not certain that the baby has as yet established its claim to life.[69] However, the *Tosafot*[70] rule leniently since we are not expert enough to decide whether the baby is not full term. This would also appear to be the *Mishnah Berurah's* ruling.[71]

The *Chazon Ish*[72] writes that there are those who rule that a baby born before term is to be considered a "*nefel*" (i.e. it is

57. עיין מג״א ס״ק יב
58. מ״ב ס״ק כא
59. ביה״ל ד״ה כל שלושים
60. ס״ק יב
61. סע׳ ט
62. כלל סח סע׳ יח
63. סי׳ צג סע׳ ד
64. סע׳ ה
65. ס״ק כג
66. סע׳ יב
67. תוס׳ שבת קכט ע״ב ד״ה כל. תפא״י ע״ז פ״ב מ״א ס״ק ו. שו״ת חת״ס יו״ד סי׳ קלא
68. שם ס״ק כח
69. שם ס״ק כט. ועיין ברמ״א יו״ד סי׳ רסו סע׳ יא וש״ך שם ס״ק טו
70. שבת קלה ע״א ד״ה בן
71. ביה״ל ד״ה או ספק
72. יו״ד סי׳ קנה ס״ק ד

NISHMAT AVRAHAM

non-viable) and discontinue treating him. However, we see that nowadays these babies, unlike those in the past, are viable, and this is probably due to a change in nature;[73] see *Rama, Yoreh Deah Siman* 156 §4. The *Minchat Yitzchak*[74] also writes that with the advances in modern medicine one may act leniently (and treat the baby on *Shabbat*). The *Shemirat Shabbat KeHilchatah*[75] writes that it is permissible to set aside Torah law for whatever the newborn infant needs even if he only has a short time to live. *Rav Auerbach zt"l*[76] adds that even if the baby was born less than seven months after conception, Torah law is set aside where there are facilities to treat him. If the baby is full term, Torah laws are set aside even if he has a mortal congenital disease and will only live a short time.

I asked *Rav Auerbach zt"l* what the *halachah* would be regarding an infant born with a serious congenital defect affecting his brain or heart who would not be able to live more than a few days or weeks. Would it be permissible to set aside Torah or Rabbinic law for his needs or would he have the same status as an infant born after eight months of gestation in the times of *Chazal* (when even Rabbinic law could not be set aside for an infant born after eight months of gestation)? He answered that, in principle, if it was certain beyond all shadow of doubt that the infant would only live a short while, only Rabbinic laws could be set aside. In spite of this, however, in a hospital, one would be obligated to set aside even Torah law for such an infant, even if his life expectancy was short. For where there are many doctors and nurses treating the baby, there is a possibility that mistakes will be made regarding the baby's true prognosis. Thus there could be a failure on their part in the future to differentiate this case from one where there is some slight chance that the infant will survive with suitable treatment. Because of this possible future baby who will have a slightly better prognosis and may not be treated because Sabbath laws were not set aside for this one, even Torah laws are set aside for this one. This is in line with the ruling of the *Shulchan Aruch*[77] that a *seriously ill* patient must have Sabbath laws set aside for him by an adult and not by a child when both are present, lest an error of judgment be made in the future. However, he continued, this discussion only applies to an infant who is both premature and has a congenital defect and who will not live more than thirty days, for whom in principle, the *Talmud* does not permit the setting aside of Sabbath laws. On the other hand, for a full-term infant with such a congenital defect, even Torah laws are set aside both in a hospital and out. However, if its heart stops beating or it stops breathing as a consequence of its disease, there is no obligation to resuscitate it.

The *Shemirat Shabbat KeHilchatah*[78] writes in the name of *Rav Auerbach zt"l* that even today the short time that a baby born as a *nefel* has to live is considered "as nothing." This means that Sabbath laws are not set aside for him as they would be for an adult who has only a short time to live. *Rav Auerbach zt"l* told me to qualify

73. ולגבי המוסג של השתנו הטבעים ראה בתוס׳ מו״ק יא ע״א ד״ה כוורא, ע״ז כד ע״ב ד״ה פרה, וחולין מז ע״א ד״ה כל. רא״ש חולין שם. שו״ת רשב״ץ מובא בב״י אהע״ז סי׳ קנו ד״ה כתוב. תרומת הדשן סי׳ רעא ובכתבים סי׳ קסז. תפא״י שבת פ״ט ס״ק א. ים של שלמה חולין פ״ח סי׳ יב. מרן הב״י אהע״ז סוסי׳ קעח. רמ״א אהע״ז סי׳ קנו סע׳ ד. החיד״א ברית עולם על ספר חסידים סי׳ תעז. שו״ת חת״ס יו״ד סי׳ קא, קנח ו־קעה. שדי חמד מערכת טי״ת כלל ה. מג״א סי׳ קעג ס״ק א וסי׳ קעט ס״ק ח. חזו״א נשים סי׳ כז ס״ק ג. ושו״ת ציץ אליעזר ח״ח סי׳ טו פ״י

74. ח״ד סי׳ קכג. וראה בשו״ת אמרי יושר ח״א סי׳ קעז ויסודי ישורון ח״ד עמ׳ רלג

75. פל״ו סע׳ יב

76. שם הערה כד

77. סי׳ שכח סע׳ יב ומ״ב ס״ק לג

78. פל״ו הערה כד

NISHMAT AVRAHAM

this statement as applying only to a premature baby.

THE FETUS. See also above, **B.** May Sabbath laws be set aside to save the life of a fetus if there is no danger to the mother? The *Rosh*[79] writes, quoting the *Ba'al Halachot Gedolot,* that a pregnant woman whom we know will miscarry if she does not eat on *Yom Kippur,* is given food, even if it is not certain that her fetus is viable. The *Ramban* (says the *Rosh*) writes that it would appear from this that Sabbath laws may be set aside if there is danger to the fetus alone. Others, however, rule that Sabbath laws are not set aside unless there is danger to the mother who craves for a particular food and the resulting miscarriage itself will endanger her. However, continues the *Rosh,* one need not search for such explanations since there is no situation where danger to the fetus does not also mean danger to the mother if she miscarries.[80] The *Ritva*[81] also rules like the *Ba'al Halachot Gedolot.* The *Ramban*[82] explains that even though the *Gemara*[83] says Sabbath laws are set aside for a one-day-old infant, this is not meant to exclude a fetus. Rather, the *Gemara's* intention is to point out that once someone dies, even one as great as King David, Sabbath laws are not set aside for him, but they are set aside for one who is alive – even a one-day-old baby. This is also the opinion of the *Rashba.*[84] The *Korban Netanel*[85] adds, in the name of the *Ramban,* that in the opinion of the *Ba'al Halachot Gedolot,* Sabbath laws are set aside even for a fetus of less than forty days after conception.[86] However, the *Korban Netanel* himself[87] disagrees with the *Rosh* and the *Beit Yosef.* The *Tur*[88] also rules that Sabbath laws are set aside if the fetus alone is in danger. However the *Beit Yosef*[89] writes that danger to the fetus always means danger to the mother as well.[90] In spite of the above opinions, the *Magen Avraham*[91] and the *Noda BiYehudah*[92] rule that Sabbath laws are not set aside in order to save a fetus. The *Maharit*[93] writes that although the ruling that one may set aside Sabbath laws to save a fetus is controversial, there is a general rule that in any controversy involving setting aside Torah law in life-threatening situations the lenient position is taken so as to save life. This is also the ruling of the *Radvaz,*[94] the *Maharsham,*[95] the *Tzitz Eliezer*[96] and the *Shemirat Shabbat KeHilchatah.*[97]

THE VERY PREMATURE BABY. A baby born after twenty-five weeks of gestation (750-1,000 grams) has an 85 percent chance of survival. If born after twenty-four weeks of gestation (about 500-750 grams) its chance of survival is about 40 percent.[98] At twenty-three weeks of gestation, survival is from 2 to 35 percent.[99] The treatment of such babies is complicated and requires a very specialized team of doctors and nurses and is also very

79. יומא פ״ח סי׳ יג
80. ראה גם ברמב״ן תורת האדם ענין הסכנה
81. נדה מד ע״ב ד״ה דכתיב
82. נדה שם
83. שבת קנא ע״ב
84. נדה שם. וראה גם בהעמק שאלה על השאילתות שאילתא קסז אות יז וביה״ל כאן סוד״ה או ספק
85. על הרא״ש יומא פ״ח סי׳ יג ס״ק י
86. ראה בשעה״צ סי׳ תריז ס״ק א
87. קרבן נתנאל על הרא״ש יומא פ״ח סי׳ יג ס״ק כ
88. או״ח סי׳ תריז
89. שם
90. וראה בב״ח שם
91. ס״ק טו
92. שו״ת מה״ת חו״מ סי׳ נט
93. ח״א סי׳ צז
94. סי׳ תרצה
95. בדעת תורה סי׳ תריז סע׳ א
96. חי״א סי׳ מג
97. פל״ו סע׳ ב
98. Am. J. Obstet. Gyn. Dec '98
99. Early Hum. Dev. Jan '99

§9: If the newborn baby's limbs are dislocated as a result of the birth they (R)**may be reset.**

SIMAN 331:
LAWS OF CIRCUMCISION ON *SHABBAT*

§1: Whatever is necessary for circumcision may be done on *Shabbat*. The foreskin is removed, the inner membrane split, (A)**blood is sucked out from the area and medication put on the wound.**

NISHMAT AVRAHAM

expensive. What is the *halachic* obligation to treat a twenty-three-week baby whose prognosis is so poor? *Rav Auerbach zt"l* told me that since such a baby has not yet established its claim to life, since the mortality is so great, and since so much must be put into his care, there is no obligation to undertake extensive resuscitative measures and Sabbath laws may not be set aside for this purpose. However, if a medical decision is made to treat it, this is permitted and Sabbath laws, even of Torah origin, may be set aside where needed. On the other hand, a very specialized unit is obligated to treat such babies and investigate ways to decrease both the mortality and the morbidity of the survivors.

THE ANENCEPHALIC BABY. The life expectancy of a full-term *anencephalic baby* is a week or less in over 90 percent of the cases and virtually all of them die within a month. The baby breathes spontaneously and has a spontaneous heartbeat. What is the *halachic* status of such a baby? May Sabbath laws be set aside for it? *Rav Zilberstein shlita*[100] rules that if the diagnosis is made during the pregnancy, the fetus may be aborted.[101] However, once born, one may do nothing to hasten its death whether actively, or even passively – by allowing it to starve for example.[102] *Rav Auerbach zt"l* wrote to me that it would appear that it would be permitted to abort such a fetus.[103] However, once born, it would appear that one may not hasten its death. The *Rav zt"l* told me that if it was a full-term baby, one would be permitted to set aside Sabbath laws for it, even those of Torah origin. On the other hand, there would be no obligation to resuscitate it if its heart stopped or it stopped breathing.

(R) may be reset: By hand.[104] If the baby was born with a dislocated hip or hips requiring either a plaster cast or, in certain cases, surgery, this may not be done on *Shabbat*. Since a delay, even that of many weeks, in no away affects the end results of the treatment, Sabbath laws may not be set aside.

SIMAN 331

(A) blood is sucked out: According to *Chazal*[1] this is necessary to prevent danger to the child. The concept of the *mohel* directly sucking blood from the open

100. מודפס משיעור לרופאים

101. וראייתו מנדה כה ע״א ורמב״ם הל׳ איסו״ב פ״י הי״א

102. ראה פתחי תשובה יו״ד סי׳ קצד ס״ק ה בשם התשובה מאהבה

103. לפי הגמ׳ והרמב״ם בהערה 108

104. מ״ב ס״ק לג

1. שבת קלג ע״ב. רמב״ם מילה פ״ב ה״א. וע״ע בחי׳ הר״ן, שו״ת חת״ס יו״ד ח״א סי׳ קלא ושו״ת שואל ומשיב מהדו״ת ח״ד סי׳ ז ו־צ שהוא חלק מן המצוה

wound has led to much opposition from doctors and others. *Rav Kook zt"l*[2] writes that if the doctors would tell us that the reason for their objection is that there is no danger to the baby should it not be done, we would still not pay any attention to them since *Chazal* have told us differently. On the other hand, if they would say that nowadays, because of a change in the nature of our bodies[3] and because of geographical changes, it is no longer applicable, this would not necessarily contradict *Chazal,* since it is possible that *Chazal*'s enactment was only applicable in the context of nature in their time. If nature has changed then it would be possible to consider this objection. But, this argument would only be acceptable if all medical knowledge would be absolutely true. However, history has shown that this is not so. There have been instances where there is some basic concept in medicine (and so too in other fields) accepted by the majority as true, only to have the next generation come and negate the whole concept; thus what one builds the other destroys. Therefore all their pronouncements are merely theoretical and must be viewed as uncertain rather than absolute. True we depend on medical opinion regarding setting aside Sabbath laws and eating on *Yom Kippur.* However, this is only because the whole Torah (except for the three cardinal sins) is set aside, if necessary, even if there is only a possibility of danger to life. Therefore since *Chazal* have defined *metzizah* as lifesaving, the opinion of all the doctors in the world will not do more than leave us with an uncertainty, and Sabbath laws are still set aside even if only for a situation of possible danger.

The *Tiferet Yisrael*[4] writes that one would have thought that since, according to the doctors, the direct sucking out of blood from the wound can actually endanger the baby, we should accept their opinion, at the very least on *Shabbat* (to avoid its desecration). However, Heaven forbid that we should stray from the opinion of our Sages and *metzizah* must be performed, even on *Shabbat.*

One may ask: Do we not find that where there is a possible danger to life according to qualified medical opinion, we act leniently even against *Chazal*? However, since the concept of *metzizah* preventing danger to the baby has been given to *Moshe Rabbeinu* at Sinai and handed down throughout the ages,[5] we cannot accept anything which contradicts this.

Must the *metzitzah* be done only directly or may it be done using a sponge or a glass pipette so as to avoid the danger of infection to either the baby or the *mohel*? This has been debated extensively in the *responsa* literature.[6] The *Har Tzvi*[7] quoting the *Chatam Sofer*[8] and the *Maharam Shick*[9] rules that where there is fear of cross-infection, a glass pipette may be used if the *mohel* has learned how to use one.[10] I was present when *Rav Auerbach zt"l* was asked by a *mohel* from the United

2. דעת כהן סי׳ קמ

3. ראה סימן של הערה 82

4. שבת פי״ט מ״ב

5. שו״ת בנין ציון סי׳ כד בשם ההפלאה. שו״ת מהר״י אסאד סי׳ ו ו־רנח. ובשו״ת מהר״ם שיק או״ח סי׳ קנב כותב דמהגמ׳ הנ״ל מוכח דהוא מהלכה למשה מסיני. אמנם שם ביו״ד סי׳ רמד כותב דאפשר שהוא מהלכה למשה מסיני

6. ראה שו״ת בנין ציון ח״א סי׳ כג ו־כד. יד אליעזר מובא מביה״ל ד״ה ופורעין. שו״ת חת״ס יו״ד ח״א סי׳ קלא. שו״ת מהר״ם שיק או״ח סי׳ קנב ויו״ד סי׳ רמד ו־רמח. שדי חמד אסיפת דינים מערכת המציצה. זוכר הברית סי׳ יב סע׳ לו. שו״ת אבני נזר יו״ד סי׳ שלח. שו״ת דברי מלכיאל ח״ד סי׳ פז. שערי תשובה או״ח סי׳ תריב ס״ק ז. שו״ת מהר״י אסאד יו״ד סי׳ רנח. שו״ת בית יצחק יו״ד ח״ב סי׳ צח. שו״ת זכר שמחה סי׳ קלד. משנה ברורה כאן ביה״ל ופורעין. שו״ת הר צבי יו״ד סי׳ ריד. שו״ת מנחת יצחק ח״ה סי׳ כד אות ב. יסודי ישורון ח״ד עמ׳ קצ. ושו״ת שבט הלוי ח״ב יו״ד סי׳ קל

7. שם

8. שם

9. שם

10. וראה גם בשו״ת חלקת יעקב ח״ב סי׳ נג

§4: A circumcision that (B)has been postponed may not be performed on (C)*Shabbat.*

§5: The circumcision of a hermaphrodite, a baby born without a foreskin, or a baby (D)born by Cesarean section, may not be performed on *Shabbat.*

§6: (E)Preparations required for circumcision that could have been arranged before *Shabbat* may not be arranged on

NISHMAT AVRAHAM

States whether he could use a pipette in certain circumstances where there was a possibility of infection, and the *Rav zt"l* permitted it.

(B) has been postponed: A baby who was even *non-seriously* ill may not be circumcised until seven full days have passed after recovery,[11] and a postponed circumcision may not be performed on *Shabbat.*[12] If he was circumcised on *Shabbat* before these seven days had passed, *Shabbat* has been desecrated.[13]

A newborn baby who must be put into an incubator is considered at least *non-seriously ill.* Therefore he may not be circumcised until seven full days have passed after he is taken out of the incubator, even if according to medical opinion he may be circumcised on the eighth day following birth; the circumcision may not be performed on *Shabbat.*[14] If, however, the baby is healthy and was only put into an incubator under a blue lamp because of *physiologic jaundice,* he may be circumcised on the eighth day, even on Shabbat.[15]

(C) Shabbat: The same ruling applies to *Yom Tov.*[16]

(D) born by Cesarean section: A woman after childbirth is ritually "unclean" by Torah law. The laws of this state of "uncleanliness" differ from those of the *niddah* – a woman's state of "uncleanliness" following menstruation. However, these laws only apply to a woman who experiences a vaginal delivery but not to one who has a child by Cesarean section; then she is only unclean like a *niddah* (because of the uterine bleeding). According to many *Tanna'im,* the commandment to circumcise a male on the eighth day after birth is linked to the mother being "unclean" because she has given birth. Since this does not apply after Cesarean section, the commandment to circumcise on the eighth day does not apply and therefore the circumcision may not be performed on *Shabbat.*[17]

A child born by forceps delivery is circumcised on the eighth day[18] if healthy.[19]

(E) Preparations required for circumcision: Before *Shabbat* one must prepare whatever dressings and bandages will be required following the circumcision. If this was not done beforehand one may not perform the circumcision with the intention of cutting the bandages to size afterwards or to bring whatever may be necessary, in a place without an *eruv.*[20]

11. יו״ד סי׳ רסב סע׳ ב
12. כאן
13. שו״ת בנין ציון סי׳ פז
14. שו״ת אג״מ יו״ד ח״ב סי׳ קכא. שו״ת ציץ אליעזר ח״ג סי׳ פב ס״ק ד
15. שמעתי ממו״ר הגרי״י נויבירט שליט״א
16. יו״ד סי׳ רסו סע׳ ב
17. מ״ב ס״ק יח
18. שמעתי מהגרש״ז אויערבאך זצ״ל
19. עיין בשו״ת ציץ אליעזר ח״ג סי׳ פג ס״ק ה
20. מ״ב ס״ק כד

***Shabbat.* Thus, if the knife was not brought before *Shabbat,* it cannot be brought on *Shabbat* even through a *carmelit,* for *Chazal* have insisted that their enactment be carried out even if the circumcision must be postponed. This is so even though circumcision is a positive commandment where the punishment for not performing it is "*karet*" (the extinction of the soul). A non-Jew may be asked to do whatever the Jew did not do before *Shabbat,* if this only involves Rabbinic law. If Torah law is involved, a non-Jew may not be asked to do it** (*see Siman* 307).

SIMAN 334:
THE LAWS OF A CONFLAGRATION ON *SHABBAT*

§12: Nowadays (A)all sacred writings written in any language or in any color of ink may be saved from a fire.

NISHMAT AVRAHAM

However, if he had already performed the circumcision in error[21] or even if he did it knowing that it was wrong to do so[22] one may nevertheless do whatever is necessary to prevent any danger to the baby.[23]

SIMAN 334

(A) all sacred writings: The *Magen Avraham*[1] writes that rescuing books of the Written Torah takes precedence over those of the Oral Torah. The *Aderet*[2] wonders what the *halachah* is with regard to manuscripts which have not yet been printed which surely can be considered Oral Torah (see *Sanhedrin* 33a)? Since they are irreplaceable do they take precedence over the Written Torah? Can this be compared to the *halachah* in *Siman* 656 that one is not obligated to spend all his wealth in order to be able to perform a positive command? One could perhaps answer that for someone who has toiled all his life to produce manuscripts containing his novellae, seeing them burn in a fire, which may not be extinguished because of the sanctity of the Sabbath, could lead to a depression severe enough to endanger his life. The *Aderet* adds that he heard that this is what happened to *Rav Charlap zt"l* – Head of the *Beit Din* in Bialystok, who died soon after such an event.

Rav Auerbach zt"l,[3] quoting the above, comments: We see that light may be kindled for a blind woman in labor in order to give her peace of mind (see above, *Siman* 330 §D) even though kindling the light is not directly part of her treatment. Similarly, one may send for a *seriously ill* patient's relatives whom he wishes to see

21. מ״ב שם

22. שעה״צ ס״ק יז

23. יו״ד סי׳ רסו סע׳ ד. שמירת שבת כהלכתה פל״ז סע׳ יג. ועיין במ״ב ס״ק כ־כב

1. ס״ק טו

2. קונטרס עובר אורח של האדר״ת, מודפס בסוף ספר ארחות חיים (ספינקא)

3. שמירת שבת כהלכתה פמ״א הערה ח וראה גם בפכ״ה הערה נ ומנחת שלמה ח״א סוסי׳ ז ד״ה ונראה. וראה בשו״ת אג״מ יו״ד ח״ב סי׳ קעד ענף א סוד״ה ולכן

SIMAN 338: PRODUCTION OF SOUND ON *SHABBAT*: WHAT IS FORBIDDEN

§1: It is forbidden to (A)use a musical instrument on *Shabbat*. However, it is permitted to knock on a door and the like if it is not done musically.

§3: A clock (B)may be wound and set before *Shabbat* so that the time may sound on *Shabbat*.

NISHMAT AVRAHAM

even if Rabbinic law must be set aside, and according to some authorities, even Torah law may be set aside.[4] This is permitted even though the patient should overcome his feelings and do without seeing them. This being so, continues *Rav Auerbach zt"l*, why is it that we do not fear for the well-being of someone who sees all his wealth go up in flames on *Shabbat* and allow him to put out the fire (an act which is only Rabbinically forbidden)? It is permitted to extinguish burning wood if it will be a danger to many and here also surely many members of the family will be affected if the house burns down. Similarly, according to the plain meaning of the *Shulchan Aruch* (*Siman* 328 §17), Sabbath laws of Torah force may not be set aside to save a limb even though this may cause him to become depressed to the point of endangering his life. Similarly someone condemned to death by *Sanhedrin* is executed regardless of the effect it may have on members of his family.

SIMAN 338

(A) use a musical instrument: One may not use a bell on *Shabbat* or *Yom Tov* even if it is not electrically activated[1] and even if the sounds produced are not musical.[2] The bell itself is *muktzeh* and may not be moved.[3] However a patient, although *non-seriously ill,* who is confined to bed, at home or in the hospital, may use a non-electric bell to call for help.[4] He may not use an electric bell unless he needs immediate medical attention and is certain that no light is lit as a result of his call. The use of an electric bell is Rabbinically forbidden according to most authorities[5] although the *Chazon Ish* rules that it is forbidden by Torah law.[6] If the patient is *seriously ill* he may use an electric bell even if a light goes on, according to all authorities[7] (see also *Siman* 278D).

(B) may be wound and set: If one forgot to wind a clock or watch before *Shabbat* and it is needed for a patient on *Shabbat* (for example, so that he may receive his medication at set times), it may be wound on *Shabbat* provided it is still going.[8] If it has stopped, a non-Jew may be asked to wind it.[9] *Rav Ovadiah Yosef*

---

4. ראה שמירת שבת כהלכתה פל״ב הערה פב

1. שמירת שבת כהלכתה פכ״ג סע׳ מה ופכ״ח סע׳ לד
2. שם פכ״ח והערה עה
3. שם
4. שם פ״מ סע׳ יט
5. שם הערה נט. וראה שם מה שכתב הגרש״ז אויערבאך זצ״ל בשיטת החזו״א
6. סי׳ נ ס״ק ט ד״ה ובפתיחה
7. שם
8. שמירת שבת כהלכתה פכ״ח סע׳ כ
9. מ״ב ס״ק טו ושעה״צ ס״ק יט. שמירת שבת כהלכתה פל״ח סע׳ י

SIMAN 340: FURTHER LAWS REGARDING *SHABBAT*

§1: It is (A)forbidden to remove hair or trim nails either by hand or with an instrument for oneself or for others. Removing one white hair from among black ones is Torah forbidden and is forbidden even on a weekday (for a man but not for a woman – author).

§2: It is forbidden (B)to remove a (C)corn or callus either by hand or with an instrument, either his or another's.

§4: One must be careful not to (D)write with his finger on a wet surface or in dust.

NISHMAT AVRAHAM

shlita,[10] however, rules that if a non-Jew is not available, and the clock is needed for the patient, one may act leniently and wind it even if it had stopped. This is because winding a clock is not forbidden by Rabbinic law (it does not fall into the category of "repairing" an instrument) but by custom only.

SIMAN 340

(A) forbidden to remove hair: A patient may not be shaved on *Shabbat* in preparation for surgery after *Shabbat* even if he is *seriously ill.* However if the surgery is urgent and will be performed on *Shabbat* or as soon after *Shabbat* as possible, and shaving him after *Shabbat* will delay the operation, it may be done on *Shabbat.* Similarly, if an urgent cardiogram or electroencephalogram cannot be done without first shaving the patient's chest or head respectively, this may be done. Since, however, Torah law forbids the removal of each and every hair,[1] one must take care to shave only the area required (see also *Siman* 328 §4C).

(B) to remove. Even if it was dry and about to fall off.[2]

(C) corn. Similarly, one may not remove a skin tag [i.e. a piece of hanging skin].[3]

(D) write. See the *Mishnah Berurah*[4] for details of the laws of writing and erasing on *Shabbat.* The *Rama*[5] rules that writing in a language other than Hebrew is only forbidden by Rabbinic law. But the *Mishnah Berurah*[6] rules that writing in any shape or form is forbidden by the Torah. He argues that the *Rama*'s ruling is based on a single authority, the *Or Zarua,* that there is no basis for this decision in the *Talmud,* and that all other authorities disagree with the *Or Zarua* and rule that writing in any language is forbidden by Torah law as stated in the *Mishnah.*[7] However, the *Sdei Chemed,*[8]

10. הערה על נשמת אברהם ח״א עמ׳ שלה. שו״ת יביע אומר ח״ו או״ח סי׳ לה
1. מ״ב ס״ק ג
2. שם ס״ק ו
3. שם ס״ק ז
4. ס״ק כב
5. סי׳ שו סע׳ יא
6. סי׳ שו מ״ב ס״ק מז וביה״ל ד״ה בכתב שלהם
7. שבת קג ע״א. וראה בשו״ת נו״ב תניינא או״ח סי׳ כט ו־לג. שו״ת חת״ס חו״מ סוסי׳ קצה. שו״ת מהרש״ם ח״ב סי׳ צג וערוה״ש סע׳ כב ואהע״ז סי׳ קכו סע׳ ב
8. מערכת כ״ף כלל קיא

NISHMAT AVRAHAM

the *Yabia Omer*[9] and the *Yesodei Yeshurun*[10] point out that there are a number of both *rishonim* and *acharonim* who rule like the *Or Zarua*. Therefore a doctor should write in a language other than Hebrew[11] or, if he writes in Hebrew he should write in script[12] (as opposed to block letters).

If a doctor must write for a *seriously ill* patient on *Shabbat* – a prescription, a referral letter to the emergency room or important details in his chart, for example – he may do so. However, he is forbidden to write anything which is not of direct benefit to the patient. He must be careful to cut down what he writes to the bare minimum – only what is absolutely necessary. Thus, writing the details of the patient's medical insurance coverage or dating the letter (if it is not essential) are not permissible. Only essential medical facts should be written, even in a request for admission or advice. It is forbidden to write one unessential word, letter or number[13] or even a period (fullstop) at the end of a sentence.[14] Wherever possible, what must be written should be dictated to a non-Jew unless this leads to delay. Wherever possible, a right-handed doctor should write with his left hand and vice versa (i.e. writing in an indirect manner).[15] If, however, this will lead to delay or illegibility, and bring about delay or less than the best possible care for the *seriously ill* patient, he should write with the hand he normally uses. And if the slow pace of writing were to lead to a delay in the doctor's availability to see other *seriously ill* patients, he must also write with his usual hand.

A doctor who, on *Shabbat*, sees a *seriously ill* patient who does not yet require emergency admission, may not write a letter of referral to the emergency room. Even if the patient does not require immediate referral but may need it later, depending on how he reacts to treatment, such a letter may not be written now to be used later if required. If the patient will later require admission, Sabbath laws should then be set aside to phone the doctor or drive to him to get such a letter. However, if there is any possibility that he may not be available then or that the ensuing delay will adversely affect the patient, he may write the letter at the first visit.[16]

A doctor who asks for a pen to write whatever is necessary for a *seriously ill* patient, may be given one even if it is probable that he will also write what is unnecessary and therefore forbidden.[17] He may not be aided if he wishes to write when there is no immediate need for writing. However, if the doctor is a non-Jew and is unable to take the pen himself, he may be given one even if he will write unnecessary information.[18]

A *non-seriously ill* patient who needs medical attention on *Shabbat* must see a religious Jewish doctor who will not set aside Sabbath laws needlessly.[19] If this is

---

9. ח״ג סי׳ כג

10. ח״ה עמ׳ לח

11. שמעתי ממו״ר הגרי״י נויבירט שליט״א

12. ראה מג״א כאן ס״ק י וסי׳ תקמה ס״ק כא. וכן שמעתי מהגרש״ז אויערבאך זצ״ל. וראה במנחת שלמה ח״א סי׳ צא אות יא. ולפי זה יהיה מותר לרופא בחדר מיון להכתיב מכתבי שחרור לגוי עבור חולים המשתחררים משם בשבת. וראה להלן הערה 30

13. תויו״ט שבת פי״ב מ״ג. שו״ע הרב סע׳ ח

14. שמירת שבת כהלכתה פל״ב סע׳ מח. ועיין באשל אברהם בוטשאטש סי׳ שכח סע׳ ב ושו״ת ציץ אליעזר ח״ח סי׳ טו פי״א ס״ק ו

15. מ״ב ס״ק כב (ז)

16. שמירת שבת כהלכתה שם סע׳ נ

17. וכותב השמירת שבת כהלכתה שם הערה קכו בשם הגרש״ז אויערבאך זצ״ל דאם מותר לחלל שבת עבור חושיב״ס, כ״ש דמותר נמי לעבור על אלאו דלפני עור

18. שם סע׳ נא

19. ד״מהיות טוב אל תיקרי רע״ ולא יכשיל את הרופא בחילול שבת – שמירת שבת כהלכתה פ״מ סע׳ ח הערה כו

NISHMAT AVRAHAM

not possible or the non-religious doctor is a specialist, the patient may go to him even though the doctor will surely write all the details of the visit as well as a prescription. However, if it is possible to ask the doctor to refrain from doing so, the patient is obligated to do so.[20] One may in these circumstances depend on the *poskim* who rule that writing in a language other than Hebrew, or even in Hebrew but in script, is only forbidden by Rabbinic law.[21] On the other hand, *Rav Auerbach zt''l*[22] writes that where the doctor will unnecessarily set aside Torah laws, the patient may only go to him if there is a possibility that he is *seriously ill*. The *Maharsham,*[23] the *Zivchei Tzedek,*[24] the *Tzitz Eliezer*[25] and the *Yesodei Yeshurun*[26] all write that a *non-seriously ill* patient should not go to a non-religious doctor on *Shabbat.*

If a Jewish doctor did write a prescription for a *non-seriously ill* patient on *Shabbat,* it may not be filled on *Shabbat.* Since the writing was unnecessary, it constitutes work done by a Jew on *Shabbat,* and one may not benefit from such work on *Shabbat.* The prescription may be filled after the Sabbath.[27] *Rav Auerbach zt''l*[28] ruled that if the prescription was wrongfully filled on *Shabbat,* the medication may still be used on *Shabbat.* The *Chayei Adam*[29] writes that on first thought it would appear that if one who did not know that it was wrong to do so, brought food through a *public domain,* the food should not be forbidden on *Shabbat.* This is because the *melachah* of carrying does not change the object carried as does the *melachah* of cooking. But, if the prohibition of carrying was violated with intent, the food would be forbidden. Nevertheless, he rules that one should act stringently as with all *melachot.* In our case, although use was made of a prescription that was written by wrongfully setting aside Sabbath laws, the medication would not be forbidden if carried through a place where there was an *eruv.*

A doctor may not write a discharge letter for a patient who is discharged home from the emergency room or from the ward on *Shabbat. Rav Auerbach zt''l* told me that the hospital management should make it possible for such a patient to remain within the hospital precincts where he can receive food and have a bed. The discharge letter could then be written after *Shabbat.* If this cannot be arranged, or if remaining in the emergency room will cause suffering for others through a shortage of beds or space to treat other emergencies, or a lack of order at the termination of *Shabbat,* a non-Jew may be asked to write the letter.[30] The patient himself may not ask for a discharge letter to be written on *Shabbat.* However, if he is a *non-seriously ill* patient and may need further treatment on *Shabbat* from his own doctor, he may ask for one if it will be

---

20. דבמומר לא שייך מסייע ידי עוברי עבירה ואין בו אפילו איסור דרבנן של ולפני עור, וכיון דשעת הדחק היא יש לסמוך על השיטות דס״ל דכל שאינו כתב אשורית, אינו אלא מדרבנן, וחושאבו״ס יש לדונו כשה״ד כי השעה דחוקה לו. גם יש לומר דהרי החולה עצמו אינו מבין אם חוליו יב״ס או לא ופעמים רבות קורה שהחולה חושב שאבו״ס ואח״כ מסתעף שמרחפת עליו סכנה, וא״כ הולך בהיתר אל הרופא או שולח אחריו לקרוא לו, ואחר שכבר הרופא לפניו וכותב לו הרפואות, הר״ז עושה הרופא מדעת עצמו, והחולה התחיל בהיתר, עכ״ל של היד יצחק ח״ג סי׳ צה מובא בשמירת שבת כהלכתה שם הערה כז

21. שמירת שבת כהלכתה שם

22. שם, ועיין מדבריו בנוגע ל״הלעיטהו לרשע״

23. ח״ב סי׳ צג

24. ח״ב בחלק השו״ת שאלה יח

25. ח״ח פי״ג ס״ק יב

26. ח״ד עמ׳ רנח מובא בשמירת שבת כהלכתה פ״מ סוף הערה כז

27. שמירת שבת כהלכתה שם

28. שם הערה ל

29. כלל ט מובא בביה״ל סי׳ שיח סע׳ א ד״ה אחת. וכנראה שמקור הדין הוא ברשב״א על שבת קל ע״ב

30. כי במקום צורך וצער לרבים, יש מקום להתיר. וראה גם לעיל הערה 12

NISHMAT AVRAHAM

written by a non-Jew. This is permitted even if he will only require the treatment on Saturday night, but will not be able to obtain the document then, thus delaying treatment.[31]

Since non-permanent writing is not considered writing by Torah law as far as *Shabbat* is concerned, can "disappearing ink" be used on *Shabbat* by the hospital staff? *Rav Weiss zt"l*[32] wrote that even writing which lasts for only a day before disappearing is considered permanent and therefore the writer will have violated Torah law. *Rav Auerbach zt"l*[33] writes that although it would appear from the *Rambam*[34] and the *Mishnah Berurah*[35] that writing which lasts through *Shabbat* only is considered permanent, it would seem that for *Rashi* permanent means forever. *Rav Auerbach zt"l* wrote me that it would be permitted even if it lasted three or four days. However, I recently heard from *Rav Neuwirth shlita* that the *Rav zt"l* had, in the latter years of his life, ruled that it was forbidden for use like any regular ink.

A non-Jew should be asked to record the important details of the history and physical of a new admission and those of the follow-up. If a non-Jew is not available and the patient is *seriously ill* and there is a possibility that because of the lack of notes in his chart he will not receive appropriate treatment on *Shabbat,* the doctor may record the important medical information with his left hand (if he is right-handed). However, if time is short as there are other patients who are possibly *seriously ill,* and who need to be examined and treated, he may write with his right hand. It is preferable to record the physical findings as line diagrams with brief notes rather than write out full sentences.[36] If the patient is *non-seriously ill,* a non-Jew may be asked to record the findings; the doctor himself may not do so even with his left hand.[37]

Documentation of operative findings (or of any other urgent procedure) should, if possible, be postponed until after the Sabbath. However, if this were to prevent optimal patient care on *Shabbat,* the notes should be dictated to a non-Jew or, if one is unavailable, they should be written with the left hand (if the doctor is right-handed). If neither is possible, the notes may be written as usual taking care to write only what is essential. Similarly, when blood and the like is sent to the laboratory, a non-Jew should be asked to fill out the necessary forms. If the patient is *seriously ill* and a non-Jew is not available, the doctor should write only what is absolutely necessary, using his left hand.

The Torah prohibition against writing includes writing on one's skin, even though it will fade away after a while.[38]

A *seriously ill* patient asked to sign a consent form before undergoing an operation or other procedure on *Shabbat,* may do so (as may a member of his family) if verbal consent in front of witnesses is not acceptable. If he must sign he should do so with his left hand (if he is right-handed) and, if it is acceptable, he should sign his initials only. He must be careful not to add any flourishes or punctuation marks. It is forbidden to sign only to obtain exemption from billing.[39]

An ECG (cardiogram) may be performed on a patient who may be *seriously ill,* preferably using a computerized model. Where possible, this should be

31. שמירת שבת כהלכתה פ״מ סע׳ מד והערה צא
32. ספר הלכה ורפואה ח״א עמ׳ רלג
33. שם עמ׳ רלה. וראה במנחת שלמה ח״א סי׳ צא אות יא
34. הל׳ שבת פ״ט הי״ג
35. שעה״צ סי׳ שג ס״ק סח
36. שמעתי ממו״ר הגרי״י נויבירט שליט״א
37. סי׳ שכח סע׳ יז ומ״ב ס״ק מז
38. רמב״ם הל׳ שבת פי״א הט״ז
39. שמירת שבת כהלכתה פ״מ סע׳ סע׳ כא

done by a non-Jew. If one is not available the instrument should be activated in an indirect manner (using the back of a finger or hand). Jelly for good electrical contact may be used if required.[40] If necessary, hair on the chest may be shaved off (see above, *Siman* 340A). A patient who needs continuous ECG monitoring over 24 hours (Holter) while at home, should do this on a weekday. However, if he must do it over *Shabbat,* he may comply, even though the slightest effort on his part causes additional recording of beats (see below on the use of a tape recorder). He may not go out with the attached instrument if there is no *eruv.* He should take care that the leads are attached to hairless or shaved parts of his body on Friday so that no hairs are pulled off on the Sabbath when the leads are disconnected. On the Sabbath, at the end of the 24-hour period, the patient disconnects the instrument without turning it off, and leaves it in a safe place until it is returned to the hospital after *Shabbat.*

An ECG may not be performed on *Shabbat* to confirm death nor may a non-Jew be asked to do so. A non-Jew may not be asked to write a death certificate on *Shabbat* for the Jewish doctor to sign after *Shabbat.* However, if not doing so will result in an undue delay in the burial, thereby resulting in disrespect to the deceased, it is permitted.[41]

A respirator patient is obviously a *seriously ill* patient. When conscious, he communicates by signs or by writing (since the tube in his throat prevents him from talking). On *Shabbat,* if it is essential for him to communicate in order to request something for his well-being, and he is unable to convey his request by signs, he may write his request, writing only the minimum number of words necessary for his request to be understood.[42]

A patient who is attached to a monitor that continuously records his cardiogram, pulse, blood pressure, and the like on a screen, may move around freely, even though this will cause changes in the tracings on the screen.[43]

A COMPUTER. It would appear that there is no Torah prohibition in typing on a computer (that has already been turned on before *Shabbat*). Since the letters that appear on the screen are the result of a continuous impact of electrons on phosphorus when each key is depressed, this is not comparable to the writing in the *Mishkan. Rav Auerbach zt"l* wrote to me agreeing, but added that entering what was written onto the hard disk or diskette would possibly be forbidden by Torah law as a *melachah* of "building." (The *Rav zt"l* told me that wherever a new article is produced, the *melachah* is one of building, since raw materials are used to make something else of far greater value, which is what happens when a house is built.) Therefore one may not feed a computer with patient details on *Shabbat* or *Yom Tov,* even if it was switched on before *Shabbat.*[44] One may, however, retrieve, preferably without printing, previous details of a *seriously ill* patient that may be essential for his present care. If possible, a non-Jew should be asked to do it. If the computer has not been switched on and is required for a *seriously ill* patient, a non-Jew should be asked to switch it on. If he is unavailable, it should be switched on in an indirect manner (with the back of a finger or hand for example). It must not be switched off after use. If a code must be

---

40. שמעתי ממו״ר הגרי״י נויבירט שליט״א ולא כפי שכתוב בשמירת שבת כהלכתה פ״מ סע׳ לא

41. שמעתי ממו״ר הגרי״י נויבירט שליט״א והסכים עמו הגרש״ז אויערבאך זצ״ל. וראה בנשמת אברהם ח״ה עמ׳ קעב סע׳ עב

42. שמעתי ממו״ר הגרי״י נויבירט שליט״א

43. שמעתי ממו״ר הגרי״י נויבירט שליט״א

44. וראה שמירת שבת כהלכתה פס״ו הע׳ה ריא

NISHMAT AVRAHAM

typed in before it can be used this may be done by typing with the back of a finger.[45] Printing is forbidden by Torah law (*melachah* of writing).[46] If it is required for the care of a *seriously ill* patient, a non-Jew should be asked to do it. If one is unavailable and it is essential to have the printout, a Jew may do it by typing the order in an indirect manner.

A TAPE RECORDER. *Rav Auerbach zt"l* wrote to me explaining that before one records on a cassette it is "dead" and of small value. It is only after the recording has been made that it turns into an object which emits the sounds of speech or music. Therefore a tape recorder may not be used to record and store patient information unless it is essential for a *seriously ill* patient. It is permissible, however, to listen to a previously recorded cassette containing essential information on such a patient.[47] Wherever possible, a non-Jew should be asked to switch the tape recorder on. If, one is not available, the doctor may switch it on in an indirect manner, but he may not turn it off afterwards. If, however, the recording is temporary and other information will be recorded in its place after *Shabbat* (automatically erasing it), the tape recorder may be used even for a *non-seriously ill* patient, provided it has already been switched on or will be switched on by a non-Jew.[48]

I asked the *Rav zt"l* if recording on a diskette is "building," why isn't there a prohibition of "building" when one writes on paper? Does he not take paper which is of little worth and transform it into something valuable? He answered that for any single act he does a person is only culpable for one *melachah*. Even though one who prunes a tree and wants the cuttings for firewood is culpable for two *melachot*, "pruning" and "reaping," that is different. For there, though he performs a single act, he has two distinct purposes in mind (see *Meiri, Shabbat* 104b).[49]

A FAX. *Rav Auerbach zt"l* told *Rav Neuwirth shlita* and myself that it would be permissible for a doctor or a member of the hospital staff to prepare a fax on Friday to have it sent by timer on *Shabbat*. *Rav Neuwirth shlita* told me that such a fax may also be sent to a non-religious Jew and not only to a non-Jew or a religious Jew. Even though he might tear off the paper from the machine on *Shabbat*, this would not be considered "putting a stumbling block in his way"[50] nor would it be classified as "cutting to size" (see *Siman* 322A), or creating something new (see "using a computer" above), since the timer was set before *Shabbat*. *Rav Auerbach zt"l* also told us that it would be permitted to leave the machine on over *Shabbat* to be able to receive faxes, if the machine will not be heard outside the room. A fax that was received on *Shabbat* may be *muktzeh*,[51] since the blank sheet of paper now has information on it giving it the status of a newly created object. Thus although one may read the fax on *Shabbat*, it is possible that one may not touch it to straighten out a crease, for instance.

X-RAY. The *Yesodei Yeshurun*[52] writes that it is forbidden for a Jew to X-ray a *non-seriously ill* patient on *Shabbat* because it involves both "kindling" and "writing." Nor may a *non-seriously* ill

45. שמעתי ממו"ר הגרי"י נויבירט שליט"א

46. כי ע"י לחיצת הכפתור הרי הוא עושה מעשה ממש, עיין חזו"א סי' לו ד"ה החורש – שמירת שבת כהלכתה שם בשם הגרש"ז אויערבאך זצ"ל

47. כתב לי הגרש"ז אויערבאך זצ"ל

48. כתב לי מו"ר הגרי"י נויבירט שליט"א

49. וראה בספר שביתת שבת עמ' יד. וראה בנשמת אברהם ח"ד עמ' נה־נז

50. ויקרא יט:יד

51. מחמת נולד

52. ח"ה עמ' פה

§6: It is forbidden to tighten a running stitch that has loosened because of (E)sewing.

NISHMAT AVRAHAM

Jewish patient allow himself to be X-rayed, even by a non-Jew. However, whether X-raying involves "writing" needs further thought, for the *Pri Megadim*[53] rules that "secret writing" (writing in milk) is not forbidden by Torah law since the writing is invisible until the paper is heated. It is, however, forbidden by Rabbinic law since it is akin to writing (see the discussion on the use of a contact thermometer in *Siman* 306B).[54] The *Shevet HaLevi*[55] rules that it is possible that taking an X-ray is only Rabbinically forbidden since the picture is automatically transferred to the plate and the technician only moves the shield away allowing this to happen. Developing the film, however, is forbidden by Torah law because of the *melachah* of "writing."[56]

May one X-ray all *seriously ill* patients on *Shabbat*? Or, to put it more strongly, is the doctor obligated to X-ray every *seriously ill* patient who is admitted on *Shabbat*? For instance, a young adult who has a clear history and physical signs of a small area of pneumonia, is in a stable condition with no suggestive signs of any complication such as an *empyema.* If he is seen on *Shabbat* may one wait for a few hours and X-ray him after the Sabbath or should one do so immediately? Obviously, treatment will be started immediately after appropriate blood tests and cultures have been taken, regardless of when the X-ray will be done. *Rav Neuwirth shlita*[57] told me that if the treating doctor X-rays every such patient immediately on a weekday, then he may do so on *Shabbat* as well. This ruling is based on the *Shulchan Aruch* (see *Siman* 328 §4) who quotes the *Ramban* "that everything that is done for a *seriously ill* patient on a weekday may be done for him on *Shabbat.*" *Rav Waldenberg shlita,*[58] on the other hand, rules that if the patient is stable, most doctors would not insist on an immediate X-ray. Since waiting until after the Sabbath will in no way prejudice his prognosis, the X-ray should only be taken by a non-Jew and this is the ruling of the *Mishnah Berurah.*[59] *Rav Auerbach zt"l* also told me that if the patient's condition was stable and there was no medical indication for an immediate X-ray, one should wait until after *Shabbat* to X-ray the patient.

If an X-ray screen must be used for a *seriously ill* patient, it may be turned on in an indirect manner. It may not be turned off after use.[60]

(E) sewing: Torah law forbids sewing on *Shabbat* if one makes a minimum of two stitches and ties a knot at the end, even if the knot is only of a temporary nature. Making two stitches without the knot is forbidden by Rabbinic law.[61] However, if he makes three stitches, even if he does not tie a knot, he transgresses Torah law.[62]

SUTURING A WOUND. A deep wound is sutured to stop bleeding and to prevent infection. There is a difference of opinion among the *poskim* as to whether suturing of a wound is forbidden by Torah or Rabbinic law. The *Shemirat Shabbat KeHilchatah*[63] writes that there is no evi-

53. כאן במ״ז ס״ק ג
54. וראה גם בשו״ת אב״נ או״ח סי׳ רג
55. ח״א או״ח סי׳ קכא סע׳ ג
56. שו״ת הר צבי יו״ד סי׳ רל
57. וראה באסיא א תשל״ו עמ׳ 3
58. כתב לי בלב אברהם ח״ב עמ׳ כד. ציץ אליעזר חי״ד סי׳ כז ס״ק ג
59. סי׳ שכח ס״ק יד
60. שמירת שבת כהלכתה פ״מ סע׳ לב
61. ועיין בשעה״צ ס״ק ס
62. מ״ב ס״ק כז ועיין שם יתר פרטי דיני תופר
63. פל״ה הערה סב

NISHMAT AVRAHAM

dence that it is forbidden by Torah law. *Rav Zilberstein shlita*[64] writes, that this was the opinion of *Rav Abramsky zt"l*. *Rav Waldenberg shlita*[65] also rules that suturing does not involve Torah law. However, *Rav Auerbach zt"l* told me that in his opinion this is possibly forbidden by Torah law and is only permitted where there is danger to life. He wrote to me that in the same way that gluing together two pieces of paper or two pieces of wood would be forbidden by the Torah because of "sewing," so too would suturing together the skin or flesh of a human being. Since the intention is to join the two edges of the wound, there is a possiblity that this would be forbidden by the Torah under the heading of "sewing." Although ultimately without sutures the wound heals and the edges join together naturally, nevertheless once it has been sutured together, the end result of the suturing is permanent. Even though one does not suture except when there is a wound and one could argue that this is not the usual *melachah* of sewing, nevertheless why is it not like writing on one's skin. Although writing on one's skin is not the usual kind of writing, the *Rambam*[66] rules that Torah law forbids it. Similarly one does not "sew" paper or wood and yet doing so is forbidden because of the *melachah* of sewing. And in suturing one sews in the same fashion that one sews a garment. On the other hand, since the two edges of the wound constitute living flesh of the same body, they are not separate like two edges of a garment and can even now be considered as joined together. Yet, this is not sufficient to permit leniency when there is a possiblity that it is forbidden by the Torah. He later wrote to me[67] that in the same way as watering seeds is forbidden by Torah law because it is like sowing even though one only pours water over them and the roots drink thirstily on their own, so *Hashem* designed our bodies in such a way that wounds heal if the edges are juxtaposed. Although in sowing one does nothing except provide the possiblity for the seeds to grow on their own, nevertheless this is what the Torah forbids as the *melachah* of sowing [*Author's note: The Rav zt"l compares watering to suturing; watering is part of the melachah of sowing in the same way as suturing is part of the melachah of sewing even though it only allows the edges to join together naturally.*]

Rav Eliashiv shlita told me that there are *melachot* which are forbidden by the Torah when done on or to a human being, such as writing on skin (see reference 66). On the other hand, there are those, such as washing one's hands or face, which are completely permitted. It is uncertain if the *melachah* of sewing applies to the human body and it is therefore probably forbidden by the Torah.

The *Shemirat Shabbat KeHilchatah*[68] writes that the tying of double knots during suturing involves setting aside Torah law for each knot. However, *Rav Auerbach zt"l* told me that this was not forbidden by the Torah since such knots are not permanent[69] even though after ten days the sutures are cut and removed without undoing the knots.

As to the use of adhesive plaster (ordinary or "butterfly") or surgical glue to close the wound, *Rav Eliashiv shlita* told me that he did not differentiate between them and suturing, and they are all forbidden on *Shabbat* except when there is danger to life.

Rav Auerbach zt"l[70] wrote to me that

64. תורת היולדת מהדורא שניה עמ׳ ריג
65. שו״ת ציץ אליעזר ח״כ סי׳ יח
66. הל׳ שבת פי״א הט״ז
67. ראה נשמת אברהם ח״ה עמ׳ מא
68. פל״ה סע׳ ד, כד ו־כו
69. עיין סי׳ שיז במ״ב בהקדמה ובביה״ל ד״ה הקושר
70. נשמת אברהם שם

using adhesive plaster or surgical glue to keep together the edges of a wound is not like sticking two pieces of paper together. One is only juxtaposing the two edges and allowing them to close naturally. However, he wrote, he still feels hesitant in his heart as to whether it is permitted. Some time later, however, the *Rav zt"l* told *Rav Neuwirth shlita* and myself, that although he still believed that suturing may be forbidden by the Torah, he now believes that the use of adhesive plaster is permitted. This is because adhesive plaster only serves to prevent the two edges of the wound from separating, and using it is not considered sewing. *Rav Abba Shaul zt"l*[71] allows the use of adhesive plaster to close a wound since this is not akin to sewing. On the other hand, he writes, suturing is like sewing.

If a wound that needs suturing on *Shabbat* to avoid infection requires five or six stitches, for example, but the patient will be left with an ugly scar, may more stitches be put in, over and above the number required to prevent the danger of infection, so that the scar will be barely visible? *Rav Auerbach zt"l* wrote to me that on first thought one may not set aside Torah law to produce a barely visible scar. There is no difference between unnecessary suturing and the addition of basically unnecessary stitches just to prevent a scar. However, he later wrote to me that it would seem to him that one could compare this to a circumcision on *Shabbat*. The *halachah* states that so long as the *mohel* is still performing the circumcision he may remove shreds of skin even those that would not render the circumcision invalid were they to remain.[72] For we are commanded to beautify our *mitzvot* before *Hashem*. Thus, here, also, since Sabbath laws are set aside in order to save life, it is permissible to produce a finished act and save the patient from an ugly scar that will cause him shame and suffering all his life. Just as a good clean wound is the final touch to the *mitzvah* of circumcision so too here, preventing an ugly scar in a *seriously ill* patient brings the *mitzvah* of saving life to completion.[73] *Rav Auerbach zt"l* added that it is possible to rest this ruling on the statement of the *Maggid Mishneh*[74] that whatever one is accustomed to do for a *seriously ill* patient during the week, one may do for him on *Shabbat,* even if not doing so will not be dangerous. *Rav Ovadiah Yosef shlita*[75] agrees with *Rav Auerbach's* basing his ruling on the *Maggid Mishneh,* pointing out that the *Shulchan Aruch*[76] rules like the *Maggid Mishneh.*

Rav Auerbach zt"l told me that it is forbidden to suture any wound of a patient who dies on the operating table on *Shabbat*. If the wound is large (such as a *thoracotomy* or *laparotomy*), wads of absorbent cotton may be put into the wound to prevent the spilling out of internal organs and to soak up the blood and prevent it spilling out when the body is taken out. I asked him whether a non-Jew may be asked to close the wound to prevent desecration of the body. The *Rav zt"l* wrote to me that one most likely could bring proof that this would be permitted since we find that *Chazal* only forbade burial on *Shabbat*[77] even by a non-Jew for the reason that it would be a desecration and shame for the deceased to be buried on *Shabbat* at the expense of Sabbath laws. But here, where the purpose is to prevent the desecration of the dead, it would be permitted.

---

71. שו"ת אור לציון ח"ב פל"ו סע' טו ובהערה שם
72. ראה יו"ד סי' רסו סע' ב
73. וראה ברש"ש יומא פד ע"ב ושמירת שבת כהלכתה פ"מ הערה פב
74. הל' שבת פ"ב ה"ה
75. בהערה לנשמת אברהם ח"ד עמ' רכה ס"ק ב
76. סי' שכח סע' ד
77. עיין ב"ק פ ע"ב תוסד"ה אומר

NISHMAT AVRAHAM

Might a Jew who is right-handed, close the wound by suturing with his left hand? We know that writing with the left hand by one who is right-handed is not a Torah offense.[78] On the other hand, if one uproots a plant, he is culpable by Torah law whether he did so with his right or left hand.[79] The *Ran*[80] asks rhetorically: Why is one only culpable if he writes with the right hand whereas if he carried an object from a *private* to a *public domain* he is culpable no matter in which hand he carried it? He answers that carrying is usually done in either hand equally, whereas a right-handed person does not usually write with his left hand. It would appear from the *Ran* that not only writing but any act which one usually does with the right hand, for example sewing, would not be a transgression by Torah law if done with the left hand. *Rav Abramsky zt"l*[81] rules that whatever one normally does with one hand only, is usually done with the stronger, the right, and not with the weaker hand. Thus if a person does do so with his left hand he is not culpable by Torah law. On the other hand, we find a discussion among the *acharonim* about the *melachah* of erasing done with the left hand. Is this considered a setting aside of Torah law or only of Rabbinic law? The *Eliyah Rabbah*[82] rules that it is possible that erasing with the left hand is only Rabbinically forbidden. The *Avnei Nezer*[83] disagrees, ruling that erasing using the left hand is forbidden by Torah law just like carrying with the left hand from a *private* to a *public domain*.[84] However, the *Da'at Torah*[85] agrees with the ruling of the *Eliyah Rabbah*. We see here an opinion like that of the *Ran*, that whatever one does only with the right hand, if done with the left, is only culpable by Rabbinic law, and this is also the view of the *Zaken Aharon*.[86] The *Kalkelet Shabbat*[87] however, rules that only with writing is it usual to do so with the right hand and writing with the left is unusual. This is not so with all other *melachot*, for example, kindling with the left hand would be culpable by Torah law since one uses the right or left hand indiscriminately. The *Chayei Adam*[88] also rules categorically that writing is the only *melachah* where we differentiate between one hand and the other, and this ruling is quoted by the *Mishnah Berurah*.[89] However the *MiBeit Meir*[90] specifically sees sewing as comparable to writing, arguing that just as writing is different, since one does not write using both hands together, and writing with the left is unusual, so too it is not possible to sew holding the needle in both hands. The *Shevet HaLevi*[91] also rules that every *melachah* that one normally does with the right hand may only be Rabbinically forbidden if done with the left. *Rav Auerbach zt"l* told me that it is not specifically stated that *melachot* other than writing have different rulings when done with the left as opposed to the right hand. However, we do find a difference if the stitches are professional or not, for instance if they are large or small, in a straight line or not.[92] Therefore in this situation where the honor of the deceased is in question, it is

78. שבת קג ע״א
79. תוספתא שבת פ״י מי״א
80. חידושי הר״ן שם ד״ה אמר אביי
81. חזון יחזקאל חידושים על התוספתא שבת פ״י מי״א
82. סי׳ שמ ס״ק יא
83. שו״ת או״ח סי׳ רט סע׳ ט
84. שבת צב ע״א
85. סי׳ שמ סע׳ ג ד״ה אסור לשבור
86. שו״ת ח״א סי׳ יז
87. כללי ל״ט מלאכות סי׳ א ס״ק ג
88. כלל ט סע׳ ב
89. כאן סוס״ק כב
90. ספר שני סי׳ יט
91. שו״ת ח״ז סי׳ סד
92. סי׳ תקמא סע׳ ה

SIMAN 343: THE LAWS CONCERNING A CHILD ON *SHABBAT*

§1: The *Beit Din* is not obligated to stop a child from eating forbidden food. However, his father is obligated to rebuke him and prevent him from doing so *(if it is food forbidden by* [(A)]*the Torah).*

NISHMAT AVRAHAM

possible that one may depend on the ruling that this would only be a Rabbinic prohibition, and allow the wound to be closed with the left hand in order to prevent desecration of the dead. [*Author's note: Although, at first sight, this ruling is against that of the Rama,*[93] *who rules that a professional who sews holding the needle in an unusual fashion has not done enough; the change must be in the pattern of stitches not in the act of sewing only. Suturing with the left hand would certainly produce an obvious change in the kind of stitches sewn.*]

DISLODGED TOOTH. A tooth that becomes dislodged on *Shabbat,* if it is put back into its socket within a short time, and held there, has a good chance of living if it was reattached permanently after *Shabbat. Rav Auerbach zt"l* told me that it would be permissible for the person to put it back into the socket until after *Shabbat* when he could then seek dental treatment. *Rav Waldenberg shlita*[94] also wrote me permitting this, since the act of "building" that is done on Shabbat is only temporary. He quotes the *Har Tzvi*[95] who permitted putting sticking powder on loose false teeth to prevent them from falling, since this was only effective for a few hours. But, he notes that a dentist must not set aside any Torah laws by, for example, using any electrical apparatus. He must not reattach the tooth permanently either since this would involve the *melachah* of "building." *Rav Waldenberg shlita* refers the reader to his discussion[96] of the controversy as to whether "building" applies to the human body.

SIMAN 343

(A) the Torah: The *halachah* forbidding a *Cohen* from ritually defiling himself by contact with a corpse, or part of a corpse, or from being in the same room with a corpse applies only to males but not to the female offspring of a *Cohen.* But it applies even to a newly born baby and obligates his parents to prevent him from becoming ritually impure. It applies equally to a newborn baby who will become ritually impure for the first time or an adult who has already become ritually impure.[1]

Concerning the pregnant wife of a *Cohen,* the *Magen Avraham*[2] quotes the *Roke'ach*[3] that she may enter a room containing a corpse because of two uncertainties: The baby may be a girl and even if it were a boy, it might be a stillbirth. This combination of uncertainties allows a leniency and she is permitted to enter the

93. שם

94. שו״ת ציץ אליעזר ח״ב סי׳ מז

95. חאו״ח בקונטרס טל הרים מלאכת בונה

96. שו״ת ציץ אליעזר שם. וראה גם בנשמת אברהם ח״ד עמ׳ ס

1. רמב״ם הל׳ אבל פ״ג ה״א וה״ד ונזירות פ״ה הט״ז. ואמנם הראב״ד בהל׳ נזירות שם חולק עיי״ש, חזר בו בספרו תמים דעים סי׳ רלו ופסק להדיא כהרמב״ם, עיין שו״ת חת״ס יו״ד סי׳ שלט ופ״ת יו״ד סי׳ שעב ס״ק ט

2. ס״ק ב

3. ח״ח סי׳ שסו

room. However, he questions the need for this reasoning since the fetus is within the mother's womb and therefore is not affected by any ritual impurity. The *Netiv Chaim*[4] answers that the *Roke'ach* was concerned with a *Cohen's* wife who was close to term. In spite of the fact that she might give birth in the room containing the corpse and the baby might be a boy, he ruled that she may enter the room because of the two uncertainties. The *Mishnah Berurah*[5] agrees with this interpretation. On the other hand the *Ya'avetz*[6] rules that she may not enter a room that contains a corpse, for when the baby's head becomes visible he immediately becomes defiled, and at that point the second uncertainty of a possible stillbirth no longer has relevance. Since there is now only one uncertainty, and the question involves Torah law, one acts severely and not leniently.[7]

At first sight this discussion does not have meaning today since most pregnant women have routine sonography (ultrasound) examinations during their pregnancy and the sex of the fetus can be clearly determined in most cases. It would appear that in such a situation a *Cohen*'s wife who is at full-term and who knows that the fetus is a boy should not enter a building containing a corpse. Thus, for instance she may not enter a hospital to visit someone if the pathology room is not completely separate from where she will visit. Similarly, she may not enter a hospital where the rules preventing defilement from a corpse are not strictly observed. Is she obligated to undergo sonography to determine the sex of the fetus, since this option is available? Morever, although a stillbirth may have once been a plausable likelihood, that is no longer true since the possibility of a stillbirth at term is very small.[8] Thus, one uncertainty – will the child be a boy or a girl – can be clarified. And the second uncertainty – maybe it will be a stillbirth – is a very weak uncertainty. The *Maharam Chalawa*[9] writes that every doubt that can be resolved cannot be considered a doubt when deciding a *halachic* question. The *Mishneh LaMelech*[10] writes that the general rule that one rules leniently in a Rabbinic law when there is a matter of doubt is only true if the doubt cannot be resolved. This is also the ruling of the *Shach*.[11]

Rav Neuwirth shlita told me that if a *Cohen*'s wife wishes to deliver in a particular hospital because she has a greater trust in the medical staff or because her own obstetrician works there, she may deliver there, even if the hospital is not particular about the rules concerning the defilement of a *Cohen* and she knows that the fetus is a boy. *Rav Eliashiv shlita*[12] told me that it is appropriate for a *Cohen*'s wife to find out the sex of the fetus, close to her delivery date. If it is a male, she should preferably choose to give birth in a hospital that is not problematic for a *Cohen,* for instance, a maternity hospital. If she must go to a general hospital, she should preferably choose one that is particular about

4. הגהה על המג״א

5. סוס״ק ג. וראה בש״ך יו״ד סי׳ שעא ס״ק א. ובנו״ב תניינא יו״ד סי׳ רז

6. ח״ב שאלה קעז

7. וראה בשו״ת הרדב״ז סי׳ ר. מנחת חינוך מצוה רסג ס״ק ג. חת״ס יו״ד סי׳ שנד. הר צבי יו״ד סי׳ רפא פתחי תשובה יו״ד שעא ס״ק א ושו״ת שבט הלוי ח״ב סי׳ רה

8. ראה בב״י אהע״ז סי׳ קכח ד״ה ואם יש, דמיעוטא דמיעוטא הוא עשרה אחוז

9. על פסחים ד ע״ב סוד״ה ולענין פסק

10. הל׳ בכורות ריש פ״ד ד״ה ועוד אני מודיע. וראה בשער המלך הל׳ מקואות פ״י כללי ספיקא דרבנן כלל ג שכותב: חפשתי ולא מצאתי דין זה בספרים של ראשונים

11. דיני ספק ספיקא וכללי דיני ספק ספיקא סוסי׳ קי אות לה. וראה בנחלת צבי סוף סי׳ קי. וכתב לי מו״ר הגרי״י נויבירט שליט״א שלכאורה קשה ממה שכתב המ״ב סי׳ תלט ס״ק ג

12. כך גם קבלתי במכתב מהג״ר יוסף אפרתי שליט״א בשם הגרי״ש אלישיב שליט״א

these laws, such as a hospital that removes a corpse immediately from within the building, as opposed to one where the mortuary is part of the main building.[13]

Is it permissible to keep a newborn *Cohen* in the hospital when there is no medical reason? It would seem that this would depend on which of two views is followed: The *Rama*[14] rules that it is not necessary to tell a completely undressed adult *Cohen* – who is sleeping and unaware – that there is a corpse in the same room. Since Torah law forbids him to be in the same room as a corpse, every minute that he knowingly remains in the room is a separate sin. Thus, he should be awakened and called to come out, so as to give him the opportunity to first get dressed. The *Shach*[15] explains that this is only so if he is in the same room, but if he is in an adjoining room the defilement is only at a Rabbinic level. Although the *Magen Avraham,*[16] the *Chochmat Adam*[17] and the *Chatam Sofer*[18] all disagree with the *Shach,* many *poskim*[19] support his ruling.

The *Mishnah Berurah*[20] rules that although it is not necessary to take a baby *Cohen* out of a room containing a corpse, it is forbidden to take him into such a room. Thus, in a hospital where a corpse or part of one is present, the baby does not becoming ritually impure, as long as the door of the nursery is closed. However every time this door is opened the baby becomes impure again, and *halachah* views this as if he is taken into the room of the corpse each time the door is opened.[21] Therefore, *Rav Auerbach zt"l*[22] rules that although the baby and the corpse are not in the same room (but are under the same roof) most *poskim* rule that he becomes ritually impure by Torah law and he is considered to have been "defiled" each time the door is opened. Therefore, in a hospital where most of the patients are Jewish, the baby *Cohen* should be taken out 24 hours after his birth, provided the doctor affirms that this will not give rise to any danger. See, however, *Chelkat Yaakov,*[23] who rules leniently.

Although, a *Cohen* is forbidden by Torah law to either come into contact with a corpse or part of one, or to be in the same room as one, this only applies to a Jewish corpse. Contact with a non-Jewish corpse or part of it is also forbidden by Torah law. However, to be in the same room with a non-Jewish corpse is only forbidden by Rabbinic law. The *Dagul MeRevavah*[24] and *Aruch HaShulchan*[25] both rule like the *Rambam*[26] that the corpse of a non-Jew does not defile unless touched.[27] The *Mechaber*[28] writes that it is proper for a *Cohen* to be careful about walking on graves of non-Jews; the *Rama* writes that it is proper to be stringent, implying that this is a Rabbinic prohibition only. Thus, in a hospital where the majority of patients are non-Jewish, one can rule leniently. For since a Rabbinically prohibited defilement from a corpse may be set aside to do a *mitzvah,*[29] it may certainly be

13. ראה "מוריה" גליון ה־ו אדר ב׳ תשנ"ז עמ׳ צב
14. יו"ד סי׳ שעב סע׳ א
15. ס"ק ב
16. או"ח סי׳ שיא ס"ק יד וסי׳ שמג ס"ק ב
17. כלל קנט סע׳ ח
18. שו"ת יו"ד סי׳ שלט
19. יד אברהם יו"ד סי׳ שעב. פני יהושע סוכה כא ע"א ד"ה והנלע"ד. והשואל ומשיב מהד"ג ח"ג סי׳ כו כותב דרוב אחרונים סוברים כהש"ך. ועיין גם בפ"ת כאן ס"ק ג
20. ס"ק ג
21. שמעתי ממו"ר הגרי"י נויבירט שליט"א
22. הערה בעמ׳ יח של לב אברהם ח"א פכ"א סע׳ ג
23. ח"א סי׳ כח
24. יו"ד סי׳ שעב סע׳ ב
25. סע׳ ה
26. הל׳ טומאת מת פ"ה הי"א
27. ועיין גם בשו"ת רעק"א מהד"ת סי׳ יח. שו"ת מהרש"ם ח"א סי׳ רטו וח"ב סי׳ רלג. ושו"ת אבני נזר יו"ד סי׳ תסח
28. יו"ד שעב סע׳ ב
29. שם סע׳ א

SIMAN 346:
THE TORAH LAWS OF *ERUVIN*

§2: Torah law only forbids one to carry something for a distance of (A)four *amot* in a public domain. Rabbinic law, however, forbids his carrying it four *amot* even in a *carmelit* and the like.

NISHMAT AVRAHAM

set aside for a baby who is considered to be *non-seriously ill.*[30]

SIMAN 346

(A) four *amot*: If a doctor was delayed at work on Friday afternoon and it is the time that the congregation "receive" the *Shabbat,* even if he himself has not yet prayed, he must empty his pockets of everything that is *muktzeh* (such as money, pens).[1] When he is ready to return home on *Shabbat,* if there is no *eruv* in the area, he must make sure that he is not carrying anything in his pockets so as not to inadvertently carry them from one *domain* to another.[2] If he has valuables with him and there is no safe place available in the hospital to store them until after *Shabbat, Rav Neuwirth shlita* wrote to me that he may take them home carrying them in an indirect manner,[3] for instance, under his hat or between his clothes.[4]

Regarding carrying medical instruments or a beeper in the street, see *Siman* 301C. See also *Siman* 318A regarding car documents when driving, *Siman* 301B regarding carrying medication in the street and *Siman* 308A regarding carrying a baby or child into the street.

CARRYING WITHIN THE HOSPITAL GROUNDS. Carrying from one apartment to another in an apartment building, or through an enclosed courtyard, is forbidden by Rabbinic law. This law was enacted because each apartment is owned individually, whereas the corridors, staircases and courtyard belong equally to all the residents.[5] Without the law one would come to carry from one kind of *private domain* (an apartment, owned individually) to another kind of *private domain* (the property owned jointly – the corridors and the like). And mistakenly people might think that one may carry from a *private domain* to a *public domain,* too. This law serves as a reminder to prevent carrying from a *private* to a *public domain.*[6] However, if all the residents have "ownership" jointly in a loaf of bread or *matzot* (of a given quantity)[7] placed in one of the houses, they may carry throughout the building and its courtyard. Since bread is considered the mainstay of our food, the common loaf joins all the residents together. It is as if they have a common meal and a common private domain. This bread (or *matzot*) is called an *eruv chatzerot* and unifies the whole building or courtyard so that all its apartments, corridors, courtyard and the like are said to have one owner, the person in whose apartment the

30. עיין במחצית השקל או״ח סי׳ שלח ס״ק א ובשו״ת חלקת יעקב ח״א סי׳ כז
1. או״ח סי׳ רנב סע׳ ז
2. שם מ״ב ס״ק נו
3. וראה בסי׳ שא סע׳ לג, מחלוקת מרן ומור״ם אם אסור או מותר להוציאם, דרך שינוי,מרשות לרשות
4. ראה בשמירת שבת כהלכתה פל״ב סוסע׳ נד
5. גזירת שלמה ובית דינו, עיין עירובין כא ע״ב. רמב״ם הל׳ עירובין פ״א ה״ב
6. רש״י שבת ו ע״א ד״ה לא עירבו. רמב״ם שם הל׳ ד ו־ה
7. סי׳ שסח סע׳ ג ומ״ב ס״ק יב

SIMAN 347: WHEN IS ONE CULPABLE BY TORAH LAW FOR CARRYING

§1: One trangresses (A)Torah law if he picks up an object in a private domain and carries it into a public domain or vice versa.

NISHMAT AVRAHAM

eruv is placed.[8] The whole area is then considered to be one private domain. *Rav Auerbach zt"l* told me that there is no need for such an *eruv* in a hospital and one may carry within its grounds on *Shabbat.* This ruling applies even if there is no *eruv* in the town, whether the owners of the hospital are non-Jews or non-observant Jews, or whether there are patients who do not eat the hospital meals but bring their own food from home.[9] *Rav Ezriel Auerbach shlita* told me that his father-in-law, *Rav Eliashiv shlita,* is of the same opinion. It is sufficient if the patients have the right to eat from the common kitchen, even if this particular patient does not make use of it. *Rav Auerbach zt"l* wrote to me that this would also apply to a religious Jew in a non-Jewish hospital since he could still eat fruits or fresh vegetables from the hospital kitchen if he so wished.[10]

SIMAN 347

(A) Torah law: The *Mishnah Berurah*[1] points out that, based on the *Talmud*'s[2] exegesis of a verse in *Leviticus,*[3] one is only culpable by Torah law if he does the whole *melachah* by himself. However, if he did a *melachah* that he was capable of doing alone but did it together with someone else, he is exempt by Torah law but has transgressed Rabbinic law. This is the ruling of the *Rambam*[4] who writes that two who wrote while holding a pen together or carried a loaf of bread together from one *domain* to another, are exempt by Torah law. The *Avnei Nezer*[5] rules that two doing the same *melachah* together (when each is capable of doing it by himself) is akin to one doing it in an indirect manner. This is also the ruling of the *Yabia Omer.*[6] On the other hand, the *Shemirat Shabbat KeHilchatah*[7] writes that the *Meshech Chochmah*[8] and the *Be'er Yitzchak*[9] rule that although they are both exempt from *karet* and from bringing a sin-offering, nevertheless they have transgressed Torah law. The *Elef Lecha Shlomo*[10] also writes that they are culpable by Heavenly law. The *Chayei Adam*[11] writes that this is worse than someone who does a *melachah* but not to the extent which would make him obligated to bring a sin-

8. סי׳ שסו סע׳ א ומ״ב שם. שמירת שבת כהלכתה פי״ז סע׳ יא ו־יג
9. וראה במ״ב סי׳ שע סע׳ ג בביה״ל ד״ה ואם היו. שו״ת מהרש״ם ח״ו סי׳ יז
10. ראה בנשמת אברהם ח״ד עמ׳ סג
1. סי׳ שמז ס״ק א
2. שבת ג ע״א. ועיין שם תוס׳ ד״ה בעשותה. וראה במשנה וגמ׳ שם צב ע״ב
3. ויקרא ד:כז
4. הל׳ שבת פ״א הט״ו
5. יו״ד סי׳ שצג או״ק ט ו־י. ומביא בשם הבכור שור שיש בזה איסור תורה. וראה גם שם או״ח סי׳ מה ה־ז
6. ח״ה סי׳ לב ס״ק ז
7. ח״ג מבוא להלכות שבת פ״א הערה עז
8. סוף פ׳ בהר ד״ה את
9. או״ח סי׳ יד
10. או״ח סי׳ קמד
11. הל׳ שבת כלל ט סע׳ ט

CHAPTER TWENTY:

The Laws of Rosh Chodesh

SIMAN 426:
THE BLESSING ON THE NEW MOON AND ITS TIMING

§1: On (A)seeing the new moon one recites the blessing: Who created the Heavens by His word etc.

NISHMAT AVRAHAM

offering.[12] The *Shemirat Shabbat Ke-Hilchatah*[13] adds that even a person doing the whole *melachah* from beginning to end with both hands (when he is capable of doing it with one) is also exempt by Torah law but is culpable by Rabbinic law (see *Tosefet Shabbat*).[14]

Based on all the above, one may conclude that when one must do a *melachah* for a *seriously ill* patient, it is better to do it in an indirect manner rather than to do it with both hands or have two do it simultaneously. *Rav Neuwirth shlita* agreed with this.[15]

SIMAN 426

(A) seeing the new moon: It is a *mitzvah* to sanctify the new moon by a special blessing instituted by *Chazal*.

The *Mishnah Berurah*[1] writes, quoting the *Maharshal*, that a blind person is obligated to do this *mitzvah* since the blessing was instituted on the renewal of the world each month. Although he himself cannot see, nevertheless, he benefits because the light of the moon enables others to see and guide him on his way when necessary. This blessing is therefore akin to the blessing: "The Creator of the luminaries" said each morning during *Shacharit*. However, in his *Biur Halachah*,[2] the *Mishnah Berurah* writes that the *Maharikash* and the *Radvaz* both disagree with this ruling of the *Maharshal*. He, therefore, concludes that it would be best that the blind person not say the blessing himself. Rather, he should ask another person who is about to say the blessing to have him in mind as well and he thereby fulfills his obligation. He may then himself say the verses that follow the blessing. This is also the ruling of the *Birkei Yosef*,[3] the *Ben Ish Chai*,[4] the *Kaf HaChaim*[5] and *Rav Ovadiah Yosef shlita*.[6]

A blind person should not recite the blessing on the sun.[7]

---

12. ועיין גם בשמירת שבת כהלכתה פל״ב הערה פז
13. ח״ג מבוא להלכות שבת פ״א סע׳ כא
14. הקדמתו לסי׳ שח ד״ה ואגב
15. ואמנם מו״ר שליט״א כותב בח״ג שם שכשצריך לדליק אור עבור חושיב״ס יעשה זאת בשתי ידיו בבת אחת, אמר לי שנכון יותר לעשות זאת בשינוי דהיינו בגב האצבע או גב היד

1. ס״ק א
2. ד״ה ונהנין
3. סי׳ רכד ס״ק ד ובמחזיק ברכה סי׳ רכט ס״ק ו
4. שנה ב פ׳ ויקרא סע׳ כד
5. ס״ק ב
6. הערה בנשמת אברהם ח״א עמ׳ שלה. שו״ת יחוה דעת ח״ד סי׳ יח הערה יב (עמ׳ קא)
7. סי׳ רכט בשע״ת סוס״ק א

§2: One looks at the new moon, (B)stands upright and recites the blessing.

§4: One may not recite the blessing until after (C)seven days have passed.

GLOSS: *One may not sanctify the new moon while standing (D)under a roof.*

NISHMAT AVRAHAM

(B) stands upright: The *Talmud*[8] relates that Meremar and Mar Zutra were carried while reciting the blessing. The *Yad Ramah*[9] explains that they could not stand because of their advanced age and therefore leaned on the shoulders of their servants in order to say the blessing standing. The *Biur Halachah*[10] learns from this that a person who is unable to stand on his own may lean on something for support during the recital of this blessing.

(C) seven days: Most *acharonim* disagree with this ruling and permit the recital of the blessing after three full days have passed from the *molad.*[11] *Rav Auerbach zt"l* told me that, in light of this controversy, a patient who knows or fears that he will not be able to wait the full seven days, as he normally does, may depend on the latter view and sanctify the new moon after three days.

(D) under a roof: The *Mishnah Berurah*[12] rules that someone who is sick, and even someone who has mild discomfort, to the extent that he is unable to go outside, may sanctify the moon looking at it through a window or through an open door. He adds[13] that this is so even if the window is closed, so long as he is certain that he is seeing the moon itself and not just a reflection. Although it would be better if the window were open, nevertheless, if it is very cold outside, the blessing can be recited with the window closed.[14] At first glance it would appear that the *Mishnah Berurah* here contradicts his ruling[15] regarding the blessing *borei meorei ha'aish* recited during *Havdalah.* There he rules that one may not, if he can avoid it, recite the blessing when he sees the *Havdalah* light through a glass lamp. *Rav Auerbach zt"l*[16] writes that according to this ruling a person wearing spectacles should, if possible, remove them for both these blessings. I wondered whether a possible answer would be that the blessing *borei meorei ha'aish* requires clear vision and the glass of the lamp hampers his vision. Spectacles, however, are worn to enhance vision and, on the contrary, without them his vision is blurred and unclear. *Baruch Hashem,* I was very happy to see that, in the new edition of his book, the *Rav zt"l* writes that seeing through spectacles is different from seeing through the glass of a lamp, since the former are worn to enhance his vision. I also found this explanation later in the *Ketsot HaShulchan.*[17]

8. סנהדרין מב ע"א
9. שם
10. סוד"ה ומברך
11. מ"ב ס"ק כ
12. ס"ק כא
13. שעה"צ ס"ק כה
14. ומוסיף המ"ב שכן כתב הפמ"ג
15. סי' רצח מ"ב ס"ק לז
16. מאורי אש עמ' 188
17. סי' צט בבדה"ש ס"ק ו

CHAPTER TWENTY-ONE:

The Laws Of Pesach

SIMAN 448:

CHAMETZ THAT REMAINED IN A JEW'S POSSESSION DURING *PESACH*: ITS LAWS AFTER *PESACH*

§7: It is forbidden for a person to give his animal to a non-Jew to feed during *Pesach* (A)knowing that it will be fed bran of barley which is *chametz*.

NISHMAT AVRAHAM

SIMAN 448

(A) knowing: If, however, he does not know that the animal will be fed *chametz*, he may give the animal to the non-Jew and need not feel apprehensive that it will be fed *chametz*.[1]

The *Mishnah Berurah*[2] writes that where there is no alternative, it is customary to sell the animal to the non-Jew and the animal is taken away by him. Or, he may sell both the animal and its shed, and have the non-Jew feed it there. The Jew may not ask the non-Jew to feed the animal *chametz* and there should be no contact between them during *Pesach*. This is also the view of the *Maharam of Rotenberg*,[3] the *Orchot Chaim*,[4] the *Noda BiYihudah*,[5] the *Chayei Adam*[6] and the *Chatam Sofer*.[7] There is, however, a view[8] that the animal and its *chametz* food must be sold to two non-Jews so that the one who buys the animal will need to buy the food himself from the second. The *Igrot Moshe*[9] rules that if a loss would otherwise be incurred, one may be permitted to sell both the animal and its food to the same non-Jew, writing in the contract that food for the animal is at the buyer's expense.

Therefore, if a doctor is engaged in animal research and the food fed to the animals is *chametz*, he must sell the animals to a non-Jew before the eve of *Pesach* and stipulate that the non-Jew is to feed them as he wishes. If this would lead to a monetary loss, he may sell him their food as well, writing up the contract as ruled by the *Igrot Moshe* above. The Jew must have no contact with them and therefore may not continue with his research during *Pesach*.[10]

1. מ״ב ס״ק לב
2. ס״ק לג
3. מובא בכף החיים ס״ק קט
4. ס״ק כא
5. מובא בשו״ת תשובה מאהבה ח״א סי׳ מב
6. נשמת אדם כלל קכד שאלה ח
7. שו״ת או״ח סי׳ סב. וראה שם שצריך גם להפקיר בפני שלושה. וראה בשדי חמד מערכת חמץ ומצה סי׳ ט ס״ק ג ובמעדני שמואל על הקיצור שו״ע סי׳ קיד ס״ק לה
8. ישועות יעקב מובא במ״ב ס״ק לג
9. או״ח ח״א סי׳ קמו
10. שמעתי ממו״ר הגרי״י נויבירט שליט״א

SIMAN 450: LAWS OF A JEWISH AND NON-JEWISH PARTNERSHIP

§6: During *Pesach* one may give a non-Jewish servant money with which to buy his own food, even though he knows that the servant (A)will buy *chametz.*

SIMAN 451: THE LAWS OF *KASHERING*

§5: Utensils that were (A)used as *keli sheni* may be *kashered* in a *keli sheni.*

NISHMAT AVRAHAM

SIMAN 450

(A) will buy *chametz*: *Rav Neuwirth shlita* wrote me about a *seriously ill* patient who cannot swallow tablets and must be given his medicine as a syrup that contains *chametz*. The medicine should be bought with the intention of not having ownership of the *chametz*, and if possible, it should be paid for after *Pesach* (see *Mishnah Berurah* 450:18). If this was not done, he should keep only what will be needed, throwing away the rest, although he knows that after *Pesach* he will need to buy more. Possibly, he should only buy each time what he needs immediately, but if he can only buy a large quantity, he should do so and throw away what is not necessary for immediate use.[1] If, however, it will be difficult to buy the medicine each time, or after *Pesach*, he may keep the remainder to be used daily including its use after *Pesach*. The *Rav shlita* continues: *Rav Auerbach zt"l* told me that if, before buying the medicine in the drug store, he intended not to take ownership of the *chametz* and he also did not pay for it, he need not worry about buying the exact amount and may even continue to use it after *Pesach*. In any event it should be put away in a place separate from other medicines and only the amount needed should be taken out each time.

SIMAN 451

(A) used as *keli sheni*: Certain types of utensils that were used for *chametz* during the year may be *kashered* (*halachically* cleansed and purged of the presence of any *chametz*) for use on *Pesach*. The way a utensil needs to be *kashered* depends on the manner in which the *chametz* was absorbed into it during the year and this depends how it was used. If it was used on a flame it is called a *keli rishon* (the first vessel) and can only be *kashered* on a flame. If, on the other hand, the *chametz* from the *keli rishon* was poured into another vessel (*keli sheni* – second vessel), this utensil may be *kashered* by pouring boiling water onto it.[1]

KASHERING OF DENTURES. The *Maharsham*[2] writes that boiling water should be poured over them before *Pesach*. The *Darchei Teshuvah,*[3] on the other hand, rules very strictly, that it would be

1. כדי לא לעבור על בל יראה ובל ימצא

1. הכשר כלים
For details see *Halachos of Pesach* by Rabbi Shimon D. Eider *shlita*.

2. שו"ת ח"א סי' קצז

3. יו"ד סי' פט ס"ק יא

SIMAN 461:
LAWS CONCERNING THE BAKING OF *MATZAH*

§4: One may fulfill his obligation of eating *matzah* during the *seder* with [(A)]*matzah* that has been soaked, provided it has not become mush. However, he does not fulfill his obligation if the *matzah* was boiled.

NISHMAT AVRAHAM

best for a person to have separate dentures for meat and milk during the year and all the more so, separate dentures for *Pesach*. The *Beit Yitzchak*[4] writes that since one does not eat food which is at a boiling point, it would be sufficient to wash his mouth. If, however, it would not be too troublesome, he should remove them if possible and pour boiling water over them [*Author's note: It would appear that he was referring to a different type of dentures that were not easily removable.*] The *Melamed LeHo'il*[5] rules that since boiling them would ruin them, one could depend on the lenient ruling and scrub them well. *Rav Wosner shlita*[6] writes that since a person usually eats and drinks from a *keli sheni*[7] food which is at a temperature of less than that which would scald him, he should refrain from eating *chametz* for 24 hours and then *kasher* them in a *keli sheni*. *Rav Ovadiah Yosef*[8] rules that it would be sufficient to scrub them well, particularly between the teeth. However, he concludes that a person who wishes to be strict with himself and either *kashers* them or pours boiling water over them is praiseworthy. The *Tzitz Eliezer*[9] quotes *Rav Tzvi Pesach Frank zt"l* who ruled that it was sufficient to clean them with spirits. See also the *Sdei Chemed*,[10] the *Yesodei Yeshurun*[11] and the *She'arim Metzuyanim BaHalachah*.[12]

When *Rav Auerbach zt"l* saw the above he wrote to me that I should write that he himself washes his dentures well, before *Pesach*, and then *kashers* them in water of about 70° C temperature (since one does not eat or drink anything hotter than this). In order not to wait 24 hours without using the dentures before doing this (as required in *kashering*), he would add a bit of kerosene to the water before boiling it (in order to spoil the taste that is being boiled out).[13] When I first wrote this, I wrote, out of deference to him, that "the Rav ruled that one should *kasher* one's dentures etc." When he saw this he said to me, "That is not what I said, I told you to write that this is how **I** kasher my dentures!"

SIMAN 461

(A) *matzah* that has been soaked: A patient or someone who is very old who finds it difficult to eat *matzah*, may break it up into very tiny pieces and eat it in this way during the *seder*.[1] If it is difficult to swallow because of its dryness, it may be

4. שו״ת יו״ד ח״א סי׳ מג אות יב
5. שו״ת או״ח סי׳ צג
6. שו״ת שבט הלוי ח״א או״ח סי׳ קמח
7. וכותב שמכיון דעיקר אכילת האדם ושתיתו מכלי שני שנפסק הקילוח דינו ככלי שלישי כמבואר ביו״ד סוסי׳ צב
8. שו״ת יביע אומר ח״ג סי׳ כד ושו״ת יחוה דעת ח״א סי׳ ח
9. שו״ת ח״ט סי׳ כה
10. מערכת חו״מ סי׳ ד ס״ק כד
11. ח״ו עמ׳ קסד
12. סי׳ קטז ס״ק ד
13. ראה יו״ד סי׳ קג סע׳ ה וסי׳ קכב סע׳ ב
1. ברכ״י ס״ק א וביה״ל ד״ה יוצא

washed down with water.[2] If even this is difficult, he may soak the *matzah* in cold water.[3] The *matzah* may not be soaked in boiling water even if the water is in a *keli sheni*. However, if there was no other way that he could eat the *matzah*, it would be permissible, provided that the water was not too hot to touch.[4] If he still finds it difficult to swallow, he may dip the *matzah* into another beverage and if this is not enough, he may soak the *matzah* in another beverage.[5] Whether he soaks the *matzah* in water or in another beverage, he must be careful not to do so for 24 hours or more for such soaking is *halachically* like boiling.[6]

KEDEI ACHILAT PRAS. The *Shemirat Shabbat KeHilchatah*[7] writes that in order to fulfill the Torah obligation of eating *matzah* on the first night of *Pesach*, a *kezayit matzah* must be consumed *kedei achilat pras*, that is within the space of 2 minutes, and at the most, 4 minutes.[8] If this is impossible because of ill-health or age, one should eat the *kezayit matzah* as best he can but not say the blessing *al achilat matzah*.[9] However, he should attempt to eat the *kezayit matzah* within 9 minutes.[10] The *Kaf HaChaim*[11] also rules that *kedei achilat pras* is up to 4 minutes. There are *poskim* who rule that one may say the blessing knowing that he will take up to 9 minutes to eat the *kezayit*. The *Rama*[12] himself refers the reader to the laws of *Yom Kippur* for a definition of *kedei achilat pras*. However, *Rav Neuwirth shlita* told me that he finds it difficult to understand why the *kedei achilat pras* for eating *matzah* at the *seder* should be compared to the eating of a *seriously ill* patient on *Yom Kippur*, since on *Yom Kippur* it is forbidden to eat whereas at the *seder* there is an obligation to eat. *Rav Ovadiah Yosef shlita*[13] defines *kedei achilat pras* as between 6 and 7 minutes, whereas *Rav Eider shlita*[14] rules that it is no more than 9 minutes and preferably within 2 minutes (see *Siman* 475A).

The *Shemirat Shabbat KeHilchatah*[15] also rules that one may not say *birkat hamazon* unless he has eaten the *kezayit matzah* within the space of 3 to 4 minutes.

Is there any *mitzvah* for one to eat *matzah* at the *seder* if he can only eat less than a *kezayit*, or if he only has less than a *kezayit*? The *Sdei Chemed*[16] rules that someone who cannot eat a full *kezayit matzah* or *maror* (or cannot eat it within 4 minutes) is nevertheless obligated to eat whatever he can. Although he himself may not pronounce the blessing of *al achilat matzah* or *al achilat maror*, he should nevertheless ask someone else who is about to say the blessing to have him in mind as well so that he thereby discharges his obligation. He writes that he himself

---

2. שו״ת בנין ציון סי׳ כט

3. מ״ב ס״ק יח, דהיינו אם יש בו כזית אפילו מאבד צורתו ואם פחות מכזית דווקא כשלא מאבד צורתו

4. מג״א ס״ק ח ומ״ב ס״ק כ. ועיין היטב במחצית השקל ובנשמת אברהם ח״א עמ׳ רס

5. מג״א ס״ק ז. חק יעקב ס״ק יב. מ״ב ס״ק יח

6. מ״ב ס״ק יז. וע״ע במגן האלף ס״ק ב ובשעה״צ ס״ק כח

7. פ״מ סע׳ צג. ואם אכל כדי שביעה עיין פמ״ג סי׳ רי א״א ס״ק א הובא במ״ב ס״ק א ושעה״צ ס״ק י שם, שנשאר בצ״ע

8. עיין שו״ת חת״ס ח״ו סי׳ טז ו־כג. ערוה״ש סי׳ רב סע׳ ח. כף החיים סי׳ רי ס״ק ח. ועיין בשיעורי דאורייתא בשיעורי המצוות סע׳ כט ושיעורי תורה סי׳ ג סע׳ טז.

9. ביה״ל ד״ה יוצא וסי׳ תעה סע׳ א ומ״ב ס״ק ט. ועיין בשדי חמד אסיפת דינים מערכת אכילה ס״ק ד ד״ה אחר זמ״ר

10. עיין סי׳ תריח במ״ב ס״ק כא

11. סימן רי ס״ק ח

12. סי׳ תעה סע׳ ו

13. חזון עובדיה ח״א סי׳ כד

14. Halachos of Pesach XX E 4.

15. פ״מ סע׳ צג

16. אסיפת דינים מערכת אכילה ס״ק ד

SIMAN 466: WHICH LIQUIDS CAUSE LEAVENING

§1: One may not chew wheat to put on a (A)sore since saliva causes leavening.

NISHMAT AVRAHAM

for the last two years had to ask his son-in-law to say the blessing for him since it was impossible for him to eat a full *kezayit maror*. This is also the ruling of the *Chida*[17] who writes that someone who has only half a *kezayit* should still eat it but without a blessing, since there is still something of a *mitzvah* in doing so. This is also the opinion of the *Chatam Sofer*,[18] the *Ben Ish Chai*[19] and *Rav Ovadiah Yosef shlita*.[20] However the *Sha'agat Aryeh*,[21] *Divrei Chaim*,[22] *Ketav Sofer*,[23] *Sha'arei Teshuvah*,[24] *Shevut Yaakov*,[25] and *Kaf HaChaim*,[26] all disagree, ruling that someone who only has half a *kezayit matzah* at the *seder* has no obligation to eat it.

SIMAN 466

(A) sore: MEDICATION ON PESACH. During the year, a person who eats forbidden food that is no longer fit for human consumption has not transgressed Torah law. However, eating *chametz* is a much more serious act. The *chametz* must reach a greater degree of decay; it must be unfit even for the consumption of an animal (such as a dog) before eating it is not considered a transgression.[1]

The *seriously ill* patient. A patient who is or may be *seriously ill* may eat or drink *chametz* if this is necessary to cure him, even if the chances of cure are not certain, provided an alternative cannot easily be found. The *Ran*[2] rules that this is not merely permissible but obligatory, since the *mitzvah* of saving life was given at Sinai and accepted on oath by all of Israel.

The *non-seriously ill* patient. Any medication containing *chametz*, no matter how small the amount,[3] is forbidden to such a patient if it is palatable. Thus syrups or lozenges containing *chametz* are forbidden[4] (see above, *Siman* 450A).

What is the *halachah* if the medication is bitter and the *chametz* in it is unfit for animal consumption? Rava (a Talmudic sage)[5] states that even though the time that *chametz* may be eaten has passed (on the morning of the eve of *Pesach*) and is now forbidden, one may derive benefit from bread that had been previously over-toasted. The *Rosh* explains this to mean that the bread was so toasted as to render it unfit for animal consumption (like moldy bread). However, this only means that he may have use from it but not, of course, eat it. Should he wish to eat it even though it is unfit for human consumption,

---

17. מחזיק ברכה סי׳ תעה ס״ק כ. ברכי יוסף סי׳ תפב ס״ק ד ושו״ת חיים שאל סי׳ יג
18. שו״ת או״ח סי׳ מט וסי׳ קמ
19. שו״ת רב פעלים ח״ג סי׳ לב
20. חזון עובדיה ח״ב סי׳ כח
21. סי׳ ק
22. סי׳ כה
23. סי׳ צו
24. סי׳ תעה סע׳ ו
25. ח״ב סי׳ יח
26. סי׳ תעה ס״ק פט

1. סי׳ תמב סע׳ ב ומ״ב ס״ק י
2. יומא פב ע״א ד״ה חוץ. יו״ד סי׳ רלח ש״ך ס״ק ה. שו״ת יביע אומר ח״ד חו״מ סי׳ ו אות ד. לב אברהם ח״ב פ״ג סע׳ ד
3. שעה״צ ס״ק ו
4. ראה שו״ת כתב סופר או״ח סי׳ קיא. שמעתי ממו״ר הגרי״י נויבירט שליט״א
5. פסחים כא ע״ב

NISHMAT AVRAHAM

his eating it shows that he regards it as being edible and therefore it is forbidden. The *Rambam*[6] writes: Something that contains *chametz* but is not at all a food or is not generally used as a food, may be kept in one's possession over *Pesach*, but not eaten until after *Pesach*. To eat it is forbidden even if the amount of *chametz* in it is minimal. This is also the ruling of the *Terumat HaDeshen*[7] and the *Shulchan Aruch*.[8] Thus the *Mishnah Berurah*[9] writes: One may benefit from it but not eat it, by Rabbinic law. Despite it being unfit for human consumption the fact that he wishes to eat it makes it forbidden since he gives it importance (*achshevei*). On the other hand, the *Ran*[10] permits it to be eaten since bread in such a state is not normally eaten. This is also the opinion of the *Ba'al HaMaor*, *Meiri*, *Ritva* quoting the *Ra'ah,* and the *Maharam Chalawa*.[11]

Their controversy concerns a healthy individual. Although there would be no *halachic* problem for a *non-seriously ill* patient to swallow tablets or capsules which contain *chametz,* according to the ruling of the *Ran* and other *rishonim,* how would the ruling of the *Rosh* and those who rule like him affect him? Since he gives importance to the *chametz* in the tablet, it should be forbidden even though he needs it as a medication and not as a food. This is how the *Sha'agat Aryeh*[12] and the *Shulchan Aruch HaRav*,[13] and probably the *Noda BiYehudah*[14] view the issue. On the other hand, the *Ketav Sofer*[15] disagrees, differentiating between food for a healthy person and medication for a patient. *Rav Auerbach zt"l* wrote to me that even according to the *Rosh* who forbids the over-toasted bread to be eaten, this is only because he burnt it. Eating it gives it importance as if the *chametz* was in its original state. However, were he to burn it to ashes and then eat it, he only attaches importance to the ashes and not to the actual *chametz*.

In contradistinction to the *Rambam* quoted above about a healthy individual, the *Rambam* writes elsewhere:[16] One may not use forbidden things as a cure except for a *seriously ill* patient. This is only where the forbidden thing is used in the normal manner, such as feeding the patient creeping creatures or insects, *chametz* during *Pesach*, or food on *Yom Kippur*. However if used in an unusual manner, for instance, if *chametz* or *orlah* is used as a salve, or if he is given something forbidden to drink mixed with something bitter, so that the mixture is no longer palatable, it is permissible even for a *non-seriously ill* patient. The *Shulchan Aruch*[17] follows this ruling.

The *Chazon Ish*[18] writes: Pills containing flour mixed with things that are not fit for human consumption can no longer be considered *chametz* since the flour can no longer be separated out nor used to leaven other flour. Nor can the patient be said to attach importance (*achshevei*) to the flour rather than to the medication. These pills therefore may be swallowed on *Pesach*. The *Shemirat Shabbat KeHilchatah*[19] follows this ruling and adds that since he swallows the pills, this is also not considered to be eating in the usual manner. He explains, quoting *Rav Auerbach zt"l*, that

6. הל׳ חמץ ומצה פ״ד הי״ב
7. סי׳ קכט
8. סי׳ תמב סע׳ ד
9. ס״ק מג
10. פסחים מה ע״ב
11. שם בסוגיא
12. סי׳ עה
13. או״ח סי׳ תמב סע׳ כב
14. מהד״ק יו״ד סי׳ לה
15. שו״ת או״ח סי׳ קיא
16. הל׳ יסודי התורה פ״ה ה״ח
17. יו״ד סי׳ קנה סע׳ ג. וראה במל״מ סוד״ה שם
18. או״ח סי׳ קטז ס״ק ח
19. פ״מ הערה קסט

SIMAN 468:
NOT TO WORK AFTER MIDDAY ON *PESACH* EVE

§1: Anyone who worked on *Pesach* eve (A)after midday used to be excommunicated, even if he did so without pay.

NISHMAT AVRAHAM

even though swallowing is considered eating, since pills are not chewed in the normal way but are only swallowed, they are probably no longer considered food. Since they also cannot be used to leaven other doughs, it is probably permitted to swallow them. *Rav Auerbach zt"l* wrote to me that the pills in consideration were not the same as those discussed by the *Chazon Ish*. The *Chazon Ish* discussed pills in which the active ingredient of the medication per se was not *chametz* but in which the flour was the binding element. However, the discussion from the previously quoted *Rambam*, *Shulchan Aruch* and others (ref. 6-11) concerned medication which was itself *chametz*, and this is an entirely different situation.

The *Igrot Moshe*[20] also rules that *non-seriously ill* patients may swallow pills of this kind since the *chametz* was disqualified as food before *Pesach* and *achshevei* does not apply to medication. This is also the ruling of the *Tzitz Eliezer*[21] and the *Yesodei Yeshurun*.[22] *Rav Ovadiah Yosef shlita*[23] also rules that a *non-seriously ill* patient may take his medications over *Pesach* provided they are not palatable. However, a patient with mere aches and pains may not take any medication that probably contains *chametz*.[24] This is also the ruling of *Rav Auerbach zt"l*.[25]

Rav Neuwirth shlita[26] writes that tablets prepared with starch made from corn flour may be taken during *Pesach*. However tablets which are coated with *chametz* may not be swallowed at all and may not be kept in one's possession since the *chametz* is visible and its taste has not been spoiled. However, the *Rav shlita* wrote to me (10 April '00): "Regarding my statement in *Shemirat Shabbat Ke-Hilchatah* Ch. 40:76 about tablets coated with *chametz* (see above), I wish to explain that I meant lozenges where one can taste the *chametz* on sucking the lozenge. However, pills that have been coated with wheat flour (assuming that there are such pills nowadays), that are swallowed and are generally bitter to taste, are unquestionably permissible during *Pesach*."

Thus, nowadays when most pills are made with corn flour and the like,[27] (and even those that do contain wheat starch, have starch which was no longer fit for animal consumption before *Pesach*), a *non-seriously ill* patient should certainly be permitted to take them unless there is an easily available kosher medication which can be substituted without harming him. There is no question that a patient should not stop taking his medication over *Pesach* without first consulting his doctor and a *posek*.

SIMAN 468

(A) after midday: The *Shulchan Aruch*

---

20. או״ח ח״ב סי׳ צב. וראה גם בח״ג סי׳ סב
21. ח״י סי׳ כה פ״כ
22. ח״ו עמ׳ ריט
23. חזון עובדיה עמ׳ סז. שו״ת יחוה דעת ח״ב סי׳ ס. וראה גם בשו״ת יביע אומר ח״ב יו״ד סי׳ יב
24. וראה גם בשמירת שבת כהלכתה פ״מ סע׳ עה שכותב לאסור בכה״ג למי שחש בכאבים קלים. וראה שם בהערה קסט בשם הגרש״ז אויערבאך זצ״ל
25. מנחת שלמה ח״א סי׳ יז
26. שמירת שבת כהלכתה פ״מ סע׳ עו
27. ראה בשו״ת רדב״ז סי׳ רמא. שו״ת מהר״ם שיק או״ח סי׳ רמא

§10: During the whole day, one may take things to or from a craftsman's workshop even though they will not be used during the Festival.

GLOSS: *It is customary not to* (B)*draw blood since it is Yom Tov eve and one should not change this custom.*

NISHMAT AVRAHAM

is referring to the *halachic midday*. The *Mishnah Berurah*[1] writes that whatever one may do on *Chol HaMoed* one may certainly do on *Pesach* eve. *Rav Neuwirth shlita* told me that a doctor or nurse may treat a patient on *Pesach* eve just as he does during *Chol HaMoed*. However, one may not make a previously arranged routine visit to a doctor if this will result in a *melachah* such as writing, nor may a doctor arrange such a visit.

Rav Neuwirth shlita also told me that a research project that was started before *Pesach* may be continued on *Pesach* eve if not doing so will adversely affect the project. One may also write a draft of a medical paper, but not the final copy.[2]

(B) draw blood: Since Hashem threatened to destroy Israel if they would not accept the Torah at Mount Sinai, *Chazal* forbade any dangerous procedure on the eve of *Shavuot.*[3] Although the main danger of bloodletting is on the eve of *Shavuot,*[4] *Chazal* forbade it on every Festival eve because of *Shavuot*. However, it is permissible on the eve of the seventh day of *Pesach*, since this is not a new Festival, which is separate from the previous six days. However, it is only forbidden if it is done to maintain good health, but if it is necessary to avoid danger, it is permissible even on *Shavuot* eve.[5]

It would appear that any procedure which will result in bleeding should be forbidden on *Shavuot* eve unless the patient is *seriously ill* and requires the procedure urgently. Thus routine surgery must not be scheduled for that day nor may blood be withdrawn for routine tests. However, if canceling surgery would mean a long wait for another available date and result in continued suffering, surgery may be performed not only on a Festival eve but even on *Shavuot* eve. Certainly it may be performed if there is a possibility that, as a result of waiting, an emergency situation may arise. The *Tzitz Eliezer*[6] discusses the question and concludes that one should generally not arrange elective surgery for a Festival eve and even more so not have blood drawn either for tests or as a donation to a blood bank and certainly one should be careful about this on *Shavuot* eve. This is also not permitted on *Hoshanah Rabbah*. If, however, the doctor insists, a *Sephardi* may be permitted to undergo a procedure in which blood will be drawn. The *Tzitz Eliezer* explains that although there are *Sephardi poskim*[7] who forbid this, nevertheless the *Pri Chadash*[8] specifically permits it and the *Rambam* and the *Beit Yosef* do not mention the problem. Therefore, if one must be lenient he may be so on a Festival eve, other than *Shavuot* eve and *Hoshana Rabbah*. However, if not having the surgery will entail a long wait for the next date, involving continued suffering, then one may permit this

1. ס״ק ז
2. מהא דמ״ב ס״ק ט
3. שבת קכט ע״ב. מ״ב ס״ק לח
4. שם
5. א״ר סי׳ תצג ס״ק יט ומ״ב כאן ס״ק לח
6. חי״ב סי׳ מו
7. הגר״ח פלאג״י בספר מועד כל חי סי׳ ח סע׳ ב. כף החיים כאן ס״ק צט
8. כאן בסוף הסימן

SIMAN 470:

THE FAST OF THE FIRSTBORN ON THE EVE OF *PESACH*

§1: Firstborn sons, either from the father or from the mother, (A)fast on the eve of *Pesach*. There is an opinion that even a firstborn daughter fasts *(this is not the custom)*.

SIMAN 472:

THE LAWS OF RECLINING AND THE FOUR CUPS

§3: One should not recline backwards or forwards or to the right but only to the left. (A)*(There is no difference whether he is left-handed or not.)*

§10: One who normally refrains from drinking wine because (B)it harms him or because he finds it distasteful, must

NISHMAT AVRAHAM

even for an *Ashkenazi,* particularly on a Festival eve, other than *Shavuot* eve and *Hoshana Rabbah*.

SIMAN 470

(A) fast: If he has a mild headache or eyeache or finds fasting difficult and weakening, he need not fast. If he will most probably be unable to fulfill the *mitzvah* of eating *matzah* or *maror* or of drinking the four cups of wine at the *seder* (after the end of the fast), it would be better for him not to fast so as to be able to fulfill these *mitzvot* properly. If he breaks his fast, he should only eat light snacks.[1]

SIMAN 472

(A) There is no difference whether he is left-handed or not: During the *seder* service the *matzot* and the four cups of wine must be consumed while reclining on the left side. This is a sign of freedom[1] and royalty.[2] *The Mishnah Berurah*[3] rules that even though he is used to eating with his left hand, he must nevertheless recline to his left and eat with his right hand. The *Biur Halachah*[4] is uncertain how one should comply with this ruling if he has no right hand or if it cannot be used. It is possible, he writes, that in such a situation there is no obligation for him to recline.

(B) it harms him: One may drink grape juice or raisin wine and thereby fulfill his obligation.[5] However, if eating *matzah* or *maror*[6] or drinking wine will make him *non-seriously ill* he is exempt from complying with these *mitzvot*.[7]

A patient who has been warned by spe-

1. מ״ב ס״ק ב. וראה גם בשו״ת החיד״א סי׳ ב ובשו״ת אלף לך שלמה או״ח סי׳ שטז

1. רמב״ם הל׳ חמץ ומצה פ״ז ה״ז

2. שו״ע הרב כאן סע׳ ז

3. ס״ק יא

4. ד״ה ואין

5. חזון עובדיה עמ׳ קכה. שמירת שבת כהלכתה פנ״ג סע׳ ב

6. חזון עובדיה עמ׳ קעג

7. מ״ב ס״ק לה וחזון עובדיה עמ׳ קכה. ועיין במ״ב סי׳ תפג ס״ק א. וראה במקראי קודש פסח ח״ב עמ׳ קטז

nevertheless force himself to comply with the *mitzvah* of drinking the four cups.

NISHMAT AVRAHAM

cialists not to eat *matzah* or *maror* or not to drink wine since doing so will make him *seriously ill*, but nevertheless does so, has performed a *mitzvah* through the means of a sin.[8] There are *poskim*[9] who go even further and rule that he has not performed a *mitzvah*, only a sin. In addition, he is not permitted to recite a blessing and were he to do so he commits the sin of angering *Hashem*.[10] The *Mechaber*[11] rules that where no wine is available, *Kiddush* is made on *matzah*. And as to the obligation of drinking the four cups of wine, the *Rama* rules that it may be fulfilled with any drink (excluding water) which is considered fitting to be served to important guests.[12] This can only be undiluted juice, but not milk or coffee (see *Siman* 272A and B).[13] *Ashkenazim* say the blessing over wine on each of the four cups (*Sephardim* only say the blessing on the first and third). However, the blessing is only said over the first and third cups when juice is used.[14] An *Ashkenazi* may not, if he does not have wine, make *Kiddush* on *matzah*, unless he has no suitable drink.[15]

If the patient feels that eating *matzah* will harm him, but his doctor says that it will not, the doctor's opinion is accepted. For though we say that "the patient's heart knows best" this is only applicable to the question of fasting and nowhere else.[16] However, *Rav Waldenberg shlita*[17] wrote me disagreeing with this view since the *Mishnah Berurah*[18] states that the rule "the patient's heart knows best" is applicable to all situations.

CELIAC DISEASE: Regarding a patient who suffers from *celiac disease* and should not eat wheat (which contains *gluten*) and thus should not eat regular *matzah*, see above, *Siman* 273C.

DIABETES: Every 100 cc. of grape juice contain about 70 calories or less. Thus he may drink the greater part of a *revi'it* of grape juice for the first three cups and a full *revi'it* for the last cup, which enables him to recite the *berachah acharonah*.[19] If he drinks 45 cc. (32 calories) for the first three cups and 86 cc. (about 60 calories) for the last, he will have consumed a total of 160 calories. *Rav Neuwirth shlita* wrote to me that he could reduce this and only drink enough to fill one cheek for each of the four cups (about 40 cc. each). And then as far as the *berachah acharonah* is concerned he could ask someone else at the table to have him in mind when he says the blessing (see *Siman* 213, *Mishnah Berurah* 9). Each machine-baked *matzah* has about 100 calories and he has to eat five *kezeitim* of *matzah* during the *seder*. In order to fulfill his obligations, he should be careful about his calorie intake during his meal and reduce it to conform to his diet. A diabetic who receives multiple injections of insulin during the day should

8. שו״ת מהר״י אסאד או״ח סי׳ קס. ועיין בשו״ת ציץ אליעזר חי״ב סי׳ מג
9. שו״ת מהר״ם שיק או״ח סי׳ רס. שו״ת מנחת יצחק ח״ד סי׳ קב אות ב
10. מהר״י אסאד שם. וכן עיין בשדי חמד מערכת חמץ ומצה סי׳ יד סע׳ יד
11. סי׳ תפג
12. שמירת שבת כהלכתה פנ״ג סע׳ ח
13. שמעתי ממו״ר הגרי״י נויבירט שליט״א
14. שעה״צ שם ס״ק ח. ועיין בשמירת שבת כהלכתה שם הערה כח
15. רמ״א שם
16. שו״ת שרידי אש ח״ב סי׳ קנח
17. נשמת אברהם כרך א או״ח עמ׳ שמב. שו״ת ציץ אליעזר חט״ו סי׳ לב
18. ביה״ל סי׳ שכח סע׳ י ד״ה ורופא אחד וראה גם במ״ב סי׳ תריח ס״ק ה
19. מ״ב ס״ק ל

SIMAN 473:
THE LAWS PERTAINING TO THE FIRST CUP OF WINE, THE *SEDER* AND THE SECOND CUP

§1: *Kiddush* is recited over the first cup of wine together with the (A)*shehecheyanu* blessing.

SIMAN 475:
THE REMAINING LAWS OF THE *SEDER*

§1: He ritually washes his hands and makes the blessing for washing hands; he then takes the *matzot* in the order in which he placed them, with the part (of the divided *matzah*) between the two whole ones. He pronounces the blessing of *hamotzi* and *al achilat matzah,* breaks off a piece from the top whole *matzah* and from the part of the *matzah* in the middle and dips the two pieces into salt.

GLOSS: *The custom is not to dip into salt on this night since any "clean bread" does not need salt.*

He eats (A)a *kezayit* from each piece while reclining.

NISHMAT AVRAHAM

adjust his dose to conform with his blood sugar level.

ARTIFICIAL FEEDING. A patient who is fed through a *naso-gastric tube* or *gastrostomy (PEG)* may not say any blessing over what he eats, neither before nor after he eats. However, he should try and hear the blessings from someone who is obligated to say them and ask him to have him in mind when he recites them.[20]

SIMAN 473

(A) *shehecheyanu* blessing: A patient who was too ill to recite *Kiddush* and the *shehecheyanu* blessing on *Yom Tov*, recites the *shehecheyanu* whenever he can during *Chol HaMoed*. In the Diaspora he recites it during the second day of the Festival and if he cannot do so then, during *Chol HaMoed*.[1]

SIMAN 475

(A) a *kezayit*: During the *seder*, every man and woman[1] is obligated to eat four *kezeitim* of *matzah*, two after the blessing *hamotzi* and *al achilat matzah* (as in the *Shulchan Aruch* here), another sandwiched with the *maror,*[2] and a fourth, the *afikoman,* just before saying *birkat hamazon* after the meal.[3] It is commendable to eat two *kezeitim* as the *afikoman.*[4]

Rav Neuwirth shlita wrote to me that a person should eat two-thirds of a machine-baked *matzah* (each *matzah* is approxi-

20. שו״ת מנחת יצחק ח״ג סי׳ יח

1. מ״ב סי׳ תעג ס״ק א

1. סי׳ תעב סע׳ יד

2. שו״ע כאן

3. מ״ב סי׳ תעז סע׳ א

4. מ״ב שם ס״ק א

SIMAN 477:
LAWS CONCERNING EATING THE *AFIKOMAN*

§1: After completing the meal each person eats a *kezayit* from the (part of the) *matzah* that was previously wrapped in a cloth, as a remembrance of the Paschal sacrifice which was eaten to complete one's satiation. It should be eaten while reclining, without a blessing. One should be careful to eat it (A)before midnight.

(*One should hurry to say the Hallel before midnight.*)

NISHMAT AVRAHAM

mately 30 grams in weight) after the blessing *hamotzi* and *al achilat matzah*, a third for the "sandwich," and another third (if possible, two-thirds) for the *afikoman*.[5] The *Chazon Ish*[6] ruled that since the first *kezayit* was a Torah obligation, it would be proper if one ate two-thirds of a machine-baked *matzah*. *Rav Eliashiv shlita* also told me that one certainly fulfills even his Torah obligation by eating 20 grams of a machine-baked *matzah*.

For someone who finds it difficult to eat a third of a *matzah* during the time of *kedei achilat pras* (see above, *Siman* 461A), *Rav Neuwirth shlita* told me that it would be sufficient for him to eat a third of a machine-baked *matzah* at the beginning and another third for *afikoman*. However, *Rav Auerbach zt"l* was not sure that he should say the blessing *al achilat matzah*. *Rav Neuwirth shlita* added that if even this was too much for him, he should eat his meal without ritually washing his hands or eating any *matzah*. After his meal he should wash his hands, without saying the blessing *al netilat yadayim*, say the blessing *hamotzi* and eat a third of a machine-baked *matzah*.[7] *Rav Ovadiah Yosef shlita*[8] writes that he should eat a *kezayit matzah* (27 to 30 grams) at the beginning (with both blessings) followed by a *kezayit maror*. For the sandwich, it is sufficient if he takes a small piece of *matzah* with a small piece of *maror* and finally, after his meal, a *kezayit matzah*.

One who ate *matzah* or drank one of the four cups during the *seder* and vomited immediately after, has fulfilled his obligation, since the food was swallowed. There is no need for him to repeat the *mitzvah*.[9] However, since he can only say *birkat hamazon* if his stomach has digested at least a *kezayit*, he must eat another *kezayit* of *matzah* so that he can recite *birkat hamazon*.[10]

SIMAN 477

(A) before midnight. Special problems may arise for those who are unable to complete the *seder* service before midnight. This includes a doctor, nurse or other health-care professional (male or female) called to see a *seriously ill* or possibly *seriously ill* patient; a doctor,

5. וכ״כ הגר״ש איידר שליט״א בספרו הלכות פסח עמ׳ 342 כשגודל המצה הוא 7 x 6 1/8 inches
6. ספר שיעורי המצוות שנת תשכ״ט בהערה
7. ראה מ״ב סי׳ תפב ס״ק ו
8. חזון עובדיה ח״א סי׳ מד
9. שו״ת תורה לשמה (המיוחס להבן איש חי) או״ח סי׳ קכה
10. שם. בן איש חי שנה א פ׳ חקת סע׳ יג. ברכי יוסף או״ח סי׳ רח ס״ק א

nurse or other health-care professional on duty at the hospital and busy attending to patients in the emergency room or floors (wards); or a patient who because of his ill-health cannot take part in the whole service. It goes without saying that a doctor, nurse or other health-care professional must first tend to their *seriously ill* or possibly *seriously ill* patients even if they will not be able to perform the *mitzvot* of the *seder* completely or partially (see *Siman* 245A).

(a) LIMITED TIME: If there is limited time he should try to:

1) At least recite *Kiddush,* drink the first cup of wine (or grape juice) while reclining and say the paragraph *avadim hayinu*. He should then ritually wash his hands without the blessing *al netilat yadayim*, recite the two blessings *hamotzi* and *al achilat matzah,* eating a *kezayit matzah* (see *Siman* 475A)[1] while reclining, within the time of *kedei achilat pras* (2 to 4 minutes). He then recites *birkat hamazon*.[2]

2) If possible, he should say the paragraph *Rabban Gamliel omer*[3] followed by the blessing *asher ge'alanu,* and then drink the second cup of wine.

3) If time permits he should eat two *kezeitim matzah*, each within the time of *kedei achilat pras*;[4] one for the *mitzvah* of *matzah* and one for the *afikoman*.[5] If he feels that he will be able to eat the two *kezeitim*, he says the blessing *al netilat yadayim* when he ritually washes his hands.[6]

At the time of eating the *matzah* he should mentally make a stipulation (referred to as "stipulation" hereafter) that when he returns, should he wish to continue his meal before *halachic midnight*, he may do so, and that the *matzah* he has just eaten (whether it be the single *kezayit* or the second of the two *kezeitim*) will be retroactively part of the meal. The *afikoman* will then be a different portion of *matzah* which will be eaten at the end of the meal. On the other hand, if he is not able to eat his meal before the *halachic midnight*, he shall be considered to have already eaten the *afikoman* before then.[7]

(b) MORE TIME: If he has more time, he should:

1) Eat a *kezayit maror* within the time of *kedei achilat pras* reciting the blessing *al achilat maror* but not the blessing *borei pri ha'adamah*.[8]

2) If possible, he should eat a further *kezayit* (and preferably two)[9] of *matzah* for the *afikoman* (see "stipulation" in (a) above), recite *birkat hamazon* and drink the third cup. If his time is limited, he should preferably eat the *kezayit maror*, thereby fulfilling a *Rabbinic mitzvah* rather than eat the *afikoman* which is only meant to remind us of the Paschal sacrifice.[10]

(c) EVEN MORE TIME: If he is able to do even more, and it is before the *halachic midnight*:

1) He should recite the rest of the *Haggadah*. If it is after *halachic midnight* and he has not yet drunk the second cup, he should recite the blessing *asher ge'alanu* without pronouncing *Hashem*'s name, and drink it. Although the *Sephardic* custom is to say the blessing *borei pri hagafen* only over the first and third cups, since he did not drink the second cup after the first (with only the recital of the *Haggadah* in between), he should say the blessing *borei pri hagafen*.

1. סי׳ תעה מ״ב ס״ק יא וביה״ל ד״ה כזית
2. או״ח סי׳ קפד סע׳ ו
3. הגרש״ז אויערבאך זצ״ל בלב אברהם ח״ב עמ׳ כא
4. סי׳ תעה מ״ב ס״ק ט
5. מהא דסי׳ תפב מ״ב סוס״ק ו
6. או״ח סי׳ קנה סע׳ ב
7. שמעתי ממו״ר הגרי״י נויבירט שליט״א וראייתו מהא דסי׳ תעז סע׳ ב
8. כף החיים סי׳ תעג ס״ק קט
9. סי׳ תעז מ״ב ס״ק א
10. שמעתי ממו״ר הגרי״י נויבירט שליט״א

NISHMAT AVRAHAM

2) As to the meal, if he has not yet recited *birkat hamazon* and, in spite of being involved in his work, has not completely forgotten about his meal, he may now continue to eat.[11] However, if he has already recited *birkat hamazon*, or if he had in the interim completely forgotten about his meal, he should wash his hands again, say the blessing of *al netilat yadayim* and recite *hamotzi* over two *matzot* as he would for any *Shabbat* or Festival meal.[12] At the end of the meal he should again eat *matzah* for the *afikoman* (see "stipulation" in (a) above), and recite *birkat hamazon*. If he had not yet drunk the third cup of wine, he should do so after saying *borei pri hagafen* and then complete the *seder* as usual.

(d) AFTER *HALACHIC MIDNIGHT*: If, however, it is after *halachic midnight,* he should act in accordance with the previous paragraph, saying the blessing *asher ge'alanu* without pronouncing *Hashem*'s name.[13] Similarly, he should eat *maror* without saying the blessing *al achilat maror*. An *Ashkenazi* says the blessing at the end of *Hallel*[14] but not a *Sephardi*.[15] He drinks the fourth cup without saying *borei pri hagafen*[16] even if he is an *Ashkenazi*, unless he had not recited the blessing on the second or third cup.[17]

(e) If he carried out no part of the *seder* before *halachic midnight*, he is obligated to do so afterwards. However, he does not say the blessings of *al achilat matzah* and *al achilat maror* and he says the blessing over wine only over the first and third cups.[18] See also above, paragraph (d) regarding the blessings of *asher ge'alanu* and the blessing after *Hallel*.

If he did not carry out the *seder* service during the night he may not do so after dawn.[19]

The above rules apply equally to the second *seder* night in the Diaspora.[20]

EXPLANATION OF THE "STIPULATION." The ruling of the *Shulchan Aruch* that one should be careful to eat the *afikoman* before midnight follows one view in a controversy between two *Tanna'im*. Rebbe Elazar ben Azariah[21] rules that the Paschal sacrifice must be eaten before midnight; Rebbe Akiva rules that it may be eaten up to dawn. Since the *afikoman* is a reminder of the sacrifice, it should be eaten at the time the sacrifice was eaten. Therefore the *Avnei Nezer*[22] rules that if one had not completed his meal close to *halachic midnight*, he should eat a *kezayit matzah* as an *afikoman* conditionally. If the *halachah* is according to Rebbe Elazar ben Azariah, this is his *afikoman*. He then waits until after midnight, completes his meal and then eats another *kezayit matzah* as *afikoman*. For one may not eat after the *afikoman* so that its taste will remain[23] until the time when it is no longer appropriate to fulfill this obligation. According to Rebbe Akiva that time is until dawn; according to Rebbe Elazar ben Azariah, until *halachic midnight*. When one eats the two *kezeitim* of *matzah*, one before and one after midnight, he fulfills his obligation no matter what. If the *halachah* is according to Rebbe Elazar ben Azariah, he has fulfilled it with the *kezayit matzah* eaten just before midnight and he may continue his meal after midnight. If the

11. מ״ב ס״ק יז. בן איש חי שנה א פ׳ בהעלותך סע׳ ב
12. סי׳ רעד מ״ב ס״ק א
13. כף החיים כאן ס״ק י
14. מ״ב כאן ס״ק ז ושעה״צ ס״ק ז
15. חזון עובדיה עמ׳ קפח
16. שם
17. שמעתי ממו״ר הגרי״י נויבירט שליט״א
18. שמעתי מהגרש״ז אויערבאך זצ״ל
19. סי׳ תפה מג״א ס״ק א
20. סי׳ תפא סע׳ ב ברמ״א
21. פסחים קב ע״ב
22. שו״ת סי׳ שפא ס״ק ה
23. סי׳ תעח מ״ב ס״ק א

NISHMAT AVRAHAM

halachah is according to Rebbe Akiva, he fulfills his obligation with the second *kezayit* eaten at the end of his meal for which dawn is its limit.

BEFORE THE HALACHIC MIDNIGHT

1. LIMITED TIME	2. MORE TIME	3. MORE TIME	4. MORE TIME
OBLIGATORY			
Kiddush; 1st cup of wine	*Kiddush;* 1st cup of wine	*Kiddush;* 1st cup of wine	*Kiddush;* 1st cup of wine
Avadim hayinu	*Avadim hayinu* *Rabban Gamliel* *Asher ge'alanu*	*Avadim hayinu* *Rabban Gamliel* *Asher ge'alanu*	The entire *Haggadah*
	2nd cup of wine	2nd cup of wine	2nd cup of wine
Wash hands without* blessing	Wash hands with* blessing	Wash hands with* blessing	Wash hands with* blessing
Hamotzi *Al achilat matzah*	*Hamotzi* *Al achilat matzah*	*Hamotzi* *Al achilat matzah*	*Hamotzi* *Al achilat matzah*
Eat *kezayit matzah* within 2-4 minutes for both the *mitzvah* and for *afikoman*	Eat *kezayit matzah* within 2-4 minutes	Eat 2 *kezeitim matzah* within 2-4 minutes	Eat 2 *kezeitim matzah* within 2-4 minutes
		Al achilat maror	*Al achilat maror*
		Eat *kezayit maror* within 2-4 minutes	Eat *kezayit maror* within 2-4 minutes
	Eat *kezayit matzah* within 2-4 minutes for *afikoman*	Eat *kezayit matzah* (if possible 2 *kezeitim*) for *afikoman*	Eat *kezayit matzah* (if possible 2 *kezeitim*) for *afikoman*
Make stipulation	Make stipulation	Make stipulation	Make stipulation
Birkat hamazon	*Birkat hamazon*	*Birkat hamazon*	*Birkat hamazon*
IF POSSIBLE** *Rabban Gamliel* *Asher ge'alanu* 2nd cup of wine		3rd cup of wine *Al hagefen*	3rd cup of wine *Al hagefen*

AFTER THE HALACHIC MIDNIGHT

5. IF THE OBLIGATORY PORTION OF THE *SEDER* WAS CARRIED OUT BEFORE MIDNIGHT

Complete the *seder* as usual with the following exceptions:
- Omit *Hashem's* Name from the beginning and end of the blessing of *asher ge'alanu*
- Recite *hamotzi* but not al *achilat matzah*
- Eat *maror* without reciting *al achilat maror*
- Recite *Hallel* (see text d)
- Drink 4th cup without blessing (see text d)

6. IF NO PART OF THE *SEDER* WAS CARRIED OUT BEFORE MIDNIGHT

Obligated to carry out the entire *seder* but:
- Without the blessings *al achilat matzah* and *al achilat maror*
- Omit *Hashem's* Name from the beginning and end of the blessing of *asher ge'alanu*
- Recite blessing over wine only on the 1st and 3rd cups (see text e)

* The blessing *al netilat yadayim* is recited only if two *kezeitim* of *matzah* will be eaten.

**Since these are important parts of the *seder,* they should be said if at all possible.

Matzah and wine must be eaten and drunk respectively while reclining on the left side.

If a doctor is called out during his *seder* and returns before the *halachic* midnight, he continues where he left off. If he returns after midnight he continues as in column 5.

SIMAN 478:
ONE MAY NOT EAT AFTER THE *AFIKOMAN*

§1: One may not [(A)]eat anything after eating the *afikoman*.

SIMAN 489:
THE ORDER OF PRAYER ON THE SECOND NIGHT OF *PESACH* AND THE COUNTING OF THE *OMER*

§8: If one [(A)]forgot to say the blessing (before counting the *Omer*) whether on the first day or any other day, he continues to count but no longer says the blessing. However, if he is uncertain if he missed a day, he continues to count with the blessing.

NISHMAT AVRAHAM

SIMAN 478

(A) eat anything: Above, at the end of *Siman* 477, I noted the controversy between Rebbe Elazar ben Azariah and Rebbe Akiva as to whether the Paschal sacrifice could be eaten all night (Rebbe Akiva) or only until the *halachic midnight* (Rebbe Elazar ben Azariah). The *Mishnah Berurah*[1] writes that there are *rishonim* who rule that even according to Rebbe Akiva, one should not eat the sacrifice (and for us the *afikoman*), in the first instance, after midnight. This being so, can a doctor, nurse or other health-care professional who came on duty at night after he or she has completed the whole *seder* at home, be allowed to eat during the night or would this be forbidden until after he has recited the *Shacharit* prayer? *Rav Neuwirth shlita* told me that if one were working all night and it would be difficult for him to do so without eating, it would not be considered "in the first instance" and he would be permitted to eat. *Rav Auerbach zt"l* confirmed this ruling.

SIMAN 489

(A) forgot to say the blessing: The Torah[1] commanded that a measure of barley be harvested on the second night of *Pesach*. A portion of this, an *omer,* was then brought as an offering to the *Beth HaMikdash* the following day. In addition, the Torah[2] commands us to count seven complete weeks, day by day, from the second night of *Pesach* until the night before *Shavuot* (a total of 49 days). This *mitzvah* is known as "counting the *Omer*." The *Levushei Mordechai*[3] discusses the case of a patient who, because of his illness, was unable to count. On recovery, would he be able to continue to count with the blessing or not? He writes that he may not say the blessing. Instead he should ask the *shaliach tzibbur* or someone else who is about to say the blessing to have him in mind as well, so that he thereby fulfills his obligation.

---

1. סי׳ תעז בביה״ל ד״ה ויהא

1. ויקרא כג: י
2. ויקרא כג:טו. דברים טז:ט
3. מהדורה קמא או״ח סי׳ צא

CHAPTER TWENTY-TWO:

The Laws Of Yom Tov

SIMAN 496: THE LAWS PERTAINING TO THE SECOND DAY OF *YOM TOV* IN THE DIASPORA

§2: There is no difference between the first and second days of *Yom Tov* except with regard to the burial of a corpse and with (A)putting ointment in an eye.

GLOSS: *Or to treat (B)other non-seriously ill conditions.*

NISHMAT AVRAHAM

SIMAN 496

(A) putting ointment in an eye: The *Shulchan Aruch's* ruling pertains to a patient with a mild feeling of discomfort in the eye with no effect whatsoever on the rest of his body and his entire well-being. In such a case, a Jew is forbidden to effect treatment on *Shabbat* or *Yom Tov*, even if he does so in an indirect manner. See *Siman* 328:17, *Mishnah Berurah* 52 and above, 328:17F. However, on the second day of *Yom Tov* this is permissible even if it is done in the normal fashion.[1] This is also the ruling of the *Minchat Yom Tov*.[2]

(B) other non-seriously ill conditions: Provided that they do not affect the entire body.[3]

THE FIRST DAY OF YOM TOV: There are two approaches among the *poskim* regarding the *halachah* of treatment on the first day of *Yom Tov*:

1) Those who forbid: The *Magen Avraham*[4] and *Pri Megadim*[5] forbid treatment as on *Shabbat* because he might "grind herbs" (see above, 328:1E). The *Ritva,*[6] however, writes that the reason is that there is no possibility of danger to the patient and it is also uncertain whether he will derive benefit from the treatment on *Yom Tov* itself or only later. The *Tzitz Eliezer*,[7] basing himself on this *Ritva,* rules therefore that where it is certain that the patient will derive benefit from the treatment on *Yom Tov* itself, for instance taking medication for pain, this would be permitted even on the first day of *Yom Tov*. On the other hand, the *Ramban,*[8] and later, the *Nachal Eshkol*[9] and the *Shemirat Shabbat KeHilchatah,*[10] write that since patient care is not *shaveh lechol nefesh*, it is forbidden by the Torah. The *Chayei Adam*,[11] *Kitzur Shulchan Aruch*,[12]

1. מ״ב ס״ק ה
2. סי׳ צח ס״ק קכב
3. מ״ב ס״ק ו
4. סי׳ תקלב ס״ק ב
5. א״א שם
6. מובא בשיטה מקובצת ביצה כב ע״א
7. ח״ח סי׳ טו פט״ז
8. תורת האדם סוף שער המיחוש
9. הל׳ מועד קטן סי׳ מג אות ד
10. פל״ג סע׳ כד ופל״ד סע׳ א
11. הל׳ יו״ט כלל כג סע׳ א
12. סי׳ צח סע׳ לג

Although only a non-Jew may treat a non-seriously ill patient on the first day, on the second day a Jew may also treat such a patient. The exception to this is the second day of *Rosh Hashanah* since the two days of *Rosh Hashanah* are considered as one long day in terms of their sanctity.

GLOSS: *Treatment that only involves setting aside Rabbinic law such as putting ointment in the eye is permissible. However, a melachah may not be done* (C)*by a Jew even on the second day of Yom Tov .*

NISHMAT AVRAHAM

Maharsham[13] and *Mishnah Berurah*[14] all rule that there is no difference between *Shabbat* and *Yom Tov* with regard to the treatment of a patient.

2) Those who permit: *Rav Horowitz,*[15] in his notes to the *Talmud*, writes that the enactment of *Chazal* regarding treatment on *Shabbat* involving the setting aside of Rabbinic law did not include a suffering patient on *Yom Tov*. *Rav Shlomo Kluger*[16] permits putting on a salve and taking medication on *Yom Tov* if there is a slight need for it. Thus he rules that where the patient is really suffering, treatment involving the setting aside of Rabbinic law may be permitted, even if treatment had not been started before *Yom Tov* . If, on the other hand, treatment was started before *Yom Tov*, it may be continued even if the suffering is not so great. The *Maharsham* quoted above disagrees with his reasoning and ruling. It would appear, however, from the way the *Mishnah Berurah*[17] explains it, that the *Shulchan Aruch* forbids putting a salve in the eye only if he has a mild discomfort in his eye but otherwise feels well. However, if it was causing him a lot of discomfort, it would then be permitted. The *Sefat Emet*[18] permits the taking of medication, if taking it will not affect his joy of the Festival. The *Avnei Nezer*[19] permits taking medication if its benefits will be felt on *Yom Tov* itself. He argues that medication is *shaveh lechol nefesh* because everyone would take it if necessary, since its purpose is to make one well again and this is a natural desire.[20] The *Tzitz Eliezer*[21] therefore rules that there is room to permit taking medication on *Yom Tov* for discomfort and certainly if treatment was started before *Yom Tov*. If he wishes to take medication for only a mild discomfort, there are precedents for this and he may do so. The *Minchat Yom Tov*[22] and the *Shulchan Aruch HaRav*[23] write that for a *non-seriously ill* patient a Jew may set aside Rabbinic law if this is done in an indirect manner; a non-Jew may do so for the Jew even in the usual manner. See also *Yabia Omer*[24]

(C) by a Jew: Even if his whole body is affected.[25] But further consideration is needed to determine whether doing so in an indirect manner would be permitted.

13. דעת תורה סי׳ תקלב
14. סי׳ תקלב ס״ק ה
15. רא״מ הורוויץ בהערותיו לשבת קלד ע״ב
16. סי׳ שכח, מובא בדעת תורה סי׳ תקלב. ונימוקיו, דאמרינן מתוך שהותרה וכו׳ ולא שייך שמא ישחוק דגם בשחיקה שייך מתוך
17. ס״ק ה
18. הוא השואל בשו״ת אבני נזר או״ח סי׳ שצד ו־שצה
19. או״ח סי׳ שצד אות ח
20. וידוע שהרמב״ם השמיט כל המושג של שוה לכל נפש מחיבורו, ועיין בערוה״ש סי׳ תצה סע׳ יט
21. ח״ח סי׳ טו פט״ז עמ׳ קעא
22. סי׳ צח ס״ק קכב
23. סי׳ תצו סע׳ ד ו־ה
24. שו״ת יביע אומר ח״ה יו״ד סי׳ כג אות ג
25. מ״ב ס״ק ח

SIMAN 502:
THE LAWS OF FIRE ON *YOM TOV*

§1: One may not (A)create a flame by the use of wood, stones, earth or water.

SIMAN 503:
ONE MAY NOT PREPARE FROM ONE DAY OF *YOM TOV* FOR THE NEXT

§2: A baker may (A)fill a caldron of water (to boil) even though he only needs a flagonfull.

NISHMAT AVRAHAM

For one acts as strictly on the first day of *Yom Tov* as on *Shabbat* since we are dealing with Torah law in both instances. But the second day of *Yom Tov* in the Diaspora is a Rabbinic enactment with respect to which one could possibly act leniently where a *non-seriously ill* patient is concerned.[26] There are indeed many *poskim* who rule leniently in such a situation; see above, *Siman* 328:17C.

It is forbidden to ask a non-Jew to perform a *melachah* unless the patient is *non-seriously ill*.[27] If the treatment involved can be delayed until the next day it should not be carried out even on the second day of *Yom Tov* even if done by a non-Jew.[28]

SIMAN 502

(A) create a flame: This includes striking a match[1] or turning on an electric light or heater.[2] As to the use of a telephone, *Rav Shlomo Zalman Auerbach zt"l*[3] writes that it is permissible to use a telephone on *Yom Tov* even for a *non-seriously ill* patient. He explains that since most *poskim* rule that the prohibition of producing light on *Yom Tov* is Rabbinic (as opposed to the *Taz*[4] who rules that it is forbidden by Torah law), even if a lamp is lit in the central exchange when the receiver is lifted off the hook, it is still permitted. Besides, although the lamp is inevitably lit, it is not of any consequence to the person using the telephone, who has no use for it. The *Rav zt"l* wrote to me adding that when Rabbinic law may be set aside as it may, for a *non-seriously ill* patient, a Jew may use the telephone on *Yom Tov* for the patient. On the basis of this ruling I wondered whether it would therefore be permissible for a Jew to drive a car on *Yom Tov* for a *non-seriously ill* patient.

SIMAN 503

(A) fill a caldron of water: Although one is allowed to cook food on *Yom Tov* which is to be eaten the same day or to carry from one *domain* to another,[1] this only applies to what is *shaveh lechol*

26. שעה"צ ס"ק ט
27. סי' שכח מ"ב י
28. מ"ב ס"ק ח בשם האו"ה כלל נט אות כו
1. שו"ת כתב סופר או"ח סי' סז

2. שמירת שבת כהלכתה פי"ג סע' ב
3. שם פל"ג הערה כג*
4. ס"ק א
1. סי' תצה סע' א

GLOSS: *However, the whole quantity must be put on the fire at the same time, as it is forbidden to add water to whatever is already on the fire since the additional labor is not for the purpose of Yom Tov.*

NISHMAT AVRAHAM

nefesh.[2] Cooking something that is only used by some, such as the sick or the fastidious, is forbidden.[3] Therefore, boiling water on *Yom Tov* to fill a hot-water bottle for a patient would be forbidden. To prepare a hot-water bottle, extra water should be added to the amount which is to be boiled for drinking or washing dishes and all of it should be put on to boil at the same time. Water for a hot-water bottle may not be added to water that has already been put on to boil for drinking.[4] *Rav Auerbach zt"l,*[5] however, rules that another kettle containing water for a hot-water bottle may be put on the fire provided that one will drink a little from the boiled water. Moreover, he writes, it is possible that one may add water for the bottle to water which is already on the stove. For since all the water blends, and he will be drinking from the mixture (which includes the water added for filling the hot-water bottle), it is permitted. It is like adding more water on a *Yom Tov* which falls on Friday which is allowed, even though there is enough water for the *Yom Tov* itself. Since the *Rama* here only forbids this because the extra effort is not for *Yom Tov,* this extra effort is surely permitted for a patient.

It would seem to me that where it is common for healthy people to warm their beds with a hot-water bottle, it would be permissible for the patient to do so as well. He may if necessary even put it on that part of his body that feels uncomfortable, if it is not obvious to all that he is doing this as a treatment.[6]

SMOKING: The *acharonim*[7] debated whether it was permissible to smoke on *Yom Tov.* This depended on whether smoking was defined as being *shaveh lechol nefesh*[8] or not. Nowadays, however, when there is overwhelming evidence that smoking is responsible for many fatal diseases (including those of the heart, lungs, stomach, arteries, and for many types of cancer)[9] there is no question that one should not smoke even on a weekday. The effects of passive smoking are also well documented. The *Igrot Moshe*[10] writes, however, that it is not possible to forbid smoking by Torah law based on the verse: "Guard yourselves well,"[11] since the disastrous effects are only felt after many years. And since it is so widespread one may apply to it the verse: "*Hashem* guards simpletons."[12] I also heard this from *Rav Ovadiah Yosef shlita. Rav Auerbach zt"l*[13] wrote to me that the *Rambam*[14] who wrote regarding extremely harmful and poisonous kinds of

2. כתובות ז ע״א. סי׳ תקיא מ״ב ס״ק א
3. ראה בשמירת שבת כהלכתה פ״ב הערה לו
4. שמירת שבת כהלכתה פל״ג סע׳ כו
5. שם הערה צו. וראה שם בח״ג תיקונים ומלואים
6. שם פל״ד סע׳ יא
7. קרבן נתנאל סוף פ״ב דביצה ומג״א סי׳ תקיד ס״ק ד שאוסרים, והפני יהושע על שבת לט ע״ב, מור וקציעה להיעב״ץ סי׳ תקיא, הפמ״ג מ״ז תקיא ס״ק ב שמתירים. וראה בשו״ת יביע אומר ח״ה או״ח סי׳ לט אות א־ג
8. כתובות ז ע״א
9. J Royal Coll of Physicians of London vol. 26 pp 352 and 357 Oct '92. Clinics in Chest Medicine March '00, the whole volume
10. יו״ד ח״ב סי׳ מט
11. דברים ד:טו
12. תהלים קטז:ו
13. לב אברהם ח״ב עמ׳ יז
14. הל׳ דעות פ״ד ה״ט

food, only states that it is proper for a person to refrain from ever eating them; he did not use the word forbidden.

However, the *Chafetz Chaim*[15] writes regarding those who excuse themselves on the grounds that smoking has become a habit that is too difficult to break: Who permitted you to become habituated to it? True *Chazal*[16] said that "one who harms himself is not liable even though he had no right to do so," but they did say "he had no right to do so." There are two reasons for this: (a) because of the verse[17] "Guard yourselves well" and (b) it is axiomatic that the whole universe belongs to *Hashem.* He created us (the people of Israel) for the purpose of proclaiming His greatness and, in His lovingkindness, He gives to each and every one of us the strength we need for His Torah and His world. How then can one act as he pleases? Surely he belongs to his Master? If, therefore, as a result of smoking he will weaken himself, he will surely be held accountable for following the dictates of his heart, knowingly and without being forced. Therefore, if he were to really be honest with himself and see the immense harm that he brings upon himself by smoking, he would surely make every effort not to become addicted to it.

Rav Waldenberg shlita,[18] however, does rule that smoking should be forbidden by Torah law. He also adds that since smoking is harmful to those in the vicinity of the smoker, they have the right to demand, in a public place, that he stop. This ruling he bases on the *Gemara,*[19] *Rambam*[20] and *Shulchan Aruch.*[21]

It is also noteworthy that the *Rambam*[22] writes: Maintaining a healthy and sound body is among the ways of *Hashem,* for when one is sick it is impossible to comprehend or learn about Him. Therefore, one should keep far away from whatever harms the body and accustom himself to only those things that keep him healthy. The *Shulchan Aruch*[23] writes: There are many things that *Chazal* have forbidden since they endanger life. Whoever does not care but instead says, "I am willing to endanger myself. Why should this affect anyone else?" or whoever is lackadaisical about them, he is given lashes by the *Beit Din;* whoever takes care to avoid them is praiseworthy. The *Be'er HaGolah*[24] adds: It appears to me that the reason the Torah warned us to guard ourselves from harm is because *Hashem* created the universe in His lovingkindness for the benefit of those whom He created, that they should recognize His greatness and serve Him by keeping His *mitzvot* and His Torah. If one endangers himself it is as if he despises His Creator's wish and neither wants to serve Him nor receive His rewards. There is no greater blasphemous disdain than this.

Finally, on a more piquant note. The *Birkei Yosef*[25] writes that his grandfather asked in a dream what Heaven's opinion is of someone who smokes. He was answered: He who smokes on *Yom Tov* is excommunicated, on *Tishah B'Av,* is cursed.

PASSIVE SMOKING: The *Igrot Moshe*[26] forbids smoking in public areas such as yeshivot and synagogues for the smoker actively harms those who are non-smokers.

15. ליקוטי אמרים פי״ג
16. ב״ק צ ע״ב
17. דברים ד:טו
18. שו״ת ציץ אליעזר חט״ו סי׳ לט
19. ב״ב כג ע״א
20. הל׳ שכנים פי״א ה״ז
21. חו״מ סי׳ קנה סע׳ לו ו־מא
22. הל׳ דעות פ״ד ה״א
23. חו״מ סי׳ תכז סע׳ ט ו־י
24. שם ס״ק צ
25. מחזיק ברכה או״ח סי׳ רי ס״ק יג
26. חו״מ סי׳ יח

SIMAN 518: CARRYING FROM ONE DOMAIN TO ANOTHER ON *YOM TOV*

§1: Since carrying from one domain to another was permitted for the purposes of eating, it was also permitted (A)even when not done for this purpose. Thus one may carry a *lulav*, child, *Sefer Torah* and other articles.

NISHMAT AVRAHAM

SIMAN 518

(A) even when not done for this purpose: The *Shemirat Shabbat KeHilchatah*[1] rules that even those *melachot* which are permitted on *Yom Tov* for the purpose of eating are forbidden when done for the treatment of a *non-seriously ill* patient (see above, *Siman* 496B) because his requirements are not *shaveh lechol nefesh.* Therefore[2] it is forbidden to carry medication necessary for a *non-seriously ill* patient from one *domain* to another if there is no *eruv chatzerot.* However, *Rav Auerbach zt"l*[3] wrote that since the need for an *eruv chatzerot* is only Rabbinical, should there not be one, the medication could be carried if it is carried in an indirect manner.

A disabled person may be taken out in his wheelchair even into a *public domain* where there is no *eruv.*[4]

1. פל״ג סע׳ כד
2. שם סע׳ כה
3. שם הערה צ
4. שם פל״ד סע׳ כז

CHAPTER TWENTY-THREE:

The Laws of Chol Hamoed

SIMAN 531: THE LAWS OF SHAVING ON *CHOL HAMOED*

§3: Even though circumstances forced a person not to be able to shave before the Festival, he nevertheless may not shave during *Chol HaMoed.* The same ruling applies to someone who could not shave before the Festival (A)because of illness but recovered during the Festival.

SIMAN 532: PARING NAILS ON *CHOL HAMOED*

§2: (A)All treatments are permitted on *Chol HaMoed.*

NISHMAT AVRAHAM

SIMAN 531

(A) because of illness: However, even a *non-seriously ill* patient may shave on *Chol HaMoed* if it is necessary for his treatment, for example in order to be able to put on a salve.[1]

SIMAN 532

(A) All treatments: *Melachot* even in the fullest sense from a *halachic* perspective are permitted for treatment, including those involved in treating a *non-seriously ill* patient.[1] This includes treatment to strengthen his resistance[2] and treatment even if there is only minimal suffering[3] or discomfort.[4] Preventive treatment is also permitted.[5] However, one may not visit his doctor or dentist for an annual checkup if he feels well, and if he knows that a *melachah* such as writing or drawing blood will be performed.[6] *Rav Auerbach zt"l* told me that a doctor may charge his usual fee as this falls under the category of that which is done to prevent a loss, which is permitted on *Chol HaMoed.*[7]

Rav Neuwirth shlita told me that research activities are permitted, if the project had been started before the Festival and discontinuation over *Chol HaMoed* will result in a loss. However, one may not write a manuscript, including a draft, even in a language other than Hebrew.

1. מג״א ס״ק יב. ועיין בביה״ל סע׳ ח ד״ה כל
1. מ״ב ס״ק ה. נשמת אדם כלל קי סע׳ יז ס״ק ב
2. ביה״ל סוסי׳ תקלא ד״ה כל אדם
3. שו״ת אג״מ או״ח ח״ג סי׳ עח
4. עיין שם בנשמת אדם
5. מאירי מו״ק י ע״ב ד״ה מקיזין
6. שמעתי מהגרש״ז אויערבאך זצ״ל. שמירת שבת כהלכתה פס״ו הערה פח. וכ״כ הגר״מ פיינשטיין זצ״ל בספר חול המועד פסקי הלכות אות טז מטעם זלזול המועד. ועיין באג״מ שם
7. עיין בסי׳ תקמב סע׳ א בהגה במ״ב ס״ק ד ובביה״ל ד״ה ודבר

SIMAN 546: LAWS OF ENGAGEMENT AND MARRIAGE ON *CHOL HAMOED*

§5: A woman may (A)pretty herself as usual on *Chol HaMoed;* she may use eye makeup, part her hair, use rouge and put lime on her face, provided she can remove the lime during the Festival.

SIMAN 548: THE LAWS OF MOURNING ON *CHOL HAMOED*

§20: The (A)days of the Festival do not count towards the seven days of mourning if the laws of mourning were not kept before the Festival.

NISHMAT AVRAHAM

One may not use a computer on *Chol HaMoed* and certainly not print out any material.[8] However its use is permitted for a patient, even one who is *non-seriously ill.*[9]

SIMAN 546

(A) pretty herself: Since these are necessary to her, they are like preparing food to be used on *Chol HaMoed;* they can be done as usual, even if they involve a lot of effort.[1] Along the same lines, one may give his eyeglasses for repair on *Chol HaMoed* since he needs them. However, he may not have the frame changed then.[2] In *Rav Auerbach zt''l's*[3] opinion one may also have his hearing aid repaired. However it would appear that this ruling would not apply to fixing a telephone that is out of order. If, however, the telephone is in the home of a sick patient or an elderly person, the *Shemirat Shabbat KeHilchatah*[4] writes that it may be repaired since it is very necessary for them.

A non-Jew may not be asked to do something on *Chol HaMoed* for a Jew which the Jew himself is forbidden to do.[5]

SIMAN 548

(A) days of the Festival: What is the *halachah* for a woman after childbirth or any other ill person who, because of their weakness or because of some other unavoidable reason, could not observe the laws of mourning before the Festival for a close relative? Normally, if a Festival starts during the seven days of mourning, the seven-day period is terminated by the Festival if the mourners observed the laws of mourning for a brief period. Similarly, if a Festival starts during the thirty days of mourning, it also terminates the thirty-

8. שמירת שבת כהלכתה פס"ו הערה ריא
9. מהא דשמירת שבת כהלכתה שם
1. ביה"ל ד"ה כל
2. שמירת שבת כהלכתה פס"ו הערה פח
3. שם
4. שם
5. סי' תקמג סע' א

CHAPTER TWENTY-FOUR:

The Laws of Tishah B'Av and Other Fast Days

SIMAN 550: THE DIFFERENCE BETWEEN TISHAH B'AV AND OTHER FASTS

§1: Everyone must fast [(A)]**these four fasts and it is forbidden to deviate from the norm.**

GLOSS: *Pregnant women and nursing mothers, however, who will have great discomfort fasting* [(B)]*need not do so. Even if they*

NISHMAT AVRAHAM

day period. In the above cases, although they were aware of their loss, they were unavoidably unable to observe any period of mourning before the Festival. Nonetheless, the Festival which starts during the seven-day or thirty-day period of mourning terminates it.[1] On the other hand, if they were unaware of their loss, either because they were not told or because they were mentally incapable then, they must observe the appropriate period of mourning if they are told or recover during the thirty-day period of mourning.[2]

SIMAN 550

(A) these four fasts: These are on the ninth of Av (*Tishah B'Av*), the seventeenth of Tammuz, the third of Tishrei (the *Fast of Gedaliah*) and the tenth of Tevet. However, *Tishah B'Av* is stricter than the other three (referred to below as the three fasts) since it marks the destruction of both Temples.[1] *Chazal* instituted these fasts to have us remember the national misfortunes that happened to the Jewish people on these days.[2] See below, *Shulchan Aruch Siman* 554 §5.

(B) need not do so: A *non-seriously ill* patient is exempt from fasting and should not act stringently.[3] Similarly, pregnant women and nursing mothers who have great discomfort should not fast.[4] The *Rama*[5] writes that on the *Fast of Esther* (not included in the above four; one can be more lenient than in the above four fasts – see *Rama, Siman* 686 §2) even one who has painful eyes should not fast if they cause him great discomfort. The *Mishnah Berurah*[6] comments on this that it is possible that since all Israel willingly accepted the above four fasts upon them-

1. מ״ב ס״ק נג בשם השו״ת שבות יעקב ח״א סי׳ פח ושו״ת חת״ס סי׳ שמב מובא בפ״ת יו״ד סי׳ שצו ס״ק ג
2. ערוה״ש יו״ד שם סע׳ ג וסי׳ שלז סע׳ ג. שו״ת שבות יעקב שם. שו״ת ציץ אליעזר ח״ד רמת רחל סי׳ כו

1. מ״ב שם ס״ק ב
2. סי׳ תקמט סע׳ א
3. מ״ב ס״ק ד
4. שעה״צ ס״ק ג
5. סי׳ תרפו סע׳ ב
6. ביה״ל כאן ד״ה מיהו

have no discomfort they are not bound to fast; nevertheless, (C)*the custom is to* (D)*act stringently. This only applies to the three fasts, but on Tishah B'Av they should complete the fast.*

NISHMAT AVRAHAM

selves, they have become obligatory. Pregnant women and nursing mothers were exempted at the outset from the three fasts as seems clear from the *Gemara* which only mentions their obligation with regard to *Tishah B'Av*. However, continues the *Mishnah Berurah,* the *Kovetz* on the *Rambam* writes that one may be lenient even with these three fasts and each case should be brought before a *posek* for his decision.[7]

The *Kaf HaChaim* writes[8] that one who is old or weak may also act leniently and not fast during the three fast days, if in a doctor's opinion the fast will harm him. Otherwise he should not act differently from the congregation. However, one who is aged and weak should not fast since the *Geonim*[9] have ruled that even on *Yom Kippur,* if it is obvious that the fast will bring him into possible danger, he is allowed to eat. Therefore this is certainly true for the three fasts.

A person who is permitted to eat during these fasts must nevertheless not derive pleasure by eating meat and drinking wine; he should eat only what is necessary for his health.[10]

Rav Auerbach zt"l wrote to me that a patient who needs to eat but also wishes to be called up to the reading of the Torah, should eat less than 30 grams every 9 minutes.[11] *Rav Waldenberg shlita*[12] commented that this was a ruling of the *Marcheshet*[13] based on the *Ra'ah,* the *Rivash* and the *Magen Avraham,* that one who eats less than this amount is considered as if he is still fasting. This being so he may even be called up during the *Minchah* service although the reading of the Torah then was instituted for those who are fasting.

(C) the custom is: If, however, they are weak, they should not do so. I was once present before the fast of Tevet when *Rav Auerbach zt"l* was asked by an old woman who had vowed many years previously to fast on all the public fast days. In her present state she was too weak to fast but wished to know whether she could annul her vow. He ruled that she need not do so since one could assume that when she took the vow she did so in order to make sure that she would not act leniently, but not that she should fast when she had no obligation to do so. Since *Chazal* did not include the weak in their enactment, her present state was automatically not included in her vow. The *Rav zt"l* explained to me that had she eaten when she could have fasted she would have transgressed the Torah law of breaking a vow. On the other hand, the undefined intention in her vow was not to include fasting in circumstances where *Chazal* from the outset did not decree a fast. The *Rash*[14] writes quoting a *Midrash* that *Hashem* wished to exempt those who returned from the Babylonian exile from any punishment for not separating tithes, provided that they would not re-sanctify the Land of Israel. However, they did sanctify the Land and

7. ועל אף שכתב הא״ר שיפרעו אח״כ, חולק עליו המ״ב בביה״ל ד״ה אין
8. כף החיים ס״ק ו
9. ספר שערי תשובה סי׳ שכה
10. חיי אדם כלל קלג סע׳ ו. הליכות עולם עמ׳ 141
11. וראה גם בא״ר סי׳ תקסח ס״ק ב
12. בהערות לנשמת אברהם כרך א או״ח עמ׳ שמב. שו״ת ציץ אליעזר חט״ו סי׳ לב
13. ח״א סי׳ יד ס״ק ד
14. שביעית פ״ו מ״א

SIMAN 551:
THE WEEK DURING WHICH *TISHAH B'AV* FALLS

§10: There is an opinion which says that those who do not eat meat during this week may nevertheless eat food in which meat was cooked. They may (A)not eat fowl or salted meat or drink freshly made wine. It is permitted to drink wine for *Havdalah* and for *birkat hamazon.*

§16: For some it is customary (B)not to have a bath from *Rosh Chodesh* Av, but others desist only during the week in which *Tishah B'Av* falls.

NISHMAT AVRAHAM

thus became obligated by Torah law to separate tithes according to Rebbe Yosi (a *Tanna*). However, according to Rebbe Eliezer (a *Tanna*) when the second Temple was destroyed, the sanctity of the Land was automatically annulled since their undefined intention had most probably been that it should remain sanctified only as long as the Temple was standing. The *Rav zt"l* explained to me that the obligation to separate tithes was Rabbinic in their case, but now, had they not done so they would have transgressed Torah law, since the sanctification brought with it a Torah obligation. This is comparable to the question at hand for here also one assumes that the old woman took her vow to include only the times when she was healthy and capable of fasting[15] (see below, *Siman* 585C).

(D) act stringently: A healthy person who is fasting and wishes to swallow a pill because of a mild headache, may do so but without water. If, however, the medication has a pleasant taste (such as a syrup or lozenge) he may not do so.[16] *Rav Auerbach zt"l* told me that a patient who has to take pills on *Tishah B'Av* and cannot swallow them without water, may drink the minimum amount necessary to enable him to swallow the pills. He does not need to first spoil the taste of the water as on *Yom Kippur* (see *Siman* 612). *Rav Neuwirth shlita* explained to me that this was permitted since *Chazal* did not institute the fast of *Tishah B'Av* for someone who was ill.

SIMAN 551

(A) not eat fowl: However, one who is unable to eat dairy foods may eat chicken. A nursing mother whose milk will be unhealthy for her child if she does not eat meat, is allowed to eat meat.[1]

(B) not to have a bath: For one who is ill, even a hot bath is permitted during the week of *Tishah B'Av* if necessary.[2] Thus bathing which is not for pleasure is permitted for any sick person, if necessary. However, on *Tishah B'Av* itself one should be careful to avoid doing so.[3]

A patient who has been instructed by his doctor to swim daily, may do so even on the day preceding *Tishah B'Av* but not on *Tishah B'Av* itself. This is true even if he is not a *seriously ill* patient but has a bad

15. והעיר לי מו״ר הגרי״י נויבירט שליט״א מהמ״ב סי׳ תקפא ס״ק יט ושעה״צ ס״ק לג
16. הגר״ע יוסף שליט״א הליכות עולם עמ׳ 141

1. מ״ב ס״ק סד
2. מ״ב ס״ק פח
3. שעה״צ ס״ק צד

SIMAN 554:
WHAT IS FORBIDDEN ON *TISHAH B'AV*

§5: Pregnant women and nursing mothers fast on *Tishah B'Av* just as they do on *Yom Kippur*. Although they are exempt from the other three fasts, it nevertheless is fitting that on those other fast days they not eat or drink for pleasure but only enough for the baby's needs (*see above, Siman* 550 §1).

§6: A woman, during the first thirty days [(A)]**after giving birth,**

NISHMAT AVRAHAM

back, for example, and swimming is for physical therapy.[4]

SIMAN 554

(A) after giving birth: The *Mishnah Berurah* writes: It is assumed that she is weak and has the status of a *non-seriously ill* patient. Therefore, even though with regard to *Yom Kippur* she has a normal status after seven days, see *Siman* 617, with regard to *Tishah B'Av* which is Rabbinic in origin, the enactment did not include the sick. The *Taz* and other *acharonim* rule that although it is certain that she or the patient mentioned later are not in danger, and have not expressed a need for food, they may be given food on *Tishah B'Av*. The *Maharshal* disagrees with the ruling of the *Shulchan Aruch,* ruling that *Tishah B'Av* is comparable to *Yom Kippur* in that after the first seven days following childbirth, unless she is also slightly ill, she must fast, even if she wants to eat. Nevertheless, many *acharonim* agree that the *halachah* is that she is allowed to eat. However, it has become an accepted custom that she does fast, as mentioned by the *Rama,* so long as she does not feel weak and has recovered from giving birth. However, if she has not completely recovered or is still slightly ill or inherently weak, she should not fast during the first thirty days. A woman after childbirth who is healthy and fasting, but who suddenly feels an unusual weakness must stop fasting.[1]

The *Aruch HaShulchan,*[2] commenting on the strict ruling of the *Rama,* writes that it is probable that this ruling was appropriate in their times when people were healthier and stronger. Nowadays, however, Heaven forbid that a woman within thirty days after childbirth be allowed to fast on *Tishah B'Av* since she is still weak and ill.

If a doctor says that an ill baby would come to harm if his nursing mother would fast and she nursed him, or if she would fast and he would be given an alternative diet, the mother may eat.[3] *Rav Neuwirth shlita* wrote to me that if the baby's total nourishment comes only from his mother, and she would not have enough milk were she to fast, she must drink regardless of the fact that she herself is healthy. Since modern medicine believes that the mother's milk has special benefits for her baby, she should drink even if she could give him other food. As to whether she may also eat, see **D** below.

4. שמעתי ממו״ר הגרי״י נויבירט שליט״א
1. מ״ב ס״ק ט
2. סע׳ ח
3. ברכ״י ס״ק ה. שע״ת ס״ק ו

and similarly, (B)a patient who must eat, (C)does not need to be assessed as to whether he should fast or not but is given to eat immediately, for *Chazal's* enactments do not include (D)situations of illness.

GLOSS: *However, (E)the custom is for them to fast, as long as (F)there is no fear that by so doing they (G)might be endangering*

NISHMAT AVRAHAM

(B) a patient who must eat: This refers to someone whose whole body feels weak, even though he has not reached the category of a *non-seriously ill* patient.

(C) does not need to be assessed: One need not stop to weigh up whether he will become *seriously ill* or not, as a result of fasting. It is sufficient that he is ill to exempt him from fasting. However, if a woman after childbirth feels that she is well enough to fast she is obligated to do so.[4]

(D) situations of illness: The *Kaf HaChaim*[5] rules that a patient who although he has recovered from his illness is still very weak, may eat if he fears that fasting may bring about a relapse. He does not need to eat by *measure* but must not eat for pleasure. On the other hand, the *Chatam Sofer,*[6] the *Maharam Shick*[7] and the *Sdei Chemed*[8] rule that if a small amount of food or drink is sufficient for him, he is forbidden to take more. It is important, however, that the decision of just how much he should eat be left to his doctor. The *Marcheshet*[9] writes: I remember that when I was ill on *Tishah B'Av* so that it was difficult for me to fast, I ate less than a *measure* each time so as not to lose the day's fast, which was instituted by the prophets and is as grave as *Yom Kippur.*

However, it would appear from the wording of the *Shulchan Aruch* that a patient may eat the usual amount of food. Moreover, since, as he writes, *Chazal* did not include the sick in their enactment, there is no concept of a fast as far as the sick are concerned. Both the *Aruch HaShulchan*[10] and the *Mishnat Ya'avetz*[11] also rule that eating less than a *measure* does not apply to *Tishah B'Av. Rav Auerbach zt"l* told me that the *halachah* is that a patient need not eat by *measure.* However, a healthy person who eats to forestall illness, if there was a plague in the town for example, or a pregnant woman who feels weak and fears that if she fasts she will take ill, should eat by *measure.*

Rav Neuwirth shlita told me that a patient who must drink for a medical reason should drink but not eat. As to swallowing a pill with water, see above, *Siman* 550D.

(E) the custom is for them to fast: This is so even if she says that she must eat. However, this ruling only applies after the first seven days after childbirth; during the first seven days she may not fast even if she says that she does not need to eat. During the first three days following childbirth (where the *halachah* is more lenient), she is forbidden to fast.[12]

(F) there is no fear that by doing so: This also applies to one who is only slightly sick, as mentioned above in **A.** See also the *Magen Avraham*[13] who writes that even

4. מ״ב ס״ק יב
5. ס״ק לא
6. שו״ת או״ח סי׳ קנז (וראה להלן סי׳ תקנט ס״ק ב)
7. שו״ת או״ח סי׳ רפט
8. מערכת בין המצרים סי׳ ב ס״ק ג
9. ח״א סי׳ יד
10. סוסע׳ ז
11. או״ח סי׳ מט
12. מ״ב ס״ק יג
13. ס״ק ט

themselves. But, those who are lenient (H)*have not transgressed.*

SIMAN 555:
LAWS OF *TEFILLIN* AND *TZITZIT* ON *TISHAH B'AV*

§1: The custom is not to put on *tefillin* or *tallit* on *Tishah B'Av* at *Shacharit,* but the *tallit katan* is worn under one's clothes without reciting the blessing. (A)At *Minchah,* we put on *tzitzit* and *tefillin* and say the respective blessings over them.

NISHMAT AVRAHAM

where it is customary to act stringently, if *Tishah B'Av* falls on *Shabbat* and is therefore postponed to Sunday, he should act leniently and not fast.[14] This is also the ruling of the *Yabia Omer.*[15] *The Biur Halachah*[16] writes that one who is slightly unwell, or a pregnant woman who feels uncomfortable, is permitted to eat when *Tishah B'Av* is postponed to Sunday.

(G) might be endangering themselves: Then it is forbidden for them to fast.[17]

(H) have not transgressed: Certainly there is no merit for one who is weak and in the category of the *non-seriously ill* to fast.[18]

SIMAN 555

(A) At *Minchah*: The *Ashkenazi* custom is as stated by the *Shulchan Aruch.* However, in many *Sephardic* communities the custom, based on the *Kabbalah,* is to wear *tallit* and *tefillin* at *Shacharit.*[1] The *Kaf HaChaim*[2] writes that this is also the ruling of the *Ramban,* the *Rashba,* the *Ari* and the *Rashash.* To this list, the *She'arim Metzuyanim BaHalachah*[3] adds the *Maharam Shick* and the *Gra.* Based on this *Rav Neuwirth shlita* told me that since it is forbidden to eat before fulfilling the *mitzvah* of *tefillin* (or any other impending positive command), see the *Magen Avraham, Siman* 692:7, an *Ashkenazi* who must eat on *Tishah B'Av* must put on *tefillin* before eating. The *She'arim Metzuyanim BaHalachah,*[4] however, writes that since the congregation does not put on *tefillin* until *Minchah* as a sign of mourning for the bitter events which occurred on the day, the patient should put on *tefillin* at *Minchah* but eat in the morning as is necessary. *Rav Auerbach zt"l*[5] wrote to me that the custom (amongst *Ashkenazim*) is not to put on *tefillin* before midday, to show that one is like a mourner on the first day, who dirties his glory with dust (taken from the verse in *Job*).[6] Even though he must eat, nevertheless he should not be adorned in his glory (referring to *tefillin*)[7] at a time when all are in mourning.

14. מ"ב ס"ק יד
15. ח"ה סי' מ אות ה
16. סי' תקנט סע' ט ד"ה ואינו
17. מ"ב ס"ק טו
18. מ"ב ס"ק טז
1. עיין בשע"ת
2. ס"ק ד
3. סי' קכד ס"ק ב
4. שם
5. לב אברהם ח"א עמ' יח
6. ראה איוב טז:טו
7. ראה יחזקאל כד:יז

SIMAN 556:
WHEN *TISHAH B'AV* FALLS ON SUNDAY

§1: When *Tishah B'Av* falls on Sunday, one says only the blessing of *meorei ha'aish* on a flame, but does not say a blessing on fragrant spices. At the termination of *Tishah B'Av*, (A)he recites *Havdalah* on wine but the blessings are not recited on a flame or on fragrant spices.

NISHMAT AVRAHAM

SIMAN 556

(A) he recites *Havdalah* on wine: A patient who must eat during Sunday, *Tishah B'Av,* recites *Havdalah* on wine on Saturday night and possibly may even be able to discharge this obligation for other members of his family. This is the ruling of the *Birkei Yosef,*[1] the *Sha'arei Teshuvah,*[2] the *Sdei Chemed*[3] and the *Orchot Chaim.*[4] However, the *Zecher Simchah*[5] rules that he should not recite *Havdalah* if he does not need to drink wine or another beverage (such as beer or fresh juice) for his health. The *Kaf HaChaim*[6] writes that only if the patient must eat on Saturday night (the night of *Tishah B'Av*) should he make *Havdalah* then; otherwise he should only do so when he needs to eat. Even then, he should not recite *Havdalah* on wine, unless he must drink it for his health, but recite it on other liquids, or else he should give the wine to a child who has reached the age of education. The *Shemirat Shabbat KeHilchatah*[7] also writes that a patient who must eat makes *Havdalah* only before he eats. The *havdalah* is made on those liquids that are permissible (see *Siman* 296A) but not on wine. If only wine is available, it should be given to a child to drink and, if this is not possible, he drinks the minimum required.[8]

On the other hand, *Rav Ovadiah Yosef shlita* told me that even a patient who only needs to drink should first recite *Havdalah* on wine before drinking. The wine should then be given to a child who has reached the age of education. If such a child is not present the patient should drink a *melo lugmav.* If he cannot, then it is sufficient if he just tastes the wine.[9] (See *Siman* 296A that in *Rav Yosef shlita's* view *Havdalah* can only be made on wine.)

The *Shulchan Aruch*[10] rules that one may drink water before making *Havdalah.* However, the *Kaf HaChaim*[11] quoting the *Geonim,* and the *Yesodei Yeshurun,*[12] quoting the writings of the *Ari z"l,* rule stringently, forbidding one to drink water before *Havdalah. Rav Neuwirth shlita* wrote to me that a patient who only needs to drink water would best act according to the ruling of the *Shulchan Aruch* and drink it as is necessary and make *Havdalah* after *Tishah B'Av.*

A patient who recites *Havdalah* Saturday night, the night of *Tishah B'Av,* does not recite a blessing over fragrant spices nor does he say the verses usually said at

1. ס״ק ב ו־ג
2. ס״ק א
3. מערכת ביהמ״צ סי׳ ב אות ה
4. ס״ק ב
5. שו״ת סי׳ סט
6. ס״ק ט
7. פס״ב סע׳ מו
8. עיין שם בהערה קיד
9. שו״ת יחוה דעת ח״ג סי׳ מ
10. סי׳ רצט סע׳ א
11. שם ס״ק ו
12. ח״ה עמ׳ תעג

SIMAN 557: THE REQUIREMENT TO SAY *NACHEM* AND *ANEINU* ON *TISHAH B'AV*

§1: When reciting the *Shemoneh Esrei* on *Tishah B'Av,* one says, "Hashem, our Master, comfort the mourners of Zion," during the blessing *bonei Yerushalayim,* and *aneinu* during the blessing *shomei'a tefillah.* If he forgets to do so, he need not rectify the omission.

GLOSS: *The accepted practice is to say nachem during the Minchah prayer only on Tishah B'Av because it was then that the Temple was torched. Therefore that is the time when we pray for comfort. A person who needed to eat on Tishah B'Av* (A)*says nachem during birkat hamazon.*

NISHMAT AVRAHAM

the beginning of *Havdalah.* He does say the blessing over a flame. If he recites *Havdalah* on *Tishah B'Av* morning, he neither recites the blessing over fragrant spices nor on a flame but only the blessing on whatever he drinks and the blessings following. He may discharge this obligation for other members of his family.[13]

It would be best for a female patient who needs to eat on *Tishah B'Av* if her husband would recite *Havdalah* for her, at the same time discharging this obligation for himself and other members of the family. As to whether he should make *Havdalah* on wine or another liquid, see above. If she is alone, she makes *Havdalah* for herself as described above for the male patient.[14]

Rav Neuwirth shlita told me that a patient with a quiescent stomach ulcer who takes a lozenge or syrup every evening as a preventative measure, should not do so on the *Shabbat* (when *Tishah B'Av* falls on Sunday) (see above, *Siman* 550D).

SIMAN 557

(A) says *nachem* during *birkat hamazon*: This is also the ruling of the *Ben Ish Chai.*[1] However the *Sha'arei Teshuvah*[2] and the *Kaf HaChaim*[3] disagree with this ruling and it would appear that the *Gra*[4] also rules that it should not be said at *birkat hamazon* since it was only instituted for the *Shemoneh Esrei.* This is also the ruling of *Rav Ovadiah Yosef shlita.*[5] The *Kaf HaChaim* concludes that since there is this difference of opinion it would be best not to say it in *birkat hamazon* lest it would constitute an interruption of the *birkat hamazon.* Instead, one should say it during the recital of the *harachaman* prayers which follow the conclusion of the four blessings of the *birkat hamazon.* However, the *Mishnah Berurah*[6] writes that all would agree that if he forgot to do so he need not rectify the omission.

13. שמירת שבת כהלכתה פס״ב סע׳ מו הערה ** ושו״ת יחוה דעת שם
14. שמירת שבת כהלכתה שם סע׳ מח
1. שנה א פ׳ דברים סע׳ כז
2. ס״ק א
3. ס״ק יא
4. בביאורו כאן
5. שו״ת יחוה דעת ח״א סוסי׳ מד
6. ס״ק ה

SIMAN 558:
MEAT IS NOT EATEN ON THE NIGHT FOLLOWING *TISHAH B'AV*

§1: On the ninth of Av, towards evening, the Temple was torched and then burned continuously until the evening of the next day. Therefore it is a praiseworthy custom not to eat meat or drink wine on the night of the tenth of Av and on the tenth of Av.

GLOSS: *There are those who only act strictly* (A)*until midday but not beyond that. If Tishah B'Av is postponed from Shabbat to Sunday, it is permitted to eat meat and drink wine on Monday, but not the evening before because of the mourning during Sunday.*

SIMAN 559:
TISHAH B'AV CUSTOMS

§3: During the night and day of *Tishah B'Av* until the *Minchah* service, one (A)**sits on the floor in the synagogue.** (*Nowadays*

NISHMAT AVRAHAM

SIMAN 558

(A) until midday: Although a woman seven days after childbirth fasts, nevertheless she is permitted to eat meat and drink wine on the night following the ninth of Av. She is certainly permitted to eat meat and drink wine if she fasted on *Tishah B'Av* that was postponed to Sunday.[1]

SIMAN 559

(A) sits on the floor: The *Rama*[1] writes: A mourner or sick person has no obligation to stand even for the president. *Rav Akiva Eiger,*[2] quoting the *Shevut Yaakov,*[3] explains that this is because there is no respect in a mourner standing; this is also true for *Tishah B'Av*. The *Chida,*[4] on the other hand, also quoting the *Shevut Yaakov,* writes that since a mourner is obligated to do all the *mitzvot,* he is obligated to stand out of respect; this is also true on *Tishah B'Av*. The *Shevut Yaakov,* explaining that it is not a sign of respect since one is sitting on the ground and mourning the destruction of the Temple, writes that he may stand if he so wishes, which is not in keeping with what the *Chida* wrote in his name. However, I found that the *Chida* elsewhere[5] corrects his previous statement. He also adds that even though a person may, if he wishes, stand up before a scholar on *Tishah B'Av,* a mourner or a sick person does not have to do so. However, both must stand up for a *Sefer Torah,* if the sick person is

1. שע"ת ס"ק ב
1. יו"ד סי' שעו סע' א
2. הגהות שם
3. ח"א סי' כו
4. הגהות יו"ד שם
5. שיורי ברכה שם

the custom is to sit on benches after leaving the synagogue following Shacharit, and to spend a long time reciting Lamentations until just before midday.)

§4: *Tachanun* (*and selichot*) **are not said on *Tishah B'Av,* nor is there *nefilat apayim,* since it is called** (B)***Mo'ed.***

GLOSS: (C)*The Torah is read etc.*

NISHMAT AVRAHAM

capable of doing so.[6] *Rav Ovadiah Yosef*[7] rules that a person is obligated to stand up for a scholar on *Tishah B'Av*.

(B) Mo'ed: For thus it is referred to in Scripture.[8] In the verse, *mo'ed* means time – a time for destruction. But since *mo'ed* can refer to a Festival – a time of joy, *halachah* puts *Tishah B'Av,* the *mo'ed,* into the same framework as the Festivals with respect to not saying *tachanun*. It also looks forward to the time of the prophecy of Zechariah (8:19) when the four fast days will become days of joy and festivals (*moadim tovim*).

(C) The Torah is read etc.: May a patient who has eaten or will eat later[9] on *Tishah B'Av* be called up to a reading of the Torah?[10] The *Chatam Sofer*[11] writes: On *Tishah B'Av* a patient who may eat must nevertheless still experience sorrow. Thus, he may only eat enough to sustain himself and if only drinking is sufficient for him, he may not eat. If it is enough that he eats once he may only eat what he needs, and may not eat again. As to the other manifestations of sorrow, he may not wear leather shoes, nor wash and anoint himself unless there is a medical reason to do so. Should all this be permitted to him, nevertheless the day of *Tishah B'Av* itself obligates the reading of the Torah both during *Shacharit* and *Minchah,* and this obligation falls on everyone including those who do not fast. *Rav Akiva Eiger*[12] ruled that someone who was permitted to eat on *Yom Kippur* could also be called up to the Torah during *Shacharit,* since this reading was instituted because of the holiness of the day. This is also the ruling of the *Mishnat Ya'avetz.*[13]

As to being called up to the Torah at *Minchah,* there are those[14] who rule strictly, reasoning that since this was only instituted for those who fast, the blessings that he would recite before and after the Torah portion may have been said in vain. On the other hand, there are those[15] who rule leniently, arguing that the Torah reading at *Minchah* was instituted for the honor of the congregation. Thus, if the patient is a *Cohen,* he should be careful to step outside the synagogue so that he will not be called up. If he does not do so and is called up but refuses out of fear of reciting blessings in vain, people might mistakenly think that the reason for his refusal is that there is a problem with his lineage. If, however, there is another *Cohen* present, he obviously has no obligation to step outside, but should make sure that the

6. שיורי ברכה שם
7. שו״ת יביע אומר ח״ג יו״ד סי׳ כו אות ג
8. איכה ב:ו
9. כי גם אם עכשיו עדיין צם, מכיון שבסופו של דבר יאכל, נמי הדין הכי וכ״כ המ״ב סי׳ תקסו ס״ק כ – שמעתי ממו״ר הגרי״י נויבירט שליט״א
10. עיין סי׳ תקסו סע׳ ו במ״ב ס״ק יט בשם המג״א
11. שו״ת או״ח סי׳ קנז
12. פסקים סי׳ כד
13. או״ח סי׳ מט
14. ט״ז. א״ר. דברי חיים. רעק״א
15. ב״ח. מג״א. חיי אדם. חת״ס

person calling up does not choose him. If he is called up and, being a scholar, he is ashamed to tell everyone that he is not fasting, it would appear that in such a situation he may rely on those who rule leniently.[16] The *Mateh Ephraim,*[17] however, permits him to be called up during *Shacharit* only but not at *Minchah. Rav Auerbach zt"l* wrote to me that a patient who must eat but wishes to be called up to the reading of the Torah, should eat by *measure.* He also wrote to me wondering what should be done in a situation when there was a congregation of ten patients none of whom was fasting. Could they read from the Torah during *Shacharit* seeing that the obligation to read the Torah is because of the day, just as it is on *Yom Kippur*? *Rav Waldenberg shlita*[18] wrote to me in reply to this question. He notes that the *Chatam Sofer* quoted above writes that even if all the ten members who made up a *minyan* were composed of the sick or did not need to fast on a postponed *Tishah B'Av* because of their close connection with circumcisions on that day (father, *sandak* or *mohel*), it would theoretically appear that they should read from the Torah even during *Minchah.* However, the *Chatam Sofer,* in practice, was unsure how to rule. Based on this, *Rav Waldenberg shlita* rules that if they all had eaten by *measure,* they certainly could read from the Torah even at *Minchah* (see below, *Siman* 618L).

As to the priestly blessing, the *Chida*[19] writes that a *Cohen* who is not fasting does not join the other *Cohanim* in the priestly blessing. *Rav Tukachinsky zt"l*[20] writes the same in the name of the *Pri Megadim* but adds, quoting the *Ginat Veradim,*[21] that if he is the only *Cohen* he may go up to recite the blessing.[22] *Rav Auerbach zt"l* told me that even if there was only one other *Cohen,* he may go up since when there are two *Cohanim* there is a Torah obligation to perform the *mitzvah.* This is only at *Minchah* since at *Shacharit* the possibility that he might have drunk enough wine to disqualify him surely does not arise.

16. מ״ב סי׳ תקסו ס״ק כא
17. סי׳ תרב סע׳ יז
18. נשמת אברהם כרך א או״ח עמ׳ שמג. שו״ת ציץ אליעזר חט״ו סי׳ לב
19. מחזיק ברכה קונטרס אחרון סי׳ קכט ס״ק א
20. לוח ארץ ישראל ג׳ תשרי
21. או״ח סי׳ א
22. עיין היטב בגינת ורדים ח״א כלל א סו״ס מט שמסקנתו אינו כן, וצ״ע

CHAPTER TWENTY-FIVE:
The Fast Days

SIMAN 566:
THE LAWS CONCERNING PUBLIC FASTS

§3: The *shaliach tzibbur* does not say *aneinu* as an independent blessing unless there are (A)ten who are fasting among those present in the synagogue, even if there are ten fasting in town.

§5: A *shaliach tzibbur* who is not fasting should not (B)lead the congregation in prayer on a public fast day.

§6: There is an opinion that on a public fast day, (C)one who is

NISHMAT AVRAHAM

SIMAN 566

(A) ten who are fasting: The *Mishnah Berurah*[1] writes that when a public fast falls on a Monday or Thursday, the Torah portion of the week is replaced by the portion beginning *vayechal.*[2] Since *Ezra* established the institution that a congregation read from the Torah every Monday and Thursday morning, this is fulfilled even though the portion for that week is not read. Therefore if there are only six people fasting in the synagogue on a Monday or Thursday and the others are unable to fast because of their illness, *vayechal* is read. At *Minchah,* and on the other days of the week at *Shacharit* also, however, there must be ten people fasting in synagogue. There is an opinion that during the four fasts (see *Siman* 550A), which were instituted by the prophets, even if there are only seven fasting in synagogue, *vayechal* may be read and *aneinu* said by the *shaliach tzibbur* as an additional independent blessing during the repetition of the *Shemoneh Esrei.* The *Kaf HaChaim*[3] advises that where possible one should try to have ten men fasting in the congregation even during the four fasts.

(B) lead the congregation: If it happened, however, that he does, he says *aneinu* in the blessing of *shomei'a tefillah,* using the phrase "on this fast day" instead of "on our fast day." The same ruling applies if he is the only person capable of leading the congregation, for it is better that there should be a *shaliach tzibbur* to lead the congregation in prayer, even though he is not fasting. Thus at least they will be able to hear *Kaddish, Kedushah* and *barechu.*[4]

(C) one who is not fasting: This includes one who is presently fasting but who intends to eat later.[5]

1. ס״ק יד
2. שמות לב:יא
3. ס״ק לב
4. מ״ב ס״ק יח
5. מ״ב ס״ק כ

not fasting should not be called up to the (D)reading of the Torah. If the *Cohen* is not fasting he should step outside and someone who is neither a *Cohen* nor a *Levi* who is fasting is called up in his stead.

SIMAN 567:

PERMISSION TO TASTE FOOD AND TO WASH ONE'S MOUTH DURING A FAST DAY

§3: It is preferable for a person who usually rinses his mouth every morning (A)not to do so on a public fast day.

SIMAN 574:

ONE SHOULD ACT ACCORDING TO THE STRICTER CUSTOM IF HE TRAVELED FROM ONE PLACE TO ANOTHER

§3: One who forgot that it was a fast day and ate (A)should not show in public that he did so. He should not

NISHMAT AVRAHAM

(D) reading of the Torah: See above, 559C. The *Mishnah Berurah*[6] writes that the non-faster may only be called up at *Shacharit* on a Monday or Thursday, even though the portion of the week is replaced by *vayechal*. However, since in any case the Torah would have been read on that day even if it were not a fast day, he may be called up. Although there are *acharonim* who disagree with this ruling, nevertheless if he was already called up, he may go up to the Torah according to all opinions. As to a *Cohen* or scholar, see above, *Siman* 559C.

SIMAN 567

(A) not to do so: However, if he feels uncomfortable it is permitted if he is careful to bend his head and mouth down so that no water enters his throat. If the discomfort is great, it is permissible to do this on *Tishah B'Av* as well, but not on *Yom Kippur*.[1] Therefore a person who must see a dentist on a public fast day or on *Tishah B'Av* may rinse his mouth when necessary during the treatment, if he is careful to bend his head forward.

SIMAN 574

(A) should not show in public: The *Minchat Elazar*[1] was asked the source for the custom that one who had to eat during one of the four fasts because of weakness, should only do so in private. Was this only an act of piety so that he should not be suspected of not wanting to fast in spite of being in good health? Or, on the contrary, was there a source for this ruling in the

6. ס"ק יט בשם המג"א

1. מ"ב ס"ק יא וחיי אדם כלל קלב סע' כ וכן משמע מהשו"ע כאן סע' א. וראה ביד אברהם יו"ד סי' קח סע' ה

1. שו"ת ח"ג סי' ג

indulge himself thinking that since he has eaten a little he may now continue to eat (*he should not do so even in private*).

SIMAN 578:
EVERY INDIVIDUAL SHOULD FAST AND PRAY WHEN HE IS IN DISTRESS

§1: In the same way as a congregation fasts and prays at a time of trouble, so should (A)an individual (B)fast and pray

NISHMAT AVRAHAM

Talmud and *poskim*? He replied: It seems to me that the source is the *Talmud*:[2] Rebbe Yehudah said: We were once sitting before Rebbe Akiva on *Tishah B'Av* which was on Friday and we brought him a soft egg which he swallowed without salt. Not that he wished to eat it but to show the students by his deed what the *halachah* was. This seems strange: How did Rebbe Yehudah know this? We cannot say that Rebbe Akiva told him so, since the *Tosafot Shantz* quotes *Rabbeinu Chananel*: "It has been handed down to us that Rebbe Akiva was *seriously ill* at the time and the doctors brought him a soft egg towards the end of *Tishah B'Av*. Rebbe Yehudah did not know the exact details of the story and relied only on what he had seen without knowing the reason." If doctors have permitted someone to eat because it is dangerous not to eat, he does not need to eat in private, even on *Yom Kippur,* since the act is public and there is no room for suspicion. That is why Rebbe Akiva ate in public. Rebbe Yehudah, however, did not realize that he ate by order of the doctors because he was *seriously ill*. As far as the four fasts are considered, although they were instituted by the prophets, we do not find that one is permitted to eat only when *dangerously ill* as on *Yom Kippur,* and the story with Rebbe Akiva was on *Tishah B'Av*. Therefore since a patient who only feels weak may not eat publicly even on one of the four fasts, one must say that Rebbe Akiva only ate publicly because he was *seriously ill*.

Rav Neuwirth shlita brought a source from the *Shulchan Aruch*: One is allowed to shave during *Chol HaMoed* under these circumstances: one who was released from imprisonment and did not have the opportunity to shave before the Festival etc. Although he is permitted to shave he may not do so publicly but only in private.[3]

SIMAN 578

(A) an individual: Since fasting is part and parcel of the process of repentance (return to *Hashem*) and humility, each and every one is obliged to examine his ways when in distress and return to *Hashem*.[1] This is also the ruling of the *Meiri* as quoted by the *Birkei Yosef*.[2]

(B) fast: This obligation lies upon everyone. Even a pregnant woman or nursing mother is obligated to fast if possible.[3]

1. מ״ב ס״ק א
2. ס״ק א
3. ברכ״י ס״ק ב בשם המאירי

2. עירובין מא ע״א
3. סי׳ תקלא סע׳ ד ו־ה

when (C)**in distress. For instance, if a member of his family is ill, lost in the desert, or imprisoned, he should fast and ask for mercy while fasting. He should not fast on *Shabbat,* a Festival, *Chanukah, Purim* or *Rosh Chodesh.***

NISHMAT AVRAHAM

(C) in distress: Not only his own distress but also that of a member of the family, if he also feels that distress.[4]

4. ברכ״י ס״ק ג בשם המאירי

CHAPTER TWENTY-SIX:

Laws Concerning Rosh Hashanah

SIMAN 585: THE BLESSING ON THE SHOFAR

§1: The *shofar* must be (A)blown while standing.

NISHMAT AVRAHAM

SIMAN 585

(A) blown: May one eat before hearing the *shofar*? The *Rama*[1] writes that it is forbidden to eat (at the termination of the *Fast of Esther*) until he has heard the reading of the *Megillah,* even if the fast was difficult. To this the *Magen Avraham*[2] adds that the same ruling applies to the *mitzvot* of *lulav, shofar* and *Keriyat Shema.* This is also the ruling of the *Sha'arei Teshuvah,*[3] the *Mateh Ephraim,*[4] the *Maharsham,*[5] the *Sdei Chemed*[6] and the *Mishnah Berurah.*[7] *Rav Shlomo Zalman Auerbach zt''l* wrote to me that the reading of the *Megillah* on the night of *Purim* is only a Rabbinic obligation (and not even an enactment of the prophets) and one has been fasting the whole day, and yet one must hear the *Megillah* before eating. Therefore, how much more so should we hear the *shofar,* which is a Torah obligation, before eating. The *Magen Avraham* adds, quoting the *Maharil,* that even a sick person (see above, *Siman* 550C) should not eat before hearing the *Megillah* unless it would possibly endanger him should he not do so. On the other hand, the *Orchot Chaim*[8] writes that closer scrutiny of the *Maharil* shows that he permitted someone who only felt slightly unwell to eat.

The *Beit Yitzchak*[9] discusses whether one may drink tea or coffee on *Rosh Hashanah* before hearing the *shofar.* He rules that it is forbidden to do so before *Mussaf.* However, a person who feels very weak may rely on the *Magen Avraham's* ruling[10] that he may taste a little food (see below) and on that of the *Eliyah Rabbah* that in such a situation, he may do so before reciting *Kiddush.*

The *Katzeh HaMateh*[11] complains: "It is surprising to me that the general public is not careful about this and, on the contrary, acts as if it was absolutely permissible to eat before hearing the *shofar* rather than only eat after hearing the first thirty blasts. They have no basis for doing so and the *acharonim*[12] have already protested against this. I have heard that they base their behavior on a *responsum* of the

1. סי׳ תרצב סע׳ ד
2. שם ס״ק ז בשם התוספתא פ״ק דשבת מ״ד
3. כאן ס״ק ג
4. סי׳ תקפח סע׳ ב
5. ח״א סי׳ א
6. אסיפת דינים מערכת ד׳ מינים סי׳ ג ס״ק כב
7. סי׳ תרצב סוס״ק טו
8. שם בסי׳ תרצב
9. שו״ת יו״ד ח״ב קונ״א סי׳ יח, מובא גם בארחות חיים סי׳ תרנב ס״ק ג
10. סי׳ תרנב ס״ק ד
11. על המטה אפרים סי׳ תקפח ס״ק ד
12. בעל האמרי אש מובא בספר זכרון יהודה דמ״ב והלבושי מרדכי או״ח סוסי׳ סה

GLOSS: *The custom is to do so* (B)*while standing on the bimah where the Torah is read.*

NISHMAT AVRAHAM

Chatam Sofer.[13] However, it will be obvious to anyone who studies the *responsum* that he only permitted someone to recite *Kiddush* before hearing the *shofar* because he was ill. To do so for no reason, and particularly to eat enough for a meal is not permissible and one should attempt to abolish this custom.''[14]

And thus writes the *Sdei Chemed*:[15] "I have heard that there are those amongst our *Ashkenazi* brothers who leave the *shul* following *shacharit* on *Rosh Hashanah* and go to their homes to drink tea before returning to hear the reading of the Torah and the blowing of the *shofar*. Although I was surprised to hear this, I did not wish to speak to them about it since I knew that once they had become accustomed to it, it would be difficult for them to abolish their custom. And, just as there is a *mitzvah* to admonish, there are times when it is a *mitzvah* to ignore and to keep silent. I have recently seen a *responsum* which writes that the saintly Rav Shimshon had all his life been accustomed to ask a weak person to recite *Kiddush* after *Shacharit* so that the congregation might fulfill their requirement to do so. Following this he himself drank tea and also gave some of the congregants to drink. I myself do so following his lead, for surely there must have been many great Rabbis present who were pious and God-fearing, yet none of them protested at what he did.'' [*One should note, however, that the discussion revolves around drinking tea with no mention whatsoever of eating, and that only some of the congregants were given to drink – A.S.A*]

However, a doctor on duty who will have no opportunity of hearing the *shofar* until much later in the day, and finds it difficult to fast until then, may recite *Shacharit,* make *Kiddush* and eat his meal. If there is no time even for this, he should at least recite the blessings over the Torah and say the first paragraph of the *Shema* before reciting *Kiddush* and eating.[16]

The above applies to men. However, a woman who feels weak and cannot wait to eat until after hearing the *shofar,* may recite *Kiddush* and eat. This is because the Torah exempts a woman from the *mitzvah* of *shofar* since it is a positive commandment fulfilled only at a particular time.[17] This is also the ruling of the *Orchot Chaim*[18] and *Chayei Adam.*[19]

As to the definition of "tasting,'' the author of the *Shulchan Aruch* writes in his *Kesef Mishneh,*[20] that eating up to a *kebeitzah* of fruit is considered tasting. However, more than this or a *kezayit* of bread is considered a casual meal and is forbidden. However, in the *Shulchan Aruch* he writes of up to a *kebeitzah* of bread[21] and the *Mishnah Berurah*[22] also permits something more than this of an intoxicating drink. There is no limit to non-intoxicating drink.

(B) while standing: One who cannot go to *shul* to hear the *shofar* with the congregation, and hears it at home, must stand

13. סוסי׳ ז ד״ה אך יפה כתב
14. וראה בספר מקראי קודש הימים הנוראים סי׳ כט ובארחות חיים סי׳ תקפט ס״ק ג
15. מערכת ראש השנה סי׳ ב ס״ק לא
16. שמירת שבת כהלכתה פ״מ סע׳ מה
17. סי׳ תקפט סע׳ ג. קיצור שו״ע סי׳ קכט ס״ק יט
18. סי׳ תקפט סע׳ ג
19. כלל קמא סע׳ ז
20. הל׳ תפלה פ״ו סוה״ד
21. סי׳ רלב סע׳ ג
22. מ״ב שם ס״ק לה. וראה גם במ״ב סי׳ תלא ס״ק ו וסי׳ תרצב ס״ק יד

§2: Before blowing the *shofar,* the blessings "to hear the sound of the *shofar*" and *shehecheyanu* are recited.

GLOSS: *There is no difference if he recites the blessings for himself or,* [(C)]*having already fulfilled the mitzvah, he recites them so that others may discharge their obligation.*

NISHMAT AVRAHAM

to hear the thirty blasts,[23] unless he is too ill or weak to do so.

(C) having already fulfilled the *mitzvah*: What is the *halachah* regarding someone who is either sick or weak who lives in an apartment on an upper floor and cannot walk down the stairs and also finds no one who will come and blow the *shofar* for him at his home? May he use the elevator to go to *shul* and to return home, if a non-Jew operates it? It would appear that this would depend on the controversy as to whether making a fire on *Yom Tov* is forbidden by Torah or Rabbinic law (see above, *Siman* 502A). According to the *Taz* who rules that the prohibition is by Torah law, and according to the *Chazon Ish* who rules that electricity is prohibited because of the *melachah* of "building"[24] (the making and breaking of electrical circuits when an elevator is operated), this would be forbidden. Although the elevator is operated by a non-Jew, asking him to operate it is forbidden on *Yom Tov* as it is on *Shabbat,* even when done for the purpose of performing a *mitzvah.*[25] On the other hand, according to most *poskim,* making a fire on *Yom Tov* is only prohibited by Rabbinic law. Asking a non-Jew to perform a Rabbinically forbidden task is permitted if it is for a sick person or a *mitzvah*[26] and he may therefore use the elevator if operated by a non-Jew.

The *She'arim Metzuyanim BaHalachah*[27] rules that women, since they are exempted from the *mitzvah* of *shofar,* may not use an elevator to enable them to go to hear it blown. A further controversy regarding a woman who will not be able to hear the *shofar* blown is whether she need annul a vow. By Torah law women are exempt from the *mitzvah* of *shofar,* as they are from any positive command that is related to a particular time (see reference 17). Nevertheless, since this is a *mitzvah* that they have voluntarily accepted upon themselves,[28] it is as if they have taken a vow to hear the *shofar.* There are *poskim*[29] who rule that she must annul the implied vow; others[30] rule that she needn't, since she intends to return to her custom when she recovers. On the other hand, it could be that even those who are stringent would agree that in such a situation one may act leniently if she cannot find anyone to nullify her vow.[31] But, if we say that she has a Torah obligation because of a vow, she is then no different from a man, and if he would be permitted to use an elevator so should she. *Rav Auerbach zt"l* wrote to me that she would probably be forbidden to use an elevator since she could nullify her vow. [See above, *Siman* 550C as to the *Rav zt"l's* opinion regarding a vow or *minhag* that one has taken upon himself. However, in another context[32] he wrote to me

23. מ״ב ס״ק ב
24. סי׳ נ ס״ק ט
25. סי׳ שלא סע׳ ו ועיין גם במ״ב סי׳ תקיז ס״ק ט
26. סי׳ שז סע׳ ג. ועיין בסי׳ תרנה במ״ב ס״ק ג
27. סי׳ קלה ס״ק ד ובקו״א סי׳ קכט סע׳ יט
28. חיי אדם כלל קמא סוסע׳ ז
29. בן איש חי שנה א פ׳ נצבים סע׳ יז עפ״י יו״ד סי׳ ריד בש״ך ס״ק ב
30. מג״א סי׳ תקפא ס״ק יב. דגול מרבבה יו״ד שם
31. שו״ת יביע אומר ח״ב סי׳ ל אות ו
32. נשמת אברהם כרך ב יו״ד סי׳ פט ס״ק א (עמ׳ כו)

SIMAN 588:
THE TIME FOR SOUNDING THE *SHOFAR*

§2: If one hears the thirty blasts over a period of nine hours, he has (A)fulfilled his obligation even if he heard them from nine different people.

NISHMAT AVRAHAM

that if a *minhag* has been accepted by many, the controversy mentioned here remains in force.] *Rav Neuwirth shlita* told me that since the *Chayei Adam* (reference 28) writes that women did not accept this *mitzvah* upon themselves should there be suffering or illness, the ruling of the *She'arim Metzuyanim BaHalachah* is correct and, moreover, there is no need for her to have her implied vow nullified.

SIMAN 588

Introduction: A person who is unable to go to *shul* is obligated to hear a total of thirty blasts of the *shofar*. In *shul,* however, a total of one hundred or one hundred and one blasts are blown during the service. The *Shulchan Aruch* is referring to such an individual who is unable to go to *shul.*

(A) fulfilled his obligation: The *Magen Avraham*[1] rules that if the interruptions were unavoidable, he has to hear the blasts all over again. The *Biur Halachah*[2] questions this: For the *Magen Avraham* himself in *Siman* 65 ruled that one should only act stringently if the interruptions were in the *mitzvah* itself, for instance, if the person's body was unclean or if the place where he was lying was unclean. This is appropriate when the *mitzvah* is to pray, to recite *birkat hamazon,* the *Hallel* or the *Megillah* since one is forbidden to say *Hashem's* Name or words of Torah in unclean surroundings. This, however, is not comparable to hearing the *shofar,* which itself is the *mitzvah.* Where, asks the *Biur Halachah* do we find that it is forbidden to perform a *mitzvah* if one's body or surroundings are unclean? Is it forbidden to wear a *tallit* in these circumstances? However, continues the *Biur Halachah,* the *Mateh Ephraim* writes that if a person started to blow the *shofar* and then became incontinent of urine, he waits until the flow stops and then returns to blowing the *shofar* from the beginning. If, however, he continued to blow while he was incontinent, or even after he found feces near him, he has fulfilled his obligation, but nevertheless should repeat the *mitzvah* without reciting a blessing. Thus we see, continues the *Biur Halachah,* that the *Mateh Ephraim* does compare the blowing of the *shofar* to the recitation of the *Shema.* One may possibly explain this to be so because one should have a positive intent when performing a commandment of *Hashem,* and this frame of mind in itself is likened to words of Torah. This may be compared to the ruling of the *Rama* in *Siman* 84 that it is forbidden to answer "*Amen*" in a bathhouse and this is no different from thinking words of Torah in these circumstances. Furthermore, the *Talmud* (*Rosh Hashanah* 33a) forbids one to clean the *shofar* with urine since this would show a lack of respect, even though the *shofar* is only the means through which the *mitzvah* is performed.

Rav Auerbach zt"l wrote to me commenting that this *Biur Halachah* needs further study, for the positive intent to

1. מג״א ס״ק ב, מובא במ״ב ס״ק ו

2. ביה״ל ד״ה שמע ט׳ תקיעות

perform a commandment of *Hashem* is only necessary at the start of the *mitzvah,* and at that time he was not incontinent. Second, he asked: Is it forbidden to wear the *tallit katan* in a bathhouse or lavatory even though it is forbidden to think Torah thoughts there? The *Biur Halachah* himself rules in *Siman* 60[3] that a person who does not have a positive intent to perform *Hashem's* commandment at the time that he performs it, transgresses a positive commandment. If so, in a bathhouse, where he may not have such thoughts in his mind about the *tallit katan* that he is wearing, he would be transgressing a positive commandment.

Rav Waldenberg shlita wrote to me[4] that many great *poskim* have previously dealt with this question. Thus, the *Halachot Ketanot*[5] wrote that although, given a choice, he is forbidden to blow the *shofar* or take the *lulav* in unclean surroundings, nevertheless, if he did so he has fulfilled his obligation. This is also true if he was unable to find clean surroundings. As to wearing the *tallit katan,* he should cover it in the bathhouse or lavatory. Thus, writes *Rav Waldenberg shlita,* according to this, someone who becomes unclean because of circumstances beyond his control, and stopped blowing the *shofar,* need not repeat the previous blasts. He quotes the *Chida*[6] who also deals with the question whether or not one may perform the act of a *mitzvah* in an unclean place without any thoughts regarding it. The *Chida* argues from the *Gemara*[7] which states that one need not stand before a scholar in a bathhouse or bathroom (lavatory) because in these circumstances it is not an act of respect. Therefore, if it wasn't for this lack of respect, one could perform such a *mitzvah* in such places. However, the *Chida* then quotes a *Zohar* that the surroundings must be clean before one can perform a *mitzvah.* Although the *Chida* writes that the *Zohar* may refer only to a place which he could have cleaned and did not, and not to a place over which he has no control, such as an unclean prison, he nevertheless concludes that the question requires further thought. *Rav Waldenberg shlita* continues, quoting the *Ikrei HaDat*[8] who rules according to the lenient argument of the *Chida* and adds that we see that the *Rama*[9] also rules that one may perform ritual slaughter in a slaughterhouse even if it is unclean, since he only warns the slaughterer to move away a distance of four *cubits* before reciting the blessing. Therefore, *Rav Waldenberg shlita* concludes that according to all the above *poskim,* he need only continue blowing the *shofar* from where he had to stop. He also points out that both the *Halachot Ketanot* and the *Chida* mentioned above hint at *Rav Auerbach zt"l's* comment that one can have the necessary intent to perform the commandment at the beginning and then actually perform it without further thought.

Rav Neuwirth shlita told me that a doctor who is occupied with patient care is exempt from the *mitzvah* of *shofar.* However, if he is able to find the opportunity to hear at least the thirty statutory blasts, he should do so, even if the opportunity arises before he has prayed *Shacharit* or *Mussaf.*

A doctor who is called to treat a *seriously* or *possibly seriously ill* patient should leave immediately even if he had just begun to hear the *shofar.* When he later has

---

3. סי׳ ס סע׳ ד ביה״ל ד״ה וי״א. ועיין בקובץ שיעורים כתובות סי׳ רנ

4. בהערה לנשמת אברהם כרך א או״ח עמ׳ שמג. שו״ת ציץ אליעזר חט״ו סי׳ לב אות יב

5. ח״ב סי׳ נז

6. ספר טוב עין סי׳ יח אות לז

7. קידושין לב ע״ב

8. או״ח סי׳ ג אות טו

9. יו״ד סי׳ יט סע׳ א

SIMAN 589:
WHO IS FIT TO BLOW THE *SHOFAR*

§2: (A)A deaf-mute, a *shoteh* and a minor are exempt. Someone who is only deaf and exempt, may not blow in order for others to fulfill their obligation.

GLOSS: *A mute may blow the shofar for others to fulfill their obligation.*

SIMAN 591:
THE ORDER OF *MUSSAF* FOR AN INDIVIDUAL

§8: If one must pray the *Mussaf* prayer on *Rosh Hashanah* without a congregation, (A)he should not do so until after the first quarter of the day has passed.

NISHMAT AVRAHAM

the opportunity, he should try to hear at least thirty blasts (if he has not already done so), and if this is not possible, at least the remainder of the thirty blasts that he has not heard. If he already heard the blessing over the *shofar* before he was called out, it is not repeated when he hears the remainder of the blasts later on.

SIMAN 589

(A) A deaf-mute: The *Mishnah Berurah*[1] rules that a person who must use a hearing trumpet is obligated to hear the *shofar*. As to one who uses a hearing-aid, see the writings of *Rav Auerbach zt"l.*[2]

The *Kaf HaChaim*[3] writes that a blind man is also obligated by Torah law to hear the *shofar,* and although *Rabbeinu Yerucham*[4] rules that his obligation is only Rabbinic, the *Radvaz*[5] and the *Pri Chadash*[6] disagree. See also the *Magen Avraham*[7] and the *Mishnah Berurah.*[8]

A woman is exempt from this *mitzvah.*[9] However, since in practice women have taken this *mitzvah* upon themselves, a woman who has the opportunity to do so should, if at all possible, listen to at least thirty blasts. This would have practical consequences for female health-care workers (doctors, nurses, etc.) on duty in a hospital.

SIMAN 591

(A) he should not do so: This *halachah* will apply to a patient who is unable to go to *shul* and prays at home[1] and to a doctor on duty who is too busy with patient care to be able to pray with the congregation.

---

1. מ״ב ס״ק ד
2. מנחת שלמה ח״א סי׳ ט אות א וח״ב סי׳ ד אות ל
3. ס״ק ו
4. נתיב יג ח״א
5. שו״ת סי׳ אלף קלא (ח״ד סי׳ נט)
6. כאן סע׳ ד
7. ס״ק א
8. סוס״ק יח
9. סי׳ תקפט סע׳ ג

1. ראה מ״ב ס״ק יג

SIMAN 594: ONE CANNOT FULFILL ANOTHER'S OBLIGATION TO PRAY WITH HIS PRAYER

§1: One may blow the *shofar* to have another fulfill his obligation of hearing the *shofar*. However, if one is unable to pray the *Shemoneh Esrei*, another is (A)unable to fulfill his obligation by praying for him.

GLOSS: *There are those who disagree and say that if he cannot pray, someone else may pray and have him fulfill his obligation thereby.*

SIMAN 600: AN EGG THAT WAS LAID ON *ROSH HASHANAH*

§1: An egg that was laid on the first day of the *Yom Tov* (of *Rosh Hashanah*), an animal that was trapped or a growth that was plucked on that day is (A)forbidden on the second.

NISHMAT AVRAHAM

SIMAN 594

(A) unable to fulfill his obligation: Even if his friend is about to pray silently but prays aloud to enable him to hear and thus fulfill his obligation. This is so although he is unable to pray himself. For one must ask for mercy himself and not through an intermediary. If, however, he is praying with a congregation, the *shaliach tzibbur* can fulfill his obligation for him, as the intermediary for the whole congregation.[1] But, if his friend prays aloud and he repeats the prayer after him word by word, he thereby fulfills his obligation,[2] provided that his friend is also praying for himself.[3] *Rav Neuwirth shlita,* however, asks rhetorically, even if his friend had already prayed, why can one not fulfill his obligation if he repeats every word after his friend? *Rav Auerbach zt"l* added that the friend should not, however, say *Hashem's* Name with the blessing.

SIMAN 600

(A) forbidden on the second: As to the taking of medications or other treatments, the second day of *Rosh Hashanah* has the same rulings as the first day.[1] This is in contradistinction to the two days of *Yom Tov* in the Diaspora, where the ruling regarding the second day is more lenient than the first day (see *Siman* 496A).

1. מ״ב ס״ק ב
2. שעה״צ ס״ק ג בשם הפמ״ג
3. כף החיים ס״ק ד

1. סי׳ תצו סע׳ ב. שו״ת אבני נזר או״ח סי׳ שצד, שצה. שמירת שבת כהלכתה פל״א סע׳ כח

§2: At the *Kiddush* on the second night (*he wears a new suit*) **he places a new fruit of the season on the table and says the** [(B)]***shehecheyanu* blessing. If such a fruit is not available** (*or a new suit*), **he, nevertheless, says the *shehecheyanu* blessing.**

NISHMAT AVRAHAM

(B) *shehecheyanu* blessing: On the second night of *Rosh Hashanah,* he says the *shehecheyanu* blessing after *Kiddush* bearing in mind that the blessing should apply both to the Festival day and to the fruit (or suit).[2] Following the blessing of *hamotzi,* he eats at least 27 grams of bread and then the fruit.[3] A male duty-doctor who lights Festival candles should recite the *shehecheyanu* blessing with the *Kiddush.* However, if he wishes to eat the fruit later in the meal, he may do so since *Chazal* instituted the *shehecheyanu* blessing to be said on seeing the new fruit of the season and not on eating it.[4]

A female doctor or nurse should light the Festival candles and recite the *shehecheyanu* blessing then. She should, if possible, light the candles immediately prior to *Kiddush* (from an already existing flame) so that the new fruit is eaten as soon as possible after saying *shehecheyanu*[5] (she may, if she wishes, make *Kiddush* later and eat the fruit during the meal – see above).[6] If she is reciting *Kiddush* she does not repeat this blessing.[7]

The above rules also apply to a hospitalized or bedridden patient.

2. מ״ב ס״ק ב
3. שמירת שבת כהלכתה פמ״ז סע׳ מד בהערה *
4. או״ח סי׳ רכה סע׳ ג. ביאור הגר״א כאן. והסכים אתי מו״ר הגרי״י נויבירט שליט״א
5. שמירת שבת כהלכתה שם הערה ** ופמ״ד הערה יד
6. כף החיים ס״ק ו
7. כף החיים סי׳ תקיד ס״ק קיב

CHAPTER TWENTY-SEVEN:

The Laws of Yom Kippur

SIMAN 612: THE PROHIBITION TO EAT ON *YOM KIPPUR* AND HOW MUCH IS CONSIDERED EATING

§1: A person who eats an amount equal to a (A)*kotevet* (a dried date) is culpable. This is a (B)little less than an egg. This

NISHMAT AVRAHAM

SIMAN 612

Introduction: A patient who is *non-seriously ill* is forbidden to eat or drink on *Yom Kippur*. On the other hand, a *seriously ill* patient may need to eat and/or drink on *Yom Kippur*. He may be permitted to eat and/or drink as usual or by *measure*. This decision will be made by a Rav, based on the objective and considered opinion of the patient's doctor.

(A) *kotevet* (date): Although the quantity for all forbidden foods carrying culpability is a *kezayit, Yom Kippur* is different. For the Torah does not use the term "eating" but rather "afflict your souls." *Chazal* knew that this referred to fasting and also that one who eats less than this quantity of food remains with the same pangs of hunger as before.[1]

(B) little less than an egg: This *measure* is the volume of two-thirds of a medium-sized egg including its shell[2] which, in today's terms, as ruled by the *poskim*,[3] is 27 to 30 grams. All these measurements are by volume.[4] However, since this is extremely difficult to measure, especially in the private home, the *poskim* give this measure of 27 to 30 grams to cover all foods and all specific gravities. *Rav Auerbach zt"l* told me in his latter years that one can recite a *berachah acharonah* (including *birkat hamazon*) on between 17 and 20 grams of food and that one fulfills his Torah obligation on the night of the *seder* if he eats this amount of machine-baked *matzah*. However, when I asked him if this would also mean that a *seriously ill* patient would only be allowed to eat that amount as a *measure* on *Yom Kippur*, he answered that one should not

1. ראה יומא עד ע״ב. מ״ב ס״ק א

2. מ״ב ס״ק ב ושעה״צ ס״ק ג

3. שמירת שבת כהלכתה פל״ט סע׳ יח. ועיין בשו״ת חת״ס או״ח סי׳ קכז ד״ה לכן נ״ל, דלענין יוהכ״פ משערים בבצים שלנו ולא אמרינן לקולא שנתקטנו הביצים

4. תשב״ץ ח״ב סי׳ רצא. שו״ת אבקת רוכל סוסי׳ נג. פרי חדש יו״ד סי׳ צט ס״ק ו. זבחי צדק סי׳ צח ס״ק ד. שו״ת יד הלוי יו״ד סי׳ ר. וראה באנציקלופדיה התלמודית ערך ביצה (ב) ד״ה קביעת השיעורים, כרך ג עמ׳ קמד.

ולגבי מחלוקת האחרונים אם נתקטנו הביצים בזמנינו או לא, עיין בצל״ח על פסחים קטז ע״א. הגר״א במעשה רב סי׳ קז. שו״ת חת״ס או״ח סי׳ קכז. חזו״א קונטרס השיעורים סי׳ לט. ספר שיעורין דאורייתא. שו״ת תשובה מאהבה ח״ג דף סח ע״ב. ספר שיעורי תורה סי׳ ג עמ׳ קעא. קובץ שיעורים ח״ב סי׳ מו סע׳ ג. פ״ת ומראה כהן ביו״ד סי׳ שכד סע׳ א. וראה גם בביה״ל סי׳ רעא סע׳ יג ד״ה של רביעית. ערוה״ש סי׳ קסח סע׳ יג. ושו״ת יחוה דעת ח״ד סי׳ נה

quantity is (C)the same for everyone whether he be a dwarf or a giant.

§2: (D)All foods eaten at one time are taken together to make up this measure, even the salt on the meat and the brine with the vegetable. However, (E)that which he eats and that which he drinks are considered separately and not added together.

§3: If he ate, stopped and ate again, so that the interval between the time he started and finished was *kedei achilat pras,* all that he ate is added together to decide whether he ate a "measure." If, however, the interval was longer than *kedei achilat pras,* the two quantities are considered separately.

NISHMAT AVRAHAM

change what has been accepted by generations of *poskim* that on *Yom Kippur* a *measure* is 30 grams (see end of **E**).

(C) the same for everyone: Although the *Shulchan Aruch* gives the *measure* for which one is considered liable by Torah law, nevertheless the Torah forbids one to eat even the smallest quantity. The *measure* has significance in speaking of a *seriously ill* patient who eats less than a *measure* each time he eats, as discussed later in *Siman* 618.[5]

(D) All foods: As explained later, the *measure* for solid foods is different from that for fluids. When a *seriously ill* patient eats solids and drinks fluids at the same time, the question of how one calculates *measures* must be considered. See **E** and **F.**

(E) that which he eats and that which he drinks: If he were to dip his bread into wine or water, their volume is added to that of the bread as if they were solids.[6] However, if he eats and drinks separately, they are not added together. But, there is a controversy about the fluid that soaks into the solid while in his mouth; perhaps it is like a condiment that makes the food palatable and is therefore considered part of it.[7]

I found it difficult to understand what the *Mishnah Berurah* meant in saying, "if he were to dip his bread into wine or water, their volume is added to that of the bread as if they were solid." Surely the bread will not swell as a result of soaking up the water or wine which will merely displace the air that it previously contained. And, since all our measurements are by volume and not by weight (see **B** above), the volume of bread will not change although its weight will. I asked a food scientist, Reb Dov (Roger) Becker to conduct a simple experiment to verify this. He dipped bread into hot coffee for one second and, although its weight increased by 70 percent its volume only increased by some 3 percent, some-

5. מ״ב ס״ק ג

6. מ״ב ס״ק ד ו־סי׳ רי ס״ק א. שדי חמד מערכת יוהכ״פ סי׳ ג ס״ק יט

7. הגרש״ז אויערבאך זצ״ל שמירת שבת כהלכתה פל״ט הערה פו

§4: As to the length of time of (F)*kedei achilat pras,* some say it is the time it takes to eat four eggs; others say the time it takes to eat three.

NISHMAT AVRAHAM

thing that was not discernible to the naked eye. After 10 seconds of soaking, the weight increased by 144 percent and its volume by 38 percent, again the latter not discernible to the naked eye. Soaking in tap water for 10 seconds produced an increase in weight of 166 percent whereas the volume increased by 15 percent only. I wondered whether this would be evidence that the volume of a *measure* does not take into consideration its air content, but does, however, take into account water or wine that has been soaked into it. The *Mishnah Berurah*[8] and the *Shemirat Shabbat Ke-Hilchatah*[9] write that the volume of a spongy food that is filled with air is measured by the food only and not the air that it holds. If, however, it is filled with water, one measures it with its hollow spaces.[10] True, the *Mishnah Berurah* writes that *matzah*[11] or bread,[12] even if spongy, need not be crushed or squashed to assess its true volume. But the eating of *matzah* or bread and eating by *measure* on *Yom Kippur,* are not comparable. The former involves a definition of "eating" – eating the required *matzah* on the night of the *seder,* or how much is required for a *berachah acharonah* – whereas the latter is concerned with "not feeling acutely hungry." *Rav Auerbach zt"l* wrote to me that since eating on *Yom Kippur* is dependent on one no longer feeling acutely hungry, the food itself, not counting the air it contains, should be less than the size of a dried date. The small and natural amount of air that is in a date, however, is part of the volume to be measured.

Thus although there may be a contradiction between the weight of a *measure* required for *matzah* or *berachah acharonah* on the one hand and that which is prohibited on *Yom Kippur* on the other, their volumes are the same. In the former the *measure* is that of the volume of *matzah* or bread as it is, whereas with *Yom Kippur,* where the concern is not "eating" but "not feeling acutely hungry," the *measure* is the food absorbed. The volumes are the same; it is the weights of the two *measures* which are different.

(F) *kedei achilat pras*: According to many *acharonim*[13] this is not a set time that is equal in all instances since there are times that food can be eaten more quickly than at others. For example it will take longer to eat something hot.[14]

Although the *Shulchan Aruch* brings the two opinions here, later in *Siman* 618 §7 he writes that *kedei achilat pras* is the time taken to eat four eggs (9 minutes).[15] The *Shulchan Aruch* here writes that this span of time is from when he starts to eat one *measure* to when he finishes eating the second. It is difficult to gauge this time accurately to be sure that one does not eat more than a *measure* in less than the allotted time.[16] Therefore these 9 minutes

8. סי׳ רי ס״ק א
9. שם
10. מ״ב סי׳ תפו ס״ק ג ושעה״צ שם ס״ק ז. מהר״ם שיק או״ח סי׳ רנט ו־רסד
11. סי׳ תפו ס״ק ג ושעה״צ ס״ק ז
12. עיין במ״ב סי׳ רי ס״ק א
13. מנחת חינוך מצוה שיג ס״ק ב ד״ה עוד צריך. תורת חסד להגאון מלובלין ח״א סי׳ לב. שדי חמד אסיפת דינים מערכת אכילה אות ג. ארחות חיים כאן ס״ק ד. וכן משמע מהמג״א סי׳ פא ס״ק ב והמ״ב שם ס״ק ג
14. שמירת שבת כהלכתה פל״ט הערה פב
15. שמירת שבת כהלכתה שם. וראה שם הערה סז שמקשה מלשון המ״ב סי׳ תריח ס״ק כא, ומתרץ שאולי כוונתו כפי שהובא כאן
16. שמירת שבת כהלכתה סע׳ יח

NISHMAT AVRAHAM

are counted from when he starts eating the *measure* to when he finishes it; in addition, he waits a further 9 minutes from the end of the first *measure* to the beginning of the eating of the second.[17] This prevents the possibility that he will eat most of the first *measure* towards the end of the 9 minutes and most of the second immediately after, thus eating more than a *measure* during 9 minutes.[18] If, however, in the doctor's opinion the patient needs to eat more often, the period of time between *measures* may be shortened, as is necessary, to a minimum of 2 minutes.[19]

A patient who is fed by naso-gastric tube or via a *PEG* may be fed as usual on *Yom Kippur,*[20] since the prohibition of eating only applies if both his throat and stomach enjoy the food.[21]

On *seder* night one acts stringently and eats the 30 grams of *matzah* within 2 to 4 minutes whereas on *Yom Kippur* the prohibition of eating (carrying culpability) is 30 grams of food eaten over 9 minutes. This is because in the former instance there is an obligation to eat, whereas in the latter, there is a prohibition against eating.[22]

It is vital to realize that a *measure* refers to quantity and not quality. The *Talmud*[23] states that the *measure* for rich meat (high calorie content) and for the leaves that grow around a vine (negligible calorie content) is identical. Therefore a *seriously ill* patient who must eat on *Yom Kippur* should be given foods with a high calorie content, thus possibly reducing the number of *measures* he will need to eat.[24] *Rav Auerbach zt"l* told me that a patient who only needs to drink, should preferably take milk with sugar, fresh juice (prepared the day before), or other substantial fluids rather than water.

DEFINITION OF A SOLID AND A LIQUID. The *measures* of a solid and a liquid are different. The *measure* for a solid is the size of a date (30 grams) to be eaten in no less than 9 minutes, whereas for a liquid,[25] the *measure* is *melo lugmav* (45 grams) to be drunk in no less than 9 minutes. How does one define foods such as porridge, sour cream or ice cream? The *Rambam*[26] writes that with the prohibition of eating forbidden foods, if *chametz* (during *Pesach*) or forbidden fat is melted in such a way that it can be gulped down, the *measure* carrying culpability is a *revi'it.* The *Radvaz*[27] rules that the *measure* for whatever is chewed or gulped down [*author's note — such as ice cream, porridge, sour cream*], is 30 grams whereas for fluids it is *melo lugmav.* This is also the opinion of many *acharonim.*[28] On the other hand, there is a controversy as to whether a raw egg is a solid[29] or a

17. שמעתי ממו״ר הגרי״י נויבירט שליט״א

18. שמירת שבת כהלכתה שם הערה סז. החזו״א סי׳ לט ס״ק יח

19. שמירת שבת כהלכתה שם לפי החת״ס ח״ו סי׳ טז וסי׳ כג. וראה גם בארחות חיים כאן ס״ק ד, שו״ת מהר״ם שיק או״ח סי׳ פה ד״ה ולפי״ז, קונטרס השיעורים להגרא״ח נאה זצ״ל ס״ק יח, ערוה״ש סי׳ תריח סע׳ יד וסי׳ רב סע׳ ח וכף החיים סי׳ רי ס״ק א שדנים בשיטות השונות להזמן של כדי אכילת פרס

20. שו״ת חלקת יעקב ח״ג סי׳ סח. שו״ת מחזה אברהם ח״א סי׳ קכט

21. אגלי טל מלאכת טוחן ס״ק סב (ב). וראה מנחת חינוך מצוה שיג. חת״ס או״ח סי׳ קכז. שו״ת אחיעזר סי׳ לא סוס״ק ד וח״ג סי׳ סא וארחות חיים סי׳ תריב סע׳ א

22. כף החיים סי׳ רי ס״ק ח

23. יומא פ ע״ב. וראה באור שמח פי״ד מהלכות מאכ״א הי״ד ושו״ת חת״ס ח״ו סוסי׳ כג

24. וכן אמר לי מו״ר הגרי״י נויבירט שליט״א

25. ראה להלן סע׳ י

26. הל׳ מאכ״א פי״ד ה״ט

27. לשונות הרמב״ם סי׳ אלף תקיח (קמה)

28. שו״ת קול אליהו ח״א או״ח סי׳ ז. בן איש חי שנה א פ׳ מסעי סע׳ ח. כף החיים סי׳ רב ס״ק סג. שו״ת זרע אברהם ח״א או״ח סי׳ ג. וכן שמעתי מהגרב״צ אבא שאול זצ״ל

29. אור שמח הל׳ טומאת אוכלין פ״ח הי״ג. שו״ת חת״ס יו״ד סי׳ יט. מטה אפרים סי׳ תריב בקצה המטה ס״ק יב. קובץ שיעורים על ביצה אות ב. שו״ת הר צבי

§6: If one ate food that was [(G)]not fit for consumption or he ate on *Yom Kippur* night when he was so full from the meal he had eaten before *Yom Kippur* that he loathed food, he is not considered culpable.

NISHMAT AVRAHAM

liquid.[30]

However, *Rav Auerbach zt"l* wrote to me asking: How do you know that sour cream is a food? It is more likely that it is a drink. Also porridge (made from flour) is probably to be considered a mixture of flour and milk where the milk is not like the brine on vegetables. Even when one sucks the juice out of a grape, even though he does not chew, nevertheless it is probably to be considered a food (there is a discussion about this in the *Mayim Chaim* of the *Pri Chadash*). There are *acharonim* who consider a raw egg to be food even when drunk and not chewed. But an egg may be different since it is usually eaten as a food. Thus it is forbidden if cooked by a non-Jew since it is not usually eaten raw. The *Ra'avad*[31] considers pomegranate and apple juice as fruit with regard to the *halachah* of ritual impurity – they also need to first come into contact with water (as does any other food) before they can become ritually impure. Nevertheless, with regard to *Yom Kippur,* they are considered to be drinks in every respect. Sucking a candy (sweet) also needs consideration. Ice cream is also probably a food although it is not chewed. In short, continues the *Rav zt"l,* I have my doubts whether the *Radvaz* (above) meant his ruling to include *Yom Kippur* where the issue is "not feeling acutely hungry." The definition perhaps depends on how something is consumed, in which case both sour cream and ice cream would be considered food.

(G) not fit for consumption: Even a *non-seriously ill* patient may swallow pills with a bitter taste, if necessary.[32] However, in order to comply with all the *poskim,* it is advisable to wrap the pill in thin paper and swallow it.[33] He may not drink water to help him swallow it. It is therefore most advisable that such a patient should practice swallowing his pills without water during the days preceding *Yom Kippur*. If, however, he is unsuccessful and it is essential that he take his pills that day, he should "spoil" the water that he will drink with his pills. *Rav Auerbach zt"l* and *Rav Eliashiv shlita* both agreed that he may do so by adding a drop of liquid soap or, where practicable, dissolving a tiny amount of the pill to be taken, in the water. There should be enough to give the water a slightly bitter taste. Less than a *measure* of this water may then be swallowed with the pills. *Rav Neuwirth shlita* wrote to me that if this was not sufficient, more than a *measure* could be taken, if necessary, since the water was "spoiled."[34]

If, on the other hand, he is a *seriously ill* patient or would become so if he did not take his pills, and he cannot swallow them

---

או״ח ח״א סי׳ קא. חזו״א טבול יום סי׳ ד סוס״ק י. שיעורי תורה להגרא״ח נאה זצ״ל דף קמג

30. הגר״ש קלוגר ספר החיים הל׳ יוהכ״פ סי׳ תריב ד״ע ע״ג. שו״ת הרי בשמים תליתאה סי׳ עג. גינת ורדים כלל א סי׳ יז. מעשה רוקח פי״ד מהל׳ מאכ״א ה״ט. שדי חמד מערכת יוהכ״פ סי׳ ג. שו״ת צפנת פענח הוצאת הגרמ״מ כשר, ירושלים תשכ״ה סי׳ יא

31. פ״א מטו״א ה״ד

32. שדי חמד מערכת יוהכ״פ סי׳ ג ס״ק ח. ישועות יעקב סי׳ תריב. שו״ת כתב סופר או״ח סי׳ קיא. פתחי תשובה יו״ד סי׳ קנה ס״ק ו. שו״ת שואל ומשיב מהדו״ד ח״א סי׳ נה. ארחות חיים סי׳ תריח ס״ק א. שו״ת אג״מ או״ח ח״ג סי׳ צא. שו״ת ציץ אליעזר ח״י סי׳ כה פכ״ב. שמירת שבת כהלכתה פל״ט סע׳ ח

33. הגרש״ז אויערבך זצ״ל בשמירת שבת כהלכתה שם

34. שמעתי ממנו שכך היתה כוונתו במה שכתב לי בנשמת אברהם

§9: If one drinks a [(H)]*melo lugmav* on *Yom Kippur,* he is culpable. This volume is measured on an individual basis and is the amount that would fill one cheek. It is [(I)]less than a *revi'it* in the average person. All liquids drunk are added together to make up this quantity.

§10: If he drank a little, waited and then drank some more, and the time interval between the beginning of drinking the first amount to the end of the second is [(J)]enough to have drunk a *revi'it,* the two amounts are added together. [(K)]There are those who say that the time interval is *kedei achilat pras* (and not the time it takes to drink a *revi'it*).

NISHMAT AVRAHAM

without water, he is permitted to take the minimum amount of water necessary to do so.[35]

A healthy person who nevertheless needs to take pills to prevent him becoming *non-seriously ill* (for example taking pills to prevent a severe attack of migraine) may take them without water.[36] If at all possible, it would be preferable to take the medication as a suppository.

All the laws concerning treatment on *Shabbat* apply equally to *Yom Kippur.*[37]

(H) *melo lugmav*: *Chazal* knew that this quantity would be enough to satisfy one's acute thirst.[38] *Rav Auerbach zt''l* wrote to me that he was not certain as to whether false dentures would reduce the amount of *melo lugmav.* Similarly, if someone had his teeth extracted before *Yom Kippur,* would this make the quantity larger; and if he had new dentures made just before *Yom Kippur,* would his *melo lugmav* be smaller?

(I) less than a *revi'it*: In an average adult, this is about 40 to 45 cc.[39] *Rav Auerbach zt''l* wrote to me that it is important to emphasize and remind a patient who needs to drink, even if only by *measure,* that he should ask his doctor before *Yom Kippur* the total amount of fluid he will need. Since it is very difficult to measure a *melo lugmav* by attempting to fill one cheek to its full, one should fill one's whole mouth as much as possible; half this quantity is certainly less than a *melo lugmav.* If possible this should be measured before *Yom Kippur.*

(J) enough to have drunk a *revi'it*: If possible, the patient should wait 9 minutes between finishing one measure and starting the next but if not, at least 2 minutes.[40]

(K) There are those who say: It would appear from the way the *Shulchan Aruch* writes that he rules according to the first opinion.[41] Although the *Pri Chadash* and the *Gra* rule like the second opinion,[42] the *Mishnah Berurah*[43] rules like the first. Therefore if 9 minutes is too long for him to wait between drinks, he should

35. שו״ת אג״מ שם
36. שמעתי ממו״ר הגרי״י נויבירט שליט״א
37. שמירת שבת כהלכתה פל״ט סע׳ לה
38. מ״ב ס״ק כג
39. שמירת שבת כהלכתה פל״ט סע׳ כ
40. שו״ת חת״ס ח״ו סי׳ טז וסי׳ כג. שמירת שבת כהלכתה שם
41. והוא דעת הרמב״ם הל׳ שביתת עשור פ״ב ה״ד
42. והוא דעת הראב״ד הל׳ תרומות פ״י ה״ג מהמ״ב ס״ק לא
43. סי׳ רי שעה״צ ס״ק יב

SIMAN 613: IT IS FORBIDDEN TO WASH ON *YOM KIPPUR*

§4: A person of delicate nature who does not feel good until he has washed his face, may do so.

GLOSS: *The custom is not to do so. One does not even wash one's eyes which has* (A)*some medicinal value. It is forbidden to wash one's mouth on Yom Kippur as explained earlier, Siman* 567:3.

SIMAN 614: WEARING LEATHER SHOES

§3: A woman, for (A)**thirty days after giving birth, or a sick person, even if not seriously ill, may wear leather shoes; so too one who has a wound in his foot.**

NISHMAT AVRAHAM

drink a *melo lugmav* each time, wait a short while and then drink again, or else drink spoonful after spoonful slowly[44]

SIMAN 613

(A) some medicinal value: However, it is permitted, if necessary for a medical reason, provided that this would also be permitted on *Shabbat;*[1] for example, if there is *danger to a limb,* or if one feels unwell in his whole body. Since washing the eyes with water does not involve a *melachah,* it would be permitted even though he is not a *non-seriously ill* patient. Although it might seem that this should nevertheless be forbidden because of *Yom Kippur,* the *Rama*[2] informs us that it is permitted. However, if he had a problem with his eye, it is forbidden to do any *melachah* even if it is only Rabbinically forbidden unless the problem is as serious as the one discussed above in *Siman* 328 §9, 20 and 21.[3]

SIMAN 614

(A) thirty days after giving birth: One who is ill, including one who has difficulty in walking without leather shoes because of a wound in his foot, may wear them.[1] It would appear that *Chazal* did not ban leather shoes for one in discomfort, although they were strict and did not allow washing for similar reasons. This is because washing has some therapeutic value[2] and the prohibition to prevent "grinding herbs" was made specifically for one who has discomfort, unless the discomfort is so great that he is in the category of a *non-seriously ill* patient. If, however, one can manage without wearing leather shoes (even if he is permitted to wear them), he should act stringently.[3] *Rav Auerbach zt"l* wrote to me: "I believe that there is no mention in our sources that a patient or woman after childbirth should try to wear non-leather shoes. It is

44. ביה״ל כאן ד״ה אם. שמירת שבת כהלכתה שם. וראה בשו״ת יביע אומר ח״ב סי׳ לא

1. מ״ב ס״ק י

2. סוף סע׳ ט כאן

3. שעה״צ ס״ק יג

1. שמירת שבת כהלכתה פל״ט סע׳ לד

2. ראה סי׳ תריג סע׳ ד ורמ״א סע׳ ג

3. מטה אפרים סע׳ ג

SIMAN 617:
THE LAWS CONCERNING A WOMAN WHO IS PREGNANT, NURSING OR HAS JUST GIVEN BIRTH

§1: [(A)]A pregnant woman or a nursing mother must fast on *Yom Kippur*.

NISHMAT AVRAHAM

therefore possible that they may wear leather shoes, since even according to the opinion that it is forbidden by Torah law to wear leather shoes, nevertheless the Torah permitted *Chazal* to decide if there were to be exceptions. However, I am unsure whether to permit this in practice."

Rav Auerbach zt"l[4] writes: If an *onen* on *Tishah B'Av* would find it difficult to deal with all the arrangements for burial while wearing non-leather shoes, he would be permitted to wear leather shoes. This holds true for one who became an *onen* while sitting *shivah* for another relative (see *Tosafot*).[5] However, if he were to become an *onen* on *Yom Kippur,* it requires further thought if he may wear leather shoes to make those preparations that are permitted (see *Siman* 71 §2). However, since nowadays non-leather shoes are available that are just as good as leather ones, it would possibly be forbidden to wear leather shoes. Thought is required, too, whether the ruling of the *Shulchan Aruch* here permitting a woman to wear leather shoes for thirty days following childbirth, holds true nowadays.

SIMAN 617

(A) A pregnant woman: It is becoming almost common practice nowadays for doctors to tell pregnant women that they must drink on *Yom Kippur*. There are those who limit their advice to women in the first or last trimester whereas others do not differentiate. This, though there is no evidence that a healthy woman with a normal, uncomplicated pregnancy and with no history of previous fasting-induced miscarriages has any higher risk of having a miscarriage as a result of fasting.[1] That she may go into labor so dehydrated (at the end of the day) that she will be at greater risk than otherwise is also a very slim possibility. *Rav Auerbach zt"l* and *Rav Neuwirth shlita* both told me that as long as she feels well she is obligated to fast. If necessary she should remain at home resting. *Rav Auerbach zt"l* commented in writing: However if she feels really unwell, it is desirable that she starts to drink by *measure*. However, as soon as she feels the first regular contractions, she should start to drink to correct her state of dehydration. *Rav Neuwirth shlita* wrote to me that if necessary, she may drink regular quantities of fluids so that her dehydration is corrected before she gives birth.

As to a woman who underwent a successful in-vitro fertilization (I.V.F.), the risk of miscarriage is higher during the first few weeks than in a normal pregnancy. Since we are unsure how the stress of a fast will affect such a pregnancy which is at a higher risk during these first weeks, *Rav Auerbach zt"l* told me that she should drink by *measure* during this time.

The *Orchot Chaim*[2] writes that accord-

4. מנחת שלמה ח"א סי' כה אות ח

5. מו"ק כג ע"ב ד"ה ואינו

1. BMJ 304:521, '92. Arch. Dis. Child. 65:1053, '90. JAMA 250:1317, '83

וראה בשמירת שבת כהלכתה פל"ט הערה לב

2. ס"ק א

§3: Anyone who smells a food and becomes so ravenous for it that it (B)shows on his face, is considered to be in danger if not given of that food. He is therefore given it.

NISHMAT AVRAHAM

ing to the opinion of the *Rosh* and the *Ran*[3] (see above, *Siman* 330Q), a woman who has miscarried twice as a result of fasting may be permitted to eat on *Yom Kippur* if there is a suspicion that this may happen again were she to fast. Even if the fetus is less than forty days old she may eat. The *Shemirat Shabbat KeHilchatah,*[4] however, qualifies this to mean that she should eat by *measure.*

The *Biur Halachah*[5] writes that if a nursing mother's baby is *seriously ill* and refuses to feed except from her breast, she should not fast even on *Yom Kippur,* if her doing so may increase the danger to the baby. This is also the ruling of the *Chatam Sofer,*[6] the *Maharsham,*[7] the *Sha'are Teshuvah*[8] and the *Katzeh HaMateh.*[9] If the baby is healthy, the *Har Tzvi*[10] writes, disagreeing with the *Chazon Ish,*[11] if the mother has just enough milk for the baby to exist were she to fast, then even though he is used to more, she must fast since there is no danger to him. The ruling of the *Biur Halachah* applies only in the situation where the baby is sick. If the baby were to become *seriously ill* without its mother's milk should she fast, she should first see whether he would be satisfied if she only drank by *measure.*[12]

The *Chatam Sofer*[13] writes that one is certainly obligated to fast even if he would have to lie in bed all day, rather than go to *shul.* If as a result of going to *shul* he would need to eat or drink any quantity no matter how small, he would be breaking Torah law.[14] *Rav Auerbach zt"l*[15] ruled that even a patient who is drinking by *measure* should stay at home and not pray with the congregation, if this means that he would require even one less *measure* of drink.[16]

(B) shows on his face: See above, *Siman* 329 §10D. The *Mishnah Berurah*[17] rules that he is only given enough to eat to set his mind at rest. However, once this has been achieved, he must fast the rest of the day. This is also the opinion of the *Katzeh HaMateh,*[18] quoting the *Rashba,*[19] the *Shoel U'Meshiv,*[20] the *Maharsham*[21] and the *Lechem HaPanim.*[22] It is interesting that although *Rav Yaakov Etlinger z"l,* in his *Aruch LaNer,*[23] disagrees with this ruling, in his *Binyan Tzion*[24] he concurs. The *Sdei Chemed,*[25] noting this apparent discrepancy, explains that in the *Aruch LaNer* he is discussing a case where he needed to eat more than a *measure* and

3. בשם הבה״ג והרמב״ן
4. פל״ט הערה לב
5. ד״ה עוברות
6. שו״ת ח״ו סי׳ כג
7. דעת תורה ס״ק א
8. סי׳ תקנד ס״ק ו
9. על המטה אפרים ס״ק א
10. שו״ת או״ח סי׳ רא סוס״ק א
11. או״ח סי׳ נט ס״ק ג
12. כף החיים ס״ק ב. וראה גם בשו״ח חת״ס ח״ו סי׳ כג
13. שם
14. יומא עד ע״א. או״ח סי׳ תריב סע׳ ה
15. שמירת שבת כהלכתה פל״ט הערה צד
16. ראה גם בשדי חמד מערכת יוהכ״פ סי׳ ג ס״ק ד
17. ס״ק ז
18. ס״ק ד
19. קדושין כא ע״ב ד״ה רב אמר
20. מהד״ד ח״א סי׳ כ
21. ח״ד סי׳ קמה אות ג
22. על הקיצור שו״ע סי׳ קלג סע׳ טו
23. על התוס׳ כריתות יח ע״ב ד״ה הא דנקט
24. שו״ת בנין ציון ח״א סי׳ לד
25. מערכת יוהכ״פ סי׳ ג ס״ק ו

§4: **(C)A woman who has just given birth should not fast during the first three days (after birth). From the third to the seventh day she is allowed to eat if she feels the need. After this she is like everyone else. These "days" are not (D)24-hour periods each from the time of birth (but calendar days). Thus if she gave birth on the seventh of Tishrei towards evening, she may not eat on *Yom Kippur* (the tenth) unless she feels the need. Although the first three full days (24-hour periods) are not completed until towards evening on Yom Kippur, nevertheless since it is the fourth day after the birth,** *(part of the seventh, eighth, ninth and the tenth of Tishrei — author's note)* ***Yom Kippur* is considered to be the fourth day.**

NISHMAT AVRAHAM

thus no longer could be considered to be keeping the *mitzvah* of "afflicting the soul" (see *Siman* 612: Introduction). However, if he ate less than this he must continue to fast.[26]

The *Kaf HaChaim*[27] rules that if a *seriously ill* patient who is permitted to eat, eats more than is necessary, he has transgressed. *Rav Auerbach zt"l* told me that it is forbidden for a *seriously ill* patient who must eat normally on *Yom Kippur* to have a candy (sweet) between meals since he is not eating it for its calorie content but for pleasure.

On the other hand, a patient who may not fast the whole day, should preferably start eating by *measure* in the morning (even though he is not hungry), rather than wait till later. By doing so he may be able to prevent a deterioration in his condition which would force him to eat more than a *measure* later.[28]

(C) A woman who has just given birth: This includes a woman who has had a miscarriage after forty days of conception.[29] However the *Maharsham,*[30] quoting *Rav Akiva Eiger,* writes that she should be given food during the first three days even though she has not asked for it, only if she miscarried at term. If she miscarried before then she is not given to eat during the first three days if she says she does not need it.

(D) 24-hour periods each: For details of this *halachah* see above, *Siman* 330H and I. The *acharonim* rule leniently[31], that is, three days are the full 72 hours from the moment of birth and not just three calendar days, where part of a day would be counted as a full day (the opinion of the *Shulchan Aruch*). Nevertheless she should eat, if possible, by *measure.*[32] The

26. וראה במקראי קודש הימים הנוראים ח״א סי׳ לט. שו״ת הר צבי או״ח ח״א סי׳ קנה

27. סי׳ תרטז ס״ק כד בשם המנחת חינוך מצוה שיג ס״ק י

28. מקראי קודש הימים הנוראים ח״א סי׳ לט בהררי קודש. הגרש״ז אויערבאך זצ״ל בשמירת שבת כהלכתה פל״ט הערה סט

29. ביה״ל כאן. שדי חמד מערכת יוהכ״פ סי׳ ג סוס״ק א

30. דעת תורה ס״ק ד

31. מטה אפרים סע׳ ד וראה שם בקצה המטה ס״ק ט. כף החיים ס״ק כב. שדי חמד מערכת יוהכ״פ סי׳ ג אות ג. מ״ב ס״ק יג. שמירת שבת כהלכתה פל״ט סע׳ טו. הגר״ע יוסף שליט״א לוית חן סי׳ צה עמ׳ קנט ושו״ת יביע אומר ח״ז סי׳ נג אות ז

32. שעה״צ ס״ק יט

SIMAN 618: THE PATIENT ON *YOM KIPPUR*

§1: If a (A)specialist doctor, Jew or gentile, says that if a (B)patient will not eat, his condition might get worse to the

NISHMAT AVRAHAM

Elef LaMateh[33] writes that it is possible that the *Terumat HaDeshen*[34] (the source of this *halachah*) and the *Shulchan Aruch* would agree that should there be even a slight possibility of danger, one would rule leniently. Thus, according to the *Shulchan Aruch* if she gave birth on the seventh of Tishrei, say at 10 A.M., since she would be starting the fourth day on *Yom Kippur* (the tenth of Tishrei), she would have to fast on *Yom Kippur*. However, according to the lenient ruling she would be allowed to eat on *Yom Kippur* until 10 A.M. and then would have to fast for the rest of the day. There is the same controversy as to whether a day is a 24-hour period or a calendar day with respect to the days from the fourth to the seventh and from the seventh to the remainder of the thirty days (see details in *Siman* 330I).

One may ask, why does the *Shulchan Aruch* rule strictly when the general consensus[35] is that we act leniently if there is the slightest chance of danger to life, as the *Shulchan Aruch* himself rules?[36] However, the *Terumat HaDeshen*[37] himself explains that since giving birth is a natural phenomenon and not an illness, it is different from any other situation of serious illness.

SIMAN 618

(A) specialist doctor: The *Mishnah Berurah*[1] writes that any Jew who says that he has knowledge of the patient's illness, and that he must eat, should be listened to, even against the opinion of the patient[2] (see also *Siman* 328 §10E).

(B) patient: The *Chinuch*[3] and the *Darchei Teshuvah*[4] both write that it is fitting to give a *non-seriously ill* patient who feels very weak to eat by *measure*. However the *Minchat Chinuch*,[5] the *Mishneh LaMelech*,[6] the *Pri Chadash*[7] and the *Ketav Sofer*[8] all disagree; for how can one permit setting aside Torah Law (eating even the smallest amount is forbidden) for a *non-seriously ill* patient. The *Sdei Chemed*,[9] *Rav Tzvi Pesach Frank zt"l*[10] and *Rav Ovadiah Yosef shlita*[11] write that perhaps the *Chinuch* meant that the patient was so weak that there was a possibility that fasting would be dangerous. However, if there was no danger he would certainly also forbid the patient to eat.

What is the *halachah* regarding feeding

33. ס״ק ד

34. סי׳ קמח

35. יומא פה ע״א תוסד״ה ולפקח. שו״ע סי׳ שכח סע׳ ה לפי התיקון של המ״ב ס״ק יז

36. סי׳ של סע׳ א

37. סי׳ קמח

1. ס״ק א

2. וראה במג״א ס״ק א בשם הרא״ש ושעה״צ ס״ק י שאין עכו״ם נאמן אם אינו בקי. וכן ראה בביה״ל ד״ה חולה ושמירת שבת כהלכתה פל״ט הערה טו לגבי רופא מומר

3. מצוה שיג

4. יו״ד סי׳ קנה ס״ק יח

5. ס״ק ה

6. הל׳ יסודי התורה פ״ה ה״ח ד״ה ודע שעדיין

7. סי׳ תסו

8. שו״ת או״ח סי׳ קיא

9. מערכת יוהכ״פ סי׳ ג אות ג

10. הימים הנוראים ח״א סי׳ מב

11. שו״ת יביע אומר ח״ב יו״ד סי׳ יב

point where he might become (C)dangerously ill, (D)he should be given to eat, and this is certainly so if there is a

NISHMAT AVRAHAM

a patient who although physically well is a *shoteh,* and is therefore exempt from all *mitzvot,* who does not eat or drink unless fed like a child? *Rav Neuwirth shlita* wrote to me that if fasting will harm him physically, he must be fed. If not, it would appear that since he is exempt from all *mitzvot,* if he were to take food and drink by himself there is no problem.[12] And if he cannot help himself? Although one may not cause even a *shoteh* to sin[13] (one may not put non-kosher food before him),[14] nevertheless eating what is forbidden is far different from eating what is kosher when one must fast.[15] The *Mishnah Berurah* rules[16] that one who is a *shoteh* may be given meat to eat and wine to drink during the week of *Tishah B'Av* – a *shoteh* may be fed kosher food on a fast day.[17] It would be preferable to feed him by *measure* if that is sufficient.

(C) dangerously ill: Even though the doctor only says that his condition might deteriorate to a point of possible danger, he is given to eat.[18]

(D) he should be given to eat: The *Haamek She'elah*[19] points out that according to the *Rif* and *Rambam,* a *seriously ill* patient is given to eat normally and not by *measure.* According to them the whole concept of eating by *measure* applies only to a pregnant woman who smelled and craved a given food (see above, *Siman* 617 §3), or to a *non-seriously ill* patient who might become *seriously ill* if not given to eat. This was also the ruling of *Rav Chaim Soloveitchik zt''l.*[20] His son, *Rav Yitzchak Ze'ev zt''l*[21] writes that he did not find any evidence to the contrary among the earlier poskim. This was also the ruling of *Rav Abramsky zt''l.*[22] However, in practice the *poskim* all rule like the *Shulchan Aruch.*[23] See also *Siman* 617B.

Incidentally, the *poskim* speak of a patient who, if he were to fast on the *Fast of Gedaliah* (the day following *Rosh Hashanah*), would probably have to eat on *Yom Kippur.* The *Aishel Avraham (Butasht)*[24] and the *Sdei Chemed*[25] nevertheless permit him to fast on the *Fast of Gedaliah.* Although the general rule is that a lighter *mitzvah* gives way to a more serious one where there is no possibility of keeping both, this is only when they are separated by no more than a day or two. However, if the interval between them is more than a few days, one perhaps should perform the lighter *mitzvah* lest he die in the interim and not have kept either.[26] The *Tzitz Eliezer*[27] rules that he should eat on the *Fast of Gedaliah* so that he will be able to fast on *Yom Kippur*[28] (see also *Siman* 683A).

12. עיין סי׳ שמג ובמ״ב ס״ק א
13. עיין במ״מ הל׳ שבת פ״כ ה״ז. או״ח סי׳ רסו במ״ב ס״ק יד. ועיין בנשמת אברהם כרך א או״ח עמ׳ רח בענין ״ספינן״
14. עיין סי׳ שמג במ״ב סוס״ק ד. שו״ת חת״ס או״ח סי׳ פג ד״ה אך לפע״ד. וע״ע סי׳ תרמ בשעה״צ ס״ק ח
15. עיין פסחים קו ע״ב תוסד״ה אישתלי
16. מ״ב סי׳ תקנד ס״ק י
17. וראה סי׳ רסט במג״א ס״ק א
18. מ״ב ס״ק ב
19. על השאילתות שאילתא קסז ס״ק יז דף שז
20. מובא במועדים בהלכה דיני יוהכ״פ פ״ב
21. חי׳ הגרי״ז הלוי הל׳ שביתת העשור
22. שמעתי מבנו ר׳ מנחם הי״ו
23. כל זה משמירת שבת כהלכתה פל״ט הערה כ
24. או״ח סי׳ תרב
25. מערכת יוהכ״פ סי׳ א ס״ק י
26. חיי אדם כלל סח ס״ק א. מחנה ישראל פ״י ס״ק ד
27. ח״י סי׳ כה פי״ד
28. והביא ראיה מהשו״ת הלכות קטנות ח״א סי׳ רצ. וראה גם בביה״ט או״ח סי׳ צ ס״ק יא ומ״ב סוס״ק כח

possibility that he might die. Even if the patient claims that he does not need to eat, (E)we follow the doctor's ad-

NISHMAT AVRAHAM

As to whether one needs to fear that he will die in the interim, the *acharonim*[29] point out an apparent contradiction in the *Rambam* if we do or do not.[30] The *Sha'ar HaMelech*[31] proves that up to seven days is a short time that one need not take into account. On the other hand, the *Aruch LaNer*[32] asks why should one not think even a year or two is a short time, since most people will not die within this time. He therefore explains that the *Rambam* does not differentiate between a short and long interval. Rather, he differentiates between a specific amount of time, even five years, since most people will not die within this interval, and an unspecified one. With the latter, even if short, one should take it into account because everyone will have to die sometime.

(E) we follow the doctor's advice: The patient may be too ill to realize the seriousness of his condition, even if he himself is a doctor.[33]

A *seriously ill* patient who, against medical advice, wishes to act strictly and fast, will be held to blame for any mishap, as the Torah says:[34] "But I will demand the blood of your souls."[35] His fasting is not an act of piety but one of shedding blood.[36] The *Shach*[37] points out that the patient has already sworn at Mount Sinai that he will keep the *mitzvah* of saving his life. *Mahari Asa'ad*[38] writes that there is no greater example than this of a *mitzvah* coming from sin, whereas the *Maharam Shick*[39] and the *Minchat Yitzchak*[40] put it that this is not a *mitzvah* but only a sin. The *Radvaz*[41] relates that when the *Riva* was ill during *Yom Kippur,* he was warned by his doctors that if he did not eat he would certainly die whereas if he ate he might live. The *Riva* said that since he was faced with only a possibility that he would live if he ate, he preferred to fast. He refused to eat and died. The *Radvaz* warns that we should not learn from what the *Riva* did, but explains that perhaps he felt that he would die regardless and thus preferred to fast. Indeed the *Mateh Ephraim*[42] writes that although one feeds a *seriously ill* patient even against his will, nevertheless, if he is close to death and wishes to fast, he should not be forced to eat. The *Tzitz Eliezer*[43] also rules that it is forbidden for a patient to act strictly. However *Rav Auerbach zt"l*[44] writes that if there is only a small possibility of danger, the patient may act strictly and fast. This ruling, he wrote to me, he bases on a passage in the *Kovetz Shiurim*[45] which argues that when the danger is small, one may act strictly in order to keep a *mitzvah*.

29. לחם משנה הל׳ נזירות פ״א ה״ד. שו״ת חכם צבי סי׳ קו. מג״א סי׳ תקסח ס״ק יג. נשמת אדם כלל סח ס״ק א

30. לחם משנה נזירות פ״א ה״ד. חכם צבי סי׳ קו. וראה גם במג״א סי׳ תקסח ס״ק יג ונשמת אדם כלל סח ס״ק א

31. הל׳ סוכה פ״ד ד״ה ועוד נראה לי

32. סוכה כד ע״א

33. מ״ב ס״ק ג

34. בראשית ט:ה

35. איסור והיתר סי׳ ס סע׳ ח. מ״ב ס״ק ה. מטה אפרים סע׳ טו

36. ר״ן יומא פב ע״א ד״ה חוץ. שו״ת רדב״ז סי׳ תתפה (ח״ג סי׳ תמד)

37. יו״ד סי׳ רלח ס״ק ח

38. שו״ת או״ח סי׳ קס

39. שו״ת או״ח סי׳ רס

40. שו״ת ח״ד סי׳ קב אות ב

41. שם

42. סע׳ ז. וראה שם באלף המטה שנשאר בצ״ע

43. ח״ח סי׳ טו פ״ג וח״י סי׳ כה פי״ד

44. שמירת שבת כהלכתה פל״ט הערה ד

45. פסחים אות לב

vice. If the patient (F)says that he needs to eat (G)he is heeded, even if a hundred doctors say that he does not need to.

NISHMAT AVRAHAM

(F) says that he needs: The *Mishnah Berurah*[46] quotes the *Radvaz*[47] that even if the doctors say that the food will harm him, we listen to the patient. The *Radvaz* himself writes that this is because a patient knows himself best. However, with regard to medication we listen to the doctor.[48] However, the *Aruch HaShulchan*[49] expresses surprise at this ruling writing that "it is a daily occurrence to see that a patient requests something that will harm him and is refused on the doctor's orders. Because it is *Yom Kippur* should that change things for the worse? Therefore, it seem to me that the great *poskim* who ruled as above were not speaking about a patient sick enough to be in bed, for in such a situation one would certainly listen to the doctor. The *poskim* were discussing someone who felt ill but nevertheless carried on as usual, although he felt discomfort in his heart, head or abdomen, for example as with someone who has tuberculosis." [*I presume that the Aruch HaShulchan is talking about someone with a chronic, stable illness that does not prevent him from getting around normally. I fail to understand why food will harm him in such a case. Nowadays, if a patient is forbidden to eat by his doctor it is either because he cannot swallow and will aspirate if he tries, or it is because of some condition of his gastro-intestinal tract, where eating would be dangerous. In all these instances, the poskim today would accept the doctor's ruling — author.*]

(G) he is heeded: This refers to a situation where the patient says that he feels that he must eat otherwise his condition will get worse. He should be reminded that it is *Yom Kippur*. If he still says that he must eat, we listen to him, since a person knows himself best, and we don't suspect him of wanting to sin deliberately.[50] *Rav Auerbach zt"l*[51] writes that when one does remind the patient that it is *Yom Kippur*, one must be careful to do so in a manner that will not cause the patient to become alarmed and frightened.

The *Binyan Tzion*[52] writes that a patient who had to eat on *Yom Kippur* does not need atonement since he did so by force of circumstances, and certainly if he only ate by *measure*. Atonement is necessary only for one who did something forbidden.[53]

✣ Summary of §2-6: the *Shulchan Aruch* and *Mishnah Berurah*

1. A doctor who has no knowledge of the patient's disease is like the man-in-the-street as far as giving an opinion about the patient's eating on *Yom Kippur*.
2. If a doctor says that the patient may fast and the patient does not know whether he should or should not, he must fast.
3. If the treating doctor, who knows the patient's disease, nevertheless says he is uncertain as to whether the patient should fast or not, the patient is given to eat even if he thinks that he is able to fast.

46. מ״ב ס״ק ד
47. שו״ת סי׳ אלף קלח (ח״ד סי׳ סו) הובא גם במג״א
48. והובא במג״א סי׳ שכח ס״ק ו. מחצית השקל כאן. חידוש רעק״א כאן. פ״ת יו״ד סי׳ קנה ס״ק ד. שדי חמד מערכת יוהכ״פ סי׳ ג ס״ק כז
49. כאן סע׳ ה-ו. וראה בתהלה לדוד סי׳ שכח ס״ק יג
50. מ״ב ס״ק ה
51. שמירת שבת כהלכתה פל״ט הערה יג
52. שו״ת בנין ציון החדשות סי׳ כה
53. מ״ב שם

§7: A pregnant woman or patient who must eat is given to eat slowly so that he does not eat (more than) a measure. He is therefore given about two-thirds of a medium-sized egg, and waits the time it would take to eat four eggs between each similar amount. As to (H)the volume of liquid, this is the amount that the patient can hold in one cheek so that both cheeks will look as if they are full.

NISHMAT AVRAHAM

4. If the patient is a doctor who is lucid, and says he does not know whether he should eat or not, even if the doctor treating him says that he may fast, he is given to eat. However, if he is of unclear mind, the opinion of the doctor treating him is accepted.
5. If two doctors cannot agree as to whether a patient should fast or not, the *Shulchan Aruch* rules that he is given to eat regardless of the religion or sex of the doctors concerned. The *Rama* adds that if the controversy was between two sets of doctors he is also given to eat, regardless of the comparative expertise of the two sets.

   However, in the opinion of the *Magen Avraham* and the *Eliyah Rabbah,* the opinion of the more expert pair is followed.[54] The *Mateh Ephraim,*[55] however, rules that the more lenient opinion may be followed and the patient given to eat regardless.
6. If a doctor says that the patient may fast and another doctor is uncertain, the patient is given to eat. However, if two doctors said that he could fast, their opinion is accepted against the uncertainty of their single colleague.
7. If both the patient and a doctor say that he can fast and a second doctor says that he must not, the patient fasts. However, if the second doctor is exceptionally knowledgeable, his opinion is accepted even though he is in the minority, and the patient must eat.
8. However, if the knowledgeable doctor says that the patient may fast and two doctors who are not as knowledgeable say that he should not, he must eat.
9. If a doctor says he must eat and two other doctors say he may fast and the patient does not express an opinion, he must fast.
10. If two say he must eat, the *Shulchan Aruch* rules that even if there were a hundred who thought that he could fast and the patient sided with them, he must eat.

    However, if the majority were more expert and also included a doctor well-known for his great knowledge, the patient may fast (see above, 5).

(H) the volume of liquid: Unlike the quantity of solid food contained in a *measure* which is the same for everyone, the volume of liquid varies from individual to individual. This should be measured by taking half the amount with which the patient can fill his mouth. Where possible the measurements of both food and drink should be made before *Yom Kippur.*[56] If this was not done, it may be done on *Yom Kippur* (see above, *Siman* 612I).[57]

54. וכן מובא בביה״ל סי׳ שכח סע׳ י ד״ה ואם
55. מטה אפרים סע׳ ג. ומוסיף שאפשר דגם הרמ״א מודה בזה שלא כתב את דינו אלא בשניהם שוים
56. מ״ב ס״ק כא
57. כף החיים ס״ק לז ו־מ

§8: He is given to drink less than the above volume and waits between each drink the amount of time it takes to eat four eggs. At the very least he should wait the time it takes to drink a *revi'it*. However, if the doctor or (I)the patient feels that these amounts are not going to be enough for him, or if there is uncertainty about this, he is given to eat and drink as much as he needs (*immediately*).

§9: A person who is seized by ravenous hunger and for whom kosher food is not available, is given non-kosher food. If there are (J)two different sorts of non-kosher foods available, one of which involves a more serious degree of prohibition than the other, he is given the food which bears the lesser degree of prohibition.

§10: A patient who has (K)eaten on *Yom Kippur* and feels well enough to recite the *birkat hamazon*, must mention *Yom*

NISHMAT AVRAHAM

(I) the patient: The *acharonim* have ruled that food and drink is put before the patient who is reminded that it is *Yom Kippur* (see above, **G**). He is then told that if he fears that it would be life-threatening for him not to eat as usual, he should do so; otherwise he should eat by *measure.*[58]

The *Mishnah Berurah* warns that a *posek* must be familiar with all of these rules so that an appropriate ruling is given immediately. See also *Siman* 328 and 330, that there is no difference between *Yom Kippur* and *Shabbat* in these matters, except that the punishment for willfully transgressing *Shabbat* is much more severe than for transgressing *Yom Kippur.*[59]

(J) two different sorts of non-kosher foods: For example, eating meat and milk that have been cooked together or placed together while still hot (even if the meat is kosher), carries two prohibitions by Torah law whereas eating non-kosher meat or pork carries one.

(K) eaten on *Yom Kippur*: A patient who must eat on *Yom Kippur,* and will be eating bread, ritually washes his hands up to the wrists.[60] If he intends to eat 54 grams of bread or more (two *kezeitim*), he recites the blessing *al netilat yadayim.*[61] However, if he will eat by *measure* he does not say the blessing even if he eats 54 grams or more.[62] He does not recite *Kiddush* on bread (nor on wine)[63] and he is also exempt from having *lechem mishneh.*[64] Many *acharonim*[65] are of the

58. מ״ב ס״ק כד

59. מ״ב שם. בשבת, איסור סקילה וביוהכ״פ, איסור כרת

60. שמירת שבת כהלכתה פל״ט הערה קא בשם הגרש״ז אויערבאך זצ״ל. וכ״כ הלבושי מרדכי מה״ת יו״ד סי׳ יא ס״ק ג

61. או״ח סי׳ קנח סע׳ ב

62. כתב לי מו״ר הגרי״י נויבירט שליט״א

63. מ״ב ס״ק כט

64. מג״א ס״ק י. מטה אפרים סע׳ יז. וראה בקצה המטה שם ס״ק טז בשם הא״ר, המור וקציעה, ספר יעב״ץ והלבוש דמ״מ אם יש לו שתי ככרות, נכון לבצוע עליהם

65. שו״ע הרב סע׳ יח. חיי אדם כלל קמה סע׳ לב. אור שמח הל׳ עבודת יוהכ״פ פ״ד ה״א. שו״ת הר צבי או״ח ח״א סי׳ קנה

Kippur* by saying (L)*ya'aleh veyavo* in the blessing *bonei Yerushalayim.

NISHMAT AVRAHAM

opinion that he should not recite *Kiddush* even if *Yom Kippur* is on *Shabbat.* However, *Rav Akiva Eiger*[66] writes that perhaps he is obligated to do so because of the obligation to recite *Kiddush* on *Shabbat.*[67]

A patient who eats or drinks by *measure* is obligated to recite the appropriate *berachah rishonah*[68] but does not repeat the blessing before each *measure.* However, after he has decided that he has finished eating or drinking for now, he should say a blessing before eating should he need to eat or drink again.[69] As to the *berachah acharonah,* if he ate at least 30 grams within 3 to 4 minutes, he is obligated to recite the appropriate blessing. If he ate at least this amount of bread, he recites *birkat hamazon* with the addition of *ya'aleh veyavo* and, on *Shabbat, retzei* as well. The *Mishnah Berurah*[70] mentions a controversy about the ruling concerning someone who drank by *measure;* he quotes the *Gra* who rules that a *berachah acharonah* should not be recited. The *Shemirat Shabbat KeHilchatah*[71] also rules that he cannot recite a *berachah acharonah.* With regard to eating by *measure,* he also should not recite a *berachah acharonah,* since we accept the view that the volume of an egg has decreased from what it was at the time of *Chazal.*[72] This being so, if he eats two-thirds of an egg (30 grams) it would not be enough to recite a *berachah acharonah.* This is also the opinion of *Rav Auerbach zt"l*[73] who wrote that since it is customary to act strictly, incorporating all the various opinions, it is impossible to eat a definite *kezayit kedei achilat pras. Rav Ovadiah Yosef shlita,*[74] on the other hand, wrote to me that since one may eat up to about 32 grams for each *measure,* there is in fact more than a *kezayit* (29 grams) in each *measure.* Therefore, he is obligated to recite a *berachah acharonah* provided that this quantity is of the bread alone and does not include anything else that was eaten with it.

(L) *ya'aleh veyavo*: The *Mishnah Berurah*[75] explains that since he was permitted to eat, *Yom Kippur* becomes like any *Yom Tov.* If it was also *Shabbat,* he says *retzei* as well.[76] However, if he forgot either of them and completed the blessing *bonei Yerushalayim,* he need not repeat the *birkat hamazon.*

Three patients who must eat as usual on *Yom Kippur* should be careful not to eat together, for if they were to eat bread they would be obligated to recite the blessing of *zimun.*[77] The *Kaf HaChaim*[78] writes that even if they did eat together, they should still not recite the *zimun. Rav Auerbach zt"l*[79] wrote that he was unsure of this ruling. For the Torah writes "and you should afflict your souls,"[80] but they

66. חי׳ רעק״א כאן
67. שמירת שבת כהלכתה פל״ט סע׳ לא
68. סי׳ רד סע׳ ט מ״ב שם ס״ק מו ושעה״צ ס״ק מ
69. ארחות חיים ס״ק ז
70. סי׳ רי סע׳ א ומ״ב ס״ק א ו־י
71. פל״ט הערה פה
72. ראה לעיל סי׳ תריב הערה 4
73. לב אברהם ח״א עמ׳ יח
74. נשמת אברהם כרך א או״ח עמ׳ שלו
75. וראה במ״ב שם ובסי׳ קפח ס״ק יט, כף החיים שם ס״ק כה ופמ״ג ס״ק י דגם לא יאמר ברכה בפני עצמה
76. מ״ב ס״ק כט. שמירת שבת כהלכתה פל״ט סע׳ לא
77. מ״ב ס״ק כט. שמירת שבת כהלכתה שם
78. סי׳ קצו ס״ק ט
79. שמירת שבת כהלכתה פל״ט הערה קה
80. ויקרא כג:לב

were forced by circumstances to eat; they should not sit together since by so doing they designate a set place to eat, and it is possible that it is not fitting to do so. For since we are to afflict ourselves, choosing a place to eat conflicts with the essence of affliction (i.e. fasting) – even though the eating itself is forced on them and does not represent a negation of fasting. And, even if they did designate a set place, perhaps on this day it is not considered to be such, and they would therefore be exempt from the *zimun* blessing. This is not to be compared with the meal eaten immediately before the fast of *Tishah B'Av* at which three should not sit together.[81] Nevertheless it is not at all certain that when patients who must eat and would have been happy to fast can be considered to designate a set place to eat when they feel sorrow because they cannot perform the *mitzvah*.

If one must say the required blessing after eating cake or of the five fruits of the Land of Israel (*me'en shalosh*), he adds: and remember me for good on this *Yom Kippur*. The *Machatzit HaShekel*[82] gives two reasons to explain why *Chanukah* and *Purim* are not mentioned in a similar way in this blessing: 1) Since a resume of the events of each follows in the *al hanissim* – a prayer of thanksgiving – it is fitting that they should be mentioned only where we thank *Hashem*, that is, in the prayer of *modim* in the *Shemoneh Esrei*, and in the *birkat hamazon*, where we thank *Hashem* for everything. 2) The concept of mentioning past historical events in the blessing of *me'en shalosh* is only mentioned in the *Yerushalmi* and that does not mention *Chanukah* or *Purim* in this context. Thanksgiving for being saved is not relevant to *Yom Kippur* nor can we expect the *Yerushalmi* to mention *Yom Kippur* – a fast day – in a passage discussing a blessing made after eating. Neither reason applies.[83]

One who had to eat on *Yom Kippur* may be called up to the reading of the Torah during *Shacharit*, and on *Shabbat*, during *Minchah* as well.[84] Although *Rav Akiva Eiger*[85] is uncertain as to whether this applies to his being called up during *Minchah* when *Yom Kippur* falls on a weekday, it would appear that in the opinion of the *Chatam Sofer*[86] it is permissible. *Rav Auerbach zt"l*[87] writes that if the patient ate by *measure*, although this is also forbidden by the Torah, he may nevertheless be called up even during *Minchah*, since he is still considered to be suffering "affliction." This is also the ruling of the *Marcheshet*.[88] The *Lev Chaim*[89] writes that he should not be called up for the reading of the last sections (the fifth and sixth – sixth and seventh if it is *Shabbat*) or for *maftir* at *Shacharit*, since they contain reference to "affliction." However, the *Sdei Chemed*[90] permits him to be called up for all sections (see also above, *Siman* 559(C).

PRAYER and CONFESSION: A patient who is too ill or a doctor who is too busy with patients to pray with a *minyan*, or even alone, should at least try to recite the blessings of the Torah, the first paragraph of the *Shema*[91] and the short *vidui* (confession of sins):[92]

---

81. סי׳ תקנב סע׳ ח ומ״ב ס״ק יט
82. סי׳ רח ס״ק יח
83. שמירת שבת כהלכתה פל״ט סע׳ לא והערה קו
84. שמירת שבת כהלכתה שם סע׳ לו
85. שו״ת, סי׳ סט (פסקים סי׳ כד)
86. שו״ת או״ח סי׳ קנז
87. שמירת שבת כהלכתה שם הערה קטו
88. ח״א סי׳ יד בשם שו״ת הרא״ה והריב״ש סי׳ רפז
89. שו״ת, להגר״ח פלאג׳י ח״ג סי׳ קלד
90. מערכת יוהכ״פ סי׳ ב ס״ק ז, כיון דהחולה זה התורה התירה לו לאכול ועושה מצוה בזה אינו יוצא מכלל תענו את נפשותיכם
91. שמירת שבת כהלכתה פ״מ סע׳ מה
92. לשון הרמ״א סי׳ תרז סע׳ ג ומ״ב ס״ק יב

SIMAN 621:
THE ORDER OF THE READING OF THE TORAH AND A CIRCUMCISION ON *YOM KIPPUR*

§3: The blessing over the circumcision is said without wine. *(There is an opinion that the blessing is said over wine and a little is then given* [A]*to the baby, and this is the custom.)*

NISHMAT AVRAHAM

חָטָאנוּ, עָוִינוּ, פָּשַׁעְנוּ – "We have sinned in ignorance, we have sinned knowingly, being unable to resist temptation, we have sinned against You rebelliously."

If he is able to, he should say the following instead:[93]

אָנָּא הַשֵּׁם, חָטָאתִי עָוִיתִי פָּשַׁעְתִּי לְפָנֶיךָ וְעָשִׂיתִי כָּךְ וָכָךְ, וַהֲרֵי נִיחַמְתִּי וּבוֹשְׁתִּי בְּמַעֲשַׂי וּלְעוֹלָם אֵינִי חוֹזֵר לְדָבָר זֶה – "Help me, O God, for I have sinned in ignorance, I have sinned knowingly, being unable to resist temptation and I have sinned against You rebelliously – (specifying here his sins). I regret this and am ashamed of my sinful deeds and will not repeat them."

If he is capable of further prayer, he should, if possible, recite at least one *Shemoneh Esrei* prayer with the full *vidui* (or at least the shorter version, above).

HAVDALAH: A patient or a duty doctor who was unable to recite *Havdalah* at the end of *Yom Kippur* or to hear it recited by someone else, should recite it as soon as possible up to sunset the following day. The blessing over a flame is only made if *Havdalah* is recited during the night following *Yom Kippur*. When *Yom Kippur* falls on *Shabbat, Havdalah* may be recited until sunset on Tuesday evening (without the blessings over spices or a flame), if there was no possibility of doing so before.[94]

SIMAN 621

(A) to the baby: The *Mishnah Berurah*[1] rules that if the circumcision is to take place in the presence of the mother, if she is ill and has been permitted to eat, she will be able to fulfill her obligation of *Kiddush* with that blessing (see, however, above, *Siman* 618K). She should be told to bear in mind that the blessing is for her, too, and she may then drink from the wine. The *Sha'ar HaTziyun,*[2] quotes the *Mateh Ephraim* that this is preferable to giving the baby to drink. *Rav Auerbach zt"l,* however, commented to me that although a *seriously ill* patient who must eat and drink as is necessary on *Yom Kippur* does so to give him strength and prevent him from becoming worse, he is, nevertheless, forbidden to eat or drink more than is necessary for his well-being.[3] For instance, he may not eat a candy (sweet) for pleasure but only for its calorie value. If so, in our days when women are not accustomed to drink wine to quench their thirst, why should the mother be allowed to drink from the wine of the circumcision? Surely she is only doing it for the *mitzvah* and does not need the wine for her health?

93. לשון הרמב״ם הל׳ תשובה פ״א ה״א
94. שמירת שבת כהלכתה פס״ב סע׳ כו
1. ס״ק יב
2. ס״ק ה
3. ביה״ל סי׳ תריח סע׳ ח ד״ה ואם. כף החיים סי׳ תרטז ס״ק כד

CHAPTER TWENTY-EIGHT:

The Laws of the Succah

SIMAN 639: LAWS CONCERNING SITTING IN THE *SUCCAH*

§1: (A)What is the mitzvah of sitting in a *succah*? One should eat and drink (*sleep and spend time*) **and live in the *succah* by day and by night for the seven days, just as he lives in his home during the year. During these seven days he makes his home his temporary residence and his *succah* his permanent one. How? He puts in the *succah* his nicest possessions and spreads, including the cups and glasses that he uses for drinking. However, pots and pans** (*after serving the meal*) **are left outside the *succah*. A lamp is lit inside the *succah;* if the *succah* is small, the lamp is left outside.**

GLOSS: *Nothing (B)that is of a lowly nature should be done in the succah so that the mitzvah does not become insignificant in his eyes.*

§3: On the (C)first night of the Festival of *Succot*, one is obli-

NISHMAT AVRAHAM

SIMAN 639

(A) What is the mitzvah: The *Mishnah Berurah*[1] refers to a controversy among the *poskim* as to whether one may contravene a Rabbinic law through a non-Jew in order to observe Torah law. See *Siman* 585C as to the use of an elevator in order to be able to keep a *mitzvah.*

(B) that is of a lowly nature: It is forbidden to urinate inside the *succah*. Although at home he perhaps does so using a urinal, this is forbidden in the *succah.*[2] However, the *Minchat Elazar*[3] permits it if this is what he does at home. A patient with an indwelling *catheter, colostomy* or *ileostomy* may sit in the *succah* (see above, *Siman* 76 §5).

(C) first night of the Festival of *Succot*: The *Mishnah Berurah*[4] emphasizes that on the first night he is obligated to eat bread in the *succah,* even if only a *kezayit* (27 grams). The same holds true for the second night in the Diaspora.[5] A patient or an older man who cannot eat a *kezayit* of

1. ס״ק א
2. מ״ב ס״ק ט בשם החיי אדם כלל קמז סע׳ ב
3. ח״ד סי׳ עג
4. מ״ב ס״ק יט
5. מ״ב סי׳ קסז ס״ק צה וכאן ס״ק לו

gated to eat in the *succah,* even if only (D)a *kezayit* of bread is eaten. The remaining days of the Festival, if he wishes to eat a meal he should do so in the *succah.* If, on the other hand, he wishes only to eat fruit or nuts he may do so outside the *succah.* This is similar to the law of eating *matzah* during *Pesach.*

SIMAN 640:

THOSE WHO ARE EXEMPT FROM SITTING IN A *SUCCAH*

§3: (A)Patients and (B)their caregivers are exempt from sitting in the *succah.* This not only includes a seriously ill patient but even someone with discomfort (C)in his head (*or*) **eyes. There is an opinion that the caregivers are only exempt (D)when the patient (E)needs them.** (*A person who has*

NISHMAT AVRAHAM

bread *kedei achilat pras* (2 to 4 minutes), should not say the blessing *leshev basuccah.*[6] An intern or duty male nurse is obligated to perform this *mitzvah* (see below, *Siman* 640D).

(D) a *kezayit* of bread: The blessing of *leshev basuccah* is recited the first night (until midnight) on 27 grams of bread or more (eaten within 2 to 4 minutes), but preferably on 54 grams. Throughout the remaining days of the Festival one may only eat less than 54 grams of bread outside the *succah* (unless illness, rain and the like prevent him from eating there — see *Siman* 640).[7] The *mitzvah* of *succah* is not fulfilled by eating cake.[8]

SIMAN 640

(A) Patients: The Torah says that one should sit in a *succah* and *Chazal* have taught us that this means to live in it as one normally lives at home. Thus, if during the year, he would not have stayed at home were he to have a particular illness or discomfort but would go elsewhere where he could find relief, here, too, he may stay outside the *succah* if it gives him relief.[1]

(B) their caregivers: Since they are involved in the *mitzvah* of caring for the sick, they are exempt from another *mitzvah.*[2]

(C) in his head: The *Mishnah Berurah*[3] explains that this is only if it is difficult for him to sit in the *succah* as a result. Since there is a possibility that going into or sitting in the *succah* may harm him, he is exempt, since we were given the Torah to live by it and not to die by it.[4]

(D) when the patient: If there are two caregivers and he only needs one at a time, one must eat in the *succah* while the other is on duty.[5] Thus a male nurse or caregiver who can leave the floor (ward) to eat elsewhere is obligated to eat in a *succah* if there is one in the hospital or near

6. מ״ב ס״ק כב
7. מ״ב שם
8. מ״ב ס״ק כא
1. מ״ב ס״ק ו
2. מ״ב ס״ק ז
3. מ״ב ס״ק ט
4. כף החיים ס״ק טו בשם הלבוש
5. מ״ב ס״ק י. וכן עיין בשו״ת שבות יעקב סי׳ נא

had (F)*a bloodletting is obligated to sit in the succah.)*

§4: One who (G)**has discomfort is** (H)**exempt from the** ***succah,*** **but** (I)**not his caregivers.** (J)*(On the first night* (K)*he is*

NISHMAT AVRAHAM

enough to allow him to eat and return to his work within the time allotted to him. The same applies to a doctor, particularly if he can be paged. A woman is exempt from the *mitzvah* of *succah.*[6]

(E) needs them: If the patient is *seriously ill,* it would appear that one may rule leniently even when the patient does not need them.[7] For example, if the patient was asleep but the caregiver must be available at his bedside should he need him at any hour, they are exempt. However, if he can find a stand-in so that he can eat in a *succah,* he is obligated to do so.

(F) a bloodletting: The *Mishnah Berurah*[8] qualifies this ruling. He says it refers to a healthy person who undergoes bloodletting as a preventive measure. However, if the blood was drawn to treat an illness, he is exempt. It would appear that this ruling only applied at the time of *Chazal* where great care was taken that one should not become cold or be in a place where there were drafts after bloodletting. Nowadays when there is no concern about cold or drafts (since the nature of things having changed), such a patient must fulfill the *mitzvah* of *succah* so long as sitting in the *succah* does not cause him discomfort. A healthy person who has donated blood is certainly obligated to fulfill the *mitzvah.*[9]

(G) has discomfort: Since normally during the year a person does not live in a place where he is uncomfortable, he is exempt from living in the *succah* there.[10]

(H) exempt from the ***succah*****:** If on the first night, however, he recovers sufficiently to be able to eat in the *succah* after midnight, he must recite *Kiddush* but does not recite the blessing *leshev basuccah* unless he eats more than 54 grams of bread.[11]

(I) not his caregivers: If they wish to eat or sleep they are obligated to do so in the *succah.* However, it would appear that if the patient hires a (male) nurse to eat and sleep close by during the year, he may do so. He is like those who guard orchards and gardens (§10 of this *Siman*) who are exempt from the *succah.*[12] But is the comparison correct? The guards cannot leave to eat in a *succah,* for the moment they would do so, the orchards and gardens would be exposed to thieves, but the nurse is not required to be with the patient every moment of the day. *Rav Auerbach zt"l,* however, wrote me that in our case too one must take into account that at any moment the patient may require the services of the nurse. *Rav Neuwirth shlita* wrote me that since the nurse was hired to be with the patient he is no different from a hired worker whom *Chazal* exempted from saying the fourth blessing of the *birkat hamazon.*

(J) on the first night: The *Mishnah Berurah*[13] writes: The *Rama* rules strictly as he did above in *Siman* 639 §5 as to what one should do if it was raining the first night. However, according to the other *poskim* who exempt a person from eating

6. כאן סע׳ א. וראה פרטי דינים במ״ב ס״ק א ובשמירת שבת כהלכתה פמ״ח סע׳ ח בנוגע לברכת לישב בסוכה
7. מ״ב ס״ק יא
8. ס״ק יב
9. עיין שם במ״ב
10. מ״ב ס״ק יג
11. סי׳ תרלט מ״ב ס״ק כו
12. מ״ב ס״ק יד
13. מ״ב ס״ק טו

obligated to eat a kezayit in the succah.) **How is this discomfort defined? If one cannot (L)sleep in the *succah* because of the wind or because of flies and the like, or because of a bad smell. This is only so if these things appeared unexpectedly after he had built the *succah*. He may not, however, build a *succah* in a place knowing that there will be a wind or smell and then say: I am in discomfort.**

GLOSS: *If he did build the succah knowing that he would be uncomfortable while eating or drinking (M)or sleeping, or if he is unable to do any of these because he is frightened of bandits or thieves, he does not fulfill the mitzvah of succah at all, even when there is no discomfort. This is because such a succah is not like his home where he is able to do as he wishes.*

NISHMAT AVRAHAM

in the *succah* if it is raining, the same would apply here. He who feels discomfort should act as is done when raining, as I wrote in the *Mishnah Berurah* above[14] that he should eat in the *succah* but without saying the blessing of *leshev basuccah*.

(K) he is obligated: It would appear from the *Birkei Yosef*[15] that only someone who feels discomfort is obligated; but if he is ill he is exempt.[16] This also appears to be the opinion of the *Eliyah Rabbah*.[17] However, the *Ben Ish Chai* rules that on the first night even if one is ill he is obligated to eat at least a *kezayit* of bread in the *succah*.[18]

(L) sleep: The *Mishnah Berurah*[19] explains that if he has difficulty eating in the *succah* he is exempt from doing so, but if he has difficulty sleeping in the *succah*, he nevertheless is still obligated to eat there.

(M) or sleeping: In places where the weather is cold he fulfills his obligation by eating in the *succah* even though it is too cold to sleep there; since there is no other alternative, it is still considered his dwelling place.[20] However, the *Biur Halachah* writes that the consensus of the majority of *poskim* is that he is exempt from eating as well if the cold bothers him. Therefore, one should be careful to be warmly clad so as not to be troubled by the cold, otherwise there would be a problem that the blessing of *leshev basuccah* may have been said in vain.[21]

14. סי׳ תרלט ס״ק לה
15. ס״ק ה
16. כף החיים ס״ק כו
17. שע״ת סוס״ק ה
18. שנה א פ׳ האיזנו סע׳ יב
19. ס״ק טז
20. מ״ב ס״ק יח ושעה״צ ס״ק כ ו־כב
21. ד״ה מפני הרוח

SIMAN 643:
THE ORDER OF *KIDDUSH*

§1: The order of the blessings at *Kiddush* are first on wine, then the *Kiddush* itself, on the *succah* and finally (A)*shehecheyanu*, since the last refers both to the *Kiddush* (the sanctification of the day) and the *succah*.

NISHMAT AVRAHAM

SIMAN 643

(A) *shehecheyanu*: If a patient was unable, or a doctor too busy, to hear or recite *Kiddush* the first night and also did not recite the *shehecheyanu* blessing, or forgot to do so, he recites the *shehecheyanu* blessing – in Israel – whenever he can, even during *Chol HaMoed;* and in the Diaspora – during the first day. If he did not recite it on the second night (in the Diaspora), although he did recite it on the first night, he should recite it whenever he can afterwards, even during *Chol HaMoed*. If he did not do so in the *Kiddush* of *Shemini Atzeret* or *Simchat Torah* (in the Diaspora), he recites the blessing whenever he can during that day.[1]

1. סי׳ תעג מ״ב ס״ק א

CHAPTER TWENTY-NINE

Laws of the Lulav

SIMAN 651: THE TAKING OF THE *LULAV* AND ITS BLESSING

§3: Even a (A)left-handed (B)man holds the *lulav* in his right hand and the *etrog* in his left, for here we follow what the majority does and are not concerned with the individual's nature. GLOSS: *There is an opinion that we take his particular nature into account so that he holds the lulav in his left hand and the etrog in his right; and this is the correct ruling. However, if he switched the lulav to the right hand and the etrog to the left, he has fulfilled his obligation. If he is ambidextrous he holds the lulav in his right hand and the etrog in his left.*

§4: A man (C)who has no hand holds the *lulav* or *etrog* in the crutch of his elbow.

NISHMAT AVRAHAM

SIMAN 651

The four species – the *lulav* (palm branch), three *hadassim* (myrtle branches), two *aravot* (willow branches) and an *etrog* (citron) are held together on each day of the Festival (except for *Shabbat*). The first three, known by the collective name *lulav,* are bound together and held in the right hand while the *etrog* is held in the left. The picking up of these four species is a Torah *mitzvah* on the first day of the Festival and a Rabbinic one on the others.

(A) left-handed man: It is only with regard to *tefillin* where the Torah says that it is to be placed on the weaker arm that we distinguish between one who is right-handed (his weaker arm is his left) and one who is left-handed (his weaker arm is his right). Since the *lulav* is made up of three species bound together, *Chazal* have given it greater importance than the *etrog,* and ruled that it should be held in the right hand. Since there is no criteria of stronger or weaker hand, both a right-handed man and a left-handed one hold the *lulav* in the right hand. The second view quoted by the *Rama,* however, compares the *lulav* to the *tefillin* and just as there the left-handed man's left hand is like the right-handed man's right, here, too, the left-handed man should hold the *lulav* in his stronger hand which is his left.[1]

(B) man: A woman is exempt from the *mitzvah* of *lulav.*[2]

(C) who has no hand: The *Sha'arei Teshuvah*[3] writes that a person without a

1. ס״ק יח
2. רמ״א סי׳ תרנח סע׳ ט
3. ס״ק יא

§5: The blessing on the four species and the *shehecheyanu* blessing should be recited while holding the three species but before he picks up the *etrog*. In this way, the blessings are said before the *mitzvah* is done. Or, he can hold the *etrog* upside down, say the blessings and then turn it right side up.

GLOSS: *The blessing should be recited* **(D)***standing.*

NISHMAT AVRAHAM

right hand holds both the *lulav* and the *etrog* in his left and if he lacks a left hand he holds both in his right, this being preferable to taking them consecutively. This is also the ruling of the *Birkei Yosef.*[4] However, the *Mishnah Berurah*[5] rules that he holds the *lulav* in his only hand (which is considered his right hand even if it is his left), and the *etrog* within the elbow of the other arm. If he cannot hold the *etrog* within his elbow, he holds them consecutively in his hand and thus fulfills the *mitzvah,* as ruled by the *Shulchan Aruch* in §12 of this *Siman*. This is also the ruling of the *Eliyah Rabbah*[6] and the *Chayei Adam.*[7] The *Sha'arei Teshuvah* concludes that he may take the *lulav* in his single hand whichever it may be and the *etrog* in the elbow of the other arm, and then holds them, one after the other, in his hand. He may also hold them first, one after the other, with his single hand and then both together, one in the hand and the other in the elbow.

If the whole of one arm is missing, he holds all four species in his remaining hand. However, since the *Mishnah Berurah*[8] quotes the *Orchot Chaim* that he does not fulfill his obligation by holding them both in one hand, he should preferably hold them consecutively.[9]

If he is completely armless,[10] or paralyzed in both arms,[11] he should not hold them in his teeth since this is not considered the "taking" required by the Torah. However, the *Birkei Yosef*[12] permits holding them in his teeth since the Torah does not specify taking in one's "hands," just as the shoe may be removed with the teeth in the *mitzvah* of *chalitzah* which may be performed in this way. However, the *Sha'arei Teshuvah*[13] writes that this ruling needs study for this is not the normal way one "takes" things; it would therefore appear that he should do so but without reciting the blessing.

(D) standing: They must also be held while standing.[14] A patient must also do the same.[15] However, if he is unable to do so, he should hold them while sitting or even lying down, with the blessing.[16] If he is paralyzed and cannot hold the *lulav* or *etrog* and asks someone else, be he a Jew, a woman or a gentile, to put them in his hands, if he can even slightly close his fingers to hold them he has fulfilled his obligation.[17]

---

4. ס״ק ה
5. ס״ק כג
6. ס״ק יג
7. כלל קמח סע׳ ח
8. ס״ק טו
9. כף החיים ס״ק מג
10. א״א ס״ק י ומ״ב ס״ק כב בשם הפמ״ג
11. שע״ת ס״ק יא
12. כאן וכ״כ הבכורי יעקב מובא במ״ב שם
13. ס״ק יא
14. מ״ב ס״ק כז
15. בן איש חי שנה א פ׳ האזינו סע׳ יד
16. מהא דמ״ב שם. ספר ארבעת המינים ח״ב עמ׳ קו בשם ספר עץ השדה סי׳ תרנא אות יט
17. וראה בנשמת אברהם כרך א או״ח כאן ס״ק ד ומה שכתב הגרא״י וולדינברג שליט״א בהערותיו עמ׳ שמו שם

§7: If one holds the *lulav* by a handle made for the purpose, he has fulfilled his obligation since holding it indirectly is also considered "taking," if it is done in a way that shows respect for the *mitzvah*. However, if not done in this way, but for example, he put the *lulav* in a pot, this is not considered showing respect for the *mitzvah,* and he does not fulfill his obligation. If he wrapped either the *lulav* or (E)his hand in a cloth and held it, some are of the opinion that he has not fulfilled his obligation.

GLOSS: *The custom is to act strictly and to remove the tefillin (on Chol HaMoed in the Diaspora – author) and rings from the hand and fingers, although halachah does not really demand this since they only partially cover the hand.*

NISHMAT AVRAHAM

(E) his hand in a cloth: This is the opinion of the *Tosafot*[18] and the *Mordechai.*[19] However, the *Ran*[20] and *Rashi*[21] rule that the cloth is considered secondary to his hand and he does fulfill his obligation.[22] The *Ben Ish Chai*[23] therefore rules that a bandage must be removed before holding the *lulav* and *etrog,* since it will be considered a *chatzitzah.* There are *acharonim* who rule that he must do so even if his hand is only partially covered.[24] It would therefore appear that if he has a band-aid on his hand he may not recite the blessing. However, *Rav Auerbach zt"l* told me that this is only true if he could remove the band-aid. However, if he cannot, he may take the four species and say a blessing since the band-aid is secondary to his hand. This is not like rings which are worn to beautify the hands and therefore are not secondary to them; they are a *chatzitzah* to the *lulav.*

If his hand is in a cast, and he can only hold the *lulav* or *etrog* with his fingers, *Rav Auerbach zt"l* told me that he should first recite the blessing and then hold the *lulav* and *etrog* in all the three different ways mentioned above in **B.** That is: 1) both together in the hand without the cast; 2) one in the uninjured hand and the other in the fingers of the injured hand; and finally 3) one after the other in the uninjured hand. All this should be done without any interruption from the time he recites the blessing until after holding them for the third time.

The *Aruch HaShulchan*[25] writes that only with ritual immersion does even a partial *chatzitzah* nullify the immersion since the whole body needs to be immersed completely. On the other hand, the *mitzvah* of *lulav* is fulfilled even though only a small part of the *lulav* or *etrog* is held. Therefore if only a part of the hand is uncovered, it is as if he holds a part of the *lulav* (or *etrog*). *Rav Ovadiah Yosef shlita* wrote to me[26] quoting the *Kappot Temarim*[27] who says that there were great men

18. תוס׳ יומא נח ע״א ד״ה מין
19. מרדכי פ״ג דסוכה
20. ר״ן סוכה מב ע״א
21. רש״י שם ד״ה דרך כבוד
22. מ״ב ס״ק לג ושעה״צ ס״ק מא
23. שנה א פ׳ האזינו סע׳ ג
24. מ״ב ס״ק לו
25. סע׳ כ
26. נשמת אברהם כרך א או״ח עמ׳ שלז
27. סוכה לז ע״א

SIMAN 652:
THE TIME FOR TAKING THE *LULAV*

§2: It is (A)forbidden to eat before taking the *lulav*. On the first day, when the *mitzvah* is from the Torah, if he forgot to hold the *lulav* and only remembered in the middle of his meal, he must stop and do the *mitzvah* even when there is sufficient time to do so after completing his meal.

SIMAN 656:
ONE SHOULD TRY TO BUY A BEAUTIFUL *ETROG*

§1: GLOSS: *One who does not have an etrog or any other object that is required to perform a mitzvah which is time related, is not required to spend vast sums of money to acquire it. Chazal have ruled that one does not need to spend more than one-fifth of one's wealth in order to fulfill a mitzvah even if it is bound to a set time. However, this is only for a positive commandment; for a* (A)*negative commandment*

NISHMAT AVRAHAM

who held the four species while wearing rings because they did so with their fingers and therefore there was no problem of *chatzitzah*. Therefore, continues the *Rav shlita*, this is all the more true for a cast which is not removed at all while doing any activity.

SIMAN 652

(A) forbidden to eat: See above, *Siman* 585A. Although it is permissible to take some light refreshment, one should not act leniently unless there is great need to do so.[1] Regarding the definition of "light refreshment" see above, *Siman* 585 end of **A.** However, if a *lulav* will only become available later in the day and a patient or duty doctor finds it difficult to fast until then, he may eat after *Shacharit* or at least after saying the blessing of the Torah, the first paragraph of the *Shema* and, on the Festival day, *Kiddush.*[2]

SIMAN 656

(A) negative commandment: According to the vast majority of *poskim,* Torah law forbids an abortion except to prevent danger to the mother's life.[1] What must an anesthetist do when, as part of his job, he must anesthetize a woman undergoing an abortion not sanctioned by *halachah*? Must he refuse and possibly risk losing his livelihood? What if the gynecologist or the woman is a gentile? Since the anesthetist is not carrying out the abortion but is helping the gynecologist, we come up against the question of his transgressing the negative commandment, "do not put a stumbling block before a blind man."[2] *Chazal* have given this verse many interpretations. One of them is that it refers to aiding another to sin.[3]

1. מ״ב ס״ק ז
2. ראה שמירת שבת כהלכתה פ״מ סע׳ מה

1. ראה נשמת אברהם כרך ג חו״מ עמ׳ רב
2. ויקרא יט:יד
3. פסחים כב ע״ב

NISHMAT AVRAHAM

One must take into account Torah and Rabbinic law with regard to this negative commandment. Torah law is transgressed when one cannot sin unless another helps him to do so. The *Gemara*[4] describes this in the context of a nazarite who sits on a bank of a river and asks someone on the opposite bank to pass him a bottle of wine. Since the nazarite cannot get the wine, which Torah law forbids him to drink, by his own efforts, the person making it available to him transgresses Torah law by putting "a stumbling block before" him. If both were on the same bank and he passed him the wine he will have transgressed Rabbinic law only. Perhaps if the anesthetist would refuse since others are available for the task and the abortion will be carried out even without his help, the transgression would only be Rabbinic. However, this is only true if the anesthetist replacing him would be a non-Jew; if he were to be replaced by a Jewish anesthetist the transgression would be a Torah transgression since a Jew will transgress a Torah commandment.[5] It would appear, therefore, that in Israel where the doctor who will replace him will most likely be another Jew, he would be forbidden to anesthetize the woman, if she or the gynecologist are Jewish, even at the risk of losing his livelihood. However, *Rav Auerbach zt"l* wrote me that the anesthetist would possibly not be transgressing a negative commandment. He explained that only the one who handed the gynecologist the instrument with which the abortion would be performed would transgress Torah law, unless the doctor could take the instrument himself or it would be handed to him by a non-Jew, when the transgression would be of Rabbinic law.[6]

The *Radvaz*[7] writes that one who is among non-Jews and can only obtain non-kosher food, even if it is only non-kosher by Rabbinic law, must spend all his money to find kosher food rather than eat non-kosher food. After he has exhausted all his money, and there is no alternative now but to eat non-kosher food because of danger to his life, he may do so, choosing the *halachically* least severe of the non-kosher foods, for instance something that is Rabbinically forbidden as opposed to something that is forbidden by the Torah. The *Pitchei Teshuvah*[8] quotes the *Pri Megadim*[9] as being unsure of the *halachah* whether one must give up all of his wealth or only one-fifth of it in order to avoid transgressing Rabbinic law. The *Sdei Chemed*[10] quotes the *Zera Emet*[11] as disagreeing with the above ruling of the *Radvaz*. However, the *Ran*[12] writes that one must give up all of his wealth so as not to transgress a Rabbinic *mitzvah* and this is also the ruling of the *Chafetz Chaim*[13] and the *Maharil Diskin*.[14] The *Gra*[15] goes even further, writing that this ruling also applies where the transgression is of a Rabbinic edict concerning a Rabbinic law[16] (see the *Gemara Shabbat* 121a where it states that it is forbidden to ask a non-Jew to put out a blaze which is not life-threatening even if this will result in

4. ע״ז ו ע״ב
5. משנה למלך פ״ד מהל׳ מלוה ולוה ה״ב, מנחת חינוך מצוה רלב אות ג, ברכ״י חו״מ סי׳ ט ס״ק ג, שדי חמד מערכת ואו כלל כו ס״ק א, בן איש חי שנה ב פ׳ ואתחנן סע׳ ב. וראה בשו״ת תורת חסד או״ח סי׳ ה
6. ראה ריטב״א ע״ז סג ע״א בסוף
7. סי׳ אלף רטז ומובא גם בחידושי רעק״א יו״ד סי׳ קנז סע׳ א
8. יו״ד סי׳ קנז ס״ק ד
9. או״ח כאן א״א ס״ק ח
10. מערכת הלמ״ד סוף כלל קז
11. ח״ג סוסי׳ לב מובא גם בדרכ״ת יו״ד שם ס״ק יז
12. חידושי הר״ן על סנהדרין סג ע״ב
13. הל׳ איסורי רכילות כלל א בבאר מים חיים סוס״ק יב
14. סי׳ קמה קונטרס אחרון
15. יו״ד סי׳ קנז ס״ק ד ובאו״ח כאן סע׳ א
16. וראה גם בשדי חמד מערכת הלמ״ד כלל קז וכן בדברי חכמים סי׳ לט ובדעת תורה כאן

the loss of all of one's wealth).[17]

The *Igrot Moshe*[18] was asked about a young widow who needed to work to support herself and her children and could not find a job unless she no longer covered her hair. He wrote that one could rule leniently in such sorry circumstances. For the transgression of a woman not covering her hair has Torah force only with respect to a married woman whereas with regard to a widow it has Rabbinic force only.[19] And with respect to its being Rabbinic it is uncertain as to whether the transgression involves a negative or a positive Rabbinic commandment. If it was a definite transgression of a negative Rabbinic commandment she would need to sacrifice all of her livelihood so as not to transgress it. If it is a positive commandment, she need only sacrifice up to a fifth of her livelihood. The uncertainty allows for a lenient ruling because we are dealing with Rabbinic law.

It would appear that an anesthetist (and all others, such as nurses, who would be assisting in the surgery) may not assist in an abortion that has not been *halachically* sanctioned, even at the risk of losing his position, and certainly so if he knows that he would be replaced by another Jew. However, if there is a reasonable doubt that the abortion may be permitted *halachically,* he would not be required to sacrifice his livelihood where there was only a possible transgression of the Rabbinic law of aiding in such a transgression. *Rav Auerbach zt"l* wrote to me that the anesthetist would need to carefully ascertain, in *Eretz Yisrael* and in the Diaspora, whether the abortion had *halachic* sanction or not.

A non-Jew is bound by the seven Noahide laws which include murder, even of a fetus.[20] Thus a Jew is forbidden, by Torah law, to aid in an abortion if either the gynecologist or the patient is non-Jewish if the abortion cannot be performed without his aid.[21] The *Rama*[22] writes that, according to one opinion, if the non-Jew can transgress without the Jew's help, a Jew does not transgress the Rabbinic law of aiding. The *Shach*[23] rules that this is permitted according to all opinions.[24] This is also the opinion of the *Chatam Sofer,*[25] the *Magen Avraham*[26] and the

17. Asking a non-Jew to do what is forbidden to a Jew is forbidden by Rabbinic edict, and putting out a blaze is forbidden by Rabbinic law only, since the purpose for doing so is not the purpose for which putting out a fire was used in the building of the *Mishkan* (see *Siman* 278A). Hence, this is a Rabbinic law twice removed (1. asking a non-Jew to do 2. what is Rabbinically forbidden) from the Torah law of putting out a flame.

18. אהע״ז ח״א סי׳ נז

19. ולכאורה צ״ע מהב״ח סי׳ כא ד״ה לא יכלו בנות ישראל, דכותב נראה דנפקא לן מדאיתא פרק המדיר וכו׳ ותנא דבר״י אזהרה לבנות ישראל שלא יצאו בפרוע ראש, דמדלא קאמר אזהרה לאשת איש אלא סתמא אזהרה לבנות ישראל, אלמא דאחת פנויה ואחת אשת איש באזהרה (והכוונה פנויה דהיינו אלמנה, עיין בב״ש ס״ק ה) וכ״כ הגר״א שם ס״ק יא: אחד פנויה מדקאמר לבנות ישראל ולא קאמר לאשה, עכ״ל. אך עיין במג״א סי׳ עה ס״ק ג ובשו״ת שבות יעקב סי׳ קג שחולקים על הב״ח, וכן ראיתי בשו״ת יביע אומר ח״ד אהע״ז סי׳ ג ס״ק ג, שגם כותב שלאשה גרושה או אלמנה פנויה אין איסור מן התורה לצאת בפרוע ראש. ועיין שם בס״ק ד מה שכותב היביע אומר על התשובה הנ״ל של האג״מ. וכן עיין במחזה אברהם סי׳ קיט ו־קכ

20. רמב״ם הל׳ מלכים פ״ט ה״ד

21. ועיין בתוס׳ סנה׳ נט ע״א ד״ה ליכא שמסתפק אם מותר לבן נח להרוג את העובר אפילו כדי להציל את היולדת. ופוסק האג״מ חו״מ ח״ב סי׳ סט, דלא הותר לבן נח להרוג עובר מפני פקוח נפש דהאם

22. יו״ד סי׳ קנא סע׳ א. ועיין גם באה״ע סי׳ ה סע׳ יד בהגה. ואמנם יש מחמירים, דהיינו התוס׳ הרא״ש והגמ״ר פ״ק דשבת והר״ן פ״ק דע״ז, התשב״ץ ח״ג סי׳ קלג והחיד״א יו״ד סי׳ קנא סע׳ א (ועיין בשדי חמד מערכת ואו כלל כו ס״ק ב ובמ״ב סי׳ שמז ס״ק ז). כותב הרמ״א שנהגו להקל כסברא הראשונה, וכל בעל נפש יחמיר לעצמו

23. יו״ד סי׳ קנא ס״ק ו

24. כשמדובר בעכו״ם או במומר

25. שו״ת יו״ד סי׳ יט, מובא גם בפ״ת יו״ד סי׳ סב ס״ק א

26. סי׳ שמז ס״ק ד

NISHMAT AVRAHAM

Pri Megadim.[27]

From the above, it would appear that the anesthetist may assist in the abortion if both the surgeon and the woman are non-Jews and the abortion will be carried out anyway; nevertheless if possible he should act strictly and refuse to help.

If a Jewish woman is undergoing a non-*halachically* sanctioned abortion, the anesthetist may not assist even if the surgeon is a non-Jew.[28] *Rav Auerbach zt''l* told me that it would be forbidden for the anesthetist to assist in such a non-*halachically* sanctioned abortion even if the fetus is less than forty days old. If, on the other hand, she is non-Jewish and the fetus is less than forty days old, it would possibly be permitted.[29]

An abortion may not be performed on *Shabbat* and it would be forbidden to assist in all the above circumstances, unless it was urgent because of danger or possible danger to the life of the mother. *Rav Auerbach zt''l* told me that both in *Eretz Yisrael* and in the Diaspora, the anesthetist must ascertain whether an operation is indeed urgent enough to be done on *Shabbat.*

Summing up

If the abortion has not been *halachically* sanctioned:

1) If the surgeon is Jewish, the anesthetist (or nurse, and other assistants) is forbidden to assist in the abortion if the woman is Jewish.
2) If she is non-Jewish he is permitted to assist regardless of who the surgeon is, if the abortion would be carried out anyway.
3) If she is Jewish, he may not assist regardless of who the surgeon is and even if the fetus is less than forty days old.
4) One may not assist in any operation on *Shabbat* unless the reason for the operation is danger or possible danger to the life of the patient.
5) See next paragraph.

Quite apart from what I discussed above, one must consider a far more important problem, the loss of a Jewish soul. *Rav Auerbach zt''l* wrote to me that according to the opinion that a Jew who performs an abortion not sanctioned by *halachah* is considered a murderer although not punishable by the death penalty, the anesthetist is guilty of aiding the surgeon and the mother in the serious sin of killing a Jewish soul. One must be prepared to spend money to save a fetus and even Sabbath laws are set aside to save its life. Even the *Yad Ramah*[30] who rules that one is not obliged to give up all of one's wealth to save a fetus, would appear to agree that he is obliged to give up one-fifth of his wealth if this would save the fetus from being aborted. All the more so, if he would only lose his position, since this would not necessarily mean a loss of his wealth. Thus the anesthetist would be forbidden to assist

---

27. סי׳ קסג א״א ס״ק ב. וראה עוד בשו״ת פני יהושע ח״א יו״ד סי׳ ג וח״ב אהע״ז סי׳ מג ובשו״ת חת״ס חו״מ סי׳ קפה

28. שמעתי מהגרש״ז אויערבאך זצ״ל שעל אף שהיא נמצאת בלי הכרה בזמן הניתוח, בכל זאת היא עוברת על לפני עור של רציחה והשחתת זרע ולא יהיה הבדל בין אם היא בלי הכרה בגלל הרדמה כללית ובין אם הניתוח בוצעה בהרדמה מקומית והיא בהכרה מלאה. עוד כתב לי הגאון זצ״ל דלגבי מה שכתוב בדין מקיף וניקף שהניקף צריך הטיית ראש כדי להתחייב, שם כדי להתחייב במלקות צריך מעשה בידים בשעת ביצוע האיסור. אך אם בוצע ההקפה בהסכמתו כשהוא בא להמקיף שיבצע את האיסור, עובר שפיר בלאו, גם אם היה בלי הכרה בשעת מעשה, עכ״ל. ועיין יו״ד סי׳ קפא סע׳ ד

29. כותב השו״ת אחיעזר ח״ג סוסי׳ סה דבן נח אינו נהרג על עובר פחות ממ׳ יום וגם בישראל אפשר דאין איסור תורה וכ״כ בשו״ת תורת חסד אהע״ז סי׳ מב אות לג. וכ״כ האג״מ חו״מ ח״ב סי׳ סט אות ג שבפחות ממ׳ יום הדין יותר חמור בישראל מבבן נח

30. על סנהדרין עג ע״א

(B)one is obliged to give up all of one's wealth before he may transgress the commandment (see below, the end of Siman 658, Gloss).

NISHMAT AVRAHAM

in the abortion. *Rav Eliashiv shlita* told me that he would be obliged to lose his livelihood rather than assist in the abortion. Since this was a part of his routine work, he would be doing it repeatedly. In such a situation he should lose his livelihood, if necessary, rather than assist in such an abortion even once.[31]

(B) one is obliged to give up all of one's wealth: A number of other examples of the *halachah* of aiding in a transgression come to mind and will be discussed:

Sonography (Ultrasound). A doctor whose expertise is in doing gynecological ultrasound examinations finds that a fetus has an obvious congenital defect. He realizes that the gynecologist who asked for the examination will recommend immediate abortion even without *halachic* sanction. What course of action is he to take? *Rav Waldenberg shlita* wrote to me that he is permitted to write his report because the abortion is only forbidden by Rabbinic law and, besides, the sonographist is not assisting the gynecologist at the time of the abortion. *Rav Auerbach zt"l* wrote to me that it is only probable and not definite that the patient will have an abortion. Although there is nevertheless a possibility that a fetus will be killed and he has assisted in this, he is not, however, obliged to lose his livelihood for it. *Rav Eliashiv shlita* told me that he is not obliged to lose his livelihood since there is no connection in time between his report and the abortion.

Determination of the moment of death. A neurologist has been asked to see a patient who meets the criteria of brain death, that is, he is in deep coma, entirely dependent on a ventilator, but with a spontaneously beating heart. The purpose of the consultation is to confirm the diagnosis of brain death so that his organs may be removed for transplantation. May he confirm brain death knowing that if he does not he risks his position and livelihood? *Rav Neuwirth shlita* wrote to me that unlike the previous example, the only reason for the consultation is to confirm the diagnosis. Therefore we have a clear and definite connection between the diagnosis and the removal of the organs (and the neurologist must refuse since a brain dead patient is considered to be alive). *Rav Eliashiv shlita* and *Rav Waldenberg shlita* both ruled that he could confirm the diagnosis because here, too, it is not actively aiding in a directly consecutive way. At the time that I wrote this *Siman* of *Nishmat Avraham* (volume 4), *Rav Auerbach zt"l,* who like *Rav Eliashiv shlita* and *Rav Waldenberg shlita,* considered a brain-dead patient as being alive, told me that since the neurologist is not directly involved with the operation and may lose his livelihood, he may confirm the diagnosis (since there is no direct connection between his report and the operation). However, when I wrote the later chapters of the volume, *Rav Auerbach zt"l*[32] defined such a patient as being a possible *gosses* and, as such, he may not be touched or moved, except for his own benefit.[33] Therefore, the neurologist may not examine him since the only purpose of the examination is to allow his heart to be removed from him while it is still beating.

31. וראה דעתו של הגרא"י ולדינברג שליט"א בנשמת אברהם כרך א או"ח עמ' צד

32. שם עמ' קמב

33. שו"ע יו"ד סי' שלט סע' א

NISHMAT AVRAHAM

Resuscitation and the decision not to resuscitate (DNR). A patient has expressed, in the presence of witnesses, or in writing, that he does not wish to be intubated or resuscitated, though *halachically,* in his case, this must be done. What should a doctor do if he is called to such a patient and finds that he has either stopped breathing or that his heart has stopped functioning and he requires intubation or full cardio-pulmonary resuscitation? If he does resuscitate him, as demanded by *halachah,* he may run the risk of losing his livelihood. On the other hand, he can comply with the DNR orders, but will transgress the Torah verse which forbids one to stand idly by where there is danger to another's life.[34] There is a controversy among the *poskim* as to whether one must be prepared to sacrifice all his wealth in order not to passively transgress a Torah commandment.[35] But this particular commandment, concerning the saving of life, is possibly more serious, and indeed the *Marcheshet*[36] rules that it is.

Rav Waldenberg shlita wrote to me ruling that since the doctor may lose his livelihood he may transgress this negative Torah command passively, based on the *Gemara Sanhedrin.*[37] This was also the ruling that I heard from *Rav Eliashiv shlita* based on the same *Gemara.* The *Gemara* states that a person is obligated to search for someone to save another when he himself cannot do so, even if he must pay for his help. The *Yad Ramah*[38] and the *Chavot Yair*[39] explain that this is only if he can then claim his expenses from the person whose life has been saved. However, if he would stand to lose all his wealth without the possibility of recompensation he is not obligated to do so, since the above commandment will only be passively transgressed.

Rav Auerbach zt''l wrote to me that although if someone performed active euthanasia on such a patient he would be guilty of shedding blood, nevertheless he is not obligated to spend all his wealth (by losing his livelihood) in order to prolong his life for a few more hours or even longer.

---

34. ויקרא יט:טז

35. ראה שדי חמד מערכת הלמ״ד כלל קז ודברי חכמים סי׳ לט שמביא מהר״ן סוכה ריש טז ע״ב בעמודי הרי״ף, שו״ת ריב״ש סי׳ שפז, שו״ת חות יאיר סוסי׳ קלט (מובא גם מפ״ת יו״ד סי׳ שנז ס״ק א), פמ״ג א״א כאן ס״ק ח, פ״ת יו״ד סי׳ קנז ס״ק ד, חידושי רעק״א על יו״ד שם, גליון מהרש״א על יו״ד שם, מנחת חינוך מצוה רל, שו״ת מהר״ם שיק סוסי׳ שג. וראה גם בדרכי תשובה יו״ד סי׳ קנז ס״ק טז ו־יח, הגהות חת״ס על או״ח כאן ושו״ת אג״מ אהע״ז ח״א סי׳ נז

36. ח״א סי׳ מג

37. סנהדרין עג ע״א

38. על הגמרא שם

39. סי׳ קסה. וכן מדייק הג״ר וולדינבירג שליט״א מהשו״ת חת״ס חו״מ סי׳ קעז

CHAPTER THIRTY:

Laws of Chanukah

SIMAN 675: THE MITZVAH IS TO KINDLE THE LIGHTS, NOT TO PLACE THOSE THAT HAVE BEEN LIT ELSEWHERE

§1: The (A)*mitzvah* is to kindle lights where they are and not to kindle them in one place and then move them elsewhere.

SIMAN 677: LAWS CONCERNING A GUEST

§1: A guest who has (A)no one at home to light for him (B)should pay his host a small sum towards the candles so as to share in the *mitzvah*.

§3: There is an opinion that even though there is someone at home who will kindle lights to include him, should he be

NISHMAT AVRAHAM

SIMAN 675

(A) *mitzvah* is to kindle lights: Therefore, a bedridden patient may not light the *Chanukah* lights while in bed and then have them taken to the front door or window of his home. Rather someone should light them there[1] or else he should light them by his bedside and they should be left there.[2]

SIMAN 677

(A) no one at home: The wife of a hospitalized patient kindles the lights at home, exempting him from the *mitzvah* even though he is far away. Thus he does not need to pay towards the lights of anyone else who is kindling in the hospital.[1]

(B) should pay his host: A blind person who lives where others will kindle *Chanukah* lights should take part in the *mitzvah* by paying towards the candles and then listening to the blessings which will include him. If he is married, his wife lights for them both. If, however, he lives alone, he should ask someone else to help him kindle them[2] but without reciting the blessing.[3] He cannot recite the blessing to include someone else.[4]

1. מהא דמ״ב ס״ק ב
2. ס״ק יד

1. לב חיים ח״ג סי׳ קמו, מובא בשערים מצויינים בהלכה סי׳ קלט ס״ק טז
2. שמעתי ממו״ר הגרי״י נויבירט שליט״א
3. שו״ת רש״ל סי׳ עז
4. שע״ת ס״ק ג

elsewhere where there are [(C)]**no other Jews, one should kindle *Chanukah* lights and recite the blessing.**

NISHMAT AVRAHAM

(C) no other Jews: If he is a patient in a non-Jewish hospital, he should kindle *Chanukah* lights. However, with regard to reciting the blessing, the *Mishnah Berurah*[5] writes that since the *Shulchan Aruch*[6] has ruled that one should not recite the blessing (*she'asah nissim*) on seeing *Chanukah* lights where he is if they will have been lit for him at home, he should not recite a blessing. Nevertheless since many *acharonim* have ruled that he may recite a blessing, if he does do so he should not be admonished. However, it is preferable to hear the blessing from someone else who is kindling *Chanukah* lights and for whom no one else will be kindling them at home. He should listen to the blessing having in mind to take part in it, answer "*Amen*" and then kindle his own lights. Or, he may kindle his lights with a blessing making sure that he does so before his wife kindles them at home.[7]

May one use electric lights for the *mitzvah* of *Chanukah*? According to the majority of *poskim,*[8] one does not fulfill his obligation by doing so. The reason for this is that since the *mitzvah* is to commemorate the miracle of *Chanukah* where oil sufficient for one day burned for eight, *Chanukah* lights must consist of a wick burning in oil (or a candle which when lit melts into a liquid). Second, each light must come from a single wick and not from the flame of multiple wicks. An electric bulb has neither a wick nor oil and its light, filling the entire bulb, looks more like that of a flame from many wicks. Third, writes *Rav Auerbach zt"l,*[9] there must be enough oil to last for at least half an hour at the time of lighting so that the flame burns continuously. With electricity, every instant is considered a new flame, especially if an alternating current is being used. *Rav Ovadiah Yosef shlita*[10] rules that in a situation where he has no choice (for instance a hospitalized patient who cannot obtain candles or oil), he may kindle electric lights (such as lamps) but without a blessing. However, he must put them in a place where lights are not normally kindled.

It would seem to me that the same ruling would apply to flashlights (torches). This is not to be confused with with the ruling above, *Siman* 263C, permitting the lighting, with a blessing, of a flashlight for the *mitzvah* of Sabbath candles. On *Shabbat* the *mitzvah* is that there should be light in the room for the honor of *Shabbat* and therefore a flashlight may be used if candles cannot be lit.

5. מ״ב ס״ק ט. בן איש חי שנה א פ׳ וישב סע׳ טו (טו). כף החיים ס״ק כג
6. סי׳ תרעו סע׳ ג
7. מ״ב ס״ק טז
8. שו״ת בית יצחק יו״ד ח״א סי׳ קכ (אולם ע״ע שם ח״ב סי׳ לא). שו״ת הר צבי או״ח ח״ב סי׳ קיד ס״ק ב. שו״ת לבושי מרדכי מהד׳ תליתאה או״ח סי׳ נט ומהד׳ תרצ״ז סי׳ יט אות ב. שו״ת ישכיל עבדי ח״ב סי׳ ט וח״ג סי׳ יז. שו״ת משפטי עוזיאל מהד״ק או״ח סי׳ ז. כף החיים סי׳ תרעג ס״ק יט. שו״ת ציץ אליעזר ח״א סי׳ כ פי״ד. שערים מצויינים בהלכה סי׳ קלט ס״ק ה. הגרש״ז אויערבאך זצ״ל בספרו מאורי אש עמ׳ צה
9. הגרש״ז אויערבאך זצ״ל בספרו מאורי אש עמ׳ צה
10. שו״ת יביע אומר ח״ג סי׳ לה

SIMAN 683

§1: [A]The complete *Hallel* is recited on each of the eight days of *Chanukah*.

SIMAN 685: THE FOUR WEEKLY PORTIONS OF THE TORAH

§7: There are those who say that there is a Torah obligation to read the Torah portion of *Zachor* and that of the Red Heifer. Therefore, anyone who lives in an outlying area where there is no *minyan* must come to a place where there is one in order to hear these portions read on the appropriate Sabbaths, to fulfill his Torah obligation.

GLOSS: *If this is not possible, [A]he must nevertheless be careful to read them at home in the cantillation used for the reading of the Torah.*

NISHMAT AVRAHAM

SIMAN 683

(A) The complete Hallel: What is the *halachah* regarding a busy duty doctor who can find a replacement for only a short while to enable him to either go home at night to kindle *Chanukah* lights (which will not be possible at work) or to attend a *minyan* in the morning?[1] The *Chochmat Shlomo*[2] speaks of a prisoner or a traveler. He rules that it is more important to pray with a *minyan* and recite *Hallel* together with them. However, *Rav Auerbach zt"l* told me that this ruling requires further study since it would appear that proclaiming the miracle of *Chanukah* by kindling lights is more important. This would be so not only if, as a result, he would have to pray by himself, but even if he knows that he would be so busy in the morning that he would not be able to pray *Shacharit* in time. Nevertheless, he should choose to be replaced in order to kindle *Chanukah* lights and, the next day, if he wasn't able to pray *Shacharit* in time, he should pray *Minchah* twice (see *Siman* 93A). He must at least try to recite the *Shema* at its appropriate time and put on *tefillin*, even if he only does so during *Minchah*.

SIMAN 685

(A) he must nevertheless be careful to read: They must be read from a text. Therefore a patient who is unable to go to the synagogue should read them at home from a Torah scroll without reciting a blessing. If he does not possess a Torah scroll he should say the portion from a *Chumash*.[1] A *posek* must be consulted as

---

1. See above, *Siman* 618D, about one who has a choice of either fasting on the *Fast of Gedaliah* or on *Yom Kippur*.
2. הגהות על שו״ע כאן. וראה גם בביה״ט או״ח סי׳ צ

ס״ק יא ומ״ב סוס״ק כח

1. שו״ת בנין שלמה סי׳ נד, מובא בשערים מצויינים בהלכה קונ״א סי׳ קמ ס״ק ה. וראה בשו״ת מנחת אלעזר ח״ב סי׳ א

CHAPTER THIRTY-ONE: Laws of the Megillah

SIMAN 686: THE *FAST OF ESTHER*

§2: One fasts on the thirteenth of Adar but if *Purim* falls on Sunday we fast earlier on the Thursday before *Purim*.

GLOSS: *This is not an obligatory fast and one may therefore act leniently where necessary, for example pregnant women or nursing mothers or non-seriously ill patients including those who only suffer painful eyes. If they are* (A)*suffering a lot they need not*

NISHMAT AVRAHAM

to whether a Torah scroll may be brought to the patient so that he can fulfill his obligation together with a *minyan.*[2]

A patient who knows that he will only be able to go to the synagogue, either to hear the *Megillah* or to hear *zachor* with a *minyan,* should choose to hear *zachor.* Although the obligation to hear *zachor* with a *minyan* is a Rabbinic one, the obligation to hear it is inherently a Torah obligation, whereas according to most *poskim* it is enough to read the *Megillah* by oneself.[3] The *Magen Avraham,* on the other hand, rules that it is better to hear the *Megillah* with a *minyan* since, in extenuating circumstances, one may fulfill his obligation to hear *zachor* with the portion read on *Purim,* if he had the intention to do so at the time. However, the *Mishnah Berurah*[4] writes that this ruling of the *Magen Avraham* requires further study since many aspects of *zachor* that we are commanded to remember[5] are not mentioned in the portion read on *Purim.*

SIMAN 686

(A) suffering a lot: The *Mishnah Berurah*[1] writes, quoting the *Yeshuot Yaakov,* that this refers to those with painful eyes. But a pregnant woman, even if she is not suffering, should not fast.[2] And although the *Eliyah Rabbah* rules strictly, he agrees that for thirty days after childbirth she should not fast. However, the above is only according to the *Rama*[3] who rules that with the other three fasts (see above, *Siman* 550A) the custom is to act strictly, but that here one may act leniently. However, according to the *Mechaber*[4] who rules that pregnant women and nursing mothers are exempt from fasting the three fasts, they are surely exempt from this one which is not as strict as the others.[5]

1. ס״ק ד
2. וכן דעת המחצית השקל
3. סי׳ תקנ סע׳ א
4. סי׳ תקנד סע׳ ה
5. כף החיים ס״ק יח

2. ראה בשו״ע ורמ״א סי׳ קלה סע׳ יד ובמ״ב וביה״ל שם
3. שו״ע סי׳ תקנד סע׳ ה
4. ס״ק טז
5. רמב״ן סוף פ׳ כי תצא

fast but should make up for it by [(B)]*fasting on another day. However, those who are healthy should not separate themselves from the congregation.*

SIMAN 689:
EVERYONE IS OBLIGATED TO HEAR THE *MEGILLAH*

§2: Both the one reading the *Megillah* and the one who hears it read have fulfilled their obligation, provided that the one reading the *Megillah* falls into the category of those who are obligated to read it. Therefore, if the reader is [(A)]**deaf,**

NISHMAT AVRAHAM

(B) fasting on another day: According to the *Yeshuot Yaakov* quoted above, it would appear that this only applies to the person with painful eyes, who really is obligated to fast with the rest of the congregation and whose exemption is only temporary. Since the *Fast of Esther* is not fixed for a specific date,[6] he must fast when he recovers. A pregnant woman or nursing mother, on the other hand, is exempt even if she is well and therefore need not fast later to make it up. However, it would appear that the *Bach* apparently disagrees with this distinction.[7] If a doctor, however, has warned someone with painful eyes and the like that fasting would harm him, he need not fast afterwards.[8]

SIMAN 689

(A) deaf: This refers to one who is completely deaf and cannot hear himself read. Although with respect to many other *mitzvot* he has fulfilled his obligation (see *Simanim* 62 and 185), *halachah* is much stricter with the *mitzvah* of *Megillah*, which is meant to proclaim the miracle of *Purim*. Or possibly there is another explanation. In the *Simanim* referred to, the man can hear but recited *Keriyat Shema* or *birkat hamazon* silently. Here he is totally deaf. The *Sha'arei Teshuvah*[1] says this *halachah* applies only to one who is totally deaf, but not to one who can hear when spoken to in a loud voice.[2] But the above has relevance to the opinion of the *Shulchan Aruch* only. However, many *acharonim* rule that the listener has fulfilled his obligation even if the reader is totally deaf. Nevertheless, all agree that, given a choice, he should not be chosen to read the *Megillah* for the congregation.[3] The *Biur Halachah*[4] sums it up by saying that someone who is totally deaf is certainly obligated to read the *Megillah* for himself, even if he does so without reading it with the proper notes.

One who has difficulty in hearing the reader should be careful to simultaneously read the *Megillah* for himself from a kosher scroll, or at the very least have a printed *Megillah* before him so that he may immediately read any words that

6. שעה״צ ס״ק יא
7. מ״ב ס״ק ה
8. כף החיים ס״ק כב
1. ס״ק ב
2. ועיין גם בשו״ת רעק״א מהד״ת סי׳ סד, שו״ת נו״ב מה״ק אהע״ז סי׳ נג ושו״ת שבות יעקב ח״ב סי׳ לג
3. מ״ב ס״ק ה
4. ד״ה חרש

a [B]minor or a *shoteh,* the listener has not fulfilled his obligation.

SIMAN 692: THE BLESSINGS OVER THE *MEGILLAH*

§4: GLOSS: [A]*It is forbidden to eat (following the Fast of Esther)*

NISHMAT AVRAHAM

he did not clearly hear from the reader.[5]

As to one who wears a hearing aid, see the *responsum* by *Rav Auerbach zt"l.*[6]

(B) minor: The *Shulchan Aruch* ruled (*Siman* 675 §3) that a minor who has reached an age of comprehension and has been taught the *mitzvah* (of kindling *Chanukah* lights) is able to discharge an adult from his obligation. Therefore, this would apply here. In extenuating circumstances where there is no one who can read the *Megillah* for an adult except such a minor, he can do so discharging the adult from his obligation.[7] However, the *Ben Ish Chai*[8] rules that the adult should nevertheless then read it himself without the blessing (or read it simultaneously with the minor).

SIMAN 692

(A) It is forbidden to eat: The *Magen Avraham* concludes that although he is forbidden to eat he may take a light snack (that is up to 54 grams of bread or liquid). Thus, it would be preferable to allow him to take a light snack before hearing the *Megillah* rather than have him hear the *Megillah* before nightfall in order to eat immediately at nightfall. However, one may not permit a light snack except in extenuating circumstances for one who is ill, for example, or for whom fasting is very difficult. The *Sha'arei Teshuvah* also rules that one may allow a sick person or a woman after childbirth to hear the *Megillah* before nightfall.[1] *Rav Auerbach zt"l* wrote to me remarking why a person who felt weak should not be allowed to eat before hearing the *Megillah* in the way of many who act leniently and eat before hearing the *shofar* (see above, *Siman* 585A).

The *halachah* forbidding one to eat at night before hearing the *Megillah* applies to the reading in the morning as well. Even if he has already prayed *Shacharit* he may not eat until after hearing the *Megillah* especially since the *mitzvah* to hear it in the morning is of greater importance than hearing it at night.[2] *Rav Neuwirth shlita* wondered whether this applied to the *mitzvot* of sending gifts of food to a friend and of sending gifts of food or money to two poor people.[3] *Rav Waldenberg shlita*[4] wrote to me that the *Moadim U'Zemanim* (see ref. 3) forbids eating before these two *mitzvot.* However, *Rav Ovadiah Yosef shlita* disagrees since eating a meal on *Purim* is itself one of the *mitzvot* of *Purim,* and rules that the custom is that the main meal for *Purim* is

5. מ"ב שם

6. מנחת שלמה ח"א סי' ט הערה 2 וח"ב סי' ד אות ל

7. מ"ב ס"ק ו

8. שנה א פ' תצוה סע' ב

1. מ"ב ס"ק יד

2. דהוא מדברי קבלה – מ"ב ס"ק טו ושעה"צ ס"ק כז

3. וראה במועדים וזמנים ח"ב סי' קפו שנשאר בצע"ג למה אין נוהגין להחמיר ולדקדק בדבר

4. הערה לנשמת אברהם כרך א או"ח עמ' שמו ושו"ת ציץ אליעזר חט"ו סי' לג אות טו

before hearing the Megillah even if [B]*it is difficult for him to continue fasting.*

SIMAN 695:
LAWS OF THE *PURIM* MEAL

§4: [A]Everyone is obligated to send a friend two portions of meat or other foods.

NISHMAT AVRAHAM

only eaten after the above two *mitzvot* have been fulfilled. Nevertheless, one may have a snack before then. *Rav Waldenberg shlita* adds that this ruling of *Rav Ovadiah Yosef shlita* is in keeping with the ruling of the *Leket Yosher* (a student of the *Terumat HaDeshen*).

(B) it is difficult for him: If he is weak by nature and prolonging the fast will harm him to the extent of making him ill, it would appear that he is permitted to eat a meal if a snack is not sufficient. However, he must ask someone to remind him to read the *Megillah* afterwards.[5]

SIMAN 695

(A) Everyone: I wondered whether one has fulfilled the *mitzvah* of sending gifts of food to a friend, if the friend is medically forbidden to eat that food – for example a box of chocolates to a diabetic (when both the sender and the recipient are aware of the diagnosis). The *Pitchei Teshuvah*[1] writes that the main reason for the *mitzvah* is to give joy. It would appear that since the diabetic will have no joy in receiving the gift and, on the contrary, will possibly even be embittered by it, the sender will not have fulfilled the *mitzvah*. *Rav Neuwirth shlita* agreed with this. However, *Rav Zilberstein shlita*[2] wrote to me that the opinion of *Tosafot*[3] that "if one does not listen to a doctor, he is not considered too much of a wrongdoer," would also apply here, since were the diabetic to eat the chocolates, it would not make him dangerously ill. Therefore, the sender fulfils his obligation. He also asked rhetorically: "If the receiver had eaten a meat meal towards the end of *Purim* and then received dairy food, would the sender not have fulfilled his obligation? It would appear that when *Chazal* instituted this *mitzvah* they did so on a general basis, obliging one to send gifts of food which most people would be happy to receive, even if a particular individual would not."

I replied to *Rav Zilberstein shlita* that I had spoken to *Rav Auerbach zt"l* who agreed with him but that nevertheless I had difficulty understanding the *halachah*. *Rav Neuwirth shlita* wrote to me that the *Sha'arei Teshuvah*[4] writes that if one sends a food gift to a friend on *Purim* with the condition that he return it to him, he has not fulfilled his obligation since the receiver will not have any joy from it. Similarly, the *Orchot Chaim*[5] writes that one who eats (kosher) bread baked by a non-Jew and sends it to someone who does not eat it, has not fulfilled his obligation since the receiver will not have any joy from it, even though in certain circumstances it is permissible to eat such bread (see *Siman* 168 §5). The *Mish-*

5. מ״ב ס״ק טז. וראה בשעה״צ ס״ק כט
1. ס״ק ז
2. נשמת אברהם כרך א או״ח עמ׳ שנג
3. ב״ק פה ע״א תוסד״ה עבר
4. ס״ק ז ועיין בביה״ל סי׳ תרצד סע׳ א ד״ה ליתן
5. כאן אות יא ד״ה ועי׳ בשע״ת

NISHMAT AVRAHAM

nah Berurah[6] also states in the name of the *Chayei Adam* that if a small gift is sent to a wealthy man, the sender has not fulfilled his obligation since the receiver will not have any joy from it. Thus we see that to fulfill one's obligation the gift must give joy. Therefore, concludes *Rav Neuwirth shlita,* whoever sends a sugared cake (or the like) to a diabetic has not fulfilled his obligation. For how is this different from the examples given above?

A hospitalized patient is also obligated to appoint someone who will perform the two *mitzvot* (gifts to a friend and to two of the poor) on his behalf. If necessary, he may exchange his food with that of another patient in the room in order to fulfil the *mitzvah* of a gift to a friend.

BLESSED BE HE WHO GIVES STRENGTH TO THE WEARY

6. ביה"ל כאן ד"ה חייב

Glossary

HEBREW AND HALACHIC TERMS

acharonim – Rabbinic authorities contemporary with or after the time of Rav Yosef Karo, the author of the *Shulchan Aruch* (16th century)

aches and pains – see introduction to Chapter 328 for definition

achshevei – elevating that which is not considered edible to the status of food by eating it

afikoman – the dessert at the end of a meal; at the Passover *seder*, a person eats *matzah* at the close of the meal in commemoration of the Paschal lamb which was eaten when the Temple existed

ahavah rabbah – the second of two blessings preceding the *Shema* in the morning service

ahavat olam – the second of two blessings preceding the *Shema* in the evening service

al achilat maror – the blessing recited over the bitter herbs at the Passover *seder*

al hamichyah – the blessing recited after eating cake made from one of the five species of grain

al hanissim – special prayer of thanksgiving added to the *Shemoneh Esrei* and to the *birkat hamazon* on *Chanukah* and *Purim*

al mitzvat tefillin – the blessing said before putting on the *tefillin* of the head

al netilat yadayim – the blessing said on the ritual washing of the hands

aneinu – prayer asking *Hashem* to answer us; included in the *Shemoneh Esrei* on a fast day

Anshei Knesset HaGedolah – Men of the Great Assembly; this is the collective name for the elders of Israel after the destruction of the First Temple

aravot – willow branches; one of the four species held together on the Festival of *Succot*

Aron HaKodesh – the Holy Ark; the place where the Torah Scrolls are kept in the synagogue

asher ge'alanu – blessing made at the conclusion of the first part of the *seder;* it precedes the drinking of the second cup of wine

asher yatzar – the blessing recited after using the lavatory

Ashkenaz – designation of the first compact area of Jewish settlement in northwest Europe; Germany

Ashkenazi(m) – Jews of German or Eastern European origin

ata chonantanu – a prayer added to the fourth blessing of the *Shemoneh Esrei* at the conclusion of the Sabbath or a Festival praising *Hashem* for differentiating between the holy and the mundane

avadim hayinu – literally: we were slaves; the beginning of the response to the Four Questions at the start of the *seder* service proper

ba'al nefesh – one who is particular about keeping Jewish law strictly

barechu – an essential part of the morning and evening service, calling on the congregation to bless *Hashem*

baruch hamavdil bein kodesh lechol – a shortened version of the *Havdalah* blessing

Baruch She'amar – the opening blessing recited before the chapters of *Psalms* during the morning service

bediavad – ex post facto

Beit HaMikdash – the Temple

berachah acharonah – blessing made after eating or drinking

berachah rishonah – blessing made before eating or drinking

Beit Din – rabbinical court consisting of three judges

bimah – platform in the center of the synagogue on which the Torah is read

birkat Cohanim – the priestly blessing recited by the *Cohanim*

birkat hamazon – the grace (blessings) after meals

birkat hanehenin – blessings recited for enjoying physical pleasures such as those derived from eating food and smelling fragrant aromas

birchot hashachar – blessings recited at the beginning of the morning service

birkat haTorah – blessings recited each morning before studying Torah

borei meorei ha'aish – blessing recited on a flame as part of *Havdalah*

borei minei mezonot – blessing recited before eating cake and cookies made from any of the five species of grain

borei nefashot – the blessing made after consuming certain foods and drinks

borei pri ha'adamah – the blessing recited before eating vegetables and certain fruits

borei pri hagafen – the blessing made on wine

brit milah – Jewish ritual circumcision

carmelit – an area which does not fit the definition of either a *private* or *public domain* but may be confused with either of them. Examples would be a street lacking the qualifications of a *public domain,* fields, or a covered *public domain.* The prohibition of carrying in a *carmelit* is Rabbinical

Chachamim – Sages of the Talmud

chalitzah – The Torah commands one to marry the widow of his brother who passed away childless. This mitzvah is called *yibum* (Levirate marriage). If there are valid reasons against a *yibum,* a *mitzvah* known as *chalitzah* is performed to release the widow and allow her to remarry at will. Part of the *chalitzah* ceremony involves the widow untying the shoelaces and removing a shoe, specially made for the purpose, worn by her brother-in-law

challah – the portion of dough separated as the priest's share; the name is also used for bread baked for the Sabbath and Festival meals

chametz – flour of the five types of grain (wheat, spelt, barley, oats and rye) which has come into contact with water and become leavened; forbidden on *Pesach*

Chanukah – the Festival of Lights commemorating the Maccabean victory over the Greeks, the reconsecration of the Temple, and the miracle of the oil which burned in the Temple candelabrum for eight days even though there was only enough oil for one day

chatzitzah – that which intervenes and does not allow contact between two entities

Chazal – our Sages (of the *Mishnah* and *Gemara*)

chazzan – cantor

Chol HaMoed – the intermediate days of the Festivals of *Pesach* and *Succot*

Chumash – each of the five Books of Moses

Cohen (Cohanim) – Priest(s); direct descendants along the male line of Aharon – the first High Priest
cubit – 48 cm. (60 cm. according to the *Chazon Ish*)
danger to a limb – see introduction to Chapter 328 for definition
dangerously ill – see introduction to Chapter 328 for definition
davar shebikdushah – e.g. learning Torah, praying, reciting blessings
dayan ha'emet – blessing made by close relatives of the deceased at the time of his death or at the funeral
discomfort – see introduction to Chapter 328 for definition
domain – There are four types of domain in *halachah*: a *private domain,* a *public domain,* a *carmelit* and a *makom petur.* Carrying an object from one to another on *Shabbat* may be forbidden by the Torah (from private to public domain or vice versa, or carrying the distance of four *cubits* in a public domain) or Rabbinically forbidden (either to or from a *carmelit,* or carrying the distance of four *cubits* in a *carmelit*). Carrying is permissible from any of the above three domains to a *makom petur* or vice versa
Elokai neshamah – the first of the morning blessings after *birkat haTorah*
emet ve'emunah – the first blessing after the *Shema* in the *Maariv* service
Eretz Yisrael – the Land of Israel
eruv – a "halachic wall" constructed to enclose a city or part of it to enable carrying on *Shabbat* (the enclosure is only possible where there is no *public domain*)
eruv chatzerot – the joining together of different apartments in a shared building by placing a jointly owned loaf of bread or *matzah* in one of the apartments.
ervah – parts of the body (male or female) which, by Jewish law, must be covered
Ezra – leader of the exiles who returned from Babylon to Israel
Fast of Gedaliah – see Gedaliah
five species of fruit – grape, fig, pomegranate, olive and date (*Deuteronomy* 8:8)
Gaon (Geonim) – highest *halachic* authorities from about the 6th to 11th centuries; also, outstanding Torah personalities of later generations
Gedaliah – Gedaliah ben Achikam, governor of the remnant left in Judea after the destruction of the First Temple. His assassination led to the final exile (see *II Kings* 25:22-25; *Talmud Rosh Hashanah* 16b)
Gemara – Talmud
gloss – annotation on the *Shulchan Aruch* by the *Rama*
gosses – one who is dying
***gramma* switch** – A device for using electricity on *Shabbat* in the context of patient care; the act performed through it involves less than an act which transgresses a Rabbinical prohibition. A "*gramma* switch" consists of a condenser slowly charged through a high resistance. In every small interval of time the voltage becomes high enough to activate the device. However, a photo resistor short-circuits the condenser allowing conduction when light strikes it; every, say, half a minute a light flashes which discharges the conductor before it can reach a voltage high enough to activate the device. When someone activates the switch, an obstruction is put between this light and the photo resistor, allowing the condenser to reach a high enough voltage to activate the device. Thus, turning on the switch eliminates the light that prevents the activation of the device. Thus there is only a doubly indirect link between the turning on of the switch and the activation of the device
guf naki – "pure body" – free from any urge to flatulate or use the bathroom

hadassim – myrtle branches; one of the four species held together on the Festival of *Succot*

hagbahah – lifting up the Torah scroll for the congregation to see the text

Haggadah – the text retelling the miracles performed by *Hashem* during the Exodus from Egypt, recited at the *seder* service

halachah(ot) – Jewish law(s)

***halachic* midday** – midway between sunrise and sunset

***halachic* midnight** – midway between sunset and sunrise

Hallel – *Psalms* 113-118, recited at the *seder* in praise of *Hashem;* also recited on *Rosh Chodesh,* Festivals and *Chanukah*

hama'avir sheinah – one of the morning blessings

hamavdil bein kodesh lechol – blessing made at *Havdalah*

hamotzi – the blessing recited over bread

Hashem – God

hashkafah – outlook on spiritual matters

hashkivenu – the second blessing after the *Shema* at the *Maariv* service

Hatzalah – Jewish emergency-call service

Havdalah – ceremony which marks the formal close of the Sabbath and Festivals

havinenu – a shortened version of the *Shemoneh Esrei* recited in times of urgency

Hoshana Rabbah – the seventh day of the Festival of *Succot;* it is one of the intermediate days

Kabbalah – Jewish mysticism

Kaddish – the prayer said by mourners in the presence of a *minyan*

karet – the "cutting off" of the soul; Divinely imposed premature death

kasher – to *halachically* cleanse and purge a vessel of the absorption of any forbidden food, including *chametz*

kavod habriot – respect for human dignity; preventing public embarrassment

kebeitzah – a measurement equivalent to the volume of an egg (54 grams)

kedei achilat pras – a span of time that *halachically* constitutes a single eating, equivalent to 2 to 4 minutes or up to 9 minutes depending on the *halachah* in question

kedei shti'at revi'it – the time it takes to drink a *revi'it*

Kedushah – verses sanctifying *Hashem,* recited by the congregation during the repetition of the *Shemoneh Esrei*

keli rishon – first vessel; that which was on the fire and is as yet hot

keli sheni – second vessel; that into which food from a *keli rishon* was poured

Keriyat Shema – the recitation of the *Shema* which begins with, "Hear O Israel . . ." (*Deuteronomy* 6:5). With it one proclaims the unity of God and the acceptance of His yoke

kezayit (kezeitim) – a measurement equivalent to the volume of an olive(s), 27 to 30 grams.

Kiddush – sanctification of the Sabbath and Festivals recited over a cup of wine

Kohelet – the Book of *Ecclesiastes*

lechem mishneh – two loaves of bread which are required for each of the Sabbath and Festival meals

lehani'ach tefillin – the blessing recited before putting on the *tefillin* of the arm

leshev basuccah – the blessing that is recited before eating in a *succah.* There are different opinions as to whether this is recited only on eating bread (*Sefardim*) or even on cookies (*Ashkenazim*)

lulav – a palm branch; one of the four species held together on the Festival of *Succot*

Maariv – the evening prayer service
maftir – additional reading at the end of the reading of the Torah on Sabbaths and Festivals
makom ervah – a part of the body that is *ervah*
makom petur – an exempted domain in a *public domain,* less than 4x4 *tefachim* square and at least 3 *tefachim* higher than the *public domain.* One may carry from and to it to any one of the other *domains*
Maran – the Master, the title usually reserved for the *Mechaber*
maror – bitter herbs eaten at the *seder* service
matzah(ot) – unleavened bread eaten during *Pesach*
measure – generally accepted to be between 27 and 30 grams of food or 40 to 45 cc. of fluid, consumed within 9 minutes. This is the maximum amount of food or fluid that may be eaten or drunk at one time by a *seriously ill* patient on *Yom Kippur* unless he has been permitted to eat as usual. This must be followed by a pause of at least another 9 minutes before the cycle may be repeated; see *Siman* 612
Mechaber – Rav Yosef Karo, author of the *Shulchan Aruch*
me'en shalosh – the *berachah acharonah* said on cakes and on the seven species of fruits of the Land of Israel
Megillah – the scroll of Esther which relates the story of *Purim*
melachah – one of the thirty-nine creative activities forbidden on *Shabbat* and *Yom Tov* by Torah law
melachah she'enah tz'richah legufah – a *melachah* that is done for a purpose other than its primary one
melo lugmav – enough liquid to fill one cheek
meshum eivah – the fear of revenge or ill will
metzizah – the procedure of sucking out a little blood from the wound immediately after circumcision
mezuzah(ot) – parchment, containing the first two paragraphs of the *Shema,* that is affixed to the doorpost of every room
Midrash – homiletical expositions on the Torah, 6th century
mikveh – pool for ritual immersion and purification
Minchah – the afternoon prayer service
minhag – custom
minor illness – see introduction to Chapter 328 for definition
minyan – a quorum of ten adult male Jews – the minimum required for communal prayer
Mishkan – the Tabernacle (House of *Hashem*) built in the desert
mitzvah(ot) – Torah or Rabbinical commandment
modim – one of the blessings of the *Shemoneh Esrei* acknowledging and thanking *Hashem*
mohel – a qualified practitioner of Jewish circumcision
molad – the first appearance of the new moon in Jerusalem
Moshe Rabbeinu – Moses our Teacher
muktzeh – that which may not be moved on *Shabbat* or *Yom Tov*
mumar – apostate
Mussaf – additional prayer recited after the *Shacharit* prayer, on the Sabbath, Festivals and *Rosh Chodesh*
nachem – a prayer asking *Hashem* to console the mourners of Zion; said during the *Shemoneh Esrei* on *Tishah B'Av* afternoon

nefel – a stillborn or a baby that will die within thirty days of birth
nefilat apayim – literally: falling on the face. The confessional prayer recited while the face is placed on the right arm, on most weekdays, after the *Shemoneh Esrei* of *Shacharit* and *Minchah*
niddah – the ritually impure state of a woman from the beginning of her menses, or other hormonal uterine bleeding, until after she has immersed herself in a *mikveh* at the appropriate time
nolad – that which is created (born) on *Shabbat* or *Yom Tov,* for example, ice produced by freezing water on *Shabbat*
non-seriously ill patient – see introduction to Chapter 328 for definition
odor with a source – odor from excrement that is still present
odor without a source – odor from excrement that has been removed or from flatulence
onen – one of the seven primary relatives of a deceased in the period before the burial
orlah – fruit which grew during the first three years after the planting of a tree – it is forbidden to have any benefit from it
parsah – a measurement of 4.0 km. (8,000 cubits)
parshah – the weekly portion of the Torah read each Sabbath
parshat hatamid – the portion of the Torah dealing with the twice-daily sacrifice offered in the Temple
parshat parah – the portion of the Torah dealing with the red heifer
parshat zachor – the portion of the Torah dealing with Amalek
patzua daka – a person whose genitalia have been injured
Pesach – the Festival of Passover celebrating the Exodus from Egypt
plag haminchah – earliest time for praying *Maariv* and for lighting Sabbath candles; 1.25 proportional (1/24 of the time between sunrise and sunset of any particular day) hours before sunset
poskim – authorities of Jewish law
private domain – enclosed area, such as a house, courtyard or car, at least 4 *tefachim* square surrounded by partitions at least 10 *tefachim* high. Carrying to and from this to a *public domain* is prohibited by Torah law
public domain – street, highway or public square with a minimum width of 16 *cubits,* open at both ends and unroofed. According to many *poskim* a *public domain* must, in addition, be frequented by at least 600,000 people each day. Carrying to and from this to a *private domain* is prohibited by Torah law
Purim – the holiday commemorating our salvation from Haman's evil decree
Rabbeinu – title usually reserved for the *Rishonim*
refa'einu – one of the blessings of the *Shemoneh Esrei,* for the healing of the sick
responsum – written response by a *posek* about questions of Jewish law
retzei – 1) one of the blessings of the *Shemoneh Esrei* asking that *Hashem* accept the prayer and restore the Temple service; 2) a special prayer added to the *birkat hamazon* on the Sabbath
revi'it – a liquid measure equivalent to 86 cc. (or 150 cc. according to the *Chazon Ish*)
Rosh Hashanah – the Jewish New Year
ruach ra'ah – evil spirit
sa'ir la'azazel – goat that was thrown over a cliff on *Yom Kippur* (see *Leviticus* 16:8,10,21 and 22)
sandak – the one who holds the baby on his lap during circumcision
Sanhedrin – a higher court than a *Beit Din;* composed of twenty-three Judges. The Great Sanhedrin was made up of seventy-one Judges

se'ah – a measurement of approximately 7.2 liters (14.4 liters according to the *Chazon Ish*)
seder – the order of the *Pesach* night ceremony recalling the Exodus from Egypt and the liberation from bondage
Sefer Torah – the scroll of the Torah
segulah – amulet, charm
selichot – prayers asking for forgiveness
Sephardi(m) – Jews of Spanish or Middle Eastern origin
seriously ill patient – see introduction to Chapter 328 for definition
seudah shelishit – the third Sabbath meal
Shabbat – the Sabbath
Shacharit – the morning service
shaliach tzibbur – one who leads the congregation in prayer
shamor vezachor – "guard and remember" – the expressions used in the Ten Commandments regarding the Sabbath
shaveh lechol nefesh – equally required by everybody. On *Yom Tov* one is allowed to do *melachot* that are concerned with the preparation of food. However, only that which is equally required by everybody is permitted; that which is required by a small group of people – such as medicines for the sick or the needs of pampered – are not permitted to be prepared
Shavuot – The Festival commemorating the giving of the Torah at Mount Sinai
shehakol – a general blessing made over foods and drinks that have no specific blessing
shehecheyanu – blessing made on new fruits and garments, on Festivals and on other joyous occasions
shel rosh – the *tefillin* worn on the head
shel yad – the *tefillin* worn on the arm
Shema – "Hear O Israel . . . " (*Deuteronomy* 6:5), the opening words of the fundamental Jewish prayer which proclaims the unity of God and the acceptance of His yoke
Shemini Atzeret – the eighth day of *Succot*
Shemoneh Esrei – the principle daily prayer said silently and also known as the *Amidah*
sheinat keva – a settled sleep in bed as distinct from a short nap
shiurim – portions. A *seriously ill* patient who must eat on *Yom Kippur* may be allowed to eat normally or with *shiurim* depending on his condition. If he eats with *shiurim,* he is permitted to eat up to 30 grams of solid food and drink up to 45 cc. of liquid with at least 9 minutes between finishing one portion and starting the next. This rule may also apply in certain cases on *Tishah B'Av.*
shivah – the seven-day period of mourning following the death of a close relative
shomei'a tefillah – one of the blessings of the *Shemoneh Esrei* in which we ask *Hashem* to hear our supplications
shoteh – someone who is so mentally impaired as to be irresponsible for his actions. He is exempt from all *mitzvot*
shul – synagogue
siddur – prayer book
Simchat Torah – the Festival of rejoicing with the Torah. In Israel, this is combined with *Shemini Atzeret* whereas in the Diaspora it is the day following
sofer – Jewish scribe who writes the scrolls of Law, *tefillin, mezuzot,* and the like
succah(ot) – a temporary dwelling which one must live in during the Festival of *Succot*
Succot – the Festival of Tabernacles

tachanun – prayers of supplication
tallit (tallitot) – prayer shawl with four fringes, worn during *Shacharit*
tallit katan – literally: a small *tallit;* worn all day, usually under the shirt
Tanach – the Books of the Torah, Prophets and Sacred Writings
Tanna (Tanna'im) – sage(s) from the Mishnaic period
techum Shabbat – the area surrounding a city up to a distance of 973 meters outside the city (1,200 meters according to the *Chazon Ish*)
tefach (im) – a measurement of 8 cm. (9.6 cm. according to the *Chazon Ish*)
tefillin – phylacteries – worn on the arm and the head during the morning service
Tehillim – *Psalms*
ten tal u'matar – the phrase in one of the blessings of the *Shemoneh Esrei* asking for rain
teshuvah – repentance
Tishah B'Av – the ninth of the month of Av when both Temples were destroyed
Tishrei – Jewish calendar month during which *Rosh Hashanah, Yom Kippur, Succot* and *Shemini Atzeret* all fall
tractate – a volume of the *Talmud*
treifah – bird or animal that may not be eaten because of a terminal defect
tzamtan – head covering used to gather in one's hair
tzara'at – a Biblical affliction which *Chazal* tell us is a punishment for the sin of speaking *lashon hara* (talebearing)
tzitzit (yot) – fringe(s) on each of the four corners of the prayer shawl
vayechal – portion of the Torah read on fast days
vayechulu – verses from the Torah (*Genesis* 2:1-3) recited as part of the *Maariv* service on Friday night and again at *Kiddush*
worthy person – one who is not suspected of any sin, or of not keeping any positive commandment
ya'aleh veyavo – prayer added to the *Shemoneh Esrei* and to the *birkat hamazon* on *Rosh Chodesh* and Festivals
yehi ratzon – "may it be Your will—"
Yom Kippur – the Day of Atonement
Yom Tov – Jewish Festival
yotzer or – the first of two blessings before the *Shema* in the morning service
zachor – the portion of the Torah commanding us to remember what Amalek did to us
zimun – a quorum of adult males who recite the *birkat hamazon* together

MEDICAL TERMS

anencephalic baby – a baby with a congenital absence of the brain and cranial vault, with the cerebral hemispheres completely missing or greatly reduced in size
angina or angina pectoris – pain coming from the heart
ascites – fluid in the abdominal cavity
balloon catheterization – *cardiac catheterization* where a balloon is used to open up a blocked coronary artery
biceps – muscle of the upper arm
cardiac catheterization – procedure to visualize the arteries of the heart (coronary arteries)
colostomy – artificial opening of the large intestine onto the abdominal wall; see also *ostomy*
empyema – the accumulation of pus in the chest cavity
episiotomy – a surgical incision made to prevent traumatic tearing during delivery
gastrointestinal – pertaining to the stomach and intestines
gastrostomy – tube put through the abdominal wall into the stomach, for artificial feeding
gluten – the protein of wheat and other grains
hemorrhoids – rectal piles
hyperviscosity syndromes – conditions leading to over-concentration of the blood
hypoglycemic attack – a drop in blood-sugar level great enough to cause symptoms
I.V.F. – in-vitro fertilization
ileostomy – artificial opening of the small intestine onto the abdominal wall; see also *ostomy*
incontinence – the involuntary passing of urine or feces
laparotomy – an operation where the abdominal cavity is opened
naso-gastric tube – tube put into the stomach via the nose, for artificial feeding
nitroglycerin pills – medication taken to treat an attack of *angina*
ostomy – operation to create an opening from an area inside the body to the outside
PEG – percutaneous entero-gastrostomy – the insertion of a feeding tube via the abdominal wall into the stomach or small intestine
phlebotomy – the puncturing of a vein for the purpose of withdrawing blood
physiologic jaundice – jaundice seen in healthy newborns as a result of an immature liver that is as yet incapable of dealing with and removing the excess bilirubin (the cause of the yellow discoloration). Disappears spontaneously in a few days; this process is hastened by placing the baby under a blue lamp
pleural effusion – fluid in the chest cavity
polycythemia vera – a disease characterized by the presence of too many red blood cells
stenting – procedure during cardiac catheterization whereby an artificial tube is inserted into a coronary artery to prevent it from becoming blocked
thoracotomy – an operation where the chest cavity is opened
urinary catheter – tube inserted into the bladder to enable urination

Bibliography

Achiezer – Rav Chaim Ozer Grodzinski, d. 1940
Aderet – Rav Eliyahu David Rabinowitz Teomim, d. 1905
Aishel Avraham (Butasht) – Rav Avraham David Werman from Butasht, d. 1841
Ari z"l – Rav Yitzchak Luria, d. 1572
Aruch HaShulchan – Rav Yechiel Michal Epstein, d. 1905
Aruch LaNer – see Binyan Tzion
Ateret Zekenim – Rav Menachem Mendel Auerbach, d. 1689
Avnei Nezer – also *Eglei Tal;* Rav Avraham Bornstein, d. 1910
Avraham ben HaRambam – Rabbeinu Avraham ben HaRambam, d. 1238
Az Nidberu – Rav Binyamin Yehoshua Zilber, contemporary
Ba'al Halachot Gedolot – author unknown. According to various Rishonim, between 6th and 10th centuries
Ba'al HaMaor – Rabbeinu Zerachiah ben Yitzchak HaLevi, d. 1186
Bach (Bayit Chadash) – Rav Yoel Sirkes, d. 1640
Badei HaShulchan – see *Ketsot HaShulchan*
Ba'er Heitev – Rav Yehudah Ashkenazi, d. 1748
Be'er HaGolah – Rav Moshe Rivkesh, d. 1671
Be'er Yitzchak – Rav Elchanan Spektor, d. 1895
Beit Shlomo – Rav Shlomo Maskala, d. 1873
Beit Yitzchak – Rav Yitzchak Yehudah Shmulkes, d. 1906
Beit Yosef – also *Shulchan Aruch; Maran* Yosef Karo, d. 1575
Ben Ish Chai – Rav Yosef Chaim of Baghdad, d. 1909
Binyan Tzion – Rav Yaakov Ettlinger, d. 1871
Birkei Yosef – see *Chida*
Biur Halachah – see *Mishnah Berurah*
Brisker Rav – Rav Chaim Soloveitchik, d. 1918
Chacham Zvi – Rav Zvi Hirsch Ashkenazi, d. 1718
Chatam Sofer – Rav Moshe Sofer Shreiber, d. 1839
Chafetz Chaim – Rav Yisrael Meir HaCohen, d. 1933; also book by the same name on laws of *lashon hara;* see *Mishnah Berurah*
Chavat Da'at – Rav Yaakov Lorberbaum, d. 1832
Chavot Yair – Rav Yair Chaim Bacharach, d. 1702
Chayei Adam – also *Chochmat Adam;* Rav Avraham Danzig, d. 1820
Chazon Ish – Rav Avraham Yeshayah Karelitz, d. 1953
Chelkat Mechokek – Rav Moshe ben Yitzchak Yehudah Lima, d. 1658
Chelkat Yaakov – Rav Mordechai Yaakov Breish, d. 1977
Chesed LeAvraham – Rav Avraham Teomim, d. 1877
Chida – also *Birkei Yosef;* Rav Chaim Yosef David Azulai, d. 1806
Chidushei HaRim – Rav Yitzchak Meir Alter of Gur, d. 1866
Chinuch – Rabbeinu Aharon HaLevi of Barcelona, d. 1299

Chochmat Adam – see *Chayei Adam*
Chochmat Shlomo – also *Elef Lecha Shlomo;* Rav Shlomo Kluger, d. 1869
Choshen Mishpat – the fourth of the four parts of the *Shulchan Aruch*
Da'at Torah – see *Maharsham*
Dagul MeRevavah – see *Noda BiYehudah*
Darchei Teshuvah – Rav Zvi Hirsch Shapira of Munkatsch, d. 1913
Derech HaChaim – Rav Yaakov Lorberbaum, d. 1832
Divrei Chaim – Rav Chaim Halberstam of Sanz, d. 1875
Dovev Mesharim – Rav Dov Berish Weidenfeld, d. 1966
Eglei Tal – see *Avnei Nezer*
Elef LaMateh – Rav Ephraim Zalman Margaliot, d. 1827
Elef Lecha Shlomo – also *Chochmat Shlomo;* Rav Shlomo Kluger, d. 1909
Eliyah Rabbah – Rav Eliyahu Shapira, d. 1712
Even HaEzer – the third of the four parts of the *Shulchan Aruch*
Gaon from Tshubin – see *Dovev Mesharim*
Gesher HaChaim – Rav Yechiel Michel Tukechinsky, d. 1951
Ginat Veradim – Rav Avraham HaLevi, d. 1730
Gra – Rav Eliyahu ben Shlomo Zalman, d. 1797
Haamek She'elah – see *Netziv*
Hagahot Asheri – Rabbeinu Israel of Krems, d. 1490
Hagahot Maimoniot – Rabbeinu Meir of Rotenberg, d. 1297
HaGra – see *Gra*
Halachot Ketanot – Rav Yaakov Chagiz, d. 1764
Har Tzvi – Rav Tzvi Pesach Frank, d. 1960
Harei Besamim – Rav Aryeh Leibish Horowitz, d. 1909
Ibn Ezra – Rabbeinu Avraham ibn Ezra, d. 1164
Igrot Moshe – see *Rav Moshe Feinstein*
Ikrei HaDat – Rav Daniel Tarani
Imrei Yosher – Rav Meir Arik, d. 1926
Kaf HaChaim – Rav Yaakov Chaim Sofer, d. 1938
Kalkelet Shabbat – see *Tiferet Yisrael*
Kappot Temarim – Rav Moshe ibn Chabib, d. 1696
Katzeh HaMateh – Rav Chaim Zvi Ehrenreich, d. 1937
Kesef Mishneh – commentary on the *Rambam's Yad HaChazakah (or Mishneh Torah)* by the author of the *Shulchan Aruch.* When one refers to "a *Rambam,*" one means his *Yad HaChazakah.*
Ketav Sofer – Rav Avraham Shmuel Binyamin Sofer, d. 1872
Kiryat Sefer – Rav Moshe MiTrani, d. 1580
Kitzur Shulchan Aruch – Rav Shlomo Ganzfried, d. 1885
Knesset HaGedolah – Rav Chaim Benveniste d. 1673
Kol Bo – Rabbeinu Aaron ben Yaakov HaCohen from Luneil, d. 1334
Korban Netanel – Rav Netanel Weil, d. 1769
Kovetz – Rav Menachem Nachum Trebitsch, d. 1846
Kovetz Shiurim – Rav Elchanan Bunem Wasserman, killed by the Nazis, 1940
Ketsot HaShulchan – Rav Avraham Chaim Na'eh, d. 1954
Lechem HaPanim – Rav Chaim Yeshaya Hilbersberg
Leket HaKemach HaChadash – Rav Yaakov Zvi Katz, d. 1964
Lev Aryeh – Rav Aryeh Grossnass, d. 1997
Lev Chaim – Rav Chaim Palaggi, d. 1868

Levush – Rav Mordechai Yaffe, d. 1612
Levushei Mordechai – Rav Mordechai Leib Winkler
Levushei Serad – Rav David Zvi Shlomo Eibeshitz, d. 1816
Likutei Maharil – Rav Yaakov ben Moshe Mulin, d. 1427
Machatzit HaShekel – Rav Shmuel HaLevi of Kalin, d. 1806
Machazeh Avraham – Rav Avraham Menachem Mendel Steinberg, d. 1928
Magen Avraham – Rav Avraham Abele Gombiner, d. 1682
Magen Giborim – Rav Mordechai Zeev Ettinger, d. 1863 and Rav Yosef Shaul Nathanson, d. 1875
Maggid Mishneh – Rabbeinu Vidal de Tolosha, d. 1356
Maharam Chalawa – Rav Moshe Chalawa, d. 1339
Maharam of Rotenberg – wrote *Hagahot Maimoniot;* Rabbeinu Meir, d. 1293
Maharam Shick – Rav Moshe Shick, d. 1879
Mahari Asa'ad – Rav Yehudah Asa'ad, d. 1865
Mahari Shtief – Rav Yonatan Shtief, d. 1958
Maharikash – Rav Yaakov Kastro, d. 1609
Maharil – Rav Yaakov ben Moshe Mulin HaLevy, d. 1427
Maharil Diskin – Rav Yehoshua Yehudah Leib Diskin, d. 1898
Maharit – Rav Yosef MiTrani, d. 1639
Maharshag – Rav Shimon Gruenfeld, d. 1929
Maharshal – see *Yam Shel Shomo,* d. 1573
Maharsham – also *Da'at Torah;* Rav Shalom Mordechai HaCohen Shwadron, d. 1911
Marcheshet – Rav Hanoch Henich Eigish
Mateh Ephraim – Rav Ephraim Zalman Margoliot, d. 1828
MiBeit Meir – Rav Meir Stalewiz
Meiri – Rabbeinu Menachem ben Rabbeinu Shlomo, d. 1315
Melamed LeHo'il – Rav David Tzvi Hoffman, d. 1922
Melechet Charash – Rav Yechezkel Chefetz, d. 1875
Meshech Chochmah – see *Or Same'ach*
Minchat Chinuch – Rav Yosef Babad, d. 1877
Minchat Elazar – Rav Chaim Elazar Shapira from Munkatsch, d. 1937
Minchat Shabbat – Rav Shmuel HaCohen Borshtein, d. 1900
Minchat Yitzchak – Rav Yitzchak Yaakov Weiss, d. 1975
Minchat Yom Tov – see *Minchat Shabbat*
Mirkevet HaMishneh – Rav Shlomo Ashkenazi from Chelma, d. 1781
Mishnah Berurah – also *Chafetz Chaim;* Rav Yisrael Meir HaCohen, d. 1933
Mishnat Ya'avetz – Rav Yaakov Bezalel Zolty, d. 1983
Mishneh LaMelech – Rav Yehudah Rozanis, d. 1727
Mishpetei Uziel – Rav Ben Zion Meir Chai Uziel, d. 1953
Mordechai – Rabbeinu Mordechai HaCohen Ashkenazi, d. 1298
Nachal Eshkol – Rav Zvi Binyamin Auerbach, d. 1778
Nachalat Binyamin – Rav Binyamin Zeev Brier, d. 1892
Nachalat Shivah – Rav Shmuel HaLevy, d. 1681
Nefesh Chayah – Rav Reuven Margaliot, d. 1971
Netiv Chaim – see *Korban Netanel*
Netziv – Rav Naftali Zvi Yehudah Berlin, d. 1892
Nishmat Adam – see *Chayei Adam*
Noda BiYehudah – also *Dagul MeRevavah;* Rav Yechezkel HaLevi Segal Landau, d. 1793

Or Same'ach – also *Meshech Chochmah;* Rav Meir Simchah HaCohen of Dvinsk, d. 1925
Or Zarua – Rabbeinu Itzchak ben Moshe, d. circa 1260
Orach Chaim – the first of the four parts of the *Shulchan Aruch*
Orchot Chaim – Rav Nachman Kahana of Spinka, d. 1900 and Rav Shalom Mordechai HaCohen Shwadron, d. 1911
Pardes Yosef – Rav Yosef Pesnivski, d. 1930
Perishah – Rav Yehoshua Falk, d. 1614
Pitchei Teshuvah – Rav Avraham Zvi Hirsch Eisenstadt, d. 1863
Pri Chadash – Rav Hizkeya ben David DiSilva, d. 1698
Pri Megadim – Rav Yosef Teomim, d. 1791
Ra'ah – Rabbeinu Aharon ben Yosef HaLevi, d. 1299
Ra'avad – Rabbeinu Avraham ben David, d. 1199
Rabbeinu Chananel – d. 1053
Rabbeinu Tam – Rabbeinu Yaakov ben Meir, d. 1171
Rabbeinu Yerucham – Rabbeinu Yerucham ben Meshulam, d. 1354
Rabbeinu Yonah – Rabbeinu Yonah ben Avraham Girondi, d. 1263
Radak – Rabbeinu David Kimchi, d. 1235
Radvaz – Rabbeinu David ben Shlomo Zimra, d. 1574
Rama – Rav Moshe Isserles, d. 1572, author of the *glosses* on the *Shulchan Aruch*
Rambam – Rabbeinu Moshe Maimonides, d. 1204
Ramban – Rabbeinu Moshe Nachmanides, d. 1270
Ran – Rabbeinu Nissim ben Reuven Gerondi, d. 1380
Rash – Rabbeinu Shimshon ben Avraham (from Shantz), d. 1229
Rashash – Rav Shimon Strashun, d. 1872
Rashba – Rabbeinu Shlomo ben Avraham Aderet, d. 1310
Rashi – Rabbeinu Shlomo Yitzchaki, d. 1105
Rav Abramsky – Rav Yechezkel Abramsky, d. 1975
Rav Ezriel Auerbach – contemporary; a son *of Rav Shlomo Zalman Auerbach*
Rav Shlomo Zalman Auerbach – d. 1995
Rav Akiva Eiger – d. 1838
Rav Yaakov Emden – see *Ya'avetz*
Rav Yosef Shalom Eliashiv – contemporary
Rav Moshe Feinstein – d. 1986
Rav Zvi Pesach Frank – see *Har Tzvi*
Rav Sherira Gaon – d. circa 1006
Rav Horowitz – Rav Elazar Moshe HaLevi Horowitz
Rav Yosef Karo – author of the *Shulchan Aruch,* d. 1575
Rav Kasher – Rav Menachem Kasher, d. 1983
Rav Shlomo Kluger – see *Chochmat Shlomo*
Rav Kook – Rav Avraham Yitzchak HaCohen Kook, d. 1934
Rav Meir of Rotenberg – see *Maharam*
Rav Isser Zalman Meltzer – d. 1954
Rav Yehoshua Y. Neuwirth – contemporary
Rav Chaim Palachi – Rav Chaim Palaggi, d. 1869
Rav Ben-Tzion Abba Shaul – author of *Or LeTzion,* d. 1996
Rav Chaim Soloveitchik – the Brisker Rav, d. 1918
Rav Yitzchak Ze'ev Soloveitchik – d. 1959
Rav Tukechinsky – Rav Yechiel Michel Tukechinsky, d. 1954

Rav Eliezer Yehudah Waldenberg – contemporary
Rav Wosner – see *Shevet HaLevi*
Rav Ovadiah Yosef – contemporary
Rav Elchanan Wasserman – see *Kovetz Shiurim*
Rav Weiss – see *Minchat Yitzchak*
Rav Binyamin Zilber – contemporary
Rav Yitzchak Zilberstein – contemporary
Raza – Rabbeinu Zerachiah Gerondi, d. 1186
Rebbe Matya ben Charash – Mishnaic sage
Rif – Rabbeinu Yitzchak HaCohen Alfasi d. 1103
Rishonim – Rabbinic authorities from after the *Geonim* to the time of the *Shulchan Aruch*
Ritva – Rabbeinu Yom Tov Ashbili, d. 1330?
Riva – Rabbeinu Yitzchak ben Asher HaLevy, one of the *Tosafot,* early 12th century
Rivash – Rabbeinu Yitzchak ben Sheshet, d. 1407
Roke'ach – Rav Elazar Rokeach, d. 1741
Rosh – Rabbeinu Asher ben Yechiel, d. 1327
Sdei Chemed – Rav Chaim Chezkiah HaLevi Medini, d. 1904
Sefat Emet – Rav Yehudah Aryeh Leib of Gur, d. 1904
Sefer HaItim – Rabbeinu Yehudah ben Rabbeinu Barzilai, d. 1125
Sefer Chasidim – Rabbeinu Yehudah ben Shmuel HaChasid, d. 1217
Sema (Sefer Meirot Einayim) – Rav Yehoshua Falk Katz, d. 1614
Seridei Eish – Rav Yechiel Yaakov Weinberg, d. 1965
Sha'agat Aryeh – Rav Aryeh Lev Ginsburg, d. 1785
Sha'ar HaMelech – Rav Yitzchak Nunis Belmonte, d. 1743
Sha'ar HaTziyun – see *Mishnah Berurah*
Sha'arei Teshuvah – Rav Chaim Mordechai Margalis, d. 1820
Shach – Rav Shabbtai HaCohen, d. 1662
She'arim Metzuyanim BaHalachah – Rav Shlomo Zalman Braun, d. 1994
Sheilat Ya'avetz – see *Ya'avetz*
Shemirat Shabbat KeHilchatah – Rav Yehoshua Y. Neuwirth, contemporary
Shevet HaLevi – Rav Shmuel HaLevi Wosner, contemporary
Shevut Yaakov – Rav Yaakov Reisher, d. 1733
Sh'lah – Rav Yeshayah HaLevi Horvitz, d. 1630
Shoel U'Meshiv – Rav Yosef Shaul HaLevi Natanson, d. 1875
Shulchan Aruch – The Code of Jewish Law by *Maran* Yosef Karo, d. 1575
Shulchan Aruch HaRav – Rav Shneur Zalman of Liadi, d. 1813
Talmud Bavli – the Oral Law, as it appears in the work compiled by Ravina and Rav Ashi, 5th century in Bavel
Talmud Yerushalmi – the Oral Law, as it appears in the work compiled by Rebbe Yochanan, 4th century in *Eretz Yisrael*
Tashbetz – Rabbeinu Shimon ben Tsemach Duran, d. 1443
Taz – Rav David HaLevi, d. 1667
Tehillah LeDavid – Rav David Ortenberg, d. 1910
Teshuvah MeAhavah – Rav Elazar Flaklish, d. 1825
Tiferet Yisrael – Rav Yisrael Lipshitz, d. 1866
Torat Chesed – Rav Shneur Zalman, Lublin, d. 1902
Tosafot – 12th to 13th century glosses on the *Talmud*
Tosfot Rid – Rabbeinu Yeshayah ben Mali d'Trani the elder, d. 1249

Tosfot Shantz – Rabbeinu Shimshon ben Avraham of Shantz, d. 1330
Tosfot Yom Tov – Rav Yom Tov Lipmann Heller, d. 1654
Tosefet Shabbat – Rav Rafael Meizlish, d. 1780
Tosefet Yom HaKippurim – Rav Moshe ben Habib, d. 1696
Terumat HaDeshen – Rabbeinu Yisrael Isserlin, d. 1460
Tur – Rabbeinu Yaakov ben Asher Ashkenazi, d. 1340
Tzitz Eliezer – Rav Eliezer Yehudah Waldenberg, contemporary
Ya'avetz – Rav Yaakov Emden, d. 1776
Yabia Omer – Rav Ovadiah Yosef, contemporary
Yad Ramah – Rabbeinu Meir HaLevi Abulafia, d. 1245
Yalkut HaGershuni – Rav Gershon Stern, d. 1900
Yam Shel Shlomo – Rav Shlomo Luria, d. 1573
Yechaveh Da'at – see *Yabia Omer*
Yerushalmi – the Jerusalem Talmud, compiled by Rebbe Yochanan, 4th century
Yesodei Yeshurun – Rav Gedaliah Felder, d. 1991
Yeshuot Yaakov – Rav Yaakov Meshulam Orenstein, d. 1840
Yoreh Deah – the second of the four parts of the *Shulchan Aruch*
Zaken Aharon – Rav Aharon Valkin
Zecher Simchah – Rav Simcha Bamberger, d. 1896
Zera Avraham – Rav Avraham Yitzchaki, d. 1729
Zivchei Tzedek – Rav Abdallah Somech, d. 1900
Zohar – major and central work on Jewish mysticism (*Kabbalah*), by Rebbe Shimon bar Yochai, 3rd century

Index

References are to the *Siman* of the *Shulchan Aruch* (Number) and to *Nishmat Avraham* on that *Siman* (letter)
***Nishmat Avraham* of *Siman* 328 of the *Shulchan Aruch* is referred to by number and letter, both within brackets.**
Example: 252A, 301J,M, 328 (1B) = *Siman* 252, paragraph A in *Nishmat Avraham, Siman* 301 paragraphs J and M and *Siman* 328 paragraph 1B in *Nishmat Avraham*

A

C

D

H

M

N

O

P

Q

R

S

T

X

Y

Z

About the Author

Abraham S. Abraham is Emeritus Professor of Medicine, Hebrew University and Hadassah Medical School, and has very recently retired from his position as Director of the Department of Medicine B at the Shaare Zedek Medical Center, Jerusalem, Israel.

He studied medicine at the Leeds School of Medicine, England, receiving his medical degree of Bachelor of Medicine and Surgery (MB, ChB) in 1960. His residency training in Internal Medicine included specialist training in Gastroenterology. He completed his Boards in 1964 (MRCP — Member of the Royal College of Physicians, London). He then went on to specialist training in Cardio-Pulmonology at the Queen Elizabeth Hospital, Birmingham, England receiving his MD (equivalent to a medical Ph.D.) from the University of Birmingham in 1968 for his pioneering work on the effects of oxygen in the treatment of patients with chronic bronchitis and emphysema. For this work he was awarded the annual prize of the American Heart Association / British Heart Foundation — to spend a year of research in the United States, which he did at the Johns Hopkins School of Medicine, Baltimore 1968/9. In recognition of his achievements in and contributions to the field of medicine, he was elected a Fellow of the Royal College of Physicians, London (FRCP) in 1977.

Abraham returned to his birthplace, Jerusalem, Israel in 1970 where he has practiced medicine for the last thirty years. For many years he has been the Director of the Department of Medicine B at the Shaare Zedek Medical Center and a teacher at the Hebrew University-Hadassah Medical School, becoming a Professor of Medicine at the latter institution, a member of the Senate of the Hebrew University, an examiner for the Israel Board in Internal Medicine and has served on a variety of national and local committees. He has published over eighty articles on cardio-pulmonary medicine, trace elements in cardiovascular disease and other subjects, in prestigious international medical journals including the New England Journal of Medicine and has, on many occasions, been included in the list of outstanding teachers at the Hadassah Medical School.

Professor Abraham has also published extensively in the field of Medical Halachah: *Lev Avraham* (2 volumes, Hebrew) and its English translation, *Medical Halachah for Everyone,* followed later by an updated and more extensive volume, *The Comprehensive Guide to Medical Halachah.* His magnum opus, the six-volume *Nishmat Avraham* (Hebrew), based on the four sections of the *Shulchan Aruch* (*Orach Chaim, Yoreh Deah, Even HaEzer* and *Choshen Mishpat*), is today the classical text for health-care personnel, laymen and Rabbis alike, encompassing medico-halachic problems and their solutions in all branches of medicine, surgery, gynecology and obstetrics. He has also published two pocket-books (both in Hebrew and in English) dealing specifically with medico-halachic problems on the Sabbath, Festivals and Yom Kippur, for health-care personnel and patient respectively.

The present book is his edited translation of the *Orach Chaim* section of *Nishmat Avraham,* and is taken from volumes one, four and five.